This book is dedicated to
Rolf C. Hagen, Canada,
with whom I have enjoyed
a 30 year personal and
business relationship

Hans A. Baensch

Photos:
Front cover:
Acanthurus leucosternon and
Amphiprion ocellaris
with the anemones
Heteractis magnifica (top)
and *Heteractis crispa* (below), (H. A. Baensch)

Back cover:
t.l. *Actinia equina* (H. Debelius)
t.r. *Nemateleotris decora* (H. Voigtmann)
b.l. *Zanclus cornutus* (E. Robinson)

Published in the United States by:
TETRA PRESS, 3001 Commerce Street
Blacksburg, VA 24060

©Copyright 1994 MERGUS®-Verlag GmbH Hans A. Baensch, 49302 Melle, Germany.

®MERGUS is a registered trademark in USA.

Library of Congress Cataloging-in-Publication Data
Debelius, Helmut
  [Meerwasser Atlas. English]
  Marine atlas : the joint aquarium care of invertebrates and tropical marine fishes /
  Helmut Debelius, Hans A. Baensch: with the collaboration of Horst Moosleitner....
  [et al.]; translated and revised by Gero W. Fischer, Shellie E. Borrer. --
  1. English ed. 1994, 1216 p. 12 x 18 cm.
  Includes bibliographical references (7 p.) and indexes.
  ISBN 1-56465-113-4 (v. 1: Hardcover)
  1. Marine aquariums. 2. Marine aquarium fishes. 3. Marine invertebrates as pets.
  I. Debelius, Helmut. II. Baensch, Hans A.. III. Title
  SF457.1.B3513 1994
  031.3'42--dc20   93-46617
                                                                    CIP
ISBN 1-56465-113-4 (U.S.A. only)
ISBN 3-88244-051-1 (For other countries)
WL Code 16820

Distribution
USA:	Tetra Sales (Warner-Lambert-Company) Blacksburg, VA 24060
Canada:	Rolf C. Hagen Inc., 3225 Sartelon Street, Montreal, Que. H4R 1E8
Great Britain:	Rolf C. Hagen (U.K.) Limited, California Drive, Whitwood Industrial Estate, Castleford WF 10 50H, West Yorkshire
Australia:	Pets International Pty. Ltd., 5 Orchard Ind. Est., Orchard Road, P. O. Box 21, Chester Hill, N.S.W.
	Pet Pacific Pty. Ltd., Unit C, 30 Skarratt Street, Auburn N.S.W 2144 P. O. Box 398, Rydalmere N.S.W. 2116

Printed in Hongkong

Helmut Debelius   Hans A. Baensch

MARINE ATLAS

The joint aquarium care of invertebrates and
tropical marine fishes

with the collaboration of:

Dr. Horst Moosleitner
Dr. Robert A. Patzner
Dr. Manfred Schlüter
Wilhelm A. Tomey

Translated and revised by:

Gero W. Fischer, Ph.D.
Shellie E. Borrer, M.S.

MERGUS

Publishers of Natural History and Pet Books
Hans A. Baensch - Melle - Germany

Foreword

For over 40 years I have been involved with aquarium fishes and other aquatic animals. Twenty of those years include marine aquaristic experience. However, my interest was truly awakened in 1970 when I learned to snorkel and SCUBA in the reefs around the island of Mauritius in the Indian Ocean. The studies in the years thereafter culminated in my first book, "Marine Aquarist Manual," which was published by TETRA. It was translated (from German) into various languages and sold over 100,000 copies worldwide. This book was considered a standard reference for the beginning marine hobbyist after its publication in 1975.

Today, 15 years later, the marine hobby has undergone profound changes. Aquarists have done an about-face concerning the joint care of invertebrates and fishes. Previously I advocated maintaining marine aquaria with only fishes and empathized with those who wanted to care exclusively for invertebrates. However, it is particularly interesting to maintain invertebrates and fishes together, but your choices of fish species and numbers thereof are severely limited.

Particularly the publications by Helmut Debelius and Dr. Robert Patzner have helped me to realize this. Their books, "Fische als Partner Niederer Tiere" (Fishes for the Invertebrate Aquarium) and "Partnerschaft im Meer" (Partnership in the Sea), have been broadly distributed and have given further impulse to this trend. Both authors could be persuaded to take part in this book. Helmut Debelius chose the various species presented in the MARINE ATLAS and classified them according to the newest taxonomic criteria. Thanks to his underwater archive, IKAN, he and fellow underwater photographers superbly illustrated this book in a manner never seen before in comparable volumes.

With zealous dedication, the facts were assembled with the help of Dr. Robert Patzner and Dr. Horst Moosleitner. The information helps the reader plan aquaria for both invertebrates and fishes. The thoroughness of the information given for each species is exemplary. Although the MARINE ATLAS is primarily directed at the aquarist, divers interested in marine biology and scientists will also find it useful, particularly the systematic layout.

It proved impossible to present all the animals suitable for an aquarium in one volume. Therefore, we presented certain fish families, such as the surgeonfishes and wrasses, as completely as possible, since there is no complete reference of them. This means that even fishes unsuitable for an aquarium are included, but they are clearly marked as such. However, the taxonomist will enjoy their listing.

The great majority of the pictured fishes can be housed with invertebrates. The second volume of the MARINE ATLAS will contain additional invertebrates other than the crustacea and anthozoans presented here. They did not fit in one volume, despite our best intentions! Damsels were not included in this book, since all 330 species of this family were recently presented in "RIFFBARSCHE DER WELT" (Damselfishes of the World) by Dr. Gerald Allen by MERGUS. However, many will be included in the third volume, which will be solely devoted to fishes.

In the plant section, W. A. Tomey from the Netherlands presents an elaborate treatise on a great variety of *Caulerpa*. Since these higher marine algae are an almost indispensable part of the biological cycle and green decoration, the chapter on marine algae is quite extensive.

We strove to present the technological and chemical aspect of the marine hobby at today's state-of-the-art-level and to entice the reader to try new methods following the newest trends.

DEAR NORTH AMERICAN READER/HOBBYIST - this book has been translated from the original German and contains references to many products (food, equipment, lighting etc.) which are not readily available in North America. Please consult your pet dealer for equivalent brands.

Melle, September, 1994
Hans A. Baensch, publisher

Table of Contents

Foreword 4
Acknowledgments 10
Introduction 12

The Aquarium
Equipment Choices 16
Invertebrate Aquarium 18
Fish Aquarium 22
Combination Aquarium 24
The Basic Algae Scrubber 34
Technical Equipment and Systems 36
Choosing a Tank 40
The Bottom Substrate 42
Aquarium Background/Decoration 44

Water
Seawater 48
Sea Salt 48
Composition of Seawater 49
Water Treatment 50
  Reverse Osmosis 50
  Ion Exchangers 54
Making Seawater 58
Salinity 60

Technology
Water Treatment in the Aquarium 63
Biological Filtration 63
  1. Aerobic Filters 63
  2. Anaerobic Filters (Denitrification Filter/Nitrate Filter) 72
  3. Algae Scrubbers 75
External Trickle Filters 76
Filtration Media 78
  1. Synthetic Filter Materials (Plastics) 78
  2. Natural Filter Materials 86
Water Movement 88
Pumps 89
Chemical–Physical Water Treatment 92
  1. Foam Fractionation 92
  2. Ozone 96
  3. Activated Carbon 98
  4. Diatom Filter 99
  5. Ultraviolet Radiation/Sterilization Lamps 99
  6. Ion Exchangers in the Aquarium 101
  7. CO_2 Fertilization/Calcium Reactor 101
  8. Temperature Control 106

Table of Contents

Illumination 109
  Quantification of Light Intensity 109
  Light Hoods 112
  Fluorescent Tubes 112
  Required Wattage 115
  Mercury Vapor Lamps (HQL) 120
  Metal Halide Lamps (HQI) 120
  Personal Safety 122
  Actinic Blue Light 124
  Photoperiod 125

Chemistry

1. Nitrogen 126
  1.1. Nitrification (Breakdown of Ammonium and Nitrite) 126
  1.2. Denitrification/Removal of Nitrate 127
  Testing 129
2. Phosphate 132
3. Silicon (Si), Silicon Dioxide (SiO_2), Silicic Acid (H_2SiO_3) 132
4. Copper (Cu) 134
5. Trace Elements 134
6. The Buffering System in Marine Water 135
  6.1. pH 135
  6.2. Carbonate Hardness (Alkalinity, Acid Binding Capacity) . . . 139
  6.3. Calcium 141
  6.4. Calcium Water (Kalkwasser) 142
7. Redox Potential 144
8. Yellow Pigments (Gilvin) 147
Analysis (Tests) 148
Controllers 152

Setting Up / Care

Setting Up and Stocking an Aquarium 156
Acclimating Fishes 160
If Fishes do Not Eat 162
Feeding Technique 164
Foods 165
  Artemia salina 166
  Brachionus 170
  Flake Food 173
  Plant Fare 173
  Feeding Stones, Mussels 176
  Frozen Foods 176
  Freeze-Dried Foods / Liquid Foods 178
Adding Minerals, Trace Elements and Vitamins 179
Catching Your Fishes (in the Aquarium) 180
Controller Maintenance and Care 182
Maintenance Activities 184

Table of Contents

The Aquarium During Vacation 185
Practical Techniques 186
Maintenance Checklist 190
Unwanted Guests 192
Fish Diseases 198
   Ectoparasites (External Parasites) 199
   Bacterial Diseases 204
   Fungal Diseases 205
   Viral Infections 206
   Diseases from Sporozoans and Protozoans 206
   Worms and Crustacea 208
Symbols Used in the Species Descriptions 212

Algae
Systematics of Algae 214
   Cyanophyta = Cyanobacteria – Blue-Green Algae 216
   Chromophyta - Flagellates 216
   Rhodophyta - Red Algae 221
   Chlorophyta - Green Algae 223
      Caulerpaceae (by W. A. TOMEY) 246

Invertebrates
Taxonomy of Sea Anemones 326
   Actiniaria - Anemones 332
   Ceriantharia - Tube Anemones 404
   Corallimorpharia - False Corals 414
   Zoantharia - Colonial Anemones 442
Taxonomy of Crustacea 462
   Decapoda - Ten Footed Crustacea 465
      Nantantia - Shrimps 468
      Reptantia - Lobsters and Crabs 562
   Stomatopoda - Mantis Shrimps 672

Fishes
Taxonomy of the Fishes Described in this Book 681
   Perciformes - Perches 684
      Acanthuridae - Surgeonfishes, Tangs 688
      Siganidae - Rabbitfishes 772
      Zanclidae - Moorish Idols 790
      Labridae - Wrasses 797
      Scaridae - Parrotfishes 926
      Serranidae - Sea Basses and Groupers 930
      Pseudochromidae - Rock basslets 958
      Grammidae - Fairy basslets 988
      Plesiopidae - Longfins 994
      Malacanthidae - Tilefishes 1012
      Cirrhitidae - Hawkfishes 1024
      Gobiidae - Gobies 1040

Table of Contents

Microdesmidae - Dart gobies 1116
Pholidichthyidae - Convict Blennies................. 1137
Callionymidae - Dragonets, Mandarin Fishes 1140
Opistognathidae - Jawfishes 1157

Bibliography 1168
General Index 1175
Index of Scientific and Common Names 1186
Picture Credits................................... 1204
Table of Conversions 1210

Aquarium bred *Amphiprion ocellaris*

Acknowledgments

We are very grateful to the many photographers who contributed to this volume; without them this lavishly illustrated MARINE ATLAS would not have been possible. Our heart-felt thanks also go to the zoologists and biologists who have helped identify many of the photographs and aided in classifying the invertebrates and fishes:

Gerald Allen
Andreas Allspach
Daphne Fautin
Antony Gill
Manfred Grasshoff
Koos den Hartog
Douglass Hoese
Friedhelm Krupp
Rudie Kuiter

Helen Larson
Raymond Manning
Horst Moosleitner
Robert Patzner
Richard Pyle
Hajo Schmidt
Michael Türkay
David Woodland
Horst Zetzsche

We also thank Dr. Manfred Schlüter for his great contribution toward the technological and chemical section of the book.

Several manufacturers of aquarium supplies, who shall remain nameless at this point, have helped us greatly with product descriptions, photographs, and drawings; our thanks also go to them.

Most product photographs were purposely kept in black and white, since, depending on the language this book is printed in, these products may change according to systems available in those respective countries. This is much easier and economical for black and white pages. Additionally, these photos are only intended as a general reference!

As authors and publisher we wanted to remain neutral. Nevertheless, it was unavoidable in some cases to be biased in front of a certain product when it was better suited or easier to operate according to our experience.

Products which have not been mentioned in this book may be as efficient as those that we have shown. But it was impossible and beyond the scope of the book to thoroughly test all available aquarium products on the market.

Chrysiptera cyanea ♂ , WAIKIKI Aquarium, Hawaii

Introduction

The sea holds a fascinating realm of species. Our mind staggers when confronted with the sheer numbers of different known species—not to mention those yet undiscovered.

As the mother of all life on earth, the ocean still retains mystery and promise in her waters. Just as it gave forth life, it nurtured that life, allowing it to grow, adapt, and evolve into a the great diverse biotope it is today. While this same ocean is a remarkably stable environment, it still exerts pressure, expecting its inhabitants to adapt or fade away. Needless to say, species within this astoundingly rich biotope have adapted in form, color, and behavior to survive. Many of these species hold interest for both the diver and the aquarist. A truly remarkable feat is bringing an infinitesimally small part of this amazing biotope into our family living room. Of course, it is much easier said than done. But with today's technology, it is certainly an accomplishable endeavor, and one aided by the information imparted in the following pages.

A freshwater aquarist who changes to seawater, or who additionally starts a marine aquarium, can largely apply his valuable experiences in fish care to marine fishes. It is therefore recommendable for every beginner to start with freshwater before attempting to keep a marine tank.

Those who failed in the marine hobby frequently abandon the aquaristic realm altogether. He/she does not want to continue. Patience. This book allows you to make a (new) beginning.

> The marine aquarium hobby is a challenge to our aquaristic capabilities. We should only get involved in this area of the hobby once we have a firm foundation of aquaristic knowledge!

This book includes both vertebrates and invertebrates. The vertebrates—represented by the fishes—occupy a full $^2/_5$ of the book and each species is individually addressed and pictured.

Invertebrates are a bit more difficult because of the sheer diversity and different phyla represented within this encompassing term. The following phyla are included under this heading: Coelenterata, Crustacea (shrimp, lobsters, crabs), Mollusca (nudibranchs, mussels, cephalopods), Echinodermata (sea urchins, sea stars), Annelida (worms), and Porifera (sponges). Within the Coelenterata we find the class Anthozoa, or "flower animals" (sea anemones and corals) which, together with the crustacea, are partially dealt with in this book.

The algae, largely represented by *Caulerpa* in this book, and invertebrates occupy another $^2/_5$ of this volume. After all, a true marine biotope includes plants and animals (invertebrates and vertebrates). While the traditional fish community aquarium has much to offer, a biotope that includes plants, vertebrates, and invertebrates and all the resulting interrelationships is a healthy, rewarding prospect.

Note that an attempt has been made to supply familiar common names to each of the species. While many persons feel the need for such names, they are in fact usually an inaccurate source of information. When you consider that this book is written for all the English speaking world, the impossibility of supplying all the known common names becomes obvious. The only true governed consistent name is that given by the International Nomenclature Society, the scientific name. The common name is one generally derived from some aspect of the organism, whether it be markings, color, behavior, etc. Often it is simply a translation of the Latin name into English. Common names certainly have their uses, but always keep in mind their many limitations.

We hope we are able to convey sufficient information to make the extended care, and perhaps even the propagation, of various animals possible. This was, and is, our greatest concern; because only through intense reproduction of particular marine organisms will we be able to promote and maintain the marine aquarium hobby over the long run.

Spawning tubeworms (*Spirobranchus giganteus*) in an aquarium. Left ♂, right ♀.

Soft corals and organ pipe corals—they will be presented in the second volume.

Damselfishes (here *Dascyllus reticulatus*) and butterflyfishes (here *Chaetodon auriga*) will likewise be found in the following volumes.

Choice of Animals and Tank

Also refer to "Technology" and "Chemistry."

Every manufacturer will swear by his system. And they all function. The basic rules of seawater aquarium maintenance must be followed by every system, and no system can prevent errors in maintenance. The only system I question is DUPLA, and only because it does not have a protein skimmer. But that can be installed additionally!

The system which you choose should have the best and most powerful protein skimmer available on the market. In addition, I have to mention that the size of the aquarium and the type of animals determine the choice of the system. If you want to keep fishes and invertebrates together, you not only need the most powerful protein skimmer, you will also need the most powerful pumps and filters.

When you start the other way around and select the aquarium, stand, and all of the remaining equipment first, the animals then have to be chosen according to the capabilities of the equipment.

Let us assume that your 100 l aquarium has a filter that handles 1 mg of N (nitrogen) per day. This limits the carrying capacity of your aquarium; you cannot have so many animals that they produce 10 mg of N per day. If this were the case, then after 100 days you would be facing a N concentration of 9 mg/l and a tank of dead animals. If you had a 500 l aquarium instead, but with the same filtration, the N concentration would still be 1.8 mg/l.

One gram of food (ca. one teaspoon of flake food) with an assumed protein level of 50% produces (protein contains 16% N):

500 mg protein	=	80 mg N	(nitrogen)
	=	100 mg NH_4	(ammonia)
	=	250 mg NO_2	(nitrite)
	=	336 mg NO_3	(nitrate)

Therefore, one gram of flake food fed to a 100 l aquarium adds 2.5 mg nitrite/l. A teaspoon of flake food can spoil a 100 l aquarium in one day. With this "game of numbers" you can easily see that the constant food ration strongly loads the water. Only a water exchange and/or a biological filter with a sufficiently large capacity can counter this load. I do not believe that anyone has flat out told you that fish food is poison for invertebrates, especially anemones and corals!

Again: if you desire a particular combination of fishes and inverte-brates, your set-up must be large enough **from the beginning**. Since no manufacturer can or will indicate how many mg N/day the filter removes, the only alternative is to give some practical examples.

The quantity of stocked animals does not depend on the quality of the set-up, but rather on the quality of salt and tap water you use and your patience to let the set-up "mature!" That is why I have put these points at the beginning of the book.

The biomass, the weight of living animals, and their feed intake decides the type of set-up and its size. The feed intake of inverte-brates and fishes is different.

Invertebrates, especially anthozoans, require much less food than, for example, crustacea. If you want your fishes to grow, they will need to be feed up to half their body weight in food every week.

It can be easily seen that:

Invertebrates and fishes should be cared for separately by the novice. If later you want to keep both groups together, the set-up must be in tune with the requirements of the invertebrates, that is, the water quality must be exemplarly maintained despite the higher food intake of the fishes. The filter set-up must be dimensioned so that the metabolites of the fishes can be by and large processed.

Fishes constantly "beg" for food, and one is inclined to react by feeding them more, resulting in more metabolites than the filters can handle. Feed (superfluous nitrogen) can turn toxic in the water and poison the invertebrates.

But not only nitrogen, which nowadays we can break down with mature biofilters, is the reason for so many mishaps. Phosphorus can also be the culprit. It, too, is introduced into the aquarium through the feed. Phosphorus can only be removed by the growth of green algae, water exchanges, or by filtering through calcium carbonate (crushed dolomite). Your set-up should compensate for the quantity of feed required by the animals.

Only small fishes (less than 8 cm long) are stocked in invertebrate tanks. Being small, they do not add much biomass. An exception is perhaps a 10 to 15 cm long surgeonfish per 500 l of water.

Invertebrate Aquaria

The biomass of invertebrates is hard to estimate/weigh. These animals frequently consist of more than 90% water. Additionally, they require very little food, since they can almost nourish themselves with the help of light and the zooxanthellae (algae) contained in their tissue. But many anemones also need proteinaceous food to grow. These anemones require a larger filter and aquarium than, e.g., disc or colonial anemones.

Stocking of invertebrates per 100 l of water:

max. of five colonial animals (small flower corals, small leather corals, colonial anemones colonies)

or

max. of fifteen 3-5 cm disc anemones,

or

one pair of boxing shrimp (*Stenopus hispidus*), or five small cleaner shrimp such as scarlet or striped cleaner shrimp, or dancing shrimp.

Invertebrate tank with blue disc anemones, *Discosoma* sp. (*coeruleus*).

Since predators that demand high feeding rates due to their high metabolism produce a lot of waste products, they should be totally omitted from the anthozoan aquarium. Starfish, sea urchins, or larger crustacea can, under certain circumstances, be kept with fishes.

A gorgeous invertebrate tank with disc anemones and *Anthelia* sp.

Invertebrates with algae

Fish Aquaria

Fish Aquarium

Fishes often tolerate a much higher waste load than invertebrates. That is why a tank with only fishes is easier to care for than one with invertebrates.

Stocking of fishes per 100 l of water:
>one 10 cm surgeonfish
>or
>one 8 cm dottyback and two 6 cm firefish
>or
>two small blennies
>or
>one or two 5 cm gobies, one 10 cm wrasse (*Coris*), and one 6 cm cleaner wrasse.

For slender fishes, 20 to 30 cm of total length can be calculated for each 100 l of water. For deep bodied or massive fishes, only 10 cm per 100 l can be calculated.

Seahorses require a species tank. Other fishes represent too much competition for food.

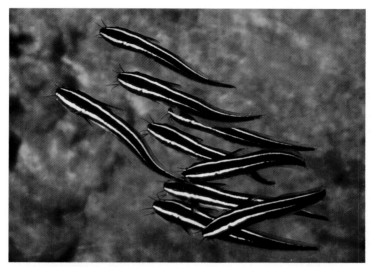

Plotosus anguillaris

Fish aquarium with the moray eel *Rhinomuraena amboinensis*

Invertebrates and Fishes

COMBINATION AQUARIUM

Stocking per 100 l of water:
one anemone with a pair of clownfishes is already plenty. And the fishes will still grow! The anemone also. If you plan on your first aquarium having invertebrates, it would be best if the tank has a volume of 150 to 200 l. One anemone, that has a diameter of 20 cm at the time of purchase, can, with correct care, reach a diameter of 30 to 40 cm in 2 years!

Amphiprion females with an initial length of 5 cm grow to be 10 to 12 cm (*Premnas, A. frenatus, A. ephippium, A. melanopus*). However, you can easily stock another 2 or 3 small fishes or shrimp with the anemone if you choose *A. ocellaris* or *A. percula* as your clownfish.

Combination aquarium

Combination aquarium with a surgeonfish, several *Amphiprion*, anemones, and sea urchins (600 liters).

Combination aquarium

Stony corals with *Pseudochromis macullochi*

Dutch "combination aquarium" with a control center and a trickle filter in the cabinet below.

Invertebrates and Fishes

Self-made aquarium cabinet with an aquarium that contains many invertebrates and
Caulerpa.

As often found: the television and aquarium next to each other. Which one is more entertaining?

This is an 800 l combination aquarium that has: one 15 cm foxface, one 12 cm *Zebrasoma flavescens*, one 10 cm *Zebrasoma veliferum*, twelve 8 cm *Chromis viridis*, two 6 cm *Amphiprion ocellaris*, one 10 cm *Chaetodon auriga*, one pair of *Stenopus hispidus*, disc and colonial anemones, sea urchins, one *Heteractis crispa* and *Caulerpa taxifolia*. This miniature reef is built with rocks and live rock and is outfitted with an undergravel filter with powerheads.

Invertebrates and Fishes

Combination aquarium. A horseshoe-shaped aquarium with cut corners, this giant set-up is in a private Dutch home. One can only dream.

Aquarium with Algae Scrubber

THE BASIC ALGAE SCRUBBER

High-tech is not only fashionable, it is necessary for heavily stocked aquaria. However, those persons who are on a budget and can limit themselves to a few animals don't have to forgo having a marine aquarium. An aquarium of a meter or larger (the bigger the better) is surely available from a freshwater aquarist, or you can purchase one for about $60.00. We do not recommend that you build one yourself, and the monetary gain of doing so is relatively small.

You will need a smaller, additional aquarium of about half the volume of the main tank to make an algae scrubber. This aquarium is illuminated with mercury vapor lamps, fluorescent tubes or whatever else is left over. Algae are grown in the second tank, that is, any type of green algae. Excellent results have been achieved with filamentous algae of the genus *Cladophora*. This algae is tough in every sense of the word. It is very tolerant and looks and feels like perlon fibers. Its distinctive advantage is the minimal light it requires (intense light is detrimental) and its uniform green growth, even on the bottom of the tank where hardly any light penetrates. *Caulerpa*, e.g., *C. taxifolia*, *C. racemosa*, etc., are also suitable, but they are more demanding in regard to light intensity and water quality.

Okay, we keep an algae aquarium into which we place a living rock which harbors many beneficial small organisms.

In the main aquarium, we work with crushed dolomite as substrate and stones as decoration. We have to have a heater. As a light source, daylight fluorescent tubes and an actinic are used. For filtering, and that is the main area of savings, one or two large foam filters, such as TETRA's Brillant pond filter, driven by an air pump are suitable. Foam filters also exist in other sizes, but you may have to special order them. The filter cartridge can be cleaned by squeezing it out about every 4 weeks, and an array of invertebrates (colonial anemones) can be fed with the contents.

The filter systems from MAXIMAL (air driven) also belong in this catagory. A protein skimmer is not necessary.

Stocking a tank of this sort commences only after the green algae in the biofilter are growing well, the foam filters are full of life (denitrification bacteria), and the smut algae growth in the principle tank has disappeared. Of course, we have to have a pump to provide circulation between the main tank and the algae tank.

An overflow pipe serves as the water return. The air-lift pump of the

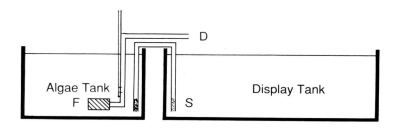

F = Brillant foam filter   D = H$_2$O discharge of the air-lift pump   S = Siphon return with a sieve

Brillant Super filter, outfitted with a foam cartridge, pumps the water. Actually, you can also set up breeding tanks for marine animals, including clownfishes, this way.

An overflow pipe serves as the water return. The air-lift pump of the Brillant Super filter, outfitted with a foam cartridge, pumps the water. Actually, you can also set up breeding tanks for marine animals, including clownfishes, this way. As mentioned at the beginning, the key to this system's success is its simplicity.

Invertebrates, namely, anemones, snails, jellyfishes, starfishes, etc., can reproduce marvelously in such tanks. The high-tech filter pumps destroy their larvae. The air driven foam filters are r..ore gentle in this regard!

An aquarium with *Caulerpa*, colonial and disc anemones and, after half a year, perhaps one pair of *Amphiprion ocellaris* or 2 to 3 colorful gobies or several small shrimp can, under certain circumstances, provide more joy than a fully stocked, expensive, high-tech aquarium which, nevertheless, is not an assured success. Once you have gathered 2 to 3 years of experience with this type of "beginner marine aquarium" and have the desire and the means to progress to the next step of powerful filter technology, protein skimming, etc., you will surely have fond remembrances of the "old" methods you previously used, and the valuable experience you gained from keeping a marine aquarium with basic methods will always be yours!

Technical Equipment and Systems		Manufacturer												
		ab	Apel	Aqua Medic	Deltec	Dupla	Eheim	Hagen	Maximal	Preis	Sander	Tetra	Tunze	Second nature
Water	Automatic refill	x	x	-	x	x	-	-	-	-		-	x	-
	Surface skimmer	x	x	-	x	x	x	-	-	-	x	-	x	-
	Protein skimmer	x	x	x	x	(-)	-	-	x	x	●	-	●	-
	Reverse osmosis	-	x	ROWA	-	-	-	-	-	-	-	-	-	x
Filter Technology	Undergravel filter	x	-	-	-	-	x	x	-	●	-	-	-	-
	High speed filter	-	x	x	x	x	x	x	-	x	-	-	x	-
	Trickle filter	x	x	x	x	●	-	x	x	(-)	x	-	x	x
	Nitrate filter	-	x	x	●	(-)	(x)	(x)	(x)	(x)	-	(x)	●	-
	Centrifugal pumps	x	x	-	x	x	x	x	(-)	x	x	-	x	-
	Air-driven filter	-	-	-	-	-	-	-	●	-	-	●	-	-
Chemistry and Technology	Automatic compact control mechanism	x	x	-	-	x	-	-	-	-	x	-	x	-
	CO$_2$ - dosage based on pH	x	x	-	x	x	-	-	-	x	x	-	x	-
	Ozone - dosage based on redox	x	x	-	x	x	-	-	-	x	x	-	x	-
	Filtered ozone-air-source	-	x	-	-	-	-	-	-	-	x	-	-	-
	Filter to add Ca (calcium reactor)	x	-	-	-	-	x	x	-	-	-	-	x	-
	Ozonizer	x	x	-	x	-	-	-	-	x	●	-	x	-
	UV	x	-	-	-	-	-	-	-	-	-	-	-	●

x = present
● = primary feature of the system
(x) = present (to be used with reservations)
- = not present
(-) = omitted (system design)

Equipment:

Glass tank (silicon-sealed)
Heater with thermostat
Thermometer
Filter
Lighting—either metal halide lights (150 W/80 cm aquarium length) or sufficient fluorescent tubes (1 tube per 10 cm of aquarium width)

Decoration:

Bottom substrate 5 to 8 cm deep; for marine anemones at least 10 cm deep; hiding places for fishes/crustacea, etc., of porous clay and live rock, dolomite rocks, calcarous algae rocks.

Maintenance:

Hydrometer
Nitrite test kit
pH test kit
KH test kit

Undergravel filter with crushed red calcareous algae as substrate.

Set-Up

NECESSITIES

Equipment:

Trickle filter and/or an under-gravel filter

Foam fractionator

Quarantine tank with thermostat controlled heater and a rapid flow filter (EHEIM®, FLUVAL®, or other)

Actinic light (can remain on 24 hr)

Timer(s)

Reverse osmosis equipment when the nitrates in the tap water exceed 10 mg/l

pH controller to automatically add CO_2

CO_2-cylinder with pressure reducer and fine-adjustment valve

Decoration:

Hiding places, even in the quarantine tank (flowerpot)

Maintenance:

Nitrate test kit (Lamotte®, TETRA®, or other)

pH meter

Phosphate test kit

Cu test kit (if the invertebrates are doing poorly)

OPTIONS

Equipment:

Tank for algae culture

A pump for water turnover and a thermostat controlled heater

An illuminated tank for a *Brachionus* culture

Aeration (membrane pump)

Power protein skimmer

UV sterilizer for algae blooms and disease

Desalinization set-up

3-chamber cannister filter (FLUVAL) for: carbon, floss, dolomite, and addition of CO_2. It should be controlled by a timer to preclude CO_2 from being added at night.

Ozonizer

Redox meter

Decoration:

Decorative background

Maintenance:

Conductivity meter

Automatic water refill

ADDITIONAL NECESSITIES:

Vibrator pump

Hoses for water exchange

Air tubing (preferably silicon!)

T's and air valves

Bottle brushes to clean the hoses

Plant forceps

H_2O_2 (hydrogen peroxide) to disinfect

Artemia and culture equipment

At least two 10 l buckets

Water container to prepare seawater

Aeration set-up with suitable diffusers

Tweezers

Magnifying lens, ∞ 3 and ∞ 10

A 50 to 60 cm long, 15 mm Ø hose to siphon off feed remains and to feed specific animals, e.g., with TetraTips.

2 nets

Glass beaker or transparent plastic container

One 2 l measuring cup (kitchen) to dilute medications or liquid foods

Glass cleaner with a stainless steel blade or a strong magnet cleaner

Water faucet with cold and hot water if possible (no copper piping)

Drain (floor drain if house is still in its planning stages!)

Several electrical outlets beside or behind the aquarium stand; preferably above the water line.

JUST IN CASE:

1 cannister filter

1 heater

1 membrane pump

Automatic feeder for vacation

Timer(s)

Tools

Medicines

Various foods

Marine salt

Teflon tape to seal pipe joints

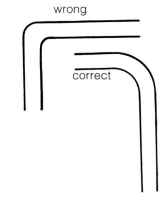

Pipes should always be angled in a large radius to avoid performance losses (pressure and quantity) of the pump

Types of Aquaria

Actually, there are only three types of aquaria to choose from:

1. Silicon Sealed Glass Tanks

The edges of the aquarium may be protected with plastic stripes.
Two types exist. In the simpler type the panes are bluntly glued together (a).
In my opinion the second method (b) is better because it is more durable. The panes are adhered "by the edge." The thicker silicone joint protects the edge to a certain extent.
The color of the silicon can be gray, clear, or brown. Black is also very attractive.

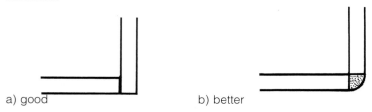

a) good   b) better

In open aquaria which are illuminated with metal halide lamps from above, the top edge of the glass pane to the water level is visible. This part of the glass can become coated with unsightly calcium scale or salt creep. The 5 to 8 cm edge is easily covered with a strip of mirrored glass or other opaque material.

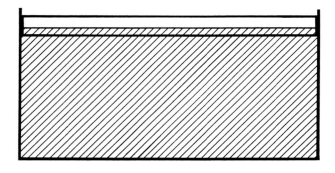

2. Acrylic (Plexiglass) Aquaria

This plastic has been developed to such an extent that it can also be used for marine aquaria. Acrylic tanks are more transparent, relatively scratch resistant, lightweight, and smooth-surfaced. Hardly any algae can adhere to their smooth surface.

3. As Part of a Complete Set-up

Most marine aquaria are bought as complete set-ups with a lower cabinet and light hood. This has many advantages, since filtration/heater cables, lamps (usually fluorescent tubes), water regulators, and the CO_2 bottle with connectors are already included and hooked up. Besides the costs, such a complete set-up is ideal.

You have the choice between many set-ups which are put together by your dealer. I cannot, and do not want to, specify the various systems.

Personally, I prefer a set-up that you yourself can put together consisting of an undergravel filter, two powerheads, and an external trickle filter beside the aquarium. This combination simply evolved when I converted my 2 m tank from freshwater to seawater.

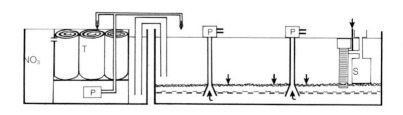

S = Protein skimmer   P = Pumps
NO_3 = Nitrate filter   T = Trickle filter (DLS)

Bottom Substrate

Depth of the Bottom Substrate

Suggestions from various companies on optimal depth of the substrate range from "nothing on the bottom" (DUPLA), through 3 to 5 cm (most other companies), to a 5 to 8 cm layer above the undergravel filter. Even 10 cm are often needed to allow tube and other larger anemones to anchor their foot properly in the substrate.

Particle Size

Fine sand, or even sand from the beach, is unsuitable in most cases. Fine sand is only appropriate for special "sand bank marine tanks" where organisms such as lugworms are kept. The disadvantage of fine sand is the generation of anaerobic (low oxygen) zones. Focal points of putrefaction quickly develop and there is no recourse other than to completely clean the aquarium.

A particle size of 5 to 8 mm for dolomite or crushed puffed clay is the best. Do not use the round spheres from the flower shop! Cover the coarse layer with a 1 to 3 cm layer of finer crushed dolomite (2 to 4 mm particle size).

Types of substrate	
Suitable	Unsuitable
Crushed marble	Quartz gravel (binds iron)
Crushed dolomite (pure calcium carbonate!)	Crushed basalt (binds iron)
Crushed puffed clay (calcium-free!)	Fine beach sand
Granite	Sand
Pebbles	Gravel
Crushed oyster shells	Crushed coral (protected)
Crushed calcareous algae	

The following comments are included for aquarists who do not live in Germany and use crushed coral as substrate. For Germany, crushed coral can only be imported with CITES certification, since grains of coral sand are "parts of protected animals."

Crushed shell or coral are conditionally suitable. Crushed coral with protein remnants of dead animals adhering to it is unsuitable; so far, it is the most frequent source of nitrite poisoning and dead animals during the "initial phases" of a beginner's tank. **If you insist on using crushed coral as substrate, it must be tested before you use it.** Believe me! If you received as many telephone calls from marine aquarists as I have, you would underline the previous lines three times (H.B.). Okay, coral slag is only bought once a sample produces no nitrite in the water after 1 week. Take a couple of handfuls and throw them into a bucket with marine water. After 8 days the nitrite content of this water is measured. It must be 0 (zero!). Only after these steps can the shell/coral slag be considered safe.

If there is the smallest trace of NO_2 present, we recommend that you do not use it. Those who insist on coral slag clean the material with sodium hydroxide (how do you dispose of it?). This caustic solution totally decomposes the protein contained in the material. A 5% solution (caution, corrosive!) is poured over the coral slag and stirred several times over the course of 2 to 3 weeks. Afterwards it must be rinsed everyday for 1 week with new water. Let it stand for one week in freshwater, and then measure the pH and nitrite again. The pH should be 7 to 7.5 (like the tap water). If the pH is above 8.5, the material/water still contains sodium hydroxide. The NO_2 value must be 0; otherwise, there is still protein in the slag.

> One part sodium hydroxide (40%) is mixed with 7 parts of water to make a 5% basic solution.

You can also use H_2O_2 (hydrogen peroxide) to clean the slag. Likewise, rinse well afterwards. This is an ecologically friendlier method because only oxygen, water, and ammonium (from the protein) remain.

A colorful bottom substrate of crushed puffed clay covered with 2 to 3 cm of crushed dolomite.

Decor

The back pane of the aquarium is only used for decorative purposes. The items placed there are not for the benefit of the animals, and the choice thereof only depends on the taste of the aquarist. The simplest decor is blue cardboard glued onto the outside of the glass. Those who want a more beautiful artistic scene will build an interior background themselves or order one made to the exact dimensions of the tank.
I have seen such backgrounds with dolomite pieces glued on. These are manufactured for lobster tanks in restaurants. Truly optically pleasing—as long as the background is clean and not covered with algae. But even then it looks better than an algae-covered glass pane. Oyster shells can also serve as a background when they are glued to the back pane (clean the shells well, see "The Bottom Substrate" on pp. 42 f.). I do not recommend slate plates if they are not glued directly onto the back wall with silicon.

The background decor should either be an acrylic plate on which the decorative material is glued or printed cardboard placed outside.
If you choose to place the decorated pane inside the aquarium, it must be firmly fastened to the back wall so small fishes do not become trapped. Worms, snails, sponges, and other animals easily become trapped behind it—an invisible source of putrefaction develops. If possible, keep even the water from passing between the back pane and the decorative wall by sealing it with silicon!
Most hobbyists totally waive the background decoration. They would rather stack live rock and/or pieces of dolomite until the rock wall almost reaches the surface. With three different colors (colored with iron), which makes this type of decor simple and relatively reasonably priced. The decor for a 500 l tank weighs approximately 100 kg. Coral skeletons, which are no longer used (nor should they be), cost many times more. Dolomite rocks weigh 2 to 3 times as much, increasing the probability that the bottom pane breaks from the weight! Please put your tank on a 1 cm thick plate of Styrofoam (can be found at hobby or hardware stores—if not available at a pet store).
Beautiful results are possible; a sample can be seen on page 279.

Dolomite rock

Calcareous algae rocks

Rocks

Pebbles

Live rocks with red calcareous algae; the shrimp are *Lysmata amboinensis*

Decor

This should not be done: pieces of coral being sold at a market (Bahamas).

Decorative coral skeletons are an integral part of the fascination and beauty of marine aquariums, and form the setting in which marine fish are displayed in all their amazing forms and colors. However, the use of coral skeletons depletes our natural resources and threatens the vitality of coral reef habitats. Tetra Coral Creations offer several practical advantages over coral skeletons, and help preserve reef habitats by eliminating the need to collect coral skeletons.

Coral Creations are ten exotic and magnificent coral replications, available in "bleached" or "natural" form, reproduced with 100% accuracy in color and detail. Each natural piece is hand-crafted to guarantee an absolutely unique finish and appearance. They are fish and invertebrate safe, more durable, easier to clean, and more impervious to medication absorption than coral skeletons.

Coral Creations are designed to be aquarium centerpieces, and are the focal point for the grace, splendor, and intrigue of the marine aquarium. Their dramatic elegance is enhanced by creating a stunning aquascape of myriad shapes and hues, a synergy that takes on a life of its own in harmony with fish and invertebrates.

Pictures on the facing page (TETRA CORAL CREATIONS):

A, B	Large brain coral (*Leptoria phrygia*): nose, natural, and bleached
C, D	Mini brain coral (*Diploria strigosa*): natural and bleached
E, F	Small brain coral (*Platygyra* sp.): natural and bleached
G	Elkhorn (*Acropora palmata*): bleached
H, I	Pillar coral (*Dendrogyra cylindricus*): 12", bleached and natural
J, K, L	Pillar coral, 6" natural, 18" bleached and natural
M, N	Open brain coral (*Goniastrea* sp.): $1/2$ helmet, natural and bleached
O, P	Flat brain coral (*Diploria* sp.): natural and bleached
Q, R	Plate coral (*Montipora* sp.): natural and bleached

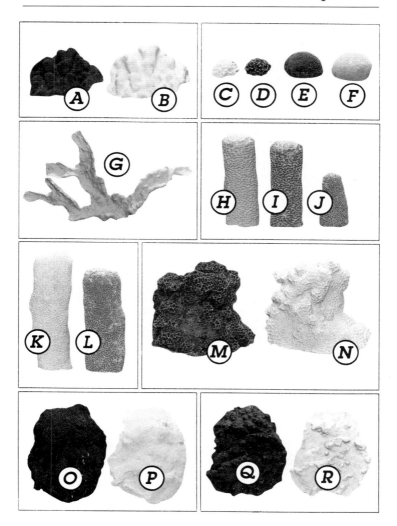

Seawater, Salt

SEAWATER (Chemical, Physical, and Biological Properties)

Marine water contains approximately 34 g of soluble salts per liter. This high salt content changes the physical and chemical characteristics of water. Seawater has a lower freezing point, a higher boiling point, and is heavier than freshwater. This difference in weight (specific gravity) can be used to determine the salinity. The salts also make seawater very corrosive. This is very important for all of the aquarium equipment. From this standpoint, metal items do not belong in the marine aquarium. Even stainless steel corrodes in time (aquarium frames). Only titanium can—e.g., in chillers and, nowadays, also in heaters—be used. Copper pipes or other copper containing materials, for example, bronze or brass, are especially detrimental.

Copper and its alloys leach poisonous Cu^{++} ions which have a deadly effect on invertebrates, even in low concentrations. Water lines or hot water heaters with an affluent or effluent line made of copper are a sure source of failure in marine animal husbandry (especially with invertebrates). Modern aquaria, and the equipment thereof, are made only of glass and plastic. These materials are absolutely inert in the face of corrosion. However, some plastics (PVC = polyvinylchloride) should not be used because of the plasticizers contained therein.

Since hardly any aquarist has a source of natural seawater of sufficient purity, synthetic seawater has to be made from its components. To make suitable seawater, two conditions have to be met: high quality synthetic sea salt and perfect water.

SEA SALT

Seawater is not composed of just table salt (sodium chloride). There are a great number of different salts dissolved therein; many are only present in trace amounts. When seawater is studied with sensitive analytical methods, nearly all the elements existing on earth can be found.

Marine water is a complex chemical compound. Not all of the components obtained by evaporating natural seawater will redissolve when water is added. The resulting solution is only conditionally suitable as aquarium water. The available salt mixes found in aquarium stores, e.g., Instant Ocean, Tropic Marine etc. contain all the necessary salts for plant and animal growth in a pure and easily soluble form. Good marine salt is initially recognized by its total solubility. No yellowish sediment should be visible after approximately 5 to 8 hr. There are differences in quality and price of synthetic sea salts. Only use marine salts that your store uses in its exhibition aquaria.

Composition of seawater

Macro Elements (mg/l)

Chlorine	Cl	18 880	
Sodium	Na	10 770	
Magnesium	Mg	1 290	
Sulphur	S	884	
Calcium	Ca	412,1	
Potassium	K	399	
Bromine	Br	67,3	
Carbon	C	28	(as HCO_3^-, CO_3^{2-}, CO_2)
Nitrogen	N	15	(as NH_4^+, NO_2^-, N_2, NO_3^-)
Strontium	Sr	7,9	
Boron	B	4,5	
Silicon	Si	2	
Fluorine	F	1,3	

Trace Elements (µg/l)

Lithium	Li	180	Beryllium	Be	0,0056
Rubidium	Rb	120	Gold	Au	0,004
Iodine	I	60	Rhenium	Re	0,004
Phosphorus	P	60	Lanthanum	La	0,003
Molybdenum	Mo	10	Neodymium	Nd	0,003
Zinc	Zn	4,9	Tantalum	Ta	0,003
Argon	Ar	4,3	Yttrium	Y	0,0013
Arsenic	As	3,7	Cerium	Ce	0,001
Uranium	U	3,2	Dysprosium	Dy	0,0009
Vanadium	V	2,5	Erbium	Er	0,0008
Aluminum	Al	2	Ytterbium	Yb	0,0008
Barium	Ba	2	Gadolinium	Gd	0,0007
Iron	Fe	2	Praseodymium	Pr	0,0006
Nickel	Ni	1,7	Scandium	Sc	0,0006
Titanium	Ti	1	Holmium	Ho	0,0002
Copper	Cu	0,5	Lutetium	Lu	0,0002
Cesium	Cs	0,4	Thorium	Th	0,0002
Chromium	Cr	0,3	Indium	In	0,0001
Antimony	Sb	0,24	Terbium	Tb	0,0001
Manganese	Mn	0,2	Samarium	Sm	0,00005
Krypton	Kr	0,2	Europium	Eu	0,00001
Selenium	Se	0,2	Radium	Ra	0,00000007
Neon	Ne	0,12	Protactinium	Pa	0,00000005
Cadmium	Cd	0,1	Radon	Rn	0,000000000006
Wolfram	W	0,1			
Cobalt	Co	0,05	Additionally, in even smaller concentrations		
Germanium	Ge	0,05			
Xenon	Xe	0,05			
Silver	Ag	0,04	Technetium	Tc	
Gallium	Ga	0,03	Ruthenium	Ru	
Lead	Pb	0,03	Rhodium	Rh	
Zirconium	Zr	0,03	Palladium	Pd	
Bismuth	Bi	0,02	Osmium	Os	
Mercury	Hg	0,02	Iridium	Ir	
Niobium	Nb	0,01	Platinum	Pt	
Thallium	Tl	0,01	Astatine	At	
Thorium	Th	0,01	Francium	Fr	
Tin	Sn	0,01	Actinium	Ac	
Hafnium	Hf	0,007			
Helium	He	0,0068			

Water Treatment, Reverse Osmosis

TAP WATER

In older literature dealing with marine aquaria, tap water was not considered very important. When the salt mix was correct, the make-up of the water was all right. I myself (H.B.) wrote "tap water and sea salt = seawater" in "Kleine Seewasserpraxis" (1974). This can no longer be said, largely because of pollutants now found in the ground water. Higher nitrate, pesticide (e.g., atrazine), phosphate, and silicic acid levels, among others, have contributed to the significant deterioration of our tap water over the last 15 years. Many hobbyists have to treat their tap water before they can use it in an aquarium. Because of the actuality of the subject, it is covered in detail in the following. Unpolluted tap water with a high carbonate hardness (KH) is best for marine aquaria.

Treating Tap Water

Until recently, only ion exchangers were used for this purpose. In these apparatus, unwanted salts are adsorbed onto the surface of artificial resin spheres and removed from the water in this manner. Unfortunately, these units have many disadvantages. Not only do they have to be regenerated regularly with chemicals (hydrochloric acid and sodium hydroxide), but they also let pesticides and uncharged substances pass through unhampered. In addition, if left unused for a prolonged period of time, they inoculate the aquarium water with unwanted bacteria. Alternative treatments are being developed for home use, and ion exchangers are being replaced.

Reverse Osmosis

A true alternative to these ion exchangers is offered by reverse osmosis, which is now available for home aquarists. Reverse osmosis technology, although known for years, was previously only used in very large set-ups, particularly to desalinate seawater. Due to advances in membrane materials, it has become possible to build compact units which can be operated at normal tap water pressures.

Reverse osmosis is a procedure in which not only salts are removed from the water (total desalination), but also uncharged substances, e.g., pesticides, bacteria, viruses, and fungi spores.

The heart of a reverse osmosis unit is the semipermeable membrane. This membrane has such small pores that only water can pass. Solutes are retained. To achieve this, the water is passed through the membrane under pressure. For small set-ups, 3 to 5 kg/cm^2 (43 to 71 lb/in^2) are sufficient. These values correspond to household pressures; large set-ups are operated at 10 to 15 kg/cm^2.

The pressure must exceed the osmotic pressure of the water—hence the name. The osmotic pressure of the solution depends on its salinity. The higher the salt content, the higher the osmotic pressure that has to be overcome for reverse osmosis. Therefore, marine desalination plants are operated at pressures of 60 to 70 kg/cm².

Reverse osmosis membranes are made of synthetic materials, e.g., polyamide/polysulfone. To achieve a larger surface within a small volume, the membrane is wound into a spiral, creating a module.

This module has an entrance for tap water and two drains, one for the resulting purified water (permeate) and one for the concentrate. The concentrate contains all the solutes that could not pass through the membrane. In small set-ups, the relation of permeate to concentrate is 1:4. Out of 5 liters of tap water, one liter of purified water is obtained. The remainder is waste. That is the disadvantage of this type of set-up. This unfavorable relationship has to be maintained because calcium deposits which block the membrane can occur if the solution becomes more concentrated. Large set-ups that first remove calcium from the water (water softening) can achieve an efficiency ratio of up to 9:1. In other words, only 10% of the water is waste.

Chlorine and turbidity-causing substances can also harm the membrane. Chlorine damages the membrane when present in concentrations above 0.1 ppm (parts per million = mg/l). Although this value is rarely exceeded in public water supplies, it can have fatal conse-

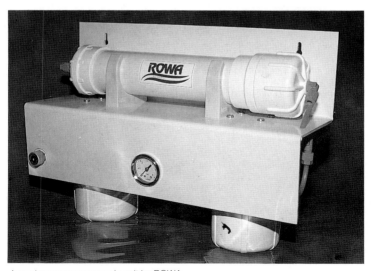

A modern reverse osmosis unit by ROWA

Water Treatment

quences. It is therefore necessary to have an activated carbon prefilter to remove the chlorine from the water. A microfilter with a 5 μm sized pore will also be needed, since public water, especially after cleaning activities, may contain turbidity-causing substances.

These filters are usually part of good set-ups. Some commercial reverse osmosis set-ups try to cut costs by omitting the charcoal filter, but if your water supply contains chlorine, your equipment should have the filter. If there is also a cleaning valve, the membrane has a life expectancy of 3 to 7 years, after which a new membrane will have to be bought. Since membranes are quite expensive (about $1/2$ the cost of the entire set-up, they should be conscientiously maintained. This is done by keeping the filter clean (charcoal filter and prefilter) and, more importantly, moist—or better yet, wet. If it has dried up once because of negligence, it turns brittle, permeable, and then ineffective. You gain nothing by using a defective membrane—it will only function as a coarse sieve.

Safety and efficiency of the equipment should be tested every 3 months. To do this, you compare the tap water with the effluent that has passed through the reverse osmosis set-up. The effluent should have a conductivity of only 30 to 70 μS/cm. The total hardness should not be above 1-2° dGH; dKH must be 0. If these values are exceeded, the membrane is defective or installed incorrectly! Carbonate hardness is easily determined, e.g., with TetraTest KH.

A carbon prefilter is extremely important—be sure to replace the carbon once a month. This cannot be repeated often enough.

A variety of membranes are available from different manufacturers. They are made of various synthetic materials:

A: Cellulose triacetate (old method)

B: Polyamide/Polysulfone (new method), also called a TFC membrane (Thin Film Composite).

Membranes of material B have a longer life expectancy. Therefore, they are the preferred choice. Set-ups that do not include information on the type and nature of the membrane should not be purchased. Some set-ups (type A) must be continuously used because cellulose triacetate is broken down by bacteria under anaerobic conditions that result when the water supply is turned off. This is impractical for the normal aquarist who only needs water for the monthly water exchange. As long as the water cannot be collected and stored, it is poured down the drain. Nevertheless, cellulose triacetate membranes are not sensitive to chlorine.

The ratio of waste water to purified water can be improved if the water is first passed though a cation exchanger (softening filter).

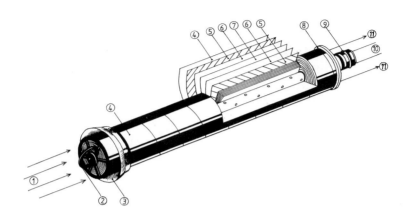

Cross-section through a reverse osmosis module

1. Water source (tap water)
2. Seal
3. Polyethylene seal
4. Vinyl casing
5. Channel for tap water
6. Membranes
7. Channel for treated water
8. Centering ring
9. O-ring
10. Permeate (treated water)
11. Concentrate (waste water)

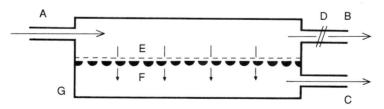

A. Tap water entrance (3-9 kg/cm²)
B. Concentrate (drain)
C. Permeate (treated water)
D. One-way valve
E. Semi-permeable membrane
F. Support structure
G. Pressure-resistant housing

53

Water Treatment

Ion Exchangers

Ion exchangers are used to prepare the tap water prior to its use in an aquarium as well as for the direct maintenance of the aquarium water. Ion exchangers consist of small artificial resin spheres. Either large numbers of acid groups (cation exchanger) or basic groups (anion exchanger) are bound to the resin structure. The ions dissolved in the water are held at these binding sites. In exchange, the ions bound to the resin are released—ion exchange!

Once a large part of the groups bound on the resin is exchanged, the resin is exhausted and must be regenerated. This is achieved by passing high concentrations of the ions originally bound at the resin through the exchanger (e.g., OH^- as sodium hydroxide [NaOH]). Due to this surplus, the ions removed from the water (nitrate, sulfate, phosphate, etc.) are released and the resin returns to its original state.

Neutral Ion Exchanger

The neutral ion exchanger only retains nitrate (NO_3) and, in exchange, releases chlorine (Cl). Sodium chloride (common table salt) makes up ca. 80% of the salts found in seawater. If the drinking water contains 50 mg NO_3/l, e.g., as found in Cologne, 14000 mg of Cl are "used up" for a 500 l tank. That is 14 g of chlorine or 3 teaspoons of salt. These quantities are insignificant in a marine aquarium. The exchange resin is available in the trade. Because of noxious side effects, neutral ion exchangers canot be used in municipal water supplies in Germany. It follows that we should also question their use in the aquarium.

Cation Exchanger

This filter exchanges calcium in tap water with sodium. The resins in this exchanger can be regenerated with table salt and are by far not as dangerous as total deionizers. The results obtained using such equipment in tandem with reverse osmosis are significantly more positive. The relationship between purified water and waste water is about 1:1.

At the beginning we said that a reverse osmosis set-up does not need to be in constant use. Those systems that need to be in constant use should not be purchased—except those to be used for a drinking or laboratory water supply.

Reverse osmosis equipment used in the aquarium hobby must withstand a limited use of one to two days a month—enough for the water exchange. Each month $1/4$ of the volume is exchanged and an additional $1/4$ must be replenished due to evaporation.

As environmentally conscious nature lovers, we should not permit ourselves the luxury of wasting precious drinking water: Germany uses over 1 million m^3 of water every day just for the WC! That is almost 2

Edertal reservoirs (in northern Hessen) each year. This dam holds 202 million m³ of water.

That is why we install a device in our toilet tanks to save up to 70% of the water for "little business." In comparison, waste water resulting from reverse osmosis hardly plays a significant role.

Recharging deionizers or mixed deionization set-ups is significantly more environmentally taxing when not left to specialized companies—which is actually required by law.

Laboratories demand a purity below 1 µS/cm. Equipment that can attain such high efficiency does not cost less than $1,500.

How does an Ion Exchanger Function?

The heart of the ion exchanger is the small spheres of resin. They have free binding sites on their surface. Depending on the type of resin, you can differentiate between cation exchangers and anion exchangers. The first bind positively charged ions; the latter bind negatively charged ions. Their function will be explained based on the Lewatit S 10061 cation exchanger.

Lewatit S 10061 is initially activated with hydrochloric acid, and the free binding sites are filled with hydrogen ions (H^+).

Now it is ready to be used.

When the resin is brought in contact with water which contains positively charged ions, they are held at the binding sites. In exchange the previously bound H^+ ions go into solution. The H^+ ions are displaced because they have a lower affinity to the resin than the other cations. The bond to the resin is loose and reversible. Only as long as sufficient binding sites are occupied with H^+ ions are the other ions retained. Once the majority of H^+ ions have been displaced from their binding sites, the resin must be regenerated.

Regeneration is accomplished with hydrochloric acid (HCl), which contains large quantities of free H^+ ions. Due to this high concentration, the cations from the water are displaced from their binding sites by the hydrogen ions. The resin is again ready to be used.

The only cations found in the treated water are H^+ ions; however, the dissolved anions were not removed.

The compounds created in this ion exchanger are strong acids, e.g., HCl (hydrochloric acid), HNO_3 (nitric acid), and H_2SO_4 (sulfuric acid). Lewatit S 10061, therefore, is also called a strong acidic cation exchanger.

The anions that remain in the water can be removed with the strong basic ion exchanger MP 62. However, MP 62 is activated with sodium hydroxide, not hydrochloric acid. The ions (e.g., Cl^-, NO_3^-, SO_4^{2-}) are exchanged for OH^- ions. These react with the previously released H^+ ions to form H_2O (water). Water treated in this manner hardly contains any ions.

Water Treatment

REGENERATION WITH HYDROCHLORIC ACID (HCL)

Lewatit S 10061 ion exchanger

active

loaded

exhausted

regenerated

Treating the Water Outside the Aquarium

If ion exchangers are the method of choice, only total deionization will simultaneously remove nitrate, phosphate, silicic acid, calcium, etc., from tap water. The water is routed through a cation exchanger and an anion exchanger. Modern apparatus unite both in one column. Lewatit S 10061 is used as the cation exchanger. When it is exhausted, it must be regenerated with hydrochloric acid. Lewatit MP 62 is used to remove anions. This resin is regenerated with sodium hydroxide. Bayer also makes a resin for total deionization columns called M 600. Effluent from these columns is practically "distilled"; deionized water is produced. This water can be used to make seawater and to replace evaporated water. Regeneration should not be done by aquarists at home, since they cannot dispose of the hydrochloric acid and sodium hydroxide properly (pollutants). Because of this necessity and the fact that uncharged substances (pesticides!) are not removed, ion exchangers are clearly inferior to reverse osmosis apparatus for total desalination in the aquarium hobby.

Summary

If the tap water needs

Only Nitrate (NO_3) Removed:

Use an ion exchanger which can be regenerated with table salt. The exchanger retains nitrate while releasing chloride. While this method is suitable for marine aquaria, it is not applicable for human drinking water, since excessive chloride is not healthy.

Complete Desalination and Toxins Removed:

A reverse osmosis set-up with a membrane of Polyamide/Polysulfone (TFC) with a carbon prefilter is needed (the carbon is replaced at least every 3 months).

The Amount of Waste Water Reduced:

Reverse osmosis is proceeded by a "softening filter." That is, a cation exchanger that binds calcium and in turn releases sodium. Many resins can be regenerated with table salt.

Now, however, we still need a pump to deliver the 3-4 kg/cm^2 of pressure needed for reverse osmosis. Plainly said, such equipment only makes sense for the professional fish breeder or fish importer.

Water Treatment

Total deionization units (mixed substrate ion exchangers) are only used when the columns are regenerated by specialized companies. Hydrochloric acid and sodium hydroxide are passsed through tne column in a ratio that in the end neutralizes them. Simply put, hydrochloric acid and sodium hydroxide combine to form table salt and water.

Making Seawater

Approximately 3.4 kg of synthetic sea salt are needed to prepare 100 l of seawater. When the aquarium is filled for the first time, the salt can be mixed therein—a separate container will be needed later (aquarium or plastic container). The water has to be aerated at least one day prior to stocking the aquarium, but several days, or even one to two weeks, are better. The best policy is to immediately refill the reservoir with new seawater after every water exchange. Then prepared seawater is always available.

Illuminating (sun) the newly made marine water is advantageous for a faster maturation process. The microbial fauna responsible for maturing the water develops significantly faster with light than in the dark. Therefore, reserve a site on a balcony or terrace for the seawater reservoir. If a dark location is selected (basement, broom closet), one to three fluorescent tubes are needed, depending on the size of the container. Do-it-yourselfers are needed here. Surely your aquarium store will also make a set-up for you. Water containers can be found in hardware stores, garden centers (rain barrel or similar), or laboratory supply stores (graduated). For larger tanks, a 1 m³ oil tank is suitable, which, of course, will need to be painstakingly cleaned if it has previously held oil. One drop of oil can pollute one thousand liters of water.

for 25 l water =   650 ml salt
for 50 l water = 1300 ml salt
for 100 l water = 2600 ml salt
or
for 100 l water = 3.25 kg salt

Measuring cup = 1 liter salt = 1250 g

WATER LIVES (with the correct salt)

Newly mixed seawater is detrimental to sensitive invertebrates and fishes. For the 10% per month minimum water exchange, seawater made from a well known marine salt needs to have been aerated and heated (to about 20°C) for one to two weeks prior to its use. Illumination can, but need not, be provided.

When starting a new aquarium, the water should be filtered and maintained at about 20°C for six to eight weeks before animals are introduced. Some salts need up to 3 months. First, *Nitrobacter* and *Nitrosomonas* bacteria need to multiply so they can metabolize nitrogen that comes from the feed and the resulting feces/urine. Newly made mixes are often so aggressive that months may be needed to establish a healthy bacterial colony. The water needs to age long enough to diminish the harshness of the chemical substances! Live rock and hardy beginner animals are usually stocked much too soon. Using a good, reputable salt can significantly increase your probability of successfully maintaining a salt water aquarium and can decrease the cycling time you must allow a new filter. Quite a few failures are not from poor tap water quality or the absence of an expensive filter (nitrate filter), but may be due to the brand of salt used.

As not all water is equal in quality, neither are brands of artificial salt mixes. A good salt will not cause anemones to slime—they remain open—or even open up if they were previously closed. They settle within hours and do not wander around. The fish dart around as if in the sea. This must be seen once. Experiment until you find a good sea salt, or consult your local pet store.

Some aquarists are surprised that nitrite and/or SiO_2 (silicon dioxide) are still found in tap water after reverse osmosis. The most commonly used salt in Germany contains these substances! SCHMIDT, Lünen, one of the pioneers in the marine aquarium hobby, tested various salts and found that Tropic Marine salt is one of the chemically purest and best suited salts for the marine hobby. The Bochum Seawater Aquarium uses HW sea salt. A definite judgement of the different sea salts cannot be given here. Even TETRA has been experimenting for several years with good success on a revolutionary salt mix—I have tried it myself. Every sea salt mix, even those produced by the same manufacturer, is somewhat different. Therefore, use the best brands your local fish store carries. He demonstrates best which brand he trusts by keeping well maintained aquaria.

Salt

SALINITY

To determine the salinity of marine water, the specific gravity or the conductivity of the water is measured.

Specific Gravity

Since seawater is heavier than freshwater, it is the salt that increases its specific gravity. Specific gravity can be measured with a hydrometer. This measuring device is placed in the water where it will sink to a particular level, depending on the salinity. The specific gravity can be directly read off a scale found on the stem of the hydrometer. Specific gravity is also temperature dependent (see table). At 25°C the specific gravity of the marine aquarium should be between 1.022 (normal) and 1.025 (Red Sea).

The precision of a good hydrometer is sufficient for aquaristic needs.

Specific gravity is the most common measurement taken by aquarists to determine salinity. Salinity of marine water can be determined much more exactly by measuring electrical conductivity. A hydrometer should always be within reach, even when a conductivity meter is used. Buy the largest hydrometer you can find. Small, slender hydrometers are frequently imprecise.

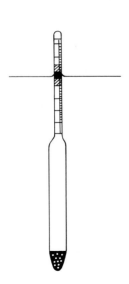

Floating hydrometer

Hydromarine (HAGEN)

Salinity of seawater in parts per thousand, measured by conductivity and specific gravity (at 25°C).			
Salt content ‰	Conductivity (mS/cm)	Specific gravity	
17.20	24	1.0110 **	
20.40	30	1.0148	
21.58	32	1.0157	
23.14	34	1.0169	
24.71	36	1.0181	
26.29	38	1.0193	
27.88	40	1.0205	
29.48	42	1.0218	
30.29	43	1.0224*	Favorable range for
31.10	44	1.0230*	the marine aquarium
31.91	45	1.0236*	
32.73	46	1.0242*	
33.45	47	1.0248*	Red Sea
34.27	48	1.0254*	
35.1	49	1.0261	
35.93	50	1.0267	
36.76	51	1.0273	
37.59	52	1.0279	
39.27	54	1.0292	
40.95	56	1.0305	
42.65	58	1.0318	

* Range for a tropical marine aquarium. The higher values are valid for Red Sea organisms.
** Half the normal salinity to treat disease, e.g., clownfish disease.

Conductivity

Conductivity meters for aquarium use are manufactured by several companies, including SANDER and TUNZE. WTW makes conductivity meters for the laboratory, which, despite their high cost (around $500), are recommended for large set-ups because of their precision. These meters measure the conduction of electrical current through water—which hobbyists can also feel when there is a defective electrical device in the aquarium. The higher the salinity of the water, the better it conducts electrical current. Conductivity is

Water

measured in siemens (S). At 25°C, marine water has a conductivity of 45-48 mS/cm (millisiemens/cm) or 45,000 to 48,000 µS/cm (microsiemens/cm). In contrast, the conductivity of distilled water—or water that is deionized by reverse osmosis—is below 30 µS/cm (microsiemens/cm).

Measuring the salinity with a conductivity meter is about 10 to 20 times more exact than with a hydrometer—but it is also more expensive by the same factor. Hydrometers can have a variation of up to ± 20%. Oily substances on the water surface, algae growth, etc., are often responsible. Cleaning the hydrometer frequently is very important!

For those who have an automatic refill system, a conductivity meter connected to the control circuits can be used to safeguard against excessive freshwater being added.

FLUCTUATIONS IN SALINITY

Water evaporates out of every aquarium. Since only pure water evaporates and the salts remain behind, the water becomes more saline. Therefore, the evaporation has to be compensated with freshwater, but this leads to fluctuations in salinity which many animals do not tolerate well. It is therefore advantageous to compensate for the evaporated water in short intervals, or to constantly add freshwater using a floating switch (e.g., TUNZE Osmolator or MINIREEF/DELTEC, automatic refill Aquastat 1000). If the salinity accidentally falls too low (e.g., salt water removed and freshwater added), the salt content needs to be increased slowly with a water exchange. Under no circumstance should synthetic sea salt be added directly to the aquarium water. This would injure the mucous membranes of fishes. Invertebrates, e.g., anemones, slime strongly and retract for days; these are symptoms of their stress. The slime is their defense against the harsh effects of newly dissolved salts.

AQUASTAT 1000

Water Treatment in the Aquarium

In the following, we want to introduce technological methods that aid in colonizing your aquarium with useful bacteria that help process wastes. Naturally, physical/chemical cleaning procedures are also discussed.

We are talking about biological aquarium filters. However, the word filter does not belong in this context. In a filter, substances are retained - filtered out. Biological "filters" biochemically transform metabolites. The safe end products are returned to the aquarium. Therefore, we are not dealing with a filter, but with a "bioreactor." This name has established itself, especially in biotechnology and wastewater technology. However, so that we do not create excessive confusion, we will continue to call the bioreactors in our aquaria "filters" or "biofilters."

Biological Filtration

1. Aerobic Filters

In an aerobic filter, all the bacteria need to be supplied with sufficient oxygen. Areas low in oxygen (anaerobic zones) have to be avoided. These filters are sites of nitrification, that is, the transformation of ammonium to nitrate with the help of *Nitrosomonas* and *Nitrobacter* bacteria. Organic wastes are also oxidized.

This is the goal of every aquarium filter, and a whole slew of various concepts exists to reach it. Most have proven themselves functional— many roads lead to Rome. However, caution is advised when proven freshwater systems are transferred without thought to seawater aquaria. The requirements—especially in regard to oxygen and ammonium levels—are significantly different here, primarily because of the higher pH (see p. 136).

1.1. Submersed Aerobic Filters

Submersed aerobic filters are covered with water. This means that the **filter material**, the surface of bacterial growth, is totally underwater. It does not come into direct contact with air. The filter box itself can be in the open, outside the aquarium.

Filtration

1.1.1. Canister Filters

The prototype of this group is the power-driven EHEIM canister filter. This filter probably has the widest distribution of all filter types in the aquarium hobby. For many aquarists, it is the exterior filter *par excellence*. The large disadvantage of these systems is the poor oxygen supply to the bacteria. All the oxygen for the bacterial metabolism must come from the surrounding water. Here, however, the maximum dissolved oxygen concentration is 7 mg/l. The effluent from a canister filter is poor in oxygen. The treatment capacity of filters in aquaria with high organic loads may be limited by the oxygen supply to the bacteria.

In moderately stocked and well planted freshwater aquaria, this economical filtration is usually totally sufficient. But this type of filtration is often unsuitable for marine animals due to their high oxygen requirements. Canister filters are well suited as a through filter for activated carbon and/or ion exchange resins, e.g., to remove nitrates. The FLUVAL's three-chamber design makes it especially suitable for this because it allows the simultaneous use of carbon as well as crushed dolomite.

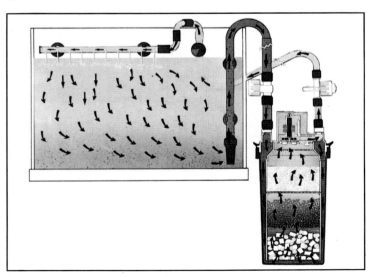

A FLUVAL canister filter with its three-chamber system

A trickle filter (left) and protein skimmer in a commercial scale set-up of an aquarium store.

Substrate Filters

1.1.2. Undergravel Filters

The undergravel filter is similar in principle to the canister filter. The filter plate creates a second bottom of perforated plastic, and the entire bottom of the aquarium is used as a filter. A 5 to 10 cm layer of substrate is placed on top. With the help of a powerhead or an air lift, a water current is produced which constantly passes through the bottom. This filtration system is very efficient because of the large surface area that bacteria can colonize. After some time, however, the bottom can slowly clog up until the aquarium must be totally cleaned. In regard to the oxygen supply, this type of filter presents the same drawbacks as a canister filter. These disadvantages have prevented undergravel filters from becoming established in Germany. In the USA, tanks with only fishes are common, and these filters are frequently used there.

Undergravel filters with strong powerheads, e.g. AQUACLEAR, function as submersed biological filters. When you see the show tanks at PREIS which have housed some of the same animals (*Xenia*) for eight years, then you have to acknowledge that undergravel filters are a better system than Germany has given them credit for. More than three years of my own experience confirms this (H.B.).

The bottom filter consumes oxygen. However, oxygen is also needed by the animals. Therefore, **always** use a strong powerhead with venturi for aeration **with** the undergravel filter. A countercurrent foam skimmer will also enrich the water with oxygen, especially when it is operated in conjunction with ozone. The installation of an undergravel filter costs perhaps 5 % of the total outlay of a set-up. You will not regret installing an undergravel filter. A favorable bottom climate and a large surface area for the bacteria colony and small living organisms (worms) are additional benefits! No other filtration system can compete in volume or surface area with this biofilter. You would have to install an equal sized tank with filtration material under or beside your show tank to achieve the same biofiltration effect.

However, undergravel filters are very sensitive to medication. A quarantine tank for future fish additions is necessary.

With the undergravel filter, we achieve strong nitrification. NH_4/NH_3 is transformed into NO_2. In "mature" zones of the filtration material, the nitirification pathway proceeds to nitrate. Anaerobic zones occur where the bottom is very dirty; even nitrate is metabolized here. However, it should not degrade to such an extent that putrid areas form, since hydrogen sulfide would be produced under those circumstances (the bottom becomes black).

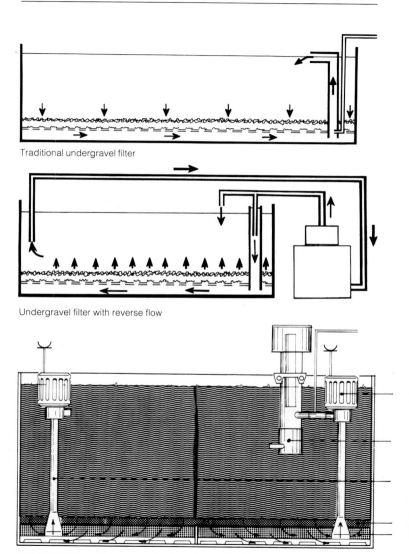

Traditional undergravel filter

Undergravel filter with reverse flow

Undergravel filter with two powerheads and a protein skimmer

Plate Filters

1.1.3. Plate Filters

For a few years the so-called plate filters were being touted as the filter system for marine aquaria. A plate filter is a submersed filter made of a row of consecutive plastic grids which are covered with layers of filter floss or foam. Due to their large cross section, the water velocity is very slow. In these calm zones, suspended matter can easily settle out. The plate filter functions as a settling chamber for detritus. The slow flow rate and the oxygen demand of the accumulated detritus lead to a marked lowering of the redox potential. Since the surface of the filter is small because of the few plates, this type of filter cannot be recommended as the only biological filter of a marine aquarium. A few (2 to 3) consecutive plates can, however, be used as a mechanical filter, but they must be regularly washed. The slow, uniform current promotes the growth of sea squirts and sponges. I (Dr. Schlüter) have seen plate filters overgrown with these animals. This is an excellent biological fine filter which also removes the last of the suspended matter. Some units offer foam cartridges with plastic grid frames in a kit format. These cartridges should be placed outside the aquarium in a separate filter box. The filter is easy to clean and has a large surface and volume. But since the cartridges have to be submersed, this system is nothing more than a modified undergravel filter.

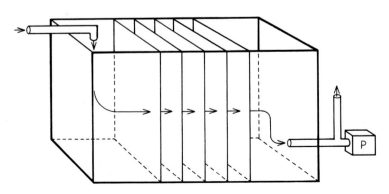

Plate filter; 5 filter plates made of thin filter floss.

Surface Filtration

Installing a surface drain—e.g., an overflow into the trickle filter—precludes a surface skin from developing and improves oxygen diffusion.

Some filter systems draw the water from the surface of the tank, especially filters that are located under or outside the aquarium. This prevents the growth of algae and bacteria on the water surface (bacterial skin). However, when the water level drops, this type of drainage will no longer work. Water levels must be constantly monitored. This is hardly the case when there is a drilled overflow in the tank and a sufficiently large reservoir in the filter system. Water should be added with an automatic system. A float regulates the replenishment of evaporated water. Dead zones on the water surface should be carefully avoided.

Whichever filter system you choose, the water surface must be incorporated into the filtration cycle. It is totally sufficient if the pump effluent gives the water surface a constant circular motion.

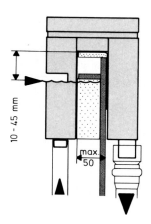

10 - 45 mm

max. 50

TUNZE
Overflow 1074

Trickle filters

1.2. Emersed Aerobic Filters

Trickle Filters (Wet/Dry Filters)

Trickle filters are biological filters that have their filter material exposed to the air. The water trickles downward on the filter material, hence their name. Two phases exist in the trickle filters: water and air. These two environments in contact assure that the oxygen supply of the bacteria which are colonizing the filter material is sufficient. The water is replenished with oxygen and returns to the aquarium enriched. This is the primary advantage of this system over submersed filters. Due to the good oxygen supply, the efficiency of a trickle filter is much greater than that of a submersed filter. In wastewater technology, where performance is sought, nobody uses a submersed filter. Trickle filters as aquarium equipment are finding more and more applications as their capabilities are recognized. Various different systems are in the trade, and they all produce excellent results. Various filter materials are used as substrate for the bacteria and are compared in the following chapter.

Trickle filter set-up at the Bochum Aquarium (Germany). It is filled with coral sand.

Internal Trickle Filters

A trickle filter can also be placed inside the aquarium.

To do so, you must lower the water level in the filter, exposing the filtration material to air so that it remains "dry." This can be done with an elaborate electronic set-up or a simple reliable mechanical set-up. In either case, the filter has a pump at the bottom that returns the water to the aquarium. Any standard aquarium can be fitted with an internal trickle filter without undergoing major changes. The primary advantage to this system is the ease on the wallet. When properly set-up, these filters work well.

Likewise in complete set-ups, trickle filters are sometimes located out of eyesight, either under or next to or behind the aquarium. A nice solution when you are not concerned with the additional space requirement.

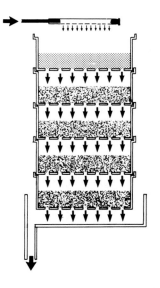

Additional Types of Filters:

1.3. Pressure Filters

Pressure filters are a hybrid between submersed filters and wet/dry filters. They are sealed submersed filters through which a pressurized water/air mixture is pumped. These are very high performance filters, but because of the elaborate mechanics, they are also very expensive. Nevertheless, in principle there are no advantages over conventional wet/dry filters.

Nitrate Filters

2. Anaerobic Filters (Denitrification Filter/Nitrate Filter)
(also see pp. 128 and 186)

Operating these filters is tricky. Some of the systems in the trade are totally unsuitable. One procedure (Nitrex) uses a PVC granulate with an extremely high proportion of plasticizers (phtalate ester). This plasticizer slowly leaches and becomes a carbon source for the bacteria. An anaerobic filter filled with this granulate can actually maintain the aquarium free of nitrates. Unfortunately, there are problems associated with the use of plasticizers. American studies have shown that they behave similar to DDT in the food web, becoming more and more concentrated as it moves up the food chain until levels in the tissue of fishes are 4000 times higher than those of the water. Therefore, for the sake of our fishes, we should not use this technique to remove nitrate.

The nitrate filter from Minireef (Holland and USA) has proven its reliability- a similar principle is used by Weidl (DELTEC), Delmenhorst. The organic carbon, which the bacteria require for denitrification, is supplied by an alcohol-containing nutrient solution added with a diffusion bag at the filter affluent. The system does not require much maintenance and is quite safe. However, because of the low flow rate in the filter, strong bacterial growth can lead to desulfhydration; the filter will smell unpleasantly of hydrogen sulfide (rotten eggs). This problem is avoided in AQUA MEDIC's denitrification filter, which is presently being developed. In this system, water is circulated within the filter. This way the occurrence of excessively low redox potentials that occur with desulfhydration are avoided. Additionally, protein skimming the treated water has proven to be very benefitial. Excessive anaerobic bacteria and alcohol are removed, and the water is again enriched with oxygen. I (H.B.) have had such a system in use for some time, and I am sure that it will find its appropriate market as soon as it is ready for mass production.

The flow rate within a denitrification filter is very low. Since, however, the water leaves the filter nitrate-free, it suffices if the entire volume of the aquarium is cycled once every one to two weeks. The nitrate concentration in the aquarium is kept at a level equivalent to the quantity of nitrate produced within one to two weeks. This quantity is harmless in aquaria with average stocking densities and feeding rates. The redox potential must be negative in a nitrate filter. You will need a redox meter which also shows negative redox values, e.g., TUNZE and SANDER. The meter by DUPLA displays negative values down to - 200. PREIS produces a meter that shows negative values, but the negative numbers are not shown with a negative sign (./. or -). When using the PREIS meter, you must remain a few minutes at the meter and watch the positive redox values fall, cross 0, and then increase again; however, this time in the negative range. These measurements are, of course, taken in the nitrate filter.

A redox value of -100 to max. -250 mV should reign in the nitrate filter. Higher negative values, from about -300 mV, lead to the growth of bacteria that reduce sulfate ions; an odor of rotten eggs develops. The amount of water entering and the turnover circulation within the nitrate filter are the secret of successful denitrification with gaseous nitrogen (which should leave the filter) as the end product. The water should be added slow enough so that the bacteria are able to metabolize the nitrate (NO_3). This rate remains more art than science and therefore is a matter of luck.

I (H.B.) maintain that nitrate is by far not as toxic as frequently said. An aquarium with invertebrates which are looking normal and healthy may have a nitrate level of 50 to 100 mg/l, and nobody can tell by looking at the animals.

It is not only nitrate which should preoccupy us, there are other unmeasurable substances which are problematic to our animals. The primary one is the salt we use and the way and extent it is aged! I am in favor of regular water exchanges, despite the nitrate filter. Phosphates and toxic compounds (gilvin, phenolic compounds) must be removed from the tank! This is especially true for aquaria with invertebrates and fishes. In the anaerobic zone of a nitrate filter, trace elements which were previously flocculated out are redissolved. This is a significant advantage of an anaerobic filter. But only the decrease in NO_3 is measurable.

Administering alcohol as a carbon source for the bacteria in the nitrate filter is discussed in the chapter "Care" (see p. 187).

TUNZE offers a complete system for the biological removal of nitrate. Unfortunately, there is no information yet available that tells us the redox value **within** this set-up. According to a verbal communication with TUNZE, other bacterial tribes transform NO_3 into N_2—and those work under **positive** redox values. Chemically, this is improbable! It is, however, possible that the TUNZE system works well because of the following reasons:

1. The aquarium is optimally stocked-many invertebrates, few fishes, algae growth, and live rock.
2. Many years of experience with marine aquatic organisms.
3. Optimal technology for current, oxygen, water replenishment, etc.

Live rocks significantly contribute to the removal of NO_3. Denitrification bacteria live within the rock. Break one of those rocks in half: it may be black and malodorous on the inside.

Nitrate Filter

However, the aquarium is optimal! The living minireef helps itself—the rest is taken care of by the algae which assimilate the nitrate. The person that proves to me that denitrification from NO_3 to N_2 is performed in a nitrate filter under positive redox potentials should be nominated for the Nobel prize!

This is probably what happens:

Nitrobacter and *Nitrosomonas* bacteria all belong to the same tribe. They are adaptive and develop along the chemical pathways that convert NH_3 to NO_3^-. With good water quality, and by this we specifically do not mean the redox value, but the chemical tolerance towards nonaggressive water, bacterial tribes develop different forms that are adapted to the prevailing redox value. Huge quantities of anaerobic bacteria are washed out of a nitrate filter. These colonize suitable zones of the aquarium (bottom, rocks) and continue working there to remove nitrite/nitrate. This is the only way to explain that a relatively small nitrate filter can maintain a nitrate equilibrium in a large tank. And this is the only way to explain that all the systems of the various companies work successfully with the appropriate adjustments by the hobbyist. On one hand we require an aerobic filter to remove NO_2—on the other, however, we also need an anaerobic filter in the bottom region to reduce previously oxidized elements.

Nitrate filter by DELTEC

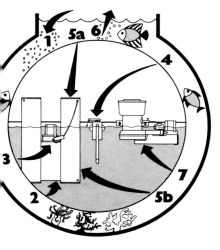

Mode of action of water treatment (TUNZE system)

1 Food
2 Cartridge filter
3 Turbelle® (powerhead) current
4 Osmomat accomplishes osmotic microbial stabilization, fertilization + surface drain
5a Oxidation stage of the biofilter
   $[NH_4 \rightarrow NO_2 \rightarrow NO_3]$
5b Reduction stage of the biofilter
   $[NO_3 \rightarrow N_2]$
6 Gaseous nitrogen (N_2) is released
7 Venturi rotational protein skimmer removes pollutants

3. Algae Scrubbers

Growing algae absorb many nutrients from the water. Nitrate, phosphate, minerals, including important trace elements, and heavy metals, are absorbed by algae and partially stored. To remove significant quantities of these nutrients, an algae scrubber can be installed beside the aquarium with finely crushed dolomite as a bottom substrate. This tank is planted with shoots of *Caulerpa*. These algae are rapid growing and nonproblematic. The water from the wet/dry filter is routed through the algae scrubber before it returns to the aquarium. The filter must be strongly illuminated to achieve sufficient algae growth. Since algae release nutrients when they die, they must be regularly trimmed. This type of water conditioning, although very effective, is only used by a few aquarists because of its large space requirement. That is why it is good to keep a large amount of *Caulerpa* sp. in an aquarium. While this is easily accomplished in the invertebrate tank, it is difficult in the fish tank. Again the rule: when keeping invertebrates, limit the number of fishes.

Trickle Filters

CONSTRUCTING TRICKLE FILTERS

Technically there are two possible types of trickle filters: interior and exterior.

External Trickle Filters

Since most aquarists are of the opinion that aquarium technology should not be visible in the aquarium, trickle filters are usually placed under or beside the tank.

This filter system demands an overflow or a stand pipe. Specialized stores can easily drill the necessary holes in the glass, even when retrofitted. TUNZE introduced an overflow based on an American design which makes holes in the aquarium itself unnecessary (see p. 69)!

The water flows from the overflow through the trickle filter and then into a sump. The sump can contain a heater, chiller, protein skimmer, or an additional mechanical filter. The water is returned to the tank with a powerful centrifugal pump. Since the water level in the aquarium falls by 2 to 3 cm if the pump fails, it is important that the sump is dimensioned to handle the extra water if necessary. Otherwise, there will be flooding. This does not happen when the trickle filters are placed laterally.

The use of an overflow in the aquarium has additional advantages. The water level in the tank remains constant; the evaporated water only lowers the level of the reservoir. To minimize fluctuations in salinity, it is advantageous to replace the evaporated water with an automated system. With a float and switch in the water chamber, freshwater can be added as needed—from a reservoir, directly from the tap or, when the tap water is substandard, after it has passed through reverse osmosis or ion exchangers.

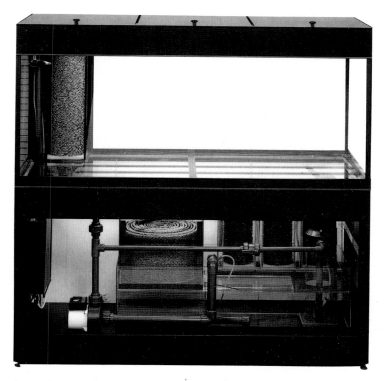

A complete aquarium set-up using DELTEC equipment. The trickle filter has a spray arm, automatic refill, etc., and is placed beneath the aquarium. The nitrate "filter" is installed within the aquarium. This is a proven, successful system.

Filter Media

1. Synthetic Filter Materials (Plastics)

1.1. Plastic Structures

The most common filler material for trickle columns in the aquarium hobby are "bioballs" (DUPLA) or biospheres (HAGEN). These are hollow spherical plastic balls. The water drips down on them so that a thin biofilm—bacterial lawn—can form. The surface of plastic structures is relatively small, so larger filter volumes are required. Air and water are very well mixed in this filter, allowing optimal oxygen enrichment. The biofilm does not adhere strongly to the material. This, however, is not necessarily a disadvantage. Old, excessively thick bacterial lawns fall off and are washed away from the trickle column, allowing new, highly active bacteria to replace them. Therefore, such a trickle filter should be outfitted with a mechanical postfilter (fiber or foam). If the circulation pump is powerful enough—turnover twice an hour—an aquarium with fishes and invertebrates may function excellently for a long time.

Besides biospheres there are other filter media with similar properties, e.g., curlerlike structures, bio-rings, blocks, etc.

Because of their relatively small surface, the plastic structures used today will have already been displaced by other designs by the time this book appears. DUPLA itself has replaced bioballs with its newly designed "Biokaskade." Personal experiences concerning their use are not yet available.

1.2. Plastic Mats, DLS, Cartridges

While plastic structures were designed for good water aeration-with a relatively low surface area—the manufacturers of filters with plastic mats approached the problem from a different angle: by providing a large surface area. With this system coarse plastic mats and fine floss or thin foam are rolled into a spiral. The coarse mat acts as a spacer between the mats of very fine material and keeps the filter from clogging up. The water flows down on the fiber mats. A biofilm soon forms on their large surface area. Because of its large surface area, huge treatment rates are achieved. This type of filter is frequently used to keep lobsters in restaurants; 20 l of filter material are sufficient to remove the metabolites of 25 kg of lobster in a 200 l aquarium! In decorative fish aquaria, these filters have a large performance reserve. However, plastic structures are more efficient in oxygenating the water than plastic mats. A protein foam skimmer should also be used in all systems.

For the first time nitrifying bacteria are pictured in an aquarium book. Rüdiger Riehl has photographed these "beneficial critters" under a scanning electron microscope at ∞ 8500 magnification. This cannot be accomplished by the layperson, but we elected to show this interesting microworld to you.

Filtration Media

1.3. Raschig Rings (Schott = glass, Eheim = clay)

Raschig rings are short tubes which are usually made of clay
(Eheim). They represent a compromise between good oxygen
enrichment and a large surface area.

A very unusually structured material has been on the market for
some time: Raschig rings of sintered glass (Siporax). This open-
pored glass material by far has the largest surface of all suitable
materials. The pore structure is ideal for bacterial colonies, and at the
same time, good oxygen replenishment is achieved due to its ring
structure.

Unfortunately the higher efficiency does not justify the high cost. That
is a pity, since this material is the most effective medium available
for trickle filters. But these rings clog up after a few months, and then
their efficiency is not any better than that of clay tubes.

1.4. Various Shaped Foamed Ceramic Structures

Foamed ceramic structures have a superior surface area per unit of
material, and they have the additional advantage that they cannot be
compressed. This material offers the largest surface after sintered
glass rings. It is pH neutral (calcium-free) and can be easily cleaned
after a few months. The disadvantages are its high initial costs and
its handling. It would be ideal to place the trickle filter media in
cartridges to make them easily exchangeable.

Calcareous algae and crushed shell are an ideal filter medium

Ceramic pieces

Bioporon

Crushed dolomite

Clay rings

Activated carbon pellets

Crushed dolomite

Sintered glass rings

BZ structures (ceramic)

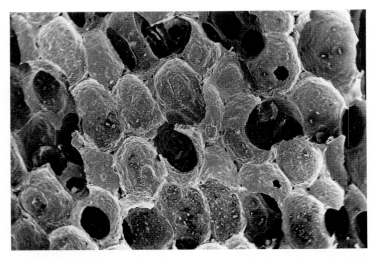

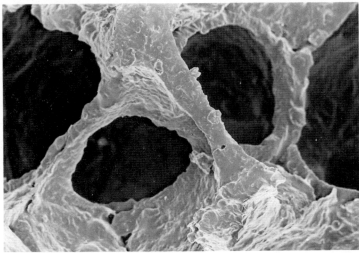

Ceramic pieces are durable, washable, and have a high flow-through rate. Following carbon and Siporax rings, they exhibit the highest filtration surface. Well suited for submersed and trickle filters. Top ∞ 40; bottom ∞ 215.

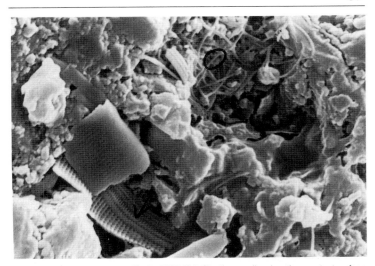

Activated carbon pellets magnified ∞ 3000. This filtration medium has the greatest surface area and the highest ability to absorb toxins—but the shortest life. Carbon is only suitable for special purposes (detoxification and pigment removal).

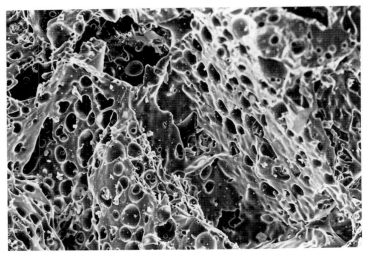

A Siporax ring magnified ∞ 2800

Filter Media

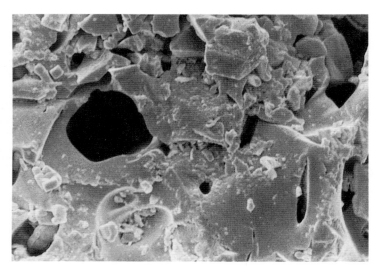

Bioporon ∞ 750

Dolomite ∞ 2060

Surface area of various filter media

1. Plastic structure	Ø 40 mm	300	m^2/m^3
2. Best plastic elements	max.	400	m^2/m^3
3. Plastic fibers	max.	1,000	m^2/m^3
4. Compressed filter fibers	max.	3,000	m^2/m^3
5. Ceramic clay tubes	Ø 5 ∞ 5 mm	1,000	m^2/m^3
6. Best porcelain structures	Ø ca. 4 mm	2,000	m^2/m^3
7. Best low-density ceramic (brittle and partially dissolves). Useful life until total closure with sediments ca. 2 years		2,500	m^2/m^3
8. Gravel, 5 mm grain		700	m^2/m^3
9. Crushed shell	max.	350	m^2/m^3
10. Schott rings (Siporax). Useful life until complete closure ca. 6 months	then	300,000 350	m^2/m^3 m^2/m^3 cannot be cleaned
11. Pumice granules. Useful life until complete closure ca. 6 months	then	600	m^2/m^3 cannot be cleaned
12. Activated carbon		ca. 500,000	m^2/m^3 cannot be cleaned
13. Porous, low-density clay material (BZ), solid structure (porous)		ca. 200,000	m^2/m^3 cannot be cleaned
Open structure, containing additional denitrification zones		from ca. 120,000 to ca. 180,000 m^2/m^3	

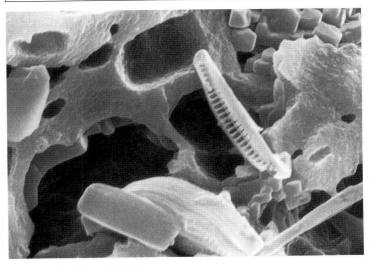

Crushed puffed clay ∞ 2150; diatom

Filter Media

2. Natural Filter Materials

2.1. Crushed Coral

Crushed coral was frequently used as filter material in submersed filters and undergravel filters. It is cleaned so that no living bacteria remain, even though this material originates from the biotope of the aquarium inhabitants. Since, like synthetic materials, it has no buffering effect on pH's above 8.0, it is inferior to those materials. Likewise, the surface to volume ratio is less favorable.

Crushed coral used as filtration material or substrate is very frequently the cause of failure. Even today unclean material is repeatedly used, and it pollutes all of the aquarium water.

Prior to using crushed coral, the material must be tested for nitrates: the material is covered with seawater (1 cup of material, $1/4$ bucket of water), left for one week, then the water is tested for nitrates.

Even if only traces of nitrate can be detected, the material is unsuitable and must be treated with sodium hydroxide and then rinsed.

Today crushed coral is protected! That is reasonable, since it does not regenerate (not in sufficient amounts to "mine" it).

Crushed shell/marble can be used instead. The nitrate test should also be performed when using crushed shell.

2.2. Dolomite

Dolomite is highly pure calcium carbonate rocks which are available graded in various sizes in the trade. It essentially has the same properties as crushed coral-therefore, it can also be used as substrate. However, the surface is rough, not smooth like crushed coral. Phosphate is bound as calcium phosphate ($Ca_3(PO_4)_2$) on newly exposed surfaces.

Because of this phosphate-binding property, filamentous algae growth is markedly inhibited. However, it will be necessary to regularly replace part of the material when the phosphate binding capacity is exhausted. Dolomite granulate is far inferior to synthetic filter materials in total surface area, making synthetic materials the substrate of choice for those who have heavily stocked fish tanks. In our opinion, the ideal filtration for the marine aquarium consists of a combination of crushed dolomite in a carbon dioxide reactor or the substrate and a trickle filter

---

Dolomite granules have a stabilizing influence on carbonate hardness. During nitrification, large quantities of H^+ ions are produced with the nitrate. These acid radicals can lower the pH in the filter to such an extent that calcium is dissolved directly from the dolomite.

with either plastic structures, DLS or porous ceramic filter pieces.

2.3. Pumice

Pumice is a calcium-free material of volcanic origin. It contains inner cavities, is very porous, and has a large exterior surface that is eminently suited for bacteria to live on. However, the material has closed pores; the inner cavities are not easily accessible to bacteria. The available surface area is much smaller than that of sintered glass (Raschig rings [Schott]) or porous ceramic bodies.

The inner cavities of pumice gravel will eventually fill with water and support microorganisms. However, water exchange is minimal, and oxygen deficient conditions prevail. Under certain conditions, denitrification processes begin. But these are uncontrollable and can become dangerous. Large quantities of nitrite may be released. Desulfhydration frequently occurs. In this process poisonous hydrogen sulfide is produced. Signs of desulfhydration reactions are easy to recognize: black zones develop within the pumice gravel (precipitation of metal sulfides).

An aquarium can be successfully kept for an extended period of time in this manner—even with denitrification. But the uncontrolled anaerobic zones in the trickle filter can turn into a time bomb.

Conclusions

All materials made and sold for trickle filters can be used for such. Each has its strengths and weaknesses. The tendency is clearly towards synthetic materials. In personal trials, the combination of synthetic and natural materials has been successful. As a continuous filter material (ca. 70% of the volume of the trickle filter), synthetic material is used—tanks that have a light biological load use plastic structures (e.g., bioballs), whereas aquaria with heavier organic loads use synthetic mats and fibers (e.g., DLS). The remaining 30% of the filter volume is filled with dolomite which, to preserve its phosphate-binding properties, is exchanged every 3 to 6 months.

Pumps

Water Movement

A current is vital for all sessile animals. A current delivers new water that supplies oxygen and food (plankton) and removes metabolites. Many invertebrates, especially filter feeders, live on reefs at sites highly exposed to current. To remain healthy, these animals need sufficient water movement in the aquarium also.

The reef aquarium should have a turnover of 4 to 6 times an hour. It is appropriate, especially in larger aquaria, to install several pumps that discharge against each other. A timed system is also advantageous— every six hours, the pump, and therefore the direction of the water flow, is changed. Besides the avoidance of dead zones, a natural tidal rhythm is simulated.

The position of the pumps in the aquarium determines where the strong and weak current will be. This allows the animals to be placed according to their individual requirements.

The pumps that provide current, and turn the water over 4 to 6 times an hour, need not discharge the water through the biological filter. A turnover of once an hour for biological filtration is a good rule of thumb. Therefore, besides the filter pump, there should also be one or two pumps solely to provide current.

The installation of an undergravel filter makes this redundant, since the pumps driving the filter also function as current pumps. Otherwise, you can use powerheads by HAGEN (AquaClear), Second nature, etc.

HAGEN Aquaclear

Pumps

The heart of every filter set-up is the pump. All life in the aquarium depends on its reliability.
A vast range of different types of pumps are offered in the trade. All of them can be used in a marine aquarium. Luckily, the stainless steel pumps of yesteryear have been replaced by more durable plastic pumps. Nevertheless, one should always have a pump in reserve— unless you already use 2 or 3 pumps. Insure that failure of a pump will not result in a catastrophe.

1. Magnetic Drive Centrifugal Pumps

These pumps have proven themselves for many years in the aquarium hobby, e.g., on canister filters. More powerful versions (HAGEN) can also be used for trickle filters since they have a sufficiently high pressure rating. From the material standpoint, these pumps are beyond reproach since the motor is totally separate from the pump section. Power is transferred through a permanent magnet. The disadvantage of this type of power transmission is the poor efficiency coefficient. All of these pumps have a higher energy requirement (current draw) than comparable pumps with a direct drive. However, the direct-drive pumps have an axis of steel which can corrode, and they have to be sealed. Since every seal becomes permeable in time, magnetic drive pumps are better.
These pumps are usually air cooled. There are, however, also submersible, oil cooled versions (e.g., EHEIM).

Circulation pump

Pumps

2. Partially Submersed Centrifugal Pumps

Centrifugal pumps, such as the powerheads by HAGEN, are placed directly above the water surface with their impeller underwater. All new models have a protected motor. Those who still use the old open pumps in their aquarium are strongly urged to exchange the old treasure with a new model. The risk of an accident is too great. Partially submersed centrifugal pumps use less electricity than magnetic drive centrifugal pumps and give a higher pumping rate. However, they operate at low pressures. But these pumps are well suited for providing current and water turnover. While these pumps are unsuitable for trickle filters, they can be used in interior filters. These pumps, too, are air cooled.

3. Submersed Water-Lubricated Pumps

The motor of submersed water-lubricated pumps is totally sealed in plastic. The only moving part, the rotor, runs on a thin film of water. Therefore, these pumps must be submersed. In output, they are comparable to the partially submersed centrifugal pumps, but use even less electricity. Since they are more economical (e.g., HAGEN, SECOND NATURE), they have displaced the partially submersed pumps previously used to provide current.
Some pumps do have a drawback when compared to partially submersed centrifugal pumps. Aquaria that use submersed pumps and are illuminated with metal halides can overheat during the summer months. A chiller may even be necessary.

Planomat

Turbelle

Vibrator membrane air pump; the untiring workhorse

Foam Fractionation

1. Foam Fractionation

Theory

Foam fractionation was not developed for the marine aquarium. It is a procedure known to sewage treatment as floatation. This term actually describes the processes in a "protein skimmer" more accurately. Floatation reactor, therefore, is a better term. During foam skimming, we take advantage of a familiar everyday phenomenon: the deposition of organic molecules on an air/water interface (border). When we put a drop of oil or gasoline on a water surface, it spreads out. A film forms which is only one molecule "thick." The reason this monomolecular film forms is the following: most organic substances are complex molecules. A large proportion of the molecule repels water (nonpolar, hydrophobic). Some attached groups, e.g., acid groups, are, however, water soluble (polar, hydrophilic). Put simply, this means the molecule has a water soluble "head" and a water repellent "tail." As can be seen from the diagram, the molecules in the air/water interface of the air bubble arrange so that the "head" is in the water, and the "tail" is in the air, that is, into the interior of the air bubble. This creates a stable foam which concentrates organic substances from the water and allows them to be removed. This monomolecular film also has numerous inorganic substances deposited within. Salts, heavy metals and trace substances are also concentrated in the foam and removed from the water.

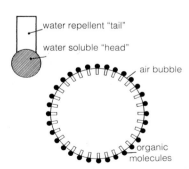

Diagram of foam fractionation:
an air bubble with deposited proteins and pollutants.

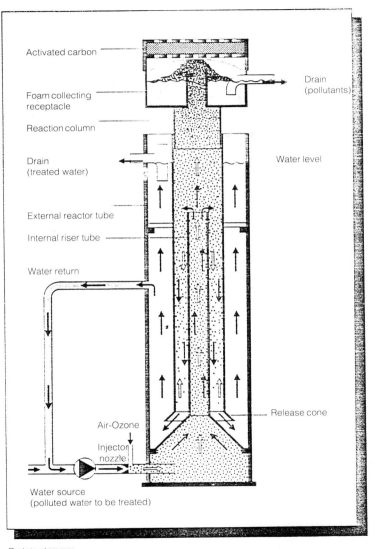

Activated carbon

Foam collecting
receptacle

Reaction column

Drain
(treated water)

External reactor tube

Internal riser tube

Water return

Air-Ozone

Injector
nozzle

Water source
(polluted water to be treated)

Drain
(pollutants)

Water level

Release cone

Protein skimmer

Foam Fractionation

Mode of Action

To work effectively, the skimmer needs a reaction column where air and water come into contact. A large air-water interface is created by injecting small air bubbles (the smaller the more effective) into the water column that is flowing by, countercurrent if possible. On top, the air bubbles burst, creating a foam that is pushed up and collected in a reservoir. This way dissolved substances and particulate matter (bacteria, plankton) are removed from the water. The efficiency of the protein skimming depends on the size of the bubbles and the time of contact. The smaller the bubbles, the more effective the skimmer. In freshwater, the excessive surface tension inhibits the formation of small bubbles. They immediately coalesce into larger ones. Unless chemicals are added, foam fractionation in freshwater is difficult.

Engineering

There are various ways to build a foam skimmer—there are simple, small set-ups, and there are very elaborate, high output devices. SANDER, a pioneer in protein skimming technology, has an appropriate device for every application. Small foam skimmers are hung in the aquarium and fitted with an air diffuser. Large exterior protein skimmers, which can treat several cubic meters of water per hour, are equipped with their own independent pumping system. Air is introduced through a venturi jet (injector) and drawn into the reaction tube as very small bubbles. This is presently the most powerful skimmer on the market. Aquaria with more than 1 m^3 of water should be equipped with this system.

A third type of foam fractionator is the power skimmer. This system uses the turbulence of the pump to beat the air into small bubbles (BIOTRONIC). The efficiency of the power skimmer is in an intermediate position between the simple skimmer that uses a wooden diffuser and the venturi skimmer. They are ideal devices for 500 to 1000 l aquaria. TUNZE likewise has a very powerful protein skimmer in its product line.

TUNZE protein skimmer

Usefulness of a Protein Skimmer

Aquarium literature rates the usefulness of protein skimmers inconsistently. There are extreme "opponents to foam fractionation" and "fanatics." For instance, SANDER installs a unit that is more than a meter high in large set-ups over 1000 l. This is even sufficient for larger aquarium stores. Objectively seen, one can hardly doubt the usefulness of foam fractionation. Those who have seen the black mess that is removed by the procedure will agree. The load placed on the biological filter is reduced by an appropriately dimensioned protein skimmer. Nitrogen-containing catabolites, which would have to be oxidized to nitrate, are removed from the tank while still in their proteinaceous state. The removal of heavy metals and trace elements is not a disadvantage either, since that controls algae growth. Additionally, the redox potential is increased and the water is aerated.

In our opinion, the protein skimmer is the most important technological component of the **marine aquarium hobby** (illumination and filtration are required by both fresh- and seawater aquarists).

The care of a protein skimmer is discussed in detail in the chapter "Maintenance," p. 184.

2. Ozone

The use of protein skimmers leads to ozonization, since these two procedures are frequently used in conjunction.

Theory

Ozone is an especially reactive oxygen molecule. It is unstable in water and quickly dissociates into oxygen:

$$2\ O_3 \longrightarrow 3\ O_2$$

Ozone $\longrightarrow$ Oxygen

In the presence of ozone, organics and some inorganic compounds are at least partially oxidized. One ozone molecule splits into an oxygen radical which can immediately react with reduced compounds.

Oxidation of nitrite:

$$O_3 + NO_2 \longrightarrow O_2 + NO_3$$

Ozone + Nitrite $\longrightarrow$ Oxygen + Nitrate

Mode of Action

Complex organics, such as gilvin (gives water a yellowish color), are broken down by ozone into components which then can either be removed with a protein skimmer or biologically metabolized. The result is crystal clear water. Some public swimming pools also use ozone to disinfect their water. Since ozone is a strong oxidizer, the redox potential is increased. However, the use of ozone in the aquarium also harbors dangers. An overdose can eliminate all life in the aquarium. The ozone generator either has to be the correct size for the tank or needs to be adjustable.

An ozonizer can also be controlled through an ORP meter and controller. After achieving the desired redox tension, e.g., 300 mV, the ozonizer is disconnected. For safety reasons, the ozone generator you buy should not be capable of overdosing the aquarium, even if you are using an automated system. The size of the ozone generators manufacturers suggest (SANDER) seem exaggerated. The next-smaller model is usually quite sufficient.

Protein skimming with ozonization is recommendable for aquaria with heavy fish loads. Aquaria with only invertebrates do well without it as long as they are not overfed.

Dosage: 5 to 10 mg/100 l of water per hour. Beginning at 20 to 25 mg/100 l, protein is denatured and cannot be removed by foam fractionation.
The room should never smell of ozone; it is detrimental to everyone's health—including humans!

Note:
Filter the discharge of the ozone generator over carbon!
Use an ORP controller.

The ozonizer needs to be preceded by an air dryer. However, such apparatus are expensive (ca. $1500). An ozonizer which usually generates 100 mg ozone/l only generates half that amount at 65% humidity. The moisture can also be removed using cartridges with silica gel (e.g., SANDER). Since most of us are too lazy to regenerate the silica gel every few days, as is normally required, an over-dimensioned ozone generator is usually bought to compensate for the drop in efficiency that results. However, this may be a catastrophic decision. An ozonizer working with humid air not only generates ozone, but also toxic nitrogenous compounds from atmospheric nitrogen and water vapor. These compounds later enter unchecked the reaction column of the protein skimmer. No ozonizer is preferable to one that is incorrectly used! A (good) protein skimmer also functions without ozone.

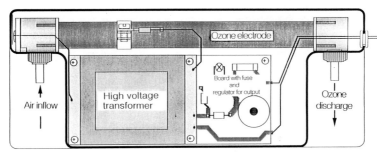

Ozonizer (SANDER)

Carbon

3. Activated Carbon

Filtering over activated carbon is another way to remove gilvin and other organic compounds from the water. These substances are adsorbed onto the surfaces of the pores in the carbon and retained. After some time the capacity of the carbon is exhausted, and it must be exchanged. This is not visible!! Carbon left in a filter past its service life (3 to 4 weeks) only acts as medium for biological filtration. Therefore, carbon should be used over **short periods of time** (7 to 10 days).
Rule of thumb: exchange the carbon filter every 2 to 3 weeks; 7 days with carbon then 14 days without carbon, then again 7 days with carbon, and so on.

Presentation
There are various grades of carbon on the market. Pelleted carbon made from carbon dust has a much greater surface area and effectiveness than broken carbon. So the higher price is justified. Some companies offer carbon which is mixed with ion exchange resins—to remove nitrates. This procedure does not work in salt water and should be avoided in freshwater tanks because of unfavorable side reactions.

Production and Activation of Carbon
To make activated carbon—usually made of beech—carbon is heated in the absence of oxygen to about $600°C$ (red glowing). All burnable hydrocarbons are turned into gas and removed. The second step is the activation. This is accomplished by reheating the carbon—this time to $900°C$ with oxygen. Pore structures are formed where dissolved organic compounds can be bound. Not all filter carbons offered are "activated." In other words, do not use the carbon sold for barbecue grills. The exact mechanism involved in binding organic substances to active carbon is still unknown. It is probable that various processes occur in parallel: mechanical filtration with sedimentation, diffusion, chemical absorption, but also biological processes. The bacteria adhering to the carbon transform or metabolize the concentrated organic substances on the carbon. Think of carbon tablets in human medicine. There, too, carbon has been used for decades as a real "medicine." The carbon removes gases and toxins from the digestive track.

4. Diatom Filters

The diatom filter is a mechanical filter that removes turbidity from the water. It is filled with diatomaceous earth, which is shells (the "skeleton") of marine diatoms. These algae have a diameter of 10 to 50 μm (0.01 to 0.05 mm). A thin cake is placed on a fiberglass mat to make a filter. Such a filter can only be used for a short time; it usually clogs up after a few days and usually cannot be cleaned. Blooms (the unchecked proliferation of bacteria or microalgae) and tomites of parasites such as *Oodinium* and *Cryptocarion* are removed with this filter. But it is only thought of as "first aid" in the aforementioned situations. It is better to either avoid or remove the source of algae or bacterial proliferation. Both result from an overabundance of nutrients in the water because of overstocking and overfeeding. Technically, a diatom filter is a canister filter, but one that is outfitted with a pump that supplies more pressure.

5. Ultraviolet Radiation/Sterilization Lamps

Ultraviolet light is suitable to disinfect the water in case of disease or to remove turbidity caused by bacteria or algae. Usually fluorescent lamps which emit special UV light (hw) are used.

Theory

These mercury vapor low pressure bulbs produce UV rays at a wavelength between 185 and 254 nm. Since UV radiation is almost totally absorbed by normal glass, UV lamps must be made of quartz glass. There are two types of glass which differ by the absorbed wavelengths:

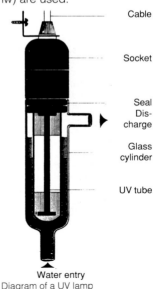

Cable

Socket

Seal
Discharge

Glass
cylinder

UV tube

Water entry
Diagram of a UV lamp

UV Sterilization

The first type, Osram HNS 5 - 20nm, is suitable for an incandescent light fixture and also lets the shortest wavelength (184 nm) pass. Wavelengths below 200 nm produce ozone from oxygen.

$$3\ O_2 \quad \xrightarrow{\hspace{3cm}} \quad 2\ O_3$$
$$\text{Oxygen} \quad \xrightarrow{\hspace{3cm}} \quad \text{Ozone}$$

Since ozone is an unwanted by-product in this context, the second type of bulb is usually used (Osram HNS 15.30 and 55 ofr). The glass used for these bulbs absorbs radiation at wavelengths below 220 nm. Therefore, ozone is not released. The radiation passing the glass (254 nm) kills algae, bacteria, protozoans, and other unicellular organisms. The radiation disrupts DNA synthesis. DNA stores all the hereditary information of the organism. Because the organism's DNA synthesis is impaired, they die during cell division.

Mode of Action

UV lamps can prevent the spread of disease. For this reason, some importers and wholesalers use UV lamps in their equipment. However, furnished aquaria often have dead corners which are not part of the filtration cycle and, therefore, are not treated with UV. The treatment's effectiveness in home aquaria is greatly diminished.

Single-celled parasites have a free-swimming stage - the tomite - in their developmental cycle. These **can** be killed using only UV rays without medication. It depends on the parasite being exposed to UV radiation for sufficient time. Since ultraviolet light only penetrates a few centimeters into the water, the water must flow close to the UV source. Therefore, the bulb is built into a glass tube so that there is a space of about 2 cm between the bulb and the tube.

The water flows through this space and returns to the aquarium by the filter pump. If the intensity of the lamp is adequate—a 30 watt UV bulb can disinfect approximately 500 l of water per hour—it suffices if the lamp is turned on 4 to 5 hours each day as a prophylaxis. The bulbs have a life expectancy of approximately 5000 hours. Thereafter only a low quantity of UV light is radiated and the bulb should be replaced. If the lamp is used 4.5 hours each day, the life of a bulb is approximately 3 years.

You cannot overdose the aquarium on UV radiation. No toxic substances are released into the water.

Ozone has already been mentioned as a way to disinfect the water. But very strong ozonizers must be used to be effective. Also, the water cannot return directly to the aquarium. Water which has been disinfected with ozone has a redox potential of approximately 700 mV and is inhospitable. A "normal" ozone generator that releases ozone into the protein skimmer has a minimal disinfecting effect and is not a substitute for a UV lamp.

The UV lamp should be installed outside the aquarium so that the organisms in the aquarium cannot be damaged by its radiation.

6. Ion Exchangers in the Aquarium

Every once in a while ion exchange resins are offered to condition marine water. Lewatit MP 62 (Bayer) exchange resin can be used. It binds nitrite, nitrate, and other anions. A decrease in the pH value is avoided by releasing hydroxyl ions (OH$^-$). MP 62 is regenerated with sodium hydroxide. Since nitrite and nitrate are not the only ions that are adsorbed, the ion composition of the seawater is uncontrollably changed. That is why the use of ion exchangers in aquaria is not recommended. But they are useful for treating tap water (see pp. 54 ff.).

7. CO$_2$ Fertilization/Calcium Reactor (also see p. 188)

CO$_2$ has been used successfully to improve plant growth in the freshwater aquarium hobby. The positive results can easily be seen.

Theory
Carbon dioxide fertilization can also be beneficial to marine aquaria. Through the addition of CO$_2$ the pH is lowered to 8.0 - 8.2. Naturally, a precise pH meter and controller are needed to prevent pH fluctuations. The growth of green algae (*Caulerpa*) and zooxanthellae are stimulated by the addition of CO$_2$. The growth of zooxanthellae has a positive effect on the growth of anthozoans. Some colonial anemones and soft corals will begin to readily spread with CO$_2$ fertilization. CO$_2$ also influences the carbonate hardness. Free carbonic acid releases bicarbonate from the decorative stones, filter substrate and bottom material:

$$CaCO_3 \ + \ H_2CO_3 \ \longrightarrow \ Ca(HCO_3)_2$$

Calcium carbonate + Carbonic acid $\longrightarrow$ Calcium bicarbonate

Practical Applications

One alternative I do not want to leave unmentioned involves the Fluval (HAGEN) cannister filter. It works well, is economical, and also combines 2 to 3 filter functions:

A Fluval filter, with its three chambers, is filled as follows:

1. Bottom chamber:
   Coarse filter material (cotton, clay rings, ceramic filtration structures, sintered glass rings).
2. Center chamber:
   Activated carbon granules.
3. Top chamber:
   Crushed dolomite.

You should place the CO$_2$ source at the filter intake so that you can count the bubbles (ca. 1 bubble per second).

Intake pipe with air hose connected to the CO$_2$ bottle

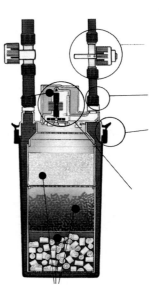

The carbon filter we require anyway, and the calcium reactor is now in the same apparatus.

Additionally, we have water current and surface movement. At least once every 4 weeks new carbon is used for one week and the water is tested to see if the KH value is still above 7 to 8. If this value is less, then the crushed dolomite of the filter should be exchanged. Of course, a CO$_2$ regulator and a CO$_2$ cylinder are also needed for this system.

CO_2 bottle, pH meter and controller, and a CO_2 metering valve

Vigorous, well-controlled *Caulerpa* growth is achieved with light and the addition of CO_2 (*Caulerpa taxifolia* is pictured)!

103

Aquaria maintained in this manner will always have enough dissolved calcium for invertebrates to build their skeletons.

A very elegant way to adjust the carbonate hardness of the aquarium water to almost any desired value is through the use of a calcium reactor. It consists of a diffusion chamber which is filled with crushed shell or dolomite granules. CO_2 is added to form an atmosphere of CO_2 through which the aquarium water cascades. A huge amount of bicarbonate dissolves in this atmosphere. It is therefore necessary to frequently control the alkalinity of the aquarium water so that it does not exceed 5 to 7 mmol/l (15-20° KH). A calcium reactor can be controlled through a pH regulator. This set-up finally solves the problem of decreasing pH values and deficient carbonate hardness. A suitable apparatus is offered by DUPLA as a CO_2 set-up. We simply adapt it: Instead of filling the reactor chamber with synthetic material or Raschig rings, we use a coarse grade of dolomite (ca. 5 mm or slightly larger). The calcium reactor is now ready to increase the pH and the carbonate hardness.

CO_2 should be added very precisely—preferably too little rather than too much. Otherwise, the result is the contrary of our goal. The added carbon dioxide may decrease the pH. Automatic monitoring and regulation with a pH controller is recommended!

pH controller (CO_2 dosifier) by TUNZE

Technology

TUNZE offers a system to increase carbonate hardness called a CO_2 hardness reactor. This system is shown in the diagram below. There are many other ways to increase the KH value (see p. 102).

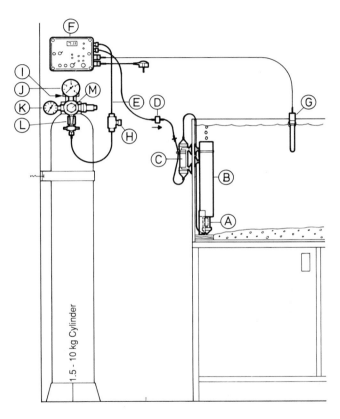

A	CO_2 connection	G	pH electrode 7072.10
B	Hardness reactor 1572	H	Precision regulator 7073
C	Bubble counter 1572.20	I	Cylinder valve
D	One-way valve 7070.01	J,K,L	Pressure reducer 7077
E	Hose 4 x 1 mm 7072.30	M	Pressure regulating screw
F	Automatic CO_2 dosifier 7072		

Heating, Cooling

8. Temperature Control

The water temperature for tropical marine organisms should lie between 25° C and 28° C. Occasional temperatures of 22° C are not harmful, but temperatures above 30° C, even if only for a short duration, are not tolerated by many animals. The oxygen content diminishes rapidly with excessive temperatures. The higher breathing rate of the fishes will be noticeable. Invertebrates close up; some mobile invertebrates, like sea stars, some tunicates (sea cucumbers), and crustacea, will seek the water surface. Sessile anthozoans are unable to do so and asphyxiate.

Heating

The water can be heated with thermostat-controlled heaters (the same ones known from freshwater aquaria). Because of the danger of broken glass and the good conductivity of marine water, using the conventional 115 V (or worse, 220 V) heaters has its risks. Low voltage heaters, such as those offered by DUPLA (24 V), are better and safer. However, due to the necessary transformers, the price for such heating devices is significantly higher.

Pay special attention that the heater is certified. These glass heaters are usually safe, especially if they have built-in overheating protection.

Certified electric appliances have the GS, VDE (Verband Deutscher Elektrohersteller, Germany), UL (Underwriters Laboratories, USA) or CSA (Canadian Standards Association) symbols for tested safety.

Thermal Standard (HAGEN)

Tank volume and required heater rating		
Tank volume	Heated room thermostat-heater rating	Unheated room additional heater
50 l	25 watts	25 watts
75 l	40-50 watts	25 watts
100 l	50 watts	50 watts
150 l	75 watts	75 watts
200 l	100 watts	100 watts
300 l	150 watts	150 watts
500 l	250 watts	250 watts

Cooling

Due to the use of large water-cooled pumps and metal halide illumination, many aquaria need to be cooled during the summer months. For Mediterranean or North Sea tanks, it is a necessity. In Mediterranean aquaria the water temperature should be around the annual median of 18°C (14 to 20°C).

Cooling seawater is much more problematic than heating. When overheating occasionally threatens tropical aquaria on very hot days, you can place ice cubes in plastic bags and hang them in the aquarium for temporary relief.

Chillers are safer. However, only chillers from the zoological trade should be used. Flow-through chillers from the beverage industry are not suitable since their heat exchangers are made of stainless steel which withstands Coca-Cola, but not the corrosive effects of salt water. After 2 to 3 years they may leak!

Only chillers with titanium or plastic coated heat exchangers are suitable to cool marine aquaria. Even coldwater aquaria can be kept with this equipment. There are such chillers for large aquaria up to 4000 l.

Cooling

Flow-through chiller

Flow-through chillers have a hermetically sealed cooling section with maintenance-free capillary injection. The water temperature is regulated with a built-in thermostat. The heat exchanger, the heart of the set-up, consists of a plastic coated copper pipe. The marine water only touches the synthetic material—no corrosion or poisoning problems can occur.

External trickle filter with a chiller and circulation pump.

ILLUMINATION

Terminology

First, something about terminology:

A lamp is the total device, that is, the reflector/transformer **and** bulb. A bulb is only the light source itself, that is, only the fluorescent tube, the incandescent bulb, etc.

In a marine aquarium, the lighting must accomplish several functions. On one hand the entire underwater scenery should be shown in "good light." This has a decisive influence on the optical effect of the tank. On the other hand, all plants require light as an energy source, including the zooxanthellae in anthozoans. The lights not only need to be of the right intensity, they also need to have the correct spectral composition; otherwise, plants are "malnourished."

Three types of bulbs are used for illumination: fluorescent tubes, mercury vapor bulbs (HQL) and metal halide bulbs (HQI). Other bulbs, such as incandescents or halogens are not suitable because of their unfavorable spectral composition.

Quantification of Light Intensity

Light intensity is measured in lux or lumens using a luxmeter. In plant biology, however, mW/m (milliwatt per square meter) is the unit used to measure light intensity. This value identifies the available photosynthetic energy (illumination intensity) for plants. The necessary illumination intensity for *Caulerpa,* for example, is 12,000 mW/m .

Illumination

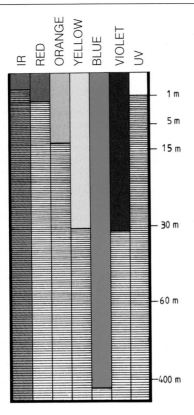

Different wavelengths of the sun's spectrum are absorbed at varying water depths. As you can easily see, blue light is vital for animals and plants that live at greater depths. This is the only light available to them in nature.

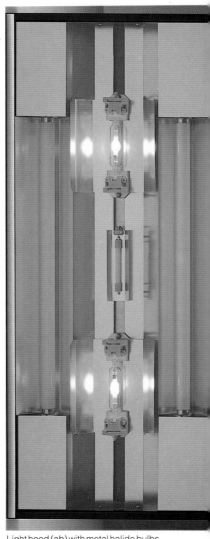

Light hood (ab) with metal halide bulbs and actinic fluorescent tubes

Table of lux/exposure times (according to Lunasix F)					
Lux	Exposure Value (EV)	Aperture (100 ASA)	Time (sec)	Description	
11	1	1.4	1	Dim light zone: smear algae, nocturnal animals	
22	2	2.0	1		
44	3	2.8	1		
88	4	2.8	$1/2$		
175	5	2.8	$1/4$	Diatoms	Moderate light zone
350	6	2.8	$1/8$		
700	7	2.8	$1/15$	"Wire algae"	
1400	8	2.8	$1/30$	Bubble algae	
2800	9	2.8	$1/60$		
5500	10	2.8	$1/125$	Moderate light zone*: zooxanthellae, *Caulerpa*	
11000	11	4.0	$1/125$		
22000	12	5.6	$1/125$	Overcast day	
44000	13	8.0	$1/125$		
88000	14	11.0	$1/125$	Mid-day sun	
175000	15	16.0	$1/125$		

* Normal light intensity measured on the water surface.

Illumination, Fluorescent Tubes

Light Hoods

Light hoods are usually part of the package when you buy a complete set-up, saving you the agony of having to choose. As these hoods usually only have two fluorescent tubes, they are more suited for freshwater aquaria than for marine tanks. Make sure the hood you choose is constructed for marine aquaria (for invertebrates if it is your desire to keep them). DELTEC offers fluorescent tubes in a component design. You install a tube for every 10 cm in width. Since the tubes have become significantly thinner, this is easily accomplished. The light output can be improved by up to 50% if the hood is interiorly reflecting (aluminum).

The number of bulbs needed depends on the width and length of the tank. There should be one fluorescent tube per 10 cm of width extending over the entire length of the tank. A metal halide lamp can illuminate a tank that is approximately 75 to 100 cm long. While fluorescent tubes should be situated as close to the tank as possible — even directly on the cover glass—metal halides should be placed 40 to 50 cm above the water level. Metal halide lamps should always be used with their glass lens. This protects the bulb from splashing water and absorbs part of the UV-A and UV-B radiation they produce. The remaining UV rays only penetrate a few centimeters, but they have a positive germicidal effect in that zone (see UV lamps, p. 99). UV-A could also have a positive effect on the animals of the upper water strata.

Fluorescent Tubes

For a long time, fluorescent tubes were an unbeatable source of aquarium illumination. They still represent an economic alternative to metal halide or mercury vapor bulbs for marine tanks up to 40 to 50 cm deep. Lamps with a spectrum similar to daylight should be used to avoid strong algae growth and to give the aquarium a natural appearance. The light coloration 11 (Osram Lumilux, daylight; Hagen, LIFE - GLO) is well suited for this.

To attain sufficient light intensity in tanks with a width of 50 cm, at least 3 tubes should be used, although 4 or 5 is better. Special natural effects can be achieved when an actinic light is added (e.g., Thorn blue, Philips 'TL'D blue; Hagen, MARINE - GLO). Blue light is not absorbed as rapidly as other wavelengths, which explains why everything in the sea appears blue-gray, even in shallow water.

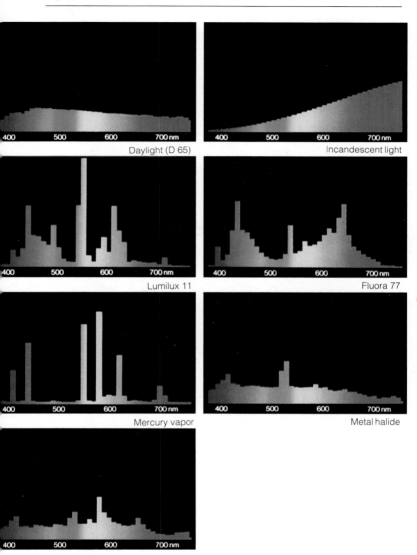

Daylight (D 65)

Incandescent light

Lumilux 11

Fluora 77

Mercury vapor

Metal halide

Metal halide . . ./NDL (neutral white de Luxe)

Illumination, Fluorescent Tubes

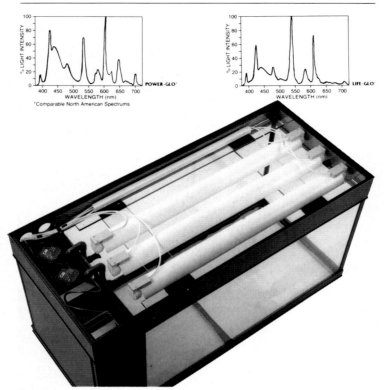

Fluorescent light fixture (DELTEC)

Illumination of marine aquaria

Water depth (height)	Life GLO + Marine GLO	Metal halide-NDL 70 watts + Marine GLO	150 watts	Metal halide-D 250 watts + Marine GLO	400 watts
to 40 cm	4+1	2+1			
to 50 cm	5+1	2+1	1+1		
to 60 cm			2+1	1+1	
to 70 cm				1+1	
to 80 cm					1+1

The table above is valid for every 80 to 100 cm tank length at a width of ca. 50 cm. The fluorescent tubes should cover the entire length of the tank! The length of fluorescent tubes, therefore, plays a significant role in determining tank length.

Required Wattage

To calculate the required number of fluorescent tubes (total wattage), we use the following formula (by PHILIPS):

$$W = \frac{H \infty S}{A \infty B \infty C}$$

W = Watts required.

H = Desired illumination intensity (mW/m²), e.g., 12,000 for good *Caulerpa* growth (see the preliminary suggestions on p.119).

S = Surface area of the aquarium (m²).

A = Growth yield (mW/W) to be taken from Table 1: Types of fluorescent tubes.

B = Illumination efficiency factor. This number represents the proportion of light that actually reaches the water.

The factor is the difference between 100 and the percent of light lost, all divided by $\frac{100 \ (100 - \% \ loss)}{100}$.

Loss of light to the aquarium hood is between 30% and 65%! The amount lost largely depends on the color and type of material it is made of. For example, in a hood made of dark wood, approximately 65% of the light is lost. Likewise, a hood constructed of clean, mirrored surfaces loses 30% at the most. There are additional intensity losses incurred when a cover glass is used. A little intuition is needed in this case to enter the correct factor in the formula.

Examples:

a) Fluorescent tubes without a hood loose 65%, since 65% of the light is radiated up and to the sides. Efficiency factor = 0.35.

b) Ideal case: hood has an interior mirrored surface and loses 30%. Factor = 0.70.

c) Interior surface of the hood is metallic silver (aluminum) and loses 40%. Factor = 0.60.

d) Hood is white or has light-colored wood inside, the loss is 50%. Factor = 0.50.

Most of the hoods today have an efficiency factor of 0.50; with black plastic hoods we have to use a factor of 0.40.

C = Water depth and pollution factor.

Illumination, Fluorescent Tubes

Table 1: Types of fluorescent tubes

Manufacturer	Type	Growth yield (A)	Color denomination
Philips	TL-D 92	240	Warm White
Philips	TL-D 93	230	Warm White
Philips	TL-D 94	220	Warm White
Philips	TL-D 95	220	Cool White
Osram	31	195	Lumilux Warm White
Osram	21	195	Lumilux White
Philips	TL-D 84	195	Cool White
Philips	TL-D 83	195	Warm White
Sylvania	CWX 184	195	Triphosphorus Cool White de Luxe
Sylvania	WWX 183	195	Triphosphorus Warm White de Luxe
Osram	41	180	Lumilux Interna
Philips	TL-D 82	180	Warm White
Philips	TL-D 86	170	Cool White
Philips	TL-D 33	160	White
Sylvania	CW	160	Cool White
Life	GLO	140	Daylight
Philips	TL-D 54	140	Cool White
Sylvania	D	140	Daylight
Duro test	True-lite powertwist	135	———
Philips	TL 34	135	Cool White
Sylvania	CWX	135	Cool White de Luxe
Duro test	True-lite	130	———
Philips	TL 27	130	Warm White
Philips	TL 32	130	Warm White
Sylvania	IF	130	Homelight
Sylvania	WWX	130	Warm White de Luxe
Power	GLO	120	Warm White
Philips	TL 47	120	Cool White
Philips	TL 57	120	Cool White
Osram	77 (Fluora)	110	Blue-Red
Penn Plax	Aquari-Lux	100	———
Sylvania	GroLux	100	Blue-Red
Marine	GLO	80	Blue

Table 2: Pollution factor			
Water Depth cm	Clean Water %	Moderately Clean Water %	Polluted Water %
0	100	100	100
10	95	90	82
20	90	82	67
30	86	74	55
40	82	67	45
50	78	61	37
60	74	55	30
70	70	50	25
80	67	45	20
90	64	41	17
100	61	37	14

Example 1

Surface area (S): An aquarium has the dimensions: L 130 x H 50 x W 50 cm. Therefore, its surface area is:
130 ∞ 50 = 6500 cm^2 = 0.65 m^2

Illumination intensity (H): We want to keep light-demanding *Caulerpa* species (requiring 12,000 mW/m^2).

Growth yield (A): We have decided to use the "90" series of Philips tubes. For this we should start with the number 220 (Lamp TL-D95; see Table 1).

Illumination efficiency factor (B): The loss to the hood is between 45% and 65%. If we assume a loss of 55% the factor in our calculation becomes 0.45.

Water depth and pollution factor (C): If we assume clean water, then Table 2 gives us 78%. This is converted to a decimal, and the number entered in the formula is 0.78.

From the formula we obtain:

$$W = \frac{H \infty S}{A \infty B \infty C} = \frac{12000 \infty 0.65}{220 \infty 0.45 \infty 0.78} = \frac{7,800}{77.22} = 101 \text{ W}$$

It is sufficient to install 3 tubes of 36 watts each.

Nevertheless, 4 tubes are recommended because too much light is better than too little. This also takes into account that the amount of light produced diminishes with the age of the tube.

Illumination

Example 2

Aquarium L 100 ∞ H 45 ∞ W 50 cm

H = We want to keep animals that need moderate light (requiring 8000 mW/m²).

S = Surface area = 100 ∞ 50 = 5000 cm² = 0.5 m²

$$W = \frac{H \infty S}{A \infty B \infty C} = \frac{8000 \infty 0.5}{A \infty B \infty C}$$

A = We will use the Life GLO tubes by HAGEN (growth yield 140).

B = Illumination efficiency factor is 0.40 (black cover).

C = 35 cm water depth; clean water. According to Table 2, the factor is 0.84.

$$\frac{8000 \infty 0.5}{140 \infty 0.40 \infty 0.84} = \frac{4000}{47.04} = 85.03 \text{ (watts)}$$

Life GLO has 40 watts, so we will need 2.12 tubes. We round this number up and use 3 tubes.

For those of you who think these calculations are too complicated, there is a simplified table on page 114 you can base your choice on. The hobbyist who wants to know exact requirements can use the previous tables to give him/her a reasonable starting point to determine the amount of wattage needed for the particular fluorescent tubes under consideration, taking all factors into account. It becomes apparent that the type of illumination, due to the very different light efficiencies (growth yields), plays a significant role in the number of tubes required.

Hardly anyone uses mW/W (defined as: milliwatts ["plant-usable wattage"] per watt [actual current draw of the bulb]) as a technical expression for illumination efficiency. We are, therefore, covering new territory. Furthermore, indications about growth yields for the various metal halide bulbs are missing. I (H.B.) would be very grateful for any information in this regard.

Invertebrate aquaria such as this one have only been possible since the advent of metal halide bulbs.

Electrical Safety/Corrosion

Metal halide spot lights are usually used for decorative purposes, e.g., for store windows. Therefore, many of these lamps are not protected against water spray. If they are used directly above a marine aquarium, they also require corrosion protection. SILL Co., sells wall lamps which are protected against splashes and lacquered against salt water. The transformer is separate, resulting in lower heat radiation for the aquarium. If the simple appearance is not pleasing to you, you can use the beautifully-shaped hanging lamps from DUPLA, which, likewise, are protected against water spray. Lamps should also have the GS, VDE, CSA or UL symbols.
Please make sure that either all outlets are above the water level or ensure that water cannot run along the cords into the outlet!!

Illumination

Actinic Blue Light (24 hr illumination)

Actinics can be left on during the night. Their electricity consumption is low, and the useful life of the tube is preserved, since turning the lamp on and off shortens its life expectancy by about the same amount as continual usage. You even save yourself a timer and have the added benefit of being able to observe the animals during the night. The fish have no problem sleeping in the pale twilight, but when disturbed, they quickly find their way back to their "bed."
These tubes are 60 cm (18 W) or 120 cm (36 W/40 W) long. Waterproof end caps should be used.
PHILIPS TLD 36 W BLUE (1.20 m long) or HAGEN MARINE-GLO is suggested for tanks 1.30 to 2.50 m long; use the shorter tube for smaller tanks. You can use OSRAM DS 11/78 (11 W) or DS 7/78 (7 W) as small emergency night lights. It is a little difficult to find a splash-proof socket with ballast. DUPLA offers these in their product line as hanging spotlights.
Blue light, with its wavelength of ca. 400 to 450 nm, is an important growth factor for deep-water invertebrates (dim light).

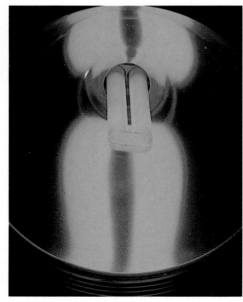

DUPLA hanging lamp with an actinic spotlight

Photoperiod

At the equatorial tropics the day length is ca. 12 hours throughout the year. Tanks that use fluorescent tubes should maintain a 12 hr day. But if metal halide lights are used, the illumination should be reduced to 8 to 10 hours. Due to the reflecting water surface, full sunlight is only available from about 9 o'clock to 3 o'clock in tropical latitudes. An actinic light and/or a fluorescent tube can remain turned on for 2 to 4 hours prior to and past the metal halide illumination to simulate dawn and dusk for the animals. As already mentioned, actinics can remain on constantly. Also see pp. 274 ff.

Hanging spotlights

Nitrogen

Don't let chemistry scare you. If the formulas shock you, then just ignore them.

1. NITROGEN

1.1. Nitrification (Breakdown of Ammonium and Nitrite)

Nitrogen is the most troublesome "waste" in the aquarium. However, it is a component of protein and other vital compounds which our fishes and invertebrates need to live. The final product of protein metabolism of aquatic animals is **ammonium** (NH_4^+). At higher pH values—the marine aquarium has a pH of 8.4—part of the NH_4^+ is present as poisonous **ammonia** (NH_3). Ammonia is toxic to all aquatic animals, even at very low concentrations.

$$NH_4^+ \;+\; OH^- \;\longleftrightarrow\; NH_3 \;+\; H_2O$$

Ammonium + Hydroxide ion $\longleftrightarrow$ Ammonia + Water

There are bacteria which transform ammonium into harmless compounds and by this process acquire energy to live. This process is called **nitrification**.
In nitrification, ammonium is transformed into nitrite, and nitrite is converted into nitrate. These transformations are carried out in two distinct steps by two different genera of bacteria:
Bacteria of the genus *Nitrosomonas* transform ammonium into nitrite.

$$2\,NH_4^+ \;+\; 3\,O_2 \;\longrightarrow\; 2\,NO_2^- \;+\; 2\,H_2O \;+\; 4\,H^+$$

Ammonium + Oxygen $\longrightarrow$ Nitrite + Water + Hydrogen ion

A lot of oxygen is needed for this reaction. Additionally, the environment of the aquarium is not greatly improved with the transformation of ammonium to nitrite. Nitrite is almost as toxic as ammonia. *Nitrobacter* then takes the nitrite and converts it into **nitrate**.

$$2\,NO_2^- \;+\; O_2 \;\longrightarrow\; 2\,NO_3^-$$

Nitrite + Oxygen $\longrightarrow$ Nitrate

Some oxygen is needed for this reaction also.
Ammonium is oxidized to nitrate through these two reactions. In the majority of aquaria, nitrate is the end product of microbial action on

nitrogen. Nitrate is by far not as poisonous as ammonium or nitrite, and the only harm it does is the way it overfertilizes the algae—including the zooxanthellae. Hence, the maximum nitrate concentrations in aquaria with invertebrates should not exceed 20 to 50 mg/l. Levels up to 100 mg/l will be tolerated for a short time. But levels above 50 mg/l indicate the need for a partial water exchange. Higher concentrations are permitted in tanks that only contain fishes, as long as red or blue smear algae do not develop. Nitrate is a scarce commodity in unpolluted seas; plants and animals compete for it to synthesize proteins. In clean seawater, the concentration is always less than 1 mg/l.

Tap water, on the other hand, contains 5 to 50 mg/l. Even these levels are exceeded in some ground waters.

Water with nitrate levels exceeding 30 mg/l is not totally safe. Baby foods prepared with this water can cause diarrhea.

1.2. Denitrification/Removal of Nitrate (also see pp. 72 and 186)

There are several ways to limit the nitrate levels in the aquarium. One way is through regular water exchanges. This, however, is only appropriate if the water you use to mix the seawater has less nitrate or has been processed through reverse osmosis. It is also possible to remove nitrate from the aquarium through, once again, bacteria. Certain bacteria metabolize nitrate.

This process is called **denitrification**.

In denitrification, nitrate is reduced into gaseous nitrogen by bacteria. Denitrifying bacteria, unlike nitrifying bacteria, do not gain energy through these processes. Instead, oxygen is removed from the nitrate and used for respiration. One also speaks of breathing nitrate. However, these bacteria can also live under aerobic conditions. Only when anaerobic conditions prevail will they change their metabolism and start using nitrate to respire.

Denitrifying bacteria, therefore, require a place where oxygen is scarce or absent. Since denitrifying bacteria and the inhabitants of our aquaria have totally opposite oxygen requirements, there are few nitrate filters that truly work.

Denitrification in Nitrate Filters

Besides an anaerobic environment, denitrifying bacteria require organic carbon as "food." Only when metabolism is running full blast will nitrate be used for respiration. Since little organic carbon is found dissolved in aquarium water, it must be added. Ethanol (the alcohol found in liquors) and many other organic compounds are appropriate as carbon sources. The dosage, however, is critical. This is discussed in the technology section. Ethanol is available from your drug store (90%). This concentration is too high! Thirty percent is more appropriate. One part ethanol is diluted with 2 parts distilled water.

> 1 part 90% ethanol + 2 parts distilled water = 30% ethanol

Determining the needed dose of "food" is not simple. A 20 to 30 l nitrate filter (for a 500 l tank) needs about one drop of 30% ethanol every two hours. A dosing system will be offered by AQUA MEDIC as soon as their nitrate filter is ready for mass production. Presently, the most effective nitrate filter is the one by DELTEC (see p. 72).

$$2\,NO_3^- + C_2H_6O \longrightarrow N_2 + 2\,OH^- + CO_2$$

Nitrate + Ethanol $\longrightarrow$ Nitrogen gas + Hydroxide ion + Carbon dioxide

Spontaneous Denitrification

Denitrification can also occur spontaneously in an aquarium, but uncontrolled denitrification is dangerous. The bacteria reduce the nitrate to gaseous nitrogen, but not in one step. There are a number of intermediates. The most important intermediate is familiar to us from nitrification: nitrite.

This poisonous compound can form everywhere in the aquarium where high nitrate concentrations and a lot of organic offal (mulm, dead plants, or animals) are simultaneously present. If the circulation pump or the filter fails, nitrite-producing anaerobic zones can develop. Finally, nitrate filters without an adequate carbon source are dangerous. Under these circumstances (lack of energy) denitrification can stop at nitrite.

Besides nitrite, there are two additional intermediates in denitrification which, however, are insignificant for the aquarium:

$$NO_3^- \rightarrow NO_2^- \rightarrow NO \rightarrow N_2O \rightarrow N_2$$

Nitrate $\rightarrow$ Nitrite $\rightarrow$ Nitric Oxide $\rightarrow$ Nitrous Oxide $\rightarrow$ Nitrogen gas

Removal of Nitrates Through Algae

Another way to remove nitrate from the water is with dense algae growth (*Caulerpa*). Growing algae use considerable nitrate. However, the algae must be removed regularly from the aquarium or the algae filter (see "Technology"). If the algae decompose in the aquarium, the nitrogen that was used by the plants as nitrate is released into the water, possibly as ammonium!

The nitrogen cycle, as it occurs in natural waters, is a "one way street" within the aquarium. This microcosm depends on organic nitrogen compounds (feed) being added continuously. In the unfavorable case, nitrate is the end product; otherwise, nitrogen gas or algae biomass represents the end of the nitrogen cycle. A partial cycle can occur when the algae are eaten by the fish. However, quantitatively, this does not play a significant role.

Testing

NH_4^+/NH_3 (Ammonium and Ammonia)

These two compounds always occur together. The relationship of both is determined by pH (see table on p. 136).
The test kits offered on the market all measure the sum of ammonium and ammonia. The upper tolerance level of NH_4^+/NH_3 is pH dependent—NH_4^+/NH_3 is more toxic at high pH's than low. Ammonium/ammonia levels are only measured when animals die or show obvious discomfort; however, corrective actions are usually too late at this point.
NH_4^+/NH_3 must be less than 0.05 mg/l; 0.01 is better. Otherwise, we have highly toxic nitrogen in the aquarium. A dead fish is somewhere! Some silicone sealers contain ammonia; at all costs, do not use this type of silicone, since it will poison the fish. Acetic acid-based silicone is what professionals use to build aquaria. Do not let your aquarium be assembled by a glass store that has no experience building aquaria. The silicone cartridge must state: suitable for aquaria. Smell the fresh silicon for yourself. It should smell like vinegar, not ammonia.

NO_2^- (Nitrite)

Available tests are well suited for freshwater. But the resolution at the lower end of the scale is often insufficient for marine aquaria. For example, Tetra's nitrite test kit only detects concentrations above 0.1 mg/l.
However, sensitive invertebrates require concentrations below 0.05 mg NO_2^-/l to survive. There are nitrite tests which can measure this lower level.

Nitrogen Cycle in the Aquarium

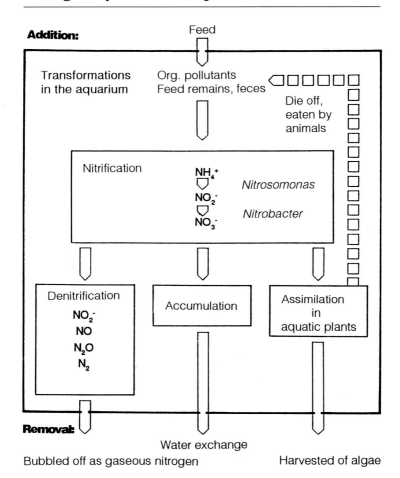

This illustrates the ideal way to remove nitrogen from the aquarium. It is undesirable to allow the nitrogen cycle to continuously increase nitrate (NO_3^-) concentrations. The unidirectional cycle presented is far removed from what happens in nature. Only judicious tank stocking and feeding, as well as water exchanges, help us control and overcome nitrate.

NO$_3^-$ (Nitrate)

Nitrate concentrations can be tested with sticks*, which are sold by EHEIM and TUNZE. TETRA has its own testing sticks from another source.

TetraTest NO$_3$ has only been on the market since the fall of 1990. It is fast and reliable. Unfortunately, values above 50 mg/l are unreadable (many aquarists work under these conditions). Fish can live in nitrate levels of 100 to 300 mg/l; freshwater fishes even tolerate concentrations of 700 mg/l of nitrate. Since quantities above 100 mg (red indicator zone) have to be avoided and/or corrected anyway, this test (TETRA) is also considered good.

You can measure higher concentrations by diluting the sample. For example, we perform the same test with the same reagents but dilute the required 5 ml sample with 5 ml of **nitrate-free** seawater. The resulting concentration is simply doubled.

* These must be "fresh," otherwise, your results will be inaccurate. An open package only lasts a few weeks. Therefore, it must be closed well and stored dry.

TETRA's nitrate NO$_3$ test

Phosphate, Silicon

2. PHOSPHATE (also see p. 186)

Phosphate is a chemical compound that is required by all living organisms—at least in trace amounts. The sea has a phosphate concentration of 0.03 mg/l.

Phosphate is similar to nitrogen in that it mainly enters the aquarium through the feed. Most of it is excreted back into the water, increasing the concentration. Phosphate is not actually toxic, but it contributes to overfertilization. This, in turn, has a negative effect on the growth of anthozoans. Biological filtration does not remove significant quantities of phosphate. But it can be chemically bound to calcium. Calcium phosphate is essentially insoluble in water under aerobic conditions. Only under anaerobic conditions will calcium phosphate redissolve.

$$3\ Ca^{2+}\ +\ 2\ PO_4^{3-}\ \longrightarrow\ Ca_3(PO_4)_2$$
Calcium + Phosphate $\longrightarrow$ Calcium phosphate

Water can be filtered over calcium carbonate ($CaCO_3$) in the trickle filter, where the phosphate will bind to calcium. A thin layer of calcium phosphate forms on the surface of the $CaCO_3$. After some time, the phosphate-binding capacity of the $CaCO_3$ is exhausted, and it must be replaced. The phosphate level can also be controlled through luxurious algae growth and by fertilizing with iron.

$$Fe^{3+}\ +\ PO_4^{3-}\ \longrightarrow\ FePO_4$$
Iron + Phosphate $\longrightarrow$ Iron phosphate (insoluble)

Various brands of test kits will chemically measure phosphate: DUPLA, TETRA, etc. Phosphate concentrations should remain below 0.3 mg/l, the lower the better. Sometimes apartment complexes pass chelating agents in the tap water to fight calcium deposits in the pipes. One such chemical is polyphosphate. Water containing this phosphate must be treated by reverse osmosis before it can be used to make artificial seawater.

3. SILICON (Si), SILICON DIOXIDE (SiO_2), SILICIC ACID (H_2SiO_3)

Silicon is a "small" problem when brown diatomaceous algae appear in the aquarium. They require silicon dioxide (SiO_2) to make their skeleton. These siliceous skeletons are mined as diatomaceous earth and used for medicinal and filtration purposes. Most tap water supplies contain excessive quantities of silicic acid. Si test kits are available from DUPLA. A good store keeper will analyze your aquarium/tap water for Si. On the other hand, silicic acid is not as important as some people think. The silicic acid, or rather the silicon dioxide, is used up after a few days. Okay, a few diatomaceous algae grow—but these will disappear again if new silicic acid is not constantly added with unconditioned tap water.

Si can be easily removed from the tap water through reverse osmosis or total deionization.

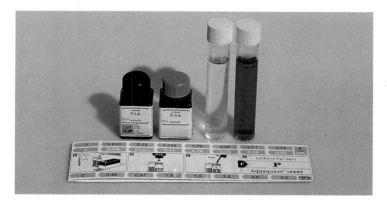

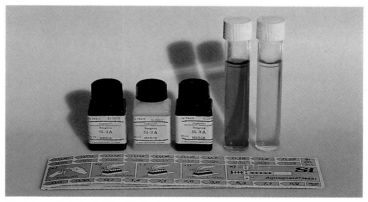

Phosphorus test (top); Si test (below)

4. COPPER (CU)

Copper tests are needed if you don't know whether or not your water pipes or hot water heater releases free Cu. Cu released from your water fixtures can harm invertebrates or *Nitrobacter* bacteria. The problem is usually solved by letting the water run for a while (5 - 10 min) or treating the water with ion exchangers or reverse osmosis. DUPLA has a simple Cu test.

The Cu content of your water source should be 0.1 mg/l or less. The water should also be tested after adding medicinal Cu. See p. 200 in the chapter on diseases.

5. TRACE ELEMENTS

Living organisms require several macroelements: namely, carbon, oxygen, hydrogen, nitrogen, sulfur, and phosphorus. But many other elements are needed in micro amounts: for example, iron and magnesium. Even some poisonous heavy metals such as cobalt, manganese, zinc and copper are needed for life processes. It is all a question of concentration.

In aquaria with invertebrates and fishes, the food and water exchanges add sufficient quantities of trace elements. Stone corals are an exception. They require regular additions of strontium, which they use in conjunction with calcium carbonate to make their skeleton. Strontium precipitates out after 36 hr in marine water and becomes unavailable. Add 5 to 10 ml of PREIS Korall/100 l of aquarium water every day to avoid a deficiency (see p. 179 in the section "Care").

Formel PREIS Korall®

6. The Buffering System in Marine Water

This chapter deals with the interaction between **pH**, **alkalinity** (carbonate hardness), elements of hardness (**calcium**), and **carbon dioxide**.

6.1. pH

pH is a measure of the concentration of hydronium ions which is an important factor of water chemistry.

Water's chemical formula is H_2O. However, some of the water molecules dissociate (separate) into hydroxide (OH^-) and hydronium (H_3O^+) ions:

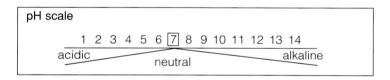

$$2\,H_2O \quad \Longleftrightarrow \quad OH^- \quad + \quad H_3O^+$$
Water $\quad\Longleftrightarrow\quad$ Hydroxide ion $\quad+\quad$ Hydronium ion

If both are present in equal concentrations, the water is neutral. If OH^- ions predominate, it is alkaline; if the majority of ions are H_3O^+, the water is acid. The pH value is the measurement of this distribution. Values of pH range from 0 to 14.

---

pH scale

      1   2   3   4   5   6 $\boxed{7}$ 8   9   10   11   12   13   14

acidic   neutral   alkaline

Most freshwater is slightly acidic (pH 6 to 7). However, there are exceptions, such as Lake Tanganyika, which have a pH above 9. The pH of seawater is quite constant between 8.1 and 8.4.
Since pH is a logarithmic function ($pH = -\log_{10}[H_3O^+]$), a one unit change in pH means a ten-fold change in the concentration of H_3O^+ ions.

pH Ranges

pH values	0	1	2	3	4	5	6	7	8	9	10	11	12	13	14
Sulfuric acid	x														
Hydrochloric acid		x	x												
Citric acid				x											
Peat water					x										
Black water					x	x	x								
Freshwater fishes					x	x	x	x	x	x					
Freshwater plants						x	x	x	x	x					
Neutral								x							
Marine fishes								7.5-8.4							
Marine plants								7.5-8.4							
Malawi/Tanganyika								7.5 - 9.2							
Red algae								7.5 - 9.6							
Blue algae							6.8 - 10								
Chlorella algae (unicellular)								7 - 9.5							
Brachionus								7.5-8.5							
Ca(OH)$_2$ solution														x	
Sodium hydroxide															x

The following table illustrates the influence of pH and temperature on the % of NH_3 in relation to the sum of ammonium and ammonia.

% Free ammonia (NH_3)							
pH	°C 22	23	24	25	26	27	28
7.8	2.8	3.0	3.2	3.4	3.6	3.8	4.0
7.9	3.5	3.75	4.0	4.25	4.5	4.75	5.0
8.0	4.35	4.7	5.0	5.3	5.6	5.9	6.2
8.1	5.4	5.8	6.2	6.55	6.9	7.35	7.8
8.2	6.7	7.2	7.7	8.1	8.5	8.9	9.3
8.3	8.3	8.95	9.5	10.0	10.5	11.0	11.5
8.4	10.2	11.0	11.6	12.2	12.9	13.5	14.0

Percentages are rounded

The higher the pH, the higher the proportion of NH_3. For example, at 25°C and pH 7.8, there is 3.4% NH_3. At a pH of 8.3, the percent of free ammonia (NH_3) is 10%. That is 3 times more, and the water is 3 times more poisonous! We easily deduce that pH and temperature have to be as low as possible. While this is theoretically correct, it creates other problems for marine animals.

Due to lower pH's (7.0 to 7.5) and consequently less unionized ammonia, freshwater has less difficulties than marine water. This is the primary reason why freshwater fishes are easier to care for than marine organisms.

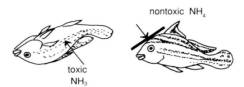

nontoxic NH_4

toxic
NH_3

The available test kits are all usable. However, MERCK® has some kits that are suitable for saltwater and others that are not. Before you purchase a test kit you must know whether you will use it for seawater or freshwater.

As long as NH_4 is present, you must beware of increases in pH, since NH_4 then transforms into poisonous ammonia! The ideal pH for the marine aquarium (in our opinion) is 8.0 to 8.2. Free CO_2 can still dissolve calcium from dolomite, etc., within this range.

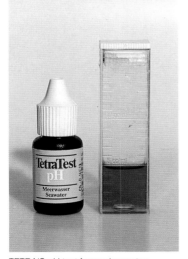

TETRA'S pH test for marine water

pH

pH 9 is 10 times more **alkaline** than pH 8! (there are 10 times more hydroxyl ions present)

pH	10	=	1000
pH	9	=	100
pH	8	=	10
pH	7	=	1
pH	6	=	10
pH	5	=	100
pH	4	=	1000

pH 6 is 10 times more **acidic** than a pH 7! (there are 10 times more hydronium ions present)

pH = the negative logarithm of the hydronium ion concentration in mol/l.

Understand? No—well, it doesn't matter. You only need to know the correct pH, the tolerance values, and the testing methods. This can probably be learned by any aquarist.

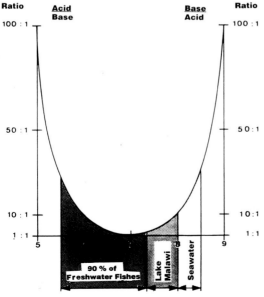

Graphical representation of the dependence of the pH value on the relationship of acid to base or base to acid. At pH 7, the acid-base relationship is 1:1 (neutral).

6.2. Carbonate Hardness (Alkalinity, Acid Binding Capacity)

pH values can be increased or decreased, respectively, by adding bases or acids. However, there are also substances that buffer such pH fluctuations. The most important buffering system in seawater is the carbonate-bicarbonate system.

$$CO_2 + H_2O \longleftrightarrow H_2CO_3 \longleftrightarrow HCO_3^- + H^+ \longleftrightarrow CO_3^{2-} + 2H^+$$

Carbon + Water ⟷ Carbonic ⟷ Bicarbonate + Hydrogen ⟷ Carbonate + Hydrogen
dioxide　　　　　acid　　　　　　　　　　　ion　　　　　　　　　　　ion

This reaction can, as the arrows indicate, proceed in both directions.

The equilibrium between NH_3^+ and NH_4^+ (see previous chapter) is similar to the equilibrium of the carbonate-bicarbonate buffer system in that it is also pH dependent. At pH 8.2, bicarbonate predominates (see diagram on the following page).
If a small quantity of acid is added, the equilibrium shifts, and bicarbonate converts to carbonic acid and carbon dioxide; however, the pH value of the water remains constant. But if a base is added, HCO_3^- is converted to $(CO_2^-)_3$. Again, there is no resulting change in pH. The water is "buffered." This buffering capacity is measured as acid binding capacity in Germany. In aquarist circles, the dKH scale (carbonate hardness) is used.

°KH can be estimated by multiplying the acid binding capacity by the factor 2.8. Acid binding capacity is measured in mmol/l (millimole per liter). This is the quantity of an acid which must be added to a certain quantity of water to lower the pH to 4.3.
°KH, in turn, can be converted to mg/l $CaCO_3$ (more commonly used in the USA) by multiplying °KH by 17.9.

In seawater, the alkalinity is approximately 2.5 to 3.2 mmol/l (7 to 9° KH). In practice, marine aquaria fare better with a KH from 8 to 14°! The higher the better? The higher the more buffer we have. However, you should not attempt to raise the KH above 14°.
Acids (e.g., CO_2 released when fishes respire) can exhaust the water's buffering system and cause the pH to fall.

Carbonate Hardness

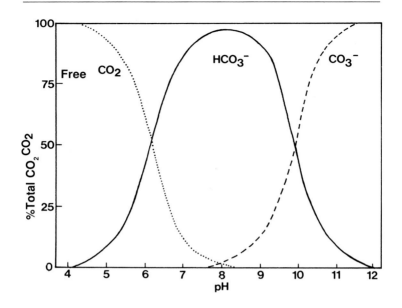

What Happens to Carbonate Hardness?

Natural seawater has a carbonate hardness of 7 to 9. Most synthetic salt mixes have additives which produce similar values, even when made with deionized water (reverse osmosis). Because of the huge volume of the sea and its buffering capacity, carbonate hardness remains almost constant, despite continuous usage and production. But within the limited water volume of an aquarium, the biochemical processes are relatively more significant, and the carbonate hardness varies. There are several "traps" for carbonate hardness. On one hand, many organisms deposit calcium as calcium carbonate in their body. Stone corals, shellfish, soft corals, and calcareous red algae use large quantities of calcium carbonate, reducing the calcium and carbonate concentrations and, therefore, the carbonate hardness. On the other hand, the large amounts of acid produced in an aquarium also destroy the carbonate buffer system. During nitrification, 4 H^+ ions are produced for every NH_4^+ ion that is converted into nitrate (also refer to the chapter "Nitrification", p. 126). The nitrate, therefore, is present as nitric acid (HNO_3), and the carbonate buffer equilibrium is pushed to the left.

$$CO_2^- + H_2O \longrightarrow H_2CO_3^- \longrightarrow HCO_3^- + H^+$$

Carbon dioxide + Water ⟶ Carbonic acid ⟶ Bicarbonate + Hydrogen ion

The CO_2 is either released from the tank or assimilated by plants - and carbonate hardness is reduced.

This is why a marine aquarium that either has a high fish density (= heightened nitrate content) or a lot of organisms that need calcium has to have regular supplements of calcium (see "Calcium Reactor" and "Calcium Water"). A normal water exchange is better!

6.3. Calcium

Elements of hardness that react with various carbonates are important. Particularly calcium will become limiting if stone corals or other animals and algae that incorporate calcium are present. The main component of the skeleton is calcium carbonate ($CaCO_3$). This compound is only slightly soluble in water with a pH of 8.2. Therefore, we recommend a pH of 8.0 to 8.2 as the ideal value in a marine aquarium. DUPLA® even recommends a pH of 7.5! However, most animals cannot tolerate this for more than a few months. Even though the aquarium may have a substrate of calcium carbonate or crushed dolomite and decorative material containing large quantities of $CaCO_3$ (live rock), it can still become limiting. Adding CO_2 or equipping the aquarium with a calcium reactor (see "Technology", p. 101) can transform enough $CaCO_3$ into $CaHCO_3$, which is highly soluble. See the following page.

$$CaCO_3 + CO_2 + H_2O \longrightarrow Ca(HCO_3)_2$$

Calcium carbonate + Carbon dioxide + Water ⟶ Calcium bicarbonate

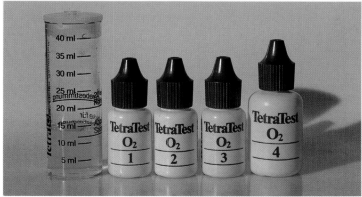

In critical situations the O_2 content of the water is also measured.

Carbonate Hardness

6.4. Calcium Water (Kalkwasser)

Another way to increase dissolved calcium in the aquarium is to add calcium hydroxide. Calcium hydroxide and water make a white calcium milk (Kalkwasser) which can be added to the aquarium after the crystals have settled.
When it is added, the following reaction occurs:

a) Excess CO_2

$$Ca(OH)_2 \quad + \quad 2\ CO_2 \quad \longrightarrow \quad Ca(HCO_3)_2$$

Calcium hydroxide + Carbon dioxide $\longrightarrow$ Calcium bicarbonate

This reaction uses carbon dioxide, so the pH rises, but if there is a CO_2 deficiency or a high pH, part of the calcium precipitates (note the fig. on p. 140).

b) Deficient CO_2

$$Ca(OH)_2 \quad + \quad CO_2 \quad \longrightarrow \quad CaCO_3 \quad + \quad H_2O$$

Calcium hydroxide + Carbon dioxide $\longrightarrow$ Calcium
carbonate + Water

Under these circumstances calcium carbonate results. It coats the bottom, forming a concrete-like mass because, as previously mentioned, it is not very soluble. Other substances, such as strontium, trace elements or phosphate, may be incorporated in the precipitated crystals and removed from the water. Neither KH nor GH are increased!

It is important that the pH does not rise above 8.2 when calcium water is added. Buffers made of sodium bicarbonate ($NaHCO_3$) and sodium carbonate (Na_2CO_3) are frequently used in an attempt to increase carbonate hardness. This procedure is unsuitable when calcium requiring animals or algae present, since no calcium is added to the water.
With these chemicals, e.g., DUPLA KH Generator, the carbonate hardness of the water is augmented but not necessarily the proportion of calcium.
Carbonate hardness can easily be maintained at a KH of above 8, for example, by weekly adding 50 cm^3/100 l of Formel PREIS Korall. This preparation contains, besides many soluble trace elements (strontium), plenty of soluble calcium bicarbonate, making calcium water (Kalkwasser) unnecessary.

The Pros and Cons of Calcium Water

Calcium water is a suspension of **10 grams of the purest laboratory grade slaked lime (calcium hydroxide, $Ca(OH)_2$) added to 1 liter of freshwater.** White calcium milk forms. After the solids settle out, the milky supernatant, the calcium water, can be added to the aquarium. For better distribution, the calcium water should be introduced close to the circulation pump. While applying the milk, the pH of the aquarium water has to be monitored. Calcium water has a pH of about 13! However, the pH should not rise above 8.2 when the milk is added to the aquarium. Therefore, it is prudent to divide the dose to minimize pH fluctuations. I would take 1 bucket of water from the aquarium and mix it with one cup of calcium water. The diluted calcium water is then siphoned into the tank or the external filter through an air hose. This way the calcium water is added slowly, and the animals are protected from pH shock.

An added side benefit to adding calcium water is that phosphate falls out of solution as calcium phosphate. This mirrors the natural processes in the sea that create limestone. Peter WILKENS, a well known author of books about invertebrates, recommends this method.

Nevertheless, it does not function in the long term. In aquaria that are treated with calcium water, the bottom and the filter material become encrusted.

Over time, aquaria treated with calcium water have a KH below 5! This method only works if corresponding quantities of CO_2 are simultaneously added. See the calcium equations on the previous page.

Pro: It works when it is done correctly.
Con: It is detrimental when done incorrectly.

Redox Potential

7. THE REDOX POTENTIAL

In chemical reactions, electrons are transferred from one substance to another. The "electron donor" substance is reduced, while the "electron acceptor" is oxidized. In a complex mixture, such as seawater, many such redox reactions occur. A relative measurement of the oxidation or reduction capability of a system is the redox potential or redox tension. Its unit of measurement is the volt or millivolt. The potential of the hydrogen electrode is defined as 0, and it acts as the reference electrode. The measured redox potential is the difference to this reference.

The redox potential can be measured with a gold or platinum coated electrode. The amplifier is by and large identical to a pH amplifier, since pH is also measured through potentiometry. Many pH meters, therefore, will also measure the redox potential. Just exchange the pH electrode for a redox electrode. The redox meter can simultaneously be coupled to a controller (one unit). Make sure you acquire a unit that can also measure negative values. This will allow you to monitor values in a nitrate filter. Measuring the redox potential of the aquarium bottom can often enable you to identify possible problem spots! When measuring the bottom, the electrode has to be safeguarded with a suitable protector (e.g., basket filter off the filter intake or similar)!
The main oxidizer in seawater is oxygen: at high oxygen concentrations we have a high redox potential; low O_2 levels yield a low or negative one. In a well maintained seawater aquarium, the redox potential is between +200 and +300 mV.
Higher redox potentials can be achieved by using ozone (see "Technology"). Ozone (O_3) is an even stronger oxidizer than oxygen. Hydrogen peroxide (H_2O_2) can also be used to heighten the redox potential. However, there are contradictory results in regard to its use in marine aquaria. Even with careful doses (Oxidator by SÖCHTING), sea anemones can be burned. But there are aquaria where H_2O_2— even at quite high doses—is successfully used. It seems that the damage is mainly due to the rapid increase of the redox potential. Due to the risk involved, using H_2O_2 in reef tanks to increase the redox potential is not recommended.

Using high redox potentials (even over +450 mV) is a controversial issue. Such heightened redox potentials do not make much sense. Smear and filamentous algae can also be controlled through nutrient poor tap water (e.g., treated with reverse osmosis) and careful feeding.

7.1. Redox Potential and pH

Redox potential and pH are interdependent. The pH is also measured in mV. Water that is equal in "oxidative force" has a higher redox potential at a low pH than at a higher pH. The following table illustrates this relationship:

pH	Redox Potential	
7.0	370	
7.6	334	
7.7	329	
7.8	323	
7.9	317	
8.0	311	
8.1	305	
8.2	300	Normal value of moderately polluted water
8.3	294	
8.4	288	
8.5	282	

Redox Potential Depending on Pollution Load and pH

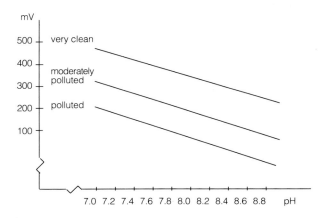

Redox Potential

A redox potential of +282 mV at pH 8.5 corresponds—if the water has an equal oxidizing force—to a redox potential of +370 mV at pH 7.0.

> Hobbyists always use the redox potential rather than the pH-corrected rH value. The latter is mainly used in the soil sciences and limnology.

Following a formula from BAUMEISTER, 1990 and other biochemical books, you can calculate the rH value from the redox potential and the pH. It is easier to use the table and the graph from the previous page.

7.2. Redox Potential and Denitrification

Nitrate filters—as previously discussed in the chapter "Denitrification"—work under anaerobic conditions. Only when anaerobic conditions prevail will the bacteria use the oxygen from the nitrate. Under these circumstances the redox potential decreases to negative values. A nitrate filter operating at top efficiency achieves a redox potential of about -200 mV. If it decreases even further, below -300 mV, it means that the nitrate has been exhausted, and the bacteria have begun to reduce sulfate:

$$C \quad + SO_4^{2-} \longrightarrow \quad CO_2 \quad + H_2O + \quad H_2S$$
Organic carbon + Sulfate $\longrightarrow$ Carbon dioxide + Water + Hydrogen sulfide

In this process, sulfate (SO_4^{2-}) is reduced to hydrogen sulfide (H_2S). This toxic compound smells unpleasantly of putrid eggs. Extremely low redox potentials need to be avoided.

8. Yellow Pigments (Gilvin)

Not only will your aquarium residents produce inorganic wastes, as previously mentioned (ammonium, phosphate), but organic wastes as well. The hard components of organic wastes (feces, plant and feed remains) are mechanically removed as detritus. When water circulation is optimal, they are retained by the mechanical prefilter (filter floss, foam).

These organic wastes are decomposed by bacteria. The resulting substances either cannot be broken down further, or their degradation is extremely slow.

Some of these endproducts turn the water yellow. These yellowing agents are not the same as humic acid of freshwater. Humic acids precipitate out on contact with seawater. The yellow substances in marine aquaria primarily consist of phenol compounds and carbohydrates from the excretions of algae, as well as nitrogenous animal excreta. While the substances excreted by the animals and plants can be poisonous, the yellow pigments themselves are harmless. However, the yellow tint of the water gives the aquarium an unnatural appearance. These yellow compounds can be easily removed from the water with either ozone or activated carbon. Ozone and activated carbon also remove colorless organic compounds which are detrimental to plant and animal growth.

You can see these yellow compounds (gilvin) with the aid of a white plate, which is partially submersed in the tank. Both the submersed half and the emersed half should appear equally white.

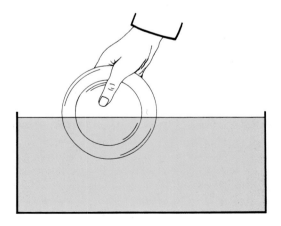

Testing

Analysis (Tests)

pH, carbonate hardness (alkalinity), ammonia, nitrite, and nitrate concentrations have a decisive influence on water quality.
How are they measured?
To analyze the water quality, three different analytical proced ures are employed in the aquarium hobby: colorimetric comparisons, titrations and electronic measurements using electrodes.

1. Colorimetric Testing

Colorimetric methods, as the name implies, allow quantitative measurements by color. Chemicals are added to a water sample which react with the compound of interest to produce a change in intensity (or hue) of a color. The color of the sample is then compared to colors of known concentrations (standards).
The pH and concentrations of nitrite, nitrate, ammonium, phosphate, and many other elements and compounds, such as iron and silicic acid, can be quantified in this fashion. The necessary, premeasured chemicals can be bought at your pet store as test kits (DUPLA, MERCK, TETRA, and many others).
MERCK offers strips for certain tests (e.g., for pH, nitrite and nitrate). These strips are impregnated with all the necessary reagents and only need to be submersed for a short time in the water sample. The reactive squares on the plastic strips change color, indicating the level of the tested item; they are read after a few minutes. The testing strips, although not as exact as drop tests, offer a fast initial reference value. To determine the concentration of the substance analyzed, the color of the sample must be compared to color-comparison standards that are supplied by the manufacturer. Each shade or hue represents a particular concentration or value.
Those who want to be more precise can determine the intensity of the color with a spectrophotometer. These apparatus are available from laboratory supply houses (e.g., MERCK, HACH). In the spectrophotometer, a ray of light is directed through the sample, attenuated by its coloration, measured and digitally represented. For hobbyist use, however, color-comparison standards are sufficient. TETRA has a beautiful and more exact alternative to the printed color standards. Its colorimetric test for pH and nitrate uses disks with colored plastic inserts.
It would be beyond the scope of this book to indicate the chemical reactions which induce these color changes; sometimes they are described in the test kit instructions. The following is an example cited from MERCK'S nitrite test (Aquamerck Nitrite, Nr. 14658; transl. from German): "The test is based on a modified Griess reaction. In the

148

3. Electronic Measurements

Significantly more elegant than both previously mentioned techniques are electronic meters. These use an electrode which is submersed in the water. Either resistance (temperature and conductivity meters), electrical tension (redox and pH meters) or amperage (oxygen meters) is measured. An amplifier converts the signals into an entity that can be displayed on an analog or digital meter. Besides the methodologies above, there are many types of electrodes that will directly measure concentrations of, among others, nitrate or ammonium, but these are very elaborate and not as precise as traditional manual methods. It would be beyond the scope of this book to explain how this equipment works. Interested persons should refer to the manufacturer's information pamphlets (e.g., WTW, SELZLE, HACH).

Various models of electronic meters are offered. Battery-powered, hand-held units are suitable for occasional measurements or if you have numerous aquaria. Stationary meters can provide constant monitoring of a single aquarium. The results can then be received by a recorder. Some meters can even be connected to a personal computer.

DUPLA's pH meter

Testing, Controllers

Controllers

If the instruments have high-low values which can be preset, they can be used as control units. If the values fall outside the pre-set range, an alarm is sounded or corrective action is induced.

Temperature

The simplest control unit is a thermostat. It turns a heater or chiller on or off when the actual temperature is higher or lower than the desired temperature.

pH

A proven way to adjust the pH is by regulating the amount of dissolved carbon dioxide. When photosynthetic plants assimilate dissolved CO_2, the pH increases. With a control mechanism regulating the addition of CO_2, its concentration in the water, and therefore the pH, can be kept constant.

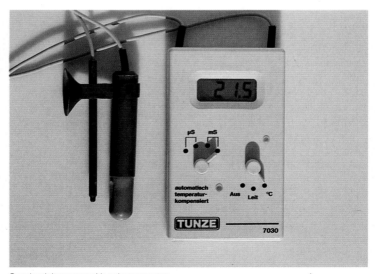

Conductivity meter with a thermometer

Redox Potential (ORP)

With the help of a redox (ORP) controller and an ozonizer, the redox potential in the aquarium can be monitored and stabilized.

Specific Gravity, Conductivity.

A rise in specific gravity, e.g., due to water evaporation, can be measured with a conductivity meter, and the addition of freshwater can be automated. However, a float which senses a decrease in the water level does the same job much more economically. But the system is not as foolproof, since it adds freshwater, regardless if the salinity is too low (e.g., when the aquarium has a leak) or not. The company "ab" has developed a very elaborate "intelligent" control system. If water is missing (sensed by a float), the electronics decide if fresh or salt water should be refilled.

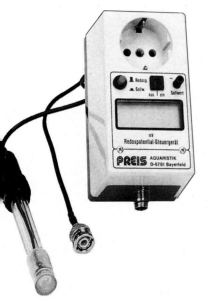

Control Centers

There is no limit to the amount of money that can be spent. You can spend over $3,000 on technical equipment to control the water chemistry in the aquarium. Of course, such a control center is a lot of fun, just like a stereo/video/CD/phono entertainment center. The beauty of such equipment lies primarily in its compactness and esthetics. There are no cables and hoses dangling everywhere. Such a set-up must be installed by a specialist.

However, money cannot buy you experience. We recommend that you begin small. Your equipment can be gradually added to in a kit-like system.

See the pictures on the following page.

Redox (ORP) controller for ozone

Control Centers

DUPLA controllers for temperature, pH, redox, etc.

ab control center, complete aquarium

Leather coral, anemones, clownfish and a foxface

Setting Up

SETTING UP AND STOCKING AN AQUARIUM

Setting Up

After the tank has substrate, a decorative back pane, and rock edifications that help hide the equipment, only water and animals are missing.

The whys and hows of water and its treatment were covered in the beginning of the book. The aquarium is filled with treated water and all of the equipment is then plugged in.

Water is added until the exterior filter set-up (pump sump) is at its operational level. Check all piping to and from the aquarium for leaks! Undetected leaks would be fatal.

If this is a new aquarium being set-up, you can **now** dissolve the marine salt in the aquarium. Approximately 3.4 kg of marine salt are needed for every 100 l water. If a suitable scale is unavailable, use a measuring cup from the kitchen (see instructions on p. 58). At 24° C the salt takes ca. 4-8 hr to dissolve. The water must be well aerated or filtered. After 24 hr the tank is clear and barren and looks like a moon landscape. Now you can move the decoration around as much as you want. You should leave enough empty space between the stone structures for "live rock," etc. Arrange the stones so that your animals have sufficient caves.

The front third of the aquarium's substrate should remain open for possible anemones which like to bury their foot into the substrate.

Stocking

When to stock the tank depends on the quality of the salt (brand) that was used. With some marine salt, you can begin stocking "live rock" as soon as 24 to 48 hr later. Together with "live rock" I would add bacterial cultures to the filter to start the biological nitrogen cycle, by HAGEN is a concentrated live bacterial culture which is highly concentrated with the proper bacteria. Before this book reaches you, there will be other companies that offer bacteria cultures to inoculate the filter material. There appear to be good results from this new research. A tried and true method is to procure a few handfuls or, better, a liter of filter material and/or substrate from a fellow marine aquarist to place in your own filter.

After a few days the first algae form. Let them. I would even put **live** oysters (1 per 100 l) into the fresh marine water. If you decide to add oysters, you will have to keep the water temperature at 20° C or below! Oysters are very hardy and a good control. Additionally, oysters "drag in" all kinds of beneficial bacteria, algae spores, sea lettuce, but also rock anemones, small limpets, small crustacea, etc.

After about 2 weeks the nitrite content should be measured. It must

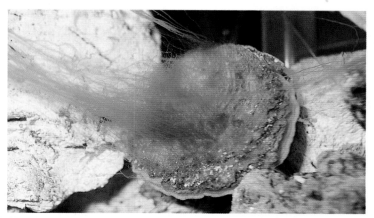

Algae-covered oysters are valuable assets during the run-in phases.

be less than 0.2 mg/l. If it is higher, remove the oysters and either place them in a separate, unheated tank to culture algae or freeze them. I would not eat them unless the nitrite content is acceptable (less than 0.1 mg/l). Of course, when an oyster dies, it has to be removed immediately; otherwise, the water is fouled.

If the aquarium includes a nitrate filter, the denitrification bacteria will have to be "fed" alcohol from the start. After 2 weeks have passed and the tank has no detectable nitrite, you can begin to place "live rocks" in the aquarium. The live rocks must truly contain life and not smell putrid. Situate them neatly within the existing decoration. Now the trial period for the filter begins. You should wait 14 days after the live rock has been introduced before adding invertebrates. Again, the prerequisite is that nitrite test results are negative. If the tests indicate the presence of nitrite, there may be foul stones that need to be removed. Only green filamentous and *Caulerpa* algae should be growing now. These remove phosphate and nitrate from the water so that brown smear algae, blue-greens and reddish blue-green algae cannot grow. After the nitrification phase (2-4 weeks or several months, depending on the artificial salt used), nitrite is no longer present, and nitrate removal should begin. Without a nitrate filter, weekly water exchanges of 10% to 25%, depending on nitrate concentration, are needed.

Setting Up

Now we can stock invertebrates and/or fishes. The number depends on the size of the tank and the filtration capacity (see pp. 16 ff.).

It is best to begin with hardy animals with a 1-2 rating in difficulty (see p. 213).

If you are caring for animals not contained within this book (starfishes, sea urchins, leather corals, soft corals, etc.), you must ask your pet store specifically if these animals really belong in your aquarium community.

Of the starfish, snake stars are particularly good scavengers for beginners. As for sea urchins (strict herbivores), I would not attempt to keep them at the beginning. Most species are quite sensitive and do not tolerate medicines. Sea urchins lose their spines when the water or food is suboptimal. Some species of leather corals are easily kept and also suitable for the beginner. However, they usually require a lot of light and plankton as food (liquid food and *Brachionus*)—they cannot live on *Artemia*. Therefore, it is better to refrain from buying these animals at the beginning.

The same applies to soft coral—after a few months they will also wane. Sea cucumbers, of which the beautifully colored *Paracucumaria tricolor* is considered especially suitable for beginners, can live on *Artemia* and/or liquid foods for one to two years, afterwards they too begin to decline. Pay special attention that fishes don't chew on their tentacles. Sea cucumbers migrate about the aquarium and can block the filter intake at any point in time. Therefore, the intake must be protected so that a sea cucumber **cannot** plug it up. The entire aquarium can be poisoned when a sea cucumber dies. The dying sea cucumber secretes a strong fish toxin (holothurin). Filter carbon rapidly removes this poison from the water and must be immediately renewed during such an unfortunate incident! The filter intake basket of my exterior filter was once climbed on by a sea cucumber. The basket fell off and the sea cucumber was sucked up piecewise by the filter. Fortunately, the sea cucumber had picked the carbon filter and nothing happened. I had put fresh carbon into the filter the day before. We are not always so lucky. My mistake: the filter intake basket was not fastened well enough.

The same applies to puffers, e.g., *Canthigaster valentini*, which also release a toxin (tetrodontoxin) upon death. Such poisonous animals do not belong in a **beginner** tank.

You must also be cautious when keeping stinging anemones and stony corals. Stings by these animals on sensitive forearm skin may require medical assistance. Therefore, be careful when working in the tank! The safest course is to make stinging animals retreat with a wooden stick or a plastic feeding pipe. I (H.B.) always wear rubber gloves to transfer such animals.

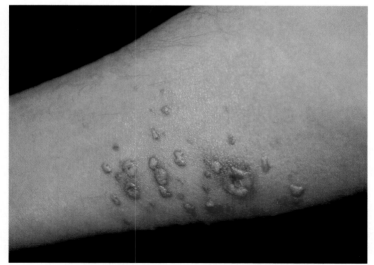

A forearm stung by a bladder coral. The wounds were treated with Braunovidon® (doctor!). The scars are still visible after 2 years.

Acclimation

Acclimation After Short Transport (up to 5 hr in a Car or Train) for Hobbyists Without a Quarantine Tank

If you don't have a quarantine aquarium, and the majority of hobbyists don't, the animals you already have prevent you from lowering the pH to 6.5. Therefore, it is important to compromise. I have yet to lose an animal using the following (modified) method to acclimate:
Immediately after the fish arrive home (or even sooner if possible), lower the pH of the receiving tank to 7.8 with CO_2. A probe should be continuously monitoring the pH of the tank. Moderate the amount of CO_2 as soon as the target pH of 7.6-7.8 is reached.
Immediately following the arrival of the fishes, measure the pH in **every** bag. Each bag is now quickly brought to a pH of 7.6-7.8 by adding "mature" marine water. Vigorously aerate each bag. The water movement will release the CO_2. The **mature** seawater is added in 20 to 30 minutes - but in small amounts or through an air hose with a valve. A partial water exchange in the bag is advantageous to remove part of the NO_2 (nitrite) and perhaps NH_4 (ammonium). The pH in the bag will slowly rise from 6.0-6.5 to 7.6-7.8. As soon as the water in the bag is roughly the same pH as the pH in the aquarium (differences of ± 0.1-0.2 are negligible), the animals can be carefully transferred into the recipient aquarium. Discard the transport water; do not place it into the receiving tank.

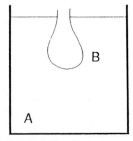
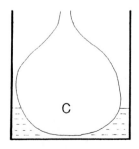

Osmosis (simplified)
A = Container with freshwater   B = Pig bladder filled with freshwater
C = Bladder filled with salt water; water diffuses through the membrane from the tank to dilute the salt water, attempting to equilibrate osmotic pressures.

Acclimation (with a Quarantine Tank)

Animals use oxygen and release CO_2 in the crowded transport containers (plastic bags). Because of this, the pH falls to about 6.5 during lengthy transport. If the animals are still alive **careful** but immediate help is needed.

Transferring the animals immediately into a new tank with a pH of ca. 8.0 to 8.4 would be lethal!

The animals have stored nitrogen gas in their blood. At a low pH of 6.5 to 6.8, the great majority of ammonium/ammonia in the blood exists as nontoxic ammonium.

If the fish or invertebrates would be placed in water with a pH of 8.0, or even 8.4, the new, higher pH would immediately transform the ammonium into ammonia, and the animals would succumb to ammonia poisoning!

> The low pH in the transport water is life insurance for the animals—do not abruptly cancel their policy.

1. Immediately after the animals arrive at the quarantine station, three values are measured in **every** transport bag:
   a) pH (with a probe if possible); b) Nitrite or NH_4/NH_3; c) Temperature.
2. The pH of the aquarium water is lowered with CO_2 to match that of the transport bag. Only then are the animals removed from the water and transferred into the aquarium. Discard the transport water. A temperature difference of up to 5°C is tolerated by most animals better than oxygen deficiency, toxic transport water or inferior pH values. Nevertheless, temperature acclimation should not be too sudden.
3. If the fish are visibly sick, follow the same procedures, but immediately treat the recipient tank with the corresponding medication.
4. Give the fish a prophylactic treatment of PREIS-Coli against intestinal worms.
5. Clownfishes are treated with PREIS-Brook; the specific gravity should also be lowered to 1.011 (ca. 30 mS): this is best accomplished by lowering the water level to half of the normal volume and replacing it with temperate water (25°C), that, depending on the quality, either comes straight from the tap, is passed through reverse osmosis or is totally deionized. The fish are very taxed by the urine and salt in the transport water during long trips. By transferring the animals into water with half the salinity of the transport bags, you allow the animals to osmotically dilute the salt concentration of their bodies; they absorb the low saline water!
6. After 24 hrs the specific gravity is increased with aged water or water

made with Tropic Marine salt and aerated for 24 hrs. This water is slowly added until the specific gravity is 1.022, the ideal value for tropical marine fishes (with the exception of those from the Red Sea).

Although surely more could be said about acclimating fishes, we will move on to comments about feeding:
If your "newcomers" are healthy, they will be hungry. You should familiarize yourself with their favorite foods. Feed them sparingly at first, especially in the quarantine tank, since the medication precludes nitrification.

IF FISHES DO NOT EAT

Fishes that do not eat are frequently death candidates. How do we get them to eat? If there is no obvious disease, the most probable culprits are intestinal worms and/or constipation. Treat them with PREIS-Coli. The fish then need to defecate. White, slimy mucus is released from the intestine.
Since marine fishes drink, you can nourish them for a while with fructose in the aquarium water. This can probably be purchased from a drugstore. Add one level teaspoon of fructose - not glucose! - per 10 l tank volume. Fructose enters the blood directly from the intestine and does not need to be metabolized by the liver.
Such a fructose feeding should only be given in the quarantine tank. A water exchange should be carried out every 2 to 3 days. If the fish have not recovered within a week, the medication needs to be repeated.
Low salinities (to 30 mS [1.016]) are increased after about 1 week. Invertebrates, particularly crustacea, do not tolerate low salinities!
I have had good results treating fishes off their feed with an osmotic shock. Many fish species can even be placed into pure freshwater for 20 min (watch the pH and temperature). They immediately defecate; analyze the feces for worms! A ∞ 10 magnifying glass is sufficient. One of my Zanclus immediately ate algae until its stomach was rounded again after a freshwater treatment. He provided me with a lot of enjoyment. Not all fishes tolerate this freshwater shock. As soon as a fish starts to breath heavily or lies on its side during treatment, add conditioned seawater, or return it to the quarantine tank.
Argus fishes frequently entice other fish species to feed by their own avid interest in food. There are other enthusiastic feeders that can be used. Who wants an argus in his marine tank? Do not purchase fishes that refuse to eat. Observe a feeding!

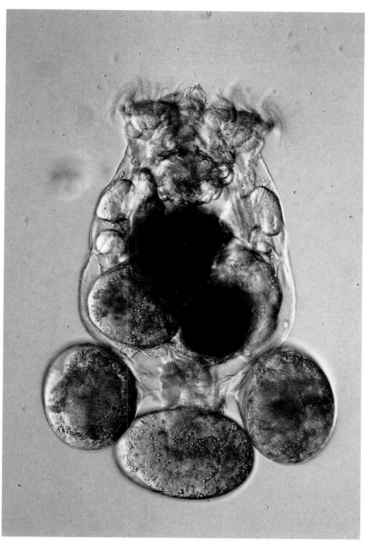

Brachionus plicatilis ♀ with eggs

Feeding Techniques

Turn the filters off for about 15 min while feeding. A timer can turn them back on.

Nitrite should be measured daily at first, or at least when the animals show signs of distress. It often takes weeks to realize that invertebrates are ill or stressed. Anthozoans close or become progressively smaller. This is a sign of either poor water quality, deficient nutrition or poor lighting. Please read about the needs of the animals in the individual descriptions that follow in this book. If you have animals which are not discussed in this volume, you have to ask the advice of your pet store for **every** animal species.

FEEDING TECHNIQUE

Liquid feeds and mineral supplements should not be added directly to the tank, but first mixed with seawater in a plastic cup and then slowly poured into the tank. Colonial anemones, bladder corals and flower corals frequently do not receive sufficient food if the liquid food is simply poured into the water.

The nutrient solution should be dispensed directly above the colony with a feeding tube that has an inner diameter of 10 to 12 mm. A turkey baster can also be used to administer such nutrient solutions close to the colony.

Individual animals (crustacea, sessile animals) can be fed with a feeding tube or plant forceps.

Tablet foods can be placed close to crustacea so they do not have to venture far from their caves.

Shellfish meat can be placed directly into the oral disk of an anemone with a pair of plant forceps.

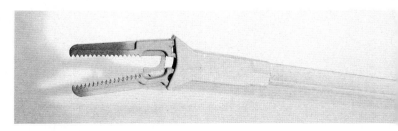

Plant forceps, an appropriate utensil to feed anemones and crustacea.

Foods

With the choice of flake, tablet, freeze-dried and frozen foods available today, not to mention fresh fish and mussel meat, most fishes and invertebrates can be kept healthy for years. There are also live foods, such as *Artemia*, which you can raise from cysts throughout the year. Some stores will also sell full-grown, live *Artemia* (brine shrimp) as well as *Mysis*. Live mussels are normally only available during the colder months, when they are marketed for human consumption.

I could easily devote a whole book to fish foods, but since it is water and not nutrition that is the main hurdle today for successfully keeping a marine aquarium, I only want to briefly mention the different types of foods. The nutritional requirements of the animals are listed in the individual species descriptions.

When choosing foods, you should concentrate on the most important kinds and only buy as much as you can use in about 3 months, which is surprisingly little. Sparse feeding is safer, especially when you only have a few small fishes in a reef tank with invertebrates.

Invertebrates live off light and CO_2 (carbon dioxide), which converts to H_2CO_3 (carbonic acid) in water. Of course, we are only talking about anthozoans which contain zooxanthellae (algae). Frequently they also feed on microscopic bacteria, Vorticellidae, ciliates (monocellular) and other microscopic plankton.

This plankton is fed liquid food in the tank. For every 100 l of water, provide one drop, e.g., PREIS-Microplan (these are **active** yeast fortified with vitamins and some trace elements), twice a week.

Once a week place vitamin A + E drops (from the drug store or your pet store) on frozen foods or inject it into mussel meat. One drop per mussel is sufficient!

Some anemone species also require solid foods, such as *Artemia* and *Brachionus*. Since these are the primary live food organisms of planktivorous invertebrates and fishes, the chapter on nutrition opens with them.

Foods

Artemia salina

The eggs of these crustacea are collected by the ton from the beaches of the salt lakes of Utah (USA) during the fall of every year. They are then washed, dried, cleaned of salt and sand, and finally vacuum packed. This type of packaging, in conjunction with cool storage, affords them a shelf life of up to 10 years! Such eggs from crustacea are called cysts. They are also found in *Cyclops* and water fleas.

Ca. $1/4$ of a million eggs weigh 1 g!

Following the freezing winter, strong spring rains come to Utah and Nevada, washing the *Artemia* cysts back into the salt lakes. Man has intervened in this natural process by harvesting these eggs for over 40 years. All this collecting seems to have had no effect on the numbers of these animals in the lakes! The ecosystem on the shore is intact and under protection. The removal of the eggs does not matter because not all the eggs are taken - this could not be done even if you tried. There are always sufficient eggs remaining in the sand to ensure the preservation of *Artemia salina*. This should be an important lesson for environmentalists. Nature can generally handle carefully harvesting by regulating itself with high reproductive rates. In the specific case of *Artemia,* this means unharvested eggs can lead to excessive numbers of animals the following year. A large number of these animals will die from lack of food and oxygen (it can get very hot in Utah during the summer).

We know the life cycle of *Artemia* and some of the environmental triggers that drive it. The salt water of the lake is diluted from 4% or 5% to approximately 1%. We use this information to make our "*Artemia* culture." One teaspoon of salt per $1/2$ l of water is exactly the correct salinity needed to hatch these small crustacea. They represent an incomparable source of live food for all decorative fishes of the world. Seawater aquarists should always have *Artemia* eggs at their disposal.

Artemia salina are available in two grades:
a) From Utah/Nevada. - These nauplii are larger when newly hatched than those from San Francisco.
b) San Francisco. - Here the eggs are "harvested" as a useful by-product of salt mining in the bay. These nauplii can be eaten by fry of smaller species, since they are smaller.

Culture

I always use two wine bottles to culture *Artemia*. This method is as old as the import of *Artemia* into Germany (ca. 1950). There are no better methods, but perhaps others that are equally suitable. Any vibrator pump such as one of the elite series by HAGEN can aerate two bottles of *Artemia*. The nauplii can be harvested from one or the other bottle **every day**.

Although the culture medium contains nitrite, the nauplii themselves do not; otherwise, the nauplii would prove lethal to our juveniles and invertebrates. It seems that *Artemia* are able to keep the nitrite out of their body.

Setting Up:
Use 1 heaping teaspoon (5 g) of iodine-free cooking salt or, even better, use the same marine salt that you use to make seawater. Put the salt in a wine bottle (clear glass if possible!) with $1/2$ a liter of cool or tepid tap water (10° to 20°C). Add a small pinch of *Artemia* eggs.
The small pinch should not be larger than a pea.

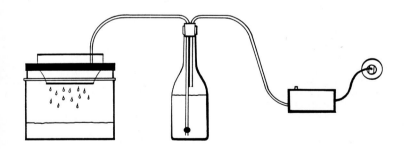

To culture *Artemia*, you will need at least one bottle, one culture chamber, air tubing, a small membrane pump, and an *Artemia* net.

Foods

Temperature:

A temperature of 20° to 26° C is needed to hatch the cysts. A heated room is sufficient.

If too many *Artemia* eggs are used, the nauplii quickly die; if too few eggs are used, these might not be enough to satisfy the appetite of our animals. The required quantity of *Artemia* eggs, of course, is determined by your food needs. In any case, do not use more than a pea-sized pinch of *Artemia* per $^1/_2$ l of water.

Harvest:

Artemia nauplii should be fed within 24 hr of hatching! Why? Because after hatching the nauplii have a yolk sac (like a chicken egg). This yolk sac is high in nutritional value. After 24 hrs the yolk sac is used up and only the empty chitin shell is left. If larger *Artemia* are wanted, they must be fed after the first 24 hr. They can be fed algae or Mikroplan (PREIS) and raised in aquaria with aeration and illumination.

Harvesting *Artemia* nauplii is difficult for many beginners. I also want to explain the process to the "caretaker" who attends the aquarium during vacation:

The egg shells (dark brown) must be separated from the orange colored small crustacea (nauplii). The shells are indigestible and can even be dangerous for fry. Older fishes spit the hard egg shell out. To remove the crustacea, turn the air supply off. Within 3 to 5 minutes the egg shells rise to the surface and the nauplii congregate on the bottom. After 5 minutes they are siphoned off the bottom with an air hose and collected in an *Artemia* net (140 μm [0.14 mm] mesh). The siphoned water is discarded and replaced with aquarium water as long as the bottle still contains nauplii. As soon as the bottle is empty, we start a new culture. This way you have live *Artemia* available **every day.**

Some aspects of *Artemia* rearing are surprising. Have you ever measured the nitrite levels in an *Artemia* culture? After 2 days the indicator turns RED; which in the NO_2 test from TETRA means a nitrite concentration above 10 mg/l, a lethal concentration for fishes. Therefore, you should never put salt water from the *Artemia* culture bottle into the aquarium! But, *Artemia* survive. At a pH of 8.5, I have measured a high nitrite content, but I have not been able to detect any NH_4/NH_3 (ammonium/ammonia).

It is interesting to note the low quantity of NH_3/NH_4 in the culture bottle. Obviously there are nitrification bacteria present that immediately transform the excretions of the nauplii into NO_2. Actually, the bacteria can only be adhering to the shells of the *Artemia*.

Nitrobacter on or in *Artemia* eggs? It could be possible. You could find this useful for the nitrification phase of newly set-up aquaria. The following experiment is worthwhile: fill the culture bottle $^1/_3$ full with seawater from your aquarium and fill it the rest of the way with tap water. Two-thirds of the wine bottle then represents ca.$^1/_2$ a liter of water with a salinity of ca. 1%. A variation of ± 20% is not important when setting up *Artemia*. With good seawater, suspended algae will immediately develop with the *Artemia* eggs; these algae can provide nourishment for the *Artemia*. Totally different algae develop when the water is made from cooking salt, but it will take several days or weeks. Light and warmth are necessary for their development.

My *Artemia* bottles sit on the bridge of an aquarium in full light! *Artemia* also hatch in the dark, but they quickly die because of lack of algae.

These algae are present in the salt lakes of Utah. *Artemia* eggs carry the algae spores, even though they were cleaned!

Rearing *Artemia* is similar to rearing *Brachionus*. Those of you who want to rear *Artemia* to offer your fishes larger live foods should study the next paragraph. But I want to say from the beginning that rearing *Artemia* is quite troublesome, requiring a lot of space and time. It is easier to feed frozen brine shrimp. Nevertheless, a true marine aquarist has reared *Artemia* to their full size of ca. 12 mm at least once. A little warm-up to raising marine fishes!

The male crustacean has large pinchers, whereas females have an egg sac. Sexual fertilization occurs.

A ♂ *Artemia salina* at ∞ 8 magnification

Foods

Brachionus

Of the ca. 50 *Brachionus* species (rotifers), only **one** lives in seawater. Trillions and trillions of sea organisms feed on this species. Unimaginable. See photo on p. 163.
These animals can be raised on a small scale for your own marine animals. The Berlin Aquarium (Dr. LANGE) has a room and a worker devoted solely to raising *Brachionus* and algae. This has allowed 14 seawater fish species to be bred in Germany.

Culture

The following method can also be used on a small scale:
Chlorella algae or others are cultivated in salinities of ca. 6% (specific gravity 1.030 and above)! This keeps *Brachionus* out of the culture. If *Brachionus* were to enter an algae culture being grown in a medium of normal salinity, they would quickly multiply and devour the algae culture.
Young *Brachionus* are reared in water that is about 3.5% saline (specific gravity 1.024) and fed with algae from the illuminated algae culture. I use my old HQL lamps from 10 years ago for illumination. Any light source will work well, even incandescents are adequate. However, 2 or 3 fluorescent tubes (daylight) and perhaps a "Grolux" are best.
The photoperiod for an algae culture should be at least 14 hr. Nevertheless, constant, 24 hr illumination is better. KH should be approximately 10° dKH; pH should be around 8.0 to 8.2.
Brachionus strains can be acquired from various *Amphiprion* breeders. Your pet store will surely have additional sources.
Before you attempt to breed your animals, you should master culturing *Brachionus.* It simply takes patience and routine. If you can breed *Artemia,* you can also successfully raise *Brachionus.* Time and patience, and luck, of course, are always needed. You have everything to gain by breeding *Brachionus*—even additional income from selling your surplus production to your pet store or other aquarists who don't have the time to do the same. *Brachionus plicatilis* grows best at a specific gravity between 1.020 and 1.024. The higher the specific gravity, the smaller the animals remain.
The *Brachionus* culture is fed judiciously every morning and evening with PREIS Mikroplan® and/or *Chlorella* algae. Two drops of Microplan® are enough to feed a 100 l tank.

Brachionus as Food

Brachionus are a "luxury food" for the community tank!? For some tunicates, such as sea cucumbers, etc., this tiny food is mandatory. If only fed *Artemia,* sea cucumbers wane and finally starve after 1 $^1/_2$ to 2 years. But this subject is covered in the following volume. *Amphiprion* larvae depend on *Brachionus* to survive the first 10 days of life! Artemia are too large. Newly hatched *Brachionus* are $^1/_{10}$ the size of *Artemia.* Still, only newly hatched *Brachionus* are suitable for fish larvae. In nature, this zooplankton is available in almost unlimited quantities. Those who have ever dived or snorkeled know that. From 10:00 in the morning to 16:00, photography is impossible. In the coral reef regions, the water teams with plankton. The photos look milky! Once again, the higher the salinity, the smaller the *Brachionus* remain. This can be used to your advantage when rearing young fishes. The most important part of cultivating *Brachionus* and feeding young fish larvae during their first 10 to 15 days is grading the *Brachionus.* The smaller the better. Plankton netting is available from various manufacturers. But the amount you want to buy and the amount they want to sell do not coincide. Manufacturers want to sell square meters, and you need square centimeters. A coffee filter can also be used to strain *Brachionus.* However, this only filters the water from the *Brachionus,* it does not grade them. A rule of thumb: the mesh size of the sieve should be equal to the Ø of the eye of the juvenile fish (eye Ø of a newly hatched *Chromis viridis* ∪ 0.08 mm). The food must be smaller. Therefore, the mesh size of the sieve should be 0.05 to 0.08 mm. *Amphiprion* have an eye diameter of 0.09 to 0.12 mm. That is just less than the best mesh size to strain *Artemia* (0.14 mm). *Brachionus,* as well as the algae culture, should be aerated. A simple diffuser or air hose that moves the water is sufficient. The medium of *Brachionus* usually has an uncommonly high ammonia concentration and, therefore, needs to have a partial water exchange once a week.

Euplotes

Some species also eat unicellular *Euplotes* (a ciliate). However, *Euplotes* is not as well suited for cultivation. It, like *Brachionus,* can live even in very polluted water. It is possible that *Euplotes* accumulates toxins, or that its nutritional value is less than that of *Brachionus* - in any case, rearing young *Amphiprion* with *Euplotes* is sporadically successful at best, and the results are inferior to those obtained using *Brachionus.*

Foods

Chlorella

A *Chlorella* culture only uses newly made salt water (well aerated and heated for 1 to 2 days). The risk is too great that water from an aquarium will contain tiny medusae, small crustacea or *Brachionus*. With the introduction of these animals, the algae culture and, subsequently, the *Brachionus* culture that depends on the algae for food, will crash. The introduced pests would live in "the land of milk and honey" until the algae were gone.

Breeding set-up for *Brachionus*. Upper row, algae cultures; second row, *Brachionus*; lower left, a foam fractionator (protein skimmer).

Flake Food

Use only the best brands of flake foods. Even today certain important vitamins (especially A + E) are missing from some feeds. Larger fishes should be fed with large flakes and smaller fishes with normal sized flakes.

H Algivorous fishes demand flake foods that contain more vegetable matter (e.g., Tetra Conditioning Food) and a lower protein content.

C Planktivores and piscivores require flake food with a higher protein content.

O For omnivores you can feed foods from both the previous groups.

Flake food should be given sparingly three times a day in allotments that are consumed in 2 to 3 minutes. An employed aquarist hardly has time for more. However, these small portions do not satiate the fishes. Planktivores—and most of the smaller marine fishes fall into this category—spend the whole day searching for food in their natural habitat. An automatic feeder can help. There are economical set-ups which can deliver premeasured portions for every feeding. But watch that the automatic feeder does not lead to overfeeding.
Once a day (one day of fast per week does not hurt) your fishes should be fed generously with *Artemia*, frozen foods, or shellfish/fish meat. Depending on their requirements, invertebrates are fed pieces of either mussels (anemones) or, for example, TetraTips (crustacea).
Nocturnal animals, which include many of the shrimp, are fed , , or whole FD* tablets, which are delivered with a feeding tube "under their noses" after the main lights are turned off.

Plant Fare (H)

Herbivorous animals (those that are identified with an H in their food section) require vegetable fare in their diet to stay healthy. For invertebrates this means unicellular algae (*Chlorella*). These can easily be propagated at home. See *Brachionus/Artemia* rearing on pp. 166 ff.
Fishes usually accept large flakes readily, e.g., Tetra Spirulina Food or similar. However, some fishes will not accept flakes, at least not until they are acclimated. They prefer to peck their food off a hard substrate or to graze. For sensitive surgeonfishes (tangs), etc., you should have algae-covered stones at your disposal in a separate illuminated tank at ca. 20°C.
Where can you get sea lettuce? If you do not live or spend your holidays

* FD = freeze dried

Foods

at the coast and cannot collect it from a river/creek estuary, buy half a dozen or a dozen **live** oysters from a fish store. You can eat the oysters or feed them to your aquarium. Thoroughly clean the **shells** of protein remains with a sharp knife and place them in the **algae rearing tank.** It soon becomes evident that the shells are seeded with a number of small animals and plants, and sea lettuce is usually among the latter. When you have too much, freeze it.

The oysters can also be frozen, providing a high protein food for extended periods of time for animals such as anemones. Instead of oysters you can also use live mussels. If you are not successful with the sea lettuce, you can feed herbivores pesticide-free, **low nitrate** lettuce (blanched!). I want to warn you about purchased lettuce. Frequently it is hopelessly high in nitrates (up to 3000 mg/kg). Pesticides do the rest to poison the sensitive liver of fishes. A woman from a zoo-logical/garden center in Holland watched as thousands of turtles were poisoned in one day with lettuce. Ill animals placed under quarantine had been separated previously and were not fed lettuce. They were the only ones that survived.

The human liver is better able to cope with lettuce than the liver of reptiles and fishes. If you have excess green algae in the aquarium, freeze them for times of need. The same can be done with *Caulerpa* and other algae.

Snail shell with oven-dried food mash. Copepods (small crustacea) sit on this food and are eagerly consumed by small fishes.

Green algae, sea lettuce (*Monostroma* sp. or *Ulvaria oxysperma*); valuable vegetable fare for algivorous fishes.

Foods

Feeding Stones, Mussels

The following is another way to present vegetable fare:
Make a mash with Tetra Spirulina Food, spinach (home-grown, if possible), chickweed, dandelion!, perhaps some vitamin A, D and E drops, etc. Place about $1/4$ of a teaspoon into each mussel shell and bake them at about 150° C (300° F). For non-herbivorous fishes we add fish meat, shellfish, beef heart, freeze-dried foods, etc., to this mash.

Frozen Foods

Mysis, Artemia salina, bloodworms, *Cyclops*, shellfish meat, squid, *Sepia* and *Calanus finmarchicus* are commonly offered frozen foods. *Calanus* is the primary food of herring in the sea. It is very fatty, so it should be fed sparingly, if at all.
There is a long list of frozen foods. One of them is enough for most marine animals. Possible combinations can be obtained from the feeding instructions (**F**) in the individual species descriptions.
Frozen foods must remain frozen; that is, the food cannot be thawed at some point and then refrozen. Never keep more than you will use in half or, better, a quarter of a year. Store at temperatures below -25° C.

FD tablets are readily accepted by larger fishes.

Fresh or frozen mussels are available throughout the year.

Sand or glass shrimp, normally used for human consumption, are a sought fish food.

Foods

Freeze Dried Foods

Many types of frozen foods are also available freeze dried. The moisture is removed from the food in a vacuum. The dry food is easily kept for long periods of time. Store cool and dry!

FD Tablets

The best known FD tablets are TetraTips. Their smooth side will adhere to the aquarium glass, where they are nibbled on until gone.
Some anemones also accept whole tablets. TetraTips can also be passed through an *Artemia* sieve; the resulting powder is a good food for all kinds of planktivores and filter organisms (mussels, sponges, etc.).

Liquid Foods

The disadvantage of liquid foods is their short shelf life once opened. Therefore, they should all be stored in the refrigerator. Most can be kept for a few weeks like this.
Hydrated yeast used to be a common prepared food. Activated yeast cells, enriched with vitamins and trace elements, are much better (e.g., PREIS Microplan®). This liquid diet feeds filter feeders and planktonic microorganisms both in the aquarium and in the filter/substrate. *Artemia salina* and *Brachionus* can also be fed these types of foods.

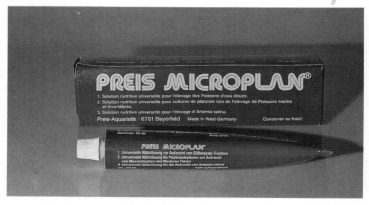

Adding Minerals, Trace Elements and Vitamins

See "Trace Elements" on p. 134.

Most nutrients are added with the food. Iron, iodine, and, for hard corals, strontium levels are often deficient.

Several companies offer complex preparations. Please be sure that vitamins A, B complex, C and E are administered through the food. For English speaking regions, TETRA has a preparation called Marine Vital that contains iodine and vitamin B supplements. Unfortunately, it is not available in Germany. DUPLA has a complete iron supplement with a corresponding test kit. PREIS has two very successful preparations: Organ Planer See and Formel PREIS Korall.

Here, too, all manufacturers swear by their products - just like they do for filters. I cannot list all the products here, but if the tanks in your pet store are healthy, ask them what products they use. Do not overdose your tank. Just like with feeding, excesses are harmful.

Iron, strontium, and iodine must be added, since they are precipitated out of the water and become unavailable.

Vitamin A and E are prescription drugs. Because they are fat soluble vitamins, they can only be added through the feed. Once or twice a week, depending on the amount of feed given, 1 to 5 drops are placed on mussel meat, frozen foods or similar. This is not necessary for fishes that are fed good quality flake foods.

Algae (*Caulerpa*) need to be fertilized when growth diminishes despite good water quality and sufficient light. Even though slowed growth is frequently desired, I just don't consider an aquarium healthy if it doesn't have good algae growth. Besides the nitrates and phosphates naturally present in the aquarium ecosystem, higher algae require CO_2 (see the chapter "Algae" on pp. 214 ff.) as well as trace elements such as iron and manganese! They should be given supplements once or twice a week.

Capture Techniques

CATCHING YOUR FISHES (IN THE AQUARIUM)

You learn to dread catching fishes from among rockwork of a fully decorated aquarium. The thought of having to take out all the beautiful "live rocks," coral, disc and colonial anemones, soft and leather corals, plus all the decoration, almost causes a headache. All of this because of a few sick fishes!? Of course, it would have been easier to have only kept invertebrates. But you wanted fishes (me too!). We must accept the consequences, forget comfort, raise the shirt sleeves, set the kid in motion (if present and old enough), pull out rocks, etc., place them in a plastic tub with aquarium water, and capture the fish. Invertebrates are **always** transferred submersed in water to the other container. Especially sea urchins! If sea urchins are lifted out of the water mouth-side up, they swallow air and can die. Sensitive anthozoans cannot be transported out of water either. The water lends support to the water-filled animal. In the air, it is flaccid and easily injured.

Now, enough stone edifications and animals have been removed from the aquarium so you can see the fishes again—if the water has not become too turbid.

You can now either chase the fish with two nets until it is exhausted, or you can use the two nets to gently "guide" it into either a glass bleaker (1 to 2 l) or an all-glass tank. The latter procedure is, of course, preferred. Before beginning with this one to two hour endeavor, please note:

The two most frequent seawater diseases, *Oodinium* and *Cryptocarion,* can be controlled, at least in their initial stages, without emptying the tank.

The simplest method is by lowering the specific gravity:

Remove half of the water from the aquarium, and refill it with water passed through reverse osmosis (approximate final specific gravity of 1.016 to 1.018). A few of the dots soon disappear—if the water is otherwise of good quality. Subsequently evaporated water is replaced with **salt water** until a specific gravity of 1.024 is reestablished.

However, if it is imperative that the fish be removed (grave illness or bite), you **have to** bite the bullet and remove the decor to catch the beast (sorry . . . fish).

try, pH or pH 7 is turned until the meter displays the value 7.0. The electrode is washed again and inserted in the pH 9 buffer solution (some manufactures use 10 or 12). With the knob for slope (mV/pH), the value 9 (or whichever buffer solution you chose as the second reference buffer) is now adjusted. After an additional cleaning and a last check with the pH 7 buffer, the electrode is ready to be used.

pH electrodes should not dry out. This is not a danger with systems that provide continuous measurements, since the electrodes are constantly submersed in the aquarium water. The electrodes of simple meters are frequently placed in a glass of water that later evaporates . . .

Those who want to provide optimal care for their electrodes will store them in 3 molar (M) KCl. Unfortunately, it is only rarely offered in the hobby trade, but it is available through laboratory supply houses. You can also purchase potassium chloride and make your own solution. A 3 M KCl solution contains 225 g of potassium chloride in one liter of water (distilled).

A plastic container (old buffer bottle) with a hole the size of the electrode in the top filled with 3 ml of 3 M KCl solution is an effective way to store the electrode. This prolongs the life of the pH electrode. Nevertheless, after some time (1 to 1 $\frac{1}{2}$ years), they can no longer be standardized and must be exchanged. pH electrodes in continuous use are exposed to other dangers. Puffers and triggerfish can crack them with their teeth. Be sure to place the electrodes in a protected area. The sump of a trickle filter is ideal. Within an aquarium, it can be protected by a basket. For instance, the meshed intake pipe of the filter will work.

Maintenance

Daily

- Feeding. You can set aside one day a week when you don't feed your fishes—except for juveniles. The best time to observe the animals is while they are feeding. If a fish does not accept food as usual, it needs special attention. I would stop all feeding for 1 or 2 days, only watching the one that refuses food. If after two days it does not come to the food, you can conclude that the fish is sick and must be removed from the tank for treatment.
- Check the water values. If you have easily readable controllers, you can note the temperature, pH and redox readings during the daily feedings.
- All animals are inspected and the fishes are counted. A sick or deceased fish in a dead corner **can** kill the others. A larger dead fish/ anemone poisons all of the water within a few days.

Weekly

- The CO_2 controller and the KH value are monitored weekly.
- Feed anemones with fresh fish or mussel meat.
- Clean the glass (only the front pane). In "see-through tanks," of course, the back pane also needs to be cleaned. Leave the algae on the lateral panes. Some fishes will use the algae as additional nourishment.
- Compensate for evaporation—if it is not performed automatically. If automated, top-up the reservoir of the refiller.
- Empty and clean the protein skimmer tray. The skimmer contact pipe must always be clean and free of oils—or the efficiency decreases. Clean it with a bottle brush in conjunction with increased air and water flow. All dirt particles are pushed out of the inside of the pipe.
- Clean the cover and outside of the tank.

Every Two to Four Weeks

- Clean the filter and piping (hoses); renew the crushed dolomite and activated carbon; thin out *Caulerpa* if necessary. "Work" the bottom with your fingers and siphon up the detritus.
- Perform a water exchange of at least 10%. Prepare new water.
- Refill alcohol for the nitrate filter (30% ethanol).
- Clean the pH/redox electrodes with pepsin and a light detergent; rinse off thoroughly with water afterwards.

> Maintenance and care of electrodes for meters and controllers is explained in detail on pp. 182 f.

Semi Annually

- Check the lights. Do the bulbs have a purchase date? I would either print the date of installation on every bulb or fluorescent tube or use a diary! Fluorescent tubes should be replaced annually—18 months at the latest! The intensity of the illumination can be verified with a luxmeter if reference values were noted when the lamp was installed.
- Calibrate the pH and controller electrodes; replace them after 18 months or when they can no longer be calibrated. The same applies for mV (redox) electrodes.
- Standardizing solutions should be replaced every 6 months and dated. One year old buffer solutions have a deviation of 0.3 pH units!
- **In the summer**, turn one heater off if you have been using two; **in the fall**, turn the second heater back on.

The Aquarium During Vacation

A mature seawater aquarium can be left alone for a week if everything is double checked before departure.

For an extended absence, the caretaker should be told how to feed the aquarium. It is best to individually package their rations **for each day** and date them. Also explain how to set up *Artemia* and how to separate the nauplii from their egg shells (see p. 168). In order to reduce the risk of a disease problem in your absence, do not introduce new fishes to the tank within 6 weeks of your departure date. Make copies of the daily and weekly checklist on pages 190-191, and go over them point by point with the caretaker. It would be a very good idea to leave the telephone numbers of one or two seawater hobbyists and/or pet stores, so that an experienced person can be consulted in case of an emergency. You should not expect your mother-in-law to become quick friends with pH values, redox measurements, CO_2 infusions and perhaps a malfunctioning controller unit. In any case, a back-up filter should be available, the CO_2 bottle filled prior to departure, and any overheating problems because of lamps, sunlight, etc., should be solved. The aquarium room should not be affected by outside temperatures, even if they climb to 30°C. Shades or drapes should keep the heat out. If it is your experience that the room where the aquarium is located can become excessively warm, installing a chiller before you leave on vacation may be warranted (see p. 107).

Ready-made seawater must be available for a water exchange. The quarantine tank should have water, a heater and filter—at least if you go to the beach for vacation. Who knows, maybe you will bring something back.

Practical Techniques

Phosphate in the Aquarium (also see p. 132)

Phosphate (entering with the food) is actually the biggest problem in a tank that houses both fishes and invertebrates. Fishes can tolerate concentrations over 1.5 mg/l.

Normal levels are 0.1-0.2 mg/l. Invertebrates with zooxanthellae cannot tolerate high levels of phosphate. Overfertilization inhibits the growth of zooxanthellae. Colonial and disk anemones wane. In contrast, larger anemones that are fed fish, mussel and crustacea meat are not affected; for example, *Stoichactus* (carpet anemone) grows great at a phosphate concentration of 1.5 mg/l.

The phosphate concentration in an aquarium can be lowered in three ways:

1. Through the growth of large quantities of algae, perhaps in a separate algae tank.
2. Decoration and substrate consisting of calcium carbonate (dolomite). It binds phosphorus, forming calcium phosphate. Part of the material must be exchanged every few months. Alpha Marin or Rowalith can be used in an external filter and exchanged every 4 weeks.
3. Two- and three-valent iron also binds phosphate. You can use iron preparations such as Duplaplant 24 or an **iron** pot scrubber (from the kitchen) that is placed in the nitrate filter where it slowly disintegrates. However, do not use a **copper** pot scrubber—although you will have no more woes from *Oodinium*, you won't have any other animals either, at least not invertebrates.

The Nitrate Filter does not Work (also see pp. 72 and 128)

The nitrate filter only functions with a corresponding energy source. The DELTEC system uses methanol in plastic bags: the alcohol slowly diffuses through the plastic. However, there are cases where the system fails and the nitrate filter suddenly produces nitrite.

The following happens: denitrification in the anaerobic nitrate filter is compromised due to lack of food. Through reduction, nitrate is transformed into nitrite (poisonous), as can be measured at the outlet of the nitrate filter. The only solution is to immediately slow the filter cycle and add a carbon source (alcohol). Although the bags are not empty, they are not releasing enough "food" for the denitrifying bacteria.

Another way to add carbon is through a tiny "dosing pump," such as the one used by SÖCHTING. A small catalyst particle (magnesium oxide) submersed in hydrogen peroxide releases oxygen. This small amount of gas causes approximately one drop of alcohol per hour to be released—exactly the correct quantity of alcohol for the nitrate filter.

The anaerobic conditions in a nitrate filter must be constantly controlled with a redox (ORP) meter. As previously indicated, the redox range within the filter should lie between -200 and -300 mV.

An elegant solution is the previously mentioned "dosing pump" you make at home. You can get the H_2O_2 from a pet or drug store. Hydrogen

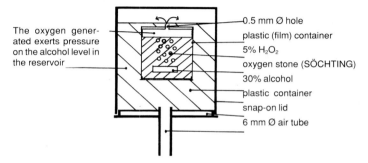

The oxygen generated exerts pressure on the alcohol level in the reservoir

- 0.5 mm Ø hole
- plastic (film) container
- 5% H_2O_2
- oxygen stone (SÖCHTING)
- 30% alcohol
- plastic container
- snap-on lid
- 6 mm Ø air tube

peroxide is usually sold in concentrations of 30%. We dilute it by mixing 1 part 30% H_2O_2 with 5 parts distilled water.

As our alcohol source, we can use methyl alcohol from DELTEC, but it is poisonous; therefore, keep away from children. Blindness results if it is drunk! Thirty percent ethyl alcohol is much less dangerous, or we simply use 32% vodka.

Besides the correct dosification of the alcohol, the unstable environment inside a nitrate filter is a constant problem. It can be solved by using a small circulating pump **inside** the nitrate filter. The water is pumped from the bottom up; this guarantees the same oxygen levels—or lack thereof—everywhere in the filter. This prevents a catastrophe when there is a food shortage in the filter. The redox value in the filter increases until it equals that of the aquarium. The bacteria stop their nitrate metabolism but do not die! And the filter does not produce NO_2. Unfortunately, this nitrate filter with a circulation pump is not presently sold in stores.

Practical Techniques

Carbon Dioxide Supply (also see p. 101)

In my tank I start adding CO_2 at about 10:00. At that time the aquarium lights have been on for 2 hr. The pH has fallen overnight to anywhere between 8.2 and 8.0. At 10:00 it is already at 8.3. Now the controller begins CO_2 supplementation. Regulate the fine adjustment valve until one bubble per second (1 one thousand, 2 one thousand, etc.) is released. This rate is enough to keep the pH from rising above 8.3 or 8.4. If the pH falls below 8.2, the controller turns the CO_2 off. The increase in pH is a result of CO_2 respiration by algae. Therefore, a decrease in the CO_2 concentration is immediately accompanied by a rise in pH.

At night I turn the CO_2 bottle totally off. If the regulator fails, the pH will not fall below 8.0 during the night if the water is sufficiently buffered (KH). If the pH should fall below 7.5, or even 7.0, through erroneous management, the water in the aquarium needs to be strongly aerated at once to vent the carbon dioxide. The fishes will quickly recover.

Excess CO_2 lowers the pH, which in turn causes fishes to be covered with *Cryptocarion*-like dots within a few hours. These white dots disappear when the pH rises.

Pseudochromis porphyreus with white dots caused by excess CO_2.

Amphipods

The third group consists of little crustacea that live in the substrate. They are black, gammarus-like, nimble individuals which attack anything edible that falls to the bottom. Juvenile fish and sick animals are ambushed and literally hollowed out. The little crustacea are relatively harmless in small numbers, but they can easily turn into a plague. Once their numbers increase and food is in short supply, amphipods will attack healthy fishes. You cannot even remove them entirely from the aquarium with fish and mussel meat. There are no known natural enemies. They can even pinch the human hand. Sensitive skin reacts by reddening and itching. Only constant trapping and feeding the tank sparingly helps. In rearing tanks and those that contain, for example, sea horses (since they are slow), only a complete break-down and cleaning solves the problem.

These crustacea are introduced with "live rock" from extraneous tanks. TetraTips are a reliable lure. Perhaps a weir basket can be used!

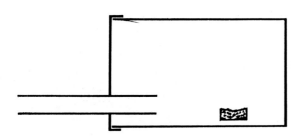

Clear cup with a glued-in weir

Unwanted Guests

Rock Anemones

There are also pronounced pests among the anthozoans. The rock anemones of the genus *Aiptasia* can—once introduced with live rock—multiply rapidly in a reef tank. Their potent toxin injures other anthozoans. Large rock anemones can also be a threat to smaller fishes. Mechanical control of these animals is practically impossible. If the are smashed, countless new polyps develop. Only chemical and biological controls remain as options. You can kill aiptasids by injecting a small quantity of hydrochloric acid into the body of the polyp using a hypodermic needle. A few drops are sufficient. These small quantities do not affect the buffering capacity of the aquarium water. The disposable syringe and the 30 % hydrochloric acid can be purchased in a drug store. However, when trying to control heavy infestations, this method turns quite laborious and cumbersome. Using fishes to biologically control them would be easier. There are a few species of butterflyfishes which devour rock anemones with pleasure (e.g., *Chelmon rostratus, Chaetodon kleinii* and *Ch. lunula*). In one to two weeks, one *Chaetodon* can totally free even a heavily infested 500 l aquarium.

Unfortunately, there is a reason why this idea was introduced conditionally. The import of these fishes is forbidden (in Germany).

This method to control aiptasids is only available to our foreign friends. The only alternative open to German hobbyists is chemical control. Feed *Artemia* and *Brachionus* sparingly as soon as rock anemones begin to multiply heavily.

By the way, rock anemones multiply significantly faster in poor water (high nitrate and phosphate concentrations) versus clean water. Good water quality is a control measure against unwanted parasites.

Aiptasia sp.

Worms (Annelida)

Bristleworms (Polychaeta)

Of this large class of worms, a number of species can be considered pests in our aquarium. Polychaeta are not uncommon on live rock, and some species will even multiply in the aquarium. Several species can grow very large; for example, *Nereis* sp. can readily attain a length of 30 cm. With their huge appetite they can cause severe damage to anthozoans. The animals are nocturnal and can be captured with large tweezers or other grasping tools. It is very painful to touch them with your hands. The worm's bristles remain stuck in the hand, making you feel like you tangled with a piece of glass wool or cactus.

Some bristleworms inhabit self-built gangways, which are hardened with bottom substrate. These usually terminate at a "victim," e.g., *Actinodendron* sp. During the day the worm sits at the other end of the tube under a stone. Bristleworms have few enemies.

The beautiful lobster *Panulirus versicolor* has a predilection for polychaetes. Unfortunately, this species is only suited as a juvenile for the reef aquarium. Once it reaches a certain size, it also preys on fishes. Smaller bristleworms that only live in the bottom substrate are readily eaten by larger bristle worms. However, since smaller polychaetes loosen the bottom substrate, they can be considered beneficial.

Hermodice carunculata, one of the large bristleworms.

Unwanted Guests

Planarians (Flatworms)

Planarians are members of the phylum Platyhelminthes (flatworms). These animals have a simple morphology, and like rock anemones, they have a high capacity of regeneration. Various types of flatworms appear in the reef aquarium, everything from colorless species that parasitize disc anemones to free-living red planarias. The latter harbor zooxanthellae in their body, similar to anthozoans. When these animals first appeared in aquaria, hardly anyone suspected what was in store for them. Many aquarists were happy about these interesting animals that would even reproduce in their tank.

However, they multiplied at an incredible rate. Initially, they only sit on the decoration, clumping into beautiful red balls in some parts. Later they cover all the stones, substrate, and anthozoans. The aquarium looks like a forest in the fall. All the other tank inhabitants asphyxiate under the mass of planarians. This worm was threatening to become the scourge of the seawater aquarist; it caused great damage, especially in tanks illuminated with strong HQI lamps. Fishes avoid flatworms. Only the mandarin fish (genus *Synchiropus*) eats them. However, a massive infestation cannot be controlled with these fishes. They can only be used as a prophylactic measure in aquaria that appear to be free of planarians. Some starfishes also seem to feed on planarians.

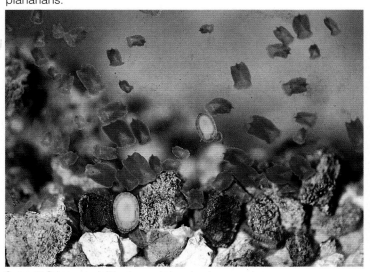

Some starfishes, e.g., brittle stars, eat planarians!

Meanwhile, CONCURAT, a chemical compound known to be effective against these worms, is making its rounds in aquarist circles. Unfortunately, it can only be obtained through a veterinarian. In some experiments it proved to be an extremely potent flatworm poison. Other animals, including tubeworms, were not affected. Within 30 min the flatworms are dead. This medication is used in animal science against intestinal worms.

Dosage: 0.8 g per 100 l aquarium water, based on the active ingredient.

> CONCURAT has not been 100% successful in controlling flatworms, and furthermore, it is much more difficult to determine the needed dosage than using Bio-Ex that ab produces (available in pet stores). However, when controlling *Convolutriluba* (= red flatworm) you need to know that these flatworms and their body fluids are highly toxic, and the filtration material will have to be cleaned after treatment. Heavy infestations demand that the filter is cleaned even **during** the treatment. Otherwise, severe symptoms of poisoning are shown by invertebrates, and fishes die within two hours. Remember, this is not from the medication, but from the toxin released by the flatworms (according to Dr. Lange, Berlin Aquarium).

Snails

Both sea snails and sea slugs (nudibranchs) can be accidentally introduced into a seawater aquarium. Both groups contain members that can be considered pests. In particular various nudibranchs imitate leather corals in shape and color and are pronounced predators of these animals. They are well camouflaged on their victim. Therefore, carefully inspect soft and leather corals when buying. Coral-feeding nudibranchs should be removed from the tank. Algae-feeding nudibranchs also exist (see "Das Aquarium", 9/90).

Some of the shelled snails also prey on anthozoans. Although they frequently have very colorful shells, you should resist the impulse that says "leave it in." Be on the safe side and remove them.

Only the limpets of the genus *Patella* are appreciated because of their algivorous diet. Look at the middle of the photo on the facing page.

In larger numbers these snails can also turn into a pest. They can reproduce at a length of 8 mm. However, these very hardy animals do little damage. They live on algae and will even eat smear algae. There are no known methods of control, and the need for such is rare. None of these snails can be found on a clean front pane, and they are seldom bothersome in other locals.

Diseases

FISH DISEASES

Fish diseases rarely appear in well established marine aquaria. However, when acquiring new fishes, there is the danger of an infection spreading quickly from the new arrival to the other specimens. But it is not always the case that the "new kid on the block" brought the disease. Many ectoparasites are latently present in nature. New animals are physically stressed from the unusual surroundings, i.e., a change in food, water and tankmates. Transportation and the less than optimal care received from catching stations and distributors also contribute to the overall weakening of the animals. Fishes subject to these conditions are easy prey to parasites. The parasites can multiply rapidly on these animals, producing a large number of tomites, which can then infest the other tankmates.

Diseased fishes in tanks with only fishes can be medicated. This is not possible with most (copper-based) medications in a reef aquarium with both invertebrates and fishes. Sick animals must be captured, transferred, and treated. Because of the jagged-edged and rough-surfaced decorations, losses are usually incurred during this process. However, NEOSAL can be used in a reef aquarium. It helps fight *Oodinium* and *Cryptocarion*.

The best prophylaxis against ectoparasitic infections is to quarantine new animals for several weeks. But since most aquarists do not have a quarantine tank, the purchase of a fish turns into a thing of trust. Only buy from reputable dealers who have maintenance systems that guarantee good water quality.

Ask your dealer:
• if he puts copper in his tanks
• if the fish eats.

Animals from aquaria which are constantly medicated with copper sulfate should not be purchased—unless you have the chance to let the animals regain their health and terminate the copper treatment in a quarantine tank.

Do not acquire fishes that don't feed. In case of doubt, ask to see the fish fed!

Do not mix and match animals without rhyme or reason. Beginners should seek advice from dealers and only acquire robust animals which are temperamentally compatible. This serves to prevent shy, tranquil fishes from being housed with aggressive tankmates that will constantly subdue them. This, too, creates a stressful situation that makes the animals prone to disease.

Even if all of these recommendations are followed, there is no guarantee that your animals will remain free of fish parasites. Therefore, it is important to quickly recognize that your animal is ill and correctly identify its illness. For the beginner, this is frequently a big problem. The most common diseases of marine fishes are presented in the following pages.

Ectoparasites (External Parasites)

The most common diseases of coral fishes are ectoparasites. The symptoms are quite similar to those expressed by freshwater fishes: white dots of various sizes, rapid breathing, clamped fins, and scraping on aquarium objects. Under "favorable" conditions, the causative agents multiply very quickly and rapidly infect the entire population. *Oodinium* and *Cryptocarion* are especially problematic in seawater.

Amphiprion clarkii infested with *Oodinium*

Diseases

Oodinium (Coral Fish Disease)

Causative Agent

The causative agent of this frequent disease of seawater fishes is the dinoflagellate *Oodinium ocellatum*. Systematically, we are dealing with a Dinophyceae of the subclass Blastodinophycideae; in other words, this is an alga! Dinoflagellates are also disease agents in freshwater. *Oodinium pillularis* is the causative agent of velvet, which labyrinth fishes and cyprinids are especially susceptible to. When you buy fishes whose treatment, arrival time, etc., is unknown, an independent quarantine tank is a necessity. If you do not have the space (or the means), you have to risk placing these animals (if possible only one species) directly into the display tank. Do not acquire new fishes within six weeks prior to leaving for a vacation!

Closely observe the newcomer and the other fishes for a few days. As soon as dots appear on their fins (*Oodinium* or *Cryptocarion*), treatment is indicated.

Life Cycle

Oodinium ocellatum is 0.02 to 0.1 mm in size. In severe cases, the fishes may be so infested that they appear as if covered by velvet.

Oodinium attacks the skin and gills of fishes. There it adheres and feeds on the tissue of the host. After a few days it forms a cyst and sinks to the bottom. The cyst undergoes 8 cellular divisions. After approximately 3 days, 256 tomites, called dinospores, emerge. These free-swimming flagellates search for a new host fish to grasp hold of. That is an easy feat in the narrow confines of an aquarium.

The tomite stage is the only phase in the life cycle of *Oodinium* which can be controlled with medication. UV radiation or a diatom filter can decrease the number of tomites and reduce the chances new infections.

The tomites are only viable for one to two days. If they do not find a new host within that time, they die. The complete life cycle of *Oodinium* takes 7 to 10 days. The first stages of the epidemic usually go unnoticed; a few parasites are hard to see on the skin of the fishes. When the first tomites hatch from the cysts, the skin and gills become heavily infested. Now quick treatment is required. Although critical, this stage is still curable.

Symptoms

According to AMLACHER (1986), the effect of the parasite primarily manifests itself by destroying gill tissue. Other affected organs are not damaged. *Oodinium* enters the epithelial tissue of the gills, forming visible white knots on the gill tissue. Severe cases lead to respiratory problems and end in death. Observe the respiration rate of the fishes.

If they respire faster than you can count, there is a problem stemming from damaged gills (or a lack of oxygen because of some other reason, e.g., pH values below 7.0).

Treatment
The treatment of choice is copper sulfate (0.8 to 1 mg/l). This medication is totally unsuitable for invertebrates, and it disrupts the biological equilibrium of the aquarium. Therefore, it should only be administered in quarantine tanks that can be totally cleaned afterwards.
MarinOomed (TETRA) is significantly milder and safe for invertebrates. The latter preparation will not even damage the microfauna (*Nitrobacter* and *Nitrosomonas*). Its formula is derived totally from plants.

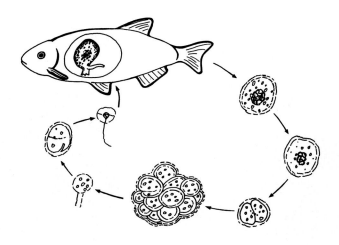

Life cycle of *Oodinium*

Diseases

Cryptocarion (Marine Ich)

Causative Agent
The causative agent, *Cryptocarion irritans*, is a ciliate. Externally it is very similar to freshwater *Ichthyophthirius multifiliis* (white spot, ich). For this reason, *Cryptocarion* is sometimes called marine ich.

Symptoms
Cryptocarion tomites attack the fishes by attaching to the skin. However, these are significantly larger than *Oodinium* tomites and, therefore, easier to see (size of a pin head). As with most ectoparasitic infestations, the animals scratch themselves on objects and have a heightened respiration rate.

Treatment
After a few days the parasites drop off and form cysts. The organism undergoes cellular divisions within the cysts. After approximately 8 days, numerous tomites emerge. *Cryptocarion* is susceptible to medication during its tomite stage.
We recommend the following procedure:
1. Prepare high quality sea salt for a partial water exchange; aerate 24 hr.
2. Remove $^1/_2$ of the tank water and discard.
3. The new seawater (or well matured water of a lesser quality brand of salt) is placed into the tank until it is $^3/_4$ full.
4. Top-up the aquarium with **freshwater** (tap water or water processed through reverse osmosis) that is free/low in nitrate until the aquarium water has a specific gravity of 1.017 to 1.018.
5. Add TETRA MarinOomed.

Lowering the salinity is usually safe for invertebrates; only crustacea such a shrimp and lobsters are sensitive.

Infestation of *Cryptocarion* on *Forcipiger*

Cryptocarion infestation on *Chaetodon falcula*

Cryptocarion infestation on *Pseudochromis porphyreus*

Cryptocarion is always latent in an aquarium (and on fish). The outbreak occurs "overnight" under stressful conditions, e.g., when the pH falls below 7.5. If the water quality problem is corrected, the disease usually disappears without further treatment.

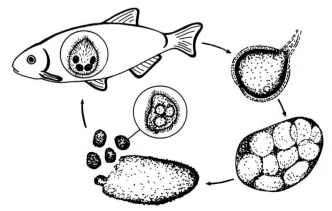

Life cycle of *Cryptocarion*

Diseases

Bacterial Diseases

Bacterial diseases of the skin and fins of marine fishes are solely caused by poor water quality.

Bacterial fin rot (*Bacteriosis pinnarum*) and skin lesions (*Vibriosis*) destroys fins and skin. They are treated with broad spectrum medications, e.g., TETRA's General Tonic (cannot be used with invertebrates) or specific antibiotics (some only available through veterinarians). Treat for 8 days in a quarantine tank.

However, it is more important to find and correct the underlying cause:

- Does the tank need a water exchange?
- Is the aquarium overstocked? Is the filter underpowered?
- Is the aquarium receiving excessive amounts of food?

An UV lamp can noticeably reduce the concentration of germs in the water and, consequently, the danger of infections. Protein skimming with ozone also diminishes the number of disease agents.

Acanthurus leucosternon, bacterial infection with skin separation due to poor water conditions.

Fish Tuberculosis

Fish tuberculosis is a very rare disease of marine fishes. The causative agent is *Mycobacterium marinum*. As in freshwater, fish tuberculosis in seawater is seldom curable. A definite diagnosis can only be made by a specialist. In advanced stages, tumors break through the skin. At that point the animals have to be removed and humanely destroyed to prevent the disease from spreading to the other inhabitants.

Fungal Diseases

Fungal diseases, caused by the fungus *Ichthyosporidium,* are frequently confused with tuberculosis. Here too, tumors will eventually break through the skin. The disease is also incurable. However, a cure can be attempted with a combination of PREIS Prebac and Cryptan! Treat for 8 days. Do not use in the presence of invertebrates.
Other fungal diseases present themselves as cotton-like coverings. Injury sites are especially susceptible to secondary fungal infections. Improved aquarium hygiene and disinfectants, e.g., MarinOomed, are effective treatments.

Chaetodon kleinii with *Ichthyosporidium*

Diseases

Viral Infections

Another nodular disease is caused by a virus (*Lymphocystis*). Both nodular diseases are incurable in their advanced stages. During the initial phases you can try removing the infected sections (carefully cut fins with nodules) or brush them with iodine. PREIS recommends treating the fishes with a combination of Prebac and Cryptan (cannot be used with invertebrates).

Ascites/Protruding Scales

These infirmities are viral in origin. Severe cases are treated with a combination of PREIS Prebac and Cryptan in a quarantine tank **without** invertebrates. Mild cases (the fish is still eating) are treated only with Prebac; nevertheless, a quarantine tank without invertebrates is still needed.

Diseases from Sporozoans and Protozoans

Occasionally, sporozoans cause diseases in seawater fishes. They can only be diagnosed by a specialist. *Haemogregarina* is a blood parasite. *Eimeria* lives in the intestine, and *Pleistophora* attacks the skin and muscle tissue. Some of these parasites only reproduce through an intermediate host, e.g., leeches, so the spread of these diseases in the aquarium is essentially impossible. Others, such as *Pleistophora,* can become very dangerous.

A nodular disease is also caused by a sporozoan (*Myxobolus*).

Queen angel with *Lymphocystis*

Scat with *Lymphocystis*

Sporozoans cannot be readily controlled with medications. You can try Prebac and Cryptan.

Clownfish Disease (The Protozoan *Brooklynella hostilis*)

Clownfish disease predominately attacks clownfishes immediately after import. Mortality can reach 90% if correct treatment is not immediately instigated.

The disease manifests itself by a whitish gray film on the skin and gills, caused by a unicellular cilitate. First symptoms often include loss of equilibrium, loss of appetite, and mucous secretions of the skin. Although the disease first looks like an *Oodinium* infestation, it progresses faster. Two to three days after the first symptoms, the infected animals die.

The only known treatment is Brook® (PREIS). An importer should have this medication on hand when importing new *Amphiprion*; otherwise, there is the risk of losing the entire batch. According to BASSLEER, 1991 (Fischkrankheiten im Meerwasser-Aquarium [Fish Diseases in the Marine Aquarium]), a combination of formaldehyde and malachite green helps. In AM 1983, Vol. 9, there is a detailed report about *Brooklynella*. It should not remain unmentioned that *Amphiprion* which are immediately placed with enough appropriately sized anemones where the fishes can hide and "bathe" can survive the disease.

The reason for the frequent infections of clownfishes is the transport water, which often has Rivanol or similar substances to preclude bacterial infections. However, this water weakens the fish so that they are an easy target for the disease vectors always latent in their bodies. The prophylactic treatment is applied in a quarantine tank whose salinity is half the norm (specific gravity 1.011 to 1.012).

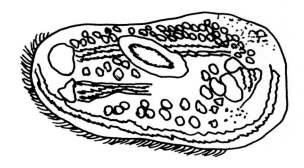

Brooklynella hostilis at ca. x 500 magnification

Diseases

Worms and Crustacea

Gill Worms (Usually Gill Crustacea)

Coral fishes can, like freshwater fishes, be struck by gill worms. *Tetraonchus* is frequently found on wimplefishes and puffers. Heavy gill worm infestations are characterized by fast breathing and spread opercula. Some larger species of gill worms can be identified with the naked eye after carefully lifting an operculum.

The gill worms can be controlled with formalin or Masoten in a quarantine tank. However, both medications are not without their risks to the fishes (and for humans!). Gyrotox (ZOOMEDICA [TETRA]) or PREIS Coly are preferable. Treat for 2 to 3 days!

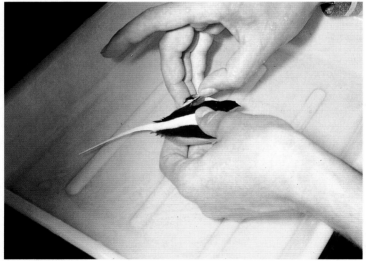

The operculum of *Heniochus acuminatus* is carefully opened. A second person should then inspect the fish with a magnifying glass.

Crustacea

Of the parasitic crustacea, fish lice (*Argulus*) and gill maggots (*Ergasilus*) can be introduced. Although these parasites are infrequently present, they are very dangerous for smaller fishes. *Argulus* is recognized by red sting sites: the crustacean can also be identified with the naked eye. Gill maggots can normally be seen with the naked eye after carefully lifting the operculum.

Use three times the recommended dosage of NEOSAL (in a bucket) for 2 to 4 minutes. The crustacea fall off and the fish is immediately returned to its tank.

Argulus

Parasitic copepod

Intestinal Worms

The symptoms for intestinal worms are mucous excretions, emaciation, cloudy eyes, pelt-like skin structure, nodules beneath the skin, and pale coloration. Treatment is performed in a quarantine tank with PREIS Coly, which is safe for invertebrates.

The importer should carry out prophylactic treatment for 2 to 3 days, especially for new imports.

Other diseases caused by helminths, which are caused by cestodes (tapeworms), trematodes (flatworms), or ascarids (roundworms), rarely appear in the aquarium. The animals have a complex life cycle requiring intermediate hosts. Only newly imported animals can harbor an infestation.

Disease

Upper left: *Pomacentrus* injured by bites. Secondary fungal and bacterial infections result. Once the tail fin has deteriorated to the caudal peduncle, the fish cannot be saved.

Above and next page upper left: When injecting an antibiotic or a vitamin B solution, the fish has to be immobilized. The fish is injected below the center of the dorsal fin, approximately 2 to 5 mm below the scales.

Lower left: Pop-eye caused by nematodes.

Upper right on facing page: The white nose on *Acanthurus leucosternon* indicates deficiency symptoms and stress.

Lower facing page: Diagnosing gill flukes on an angel: the thorned operculum is lifted with a soft plastic ring.

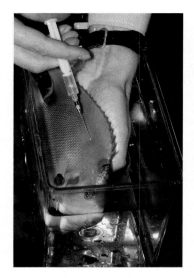

Symbols Used in the Species Descriptions

Fam.:	Family
Subfam.:	Subfamily
Syn.:	Synonym = different names for the same species. In this book we mention synonyms in exceptional cases, especially when the species has also been mentioned in the scientific literature under an erroneous name, e.g., *Chromis viridis,* whose synonym is *Chromis caerulea.*
Common name:	The most commonly used trade names have been listed. Frequently, a new common name is suggested, or it is entirely omitted. Should you have knowledge of a common name, please write us. It will be included in the next edition. Next to the Latin name, the name of the describer and the year of the description are listed. If both describer and year are in parenthesis, the species was initially classified under a different genus.
Hab.:	Habitat. This refers to the species' natural geographic origin.
Sex:	Sexual differences. ♂ = male, ♀ = female.
Soc.B./Assoc.:	Social Behavior/Association. An indication on how the organism interacts with other species and animal groups and, when possible, what animals it can and cannot be housed with.
M.:	Conditions recommended for maintenance. Deviations to normal conditions are given. Additional information can be obtained from the data line at the bottom of every species description. Because marine organisms (except those from the Red Sea) should always be maintained under similar conditions, indications about pH, redox, or carbonate hardness are not specifically given.
Light:	Light requirement. Sunlight zone = 30,000 to 50,000 lux; moderate light zone = 10,000 to 20,000 lux; dim light zone = 500 to 1,000 lux. These values are measured at the water surface of the aquarium.
B./Rep.:	Breeding/Reproduction. Indications are given on breeding the various species to the best of our knowledge. There are no breeding reports for the majority of animals, and we ask for information dealing with possible breeding successes.

Symbols Used in the Species Descriptions

F:	C = Carnivore (meat eater) H = Herbivore (plant eater) O = Omnivore (meat and plant eater) More specific recommendations are given in the individual animal descriptions. Note that FD = freeze dried.
S:	Specialties. Deals with subject matter not corresponding to any other category.
T:	Temperature.
L/Ø:	Length/Diameter. For fishes and crustacea the total length, including the tail, is given. For anthozoans we think it is more appropriate to indicate a diameter.
TL:	Tank length. Although aquaria outside Europe are usually sold by volume, length gives a better feel for the size of the aquarium, since tall models generally offer less "living space" per unit volume.
WM:	Water movement: w = weak, m = moderate, s = strong.
WR:	Water region: b = bottom, m = middle, t = top.
AV:	Availability: 1 = regularly in the trade, 2 = intermittently in the trade, 3 = rarely in the trade, 4 = not available (possibly a protected species).
D:	Degree of maintenance difficulty. 1 = Species for beginners. These are aquarists which begin the hobby without prior experience. Organisms in this group are to very robust species that tolerate all but the most blatant maintenance errors. 2 = Beginners with half a year of experience. 3 = For advanced hobbyists with approximately 2 years experience in marine aquarium maintenance. 4 = For advanced hobbyists with specialized knowledge. Poisonous animals, while not necessarily difficult to maintain, are listed under this category. Mostly, however, it identifies animals with special dietary difficulties, and/or those that require optimal water conditions. A beginner should initially refrain from buying these species.

Algae in the Sea and the Aquarium

There are many divisions of aquatic algae. To a certain extent these divisions evolved independently. Only green algae can be considered direct ancestors of "higher" plants.

Division/Class	Important Representatives
CYANOPHYTA (CYANOBACTERIA)	Blue-green algae; blue-green, red, and black smear algae
CHROMOPHYTA	
CHRYSOPHYCEAE	Golden-brown algae; unicellular flagellates, e.g., *Isochrysis galbana*
XANTHOPYCEAE	Yellow-green algae; flagellate algae
BACILLARIOPHYCEAE	Diatoms; e.g., brown smear algae
PHAEOPHYCEAE	Brown algae; e.g., rockweed (*Fucus*), kelp
DINOPHYCEAE	Dinoflagellates; many planktonic algae, parasites (*Oodinium*), zooxanthellae, golden algae
RHODOPHYTA	Red algae; complex red algae, red calcareous algae
CHLOROPHYTA	Green algae; filamentous algae, *Caulerpa*, calcareous green algae

The above classification of algae was taken from a work by BOHUSLAV FOTT (Algenkunde, 2nd edition, 1971). Other authors, e.g., F. E. ROUND (Biologie der Algen, 1975), consider CHRYSOPHYCEAE, XANTHOPHYCEAE, BACILLARIOPHYCEAE, PHAEOPHYCEAE, and DINOPHYCEAE as divisions rather than classes (CHRYSOPHYTA, XANTHOPHYTA, BACILLARIOPHYTA, PHAEOPHYTA and DINOPHYTA).

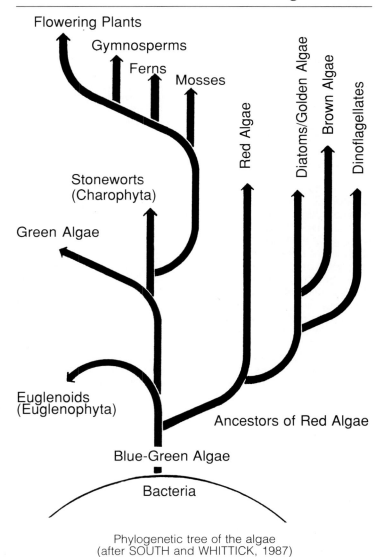

Phylogenetic tree of the algae
(after SOUTH and WHITTICK, 1987)

Algae in the Sea and the Aquarium

CYANOPHYTA = CYANOBACTERIA   Blue-Green Algae

The classification of blue-green algae in the plant kingdom is rather precarious. The microbiologists claim them as Cyanobacteria, that is, photosynthesizing bacteria, while phycologists and botanists classify them as Cyanophyta, or blue-green plants. Blue-green algae lack both a true nucleus and double membranes around the cell's chloroplasts. Consequently, they actually have more in common with bacteria than with algae.

Some blue-green algae, particularly freshwater forms, are able to fix atmospheric nitrogen. They do not require ammonium or nitrate to grow.

There are both unicellular (e.g., *Micrococcus*) and filamentous (e.g., *Oscillatoria, Spirulina*) blue-green algae.

The most common blue-green algae in the marine aquarium are the infamous blue-green, red, and black smear algae. They grow on stones and substrate, coating everything like a carpet and asphyxiating all life beneath them. These sheets are made of intertwined filaments. Large amounts of blue-green algae are caused by excess nutrients, especially nitrate and phosphate.

The presence of blue-green algae indicates poor water quality. In nature, too, they grow in heavily polluted areas rich in organics. This is why they are prevalent around sewage discharges. Blue-green algae grow poorly in clean water with a high oxygen content, i.e., a high redox potential. They should be removed by siphoning them up. Afterwards, watch the nutrient levels. Usually, less food added to the system controls their growth! Blue-green algae, particularly the brown smear algae, were previously called crevice algae. This name and the Latin name Schizophyta are considered antiquated.

CHROMOPHYTA   Flagellates

CHROMOPHYTA includes various types of algae that are yellowish to brownish in color.

CHRYSOPHYCEAE   Golden-Brown Algae

Mostly golden-brown flagellates. These unicellular organisms are an important part of marine plankton. The flagellate *Isochrysis galbana* is cultured to feed fish larvae, rotifers, and molluscs. CHRYSOPHYCEAE play a subordinate role in aquaria.

Algae

XANTHOPHYCEAE   Yellow-Green Algae

XANTHOPHYCEAE are a class of yellow-green to green flagellates. The two flagella are different lengths. Most representatives remain very small. Although there are marine forms, they do not play a significant role in the aquarium.

BACILLARIOPHYCEAE   Diatoms

Diatoms are a large class of unicellular algae. Their cell wall is composed of silicon dioxide (SiO_2) and comes in a variety of shapes. Diatoms are microscopic works of art. Their shape and cell wall markings are exquisitely fine and beautiful. Frequently they are erroneously called brown algae.

The walls of the diatom consist of two overlapping halves, one inside the other. They fit together rather like a petri dish. The larger half, the epitheca, and the smaller half, the hypotheca, form the whole. During asexual reproduction, the two halves separate and a new opposing piece is formed. The old shell halves, however, are always the bottom (epitheca); only the smaller top half is new. Since the old hypotheca does not grow, the diatom population becomes progressively smaller (in size—not number). A critical size (too small) is reached after a number of cellular divisions and sex cells (auxospores) are formed. These unflagellated auxospores fuse into a zygote. The zygote grows to a large size and than secretes a cell wall. The original size of the diatom, which was progressively diminished through cellular division, is reestablished.

Diatoms appear as brown smear algae in aquaria. Examine them with a microscope! Diatoms have to have free silicic acid in the water to grow. When the aquarium is filled with tap water which contains high concentrations of SiO_2, the plague is never ending. Only removing the silicic acid with an ion exchanger or, preferably, reverse osmosis will help. Using desalinated water will quickly insure that diatoms will disappear without further ado. The silicon concentration of new water should not be higher than 1 mg/l.

Diatoms play an important role in nature. Together with the dinoflagellates, they represent a large part of the marine plankton. Especially notable are the genera *Sceletonema, Thalassiosira,* and *Asterionella.* Massive quantities of these algae are cultivated to feed zooplankton, fish larvae, and molluscs.

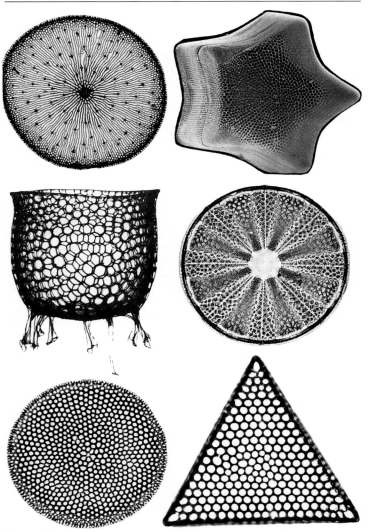

Diatoms. Left column from top to bottom: *Coscinodiscus* sp., ∞ 500; *Stephanopyxis* sp., ∞ 700; *Coscinodiscus* sp., ∞ 280. Right column from top to bottom: *Triceratium pentacrinus*, *Actinoptychus* sp., ∞ 400; *Triceratium favus*, ∞ 500.

Algae

Diatom cell walls withstand biological decomposition and can remain intact throughout millions of years. In some areas it is possible to mine these diatoms and use them commercially. The highly pure powder made of diatom shells, diatomaceous earth, is used in medicine and animal nutrition. Diatomaceous earth makes an extremely effective filter material. The beverage industry uses diatomaceous earth to filter particulate, turbidity-causing matter from wine and beer. Diatom filters made for aquaria do the same. These filters contain nothing more than refined cell walls of fossil diatoms.

PHAEOPHYCEAE   Brown Algae

The most familiar brown algae are the seaweeds found along many coasts (e.g., *Fucus versiculosus*, rockweed). The largest known algae, and perhaps the largest plants on earth, are contained within this class. The species *Macrocystis pyrifera*, which grows along coasts in the southern hemisphere, reportedly reaches a length of more than 400 m. Specimens 60 m long are common.
Brown algae store iodine and are therefore used in medicine (e.g., parkelp). They are of great economic importance along the west coast of North America. There, the large seaweed beds of *Macrosystis* and *Laminaria* are harvested.
Various components of the algae are separated and used commercially. Algin, a component of the cell walls, is a prime example. It is used in the cosmetic and food industries as an emulsifier, and it is used to make dyes.
Brown algae are rarely grown in aquaria. A notable exception is the California Aquarium at Monterey Bay. A complete kelp forest is being cultivated there using several million liters of water in an 11 meter tall "aquarium."

DINOPHYCEAE   Dinoflagellates

In the sea - and therefore in the marine aquarium—we encounter the dinoflagellates in a variety of forms. They play a very important role in the functioning capacity of the marine aquarium, both in positive and negative ways!

Algae in the Sea and the Aquarium

Anatomy

Dinoflagellates have an armored cell wall made of clearly defined cellulosic plates. These plates frequently have appendages, spines and perforations. When the cell wall goes through ecdysis and sheds its armor, a thick pellicle covers the cell. The typical coloration (yellow to dark brown, green, or blue) is caused by a combination of various pigments. However, relatively colorless predatory species also exist. They can overpower and ingest comparatively large algae and unicellular organisms.

Dinoflagellates move using their two flagella—one longitudinal flagellum for forward motion and a transverse flagellum for rotation. A forward, spiral trajectory results.

Habitat

Dinoflagellates are the main component of plankton and as such are important producers of organics compounds. In the seas, where plankton is the basis of the food chain, dinoflagellates together with diatoms and coccolithophores are the main components of plankton. A liter of water from cold, nutrient-rich seas can contain as many as 200,000 dinoflagellates—in the tropics this number diminishes to 2,500.

A known representative of the dinoflagellates is *Gymnodinium*. This alga multiplies massively during certain seasons. The reddish color of *Gymnodinium* turns the sea red. These are the causative agents of red tide, and they contain toxins which are dangerous for humans. This is why oysters, mussels, and other filtering organisms are banned in the northern latitudes from July to September. It is during these months that a heavy proliferation of *Gymnodinium* is most likely.

Planktonic members of this class play a subordinate role in our aquaria. Our filtration methods maintain the water essentially free of plankton.

Fish Parasites

Some members of the class Dinophyceae are parasites. The best known example is *Oodinium*, the causative agent of coral fish disease (see pp. 200-201). The parasite only has the typical dinoflagellate shape during its free-swimming tomite stage. Due to its small size (ca. 0.05 to 0.1 mm) a microscope capable of ∞ 300 will be needed to view these organisms.

Zooxanthellae (sometimes called golden algae)

The algae most aquarists know as zooxanthellae are also members of the Dinophyceae. These algae live in tissues of sponges, polyps, anemones, corals, and some molluscs. They can be cultivated outside their host. When they are free-living phytoplankton, they adopt the typical dinoflagellate shape.

Incredible quantities of zooxanthellae live in reef-building corals. A cubic centimeter of coral tissue may contain 30,000 algae cells. This represents up to 5% of the coral's total biomass! As you can see, coral reefs are a mixture of autotrophic and heterotrophic communities. These animals can bind ca. 3,500 g of carbon/m^2/year. By assimilating CO_2, the zooxanthellae play a significant role in calcium secretion of corals thereby contributing to reef formation. In this process they remove carbon dioxide from the bicarbonate found in seawater.

$$Ca(HCO_3)_2 \longrightarrow CO_2 + CaCO_3 + H_2O$$

Calcium bicarbonate ⎯⎯⎯> Carbon dioxide + Calcium carbonate + Water

The remaining calcium carbonate is insoluble and can be used by the coral polyp to build its skeleton. Without zooxanthellae, this process would not be possible. But it is not only stony corals that require calcium. Leather and soft corals also incorporate calcium as crystals and supportive needles in their tissue.

RHODOPHYTA   Red Algae

This division consists of more than 4.000 species. The red pigment contained in these algae is called phycoerythrin. Calcareous red algae are important organisms of certain reefs. Some even make the formation of reefs possible through their ability to fortify it.

Leafy forms of red algae have only been kept in aquaria since 1980. Because of their colorful contrast to green *Caulerpa*, white dolomite rocks, and the normally white substrate, they are a very appreciated addition. Improved salt mixes, protein skimmers, and filtration technology have allowed their cultivation in aquaria. The variety of forms found in this division is incredible: seaweedlike, filamentous, foliose, clustered, lattice-shaped, pearl lace-shaped, mosslike, spongelike, and spherical and bladderlike (e.g., *Ventricaria*). They far outdistance all other algae groups in diversity.

Algae in the Sea and in the Aquarium

The most popular red algae are those that either have foliose structures or resemble seaweed. However, herbivorous animals, particularly surgeonfishes, show an equal fondness for these species. If your tank houses one of these fishes, you will probably not be able to successfully grow these red algae. The algae may revive from remains in rock crevices if the fish is promptly removed and water conditions are favorable.

RHODOPHYTA is a very old group that only has one class, the RHODOPHYCEAE. They represent their own branch of algae that has developed in parallel to the other algae phyla, but is no longer related to them. They are large seaweeds. Like the brown algae, they have important commercial applications. Agar and carrageenan are extracted from the water soluble fraction of the cell walls of these algae. Agar, a commonly used growth medium for bacteria, and gelatin, often used in foods, are two products derived from red algae. These algae are found in all waters, both warm and cold, that do not fluctuate widely from the annual mean temperature.

In the aquarium, red algae frequently grow on live rocks. Due to their bizarre thalli, they are very popular and desired. Unfortunately, most species are very sensitive and soon vanish.

Calcareous red algae from the genus *Lithothamnion* grow crustlike over hard objects such as rocks along coasts. *Lithothamnion* will also grow in a clean reef aquarium. It can progressively cover all the decor and the bottom with a red-violet crust. The surfaces colonized by *Lithothamnion* prohibit the growth of green filamentous algae. Aquaria thoroughly overgrown with *Lithothamnion* offer the greatest degree of biological stability.

Red algae are reef builders; they store calcium carbonate. Aquaria that have plenty of calcareous red algae growth must have a constant source of soluble calcium bicarbonate; otherwise the buffering capacity of the water, the carbonate hardness, can fall to deficient values (below KH 7).

Chlorophyta

Green Algae

Chlorophyta, the green algae, contains many freshwater as well as marine species. Phylogenetically, they are the predecessors of higher land plants. Of all the discussed divisions of algae, these are the only ones that can be considered directly related to higher plants.

The structural variability of green algae extends from unicellular planktonic species to more complex plants like the stoneworts (Characeae) that resemble flowering plants. The greatest number of unicellular green algae are found in freshwater; the sea primarily contains thallose forms. Green filamentous algae frequently grow in marine aquaria. Years ago many aquarists were happy when these algae spread in their tanks—they displaced the undesirable blue-green algae and diatoms. However, rich filamentous algae growth requires high nutrient concentrations that exceed levels suitable for sensitive invertebrates. Additionally, invertebrates are often smothered by the rapid-growing algae lawns. Many anthozoans, e.g., *Xenia* and various tube corals, can only be maintained in aquaria free of green filamentous algae. However, these are the hardiest of all unwanted algae, and once they are established, can only be controlled mechanically. Low nitrate and phosphate concentrations prevent exuberant filamentous algae growth.

If green filamentous algae are cultured to feed, for example, surgeonfishes, a separate (small) tank with intense illumination should be set up. A large variety of thallused green algae grow on almost all rocky coasts. *Ulva lactuca*, sea lettuce, is a tender, edible species that grows in the Atlantic. It needs unheated aquaria for continued growth. You can easily seed your aquarium with a live oyster. I ended up having to harvest sea lettuce after I kept some oysters for several months (H.B.).

For the aquarium, green algae from the family Caulerpaceae have become very important. Hence, the entire chapter dedicated to *Caulerpa*.

Cyanophyta

Red blue-green algae on stones

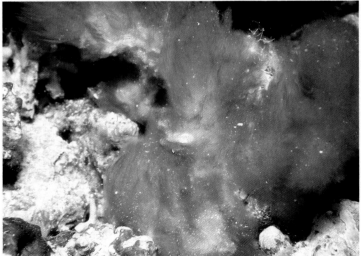

Brown blue-green algae

Green blue-green algae

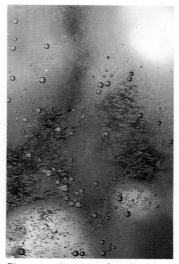

Blue-green algae eaten from the glass

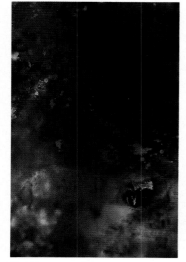

Red blue-green algae

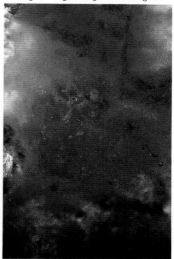

Brown blue-green algae (smear algae)

Phaeophyta

Fucus sp., rockweed from cooler latitudes

Hab.: All coasts of cold and temperate seas at depths of 0 to 2 m. Found deeper in regions that have higher tidal fluctuations. Regularly in intertidal zones. It is necessary that part of the plant is occasionally emersed, and it can even tolerate exposure to strong solar radiation or frost.

M.: Can only be maintained for a few weeks in an aquarium. In the sea, seaweed offers protection and feeding sites for many animals. It is used as fertilizer.

Right hand photo:
Giant seaweed or kelp (*Macrocystis pyrifera*) is found from the Californian coast to the coast of Chile. It is one of the largest plants. Kelp is regularly harvested to make gelatin. Garibaldi (*Hypsipops rubicundus;* see photo), sea otters, mussels, oysters, shrimp, and many fishes live among kelp. Diving in these seaweed forests is an unforgettable experience.

Macrocystis pyrifera, kelp

Phaeophyta

Sargassum fillipendula, seaweed from temperate latitudes

Dictyota bartayresii
Fluorescent blue alga, forked sea tumbleweed

LAMOUROUX
Fam.: Dictyotaceae

Hab.: Tropical Atlantic, from west Africa to the Caribbean. Found at depths of up to 40 m (lower right). The upper right aquarium photo shows a specimen of unknown origin.

M.: As shown in the upper photo, this tender, frail brown algae has been kept in aquaria. The alga only develops under extremely favorable water conditions, sometimes from live rock. Since it is easily damaged in transit, it can hardly be introduced by any other method. It will quickly decompose if water conditions change. The picture to the right shows this alga in the sea at Lanzarote (Canary Islands) at 20 m depth. While these two algae probably belong to the same genus, it is doubtful that they are the same species. An invertebrate tank—no fishes—with zooxanthellae animals is recommended. In order to insure high water quality, exclude carnivorous anemones.

S.: The beautifully iridescent sheen is typical for this species (genus?). Under blue light the blades have a fluorescent haze.

T: 18°-28°C, **L:** 10 cm, **TL:** 60 cm, **WR:** b, **D:** 3-4

Dictyota bartayresii, aquarium photo

Dictyota bartayresii, Lanzarote (Canary Islands)

Rhodophyta

Gracilaria sp.

Gracilaria curtissae (?)   AGARDH
Ruby red alga   Fam.: Gracilariaceae

Hab.: Tropical seas at depths of 4-10 m.

M.: In marine aquaria that are decorated with live rocks, this red alga appears quite frequently when water conditions are favorable and there are no herbivores to disrupt its growth. It will do best in an invertebrate tank. It does not appreciate being kept with *Caulerpa*. The green algae seem to use the (low) nutrient content which they themselves need for growth. Higher concentrations of nitrate and phosphate, which are tolerated by some *Caulerpa*, inhibit their growth.

S.: The ruby red alga, whatever its scientific name may be, is one of the most beautiful plants for marine aquaria. Adapt the animal community accordingly. The number of fishes should be limited, and they should be restricted to planktivorous species. Shrimp and anemones can also be kept.
Ruby red algae may need to be pruned occasionally. Do not damage the center leaves (heart) in the process—lest the entire plant should perish.
Depending on origin, these plants are pink to straw-colored. Red and brown forms are also found within this genus.

T: 20°-28°C, **L:** up to 40 cm, **TL:** 100 cm, **WR:** b, **D:** 3

Halymenia sp. cf. *floresia*
Red seaweed alga   Fam.: Grateloupiaceae

Hab.: The foliose red algae of the genus *Grateloupia* and *Halymenia* are favorites of marine plant connoisseurs. The differentiating characteristics are often so minute that only an experienced phycologist can make a positive identification. Various species of the genus inhabit tropical waters of the Indo-Pacific and Caribbean; usually found at depths between 5 and 40 m.

M.: Moderate light. Needs extremely clean water. Preferably kept in invertebrate tanks. If fishes are kept with the invertebrates, limit them to planktivores—especially those that will not nibble on the algae.
Red algae that have racemose growth appendages on the thalli belong to other genera, e.g., *Laurencia*.

T: 22°-28°C, **L:** 10-20 cm, **TL:** 120 cm, **WR:** b, **D:** 2-3

Rhodophyta

Halymenia sp. ?, *Laurencia* sp. ?

Grateloupia filicina

Halymenia sp. *floresia* (?)

Wrangelia argus, red bunch algae

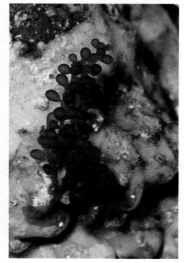

Botryocladia uvaria

233

Beach of red calcareous algae ("Coral Beach") on the west coast of Ireland. These algae grow at depths of 5 to 50 m under the influence of the Gulf Stream.

Liagora sp. cf. *ceranoides* (perhaps *Polysiphonia* sp.)
Calcareous red alga   Fam.: Helminthocladiaceae

M.: This species cannot be positively identified from the photo. Therefore, we can only call it a stalked calcareous red alga. The calcium carbonate deposited in the cell wall of these algae make them so similar to true corals, that people tend to call them corals. The Latin family name, Corallinaceae, also indicates the similarity. Two examples: along the southern Irish coast there are two "coral sand beaches," at least they are called coral beaches. Trondheim Fjord (Norway) definitely lacks corals because of the cold temperatures. However, you can find spherical and hard ring-shaped calcareous structures which are very similar to coral stalks. When angling, you may find such pieces on your hook. The branched structures harbor a multitude of crabs, brittle stars, and other invertebrates. We are dealing with either *Neogoniolithon* (previously *Goniolithon*) *spectabile* or a similar species. There is little information concerning keeping these plants in an aquarium. These calcareous red algae are very brittle and therefore not harvested and exported. Keeping them in a species tank should be interesting, but only for aquarists that live near their natural habitat.

Red algae that secrete a calcium carbonate skeleton usually colonize sandy bottoms in strong tidal zones. The encrusting species can be found on all sections of the reef and along rocky coasts. Some species are even found on calcium-containing substrates such as dead mussel shells, e.g., *Titanoderma* (previously *Lithophyllum*) *prototypum*.

T: 5°-25°C depending on origin, **L:** to 15 cm, **TL:** 60 cm, **WR:** b-m, **D:** 3

Rhodophyta

Corallina officinalis, see lower right hand page for text

Amphiroa hancockii, a "beach forming" red calcareous alga—an excellent filtration material and bottom substrate (Atlantic and Caribbean coasts).

Hydrolithon boergesenii
Encrusting calcareous red alga

FOSLIE
Fam.: Corallinaceae

Syn.: *Goniolithon boergesenii, Spongites* sp.

Hab.: All tropical seas at depths of up to 30 m.

M.: This red alga can form a 5 mm thick layer over rocks and dead pieces of coral. This is a desirable aquarium plant because other algae will not grow on it. When it dies—due to poor water conditions—then smear algae will grow on top. Dramatically improve the water quality with a water exchange, carbon filtration, etc., and clean the encrusted stones with a soft brush under a stream of seawater.

Light: Moderate light.

S.: A necessity for invertebrate tanks over the long run. Acquisition is assured with live rock. This alga is very useful as a reef builder because of its ability to form velvetlike coatings that reinforce dead reef sections. Another similar calcareous red alga is *Sporolithon episporum*. It only differs in coloration and structure; it typically is smoother and browner.

T: 20°-30°C, **L:** 0.5 to 5 mm, **TL:** 40 cm, **WR:** all, **D:** 2

Corallina officinalis
Coral weed, tufted red calcareous alga

LINNAEUS
Fam.: Corallinaceae

Hab.: Tropical Indo-Pacific; under rock overhangs in moderate current (inner reefs).

M.: Moderate light of 3,000 to 5,000 Lux. Extremely clean, unpolluted water is needed. Only suitable for tanks with invertebrates (zooxanthellae animals). Under favorable water conditions, the alga is pliable. At nitrate levels above 20 mg/l, the branches turn hard and brittle.

T: 22°-28°C, **L:** about 6 cm, **TL:** 80 cm, **WR:** b-m, **D:** 3

Chlorophyta

Halimeda opuntia
Cactus alga

(LINNAEUS) LAMOUROUX
Fam.: Halimedaceae

Hab.: Tropical Indo-Pacific and Caribbean to depths of 25 m. There are several very similar species in this genus. However, *H. opuntia* is the most common.

M.: *H. opuntia* will prosper in well maintained marine aquaria when calcium is regularly added (calcium water). KH 8°-12°. Nitrate and phosphate values have to be monitored. An aquarium with these calcareous algae will surely certify the expertise of the aquarist. When this species grows, everything else will follow. *Halimeda* does not tolerate rigorous pruning!

Light: Sunlight to moderate light.

S.: This alga contributes significantly to sedimentation. Calcareous sand beaches in some tropical areas may in part be formed by remains of this algae as well as crushed corals!

T: 20°-28°C, **L:** 10-20 cm, **TL:** 60 cm, **WR:** b, **D:** 3

Codium repens or *Neomeris annulata*
Finger alga

Fam.: Codiaceae

Hab.: *Codium repens* comes from the Caribbean (to 10 m depth). *Neomeris annulata* is from the Indo-Pacific. Both algae are difficult to identify by photo if the origin is unknown. The pictured plants are probably *Neomerus annulata*.

M.: In nature the algae grow beneath the surf zone (2 to 4 m depth) to depths of approximately 10 m, frequently under rock overhangs in moderate light of 2,000 to 5,000 Lux.

S.: Very sensitive to poor water quality. Should not be kept in aquaria that contain fishes. The diameter of the alga bunch can reach 40 cm.

T: 22°-28°C, **L:** 8-10 cm, **TL:** 100 cm, **WR:** b, **D:** 3

Codium repens

Halimeda opuntia, Maldives

Halimeda opuntia in an aquarium

Chlorophyta

Bryopsis plumosa
or *Clorodermis fastigiata*
Sea moss

(HUDSON) C. AGARDH

Fam.: Bryopsidaceae

Hab.: Caribbean. *Chlorodermis* is very similar but from the Indo-Pacific. Depths of 1 to 5 m in the breaker zone and tidal pools.

M.: This alga requires a lot of light. It is insensitive to fluctuations in salinity and will tolerate higher phosphate and nitrate values.
This alga is not held in high esteem by aquarists because it will cover all the tank's decor when favorable conditions prevail. Excessive nutrients or light must be controlled to curb its growth. A surgeonfish could be a solution.

S.: This alga is readily eaten by some sea turtles.

T: 20°-30°C, **L:** 5-12 cm, **TL:** 40 cm, **WR:** b, **D:** 2

Clodaphora profilera
Brush alga

(ROTH) KÜTZING
Fam.: Cladophoraceae

Hab.: Around the tropics to 10 m depth. Grows on rock and coral stones up to the beach, even in moderately polluted waters. Frequently found in fairly clean harbors.

Light: Moderate light to sunlight.

M.: Surgeonfishes are reluctant to eat this alga, but they still prefer it over foliose caulerpas. When caring for this alga in conjunction with surgeonfishes, place the algae among the substrate so that the surgeonfish cannot devour every last piece of it.

S.: A hardy, undemanding alga which can also be cared for in tanks that do not contain herbivorous fishes.

T: 20°-28°C, **L:** 5 cm, **TL:** 60 cm, **WR:** b, **D:** 2

Chlorodermis fastigiata

Clodaphora profilera

Chlorophyta

Chaetomorpha linum　　　　　　　　　　　　(O. F. MÜLLER) KUETZING
Wire alga, perlon alga　　　　　　　　　　　　　Fam.: Cladophoraceae

Hab.: In tropical and subtropical areas (Caribbean, Indo-Pacific).

M.: This alga feels like coarse steel wool and looks like perlon fibers. Any light from 500 to 2,000 Lux is acceptable. Lower sections of the algae mat do not receive hardly any light (10 Lux!). This alga provides hiding places for young fishes and invertebrate larvae. Carpets of 1 x 2 m are formed. Place in a shaded site in the aquarium. Excessive illumination causes it to turn yellow then decompose. It is not eaten by surgeonfishes, etc. It is unknown whether or not sea urchins will feed on it.

S.: This alga only grows under favorable water conditions. However, low light levels are required, making it suitable for either an algae scrubber or the sump tank of the trickle filter. Growth ceases at phosphate values above 3 mg/l. Nitrate levels up to 100 mg/l are tolerated.

T: 22°-28°C, **L:** 10-30 cm, **TL:** 40 cm, **WR:** b, m, **D:** 2-3

Filamentous Green Algae

These algae form in every aquarium that has sufficient light and tolerable water conditions. An ideal alga for the algae scrubber and to provide vegetable fare for surgeonfishes, etc. Introduce fist-sized stones in the algae scrubber to always have an algae stone for algivores. This alga is not appreciated in the aquarium itself, since it will eventually cover all the decor. Sufficient *Caulerpa* growth slows filamentous algae growth and eventually brings it to a halt. Filamentous algae grow optimally with mercury vapor bulbs. Metal halide illumination is not assimilated as well.

S.: Under strong light, this alga generates a lot of oxygen. Note the oxygen bubbles in the photo.

T: 18°-30°C, **L:** up to 25 cm, **WR:** b, **WM:** t-m, **D:** 1

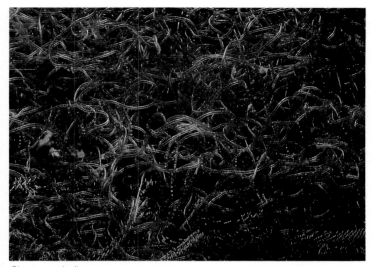

Chaetomorpha linum

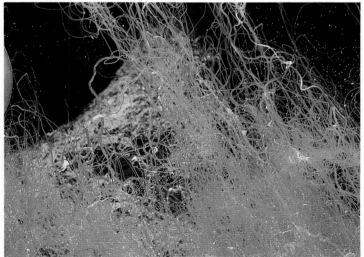

Filamentous green algae

Various Calcareous Green Algae

left: *Neomeris annulata*, finger alga   Fam.: Halimedaceae
center: *Udotea spinulosa*, mermaid's hard fan
right: *Rhipocephalus phoenix*, poplar alga

Hab.: Caribbean, at depths of 1 to 30 m.

M.: These algae grow on coral and calcareous sand substrates, frequently among seaweed lawns in shallow waters. Their dimensions, 5 -15 cm, make them fitting plants for marine aquaria.

Calcareous green algae are incredibly sensitive to polluted water. In bays where sewage is released (hotels), they disappear (usually unnoticed), while seaweeds grow exuberantly. Light values of 20,000 to 50,000 Lux and wave movement are found in their natural habitat; high and low tide currents are factors which cannot be provided in the aquarium. These algae may live several weeks, perhaps as long as several months, in the aquarium. After this time has elapsed, they begin to wane. This process is accelerated if the tank contains fishes.

S.: Those who live at the coast and constantly exchange the seawater can grow a really decorative underwater lawn with these algae.

T: 22°-28°C, **L:** 5-15 cm, **TL:** 60 cm, **WR:** b, **D:** 3

Green Algae

Ventricaria ventricosa
Bubble alga

(TAYLOR, 1960)
Fam.: Valoniaceae

Syn.: *Valonia ventricosa.*

Hab.: 1 to 80 m depth in tropical and subtropical seas.

M.: This alga resembles glass marbles. Depending on light penetration, it can be blue-green to grass-green. Usually bottle-green. With unsuitable water conditions, the color fades until a vitreous shell remains which will decay later. The CO*-filled cells adhere to hard substrates with hair-fine threads (rhizoids), similar to *Caulerpa*. Impeccable water quality is needed to maintain them (sea salt composition). Phosphate- and nitrate-free water is a necessity. It is pleasurable to see this alga growing in all its forms and colors.

S.: One of the largest unicellular organisms on earth.

T: 20°-28°C, Ø: to 5 cm, **TL:** 40 cm, **WR:** b, m **D:** 3

* CO = carbon monoxide = a toxic gas

Table of Contents for *Caulerpa*

Introduction: A Short Historical Overview 247
Morphological Descriptions 248
Systematics 250
List of the Species, Varieties, and Forms 252
Morphology and Taxonomy 258
The Geographic Distribution of *Caulerpa* 262
Live Rocks as a Means to Introduce *Caulerpa* into the
    Marine Aquarium 264
Morphology of *Caulerpa* 265
Cytology of *Caulerpa* 266
Sexual Propagation in *Caulerpa* 267
        Can Bleeding Plants be Avoided? 268
Vegetative Propagation 269
Conquering the Substrate 270
Care of an Exuberantly Growing *Caulerpa* Stand 270
Growth and Life Cycle of *Caulerpa* in the Sea 271
Life Expectancy of *Caulerpa* in the Marine Aquarium 271
The Influence of Abiotic and Biotic Factors of *Caulerpa* 272
Temperature in the Sea and the Aquarium 273
Light 274
        The Spectrum 274
        Day Length and Photoperiod 274
The Relation of Substrate and Illumination on the Shape and
    Development of *Caulerpa* 276
Suggestions 277
Illumination of *Caulerpa* and other Marine Algae and its Effect
    on pH and Oxygen Levels in the Water 278
Colonizing the Substrate 280
        Known Supporting Substrates for *Caulerpa* 280
When *Caulerpa* are the Dominant Species Along Dead Reefs 282
Value and Influence of *Caulerpa* on the Aquarium Environment 283
Caulerpa as Food for Fishes and Invertebrates 284
Production of Colloids and Their Importance 285
Caulerpicin, a Deadly Toxin 286
Antibiotics Derived from Marine Algae 286
Characteristics of the Antibacterial Substances and Their Activity 287
Growth Inhibitors, a Reality? 288
Growth Stimulators Produced by Algal Communities 289
The Interaction between *Caulerpa* and Bacterial Cultures 290
Do growing *Caulerpa* Cause a Mineral Deficiency? 291
Transport from the Tropics 291
Artificial Seawater and Transferring *Caulerpa* into a new Environment 291
Salinity and Dissolved Substances 292
Is *Berthelina chloris* a Specialized Lethal Parasite? 292
        Fatal Damage 294
        Reproduction of the Snail 294
        Prevention is Better than Healing 294
Illustrations of *Caulerpa* 295
Literature for the *Caulerpa* Chapter 1172

Caulerpas

INTRODUCTION

The most recent published overview of this genus, "Monographie des Caulerpes," was written by Anne WEBER-VAN BOSSE and published in 1898.

For aquarists, this chapter is particularly interesting since *Caulerpa* are the plants *par excellence* for the marine aquarium. Every day more and more aquarist are caught up in the excitement of maintaining an aquarium with plants, fishes, and invertebrates.

A Short Historical Overview

Ms. A. van Bosse was surrounded for most of her life by scientists and studied botany with Prof. HUGO DE VRIES in Amsterdam. After finishing her studies, she participated in the famous Siboga Expedition (1899-1900) and later married Prof. Weber, a zoologist.

Her constant interest in the mysterious world of lower plants, such as algae, culminated in January 1898 when "Monographie des Caulerpes" was published. There has not been another comprehensive scientific review of *Caulerpa* published since.

She frequently based herself on the important publications of the Swedish botanist C. A. AGARDH (1785-1859 Karlstad), whose two books dealing with algae, "Species algarum rite cognitae" (1820-1828) and "Systema algarum" (1824), are the foundation of phycology. His son, J. G. AGARDH, continued in his footsteps by becoming a professor of botany in Lund. He, too, largely specialized in studies of marine algae. He wrote his results in "Species, genera et ordines algarum" (1848-1876) which is frequently referred to by Mrs. WEBER-VAN BOSSE.

Many of the letters exchanged between Ms. Weber-van Bosse and J. G. Agardh are stored in the Imperial Herbarium in Leiden (Netherlands). Contained within are frequent references to *Caulerpa*. One would expect nowadays that a publication such as "Monographie des Caulerpes" from January 1898 would be displaced by many subsequent publications, but in actuality, the work by Ms. WEBER-VAN BOSSE is still used for comparative studies and identification of many species.

The conscientious descriptions, the thoroughness with which the drawings were made, the use of the pleasant sounding Latin, and all of this even though they lacked all modern equipment and materials, illicits awe and great respect from today's scientists.

Caulerpaceae

J. G. ARGARDH recognized in January 1872 that the Caulerpaceae are hard to identify because of the intraspecific differences and interspecific similarities.

To simplify the situation, he recommended a classification which was based more on the shape of different *Caulerpa* species than on particular characteristics of their reproduction.

This method is still being used, just as "Monographie des Caulerpes" by Ms. WEBER-VAN BOSSE is still used. The following is his system of classification in which he used morphological descriptors recognized in higher plants:

Vaucheriodeae	= filamentous	*Caulerpa filiformis* *Caulerpa fastigiata*
Charoideae	= verticillate	*Caulerpa murrayi* *Caulerpa pusilla* *Caulerpa verticillata*
Bryoideae	= mosslike, muscose	*Caulerpa webbiana* *Caulerpa elongata* *Caulerpa pickeringii*
Phyllantoideae	= leaflike, foliiform	*Caulerpa prolifera* *Caulerpa brachypus* *Caulerpa parvifolia* *Caulerpa anceps* *Caulerpa stahlii* *Caulerpa biserrulata* *Caulerpa subserrata*
Filicoideae	= fernlike, filiciform	*Caulerpa remotifolia* *Caulerpa scalpelliformis* *Caulerpa pinnata* *Caulerpa taxifolia* *Caulerpa falcifolia* *Caulerpa ashmeadii* *Caulerpa plumaris* *Caulerpa selago*

Caulerpas

Hippuroideae	= fir-frond-shaped	*Caulerpa alternifolia* *Caulerpa trifaria*
	= equisetum-shaped	*Caulerpa harveyii* *Caulerpa obscura* *Caulerpa cliftonii*
Lycopodiodeae	= ground-pine-like	*Caulerpa lycopodium* *Caulerpa brownii*
Thuyoideae	= scale-shaped, scuamiform	*Caulerpa freycinettii* *Caulerpa bartoniae* *Caulerpa urvilliana* *Caulerpa cupressoides* *Caulerpa lessonii* *Caulerpa distichophylla* *Caulerpa plumifera*
Araucariodeae	= needle-shaped, aciculiform	*Caulerpa hypnoides*
Paspaloideae	= cristiform	*Caulerpa paspaloides*
Sedoideae	= crassulaceous, sedumlike	*Caulerpa racemosa* *Caulerpa peltata*
Vesiculiferae	= physophorous vessicle-bearing	*Caulerpa simpliciuscula*
Pedicellatae	= forms with small assimilators and stalks	*Caulerpa lentilifera* *Caulerpa agardhii* *Caulerpa papillosa* *Caulerpa ethelae* *Caulerpa okamurai*
Opuntiodae	= cactus-shaped, opuntia-shaped	*Caulerpa sedoides* *Caulerpa ambigua* *Caulerpa fergusonii* *Caulerpa articulata* *Caulerpa holmesiana*

Caulerpaceae

While this classification is still valuable, the number of species within the morphological descriptions should be significantly increased, since many new species have been discovered and described after this publication. The great majority of publications on *Caulerpa* are found in the scientific literature on marine algae, which makes the search for the articles difficult and time consuming.

As far as the author could determine, there are now 75 recognized species of *Caulerpa*. However, a number of these may not be autonomous. Discerning the habitats of each species also requires tedious searching through the scientific literature for pertinent information. But the search was done and an alphabetic species list that includes habitats was compiled. The habitats are probably far from complete since the localities are occasionally widespread.

In botany nomenclature it is customary that whenever a new name of a variety and/or form is published, a variety or form with the name of the species is added automatically.

For example, in *Caulerpa brownii* there is also a *Caulerpa brownii* var. *brownii*.

It is customary to place this so-called tautonym (automatically formed taxon) prior to other varieties or forms. We elected not to list our species in this manner because it would have disrupted the alphabetical order of the species.

SYSTEMATICS

Rechnum Plantarum = Plant Kingdom

Division: Chlorophyta, division of the green algae which only has one class, the Chlorophyceae.

Class: Chlorophyceae or green algae in which chlorophyll is the primary pigment. Some representatives of this class live in freshwater, and others inhabit the upper strata of intertidal zones in the seas. Some even live on humid rocks, trees, etc.

Subclass: Eusiphoniidae have complementary pigments such as carotene (orange) and xanthophyll (yellow).

Order: Bryopsidales: *bryon* (Gr.) = moss + *obsis* (Gr.) = appearance; (Siphonales: *siph.* (Gr.) = tube; *kladas* (Gr.) = branch) similar to branched mosses. Dense stands of these plants actually look like branched mosses from a distance. The order is comprised of eight families.

Family: Caulerpaceae

This family only contains one genus: *Caulerpa* LAMOUROUX. The presence of trabeculae clearly distinguishes this family from other algal families. These are fibrous growths of the cell wall that grow inward and serve to mechanically strengthen the tubes. Like Udoteaceae, Caulerpaceae have two types of plastids: chloroplasts (green) and colorless, starch-containing amyloplasts. Rhizoids lack chloroplasts. The micromorphology of the fronds and the creeping stolons show a great deal of similarity (DAWES & RHAMSTINE, 1967). Plants "turning glassy/transparent" or "bleeding empty," is the scourge of aquarists that keep *Caulerpa.* However, this event can be considered a typical occurrence.

Genus: *Caulerpa*   LAMOUROUX, 1809

Caulerpa (*kaulos* (Gr.) = thallus, stalk or stipe; *herpo* (Gr.) = creep). Green leafy algae from warm seas with creeping stolons that do not have internal divisions segregating the algae into individual cells. Exteriorly, the thallus looks like a higher plant that has roots, stems, and leaves, but it is not anatomically equal. What is a thallus? It is a plant body that is not differentiated into stems and leaves. *Caulerpa* is divided into more than 72 highly variable species based on their morphology. Added to this are 56 varieties. In the plant world, a variety frequently shows individual genetic characteristics which, together with differences in geographic distribution, make breeding within the species impossible.

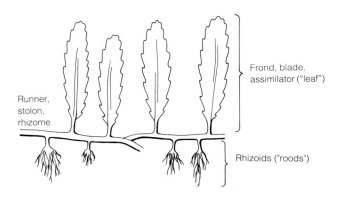

Runner, stolon, rhizome

Frond, blade, assimilator ("leaf")

Rhizoids ("roods")

Fam.: Caulerpaceae

Genus *Caulerpa*[*] Lamouroux, 1809

Species	Variety	Form	Habitat
1.*agardhii*	—	—	Ellice Islands, Australia, New Zealand.
2.*alternifolia*	—	—	Australia, New Zealand, Bracebridge.
3.*ambigua*	—	—	West Africa, Atlantic Ocean, Bonin Islands, Japan, Honshu, Matsumoto.
4.*anceps*	—	—	Japan, Okamura, Society Islands.
5.*arenicola*	—	—	Philippines, Visayan Islands (Siquijor, Negros Oriental).
6.*articulata*	—	—	New Zealand, Australia, Tasmania.
7.*ashmeadi*	—	—	Florida, Mexico, Brazil, Virgin Islands (Taylor).
8.*bartoniae*	—	—	Japan, east African coasts.
9.*bikinensis*	—	—	Bikini Atoll.
10.*biloba*	—	—	Costa Rica, Puerto Vargas, Cuhuita National Park.
11.*biserrulata*	—	—	Cape York.
12.*brachypus*	—	—	Japan (Janega).
13.*brownii*	—	—	Pacific Ocean, New Zealand, Tasmania.
"	1.*brownii*	—	
"	2.*minor*	—	
14.*cactoides*	—	—	New Zealand, Australia, Tasmania.
15.*charoides*	—	—	India, Gujarat, eastern Atlantic Ocean.
16.*clavifera*	—	—	Bahamas, west Africa, Atlantic Ocean (Mauretania).
17.*cliftonii*	—	—	Australia, Tasmania, New Zealand.
18.*crassifolia*	—	—	Bahamas, west African Atlantic.
19.*cupressoides*	—	—	Tropical and subtropical coastal waters, Atlantic, eastern American coast, Indian Ocean at Sri Lanka, Cuba, Key West, Manga Rave Islands.
"	3.*alternifolia*	—	
"	4.*canariensis*	—	
"	5.*cupressoides*	—	
"	"	1.*cupressoides*	
"	6.*disticha*	—	Guadeloupe, Bahia, Barbados, Society Islands, Florida.
"	7.*elegans*	—	
"	8.*ericifolia*	—	Bermuda, Mount Rouge Bay, Jamaica.
"	9.*flabellata*	—	
"	10.*lycopodium*		
"	"	2.*alterniflora*	
"	"	3.*amicorum*	
"	"	4.*anticorum*	
"	"	5.*disticha*	Indian Ocean, west Atlantic Ocean, Guadeloupe, Australia, Florida (Lake Worth).
"	"	6.*elegans*	

19.*cupressoides*"	"	7.*intermedia*	
"	"	8.*lycopodium*	
"	11.*mamillosa*	—	
"	"	9.*mamillosa*	
"	"	10.*thyoides*	
"	12.*serrata*	—	
"	13.*turneri*	—	
20.*denticulata*	—	—	West African Atlantic.
21.*distichophyla*	—	—	Pacific Ocean, Australia, New Zealand.
22.*elongata*	—	—	Indian Ocean, Sulawesi, Indonesia.
23.*ethelae*	—	—	Pacific Ocean, Waterloo Bay, Port Phillip Bay.
24.*falcifolia*	—	—	Tanga Tahu, Port Denison, Australia.
25.*fastigiata*	—	—	Bermuda, Bahamas, Florida, Cuba, Hispaniola, Barbados, Guadeloupe.
"	14.*confervoides*	—	Honduras, Panama.
"	15.*fastigiata*	—	Brazil.
26.*fergusoni*	—	—	Sri Lanka, Indian Ocean.
27.*filiformis*	—	—	Pacific Ocean, Society Islands.
28.*flagelliformis*	—	—	Southwest African Atlantic, Natal, Knysna Lagoon.
"	—	11.*flagelliformis*	
"	—	12.*ligulata*	Southwest Africa, Cape of Good Hope, Simonstown, Isipingo, Durban, Mediterranean, Cadiz.
29.*floridiana*	—	—	Florida.
30.*freycinettii*	16.*deboryana*	—	Egypt, Red Sea, Port Sudan.
"	17.*freycinettii*	—	
"	"	13.*angusta*	Guadeloupe, New Caledonia, Malaysia, Sumatra.
"	"	14.*formulata*	
"	"	15.*freycinettii*	
"	"	16.*serrulata*	
"	18.*integerrima*	—	Red Sea, Persian Gulf.
"	19.*pectinata*	—	Red Sea, Mariana Islands.
31.*herveyi*	—	—	New Zealand, Society Islands.
32.*holmesiana*	—	—	Southern Africa, Cape of Good Hope.
33.*hummii*	—	—	Venezuela.
34.*hypnoides*	—	—	Tasmania, New Zealand, Australia, Pacific Ocean, Israelite Bay, Port Elliot, Georgetown, Port Phillip.
"	20.*flexilis*	—	
"	"	17.*flexilis*	
"	"	18.*novozelandiae*	
"	21.*hypnoides*	—	
"	"	19.*compacta*	
"	"	20.*hypnoides*	
"	"	21.*lanceolata*	
"	22.*lana*	—	

Caulerpaceae

34.*hypnoides* 23.*mulleri* —
  " " 22.*densa*
  " " 23.*mulleri*
35.*juniperoides* — —
36.*lanuginosa* — —
37.*lentiliflora* — —   Red Sea, Port Sudan.
  " 24.*killnerii* —   Timor, Atapupu, Flores, Lombok.
  " 25.*lentiliflora* —
38.*lessonii* — —   Indian Ocean, Caroline Islands, Oualan Islands.
39.*longicaulis* — —   Southern American Atlantic.
40.*lycopodium* — —   Indian Ocean, southeastern USA (Florida, Key West).
  " 26.*delicata* —
  " 27.*lycopodium* —
41.*mexicana* — —   Brazil, Trinidad, Gulf of Mexico, African Atlantic, Red Sea, Mediterranean, likewise for the forms.
  = *sertularoides*
  " " 24.*laxior*
  " " 25.*mexicana*
  " " 26.*pectinata*
42.*microphysa* — —
43.*murrayi* — —   Victoria Banks, Pacific Ocean, Brazil, western Atlantic.
44.*obscura* — —   Tasmania, New Zealand.
45.*okamurai* — —   Japan, Shimane, Ogasawara-gunto, Matsumoto.
46.*olifovilla* — —
47.*ollivieri* — —   Gulf of Mexico, Mediterranean.
48.*papillosa* — —   Queenscliff, Port Phillip, Pacific Ocean.
49.*parvifolia* — —   Japan, Kaima, Australia.
50.*paspaloides* — —   Martinique, Bahamas, Florida, California, likewise for the forms.
  " 28.*laxa* —
  " 29.*paspaloides* —
  " " 27.*compressa*
  " " 28.*flaabellata*
  " " 29.*paspaloides*
  " 30.*wurdemannii* —   Western Atlantic, Florida, Key West, Yucatan.
  " " 30.*obovata*
  " " 31.*wurdemannii*
  " " 32.*zosterifolia*
51.*peltata* — —   Bermuda, Florida, Mexico, Japan.
  " 31.*exigua* —   Red Sea, Indian Ocean, Canary Islands, Indonesia (Ujung Pandang), Sulawesi, Pulau Seribu, Flores.
  " 32.*macrodisca* —   Durban (South Africa), Society Islands, Tongatapu.

51.*peltata*	33.*peltata*	—	
"	34.*stellata*	—	Anabas Archipelago, Wataram, Ujung Pandang, Fiji Islands.
"	"	33.*imbricata*	
"	"	34.*peltata*	
52.*pickeringii*	—	—	Tuamoto Islands, Tahiti, Society Islands, South Sea.
53.*pinnata*	—	—	West African Atlantic.
—	—	35.*mexicana*	Mexico, Indian Ocean, Red Sea, Society Islands, Sri Lanka, Gran Canaria.
—	—	36.*pectinata*	Bermuda, Guyana south to the Brazilian coast.
—	—	37.*pinnata*	All tropical seas.
54.*plumaris*	—	—	West African Atlantic, Senegal, Indian Ocean, Sri Lanka, Indonesia (Flores), Florida.
"	"	38.*farlowii*	
"	"	39.*flagellata*	
"	"	40.*plumaris*	
55.*plumifera*	—	—	
56.*prolifera*	—	—	Florida, Bermuda, Panama, Bahamas, Cuba, Mediterranean, Tunisia.
"	"	41.*dichotoma*	Canary Islands, Gulf of Naples, Monaco, Italy, France, Indian Ocean.
"	"	42.*prolifera*	
57.*pusilla*	—	—	Bermuda, Guadeloupe, Barbados, Brazil, Pernambuco.
58.*racemosa*	—	—	West Atlantic.
"	35.*chemnitzia*	—	
"	"	43.*chemnitzia*	Puerto Rico, Bahamas, Caribbean, Indian Ocean, Philippines, Indonesia, Malaysia, Sri Lanka, eastern Mediterranean, Egypt, Cyprus, Lebanon, Red Sea, Persian Gulf, Katar, Malabar, Guadeloupe, Samoa, Indonesia (Pulau Seribu);
"	"	44.*turbinata*	
"	36.*clavifera*	—	Red Sea, Persian Gulf.
"	"	45.*clavifer*	Indian Ocean.
"	"	46.*macrophysa*	Indian Ocean, Djakarta, Pulau, Maribu;
"	"	47.*microphysa*	Indian Ocean, Sulawesi, Ujung Pandang.
"	"	48.*reducta*	Toud Islands, Port Denison, Indonesia, Sulawesi.
"	37.*corynephora*	—	
"	"	49.*complenata*	
"	"	50.*corynephora*	
"	38.*gracilis*	—	
"	39.*laetivirens*	—	
"	"	51.*cylindracea*	

Caulerpaceae

58. *racemosa*	"	52. *cylindracea macra*	
"	"	53. *laetivirens*	
"	"	54. *laxa*	
"	40. *lamourouxi*	—	
"	"	55. *lamourouxi*	
"	"	56. *requienii*	
"	41. *macrophysa*	—	
"	42. *occidentalis*	—	
"	43. *racemosa*	—	
"	"	57. *racemosa*	
"	44. *uvifera*	—	
"	"	58. *compressa*	
"	"	59. *condensata*	
"	"	60. *cylindracea*	
"	"	61. *intermedia*	
"	"	62. *uvifera*	South Africa, Durban, Isipingo.
"	45. *zeyherii*	—	Fiji Islands.
59. *remotifolia*	—	—	Philippines, central Visayas, Solongon, Siquijor Island.
60. *reyesii*	—	—	West African Atlantic, Pacific, Japan, Oki Gunto Islands, Australia, Tasmania (Pacific), Indian Ocean, Sri Lanka, Mauritius, Red Sea.
61. *scalpelliformis*	—	—	
"	"	63. *denticulata*	
"	"	64. *intermedia*	
"	"	65. *scalpelliformis*	
62. *sedoides*	—	—	New Zealand, Tasmania, Australian coast.
"	46. *crassicaulis*	—	
"	47. *sedoides*	—	Red Sea, New Guinea.
63. *selago*	—	—	New Caledonia.
64. *serrulata*	—	—	New Caledonia.
"	"	66. *angusta*	
"	"	67. *boryana*	
"	"	68. *lata*	
"	"	69. *occidentalis*	
"	"	70. *pectinata*	
"	"	71. *serrulata*	
65. *sertularioides*	—	—	
"	"	72. *brevipes*	West African Atlantic, Caribbean, Bahamas, Virgin Islands, Lesser Antilles, Venezuela.
"	"	73. *corymbosa*	
"	"	74. *farlowii*	
"	"	75. *longicela*	
"	"	76. *sertularioides*	West African Atlantic.

66. *simpliciuscula*	—	—	Solomon Islands, Australia, Port Phillip, Tasmania.
"	48. *simpliciuscula*	—	Java Sea.
"	49. *vesiculifera*	—	Japan, Okamura, Bonin Islands, Ogasawara-gunto.
67. *stahlii*	—	—	West African Atlantic, Senegal, Indian Ocean, Sri Lanka, Sandwich Islands, Flores, Timor.
68. *subserrata*	—	—	
69. *taxifolia*	—	—	West African Atlantic.
"	50. *crassifolia*	—	Australia, Tasmania.
"	51. *taxifolia*	—	Torres Strait.
70. *trifaria*	—	—	
71. *urvilliana*	—	—	Society Islands.
"	52. *urvilliana*	—	New Caledonia.
"	"	77. *mircrodonta*	New Caledonia.
"	"	78. *serrata*	Torres Straits.
"	"	79. *disticha*	Viti Archipelago, New Hebrides, Australia.
"	"	80. *urvilliana*	
"	53. *vitiensis*	—	West African Atlantic (Angola).
			West African Atlantic.
72. *veravalensis*	—	—	
"	"	81. *asplenoides*	India, Gujarat, Caribbean, Grenada, Antilles, Martinique, Venezuela, Brazil, Trinidad, Bahamas, Indonesia.
"	"	82. *veravalensis*	
73. *verticillata*	—	—	Indian Ocean, Sri Lanka, Caribbean (gulf), Cuba, Guadeloupe, Society Islands, Tongatapu.
"	"	83. *charoides*	
"	"	84. *verticillata*	Caribbean, Florida, Jamaica, Virgin Islands, Barbados, Costa Rica, west African Atlantic.
74. *vickersiae*	—	—	
"	54. *farcifolia*	—	
"	55. *luxurians*	—	Indian Ocean, Mauritius, Jamaica, Puerto Rico, Virgin Islands, Brazil, Guadeloupe, Caribbean islands.
"	56. *vickersiae*	—	
75. *webbiana*	—	—	
"	"	85. *disticha*	
"	"	86. *tomentella*	
"	"	87. *webbiana*	

Total:
75 species, 56 varieties, 87 forms

Caulerpaceae

Due to the worldwide increase in seawater hobbyists and the improved knowledge at their hands, hobbyists and science are turning their attention to the leafy marine algae. Algae used to be near impossible to grow in the artificial confines of an aquarium. Today, not only can they be grown, they often have to be removed by the bucket load. We have come a long way!

In the earlier years of the marine hobby, *Caulerpa prolifera* was the only success story. Attempts to keep other beautiful species of *Caulerpa* met with failure. Even though this species is gradually being displaced by numerous others, it is still considered to be the "bread and butter plant" of marine aquarists. Little is known concerning the biology of marine algae within the aquarium hobby; even less is known about the importance of its role within the community of the aquarium. While this chapter does not pretend to end this dilemma, it does attempt to provide more information about *Caulerpa* to aquarists. Few species of algae draw as much attention as those of the genus *Caulerpa*. Not only have they proven their worth to the aquarium hobby, but they are economically important in some countries. Whether strolling along a tropical beach, snorkeling in coral reefs or mangrove forests, or simply walking along the high tide line of foreign lands, you will encounter *Caulerpa* throughout.

Most species are brought home by globe trotters and fanciers, or they are accidentally introduced with live rock. *Caulerpa prolifera* was, and still is, taken home from the Mediterranean and the Adriatic Sea by vacationers. Tropical forms come from the Pacific, the Indian Ocean, the Caribbean, the Red Sea, and the Persian Gulf. Aquarists are particularly smug about species that grow spontaneously from incidental imports on live rock. The drawings and color photographs may help you identify them, and the information on their natural habitats can aid in their cultivation.

In the case of *Caulerpa*, descriptions of varieties are frequently unclear. Identification is often done using pieces and sections rather than whole healthy plants, and the character of the plant is often lost. Furthermore, plant descriptions are often carried out far removed from the plant's origin, and little information is available about its natural biotope. Information concerning a plant's natural biotope is especially important for correct species identification.

The growth form, the way the plant anchors itself to the substrate, and the length of the stolons are the main characteristics taken into account when identifying varieties.

In *Caulerpa*, contrary to higher plants, it is almost impossible to know which morphological characteristics are constant and which are influenced by their environment. Other characteristics such as the shape of the chloroplasts within the cells, the presence or absence of pyrenoids and their structure (pyrenoid = a pigmentable body where starch (amylase) is stored that is present in green chromatophores of algae and protists with iron hematoxylin), and biochemical differences have not been studied in many species, varieties, and forms.

Many marine aquarists cannot believe their eyes when the *Caulerpa* they planted in another aquarium ends up looking totally different. This is a prime example of how this highly polymorphic group acclimates to its environment. An excellent example is *Caulerpa racemosa* which—depending on the shape of the thalli (plant body without roots, stems or leaves)—is known by the following common names: grape caulerpa, club caulerpa, trumpet caulerpa, and disc caulerpa. This does not even take into consideration the sometimes beautiful semi-scientific names that are thought-up.

This helps illustrate the morphological plasticity of the genus. The most important factors which influence this in nature and the aquarium are:

1) The intensity and quality of the light as well as the photoperiod.
2) The amount of current, its pattern, and the relative resistance that *Caulerpa* offers to the water movement.
3) Drying, as it pertains to forms which are periodically emersed from the water.
4) The nature of the substrate where *Caulerpa* is growing.
5) The geographic habitat of the species, the associated temperature, salinity, and available dissolved nutrients.

Several of these factors also govern the shape and form *Caulerpa* assumes in the marine aquarium. The same species on different sides of the aquarium, i.e., one close to the filter inlet and the other near the outlet, can adopt a different form, as can a plant anchored to stones versus one creeping along the substrate. **These factors also influence the growth form that certain species of *Caulerpa* assume in their natural habitat which will persist until influencing parameters change.**

Caulerpaceae

Differences in availability and quality of nutrients may also cause the advent of new forms. This gives rise to the term ecological races. In many cases, the division between race and true species is unclear in *Caulerpa*. This is probably the reason it is thought that there are far fewer autonomous species than presently acknowledged.

Actually, there is no other known environment that is as stable as the sea—human influences aside. The formation of ecological races is probably more a consequence of the distribution of true species throughout the seas than a local adaptation to a changing environment. Therefore, it is tempting to consider *Caulerpa* variants with the same basic form, as they indeed appear throughout the world, as a single species. These environmentally influenced phenotypes make it very difficult to determine what characteristics are genetic, thereby pointing to a new species' genotype, and which characteristics are the result of environmental pressures.

The geographic distribution also offers scant clues, since most of the short-lived gametes are, nevertheless, distributed over large distances. Additionally, *Caulerpa* exhibits remarkable regenerative powers, and small drifting pieces can grow to be giant fields far distant from the parent site. All things considered, it seems clear that the number of true species is fewer than presently accepted figures indicate. A number of *Caulerpa* species grow exuberantly in aquaria. Yet there are still species whose growth does not meet our expectations. More knowledge about the natural biotopes of these algae can only help us understand why.

Note the list of geographic distributions. Some species are more or less restricted to coastal regions and around the islands of the South Pacific, and almost all other species around the world have habitat variants. Many species are found between 10° and 30° latitude (tropical to subtropical zone). Ms. WEBER-VAN BOSSE wrote the following about these variants: "Toute ces forment livrent continuellement passage de l'une à l'autre," which freely translated means 'all these forms pass continuously from one to the other.'

This could be the basis to unite many varieties and numerous forms under one name. These ecological races, which are even noted in the open sea, can also be seen when the algae are cultivated in an aquarium. With the help of modern cultivation techniques, you can prove that the habit (morphology) of all *Caulerpa* species strongly deviates, depending on the environment.

Transplanting *Caulerpa* into another aquarium where one environmental factor deviates from the conditions the plant was originally growing under unavoidably induces an adaptation or other growth form, whereby the original form soon becomes unrecognizable. Remarkably, this can even be demonstrated within a large marine aquarium. The same *Caulerpa* species growing throughout the tank will develop conspicuous shape and growth variations. Different substrates, different zones of lighting, current, etc., are to blame. Describing the individual varieties and forms as is customary in literature only seems to make sense to characterize the growth forms of *Caulerpa* species in relation to their environment. Taxonomically they are worthless.

Many variety and/or form descriptions lead in time to fictitious names, confusing the situation. As an example, I mentioned *Caulerpa racemosa* FORSKÅL, 1775, var. *clavifera* f. *acrophysa*. The species name *racemosa* is frequently omitted and substituted with the variety or form name. Many of these so-called names, e.g., *Caulerpa uvifera, C. clavifera, C. macrodisca,* etc., became well established among marine aquarists.

Caulerpa racemosa var. *peltata*

Caulerpaceae

THE GEOGRAPHIC DISTRIBUTION OF *CAULERPA*

As already mentioned, *Caulerpa* are distributed throughout the warm seas. The northern boundary is the coast of France and the Iberian Peninsula, where the temperature never falls below 12°C. The Atlantic as well as the Indian Ocean form an immeasurable area, and research by marine algae specialists will still hold surprises. These studies may uncover yet more species.

Mediterranean: 5 species:

Caulerpa prolifera, Caulerpa ollivieri: from the Côte d' Azur and the coast of Spain. They are endangered in their natural habitat because of water pollution and tourists. Gulf of Lions and Genoa.
Caulerpa racemosa, Caulerpa sertularioides, Caulerpa scalpelliformis: eastern Crete, Cyprus, Gulf of Sidra (Egypt), but it has also been found by divers along the coast of Turkey.

Atlantic/America side: approximately 20 species, among others:

Caulerpa prolifera: the coast of the Americas, the Caribbean Sea, the Gulf of Mexico, and the islands south of this line are especially rich in *Caulerpa* species.

Atlantic/African side: possibly 8 species:

The mobile sand beaches and sand banks along the western coast of Africa are mostly unsuitable for *Caulerpa* growth. *Caulerpa* species have been found in the waters around Tenerife by vacationing aquarists. Additionally, there are some reports of *Caulerpa* growing in the coastal waters of Guinea, Nigeria (Pt. Harcourt), and Cameroon. NIEL mentions 2 species from the Canary Islands and 4 from Cape Verde (*C. prolifera, C. racemosa, C. taxifolia, C. sertularioides, C. webbiana,* and *C. cupressoides* (Lanzarote)).

Indian Ocean: 15 species:

Since many fish species found in the aquarium hobby originate from the Indian Ocean, it is only logical that plants from the same biotope garner serious regard. Many *Caulerpa* species are collected in several Asian countries for human consumption; namely, *Caulerpa racemosa* in the Philippines. *Caulerpa* species have been found along the coasts of India, Pakistan, Burma, Thailand, Madagascar, the Seychelles, Sri Lanka, and the Maldives. Further south, Indonesia, Malaysia, and the Philippines are also noted locals.

Pacific Ocean: approximately 25 true species and a multitude of varieties:

The Pacific, from southern Japan to Tasmania, and the Californian Peninsula (USA) to Panama, has the highest species diversity. Many islands of this area, e.g., Hawaii, Indonesia, the Philippines, the Marshall and Caroline groups, Polynesia, etc., are rich in *Caulerpa* species. Six species are known from the west coast of the Americas. Future studies will undoubtedly reveal additional species, particularly from this region.

Red Sea: about 10 species:

The Red Sea is famous for its relatively high temperature and salinity. The salinity increases as you proceed north. At the coastal town of Massawe (Ethiopia), the salt content is 3.6%. Around the tip of the Sinai Peninsula, it reaches 4.1%. The average temperature of the surface waters is between 25°C and 28°C. Temperatures in the south can climb to 31°C (Port Sudan, Sudan). The temperature falls to about 18°C in the northern region around the Suez Canal.

The number of species indicated for the various seas and oceans is probably going to increase as numerous scientists become intensely involved in marine biology projects. Because diving equipment is constantly improving, our capabilities for movement and observation are much better than ever before. Just recently, a few new species such as *Caulerpa biloba, Caulerpa arenicola,* and *Caulerpa reyesi* were described.

Caulerpaceae

Live Rocks as a Means to Introduce *Caulerpa* into the Marine Aquarium.

The popular name "live rock" already indicates the life found on or in these rocks. It seems that the legion of small invertebrates (meiofauna) and plants that grow on them have significant influence on the water quality in a marine aquarium. These organisms make the water "friendly" and help maintain a constant high water quality. The mysterious communities in live rocks probably have greater importance on the nitrogen cycle and the basic balance of the seawater than previously supposed. Since the advent of commercial importation of live rock and its use as decorative material for marine aquaria, a sound biologically functioning living community has become possible—which previously seemed unattainable. Additionally, live rock has been shown to often carry innumerable traces of plant organisms such as red, brown, golden, and green algae, which includes the *Caulerpa* species. These plants are commonly invisible to the casual observer. Virtually all *Caulerpa* species and other algae are seeded in marine aquaria from live rock. Unknown organisms are still being discovered by hobbyists. The effect of these organisms on the bottom substrate, the filter medium, and the entire biomass of the aquarium diminishes the aggressive nature of marine water for fishes and stimulates desirable metabolic pathways and cycles to predominate. This in turn incites *Caulerpa* and filamentous algae to prosper, but the latter can be better controlled. Live rocks from the Indo-Pacific region as well as from Caribbean waters can be qualitatively good; however, quite a bit depends on the original appearance and condition of the rock and how it was maintained after collection. Mousey-gray stone formations can hardly be called upon to resurrect and establish new growth in a marine aquarium. Only live rocks covered with small organisms and red, terra cotta, wine red, pink, and blue crust algae, and similar, should be considered. Nevertheless, always keep in mind that from the time the rocks are collected until they reach retail stores, the rocks will have to have been tended.

This means that heavy water exchanges have to be carried out from the collection site to the exporter, and larger stones that are sensitive to air have to be handled with this in mind. The exporter needs to have a good pressure pump to hose the live rocks down. This removes dead organisms and allows the living meiofauna to recover and adapt to new conditions. Although this implies that a substantial proportion of the meiofauna and plants will have been damaged, under good care they will quickly recover. Their original beauty will never be regained!

MORPHOLOGY OF *CAULERPA*

Morphology (*morphe* (Gr.) = form + *logos* (Gr.) = study) is the study of the form and structure of living organisms. Anatomy refers to the interior and exterior form, while cytology is the study of organic cells and tissues.

As a species, *Caulerpa* is easily differentiated from other green leafy algae. The thallus (green stalk; plant body undifferentiated into true stems, roots, or leaves) is divided into 3 organs, each of which plays a distinct role, even though they are largely the same structurally:

1) Tubular stalks or runners (stolons). The stalk segments are normally slightly hollow, smooth, and frequently branched. Each branch can grow in any direction. New segments of the stalks originate from any leaflike organ. Even tiny pieces of fronds are capable of producing a stalk or runner. In nature, sometimes giant fields are created when the stolons creep along the bottom (hence the name: creeping shoot algae).

2) Rootlike holdfasts (rhizoids). The rhizoids appear similar to small bunches of root hairs and—although structurally different—serve the same role in algae, mosses, aquatic cryptogams (non-flowering plants), and certain epiphytes. Rhizoids come off the side of the stolon that is closest to the substrate. These thin, profusely branched filaments enter the substrate and securely anchor the plants, serving much the same function as roots in higher plants. They probably also absorb nutrients.

3) Leaflike organs, assimilators, fronds or blades. Numerous finely branched assimilators grow from the runners. A hopeless tangle sometimes results. Whereas assimilators naturally come in a variety of shapes and sizes depending on the species, quite strangely, the same can be said about assimilators within one species or even on one plant. This, as mentioned earlier, is the result of environmental influences such as temperature, salinity,

current, substrate, illumination, water depth, and nutrient availability. It is normal to find various forms of the same species in separate geographic zones that have differing biotopes.

Expressions such as relative forms of shallow water (high tolerance), optimal forms growing under optimal living conditions, and forms of a low tolerance (usually growing at greater depths) are used. A comparison of forms among the individual *Caulerpa* species shows a consensus on the influence of depth; it appears that an equal response is seen in coral colonies.

CYTOLOGY OF *CAULERPA*

Cytology (*kyton* (Gr.) = cave, cell + *logos* (Gr.)= study) is the study of cells.

Green algae differ from higher plants by the absence of true organs such as roots, leaves, stems, flowers, and seeds. While true veins and cross walls are absent in the assimilators, they have a fibrous tissue that provides enough support to allow *Caulerpa* to withstand changes in osmotic pressure and maintain its shape. A cuticle and a cell wall surround the slimy cytoplasm that is rich in organelles. It is beyond the scope of this book to explain the function of the cytoplasm and each of the organelles found therein. However, the presence of pyrenoids has to be mentioned. These particles have strong light refracting properties. They are found in the chloroplasts of many algae. The chloroplasts, which are usually located along the cell wall, capture energy from light. Varieties that grow at great depths often compensate for the shortage of light by having a "leaf" with a large surface area.

SEXUAL PROPAGATION IN *CAULERPA*

Like many plants and virtually all algae, the green algae of the genus *Caulerpa* can reproduce both sexually and asexually (vegetatively). The vegetative manner is familiar to all aquarists that have kept these algae. *Caulerpa* forms creeping runners (stolons) which continue to grow, even when separated from the mother plant.

Sexual reproduction is also possible in *Caulerpa*. It occasionally occurs in the aquarium, and the event is totally misconstrued by most aquarists:

Suddenly, without apparent reason, a large part of the algae in the aquarium dies—only a collapsed whitish skin remains. Simultaneously, the water becomes very cloudy; however, the water usually clears within a few hours. Why? Could it be because of overfertilization?

What Happened?

The algae of the family Caulerpaceae consist of a tube-shaped (siphonous) thallus. When growing, no cross walls are formed. The resulting cell is multinucleated and has many chloroplasts. Such plants are coenocytic. Prior to sexual reproduction the individual nuclei undergo meiosis. This yields 4 gametes for every nucleus. These are separated by cell walls.

As if commanded, these gametes are expelled simultaneously by the entire algae population (sporulation). What remains is a dead spent shell of cellular walls. The gametes are unicellular and flagellated. They look like unicellular green algae (e.g., *Chlamydomonas* or *Dunlaniella*). The water turns cloudy and green from the overwhelming number of gametes. The aquarium looks as if it is undergoing an algae bloom. The gametes fuse, adhere to the substrate, and produce an new plant.

Sexual reproduction is rarely fruitful in aquaria for two reasons. First, strong filtration, particularly when the aquarium has a protein skimmer, kills the gametes. Secondly, filter feeders—tubeworms, bivalves, and anthozoans—take advantage of the situation and feed on the copious amounts of gametes.

For the aquarist, this phenomenon is no cause for jubilation. The massive die-off of gametes causes a surge in the nutrient concentration of the water.

Caulerpa taxifolia and *C. sertularioides* are two pinnate species that rarely sporulate in the aquarium. Some species, such as *C. prolifera*, are more prone to sporulation and may go through the process every 6-8 weeks.

Caulerpaceae

Can Bleeding Plants be Avoided?

Until recently there was no way to prevent *Caulerpa* from bleeding during or after harvesting or pruning. However, DAWES and GODDARD discovered that *Caulerpa* minimized damages sustained from grazing fishes by producing a wound plug within seconds. Their discovery, and several exhaustive studies that followed, culminated in two interesting publications (see bibliography). When armed with information from these studies, it is fairly easy to prevent *Caulerpa* from bleeding while being thinned out.

> Briefly apply firm pressure to the stolon you want to trim. Hold it and give the plant time to produce a wound plug. You are then free to pinch the stolon off distally to where you applied pressure!

As long as *Caulerpa* is healthy, this method will prevent most plants from bleeding empty.

When pruning *Caulerpa*, bacteria frequently infect the wound. These usually disappear on their own. If pruned too often, many species of

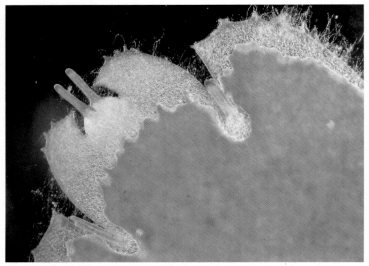

The "bleeding" begins at the edges of *Caulerpa*—the gametes are released.

Caulerpa develop into degenerate forms with wartlike structures. However, given enough time to recover, the ugly outgrowths spontaneously disappear, and the normal growth form returns. If the plant is severely weakened or the injuries are too serious, it will be unable to produce an adequate wound plug, if it even makes the attempt. Very succulent species are more sensitive to rough handling. Those who consider *Caulerpa* an important part of their biotope should thin their stands carefully. By the way, vitreous thalli also appear during sexual reproduction (see previous page).

Vegetative Propagation

A single piece of frond is often enough to produce a beautiful stand in the aquarium. Could this be the reason *Caulerpa* are so popular? Vegetative propagation rejuvenates the stand without the loss in biomass associated with sexual reproduction. When conditions remain unchanged over extended periods of time in the aquarium, few, if any, morphological changes will manifest themselves; however, if the environment looses *status quo,* variform *Caulerpa* often result. Many different shapes of *Caulerpa racemosa* were produced in the laboratory using various illuminations. Exceeding normal lighting (for the initial form) seemed to foster—up to a certain point—the demise of the stolons, whereby the remaining sections produced new plants which were adapted to the new environmental parameters. In nature, a loose substrate means the stolons are frequently long, and the thalli are widely spaced. A hard substrate, on the other hand, seems to favor short stolons and very dense blades. This can also be easily observed in the aquarium. If you carefully thin the stand and gradually change the quality/intensity of the illumination and the photoperiod, a decorative *Caulerpa* stand can survive many years. Sometimes *Caulerpa* will—regardless of species—grow exuberantly. Rigorous pruning may be needed. Careful! The resulting shock may kill the entire stand, obligating you to start completely anew. Moderate pruning is recommended.

Caulerpaceae

Conquering the Substrate

Although fertilized eggs (zygotes) have not been observed, it is almost unimaginable that sexual propagation in *Caulerpa* is absent. If so, then why are gametes formed? Zygote formation and the subsequent settling, germination, and juvenile plants are well documented for some of the economically important algae. There is no foundation to think that *Caulerpa* are an exception. It seems reasonable to further deal with the colonizing substrate.

Many aquarists do not realize that certain mature algae anchor strongly to a substrate; some red algae are known for their strong anchoring. Fortunately *Caulerpa* species are an exception.

How does this happen in young plants that develop from zygotes? These zygotes are photophilous at first, migrating with the current to well illuminated superficial waters where they are likely to come in contact with an appropriate substrate. However, the zygotes will progressively turn photophobic and begin to move away from the light towards dark substrates or dark colored objects such as rocks, bivalves, dark sand, etc. During migration, the zygote has formed a phycocolloid that permits the cell to adhere to the new substrate. If the substrate and the environment are suitable, a small phylloid and a rhizoid develop. The rhizoid enters the substrate and anchors the young plant, and a new generation of *Caulerpa* is ready to begin. The primary function of rhizoids (rootlike structures) is to quickly and effectively anchor the alga. Marine algae utilize their entire surface to absorb nutrients from the water. Research with the same *Caulerpa* on various substrates, but in the same habitat under equal illumination, has shown clear differences in growth, expressed in dry weight. This study casts doubts that rhizoids—contrary to popular belief—only serve to anchor the plant. It is possible that small amounts of soluble matter from the substrate may be absorbed.

Care of an Exuberantly Growing *Caulerpa* Stand

A healthy stand of *Caulerpa* demands constant care. This includes the time consuming task of pruning. A number of coral reef fishes graze on most of the soft, easily damaged *Caulerpa* species. Many aquarists try to balance *Caulerpa* growth with a few of these species to minimize the time spent pruning. Within a few weeks, the damages incurred are so great that the decorative value of the plants is lost.

As the favorable influence of *Caulerpa* on the aquarium environment is realized, the interest in this genus grows. But the amount of care needed is a frequent deterrent to maintaining these algae. Keeping a decorative stand under control can only be achieved by regular care and selective thinning by hand. Herbivorous fishes cannot create an aesthetically pleasing plant. Quite the opposite in fact: short, but not beautiful!

GROWTH AND LIFE CYCLE OF *CAULERPA* IN THE SEA

When *Caulerpa* species grow in regions that have definite seasons, such as summer and winter, the plant's growth will exhibit a corresponding growth rhythm. New sprouts emerge in the spring from the remnants of the overwintering population. These plants can grow 1-2 cm per week. In tropical waters, growth is frequently much faster. But this rapid growth is often matched by rapid aging. This means that the oldest part of the colony dies as the newer sections continue creeping. You could say that the difference between decay at the back and growth at the front is 6-14 weeks. This seems to be directly related to temperature and available nutrients and is certainly species dependent. *Caulerpa webbiana*, a slow growing leatherlike species, has much older thalli than, for example, *C. racemosa*.

LIFE EXPECTANCY OF *CAULERPA* IN THE MARINE AQUARIUM

Life expectancy of *Caulerpa* can be considered limitless since colonies that have sufficient nutrients and light for metabolism constantly renew themselves. The thin-skinned succulent species, however, die faster than leathery, tough species. I suspect that tropical forms have a shorter life expectancy than hardier forms from cooler waters. Marine aquaria which have profusely growing *Caulerpa* sometimes undergo "stolon yellowing," followed by the rapid demise of the entire colony. It seems that the cause is due less to disease than to a mineral deficiency. Nutrients such as cobalt, copper, iodine, iron, manganese, nitrate, phosphate, vanadium, zinc, and perhaps vitamins together with chelators may be needed to reestablish growth.

Caulerpaceae

We have learned that a few drops of juice pressed from newly harvested healthy *Caulerpa*, preferably from another aquarium, make an excellent chelating agent. This helps maintain nutrient preparations in solution for *Caulerpa*. Excellent results have already been achieved using the above mentioned method with various nutrient products available in the trade.

THE INFLUENCE OF ABIOTIC AND BIOTIC FACTORS ON *CAULERPA*

Ecological factors are known to have great influence on animal as well as plant life. The distribution of *Caulerpa* is strongly influenced by its environment, particularly climatic factors such as light, temperature, water movement, salinity, etc. The latter two play an important role in the presence of *Caulerpa*. Here we distinguish between physical or chemical factors. An important physical characteristic is the texture of the substrate (e.g., the size of the grain), the rolling movement as a consequence thereof, and its stability. For *Caulerpa,* the following chemical factors seem to be important: calcium content, salinity, acidity or pH (which is significantly less stable in the aquarium than the sea), and the concentration of trace elements. *Caulerpa* grow best on sites whose topographical characteristics closely match their needs. Additionally there is a complex of biotic influences from organisms in the same biotope. They can be classified into 3 groups:

1) Influences of other plants (macro and micro), disease agents, competing species (frequently found in aquaria).
2) The influence of animals that use *Caulerpa* as food and possibly serve as an element in their distribution.
3) Human influences: direct and indirect exploitation through water pollution, toxicants, etc.

Caulerpa's sensitivity to all these factors can be seen daily in our aquaria.

TEMPERATURE IN THE SEA AND THE AQUARIUM

Caulerpa from temperate regions or from tidal pools have a large temperature tolerance. *Caulerpa prolifera* and *Caulerpa ollivieri* are two examples thereof. In relation to water temperature they are hardy species that can thrive indefinitely, even with wide temperature variations. If this range is exceeded, these species temporarily disappear. The remaining stolons that survive in the substrate resume growth when conditions become favorable. *Caulerpa prolifera* is one of the hardiest flora grown in marine aquaria. The optimal temperature for *Caulerpa* and other algae from the Mediterranean and Adriatic Sea is 23°C, but temperatures between 19°C and 30°C are also endured.

True tropical forms which grow constantly submersed usually prove to be less forgiving of temperature variations. Fluctuations of 5°C may be fatal for some of these species. It is unknown what impact the condition of the plant plays in being able to withstand temperature fluctuations. Certain adaptations have been made by some species to deal with adverse environmental conditions. In the case of forms that live along tropical coasts, NIEL mentions the dense spheres from *Caulerpa racemosa* as a way to counter excessive evaporation when they are exposed to the sun's drying effects during low tide. He also hypothesizes that *C. sertularioides* and *C. taxifolia* shade themselves by widening the tips of their fronds—which are normally finely pinnate—while the rhizoids remain cooly encased in the mud. These two species have ecological races, but it seems questionable whether this is a consequence of solely temperature, since different ecological races seem to have different allowable temperature ranges. It is possible that this depends on the environment that the species is adapted to. What influence the thermal effects have on assimilation and growth is being investigated due to the economic importance of some *Caulerpa* species. A few species are presently being cultured in shallow aquaculture. In aquaria, the best results are achieved when the intensity of the illumination and temperature correspond to each other. In other words, the stronger the illumination the higher the temperature must be for a luxurious, stable plant.

This is usually the natural progression of events in home aquaria, since the room is normally heated and the aquaria are further heated by fluorescent tubes, transformers, and other electrical equipment. A permanent, stable algae culture demands at least an 8 hour "night." A corresponding permissible temperature drop occurs automatically.

Light

The Spectrum

Very little has been done to try to define the effect of different spectral compositions on particular *Caulerpa* species in nature. The spectral composition of light changes with the seasons and the time of day. This is quite the contrary to what is found in marine aquaria. The light sources constantly emit the same light spectrum, yet *Caulerpa* species grow fabulously in aquaria also. The spectral composition changes the most when certain types of tubes are turned on or off. These changes can be good or bad. If you have good *Caulerpa* growth and are happy with your results, do not change the illumination.

Day Length and Photoperiod

Temperate latitudes have seasonal variations in day length (short during the winter and long during the summer). *Caulerpa* from temperate latitudes are more sensitive to photoperiods than tropical species which are accustomed to a fairly constant day length. While *Caulerpa prolifera* almost disappears from the Mediterranean during the winter, species such as *Caulerpa racemosa* from Java grow strongly year-round. The frequently adopted thought that a 12 hr tropical day means 12 hr of illumination is incorrect. Since the sun's rays are strongly reflected at dusk and dawn, very little sunlight penetrates the water surface during these hours.
The quantity of sunlight is also strongly attenuated as it passes through the water to the depth where *Caulerpa* is growing. In short, the light at sunrise and sunset has little influence on organisms in the water. These organisms depend on radiation hitting the surface so that light refraction and reflection are kept to a minimum. The greatest proportion of the sun's rays penetrate the water surface at angles between 50 and 130 degrees. Aquaria are almost always illuminated from above, and the amount of light that falls on and penetrates the surface is optimized by the hood and sometimes

special shaped reflectors. Taking all of the above into consideration it is somewhat interesting to note that many people advocate 12 hr of light per day for tropical tanks. This not only makes maintenance of a marine aquarium expensive, but it also has a detrimental effect on the community within. TAYLOR and TANYKA even report that photosynthesis stops during peak illumination times during the tropical day. Shortening the duration of effective illumination to 7-9 hr per day gives excellent results and corresponds to the radiation available in nature, even though true sunlight is irreplaceable.

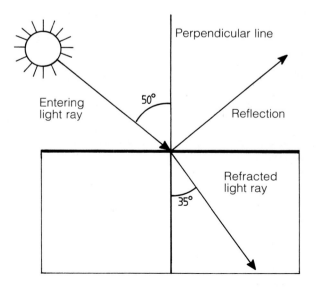

Caulerpaceae

THE RELATION OF SUBSTRATE AND ILLUMINATION ON THE SHAPE AND DEVELOPMENT OF *CAULERPA*

In nature, *Caulerpa* species live on a wide variety of substrates: stones, rocks, sand, mud, etc. But in the aquarium, there are actually few substrates available: hard substrates in the form of live rock, dolomite, puffed clay rocks, or finely crushed dolomite. Regardless of which form of *Caulerpa* you grow, if it is floating—like in an algae scrubber—the plant turns looser, longer, and more flaccid than plants attached to a substrate, even under intense illumination. This indicates that rhizoids are more than merely anchoring organs. Rhizoidal filaments can enter deep into porous rocks and adhere to grains of sand. Research on rhizoids showed that they contain many storage compounds such as amylum (starch). Additionally, the substrate itself seems to interact with the growing *Caulerpa*. When it is sufficiently porous, organic substances break down within. The resulting products seem to be assimilated by the rhizoids. The shape and length of the fronds and internodes, the length of the horizontal axis, and the overall turgor of the plant are also determined by the substrate. When *Caulerpa* grow on piles of live rock close to the water surface, and thus close to the light source, we see a short, stout form with heavy, thick axes and runners (see the picture on p. 277, *Caulerpa racemosa*). An elongate, looser form with more upright fronds is obtained from runners of the same species as they creep over stones until the bottom substrate is reached. When the rhizoid reaches the different, often deeper, bottom substrate, the rhizoid becomes shorter, and the "root hairs" become broader and more finely branched. The plasticity of the rhizoids in response to environmental conditions allows the roots to garner nutrients and affix the plant to various substrates.

Some species even grow well in areas of reduced light. But these shaded areas are often in short supply in many marine aquaria. This is sad since very interesting photophobic communities can develop in these sites.

The rhizoids can also effectively use nitrogen products produced by anaerobic bacteria. However, keep in mind that anaerobic bacteria are inhibited by a strong reverse flow through the substrate (a frequently recommended method of filtration).

Rhizoids of *C. racemosa*

SUGGESTIONS

When the shape and length of the fronds (leaves) on new sections of the thalli are hardly distinguishable from the initial form, there is sufficient light. If the new fronds are elongated, more delicate, and flaccid, there is a problem with either the quality or the quantity of light provided. This can be solved by replacing old tubes, using additional tubes, or extending the photoperiod. In general, a photoperiod of 9 to 10 hr per day* is sufficient. In some marine aquaria, the color of the water diminishes the efficiency of the illumination. A partial water exchange may remedy the situation, but removing pigments by filtering over activated carbon is also an effective alternative. Experience will tell you how to best deal with these problems.

* with fluorescent tubes (7 to 9 hours using metal halides)

Caulerpaceae

Good sensible illumination is very beneficial, not least of all because of the photosynthesis of green leafy algae such as *Caulerpa*. A lot of oxygen is produced during photosynthesis. It is sometimes released as tiny visible air bubbles; however, the bubbles may be so small that they immediately dissolve.

A number of chemical reactions, including the dissociation of CO_2 (dissociation is the cleavage of a chemical compound into atoms, ions, and radicals), lowers the concentration of CO_2, and bicarbonates are transformed into carbonates. An increase in pH of the aquarium water is unavoidable.

When there is insufficient light, photosynthesis is retarded and may even come to a complete halt. Photosynthesis, and thereby the production of O_2, is impossible without light, but respiration continues. *Caulerpa*—like all green plants—first use O_2 reserves from their tissues for respiration. When this source is exhausted, O_2 from the environment is used. Under these circumstances the reaction proceeds in the other direction and the pH decreases.

The wide pH fluctuations that are a natural by-product of healthy *Caulerpa* colonies can be extremely detrimental to animals. Strong water movement, which may be provided to aerate the water, has a stabilizing effect and prevents problems from occurring during the night. During the day, the increasing pH should be countered by adding CO_2.

Metal halide lights on *Caulerpa taxifolia*. The decoration was built with PREIS rocks (brown), AQUA MEDIC calcareous algae rocks, and live rocks. The large sphere is a skeleton of a calcareous red algae collected from Trondheim Fjord, Norway. The gastropod shell (*Strombus gigas*) comes from the Caribbean. The green calcareous algae in the center of the photo is *Halimeda opuntia*.

Caulerpaceae

Position and structure of the bottom or the substrate can, to a certain degree, determine the shape and development of the plants. The color and structure of the substrate determine the amount of light that will be reflected. This light contributes to the overall quantity and type of light that *Caulerpa* receives. The chemical composition of the substrate is probably of little interest to *Caulerpa,* since most nutrients are assimilated from the surrounding seawater. Species that have a long runner with an erect axis branching off (e.g., *Caulerpa paspaloides*, which does not have fronds on the lower stolons) are better suited to conquering a moving substrate than short-stemmed species. These plants have developed an ingenious way to prevent themselves from becoming buried in the sand. Static, rough, and hard surfaces are usually overgrown with smaller, shorter forms which have a very dense rhizoid system.

Caulerpa occasionally engages in a bit of environmental manipulation. In central Java this can be easily observed in the coastal region of Gunung Kidul and Baron. There the water is crystal clear. Within the dense stands of *Caulerpa*, we see a quantity of mud retained among the many creeping stalks and rhizoids. This is an unexpected sight in this clear water. You could deduce that a exuberantly growing *Caulerpa* mat creates its own nutrient reservoir by slowly but surely collecting and holding it fast. Substrate formed in this manner is excellent for colonizing bacteria that are very important for *Caulerpa* and other algae.

Along shallow coastal waters, *Caulerpa* has developed ways to prevent total desiccation. It simply grows among algae that are structurally more capable of maintaining their water content.

Known Supporting Substrates for *Caulerpa*

Natural Substrates
Sand/mud, coral sand, mangrove roots with coarse structure, crustlike structures of animals as well as plants, rough-surfaced rocks, calcium deposits between barnacles, and tubeworms.

Artificial Substrates
Ship wrecks, concrete jetties, metal buoys, rubber bumpers and car tires that are used to protect ships, pipes and plastic lines, ship and nylon ropes, and aquarium glass. As soon as climate, current, or numerous other factors create the slightest gouge, scratch, abra-

sion, etc., on these surfaces algae such as *Caulerpa* can colonize it.

Epiphytic/Epizoic
There are various examples of epiphytic *Caulerpa*. In the coastal region between Mombasa and Malindi, *Caulerpa sertularioides* occurs on scattered colonies of the calcareous algae *Halimeda* that have a heavily calcified base. On the coast of Mataram and Lombok, I found *Caulerpa racemosa* and *C. sertularioides* so entangled that it was impossible to determine which was growing on the other. The shallow waters of Taman Laut along the coast of Ambons (Molucca Sea) are home to vast quantities of two soft leather corals, *Sarcophyton trocheiophorum* and *S. ehrenbergi*. *Caulerpa racemosa* can be found along the base of these corals. These leather corals, and consequently *C. racemosa,* seem to prefer sites where hard coral reefs are destroyed by the local population. These people harvest the coral and burn it to make quicklime.
Live sponges as well as the six-rayed *Zoantharia* species also seem to offer a suitable substrate and are often overgrown with *Caulerpa racemosa* and *Dendrophyllia gracilis*.
Caulerpa species generally only grow on sites which either never or very rarely dry out. But there are exceptions. *C. racemosa* varieties, e.g., from around the coastal regions of central Java, are totally exposed to the air when the water level becomes extremely low. Extensive colonies are lost, but they recover and form new colonies within a year. Along other shallow coastal regions other *Caulerpa* species often become exposed to the air, but the spray from the breaking surf is enough to keep them from drying out. A number of *Caulerpa* species have leaves with a soft axis that bends as the water level falls. The fronds lie flat on the remaining water and return to their erect position when the level rises and the water becomes deeper. This is also a preventive measure to keep the algae from drying out.

Drifting Colonies
Sometimes *Caulerpa* colonies are found drifting. Stolons, blades, and rhizoids form a compact mass. The interior of such a dense plant mass probably would not dry up if washed up on the beach during low tide. High tide will then carry the mat back out to sea. It is not rare that old parts of a *Caulerpa* plant become overgrown by other species of algae, e.g., red algae, which also protects *Caulerpa* from desiccation.

Caulerpaceae

Around the Indonesian islands of Lombok, Sumba, and Sumbawa (Mataram Bay), there are extensive sections of dead or destroyed coral reefs which are now 2-3 meters below the water's surface. Coral is harvested for the native lime kilns to produce quicklime. Some regions are totally covered by a dense mat of *Caulerpa racemosa,* but only where sufficient light penetrates. There are no traces of *Caulerpa* in dark caves and crevices. These areas support brown and red algae. Protected bays are a particular haunt of *Caulerpa.* Large quantities of these algae are found there. Sand and dead coral on the leeward side of reefs are covered in *Caulerpa.* This is another apparently suitable environment for these algae. An interesting community lives within these algae mats. Since these areas are little investigated, a whole realm of new organisms for the aquarium may be discovered. The coarse structure of dead coral stalks seems suitable for primary succession of pioneer vegetation such as *Caulerpa racemosa* or *C. sertularioides.* The *Caulerpa* then attempt to reach the bottom substrate from these structures. The lee side of these structures provides a calm place in strong currents. The runners on this side reach the sand and colonize the bottom, some being as much as a few meters long and 4-6 mm thick. But this is species dependent. A similar sequence of events can be observed in aquaria. Strong runners of *C. racemosa* can be 5 to 7 mm thick! The tough, anchoring rhizoids quickly enclose everything they encounter on the bottom: grains of sand, shells, parts of sea urchins, and other exoskeletons. Weight, volume, and shape of these remains—coalesced by the rhizoids of *Caulerpa*—form a "weighted carpet." This ballast prevents the algae from being swept away in the current.

An exuberant living community of very small invertebrates can be found within this tangle. These may contribute to anchoring the clump and use it for shelter at the same time. Colonization on loose dynamic substrates in current-ridden waters is only guaranteed by rapid growth from the base up, whereas a network developes that can withstand the movements and the forces of the current.

Caulerpas

VALUE AND INFLUENCE OF *CAULERPA* ON THE AQUARIUM ENVIRONMENT

1) Modern marine aquaria almost demand a variety of marine algae, even though there is a trend towards specialization in the marine hobby. The role of *Caulerpa* species in a so-called reef aquarium is rather small, and their esthetical and biological values are less pronounced.

2) Algae offer favorable surroundings for a stable microfauna to develop. In turn, this community helps metabolize food particles and enhances the food chain: for example, the mandarin fishes (Synchiropidae) will live off this microfauna.

3) *Caulerpa* species and several other chlorophytes represent an important source of food for many fishes. Additionally, a thriving stand of *Caulerpa* contributes to the good health and continued vitality of the entire animal community in a marine tank.

4) These leafy algae not only produce organic acids which are released into the water, but also necessary substances such as vitamins and amino acids. Healthy stands of *Caulerpa* imply that pH levels will fall during the night, but not so drastically as to be problematic. But this, of course, depends on the amount of plants in relation to the water volume and movement.

5) Perhaps more important than the production of vital compounds is the extent that *Caulerpa* assimilate nitrogenous compounds and phosphates. Ammonia, which represents the initial step in the nitrogen cycle, and nitrate, the endproduct of the same cycle, are the most common sources of nitrogen for plants. This is the basis of the algae scrubber. Algae use these nutrients from the water to anobolize proteins, and the by-product is cleaner water. This is why most *Caulerpa* flourish in the nutrient rich water of marine aquaria to such a degree that large quantities can be harvested and removed.

6) *Caulerpa* and other algae are a legitimate, proven way to remove ammonia and nitrate from the system. Algae scrubbers are the solution for reef aquaria because many of the inhabitants of these tanks are herbivorous. Algae scrubbers consist of a separate tank either beside or below the display tank. The water passes through the scrubber as part of the filtration circuit. The algae are thereby protected from the herbivores of the tank who would browse on the algae and disrupt their filtering capacity. However, algae scrubbers are a costly addition to the aquarium. The functional capacity of the *Caulerpa* biomass depends on the lighting, which

is usually artificial. During the illumination period when *Caulerpa* is strongly assimilating nutrients, the algae remove a lot of carbonic acid from the water. The pH value may rise significantly at this time. Therefore, pH regulation through the addition of CO_2 or the quantitative control of light using a pH controller and timers is particularly important in the algae scrubber.

CAULERPA AS FOOD FOR FISHES AND INVERTEBRATES

It is a well recognized fact that vegetable fare is an important staple for a number of fishes and invertebrates. This is further supported when you read the ingredient lists on your fish foods. Coral fishes demonstrate their need for vegetable fare quite strongly—just look at your once beautiful *Caulerpa* stand. Algae are often "grazed" to such an extent that the plants cannot recover. This balance of natural fresh vitamins maintains herbivores, e.g., angelfishes and surgeon-fishes, in good condition. Many marine aquarists that are confronted with an aquarium that has been eaten bare will build a special illuminated algae scrubber where they cultivate *Caulerpa*. They kill two birds with one stone. The *Caulerpa* filter detoxifies and conditions the water, and the "excess" algae is fed to the fishes. A nice nutrient cycle is established.

In modern public aquaria, *Caulerpa* is also raised because of its healing qualities. Ill fishes will sometimes recover quickly in water that contains fresh squeezed *Caulerpa* juice. This method is used in the modern Hasanal Aquarium in Brunei (Indonesia).

Caulerpa Species	
Relished by fishes	Not relished by fishes
C. pinnata	*C. cupressoides*
C. racemosa*	*C. "macrodisca"*
C. racemosa var. *uvifera*	*C. urvilliana*
C. scalpelliformis	
C. sertularioides	

* also for human consumption

PRODUCTION OF COLLOIDS AND THEIR IMPORTANCE

When provided with good lighting, *Caulerpa* and other green algae not only produce a lot of oxygen that hastens the oxidation of catabolites, but they also produce phycocolloids which seem to play a significant role in the marine aquarium. Phycocolloids are large, noncrystalline molecules that are also known as seaweed gums. They are gluelike compounds that seem to be very important for marine organisms. They are used in water conditioners for aquaria and in instant foods and pharmaceutical preparations for humans. Their large capacity to hold water molecules makes them an appropriate gelling, emulsifying, and thickening agent. Low concentrations of these substances are used in aquaria (both fresh and salt water) as a coating agent. When minimal quantities of a phycocolloid are added to an aquarium (marine and freshwater), a thin emulsion results whose stability depends on the surface tension, the resulting adhesion (stickiness), and the electrical charge of the molecules. These small colloidal particles are called micelles. In molecular colloids (e.g., originating from organisms such as marine algae) the micelle consists of a polysaccharide which can adhere a large quantity of water molecules to its surface. All the connected micelle form a sol (liquid state of colloids in contrast to gel = gelatinous state of colloids) which changes in color and is adhesive, hence the name (colle = glue). The phycocolloids from marine algae are sensitive to salts such as those containing chlorine. These salts change the colloid's equilibrium in water, affecting the micellar colloids, and may even coagulate them. Organic and mineral colloids are numerous in nature. Some are even artificially made. Since colloids easily diffuse through living tissue, they are eminently suitable to use in water conditioners, prophylactic preparations, and medical products.

The previous lines underscore the biological significance of cultivating *Caulerpa* in an artificial system like an aquarium. It offers the fishes subtle yet useful protection and makes them less sensitive to skin irritations caused by chemicals (e.g., newly made seawater). It is also helpful in fighting skin and gill diseases.

Caulerpaceae

CAULERPICIN, A DEADLY TOXIN

Another aspect of keeping *Caulerpa* is the deadly poison, caulerpicin, they produce. So far it has been occasionally found in Hawaii and the Philippines. It has been known to enter the food chain of humans and other animals (D. & A. SANTOS, 1966/1970). Its chemical composition has been analyzed (SANTONS & DOTY, 1971). Because *Caulerpa* is often eaten with rice in these countries, humans may also be affected by this poison. Sudden, mysterious deaths of fishes in an aquarium may be explained by this toxin. It is not known if the excretion of caulerpicin is seasonal (like the red tide).

ANTIBIOTICS DERIVED FROM MARINE ALGAE

It has long been known that various marine algae contain medicinal substances. Several have a significant antibiotic effect towards fungi and saprobic (putrefying) and pathogenic (disease causing) microorganisms from the marine bottom. These antibiotic substances are broad spectrum antibiotics and particularly useful against microbes that are resistant against "classic" antibiotics. This helps explain why aquaria with dense algae growth or an algae scrubber traditionally have fewer disease problems. Sick animals introduced from other tanks into an aquarium with an algae scrubber or a healthy stand are sometimes spontaneously healed, even after standard treatments have failed. After the German microbiologist HARDER pointed out the bacteriostatic effect of substances from marine algae in 1917, these substances have been frequently researched. Extraction methods have been documented for each of the following classes of algae: Rhodophyceae (red algae), Phaeophyceae (brown algae), and Chlorophyceae (green algae, of which *Caulerpa* is a member).

CHARACTERISTICS OF THE ANTIBACTERIAL SUBSTANCES AND THEIR
ACTIVITY

It must be noted that many of these substances have not yet been
identified, but others are well known. For example:

Acrylic acid -   a highly soluble, unsaturated acid that is
                        produced by oxidizing acrolein.
Carbonyl compounds-   liquid and evaporative complex compounds
                        formed with a carbonyl group bonded to
                        iron, nickel, or cobalt.
Terpenes -   unsaturated hydrocarbon liquid found in
                        essential oils. Many compounds exist with
                        highly differing chemical structures.
Fatty acids -   various kinds and structures.

KATAYAMA (Japan) was the first scientist (1953) that isolated the
above mentioned substances from marine algae. They proved to be
particularly active against *Escherichia coli* (*E. coli* bacteria) and
Staphylococcus aureus. But only a fraction of carbonyl compounds
and terpenes were toxic to certain annelids (worms). The latter
observation is very relevant to marine aquarists, since after massive
"bleeding" of a large *Caulerpa* stand following spontaneous gametogenesis or mechanical injury, tubeworms frequently begin to act
strangly. Tubeworms will crawl half out of their tube where they
remain stuck or even abandon the tube entirely. In the first case, it
has been determined that occasionally the worm returns to its tube
and lives, but more frequently, the movements decrease and the
worms die. It is enticing to think that there is a correlation between
the mysterious and inexplicable die off of the tubeworms and the
excretion of algae juices. Acrylic acid is a strong antibiotic with a
broad bacterial spectrum. Its antibiotic effect seems to be directly
proportional to the acidity of the water until the optimal pH of 5-6 is
reached. Such a low pH is hard to imagine in a natural marine
environment. The alkaline environment will constrain its effect to the
direct surroundings of the alga producing the acid. The alkaline pH
value of the marine water will eliminate the antibacterial effect further
away. Other fatty acids and terpenes have certain influence on
oceanic waters, and it is possibly that they are even released into the
atmosphere. Algae produce volatile compounds (aerosols), bro-
mides, phenolic compounds, hydrocarbons (carbohydrates), pro-

teins, and fatty acids whose chemical character is so complex that they have yet to be identified.

Based on the antibiotic properties, the advantages of a lush stand of *Caulerpa* and other genera in a marine aquarium seem to outweigh the disadvantages, even if they are a time consuming proposition to maintain.

GROWTH INHIBITORS, A REALITY?

HEERING, 1969 (Capetown, South Africa) discovered that certain marine algae are capable of producing growth inhibitors, enabling the algae to synchronize nutrient availability with nutrient requirements. These growth inhibitors are called autoinhibitors. Extremely low concentrations are needed to fulfill their goal. Higher concentrations will cause mass mortality. This growth check was seen in laboratory experiments using certain microalgae. Because *Caulerpa* appear to maintain incredibly fast, even exuberant, growth in aquaria, it seems questionable whether *Caulerpa* produce these autoinhibitors. Most aquarists will confirm these observations. Despite the incredible growth rates of *Caulerpa* in aquaria, it cannot be denied that there are occasions—although rare—when the entire stand is suddenly decimated. Another element that points to the presence of autoinhibitors is the futility of trying to counter the die off. It seems that no matter what you do—either trying to establish new growth from the remains or taking cuttings from another aquarium—it is next to impossible to establish new growth in the same water. A total or partial water exchange is called for. It also appears that unfavorable conditions such as extended transport in small volumes of water stimulates macroalgae—for instance, *Caulerpa*—to produce autoinhibitors. These plants will never resume growing. This is why scientists and hobbyists transport *Caulerpa* only in inflated plastic bags or thermos bottles with colloids added to the water. This technique automatically implies that the plants are usually in the dark for 24 hr. This is harmless for an additional 48 hr. This "darkness shock" seems to have a growth stimulating effect when the plants are again exposed to light.

The environmental impact of a sudden die off of *Caulerpa* and other leafy algae usually does not cause problems in the faunal community of the aquarium. However, it is a "different kettle of fish" when smear algae die. This frequently poisons the water to such an extent that faunal fatalities may be sustained.

GROWTH STIMULATORS PRODUCED BY ALGAL COMMUNITIES

It is known that live algae produce compounds that can change the composition of the water. There is little information on how to use extracts of higher microalgae to fertilize newly set up marine aquaria. Squeezing *Caulerpa racemosa* has a growth stimulating effect on itself as well as other species of algae. HEERING points out that this does not necessarily follow in all species. Higher growth rates are induced in some, whereas others are totally oblivious to the presence of these compounds.

Due to a significantly higher production of polysaccharides and polypeptides, brown and red algae are more commercially relevant than green algae. Additionally, the former two are capable of returning up to 60% of the stored substances in their tissues to the water, thereby returning them to the cycle. *Caulerpa* is also capable of returning a large percentage of its stored nutrients to the environment, which probably has a great impact on the environment of the aquarium. It is interesting to note that older stands produce fewer growth stimulating compounds. This means you should always rejuvenate the *Caulerpa* stand.

Decreasing the light intensity, that is, decreasing the wattage per tube, the number of tubes, or the photoperiod, fosters strong secretions. Increasing the photoperiod or the intensity of light minimizes the secretions.

The secreted substances probably chelate metals, making them soluble and available to *Caulerpa*. Additionally, it cannot be excluded that many other soluble substances such as phosphates can be use advantageously by *Caulerpa* when combined with its secretions. The substances produced by the algae foam in aerated water. Old stands produce less foam than new stands.

Caulerpaceae

The Interaction Between *Caulerpa* and Bacterial Cultures

Bacteria obtain most of their energy for growth and propagation from carbohydrates, but nitrogenous compounds from proteins are also used. When energy comes from proteinaceous material—and the bacterial population is still unbalanced—the metabolites can be toxic. However, when the energy comes from carbohydrates, the metabolites will be harmless acids. Fish foods introduce protein to the aquarium. Carbohydrates come from algae excretions, mainly from *Caulerpa* in the marine aquarium. Various hobbyists have tried to stimulate bacteria colonies to grow by providing them with different carbohydrates ranging from simple sugars to various alcohols. It was successful. Large quantities of various bacteria grew and proliferated until the population stabilized with the bacteria most suitable for that particular environment. We not only have to thank improved technology and illumination for the way we success-fully grow *Caulerpa* in modern marine aquaria. The final products of bacterial metabolism such as nitrate deserve their just dues also. Consider the filters as water treatment plants that use bacterial colonies living in the substrate to provide the necessary nutrients for *Caulerpa.*

Caulerpa species and, of course, all other marine algae are conse-quential in establishing and maintaining good water quality:

a) To bind and absorb heavy metals.
b) To neutralize toxins.
c) To produce growth stimulating substances.
d) To foment protein skimming.
e) To adhere and flocculate suspended inorganic particles.
f) To produce compounds against pathogenic bacteria.
g) To provide a buffer against the tendency of the pH to fall.

A number of other interesting aspects could be added to this list. It could also include the protection to the skin, intestines, and gills of fishes that is granted by the plant's excretions.

Do Growing *Caulerpa* Cause a Mineral Deficiency?

Due to luxuriant growth of a permanent stand of *Caulerpa*, many persons often question the effect of *Caulerpa* on mineral depletion in the aquarium. There is no doubt that *Caulerpa* and almost all other algae use minerals and trace elements. However, such small quantities are used that a true mineral deficiency is almost impossible. Unavoidably, evaporated salt water will have to be replaced with freshwater. Additionally, coral sand, live rock, crushed oysters, other natural filter substrates and, naturally, the fish food will introduce sufficient trace elements into the marine water to maintain mineral concentrations.

Transport from the Tropics

Collection and transport techniques of *Caulerpa* from warm seas have been improved. If possible, collect the *Caulerpa* shortly before leaving. Clean the stolons well and remove sessile animals and other organisms. Pack the *Caulerpa* in a plastic bag with just enough water to dampen the plant. Inflate the bags to prevent the plants from being smashed. Pack the bags in a Styrofoam or cardboard box and place the boxes between the clothing in your luggage. The salinity and temperature of the natural biotope will give you a starting point on what water conditions to use when introducing the plants into your home aquarium.

Artificial Seawater and Transferring *Caulerpa* into a New Environment

Successfully cultivated *Caulerpa* in Dutch marine aquaria proves that most *Caulerpa* have an excellent capacity to adapt to various compositions of aquarium seawater. For the most part, they live in artificial seawater mixes that are simply dissolved in tap water. Freshly made artificial seawater can be particularly aggressive to living organisms, and *Caulerpa* may totally decompose in response. When transferring *Caulerpa*—regardless of species—using biologically mature water will minimize difficulties.

Caulerpaceae

SALINITY AND DISSOLVED SUBSTANCES

Within certain boundaries, you do not need to concern yourself with trying to match the salinity of your aquarium with the salinity found in the plant's natural habitat. It seems the effect of this aspect of water quality on growth and development of *Caulerpa* is unimportant. A wide range of salinities are found in marine aquaria. Almost regardless of what that value is, *Caulerpa's* growth will exceed all expectations once it has adapted to its environment (salinity). In general, the seawater in tropical marine aquaria tends to have a higher specific gravity than what you might find in these plants' natural habitat. But various species of *Caulerpa* such as *C. racemosa* (grape caulerpa), *C. certularioides* (feather *Caulerpa*), *C. verticillata,* and *C. scalpelliformis* will even thrive in lower salinities. When *Caulerpa* fails to grow, many hobbyists blame the differences in salinity instead of other water parameters. But adjusting the salinity to better "meet the plants' requirements" should be one of the last resorts. The most common cause of failure are fishes and other organisms within the community that graze the algae and/or different concentrations of metabolites. When *Caulerpa* has adapted to higher concentrations of metabolites, it can decompose if suddenly placed in clean—that is, better—water, even if the salinity is the same!

IS *BERTHELINA CHLORIS* (DALL, 1918) A SPECIALIZED LETHAL PARASITE?

About 2 years ago I received a bunch of *Caulerpa prolifera* through the mail from a fellow hobbyist. He requested that I check to see if there was a relationship between the presence of what appeared to be tiny bivalves on the plant and the die off of large stands of *Caulerpa*. I introduced the sample into a small aquarium where I had the same species successfully growing. Initially everything grew well, but the small shellfish quickly proliferated and almost exclusively lived on the *Caulerpa*. Although growth was more than satisfactory, the fronds sustained holes and other infirmities from being eaten on. These damaged areas always corresponded to where the small green shellfish were sitting. However, the damage remained in check until 3 *Caulerpa* developed a vitreous appearance within a few days. Simultaneously the water became turbid.

When the "fog" cleared two days later and the damage could be assessed, it appeared that the *Caulerpa* had almost disappeared with the exception of a few fragments which, to our amazement, were covered with a huge quantity of small green bivalves, even though a few months ago there were only 10 of these animals.

The original number of these creatures versus what is now seen in the decimated tank show the awesome reproductive potential of these animals. *Berthelina chloris* (DALL, 1918), the *Caulerpa* parasite, is especially inconspicuous because these small, flat, 8 mm long snails with a bivalve shell are exactly the same color of the *Caulerpa* they happen to be living on. It is well camouflaged among the jumble of thalli. At first glance these organisms look like a small two-shelled mussel, but today we know that it is a small snail. It has become known in the aquarium hobby as the infamous *Caulerpa* parasite! It belongs to the family Juliidae, subclass Opisthobranchia, and hails from the Caribbean and the coast of Mexico where it lives on stands of *Caulerpa.* These thin-shelled organisms probably have many enemies in their natural biotope that keep their numbers in

The *Caulerpa* parasite *Berthelina chloris* (DALL, 1918) feeds on *Caulerpa racemosa.*

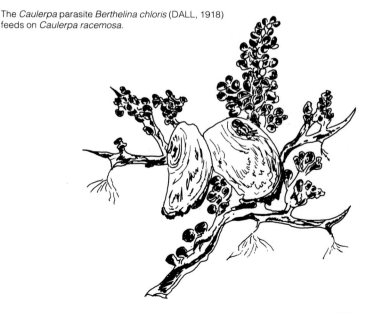

check. But in marine aquaria that lack their natural predators, they can multiply almost explosively. The body, which has acquired the color of the *Caulerpa* it happens to be feeding on, can be seen through the greenish yellow, thin, transparent shells. The body contributes substantially to the overall coloration of the organism. They move about undetected among the *Caulerpa.*

Fatal Damage

Fronds as well as stolons have holes pierced through them. The *Caulerpa* bleed, and this is how *Berthelina chloris* is able to easily suck the plant juices from *Caulerpa.* It is known that some species of *Caulerpa* produce a wound plug within a few seconds. As long as the plant is healthy, the plug will prevent the plant from bleeding. It is possible that *Berthelina* counters this defense by unknown methods.

Reproduction of the Snail

Sexually mature animals are almost always found in pairs, and copulation is regularly observed. *Berthelina chloris* seems to be very productive; 150-300 eggs in a transparent white gelatinous mass are occasionally seen in the aquarium. This is how the population multiplies so fast, and why *Caulerpa* has almost disappeared by the time the snails are discovered. After hatching, they are quickly distributed by the current. They use a sticky mucus they produce to adhere to any and all surfaces in their search for *Caulerpa.*

Prevention is Better than Healing

Normally, *Berthelina chloris* is only found on *Caulerpa* or green algae. But there are also indications that after a *Caulerpa* stand dies, red algae are also sought. It seems that contamination can only be avoided by placing newly acquired *Caulerpa* in a quarantine tank until you are positive that the plants are free of *Berthelina.* There are also rumors that this small *Caulerpa* parasite can be controlled with UV radiation. I have not experimented with this possible method of control. It is also possible that there are fishes that will feed on these snails. Small puffers or boxfishes may clean the tank of *Berthelina chloris.* Once this parasite is present, it seems impossible to rid yourself of it. Therefore, in this case, prevention is the secret!

Caulerpa brachypus
Miniature caulerpa

Fam.: Caulerpaceae

Hab.: Japan (Janega).

M.: This *Caulerpa* resembles a smaller version of *Caulerpa prolifera*. It will only prosper under extremely good water conditions and light from 5,000 to 8,000 Lux. It cannot be kept in aquaria with herbivores, since its tender fronds are considered a delicacy of fishes such as surgeonfishes. Those who successfully cultivate this alga in surplus quantities should pass it on to other aquarists. It is extremely rare in European aquaria.

S.: *Caulerpa* all have similar maintenance requirements. This small *Caulerpa* is the most sensitive, exacting species. Use TROPIC MARINE salt!

T: 23°-28°C, L: up to 30 cm, TL: 40 cm, WR: b, m D: 3

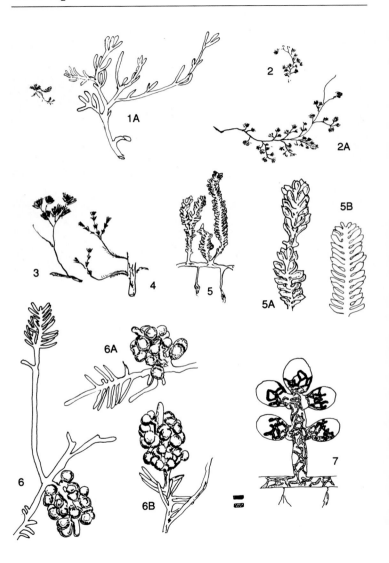

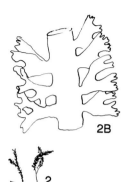

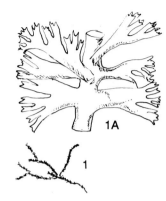

1. *Caulerpa webbiana*; stolon—actual size
1A. *Caulerpa webbiana*—greatly enlarged
2. *Caulerpa webbiana*
2A. *Caulerpa webbiana*—greatly enlarged
3. *Caulerpa elongata*
4. *Caulerpa pickeringii* from Tuamotu—actual size
5. *Caulerpa pickeringii* from Tahiti—actual size

Left Page:

    1. *Caulerpa fastigiata*
    1A. *Caulerpa fastigiata*—greatly enlarged
    2. *Caulerpa murrayana*
    2A. *Caulerpa murrayana*—greatly enlarged
    3. *Caulerpa verticillata*—actual size
    4. *Caulerpa pusilla*—actual size
5A. + 5B. *Caulerpa reyesi*
6A. + 6B. *Caulerpa biloba*
    7. Gametogenesis of *Caulerpa okamurai;* dark aggregations are concentrations of female gametes; light aggregations are concentrations of male gametes.

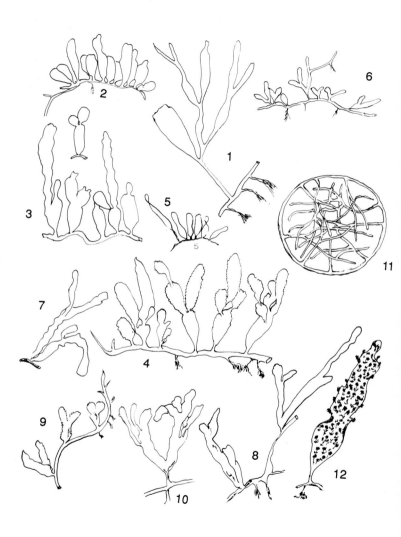

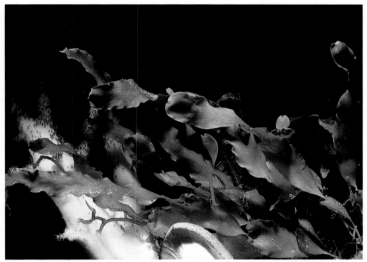

Caulerpa prolifera, the most common green alga seen in marine aquaria.

1. *Caulerpa prolifera*
2. *Caulerpa brachypus*
2A. *Caulerpa brachypus*—blade
3. *Caulerpa stahlii*—actual size
4. *Caulerpa stahlii*
5. *Caulerpa parvifolia*—actual size
6. *Caulerpa anceps*⎤
7. *Caulerpa anceps*⎟ several forms from the Society Islands in the Pacific Ocean
8. *Caulerpa anceps*⎟
9. *Caulerpa anceps*⎦
10. *Caulerpa anceps*—from Japan
11. Cross-section of a stolon. The internal projections of trabeculae of caulerpas serve to mechanically reinforce the cell. The cells have chloroplasts and amyloplasts.
12. A full-grown, mature phylloid about to release its gametes through papillae located on very thin stalks. They can be easily seen in the aquarium on *Caulerpa prolifera*, but are only noticed by a few hobbyists.

Caulerpaceae

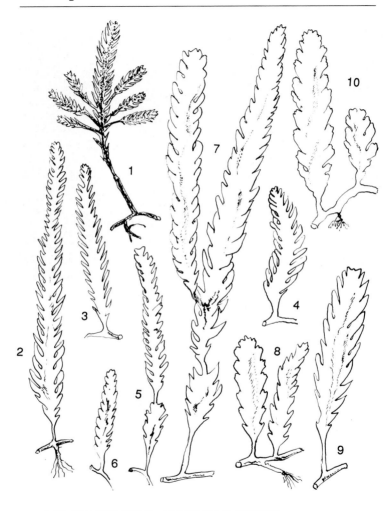

1. *Caulerpa scalpelliformis*—several forms; $^2/_3$ actual size
2 – 4. *Caulerpa scalpelliformis*
5 – 6. *Caulerpa scalpelliformis*—from Sri Lanka
7. *Caulerpa scalpelliformis*—from Mauritius
8 – 10. *Caulerpa scalpelliformis*—from the Red Sea

Caulerpas

Caulerpa scalpelliformis in the aquarium (the serrated edges of the fronds frequently turn entire).

Caulerpa sertularioides (feather caulerpa) and *C. racemosa* (center)

Caulerpaceae

Caulerpa pinnata

Caulerpa plumaris, south coast of Australia

Caulerpa taxifolia

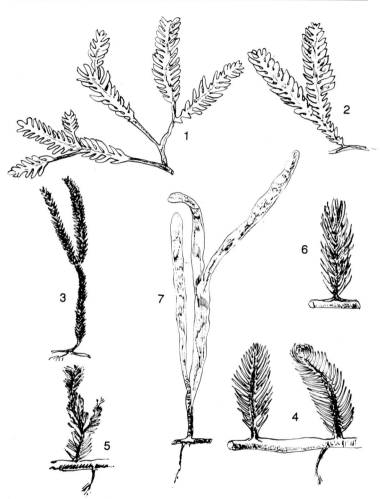

1. *Caulerpa pinnata*⌉
2. *Caulerpa pinnata*⌋— several forms; ²/₃ actual size, one form is found in Mexico
3. *Caulerpa pinnata*⌋
4 – 6. *Caulerpa plumaris*—several forms
7. *Caulerpa flagelliformis*

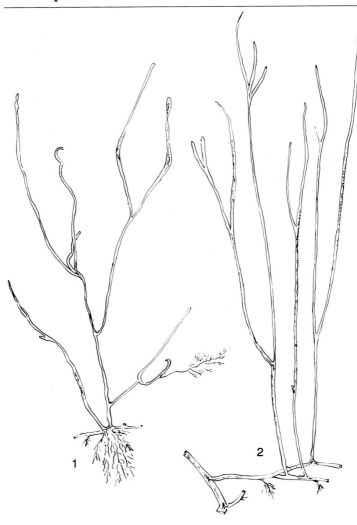

1. *Caulerpa flagelliformis*—coast of Morocco
2. *Caulerpa flagelliformis*—Gulf of Cadiz, southern Spain

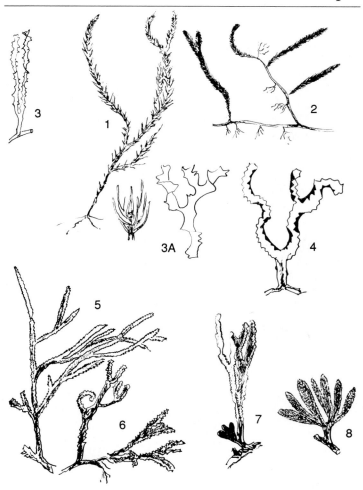

1. *Caulerpa alternifolia*
2. *Caulerpa brownii*
2A. *Caulerpa brownii*
3. *Caulerpa freycinetti*
3A. *Caulerpa freycinetti*

4. *Caulerpa freycinetti*—more serrated
5. *Caulerpa freycinetti*
6. *Caulerpa freycinetti*—Red Sea
7. *Caulerpa freycinetti*—Red Sea and Persian Gulf
8. *Caulerpa freycinetti*

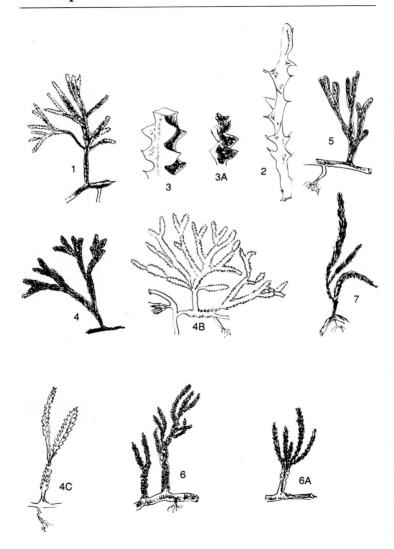

Caulerpa urvilliana

Caulerpa cupressoides

1. *Caulerpa urvilliana*
2. *Caulerpa urvilliana*—growing tip
3. *Caulerpa urvilliana*—enlarged; see segment (3 + 3A)
4. *Caulerpa freycinetti*—²/₃ actual size
4B. *Caulerpa freycinetti*
4C. *Caulerpa freycinetti*—frequently occurring aquarium form
5. *Caulerpa freycinetti*—smooth variety—²/₃ actual size
6. *Caulerpa cupressoides*—actual size, physophrous (vesicle) form
6A. *Caulerpa cupressoides*—actual size, form with more spines
7. *Caulerpa cupressoides* var. *lycopodium*—²/₃ actual size

1. *Caulerpa hypnoides* $^2/_3$ actual size

1. *Caulerpa paspaloides* f. *flabellata*
2. *Caulerpa paspaloides* var. *laxa*
3. *Caulerpa paspaloides* f. *compressa*

Caulerpaceae

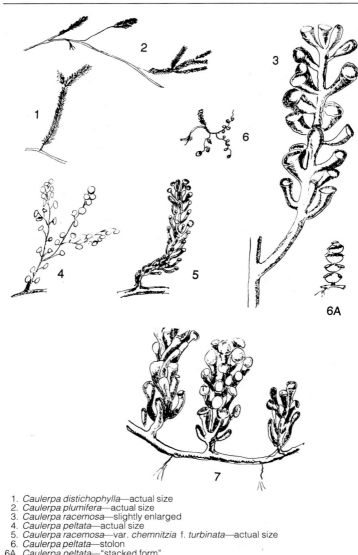

1. *Caulerpa distichophylla*—actual size
2. *Caulerpa plumifera*—actual size
3. *Caulerpa racemosa*—slightly enlarged
4. *Caulerpa peltata*—actual size
5. *Caulerpa racemosa*—var. *chemnitzia* f. *turbinata*—actual size
6. *Caulerpa peltata*—stolon
6A. *Caulerpa peltata*—"stacked form"
7. *Caulerpa racemosa* var. *chemnitzia*—actual size

Caulerpa paspaloides, Florida coast

Caulerpaceae

1. *Caulerpa racemosa*
2. *Caulerpa racemosa*
3. *Caulerpa racemosa* Typical morph in nature; the very smooth morphs without blister-
4. *Caulerpa racemosa* like enlargements are so far little known from aquarium cultivars
5. *Caulerpa racemosa* (see p. 313 top).
6. *Caulerpa peltata*—forms from the open sea.
7. *Caulerpa peltata*—forms from aquaria and aquaculture.

Caulerpa racemosa (elongated because of insufficient light)

Caulerpa racemosa, a common aquarium form

Caulerpa peltata var. *macrodisca*, coast of Ireland

Caulerpa peltata var. *peltata*, aquarium form

Caulerpa peltata var. *macrodisca*

Caulerpa peltata var. *macrodisca*

Caulerpaceae

1 – 12 *Caulerpa racemosa*
The extreme variations in shape and appearance that become evident as *Caulerpa* adapt to environmental conditions are seen when *Caulerpa racemosa* is grown in the aquarium. Both the shape of the vesicles and their arrangement vary according to environmental conditions such as: substrate, nutrients, origin, current pattern, and intensity, angle, and reflection of light.

Caulerpa racemosa

Caulerpa racemosa, natural form: underwaterphoto from Java

1–6 *Caulerpa racemosa*—several growth forms from nature

Caulerpa paspaloides, young shoots

Caulerpa racemosa, aquarium photo

Caulerpaceae

Caulerpa racemosa; the fleshy stolons are a result of the intense illumination the plant receives by growing just beneath the water's surface.

Caulerpa racemosa is capable of producing a great variety of shapes. This specimen was found growing on a rocky substrate on the northern coast of Java.

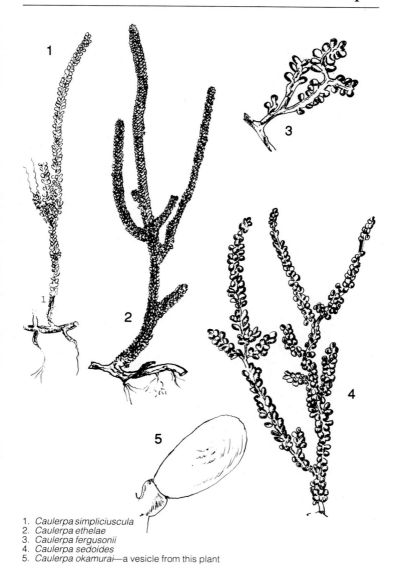

1. *Caulerpa simpliciuscula*
2. *Caulerpa ethelae*
3. *Caulerpa fergusonii*
4. *Caulerpa sedoides*
5. *Caulerpa okamurai*—a vesicle from this plant

Caulerpaceae

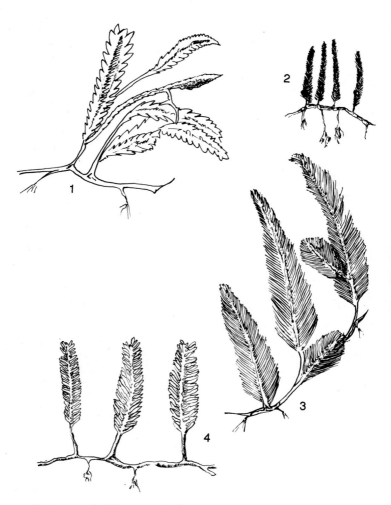

1. *Caulerpa sertularioides*—aquarium form
2. *Caulerpa mexicana = C. sertularioides* (GMELIN) HOWE
3. *Caulerpa taxifolia* AGARDH
4. *Caulerpa floridana* TAYLOR

Caulerpa floridana

Caulerpa sertularioides

Caulerpa mexicana = C. sertularioides

Right: Caulerpa *nummelaria* (REINKE); the small assimilator discs, which sometimes are sessile on the stolon, have a cuplike shape and frequently have an undulant rim. An exceptionally beautiful species. Left: *Caulerpa verticillata*, Caribbean form.

Entacmaea quadricolor, aquarium photo. This species is easily recognized by its enlarged tentacle tips.

Taxonomy

Phylum: CNIDARIA		Cnidarians
Class: ANTHOZOA		Anthozoans
Subclass: HEXACORALLIA		Six-Tentacled Anthozoans

Order	Actiniaria	Anemones
Superfamily	Endomyaria	
Family	Actiniidae	GOSSE, 1858
Genera	*Actinia*	BROWNE, 1756
	Anemonia	RISSO, 1826
	Condylactis	DUCHASSAING & MICHELOTTI, 1866
	Cribrinopsis	CARLGREN, 1921
	Entacmaea	RÜPELL & LEUCKAART, 1828
	Macrodactyla	HADDON, 1898
	Urticina	VERRILL, 1922
Family	Actinodendronidae	HADDON, 1898
Genus	*Actinodendron*	BLAINVILLE, 1930
Family	Andresiidae	STEPHENSON, 1922
Genus	*Andresia*	STEPHENSON, 1921
Family	Phymanthidae	ANDRES, 1883
Genus	*Phymanthus*	MILNE-EDWARDS, 1857
Family	Stichodactylidae	ANDRES, 1883
Genera	*Heteractis*	MILNE-EDWARDS, 1857
	Stichodactyla	BRANDT, 1835
Family	Thalassianthidae	MILNE-EDWARDS, 1857
Genera	*Cryptodendrum*	KLUNZINGER, 1877
	Heterodactyla	MILNE-EDWARDS; 1857
Superfamily	Acontiaria	
Family	Aiptasiidae	CARLGREN, 1924
Genera	*Aiptasia*	GOSSE, 1858
	Bartholomea	DUCHASSAING & MICHELOTTI, 1866
Family	Metridiidae	CARLGREN, 1893
Genus	*Metridium*	OKEN, 1815
Family	Nemanthidae	CARLGREN, 1940
Genus	*Nemanthus*	CARLGREN, 1940
Family	Sagartiidae	GOSSE, 1858
Genera	*Sagartia*	GOSSE, 1855
	Sagartiogeton	CARLGREN, 1924
Family	Isophellidae	STEPHENSON, 1935
Genus	*Telmatactis*	GRAVIER, 1918
Superfamily	Boloceroidaria	
Family	Aliciidae	DUERDEN, 1897
Genera	*Alicia*	JOHNSON, 1861
	Lebrunia	DUCHASSAING & MICHELOTTI, 1860

	Triactis	KLUNZINGER, 1877
Family	Boloceroididae	CARLGREN, 1924
Genus	*Boloceroides*	CARLGREN, 1899

Order   Ceriantharia   Tube anemones

Family	Cerinathidae	MILNE-EDWARDS & HAIME, 1852
Genera	*Cerianthus*	DELLE CHIAJE, 1832
	Pachycerianthus	ROULE, 1904
Family	Arachnactidae	McMURRICH, 1910
Genus	*Arachnanthus*	CARLGREN, 1912

Order   Corallimorpharia   False corals

Family	Discosomatidae	DUCHASSAING & MICHELOTTI, 1864
Genera	*Amplexidiscus*	DUNN & HAMNER, 1980
	Discosoma	RÜPELL & LEUCKART, 1828
	Metarhodactis	CARLGREN, 1860
Family	Ricordeidae	WATZL, 1922
Genus	*Ricordea*	DUCHASSAING & MICHELOTTI, 1860
Family	Corallimorphidae	HERTWIG, 1882
Genus	*Corynactis*	ALLMAN, 1846
	Pseudocorynactis	DEN HARTOG, 1981

Order   Zoantharia   Colonial anemones

Family	Zoanthidae	
Genera	*Palythoa*	LAMOUROUX, 1816
	Parazoanthus	HADDON & SHACKLETON, 1899
	Zoanthus	LAMARCK, 1801
Family	Epizoanthidae	
Genera	*Epizoanthus*	GRAY, 1867

Phylum: Cnidaria (Coelenterata)
Class: Anthozoa

Anthozoans, hydrozoans, and jellyfish compose the phylum of coelenterates, whose members typically have intrinsic nematocysts (stinging cells). These unicellular predation and defense organs react to tactile stimuli by shooting a barbed tube into the skin of the adversary and simultaneously injecting a strong poison. This chases aggressors away and immobilizes small prey organisms which can be easily captured thereafter. Besides normal nematocysts, they also have adhesive cells (spirocysts) to entangle the prey, allowing it to be guided to the mouth with the tentacles. At present there are approximately 6,500 known species of anthozoans. They range in size from a few millimeters to one and a half meters. Anthozoans are solely marine inhabitants that possess a cylinder-shaped body, which is usually adhered to the substrate with a pedal disc, and one to several rows of tentacles, frequently arranged in concentric circles. The interior space is divided into wedge-like sectors by vertical walls (mesenteries); the deeply recessed, slit-shaped mouth is located in the center. At least one, but usually both sides of the mouth have a ciliated groove (siphonoglyph) that constantly introduces fresh water to maintain oxygen levels and the animal's hydrostatic skeleton. Normally the water flows in through one corner of the mouth and out the other. These animals only have 2 layers of cells. An external (epidermis) and internal (gastrodermis) layer; between these two layers is a gelatinous mass (mesogloea) that is secreted by the cells. The gastrodermis segregates the interior cavity and takes care of digestion, respiration, reproduction, and even forms a circular musculature. The epidermis contains longitudinal muscles (retractor muscles) which can contract the animals. In many species the epidermis excretes an exoskeleton. No specialized sensory organs are present; however, both cell layers have a net of nerve cells which react to stimuli. Sexual reproduction consists of either the release of sperm and eggs to the open water or internal fertilization and larval release. Asexual division can also be observed. Frequently it is incomplete and leads to large contiguous colonies. Anthozoans are comprised of highly variable forms well-known to aquarists and divers. While anthozoans are principally located in the shallow waters of tropical seas, they also inhabit polar waters. Some inhabit the deep sea, and others have abandoned their sessile life and become planktonic.

A short overview on the various orders follows: the subclass of the six-tentacled anthozoans (Hexacorallia) has members with six tentacles or a multiple thereof and includes the sea anemones (Actiniaria), stone corals (Madreporaria), black corals (Antipatharia), tube anemones (Ceriantharia), false corals (Corallimorpharia), and colonial anemones (Zoantharia).

328

An aquarium photo of an "inflated" *Heteractis magnifica*. This is the way these animals move with the current (observed along the coast of Kenya). Note the clownfish *Premnas biaculeatus*.

Class: Anthozoa

Sea anemones usually live singly, can attain a size of 150 cm, and lack hard skeletal components. Over 1,000 species are known, a few of which are presented in this book.

In contrast, **stone corals** secrete a calcium carbonate exoskeleton made of small aragonite crystals formed by the epidermis on the lower half of the column and the pedal disc. The animals rarely live singly. They generally live in colonies that form hard round shapes or antler-like branched stalks. There are numerous species that contribute to coral reef building in tropical seas where, under favorable geologic and climatological conditions, they can give rise to calcium formations anywhere from several meters to 1,000 meters high and many kilometers wide. Approximately 2,500 species of stone corals exist, which makes them the largest order of anthozoans.

The **black** or **thorny corals**, as they are called among divers, build fan-to bush-shaped colonies. The tender polyps do not secret a calcium skeleton, but a keratinlike substance that is frequently black and has small thorns. A thin, vulnerable layer of polyps forms around this axis. Thicker trunks have been used to manufacture jewelry. Nowadays this is not done (?), since black corals are protected! There are more than 100 species of black corals.

Only about 50 species of **tube anemones** are known. They live individually and do not form a skeleton. Instead, they construct a tube around their elongated body that may be 75 cm long. The tube consists of secreted mucus with foreign matter such as sand adhered onto it. They only extend their long threadlike tentacles out of the tube to capture prey. When in danger, they are quickly retracted.

Colonial anemones form extensive, crustlike colonies which constantly grow from runners extending off their pedal disc. In the gelatinous intermediate layer, they introduce foreign matter such as sand and foraminiferans, creating a skeleton of sorts. There are about 300 species. Many grow on top of other sessile marine animals such as sponges and dead corals.

The second subclass of the anthozoans are the octocorals (Octocorallia = Alcyonaria) who have 8 tentacles or a multiple thereof. Many have a skeleton of fine calcium spicules (0.01-10 mm), which are either distributed singly about the body, arranged in groups, or form an interior axis. Leather corals, soft corals, horny or gorgonian corals, blue corals, and sea pens are octocorals. **Soft corals** (Stolonifera and Alcyonacea) have polyps arising from a soft, fleshy substance. Their general shape may vary from planar to lobed, fingerlike, or mushroom-shaped. The calcium spicules contained within are species specific, which means they are used to identify the animals.

The **gorgonians** (Gorgonacea) are comprised of approximately 1,200 species which either have a skeleton of glued calcium spicules or an interior axial rod made of calcium and horny material. A cortex of living polyps surrounds the skeleton. These corals may grow up to 3 m in height and are often intensely colored.

There is only one species of **blue coral** (Heliopora). It builds a plateau-shaped exoskeleton of fiberlike aragonite.

The **sea pens** and **sea pansies** (Pennatulacea) are comprised of about 300 species. Their colonies can grow up to 2.3 m in height. They are not firmly fastened, merely loosely attached to soft substrates. The main axis is made of a primary polyp and dimorphic secondary polyps that emerge pinnately. The base is frequently enlarged like a bulb. Most species are nocturnal and hide in the sand during the day.

The octocorals and stony corals will be covered in the second volume.

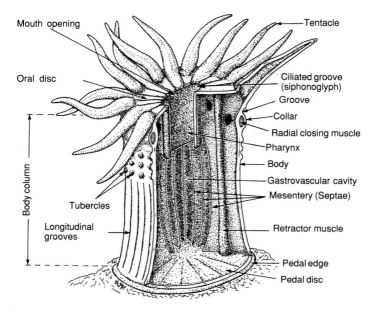

Anatomy of a sea anemone

Order: Actiniaria

Actiniaria are solitary, non-skeleton forming anthozoans called sea anemones. They have a pipe-shaped column whose epidermis may be smooth, tuberculate, or blistered. Sometimes various regions are separated from each other by depressions or ridges. On the basal end of the body is a foot, which can be bulb-shaped or flattened into a pedal disc. It serves to anchor the animal in sand or onto a hard substrate. The pedal disc creates suction pressure by arching in the center. An almost unbreakable hold is attained. Numerous (usually a multiple of 6), partially retractable tentacles frame the oral end of the body. They are arranged in either one or several rows; they rarely radiate like the spokes of a wheel on the body surface of the mouth disc (radial symmetry). The tentacles are usually simple and fingerlike (digital). However, in some species the tentacles are warty, blistered, or have other structures; they may even be branched.

The oral disc itself is usually circular and even, but it may be funnel-shaped or undulate. It may be transparent or pigmented. Frequently it is indicative of the interior morphology of the animal, since the colored vertical divisions (mesenteries) usually radiate from the disc into the otherwise empty interior (septum). Not only the interior body is divided like the slices of a pie, but also the mouth disc. The oral opening is usually slit-shaped, located at the center of the disc, and connected to the pharynx.

The gamete-producing gonads are located on the mesenteries which divide the gastrovascular cavity. The sexes are separate in most anthozoans, but in some cases, they are hermaphrodites. Fertilization is frequently accomplished in the open water after the animals simply release their eggs and sperm. Occasionally there is internal fertilization followed by the release of ciliated larvae. The larvae will drift in the plankton until they find a suitable site. Besides sexual reproduction, there is also asexual division, as found principally during the summer in rock anemones.

The majority of the nematocysts, the animal's defense mechanisms and hunting weapons, are located on the tentacles. The tiny barbed harpoons are shot forth upon tactile stimulation. They penetrate the skin of the victim or opponent and simultaneously inject a toxin. Some species produce threadlike structures within their body, so-called acontia, which also contain nematocysts. When threatened, they press these filaments out through specific body openings. These filaments adhere to the enemy and cause burns.

When severely disturbed, exposed to adverse environmental conditions, or simply resting, anemones use their strong musculature to contract. Some disappear underground or in a rock crevice. Others retract their tentacles within their body and form a knoll or hemisphere. Acquiring food is accomplished in various ways. Some species, such as *Actinia plumosa*, limit themselves to capturing small planktonic organisms from the water and transporting them to their mouth using mucous and cilia. Other species, particularly those with well developed nematocysts, are true predators (such as *Actinia*, *Anemonia*, *Calliactis*, and *Stichodactyla*). They immobilize small crustacea, molluscs, and fishes that bump into them and guide them towards their mouth using their tentacles. All indigestible parts are expelled through the mouth opening.

Actinodendron anemones have symbiotic algae inside of their body, especially in the branched tentacles. The algae's metabolic products are used by the anemones. They require little animal food to supplement what they gain from their symbiotic algae.

Actinia equina

Fam.: Actiniidae

About the Genus *Actinia*

Members of this genus have a smooth body that is distinctly separated from the tentacles of the mouth disc by a ridge and an adjacent furrow. Simple or lobed "edge vesicles" (acrophages) containing nematocysts are located in the furrow. The tentacles are simple, fingerlike (digital) and contain longitudinal musculature formed by the epidermis.

Actinia cari
Green sea anemone
DELLE CHIAJE, 1825

Hab.: Mediterranean; from the low tide line to 8 m depth.

Sex.: None.

Soc.B./Assoc.: Lives singly. In shallow waters it prefers a smooth rock in a shady local or rock edifications. At greater depths they will also live on the upper side of stones.

M.: Requires shaded rocks to adhere. Does not attach quite as strongly as *A. equina*; therefore, it is more sensitive to turbulence.

Light: Shaded areas in the sunlight zone.

B./Rep.: *Actinia cari* has separate sexes and releases its eggs (oviparous) during the summer.

F.: C; exclusively a nocturnal predator. It will eat shrimp, mussel, and fish meat, frozen foods, etc.

S.: *A. cari* is easily recognized by its brownish to greenish coloration and the black-brown concentric circles on its smooth body. When compressed, it is quite flat, not semispherical. You can count 192 tentacles when they are completely relaxed.

T: 15°-20°C, **Ø:** 5 cm, **TL:** from 30 cm, **WM:** m, **WR:** b, **AV:** 2-3, **D:** 3

Actinia equina
Red sea anemone, horse anemone
LINNAEUS, 1766

Hab.: Mediterranean, east Atlantic, and northern Scotland. From the high tide mark to 2 m depth.

Sex.: None.

Soc.B./Assoc.: Lives singly or in groups. Usually found on shaded vertical rock walls, but also in tidal pools exposed to rain as well as sun and cold.

M.: It is insensitive to temperature and salinity fluctuations; tolerates drying out for short periods of time. Slight illumination is enough. It congregates close to the water surface in the aquarium.

Light: Shaded areas within the sunlight zone.

B./Rep.: The larger form (see **S.**) has separate sexes and releases its eggs into the water (oviparous); the eggs mature throughout the year. The second form fertilizes the eggs internally and releases larvae into the water (viviparous). The larvae are only released in June and July.

F.: C; mussel and fish meat as well as frozen foods.

S.: This species is very variable in form and coloration. Its color ranges from purple to brownish red with bluish edge vesicles. There are two very different forms: one is purple, has 192 tentacles, and reaches a size of 7 cm. The second is brownish red, has 124 tentacles, and reaches a size of 3 cm. Since it only opens at night, it is usually found contracted into a hemisphere.

T: 16°-20°C, **Ø:** 7 cm, **TL:** from 30 cm, **WM:** s, **WR:** b, **AV:** 1, **D:** 2

Actinia cari; the clownfish does not belong there!

Color variants of *Actinia equina* (aquarium photograph)

Fam.: Actiniidae

About the Genus *Anemonia*

The genus *Anemonia* is comprised of sea anemones that have a smooth, soft wall. The tentacles are long, only slightly contractile with longitudinal musculature that originates from the epidermis. Number and arrangement of the septae is usually irregular.

Anemonia sulcata   (PENNANT, 1777)
Oplet, sea anemone

Hab.: Mediterranean and east Atlantic from Bergen to Madeira. From the low tide line to a depth of 30 m.

Sex.: None.

Soc.B./Assoc.: At least younger specimens are social towards conspecifics and can form lawns. Many animals, especially crustacea, can live in community with them. These include three species of *Periclimenes* cleaning shrimp, the spider crabs *Inachus phalangium* and *Maja verrucosa*, and the mud crab *Pilumnus hirtellus*. Most of these crustacea are protected from the nematocysts of the anemone, but not the drifting shrimp *Leptomysis lingvura*. This is because its behavior is to swim nimbly among the tentacles. Even a fish can live symbiotically with this anemone: the goby *Gobius bucchicchii* is protected from the nematocysts like clownfishes of tropical seas and can even swim from one oplet to another.

M.: Needs a rocky bottom with crevices to adhere to.

Light: Sunlight.

B./Rep.: Reproduction is usually sexual (the animals have separate sexes). The eggs are released into the water (oviparous). They usually spawn during the summer. Additionally, type 1 (see **S.**) in particular undergoes asexual reproduction through longitudinal division. This method of reproduction is to be suspected when you notice numerous animals with a reduced number of tentacles.

F.: C; small crustacea, mussel and fish meat, frozen foods.

S.: There are several forms of the sea anemone that are considered separate species by some authors. They not only vary in coloration between shades of green and brown, sometimes even with purple tips on the tentacles, but also in size, number of tentacles, and type of nematocysts. The colors depend on the illumination and, correspondingly, the quantity of symbiotic algae (zooxanthellae) in their tentacles. At least two types (or species) can be distinguished: type 1 inhabits very shallow waters to a depth of 5 m, usually attaches to rocks that are grazed by sea urchins, and lives in community with numerous conspecifics. Its number of tentacles fluctuates between 70 and 192, and it is significantly smaller than type 2. The latter prefers deeper water, grows significantly larger, and frequently has 384 tentacles. It tolerates life in higher growth and even colonizes coral substrates at about 30 m depth. While the shallow form always has green tips on its tentacles, type 2, the deep water form, usually has purple tips.

T: 18°-24°C, **Ø:** 25 cm, **TL:** from 80 cm, **WM:** s, **WR:** b, **AV:** 1, **D:** 2

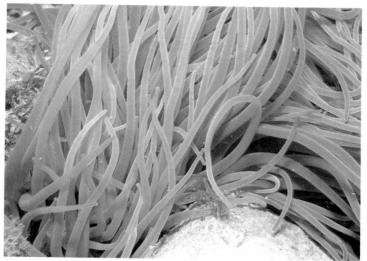

Anemonia sulcata

Anemonia sulcata (aquarium photo)

Fam.: Actiniidae

About the Genus *Cribrinopsis*

The sea anemones of this genus have a variable number of epidermal tubercles. The tentacles are simple, short, thick, and cylindrical rather than conical.

Cribrinopsis crassa   (ANDRES, 1884)
Thick-tentacled anemone

Hab.: Mediterranean. At 30 to 50 m depth.

Sex.: None.

Soc.B./Assoc.: It lives singly on secondary hard substrates.

M.: *C. crassa* requires either cave or crevice-riddled rock edifications or stones lying on the sand where they can excavate a cave.

Light: Moderate light.

B./Rep.: *C. crassa* has separate sexes and primarily releases its eggs (oviparous) into the open water in June and July.

F.: C; crustacean, mussel, and fish meat and frozen foods.

S.: Unfortunately, its beautifully colored body is rarely visible. The pedal disc is orange with small red spots, and the body is yellow with 48 rows of suction tubercles. The thick tentacles have lilac tips and a light ring near the center. Since this anemone inhabits a relatively narrow depth range, few differences in coloration have been observed. Animals in clear water are usually more intensely colored than those from turbid waters. *Cribrinopsis crassa* appears somewhat similar to *Condylactis aurantiaca*, but the latter only colonizes soft substrates, and its tentacles, especially those on the outer ring, gradually narrow to a point.

T: 18°-22°C, Ø: 20 cm, TL: from 80 cm, **WM:** m, **WR:** b, AV: 3, D: 2

Cribrinopsis fernaldi   SIEBERT & SPAULDING, 1976

Hab.: West coast of the USA. At depths of 5 to 20 m.

Sex.: None.

Soc.B./Assoc.: Singly.

M.: Does not burrow in the substrate.

Light: Moderate light.

B./Rep.: Separate sexes.

F.: *Mysis* and *Artemia*.

S.: Appreciated host for anemone shrimp.

T: 12°-17°C, Ø: 15 cm, TL: from 80 cm, **WM:** m, **WR:** b, AV: 3, D: 3

Cribrinopsis crassa

Cibrinopsis fernaldi

Fam.: Actiniidae

About the Genus *Condylactis*

These sea anemones are large. The body is smooth with small tubercles superiorly and a distinct groove along the very top. The tentacles are thick, long, and quite cylindrical. Particularly those of the outer ring terminate conically into blunt ends.

Condylactis aurantiaca   (DELLE CHIAJE, 1825)
Golden anemone

Hab.: Mediterranean; at depths of 3 to 12 m (even 80 m).

Sex.: None.

Soc.B./Assoc.: Lives singly on sandy and muddy bottoms.

M.: Needs at least 10 cm of sand substrate to anchor itself. It does not need hard substrates.

Light: Sunlight.

B./Rep.: *C. aurantiaca* has separate sexes and releases eggs and larvae into the water; it is therefore oviparous as well as viviparous. Mainly spawns in the spring (April to June).

F.: C; feeds on mussel, crustacean, and fish flesh, frozen foods, etc.

S.: The hidden body is smooth and orange with 12 indistinct whitish longitudinal stripes. The upper third is brownish to bluish with small white suction tubercles which hold small stones and grains of sand. The oral disc frequently has light and dark red radial lines. In contrast to *C. crassa*, the tentacles are significantly thinner and at least those of the outer ring terminate conically into blunt violet tips. Depending on substrate, lighter and darker specimens occur. Depending on the density of symbiotic algae in their tentacles and oral disc, these structures occur in a range of colors from dark brown-green to brown-gray or brown. At greater depths, the dark and light striations are more pronounced.

T: 18°-24°C, **Ø:** 30 cm, **TL:** from 100 cm, **WM:** s, **WR:** b, **AV:** 1, **D:** 2

Condylactis aurantiaca

Condylactis gigantea
Giant golden anemone

(WEINLAND, 1861)

Hab.: Caribbean and west Atlantic from the Bermudas to Brazil; from the surface to a depth of at least 30 m.

Sex.: None.

Soc.B./Assoc.: Lives in lagoons and inner reefs either individually or in very loose groups, but never in connected "fields." Numerous shrimp live in community with *C. gigantea*, especially *Periclimenes pedersoni* and *Thor amboinensis*.

M.: It requires rock crevices or holes to hide in and fasten onto.

Light: Sunlight.

B./Rep.: Not known.

F.: C; fish, mussel, and crustacean meat, shrimp, frozen foods, and many others.

S.: Only the up to 10 cm long, numerous, and often colorful tentacles appear above the substrate. They are much thicker at the base, become thinner distally, and terminate in a bulblike tip. Clusters of nematocysts can be seen as light dots and faint cross striations along the greenish, whitish, or bluish tentacles. The tips may be violet, purple, or a luminous yellow.

T: 20°-24°C, **Ø:** up to 40 cm, **TL:** from 50 cm, **WM:** s, **WR:** b, **AV:** 2, **D:** 2-3

Condylactis gigantea, Panama (Caribbean)

Fam.: Actiniidae

Condylactis gigantea

ABOUT THE GENUS *ENTACMAEA*

Members of this genus have a well developed pedal disc. The body is smooth, and its upper edge is clearly separated by a deep groove. However, it does not have edge blisters. The inner ring of tentacles within this genus are typically longer than those on the outer ring. The animals are highly contractile.

Entacmaea quadricolor is a sea anemone that can easily be cared for in home aquaria. When placed in small groups, the four-colored anemone tolerates disturbances associated with aquarium maintenance and its symbiotic clownfishes better. In contrast to other symbiotic anemones, *Entacmaea* does not anchor itself deeply into the substrate; it is rather similar to *Heteractis magnifica* (p. 329, 368) in this regard. Small, flat and, if possible, smooth indentions are preferred. Unfortunately, these anemones frequently start to wander without showing signs of unease. Because of this, they are only suitable for very large reef aquaria. Unlike *Heteractis magnifica*, this genus looks for a substrate to colonize. If the animals settle on solitary rocks, they may roam about on them without detaching themselves. Do not place these anemones directly in the current.

Entacmaea quadricolor

Entacmaea quadricolor

Fam.: Actiniidae

Entacmaea quadricolor
Four-colored anemone

(RÜPPELL & LEUCKART, 1828)

Hab.: Indo-Pacific, from the Red Sea to Samoa. Found along shallow coral reefs from the low tide line to at least 40 m depth.

Sex.: None.

Soc.B./Assoc.: Dense colonies of smaller specimens can sometimes be found in shallow waters; animals that live at more profound depths live singly. Depending on its geographic location, it provides shelter for a variety of clownfishes; *Amphiprion bicinctus* in the Red Sea, *A. allardi* and *A. clarkii* in the Indian Ocean, and *A. ephippium, A. frenatus, A. melanopus* and others in the Pacific. *Premnas biaculeata* and *Dascyllus trimaculatus* will also inhabit this anemone.

M.: Requires deep holes and cracks in rocks as hiding places and anchor points.

Light: Sunlight.

B./Rep.: Sexual.

F.: C; fish, mussel, and crustacean meat.

S.: Oral disc and tentacles contain symbiotic algae which are responsible for its coloration. The tentacles themselves are particular: frequently they have blisterlike ends or a spherical to pear-shaped enlargement just below the tips. It was previously thought that there was an additional species, *Entacmaea helianthus*, with "normal" tentacles. However, D. F. DUNN proved in 1981 that *E. helianthus* formed the aforementioned enlargements on its tentacles and "transformed into another species" when associated with clownfishes.

T: 22°-26°C, **Ø:** 50 cm, **TL:** from 120 cm, **WM:** s, **WR:** b, **AV:** 2, **D:** 2-3

Entacmaea quadricolor and *A. melanopus*, Palau

Entacmaea quadricolor

Entacmaea quadricolor

Fam.: Actiniidae

About the Genus *Macrodactyla*

The genus *Macrodactyla* includes sea anemones with a pronounced base and an elongated body with tiny dots and tubercles in the upper third. The tentacles are long.

Macrodactyla doreensis
Corkscrew anemone

(QUOY & GAIMARD, 1833)

Hab.: Indo-West Pacific; from Mauritius to Japan. At 1 to 15 m depth.

Sex.: None.

Soc.B./Assoc.: Lives singly. When exposed to current, it will either compress its tentacles like a corkscrew or disappear into the substrate. Two species of clownfishes inhabit its tentacles: *Amphiprion perideraion* and *A. clarkii*.

M.: Requires a 10 cm layer of sand or rubble as substrate so it can hide its body and lay its long tentacle-fringed oral disc on the surface.

Light: Sunlight.

B./Rep.: Unknown.

F.: C; small fishes, mussel and fish meat, crustacea, and frozen foods.

S.: It places its pedal disc on a covered hard surface, usually in the sand between or in front of coral reefs. Its body is inferiorly orange to red; it widens funnellike towards the top and is gray-brown to violet-brown with non-adhesive white tubercles in longitudinal rows in this region. The oral disc is purple-gray to purple-green (depending on the quantity of symbiotic algae). The mouth is small with "lips." The tentacles are roughly equal, but those towards the center are slightly longer than those along the periphery. Pairs of white stripes may extend radially from the mouth, one to the right and the other to the left side of the tentacle's insertion point.

T: 22°-27°C, Ø: 50 cm, **TL:** from 120 cm, **WM:** m, **WR:** b, **AV:** 2-3, **D:** 3

Macrodactyla doreensis, aquarium photo

ABOUT THE GENUS *URTICINA*

These sea anemones (previously *Tealia*) are compact. The largest species reach 35 cm in diameter, and all are known for their variable coloration which includes shades of red, brown, yellow, and green. Some of these hues are present in every animal in the form of longitudinal or cross-stripe designs or faint dots and spots. Therefore, rarely are two specimens ever identical. This confounds their identification and places the validity of some species in doubt.

Urticina felina, Atlantic

Fam.: Actiniidae

Urticina felina   (LINNAEUS, 1758)
Feline sea dahlia

Hab.: Shallow, dynamic zones of the cool northeastern Atlantic and the North and Baltic Seas. At depths of 1 to 30 m.

Sex.: None.

Soc.B./Assoc.: Because it stings, it requires a lot of room and must be placed at least 20 cm from any other anemone or coelenterate; however, it can be kept in a colony. It can be associated with crabs such as swimming and shore crabs, hermit crabs, and pocket crabs as long as they are not too large. Starfishes and sea urchins can also be part of the community, as they are in nature.

M.: Its foot adheres to any hard substrate as long as it is not densely covered with algae.

Light: Sunlight.

B./Rep.: Not known.

F.: C; *U. felina* has a "hardy" appetite and can be easily satisfied with animal fare such as mussel and crustacean meat. Its nematocysts can even overpower relatively large crabs, shrimp, and small fishes.

Urticina felina

S.: The body column is normally short (about 5 cm) but can stretch to 15 cm. Its coloration fluctuates between green and red. It has reddish longitudinal lines and suction tubercles which serve to fasten articles such as sand, small stones, and broken pieces of snails and shellfish shells. When retracted, this anemone looks like a hemispherical, tuberculated elevated hump covered by the aforementioned foreign matter. The oral disc is equally red or green but with a yellowish tinge. It often has reddish radial bands. The mouth itself is frequently an intense yellow. The tentacles are short and thick with pointed tips and are either equally or lighter colored than the oral disc. Their color ranges from red and green to orange and cream-white. This anemone was previously classified as the variety *U. felina coriacea* to differentiate it from the following variety, *U. f. lofotensis*.

T: 15°-19°C, Ø: 15 cm, **TL:** from 50 cm, **WM:** m, **WR:** b, **AV:** 1, **D:** 2

Fam.: Actiniidae

Urticina lofotensis   (DANIELSSEN)
Sea dahlia

Hab.: Northeastern Atlantic, the North and Baltic Seas as well as the northeast Pacific from Alaska to California. At depths of 0 to 600 m.

Sex.: None.

Soc.B./Assoc.: Should either be kept alone or at least 20 cm from other actinides, similar to *U. felina*.

M.: *U. lofotensis* prefers cooler, quiet waters and adheres to stones, rocks, pillars, or mussels.

Light: Sunlight to dimly lit zones.

B./Rep.: Not known.

F.: C; fish, shrimp, and mussel meat and frozen foods.

S.: This species was previously considered a subspecies of *U. felina*. However, contrary to *U. felina*, this species differs by having less conspicuous tubercles which do not adhere foreign particles, so the body remains nude. *U. lofotensis* attains a larger size; it is about 12 cm along its base, is taller than it is broad, and its more numerous tentacles are at least 6 cm long and arranged in 4 rows. The coloration is variable, but bright red hues predominate. When this nocturnal anemone retires, only a red spherical shape covered with numerous bright spots and an indented center remains visible. These dots can be white, bluish, or pink and are usually arranged in rows.

T: 10°-18°C, **Ø:** 15 cm, **TL:** from 50 cm, **WM:** m, **WR:** b, **AV:** 2, **D:** 3

Urticina piscivora   (SEBENS & LAAKSO, 1977)
Piscivorous sea dahlia

Hab.: East Pacific coast of North America. At depths of 1 to 30 m.

Sex.: None.

Soc.B./Assoc.: This very toxic anemone requires a significant distance from other anemones and conspecifics; it is best kept alone.

M.: Requires cool water and a hard rocky bottom as substrate.

Light: Sunlight to dim light zones.

B./Rep.: Not known.

F.: C; besides crustacea and other invertebrates, it also eats fishes (note the scientific name).

S.: This is probably the largest species of the genus. It has a broad foot which serves to anchor it to rocks or large seaweeds and a very broad, extendable body. The tentacles form a sizeable circle that leaves the large mouth free. It has a distinctly colored mouth and throat from which lines radiate to the tentacles. These lines are usually yellow.

T: 10°-15°C, **Ø:** 30 cm, **TL:** from 100 cm, **WM:** m, **WR:** b, **AV:** 2-3, **D:** 3

Urticina lofotensis, California

Urticina piscivora, British Columbia

Fam.: Actinodendridae

About the Genus *Actinodendron*

These sea anemones look more like colonies of soft corals than actinides. They have bushy, branched, long tentacles; their foot and body are buried in the sand and therefore invisible. They can retract their entire body into the sand.

Actinodendron arboreum
Tree anemone   (QUOY & GAIMARD 1833)

Hab.: Indo-Pacific. Only on sandy bottoms among coral reefs at depths of 1 to 30 m.

Sex.: None.

Soc.B./Assoc.: Lives singly; in nature they live at least 1 m from their nearest neighbor. *Lissocarcinus laeve,* a relatively uncommon swimming crab, and *Periclimenes brevicarpalis,* a slightly more common shrimp, are two crustacea that find protection within this anemone's tentacles. While *Lissocarcinus* burrows into the sand when the anemone retracts, the shrimp hovers above the substrate before swimming to the next available anemone. There it immediately seeks protection within the tentacles.

M.: Needs a sandy substrate at least 20 cm thick to enable it to totally retreat within.

Light: Sunlight.

B./Rep.: Not known.

F.: C; the tentacles and the part of the body exposed to the sun have symbiotic algae (zooxanthellae) which provide part of this anemone's nutrition.

S.: These anemones have a greenish brown transparent body that is broadened funnellike in the upper third. They can rise above the bottom by taking in water. The main tentacles are pyramid-shaped and have lateral, short, pointed tentacles. They have a potent toxin. When touched, the anemone quickly expels water, and in a second, it disappears so deep in the sand that nothing remains visible other than a small indentation over its hiding place.

T: 22°-26°C, Ø: 50 cm, **TL:** from 120 cm, **WM:** m, **WR:** b, **AV:** 3, **D:** 3

Actinodendron plumosum
Pinnate anemone   HADDON, 1898

Hab.: Indo-Pacific. At 3 to 20 m depth.

Sex.: None.

Soc.B./Assoc.: Lives singly on sandy bottoms and coral rubble.

M.: A 15 cm layer of sand or light coral rubble is needed to enable the anemone to hide within.

Light: Sunlight.

B./Rep.: Not known.

F.: C; small, finely minced pieces of mussel, crab, and fish flesh, small crustacea, etc.

S.: The body of this anemone shows numerous fine longitudinal grooves which divide the body column in partitions, every other one of which usually terminates in a tentacle. These tentacles are significantly thinner and longer than those of the previous species. The lateral branches off the main tentacles are finely branched. Like the previous species, this one also has a potent toxin and is reputed to even eat fishes. When in danger, *A. plumosum* also retires deep into the sand substrate.

T: 22°-26°C, Ø: 20 cm, **TL:** from 80 cm, **WM:** m, **WR:** b, **AV:** 3, **D:** 3

Actinodendron arboreum

Actinodendron plumosum, aquarium photo

Fam.: Andresiidae   Sea Anemones

The genus *Andresia* is comprised of anemones with a roundish or circular foot that lies unattached in soft substrates. The foot can be inverted. The body is smooth and usually translucent, which allows you to see the numerous complete septae and use them for identification. The tentacles are long, and their ability to retract is highly limited. They, of course, are arranged in rows of 6.

Andresia parthenopea   (ANDRES, 1884)
Burrowing anemone

Hab.: Mediterranean; on soft bottoms, especially at depths between 30 and 60 m.

Sex.: None.

Soc.B./Assoc.: Lives singly. Sometimes found in community with spider crabs (*Inachus*), small triangular crabs with long legs and chelae.

M.: Requires at least 20 cm of sand or mud to anchor its round pedal disc.

Light: Sunlight to moderate light.

B./Rep.: Has separate sexes and reproduces in July and August (oviparous).

F.: C; mussel and fish meat and small crustacea. Besides the pictured hunting position, you can find animals which rest all their tentacles on the bottom in totally calm, profound depths; they catch food that descends vertically.

S.: The 48 tentacles are attached to roundish, distinctly colored swellings on the oral disc. The tentacles are generally longer than the diameter of the disc. The coloration of the oral disc and its tentacles depends on the illumination, although symbiotic algae (zooxanthellae) are absent. The color varies between pronounced brown and reddish brown hues along intensely illuminated sites; multicolored forms are found in deeper regions; spotted, gray-white, or transparent animals occur on muddy bottoms.

T: 16°-24°C, **Ø:** 25 cm, **TL:** from 100 cm, **WM:** m, **WR:** b, **AV:** 2-3, **D:** 3

Andresia parthenopea

About the Genus *Phymanthus*

Sea anemones of the genus *Phymanthus* have suction tubercles on the upper half of their body, an unmarked pedal disc, and a large oral disc with one or two concentric circles of tentacles up to half way inside; the remaining tentacles are close to the edge.

Phymanthus pulcher   (ANDRES, 1884)

Hab.: Mediterranean. In depths of 20 to 50 m (70 m).

Sex.: None.

Soc.B./Assoc.: Lives singly on mixed bottoms of rocks and sand, especially on secondary hard bottoms.

M.: The disc holds and adheres to hard surfaced crevices which can be below rubble and coarse sand. Only the oral disc and tentacles are visible. When disturbed, it quickly retracts and totally closes. It fastens itself very strongly to the substrate.

Light: Sunlight to moderate light.

B./Rep.: They have separate sexes (oviparous) and reproduce from August to October.

F.: C; mussel and crustacean meat, small crustacea, and frozen foods.

S.: The interior half of the oral disc is void of tentacles, covered by tubercles, and has gray white spots. The 96 short tentacles have laterally symmetrical, semispherical protrusions which make them resemble a string of pearls. They are gray with light lines and transverse dots. Twelve almost vertical tentacles are attached approximately $1/3$ of the way inside the oral disc. The animals' coloration is greatly variable and hardly any animal is the same. On bright locals, gray-green to gray-brown forms predominate; on dark sites, the specimens tend to have bright multicolored designs.

T: 20°-24°C, **Ø:** 20 cm, **TL:** from 80 cm, **WM:** m, **WR:** b, **AV:** 2-3, **D:** 3

Phymanthus pulcher

Fam.: Stichodactylidae

The symbiosis between clownfishes and sea anemones fascinates every observer, be he scientist, diver, or aquarist. Every anemone represents a clownfish's territory. It is rarely abandoned, and the protection of the tentacles is rapidly sought when danger encroaches. It was quite simple for marine scientists to find the sessile research object (anemone) and perform long range studies on both the host animal and its inhabitant. Underwater photographers were always enchanted by the beauty of each of the symbionts. There are few living communities in the sea as well-known to the layperson. Extensive studies of clownfishes have made their taxonomy fairly stable. But some families of sea anemones have just recently been classified according to information that became available in the 1980's.

The sea anemones of the order Actiniaria live in all the oceans on earth, from the poles to the equator and the deep sea to the shores. However, only 10 of the approximately 1,000 known species of anemones harbor clownfishes from the genera *Amphiprion* and *Premnas*. These 10 symbiotic anemones live in parts of the Indian and Pacific Oceans that are subject to tropical currents. That corresponds to the latitude of Tokyo, Japan, in the north and Sydney, Australia, in the south. Not one species from this family lives in the Atlantic Ocean. All **28 species** of clownfishes inhabit only **10 species** of sea anemones.

These anemones only exist in shallow waters to a depth of 50 m; this corresponds to the maximum depth divers should descend using compressed air. The reason host anemones cannot live below 50 m is obvious: one of their bases for life, the unicellular zooxanthellae algae contained in their tentacles and the oral disc, depends on light. This anemone's "place in the sun" is not only found directly on the coral reef, but also on sandy surfaces, seaweed lawns, and muddy bottoms near a reef.

Like all animals of the phylum Coelenterata, sea anemones use their poison to catch prey. Food in the form of plankton is brought to these sessile animals in the current. They have no need to actively hunt. However, small fishes, sea urchins, and various crustacea have also been found in the anemones' digestive track. Although the energy obtained from their photosynthetic zooxanthellae is sufficient to survive, anemones require animal foods to grow and multiply.

So far it has been impossible to determine the age of a sea anemone. The exception, of course, are those that have been raised in an aquarium. A small anemone is not necessarily young, because

Heteractis magnifica with *Amphiprion bicinctus*, Red Sea

Fam.: Stichodactylidae

coelenterates only grow if they receive good food and will shrink when there is a shortage thereof. Scientists have kept measurements on several individual symbiotic anemones for several years in their natural biotope. There was no significant difference in size throughout this time. Additional studies proved that sea anemones may live for decades if not centuries: a coldwater anemone studied in New Zealand is probably more than 300 years old. Large, giant anemones of the family Stichodactylidae definitely live longer than humans. They are well protected from predators by their venom, and it is unknown exactly what will cause their demise.

The typical reproduction scheme of coelenterates is similar to most marine animals: eggs and sperm are released into the water, the eggs are fertilized, and the resulting zygotes drift in the plankton until they find a suitable site to colonize. It is not known exactly if the 10 symbiotic anemones follow this pattern. Some species have internal fertilization. In this case, the sperm enter the female's body when it pumps in fresh water. Small anemones are then expelled through the mouth. Asexual reproduction has only been observed in symbiotic anemones living in extremely shallow waters. *Entacmaea quadricolor* is a species that reproduces through asexual reproduction: the polyp divides along its longitudinal axis, forming a new animal. All offspring of the original anemone form a community of genetically identical individuals (clones). This is why you can find large tentacle fields of this anemone on the reef, which, although not one animal, are claimed by a clownfish as such, and the entirety is defended as its territory.

In contrast to their fish partners, the 10 symbiotic anemones are not closely related. They belong to 3 families within the order Actiniaria. Not all members of these families are symbiotic. The largest family of anemones, the Actiniidae, also inhabit cold waters void of clownfishes. Likewise, not all species of the exclusively tropical families of the giant and carpet anemones (Stichodactylidae and Thalassianthidae, respectively) live in symbiosis with clownfishes.

All present publications about identifying anemones have been technical. They deal with the characterization of musculature, the size and distribution of nematocysts, tentacle morphology, and comparative internal anatomy. Identification meant killing the animals and dissecting them to gather the meristic data. Nowadays it is possible to identify many sea anemones in their natural habitat, although some scientists continue to consider the analysis of nematocysts necessary. The stinging cells (nematocysts) are usually composed of elongated capsules from which "poison darts" are shot in response to tactile stimuli. These nematocysts are only a few microns long. We still largely distinguish the various species of anemones based on the structure of the barbed nematocysts (calcium needles). The preparation of such calcium needles for microscopic examination is difficult and tedious. That is probably why it has taken so long for scientists to work through the 10 species of host (symbiotic) anemones and determine correct names for them.

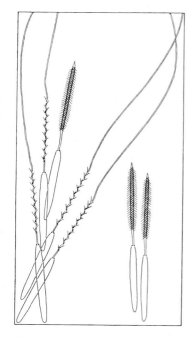
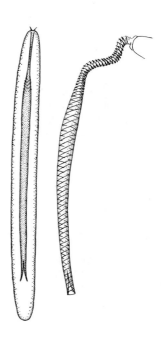

Nematocysts (stinging cells) of various anemones

Fam.: Stichodactylidae

The drawings on the previous page not only show the basic morphology of nematocysts, they also give a general idea of the possible variations these structures can assume. Since the structures are constant within a species, they are an important tool for taxonomists. After examining these organelles, you will not be surprised to learn that fishes avoid anemones that posses such defense equipment. Not even human skin is impervious to their effect.

Heteractis magnifica with *Amphiprion perideraion*

Aquarium with *Heteractis* and *Stichodactyla* anemones

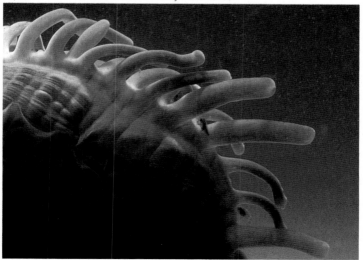

Amphiprion ocellaris (7 day old juveniles) in *Heteractis magnifica*

Fam.: Stichodactylidae

The genus *Heteractis* is comprised of anemones that have relatively few, uniform, moderately-long tentacles which are normally digital (but slightly enlarged on the tips). The foot is well-developed and somewhat wider than the body column itself, but more slender than the oral disc. The diameter of the oral or pedal disc is a good indication of the length of these anemones. The superior body has tubercles, whereas the inferior half is smooth.

Heteractis aurora   (QUOY & GAIMARD, 1833)
Sand anemone, glasspearl anemone

Hab.: Indo-Pacific from the Red Sea to the Eniwetok Atoll of Japan (N) and Mauritius (S); at 1 to 5 m depth.

Sex.: None.

Soc.B./Assoc.: Lives singly in rocky crevices of reef terraces or on sand. Its tentacles provide protection for numerous species of clownfishes as well as *Dascyllus trimaculatus*.

M.: Requires 20 cm of sand with a hard substrate underneath to anchor itself. It is weakly adhesive. Totally retreats into the substrate when disturbed.

Light: Sunlight.

B./Rep.: Not known.

F.: C; mussel, fish, and crustacean meat.

S.: It is extremely polymorphic and has been described under a wide variety of names. The upper part of the body is gray-green to chestnut brown, depending on the density of the symbiotic algae (zooxanthellae), while the inferior half of the body is golden yellow. The body column has rows of light suction tubercles. The tubercles are smallest along the top. A special characteristic are the white elevated spots on the 4-6 cm long tentacles. These can be individual or coalesced into designs. Larger white spots form raised areas; if these encircle the tentacles, thick and thin segments alternate.
The most common synonym is *Bunodes koseirensis*; the trade name *Radianthus koseirensis* is a "*nomen nudum.*"

T: 22°-26°C, **Ø:** 30 cm, **TL:** from 100 cm, **WM:** m, **WR:** b, **AV:** 2, **D:** 3

Heteractis aurora

Heteractis aurora with *Amphiprion clarkii*

Fam.: Stichodactylidae

Heteractis crispa (EHRENBERG, 1834)
Leather anemone

Hab.: Indo-West Pacific from the Red Sea to Tuamotu. At depths of 3 to 40 m.

Sex.: None.

Soc.B./Assoc.: Lives singly; it acts as host to *Dascyllus trimaculatus*, shrimp (especially *Periclimenes*), and a variety of *Amphiprion* species.

M.: Requires deep crevices or coral blocks for its body; only the oral disc and the tentacles are exposed. Specimens less than 8 cm in Ø should not be put with clownfishes. The fishes cause too much stress, and the anemone wanes and refuses food.

Light: Sunlight.

B./Rep.: Not known.

F.: C; mussel, fish, and crustacean meat and frozen foods.

S.: Its foot does not adhere strongly to hard substrates and can be removed with relative ease. Like the inferior half of the body, it is whitish to cream. Infrequently, the foot is either brown or yellow spotted. The upper half, depending on the concentration of symbiotic algae (zooxanthellae), is gray to violet brown with longitudinal rows of tubercles to which sand and mud are adhered. The oral disc and the 15 cm long pointed tentacles can be whitish, violet, or greenish and are rather similar to the Mediterranean oplet. Even specimens with violet, pink, or blue tentacle tips have been found. Frequently the tentacles are covered by a white reticulation that looks like frost. They are the most commonly imported tropical anemone and are suitable hosts for most tropical clownfishes. However, many aquarists prefer species specific anemones.

T: 22°-26°C, **Ø:** 30 cm, **TL:** from 100 cm, **WM:** m-s, **WR:** b, **AV:** 1-2, **D:** 2-3

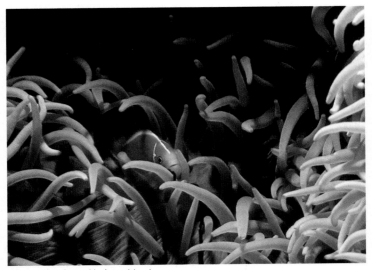

Heteractis crispa with *A. perideraion*

Heteractis crispa with *A. perideraion*

Fam.: Stichodactylidae

Heteractis crispa, aquarium photo

Heteractis crispa, Maldives, with *A. clarkii*

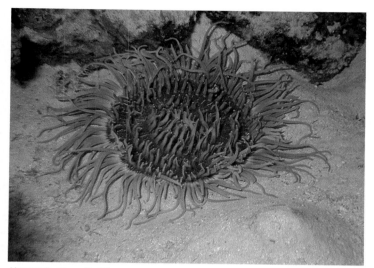

Heteractis crispa, Red Sea

Heteractis crispa, Red Sea, with *A. bicinctus*

Fam.: Stichodactylidae

Heteractis magnifica (QUOY & GAIMARD, 1833)
Magnificent anemone

Hab.: Entire Indo-Pacific; from the Red Sea to Samoa. At depths of 1 to 10 m.

Sex.: None.

Soc.B./Assoc.: Lives singly or in groups so dense that their tentacles form giant "fields." Host for *Dascyllus trimaculatus*, several shrimp such as *Neopetrolisthes ohshimai*, and numerous clownfishes. In the Red Sea, it is inhabited by *Amphiprion bicinctus*; *A. akallopisos, A. nigripes*, and *A. ocellaris* are symbionts in the Indian Ocean; *A. akindynos, A. chrysopterus, A. leucokranos, A. percula*, and *A. perideraion* live within its tentacles in the Pacific. It is interesting to note that only one certain clownfish lives in symbiosis with this anemone at any particular locale. For example, in the central Indian Ocean (Sri Lanka, Maldives) only *Amphiprion nigripes* lives in *H. magnifica*, not *A. clarkii*, even though it is also present in the same region.

M.: Requires bare rocks on the bottom to adhere to. Contrary to most other species that hide in the substrate or in crevices, *H. magnifica* prefers higher sites on the reef. This means the body is often visible. In the aquarium it frequently sits on one of the panes.

Light: Sunlight.

B./Rep.: Not known.

F.: C; frozen foods as well as meat of fish, mussels, and crustacea.

S.: The body always has an intense color, ranging from avocado green, greenish brown, and white to sky blue and violet. Its surface may be smooth or covered with blisterlike swellings, the result of longitudinal and cross grooves. Normally you see very little of the column, since its uppermost part covers the base and the tentacles can cover a square meter of area. These tentacles are up to 8 cm long, obtuse, and usually have an iridescent spherical tip which is mostly yellowish green. When disturbed, in danger, or not feeling up to par (an aquarium with unfavorable climate or water quality), the anemone can enclose its tentacles so that only a colorful sphere remains. Small tufts of tentacles may protrude from the sphere. It is cute to observe how the symbiotic clownfishes remain snuggled among the few remaining tentacles.
For many years it was classified as *Radianthus ritteri*.

T: 22°-27°C, Ø: up to 100 cm, **TL:** from 100 cm, **WM:** s, **WR:** b, **AV:** 1, **D:** 2-3

Heteractis malu (HADDON & SHACKLETON, 1893)
Hawaii anemone

Hab.: East Pacific, especially around the Hawaiian Islands. At depths of 2 to 20 m.

Sex.: None.

Soc.B./Assoc.: Lives singly; it is only inhabited by *Amphiprion clarkii*. Can be housed with small coral reef fishes, shrimp, and echinoderms.

M.: Requires at least 10 cm of sand or gravel along the bottom. Quick as a flash, it will withdraw within.

Light: Moderate light.

B./Rep.: Has not been successful in an aquarium.

F.: C; mussel and fish meat and frozen foods (defrosted).

S.: The body has tubercles on the upper third. The tentacles are short (max. 4 cm) and variably colored: green-brown interior tentacles and light peripheral tentacles.

T: 18°-24°C, Ø: 20 cm, **TL:** from 80 cm, **WM:** m, **WR:** b, **AV:** 2-3, **D:** 2-3

Heteractis magnifica with *A. nigripes*

Heteractis malu, Oahu, Hawaii

Fam.: Stichodactylidae

Heteractis magnifica with *A. perideraion*

Heteractis magnifica with *A. clarkii*, Western Australia

Heteractis magnifica constricted into a sphere

Heteractis magnifica with *A. ephippium*

Fam.: Stichodactylidae

The body of these anemones is generally much broader than it is tall. The irregular foot is well-developed and adheres strongly to substrates. The body is inferiorly smooth, extremely broadened, and covered with tubercles superiorly. The oral disc is repeatedly folded and only slightly retractable. It is usually completely covered by numerous short, blunt tentacles which may be somewhat longer near the mouth.

Stichodactyla gigantea   (FORSSKÅL, 1775)
Giant anemone

Hab.: Indo-Pacific; from the Red Sea to the Solomon Islands. At 2 to 20 m depth.

Sex.: None.

Soc.B./Assoc.: Lives singly on coral rubble among reefs; harbors at least 6 species of *Amphiprion*, *Dascyllus trimaculatus*, and numerous crustacea such as *Thor amboinensis*, *Neopetrolisthes ohshimai*, and *Periclimenes brevicarpalis*.

M.: Requires a substrate with rock crevices partially filled with coral rubble to hide its body.

Light: Sunlight.

B./Rep.: Not known.

F.: C; fish, crustacean, and mussel meat and frozen foods. Feed at least once a week with a feeding tube or a pair of large plant forceps.

S.: The body is inferiorly smooth and light, but tubercular and darker superiorly due to symbiotic algae. There are as many as 10 tubercles in one longitudinal row. The oral disc is very convoluted; the central part is almost void of tentacles. However, this is hard to see because of the heavy folds. All the tentacles are about the same length and somewhat contractile with blunt ends. Those towards the outside are 2 cm long, whereas those on the inside are up to 5 cm in length. Sometimes you can see all the tentacles vibrate. These tentacles are so adhesive that they break off with part of the oral disc before their bond breaks. Very toxic.

T: 22°-27°C, Ø: 50 cm, **TL:** from 100 cm, **WM:** m, **WR:** b, **AV:** 2, **D:** 2-3

Stichodactyla gigantea, Indonesia, with *A. ocellaris*

Stichodactyla gigantea, Papua N.G., with *Amphiprion percula*

Fam.: Stichodactylidae

Aquarium Maintenance

Tropical anemones, especially symbiotic host anemones of the family Stichodactylidae, are relatively sensitive and should be kept in rock crevices, which is how they are found in their natural biotope. These anemones require temperatures between 24° and 28°C, a specific gravity of 1.018 to 1.023, and a distance of at least 20 cm from other anemones. In smaller tanks you should limit yourself to one giant anemone. Feeding them small crustacea, small pieces of mussels, and crustacean meat with a feeding tube 2–3 times per week is sufficient and avoids overfeeding. Colorful species require vitamin-rich natural foods to maintain their colors. If possible, metal halide illumination or natural sunlight should be provided to keep the symbiotic algae healthy. The tank can be stocked with one or two clownfish, preferably a species it plays host to in nature. However, foreign associations are possible.

> Anemones associated with clownfishes should have a diameter (→) at least 3 times larger than the length of the fish.

Stichodactyla haddoni   (SAVILLE-KENT, 1893)
Haddon's anemone, carpet anemone

Hab.: Indo-Pacific, from the Red Sea to the Fiji Islands. At 4 to 40 m depth.

Sex.: None.

Soc.B./Assoc.: Lives singly on reefs and soft bottoms; harbors numerous species of *Amphiprion* (sometimes several species simultaneously, such as *A. sebae* and *A. clarkii* in the Indian Ocean), *Dascyllus trimaculatus*, crustacea such as *Neopetrolisthes ohshimai*, and at least one *Periclimenes* shrimp.

M.: Colonizes sand at least 20 cm deep or rock crevices with sand or rubble.

Light: Sunlight.

B./Rep.: Unknown.

F.: C; crustacean, mussel, and fish meat. Feed pieces of food 2-3 times a week with a feeding tube.

S.: Its undulant mouth area is covered with tiny, spherical, short-based tentacles that usually lie in radial groups. Interiorly, only one or two tentacles form a "group"; exteriorly, up to 5 are next to each other. Light and dark groups frequently alternate. The tentacles have a strong poison, stick to the skin, and easily break off. The body is a translucent white, yellow, or light green. The column is wide open on the upper edge. The upper part is pink, yellowish, or violet and covered with small tubercles. The wavy oral disc either lies directly on the substrate or is somewhat elevated. It may reach a diameter of 75 cm and have a narrow zone around the mouth free of tentacles. The body above the bottom contains symbiotic algae (zooxanthellae) which provide part of the animal's nourishment and make it possible for it to achieve its extraordinary size.

This anemone is very toxic, but does not cause undue irritation to human skin. When under severe attack, the anemone can exude a milky liquid that immediately transforms the aquarium into an opaque broth. This phenomenon was observed when a 40 cm foot was dug up to transfer the animal. It was not possible to determine whether the secretion was regurgitated stomach contents (digested fish) or a specialized defense secretion (H.B.).

T: 22°-26°C, Ø: 75 cm, **TL:** from 150 cm, **WM:** m, **WR:** b, **AV:** 1, **D:** 2

Stichodactyla haddoni, aquarium photo

Stichodactyla haddoni with *A. frenatus*

Stichodactyla haddoni, Indonesia

Stichodactyla haddoni, Red Sea

Stichodactyla haddoni with *A. polymnus*, aquarium photo

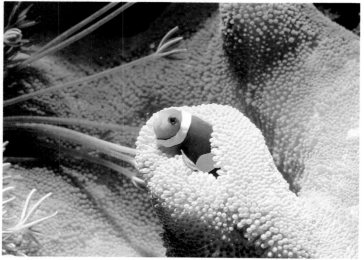

Stichodactyla haddoni and *A. ocellaris*, Indonesia

Fam.: Stichodactylidae

Stichodactyla mertensii   BRANDT, 1835
Merten's anemone, non-stinging carpet anemone

Hab.: Indo-Pacific; from the Comoros to the Fiji Islands. At depths of 1 to 20 m.

Sex.: None.

Soc.B./Assoc.: Lives singly. In contrast to *S. gigantea*, this species is not toxic. In many regions, *S. mertensii* is recognized by the accompanying clownfishes: clownfishes (*A. clarkii*, *A. chrysopterus*, and *A. tricinctus*) living within *S. mertensii* are dark (melanistic). Fishes transferred to other anemone species lighten. That is, the yellow component is masked with black when the fish associates with *S. mertensii*. In the Red Sea, *A. bicinctus* colonizes *S. gigantea* instead of *S. mertensii*. Crustacea such as *Neopetrolisthes ohshimai* also live in this anemone.

M.: It requires deep rock crevices or a vertical hole for its body. Only the tentacle-covered oral disc remains above the substrate.

Light: Sunlight.

B./Rep.: Not known.

F.: C; fish, crustacean, and mussel meat and frozen foods.

S.: This carpet anemone is difficult to distinguish from *S. gigantea* based on the type and length of the tentacles. It, too, has tentacles that are about 2 cm long on the periphery and up to 5 cm long towards the mouth. The regular, blunt, fingerlike (digital) tentacles are normally a uniform brown. Individual, somewhat stiffer tentacles with yellow tips have been found on selected specimens. *S. mertensii* can simultaneously vibrate all its tentacles. By touching the tentacles, you immediately notice the difference between this species and *S. gigantea*. *S. mertensii*'s tentacles are not sticky. Additionally, the oral disc is less undulate. When fully extended, the disc lies more or less on the substrate and the edge is only slightly curled. When they retract, the edge folds strongly upward. The surface of the mouth is only visible when the tentacles are somewhat relaxed. It is white to pink-brown (depending on the amount of zooxanthellae), but the area near the edge is sometimes a darker color with a greenish tinge. The central mouth is elongated and may protrude conically above the oral disc, but it is usually invisible. The white foot is very irregular and totally adapts to the shape of the substrate it is adhered to. The column is very extendable and extremely stretched superiorly. The body column is thin and easily torn. The inferior section is white with irregular red-orange to purple spots, while the upper section turns progressively gray to gray-green (zooxanthellae) and has tubercles. The tubercles near the top have a cross section of 1-2 mm, whereas those further below are 5 mm in diameter. They adhere to the surrounding rocks, but do not adhere sand! With a diameter of 1.5 m, *S. mertensii* is the largest anemone. The mammoth size of this anemone makes it easily recognizable in nature, even though its tentacles are similar to those of *S. gigantea*.

T: 23°-27°C, **Ø:** 150 cm, **TL:** from 250 cm, **WM:** m, **WR:** b, **AV:** 2-3, **D:** 3

Stichodactyla mertensii with some *A. clarkii*, Australia

Stichodactyla mertensii from Mauritius

Stichodactyla mertensii, Mauritius, with *A. chrysogaster*

Fam.: Thalassianthidae

ABOUT THE GENUS *CRYPTODENDRUM*

This genus only contains one species, *Cryptodendrum adhaesivum*. It typically has variable tentacles; that is, it has both branched and nap-edged tentacles.
The two tentacle forms differ in coloration, too.

Cryptodendrum adhaesivum with *Amphiprion clarkii*

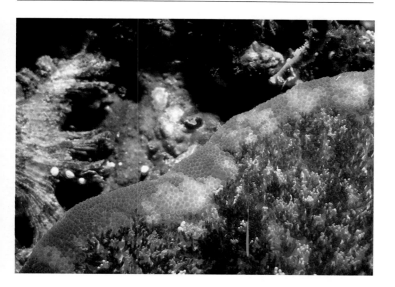

Cryptodendrum adhaesivum
Nap-edged anemone

KLUNZINGER, 1877

Hab.: Indo-Pacific from the Red Sea to the Marquesas. From the tidal zone to 5 m depth.

Sex.: None.

Soc.B./Assoc.: Lives singly; harbors at least two species of shrimp from the genera *Thor* and *Periclimenes*. Only in the Indian Ocean does it harbor a clownfish, *Amphiprion clarkii*.

M.: Adheres to rock crevices or beneath stones where coral gravel or sand is piled up.

Light: Sunlight.

B./Rep.: Unknown.

F.: C; finely minced pieces of mussel, fish, and crustacean meat.

S.: The bulging nap edge of the oral disc makes this species impossible to confuse. Its interior is covered with tiny, usually multibranched tentacles. The superior half of the body has rows of strongly adhesive tubercles. Coloration is extremely variable. The body of some forms is yellowish inferiorly with brown dots and reddish violet with yellow tubercles superiorly. Others are totally white with orange spots and tubercles, whereas a few are brown or orange with various colored dots or stripes and green or white tubercles. The mouth is small, approximately 1 cm in diameter, and the lips are frequently a contrasting color like yellow, white, green, or violet.

T: 23°-27°C, **Ø:** 30 cm, **TL:** from 100 cm, **WM:** m-s, **WR:** b, **AV:** 2, **D:** 3

Fam.: Thalassianthidae

About the Genus *Heterodactyla*

These anemones also have variable tentacles that are either finely branched or filiform. They may or may not bear clusters of peduncled spherical or club-shaped bodies.

Heterodactyla hemprichi   EHRENBERG, 1834
Hemprich's anemone

Hab.: Red Sea and Indian Ocean. At depths of 3 to 20 m depth.

Sex.: None.

Soc.B./Assoc.: Lives singly in symbiosis with *Periclimenes brevicarpalis.*

M.: Its foot adheres to hard substrates in rock crevices or beneath corals; it needs to be offered a similar site in the aquarium.

Light: Sunlight.

B./Rep.: Separate sexes.

F.: C; fish, crustacean, and mussel meat.

S.: *H. hemprichi* is easily recognized by its variable tentacles and the deeply folded oral disc. The body column is yellowish, has violet speckles inferiorly, and indistinct suction tubercles superiorly. It supports a very wide oral disc that has pronounced undulations and folds. Its edge is gray to yellow; the disc itself is blue-gray, striated towards the periphery, and virtually covered by tentacles. The dense filiform tentacles you see are actually branches off the main tentacles, and each main tentacle has 10 or more branches. Additionally, the edge of the mouth disc has groups of 7-10 spherical structures usually on branched peduncles in regular intervals between the filiform tentacles. They are frequently a conspicuous blue-violet with greenish yellow indentions on their tips. These structures house the anemone's clusters of nematocysts.

T: 23°-27°C, **Ø:** 15 cm, **TL:** from 80 cm, **WM:** m, **WR:** b, **AV:** 2-3, **D:** 3

Heterodactyla hemprichi from the Maldives

ABOUT THE FAMILY AIPTASIIDAE

The most important characteristics of this family include the flat pedal disc, the smooth body, and closable openings therein (cinclides). Small stinging and adhesive threads (acontia) can be expelled as a defense mechanism through the cinclides.

ABOUT THE GENUS *AIPTASIA*

This genus is comprised of anemones with cylindrical to trumpet-shaped columns (bodies). The openings to expel acontia (cinclides) are usually located near the center of the body. The tentacles are either in multiples of 6 or in irregular arrangements. The coloration is predominately determined by the symbiotic algae found in its upper body, oral disc, and tentacles.

Aiptasia mutabilis, Mediterranean

Fam.: Aiptasiidae

Aiptasia mutabilis   (GRAVENHORST, 1831)
Rock anemone, trumpet anemone

Hab.: Mediterranean, east Atlantic from Plymouth to the Gulf of Guinea. At 1 to 50 m depth.

Sex.: None.

Soc.B./Assoc.: Usually lives singly; however, in quiet shallow zones, it may reproduce asexually (cross division) and form colonies during the summer.

M.: Lives in rock crevices or under stones. Like habitats should be offered in the aquarium.

Light: Sunlight.

B./Rep.: *A. mutabilis* has separate sexes and releases eggs and sperm into the open water (oviparous).

F.: C; fish, mussel, and crustacean meat.

S.: The body is inferiorly opaque and is usually ochre with yellowish white spots. As you ascend, the body turns brown to brown-violet, translucent, and spotted. The septae are visible as white longitudinal lines. The discharge openings (cinclides) for the acontia are located above the center of the body and are usually in groups of three, one above the other. The 136 tentacles run together conically, are about as long as the diameter of the oral disc (ca. 6 cm), translucent, and finely speckled; their epidermis has irregular, reticulate white bands or rings. There are two forms. The typical, larger form corresponds to the one described above and is found in a variety of colors. It usually lives singly, hidden in rock crevices or beneath stones and prefers more profound sites down to 50 m depth. There is a shallow water form (previously classified as the autonomous species *A. couchi*) which rarely inhabits depths greater than 5 m and is very resistant to salinity fluctuations. It enters higher salinity (hypersaline) locals as well as brackish water lagoons. The coloration corresponds to the concentration of zooxanthellae present in the tissues and fluctuates with the season. They tend to be dark green in the winter and almost a transparent greenish red in the summer.

T: 18°-24°C, **Ø:** 15 cm, **TL:** from 80 cm, **WM:** m, **WR:** b, **AV:** 1, **D:** 2

Aiptasia mutabilis

Aiptasia diaphana   (RAPP, 1829)
Small rock anemone

Hab.: Mediterranean; also reported from the Suez Canal and the Gulf of Aqaba. At depths of 0 to 5 m.

Sex.: None.

Soc.B./Assoc.: Lives both singly and as connected colonies; groups spontaneously appearing in the aquarium can be kept.

M.: Needs stones or rocks to adhere to.

Light: Sunlight.

B./Rep.: Although *A. diaphana* has separate sexes and releases eggs and sperm into the water during the fall (oviparous), this totally deficient method of propagation is substituted by asexual reproduction May through October when water temperatures reach 20°C. Small parts separate from the base of the extremely broad foot (pedal laceration) and even these pieces are capable of subdividing. Each segment that divides grows into a new anemone. This process gives rise to extensive fields of these animals, especially in shallow (0-1.5 m), quiet lagoons. Because of its high rate of propagation, the small rock anemone turns into a feeding competitor for other invertebrates in the aquarium (see also "Unpleasant Guests in the Aquarium," p. 194).

F.: C; finely grated mussel, fish, and crustacean meat, etc.

S.: This small anemone can easily be confused with the shallow water form of *A. mutabilis*. But at least in nature, this species has significantly longer, thinner tentacles, seems to prefer polluted waters such as channels and ports, is differently colored, and has a deviating tentacle arrangement. It is sensitive to low salinities and will not enter brackish lagoons.

Continued on the next page.

Fam.: Aiptasiidae

Continued from previous page:

The lobed, gray-green, transparent foot can grow to a diameter of 2 cm. The body is cylindrical, up to 4 cm in height, brown-green inferiorly, but a lighter gray-white with yellow-white mottling superiorly. Usually there is only one cinclide (two at the most, one on top of the other) above the center of the body. Frequently there are additional openings just above the foot. Fully developed *A. diaphana* have 96 conical tentacles which are at least twice as long as the diameter of the oral disc (2 cm), but can be extended even more. They are translucent, greenish brown, mottled, and often have a bright spot on the tip. The oral disc itself is as clear as glass, and some of the septae appear as a cross in the center. The appearance of *A. diaphana* undergoes major changes with the season. The coloration is totally dependent on the concentration of symbiotic algae. In the warm season from May to October, they are greenish to yellowish brown or red. From November on, they become a silvery gray-green. In December when temperatures fall below 12°C, its tentacles fall off; at 8°-9°C many of the animals die. Regeneration of tentacles commences at 15°C. The animals turn reddish yellow to yellow orange in the spring. At the beginning of June (ca. 20°C), they regain their summer coloration and long thin tentacles. This anemone is voraciously consumed by some butterflyfishes, e.g., *Chaetodon lunula, Ch. kleini,* and *Chelmon rostratus*.

T: 18°-24°C, Ø: 2-8 cm, TL: from 40 cm, WM: m, WR: b, AV: 1, D: 1

Aiptasia sp.
Trumpet anemone

The species pictured below largely corresponds to the above description and, therefore, may in fact be *A. diaphana*.

Bartholomea annulata, Caribbean

Fam.: Aiptasiidae

About the Genus *Bartholomea*

This is a particularly common anemone from the Caribbean whose geographical distribution extends from the Bermudas to South America. It is easily identified by its almost 200 transparent tentacles. The nematocysts are recognizable therein as bright yellowish-green to brown curls and incomplete spirals. The background coloration of the anemone is the result of zooxanthellae in its tissue.

Bartholomea annulata (LESIEUR, 1817)
Corkscrew anemone, ringed anemone

Hab.: Caribbean and western Atlantic from the Bermudas to the coast of South America. At depths of 1 to 40 m.

Sex.: None.

Soc.B./Assoc.: Solitary living animals; a large number of crustacea live in community with *B. annulata*, especially members of the genus *Alpheus* (*A. armatus*), *Periclimenes* (*P. yucatanicus*), and *Heteromysis* (*Heteromysis actinae*). The photo shows some tentacles of this anemone extended out of a crevice and a symbiotic *Periclimenes* shrimp.

M.: Leads a reclusive life in crevices and holes in reefs, rocky regions, or isolated hard substrates in seaweed lawns. Don't be surprised when this anemone emerges from a large empty conch shell such as *Strombus gigas*. When the anemone is relaxed, all its tentacles are above the substrate; however, it can retract totally below.

Light: Sunlight.

B./Rep.: Sexual reproduction.

F.: C; fish, mussel, and crustacean meat and many others.

S.: Its almost 200 transparent tentacles are distinctive. The nematocysts are visible as light yellowish-green to brownish curls and incomplete spirals therein. The coloration of the anemone is a result of the symbiotic algae (zooxanthellae) in its tissue. *B. annulata* becomes quite large, and its oral disc, including the tentacles, grows to be over 30 cm in diameter.

T: 22°-26°C, Ø: 30 cm, **TL:** from 100 cm, **WM:** m, **WR:** b, **AV:** 2-3, **D:** 3

Bartholomea lucida DUCHASSAING & MICHELOTTI, 1860
Knobby anemone, lucid anemone

Hab.: Only known from the Bahamas and the Caribbean. It prefers depths of 2 to 30 m.

Sex.: None.

Soc.B./Assoc.: Lives singly. Rarely harbors symbiotic crustacea.

M.: It prefers clean, oxygen-rich water. Normally hides in crevices and holes until only the knobby tentacles remain visible. Although the specimen pictured here has an exposed body, this is not a typical stance.

Light: Sunlight.

B./Rep.: Not known.

F.: C; meat, particularly from mussels, crustacea, and fishes.

S.: This Caribbean species is easily recognized by the peculiar whitish knots along its tentacles. These knots are groups of nematocysts. Otherwise, the tentacles are pale brown and transparent. As with the species above, *B. lucida* is only capable of mild stings; therefore, it is relatively harmless to man.

T: 20°-24°C, Ø: 25 cm, **TL:** from 120 cm, **WM:** m, **WR:** b, **AV:** 2-3, **D:** 3

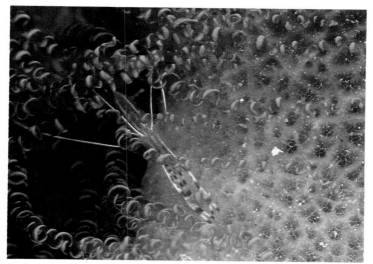

Bartholomea annulata

Bartholomea lucida

Fam.: Metriidae

About the Genus *Metridium*

The sea anemones belonging to this genus have a broad, strongly adhering pedal disc, a long, smooth body which is separated from the oral disc by a collarlike fold, and many (over 1,000) fine tentacles.

Metridium senile   (LINNAEUS, 1761)
Plumose anemone

Hab.: Cool to cold seas around the North Pole and in the north Atlantic, the North and Baltic Seas, and the northeast Pacific. From the low tide mark to 20 m depth.

Sex.: None.

Soc.B./Assoc.: Usually lives in large loose to dense groups.

M.: Adheres to hard substrates such as rocks, stones, wood pilings, and other solid objects which can be easily offered in the aquarium. Lives for several years.

Light: Sunlight.

B./Rep.: Reproduces sexually and asexually. The latter is achieved by division along the longitudinal axis or by pedal laceration, in which small pieces of their pedal disc are left behind as the anemone crawls along the substrate. These pieces grow into complete anemones.

F.: C; primarily feeds on zooplankton captured with a mucuslike substance that covers their entire body. Cilia move this layer and the captured zooplankton towards the mouth opening. Non-edible inorganic matter is expelled by the cilia.

S.: Despite the extremely variable coloration (white, yellow, orange), this anemone is always identifiable by its deeply folded oral disc, numerous slender tentacles, and well-developed collar. The collar is a broad spinelike structure that runs around the column below the tentacles. It is sometimes covered by the tentacles and hidden from sight.

T: 15°-19°C, Ø: 25 cm, **TL:** from 60 cm, **WM:** m, **WR:** b, **AV:** 1, **D:** 2-3

Metridium senile from Ireland

Metridium senile from Norway

Fam.: Nemanthidae

About the Genus *Nemanthus*

At first sight, anemones of this genus do not even seem to be actiniarians since they form corallike colonies. These, however, are not the result of polyps dividing off the oral region, but outgrowths from the pedal disc.

Nemanthus nitidus   WASILIEFF, 1908
Jewel anemone

Hab.: Tropical and temperate waters of the Indo Pacific Ocean.

Sex.: None.

Soc.B./Assoc.: Colonial animals.

M.: Frequently overgrows coral skeletons, especially gorgonids. The only successful means to transfer these animals is to transfer a piece of substrate with its accompanying animals.

Light: Sunlight to moderately lit zones.

B./Rep.: Sexual and asexual reproduction. The latter method entails separating the juveniles from the lower body region. Colonies are arranged according to the substrate, not any higher order.

F.: C; *N. nitidus* feeds on zooplankton it catches with a funnellike capture apparatus consisting of its oral disc and tentacles. Plankton substitutes make aquarium maintenance possible.

S.: The oral disc and tentacles are usually a totally translucent white. Only the oral disc has a radial design. When magnified, you can see that the small light dots and spots on the tentacles are nematocysts. The column (body) occurs in many different colors. The hues can range from translucent white to an intense golden yellow, ochre, brown, or other color. Some scientists think the different color variants represent independent species or subspecies.

T: 15°-18°C, **Ø:** 3 cm, **TL:** from 50 cm, **WM:** m, **WR:** b, **AV:** 3, **D:** 3

Nemanthus nitidus from the Red Sea

Nemanthus nitidus from the Maldives

Fam.: Sagartiidae

About the Family Sagartiidae

This family encompasses anemones that have a shallow pedal disc, a smooth body with adhesive tubercles or other appendages, and rows of tentacles in multiples of 6. All have stinging threads (acontia) inside their body which can be released through openings in the column.

Sagartia troglodytes (PRICE, 1847)

Hab.: Mediterranean (rare), east Atlantic, and the North Sea. Normally found along the coast somewhat below the tide zone; however, it has also been found in depths up to 50 m.

Sex.: None.

Soc.B./Assoc.: Solitary animal.

M.: *S. troglodytes* lives in shallow water either on stones or mussels such as *Mylilus galloprovincialis*. However, it also lives buried in coarse and fine sand so that only the oral disc and the tentacles remain above the substrate. As can be deduced, these animals are not picky about their substrate, but they do require moving, oxygen-rich water.

Light: Sunlight.

B./Rep.: Sexual.

F.: C; small crustacea and finely minced meat from crustacea and mussels.

S.: This anemone occurs in a variety of colors. *S. elegans* is very similar except that it has monochrome tentacles, while *S. troglodytes* has 192 patterned tentacles. The foot is strongly adhesive, the body column grows up to 4 cm tall, and the epidermis is covered with numerous suction tubercles that frequently adhere little stones and pieces of shells. Several varieties are differentiated based on the color of the column and the design of the oral disc and tentacles, e.g., var. *decorata* has a yellow body and pronounced yellow-brown patterns on the tentacles and var. *ornata* has a green body and faint designs on the visible sections.

T: 15°-20°C, Ø: 4 cm, **TL:** from 30 cm, **WM:** s, **WR:** b, **AV:** 2, **D:** 3

Sagartiogeton undulatus (MÜLLER, 1788)

Hab.: In shallow waters of the Mediterranean, Black Sea, eastern Atlantic, and North and Baltic Seas. At depths of 1 to 15 m.

Sex.: None.

Soc.B./Assoc.: Usually lives singly.

M.: They frequently colonize empty mussel shells on fine sand or mud bottoms in protected areas of the sea. Numerous animals found in river deltas and lagoons seems to indicate its preference for lower salinities.

Light: Sunlight.

B./Rep.: Sexual.

F.: C; it captures small planktonic organisms with its long tentacles. For aquarium maintenance, a suitable plankton substitute has to be found.

S.: *S. undulatus* has 170-190 transparent, 5-7 cm long tentacles. The yellowish white oral disc has jagged lips which are yellow or yellow-ochre like the pharynx. The body is smooth, yellowish white, and either speckled or longitudinally striped red-brown; the upper openings for the acontia (cinclides) have a red-brown circle around them.

T: 16°-22°C, **Ø:** 10 cm, **TL:** from 50 cm, **WM:** m, **WR:** b, **AV:** 2, **D:** 3

Sagartiogeton undulatus, North Sea

Fam.: Isophelliidae

About the Family Isophelliidae

This family is comprised of species that have a flat pedal disc and acontia. The body is generally textured and divisible.

About the Genus *Telmatactis*

Sea anemones of this genus have a long, more or less cylindrical body column. It is indivisible. The lower part, called the *scapus,* has "bark" and small false tentacles; the upper body, the *scapulus*, is short and smooth. The tentacles are in circles of 6.

Telmatactis cricoides   (DUCHASSAING, 1850)
Club anemone

Hab.: Southwest and east Atlantic, from the Caribbean to west Africa, the Canaries, and Madeira.

Sex.: None.

Soc.B./Assoc.: This anemone often lives in partnership with various crustacea: shrimp such as *Thor amboinensis* and *Lysmata grabhami* as well as the arrow crab *Stenorhynchus lanceolatus*.

M.: Depending on origin, the temperature is important. While animals from the east Atlantic have to be maintained between 18°-23°C, Caribbean animals need temperatures between 20°-27°C. Provide rocks and a sandy bottom. They like to bury themselves.

Light: Sunlight to moderate light.

B./Rep.: Unknown.

F.: Pieces of fish and mussel, *Artemia*.

S.: Does not sting strongly, but the tentacles do stick to the fingers. The crustacea mentioned above seem to be immune to its stings (see DAS AQUARIUM, 10/1991). The pictures show the wide range of colors these animals assume.

T: 23°-27°C, Ø: 15 cm, TL: 100 cm, **WM:** m, **WR:** b, **AV:** 3, **D:** 3

Telmatactis cricoides, 15 m depth, Lanzarote, Eastern Atlantic

Telmatactis cricoides, Bonaire, Caribbean

About the Superfamily Boloceroidaria

This superfamily contains highly divergent anemones. Two families, Aliciidae and Boloceroididae, are presented here. All have a smooth body that is sometimes divided in two parts, a broad pedal disc, and a lack of distinct musculature on their base. The tentacles do not have nematocyst batteries over their entirety. They can be sealed against the interior of the body by a "skin."

About the Family Aliciidae

Anemones of this family have a broad pedal disc. The column is clearly two-part: the inferior section (*Scapus*) has blisterlike partially peduncled or branched appendages dotted with nematocysts; the upper half of the column (*Scapulus*) is smooth, only the longitudinal musculature is visible as stripes. The tentacles are very long and have nematocysts only in their proximal half.

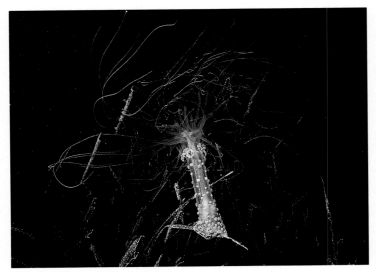

Alicia mirabilis from the Mediterranean

Alicia pretiosa
Berry anemone
(DANA, 1849)

Hab.: Red Sea. Often confused with the Mediterranean species, *A. mirabilis*. At depths of 2 to 30 m.

Sex.: None.

Soc.B./Assoc.: A nocturnal, solitary animal. During the day it contracts into small cup-shaped mounds on the substrate or aufwuchs. At night it expands into a very tall anemone.

M.: It needs elevated sites, which it seeks and finds for itself. Its foot has a ciliated pedal disc which easily detaches and allows *A. pretiosa* to move about. Usually the anemone bends towards the bottom where it fastens itself with half open tentacles, releases its pedal disc, and adheres it further along the substrate which may include elevated sites such as stone corals or gorgonians. Sometimes it will detach and retract its foot, assume a spherical shape, and drift in the current.

Light: Dim light.

B./Rep.: Sexual.

F.: C; uses its long tentacles to catch zooplankton from the current.

S.: The body is very expandable, transparent, and virtually covered with blisterlike nematocyst batteries. The transparent tentacles are extremely extendable and immediately contract spirally into balls when disturbed. The tentacles can be brought to the mouth. The coloration fluctuates between white, brown, and green. Younger animals have shorter tentacles and smaller tubercles. This anemone is extremely sensitive to light and may entirely close when illuminated with a lamp or a flash. In these instances, the oral disc and the upper part of the body are contracted to such an extent that the entire exposed surface is covered by stinging vesicles.

T: 22°-26°C, **Ø:** 5 cm, **TL:** from 50 cm, **WM:** m, **WR:** b, **AV:** 3, **D:** 3

Fam.: Aliciidae

Lebrunia danae from the Caribbean

Lebrunia danae   (DUCHASSAING & MICHELOTTI, 1860)
Stinging anemone, branching anemone

Hab.: Caribbean and the tropical western Atlantic, from the Bermudas to Brazil. At depths from 2 to 60 m.

Sex.: None.

Soc.B./Assoc.: Loner; lives in symbiosis with the cleaner shrimp *Periclimenes pedersoni*, although this relationship is generally limited to specimens living at more profound depths.

M.: Rock crevices or deep holes are its preferred attachment sites. Be sure these are offered in the aquarium.

Light: Sunlight.

B./Rep.: Sexual.

F.: C; minced crustacean, mussel, or fish meat.

S.: This extraordinary anemone not only hides its foot and body deep within a rock crevice or a coral reef, but also its oral disc and tentacles! The oral disc and its tentacles emerge from the crevice but are hidden by so-called pseudotentacles. These originate right below the oral disc as bunches of finely branched threads attached to oval or round edge vesicles typically found in this family. The pseudotentacles are densely covered with potent nematocysts and can cause unpleasant "burns" on humans. The folded edge of the oral disc creates a dense lawn of cream to brownish colored false tentacles that totally covers the anemone.

T: 22°-27°C, **Ø:** 30 cm, **TL:** from 100 cm, **WM:** m, **WR:** b, **AV:** 2-3, **D:** 3

Triactis producta with the featherduster *Sabellastarte indica*

Triactis producta
Boxing crab anemone

KLUNZINGER, 1877

Hab.: Tropical Indo-Pacific. The first described specimen was from the Red Sea. At 2 to 20 m depth.

Sex.: None.

Soc.B./Assoc.: It is either found on the chelae of the boxing crab *Lybia leptochelis* or alone on the substrate.

M.: The crab lives beneath coral and stones within the narrow depth of 0 to 2 m. These anemones are essential for the survival of the boxing crab. However, the anemone does not need the crab, even though it gains a wider distribution range by being attached to it. Larger anemones live alone on various substrates, including shaded rock crevices and caves as well as along the foot of fire corals.

Light: Sunlight.

B./Rep.: Besides sexual reproduction, the oral disc buds laterally, giving rise to new anemones.

F.: C; this anemone has extremely potent nematocysts and captures zooplankton. Small crustacea and other plankton substitutes suffice as food.

S.: Specimens living on the pinchers (chelae) of crabs are small and usually pink. Large anemones are brownish red with pink tubercles around the oral disc. *T. producta* is nocturnal and grows to be at least 2 cm in diameter. During the day, it constricts into a clump and can be mistaken for a coral polyp.

T: 22°-27°C, **Ø:** 2 cm, **TL:** from 40 cm, **WM:** m, **WR:** b, **AV:** 3, **D:** 3

Boloceroides mcmurrichi   (KNIETNIEWSKI, 1898)
Swimming anemone

Hab.: Indo-Pacific; it is particularly common in the northern most part of the Red Sea near Aqaba. At 1 to 30 m depth.

Sex.: None.

Soc.B./Assoc.: Lives singly or forms colonies.

M.: In the sea it lives on the underside of table corals, among sponges, on mangrove roots, etc. It even adheres to the long spines of diadem sea urchins.

Light: Sunlight.

B./Rep.: Besides sexual propagation, it reproduces asexually by dividing and forming colonies. This means there is a great variation in the number of tentacles among specimens.

F.: C; crustacean, fish, and mussel meat, minced if possible.

S.: This is a peculiar, somewhat deviating anemone that, nevertheless, belongs to the Boloceroididae. It reaches a size of 5 cm and is capable, as the name indicates, of swimming. Its body is not very developed, and the pedal disc adheres so weakly that strong currents or water movement cause it to separate from the substrate. Even water currents caused by large fishes or divers swimming near are sufficient to uproot them. Although you commonly read that they swim by beating their tentacles, this is incorrect. Usually they drift motionless with their tentacles extended.

T: 22°-27°C, **Ø:** 5 cm, **TL:** from 50 cm, **WM:** m, **WR:** b, **AV:** 2-3, **D:** 3

Cerianthus membranaceus fuscus, Lanzarote

Arachnanthus sp. cf. *nocturnus*, Lanzarote, 15 m depth

About the Order Cerianthria

The tube anemones are represented worldwide by approximately 50 species. Some beautiful specimens may even have a body tube over 70 cm long. Their lovely colors and hardiness make them prized aquarium animals. Their health and prosperity depends on the presence of an 8-10 cm layer of coarse sand substrate. Within this thick layer, they construct a long slime tube. Tube anemones are capable of slowly crawling along the surface and digging into the substrate. Otherwise, they are always found in their tube. Large specimens have long tubes that reach deep into the substrate. When threatened, the animals can disappear into the tube instantly. Tube anemones are inhabitants of the upper strata of the marine bottom and live solitarily. Only the upper part of the body with its oral disc and crown of tentacles is visible. Unlike anemones, the elongated slender body does not have a pedal disc. The foot is rather pointed but can, through hydrostatic pressure (turgor), widen into a bulblike structure. These movements serve to burrow and anchor the foot into the substrate. The slit-shaped mouth is surrounded by an interior (oral) and an exterior (marginal) crown of up to several hundred tentacles. In their extended state, they are long and filiform. The tentacles are arranged in pairs of one oral and one marginal tentacle.

All members of this order are only capable of sexual reproduction. That means they do not divide like many other anthozoans. Most species are hermaphrodites, meaning each animal is both male and female. Both eggs and sperm are produced, but they do not mature simultaneously in one animal. Two animals are always needed to produce a zygote. Brood care is unknown. Many species have developed a special tentacled larval stage that has an extended planktonic phase. By beating its tentacles back and forth, it can actively swim and capture food.

In aquaria, tube anemones will demand a large area. Stone corals, leather corals, and colonial anemones should not be placed in their vicinity, since the tube anemone's poison may either outright kill them or cause fatal injuries. They do not get along with most fishes. Large, active fishes disturb tube anemones; smaller fishes are frequently stung. Under no circumstance should they be associated with sea horses or pipefishes. These delicate, slow-moving fishes will invariably come in contact with their dangerous tentacles. Despite these concessions, these animals will provide you with a lot of joy. So far, it is unclear what age they attain. In the aquarium of Naples many of the original tube anemones introduced when the institute was founded are still alive. That was more than 100 years ago!

Pachycerianthus fimbriatus

405

Fam.: Arachnactidae, Cerianthidae

Arachnanthus nocturnus   DEN HARTOG, 1977
Banded tube-dwelling anemone, nocturnal tube anemone

Hab.: Coast lines of the Caribbean islands. Over sand bottoms at 5 to 20 m depth.

Sex.: Do not exist, since the animals are hermaphrodites.

Soc.B./Assoc.: Loners that should not be associated with very small fishes because of their strong venom.

M.: They require a sandy bottom at least 8 cm deep for their tube. When the animals have difficulty constructing a tube, you can provide them with a section of acrylic tubing placed at an angle into the sand. However, you have to be careful that the tube is unobstructed at the inferior end and that there are no sharp edges. With good water and a high oxygen content, the animals can be kept for several years. Avoid water currents. The surface of the substrate has to be clean, or they will not emerge.

Light: The animals are nocturnal and rarely come out during the day.

B./Rep.: Has not been successful in an aquarium.

F.: C, FD; they are actually planktivores; however, in the aquarium they readily take small pieces of frozen foods such as *Artemia*, water fleas, chopped mussel and shrimp meat, and crumbled tablet foods (Tetra Tips). Two or three feedings per week are sufficient.

S.: Nocturnal animals which are sensitive to sudden illumination.

T: 22°-28°C, Ø: 20 cm, **TL:** from 80 cm, **WM:** w, **WR:** b, **AV:** 2, **D:** 1-2

Cerianthus lloydii   GOSSE, 1859
North Sea tube anemone

Hab.: They live along clean coastal sections of the North and Baltic Seas at depths of 20 to 40 m, occasionally even at depths down to 700 m.

Sex.: Do not exist, since the animals are hermaphrodites.

Soc.B./Assoc.: Only keep with fishes in larger tanks. You can readily associate conspecific specimens (see picture), but not others.

M.: Based on its distribution, it is only suitable for coldwater aquaria. It relishes a deep sandy layer (ca. 10 cm) to bury its tube. Current should be avoided to keep the animals from being swept from their tube. If this happens, they float away and cannot reestablish contact with the substrate. They are sensitive to temperature fluctuations. Conspecifics should be placed so that only the tips of their tentacles touch.

Light: Dim light.

B./Rep.: They have a planktonic larval stage that lasts for 3-4 months. The larvae have an internal yolk sac which probably serves to maintain them in suspension. *C. lloydii* larvae captured with plankton have been repeatedly reared.

F.: C, FD; frozen plankton, water fleas, mosquito larvae, and similar items. For variety, feed broken tablet and flake foods.

S.: Often forms dense, lawnlike colonies. They were previously classified as *C. borealis*, which inhabits the region from Canada to Cape Hatteras.

T: 10°-18°C, Ø: 2-3 cm, **TL:** from 80 cm, **WM:** w, **WR:** b, **AV:** 2, **D:** 2

Arachnanthus nocturnus

Cerianthus lloydii

Fam.: Cerianthidae

Cerianthus membranaceus
Large Mediterranean tube anemone

(SPALLANZANI, 1784)

Hab.: Mediterranean, on rocky and sandy bottoms starting at a few meters depth.
Sex.: Not applicable because the animals are hermaphrodites.
Soc.B./Assoc.: In their natural habitat, they are always found singly, but several specimens can be kept in an aquarium. They are usually disturbed by fishes.
M.: Not suitable for tropical aquaria. Although the temperature can reach 24°C, it should be decreased below 20°C for a few months each year (winter). As with all tube anemones, a deep sandy bottom and sufficient room for its large tentacles is needed. Longevity follows good maintenance. Some specimens in the public aquarium of Naples are over 100 years old!
Light: Moderate light.
B./Rep.: Another Mediterranean species, *C. dornii,* is one of the few captive bred tube anemones.
F.: C, FD; feed small pieces of frozen and dry foods 1-2 times per week.
S.: There are many color variations. In the Mediterranean there are at least 5 very similar species. These animals are being reclassified.

T: 15° to 24°C (see above), **Ø:** 25 cm, **TL:** from 100 cm, **WM:** w, **WR:** b, **AV:** 1-2, **D:** 1-2

Cerianthus membranaceus

Cerianthus membranaceus, aquarium photo

Cerianthus membranaceus

Fam.: Cerianthidae

Cerianthus maua
Banded tube anemone

(CARLGREN, 1900)

Hab.: Red Sea, individual specimens occur on sand bottoms at depths of 5 to 30 m.

Sex.: Not applicable since the animals are hermaphrodites.

Soc.B./Assoc.: If possible, do not associate with fishes, since small fishes are frequently stung and larger fishes may disturb the anemone.

M.: Provide about 10 cm of sandy substrate they can use to bury their tube. There must be enough space to spread their long tentacles. Conspecifics can be placed so that the tips of their tentacles touch. Avoid currents. Since the animals have a high oxygen requirement, RUFFUS recommends a careful daily addition of 1 to 2 ml of 15% hydrogen peroxide per 100 l of water (TI 45, 1979, pp. 40 f.; or DATZ 9/1976, pp. 310 ff.). This is a fairly dated article; today an ozonizer can be used.

Light: Moderate light.

B./Rep.: Has not been successful in an aquarium.

F.: C, FD; small pieces of fish, shrimp, and mussel meat, frozen foods, and an occasional crushed tablet (TetraTips) can be fed directly to the short oral tentacles.

S.: A nocturnal animal which occasionally emerges during the day. With consistent high water quality, the animals can be maintained for years. When buying this species, check the animals closely for injuries; very polluted tubes have to be removed prior to introducing the anemone.

T: 22°-28°C, **Ø:** 20 cm, **TL:** from 100 cm, **WM:** w, **WR:** b, **AV:** 3, **D:** 1-2

Pachycerianthus soletarius
Dwarf tube anemone

(RAPP, 1829)

Hab.: Mediterranean, probably endemic. Depth distribution begins in shallow water.

Sex.: None; the animals are hermaphrodites.

Soc.B./Assoc.: They are frequently found in close proximity to each other. Sufficiently large tanks can include fishes.

M.: At least 8 cm of coarse sand, crushed shell, or coral. Current has to be avoided when introducing the animals, lest they are uprooted and drift in the water. After the tube is formed, they can tolerate a slight current.

Light: Dim light.

B./Rep.: Has not been successful in an aquarium.

F.: C, FD; feed water fleas, *Artemia*, or pieces of frozen and tablet foods twice a week. When there is current, you must ensure that large pieces of food intended for fishes do not reach the tentacles. They are poorly digested. Perhaps the pump should be turned off when feeding. Do not overfeed!

S.: Smallest species found in the Mediterranean. The color is characteristic for the species.

T: 15°-20°C, **Ø:** 7 cm, **TL:** from 80 cm, **WM:** w-m (see above), **WR:** b, **AV:** 3, **D:** 1-2

Cerianthus maua, Red Sea

Pachycerianthus soletarius

Fam.: Cerianthidae

Pachycerianthus sp.

Hab.: Singapore and the Philippines. Solitary specimens are scattered along clean coastal regions on sandy bottoms at depths of 5 to 30 m.

Sex.: None; the animals are hermaphrodites.

Soc.B./Assoc.: Keep singly if possible. They are magnificently suited for invertebrate tanks, but less appropriate for tanks containing fishes.

M.: Large specimens require a sandy bottom at least 10 cm deep and sufficient space to spread their long tentacles.

Light: Dim light at first (cover the section of the aquarium that holds the anemone); after acclimation, they can tolerate moderate light.

B./Rep.: Has not been successful in an aquarium.

F.: C, FD; feeding twice a week is sufficient. All small pieces of food are readily accepted, including frozen and dry foods. The animals only open at night, but you can try to entice them to open during the day with mussel milk (the juice of mashed mussels) placed directly into their tube with a syringe or feeding tube.

S.: These animals are easy to care for. Even though they are nocturnal, you can entice them out more and more during the day. It they are provided with good care and not overfed, they will live for years.

T: 22°-28°C, **Ø:** up to 30 cm, **TL:** from 100 cm, **WM:** w, **WR:** b, **AV:** 1, **D:** 1

Most tube anemones are classified into a genus based on external characteristics. For species identification, their nematocysts (cnidae) usually have to be examined under a microscope.

Pachycerianthus sp.

412

Pachycerianthus sp., aquarium photo

Class: **Anthozoa**
Order: **Corallimorpharia**

ABOUT THE ORDER CORALLIMORPHARIA

The anthozoans of this group are often called "false corals." Their internal morphology corresponds more to a skeleton-forming coral than to a skeletonless anemone. Their systematics are still under discussion. As recently as 1937 they were separated from true anemones and placed in their own order. Unfortunately, this group has been neglected in the literature. WILKENS (1987) provides a useful summary thereof.

In recent years, coral anemones have become progressively more appreciated in the marine aquarium hobby. They have two points in their favor: they are extremely attractive, and they are relatively easy to keep. They get along with many invertebrates and fishes. However, excessive concentrations of phosphates and nitrates are detrimental. Both of these compounds are removed from the water by growing plants, so introducing plenty of plants is advisable. The various *Caulerpa* species are well suited for this task. When illuminating the aquarium, the species' natural habitat must be considered. For example, species from greater depths cannot tolerate metal halide lights, or do so only for short periods of time. But species from shallow waters require intense illumination. Since species identification is generally impossible for the layman, you will have to get information about the natural biotope of every purchased species from your dealer. Importers should have their exporters (sources) print the capture depth and lighting conditions on each bag.

Collecting Data for Invertebrates		
depth	————	m/ft.
	☐	dim (caves)
light ⌐	☐	moderate
⌐	☐	sunlight
Please fill-in/check the appropriate information!		
Importers: Please send this to your sources.		

Coral anemones have three methods of reproduction:

Sexual reproduction: Eggs and sperm are released, unite, and result in free-swimming larvae. Initially they are planktonic. Later they adhere to the substrate.

Budding: So-called daughter individuals are formed which divide off the pedal disc.

Division: Similar in principle to budding. The anemone divides exactly along its center, and two animals are formed.

Today's filtration methods tend to make the aquarium an inhospitable environment for free-swimming larvae. Only asexual budding or division are successful methods of reproduction in captivity.

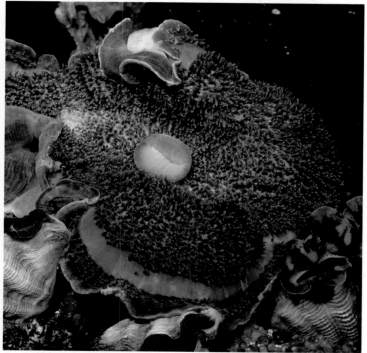

Amplexidiscus fenestrafer, see p. 432

The elephant ears of the genus *Amplexidiscus* are appreciated specimens that can be maintained in captivity. The specimen pictured above has been kept for more than four years in an aquarium. During this time, it more than doubled in size. It was fed thawed *Artemia* and krill with a syringe.

Metarhodactis sp., Mauritius

Disc Anemones

Disc or coral anemones are frequently secondary colonizers on dead reef sections. They are often the first symptom of man-made pollution in the sea. However, reefs can also be damaged by natural catastrophes, creating an appropriate substrate for coral anemones. Due to their ability to tolerate changing environmental conditions, disc anemones are well suited to captivity.

Fam.: Discosomatidae

Metarhodactis sp.
Folded elephant ear

Hab.: Tropical Indo-Pacific.

Sex.: Cannot be distinguished by external characteristics.

Soc.B./Assoc.: They get along with many invertebrates, but not with shrimp from the genus *Saron* or *Rhynchocinetes*. Can also be associated with most small fishes.

M.: Reef aquarium with moderate current. Most species will not tolerate direct metal halide illumination.

Light: Moderate light.

B./Rep.: Asexual reproduction by budding or division.

F.: FD; plankton substitutes and mussel milk. Feed moderately!

S.: Under favorable conditions, they can propagate to such an extent that they cover large surfaces. This only occurs in invertebrate tanks. Daily feedings needed in tanks containing fishes boost nitrogen levels beyond what these animals will tolerate.

T: 22°-28°C, Ø: 5-10 cm, **TL:** from 100 cm, **WM:** m, **WR:** m-t, **AV:** 2, **D:** 2

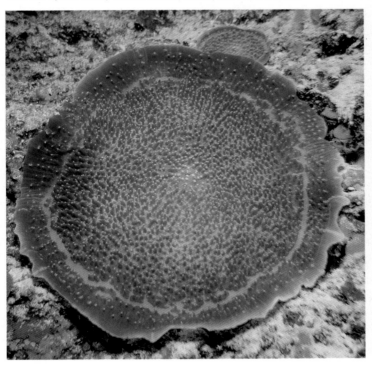

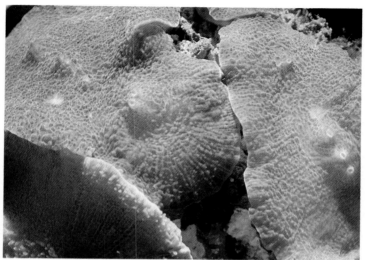

Metarhodactis sp.

Metarhodactis sp.

Fam.: Discosomatidae

Discosoma sp., yellow-fringed disc anemone

Discosoma sp.
Disc anemone, mushroom anemone

Hab.: Tropical Indo-Pacific.

Sex.: Not distinguishable from external characteristics.

Soc.B./Assoc.: They can be housed with shrimp from the genera *Periclimenes, Stenopus,* and *Lysmata,* but not *Saron* and *Rhynchocinetes*. The latter two pull on the anemone's short tentacles. All small fishes with the exception of the pygmy angelfishes are recommendable.

M.: Reef aquarium with *Caulerpa*. Filamentous green algae should be avoided at all costs. Illumination depends on where the animals came from: shallow water animals need strong illumination, whereas deep water animals will need subdued lighting. Many species fluoresce in blue light! Such species usually originate from dimly lit areas and should therefore be placed accordingly in the aquarium. Place nonfluorescing species closer to the water surface; they need more light.

Light: Sunlight to moderate light, depending on what depths it was collected from (ask your dealer).

B./Rep.: In the aquarium, only by budding or division.

F.: FD; plankton substitutes and mussel milk. Shallow water species contain zooxanthellae and do not need to be individually fed.

S.: Under favorable conditions, most *Discosoma* species multiply readily.

T: 22°-28°C, Ø: 3-10 cm, **TL:** from 100 cm, **WM:** m-s, **WR:** m-t, **AV:** 1-2, **D:** 2

Discosoma sp. *(malaccensis)*

Discosoma sp., aquarium photo

Fam.: Discosomatidae

These photographs of *Discosoma* anemones were taken in their natural biotope. Asexual division or budding can give rise to large "fields." Although they are sensitive to elevated phosphate or nitrate levels in the aquarium, they are more numerous in regions around large populations where you would expect concentrations of these compounds to be higher. Several years worth of observations have shown that disc anemones propagate particularly well where stone corals have died off because of environmental pollution, for example, channel entrances and around industrial discharges. Disc anemones primarily inhabit tropical seas such as the Indo-Pacific, Red Sea, and Caribbean. However, there are a few representatives found in subtropical regions.

Discosoma nummifere, Red Sea (in a cave)

Discosoma sp., Maldives: secondary colonizer of dead reef sections. The taller, treelike leather corals (*Sinularia asterolobata*) will be presented in the second volume of the Marine Atlas.

Fam.: Discosomatidae

Discosoma sanctithomae (DUCHASSAING & MICHELOTTI, 1860)
Warty corallimorph, St. Thomas false coral

Hab.: Caribbean.

Sex.: Cannot be determined externally.

Soc.B./Assoc.: This species usually gets along well with various invertebrates and small fishes (also see p. 440).

M.: Reef aquarium with a weak current. Do not expose them to direct metal halide lighting.

Light: Moderate light.

B./Rep.: The animals divide in half (division).

F.: C, FD; chopped frozen foods and *Artemia*. These animals have never been seen capturing fishes or crustacea.

S.: Aquarium specimens of *Amplexidiscus* elephant ears have been observed preying on small to medium sized fishes and various crustacea by covering them and digesting them exogastrically (outside the stomach).

T: 22°-28°C, **Ø:** 5 cm, **TL:** from 100 cm, **WM:** w-m, **WR:** m, **AV:** 2, **D:** 2

Discosoma sanctithomae

Discosoma sanctithomae, an atypical form

Fam.: Discosomatidae

Discosoma neglecta

Discosoma sp., Indonesia

Discosoma sp. (*plumosa*), carpet disc anemone

Discosoma sp. (magnified)

Discosoma sp. (*ferrugatus*)

Discosoma sp. (*marmoratus*)

Discosoma sp. (*striatus*), mushroom anemone, aquarium photo

Discosoma sp. "*coeruleo-striatus*," Indonesia

Fam.: Discosomatidae

Discosoma sp. (*coeruleus*), east Africa

The blue-green disc anemone pictured here is frequently imported from the eastern coast of Africa, mainly from Kenya. Since it inhabits shallow water regions there, it demands high quality lighting (metal halide - NDL).

Actinodiscus/Discosoma
Disc anemones, photos on page 421 (lower) and page 428-431

Hab.: Entire Indo-Pacific, from east Africa to Polynesia

Sex.: None

Soc.B./Assoc.: Very robust when compared to other anthozoans. Even strong stinging animals such as stone corals or rock anomones are pushed back or maintained at a distance. The beautiful *Acropora* stone corals are stung.

M.: Weack current; maintain large colonies. When doing so, the diffent color morphs can be mixed randomly. All Species (?) tolerate metal halide illumination and reproduce prolifically by pedal laceration. The animals tolerate unfavorable water values, but need water low in phosphate and nitrate to display their beautiful colors. Most animals live at

Discosoma sp. (*punctatus*), Indonesia

This beautiful disc anemone hails from Indonesia. To the delight of snorkelers, it makes its home in shallow water. In the aquarium, you must provide enough illumination to keep the symbiotic zooxanthellae alive.

about 10 m depth and fluoresce. This iridescent coloration is caused by UV protecting substances. *Actinodiscus* cf. *nummiformis* (photo on the top of p. 428), however, should be placed in a darker region.

Light: Sunlight to moderate light areas. These disc anemones are usually more beautiful colored when illuminated with fluorescent tubes.

B./Rep.: The animals regulary produce small daughter anemones by pedal laceration. A large anemone will annually produce about 40 daughter anemones, which gradually move out of the shade of the mother polyp.

F.: Feeding is not necessary. Usually the animals are incapable of digesting hard food items.

T: 20-29°C, Ø up to 15 cm, **TL:** from 50 cm, **WM:** w-m, **AV:** 1, **D:** 2

Fam.: Discosomatidae

The genus *Amplexidiscus* is known to most snorkelers and divers in tropical regions. The elephant ears, as they are commonly called, are encountered in all shallow waters less than 20 m deep in the Indo-Pacific. These animals have developed an interesting method of food procurement: once planktonic organisms or careless small fishes have settled themselves within reach of its tentacles, this anemone encloses its victim within the confines of its plate-shaped body to circumvent escape. When greatly disturbed, these anemones expel mesenteric filaments (lower right hand photo).

Large elephant ear in an aquarium (*Amplexidiscus fenestrafer*)

Amplexidiscus fenestrafer   DUNN & HAMNER, 1980
Elephant ear

Hab.: Indo-Pacific.

Sex.: Not recognizable from external characteristics.

Soc.B./Assoc.: They get along well with most crustacea and small fishes (see p. 440). If you wish to combine them with large fishes, only the herbivorous surgeonfishes can be recommended, as they control filamentous green algae.

M.: Reef aquarium with a slight current. The type of illumination depends on their origin.

Light: Moderate light.

B./Rep.: Usually the animals divide in half; they rarely bud.

F.: C, FD; substitute plankton and finely chopped frozen foods given with a feeding tube.

S.: Most, but not all, are passive predators.

T: 22°-26°C, Ø: 5-10 cm, **TL:** from 100 cm, **WM:** w, **WR:** m, **AV:** 2, **D:** 2

Amplexidiscus fenestrafer, Photo from the Maldives

Amplexidiscus fenestrafer with expelled mesenteric filaments, Photo from the Philippines

433

Fam.: Ricordeidae

Ricordea florida DUCHASSAING & MICHELOTTI, 1860
Florida disc anemone, Florida false coral

Hab.: Caribbean islands.

Sex.: Not distinguishable from external characteristics.

Soc.B./Assoc.: Colonial animals. Can be associated with most crustacea, small fishes, and surgeonfishes (see p. 440). Since pygmy angelfishes constantly pick on their tentacles, they should be avoided.

M.: Reef aquarium with moderate current.

Light: Sunlight. This shallow water form tolerates strong metal halide lighting very well. Actually, it will only open when provided with strong illumination.

B./Rep.: Either through division, which begins at the mouth opening, or by budding along the pedal disc.

F.: C, FD; feed substitute plankton twice a week.

S.: In the trade, forms from the Indo-Pacific are likewise identified as *Ricordea florida*. These species can be distinguished rather easily from the much more beautiful species from the Caribbean. Species from the Indo-Pacific (top of p. 435) have tentacles arranged around the raised mouth opening; *Ricordea florida* does not. Additionally, *Ricordea florida* is more beautiful colored and usually has short, spherical, white or shiny green tentacles. These rare imports almost exclusively come from Belize.

T: 22°-27°C, Ø: 6 cm, **TL:** from 100 cm, **WM:** w-m, **WR:** m-t, **AV:** 2, **D:** 2-3

Anemones with knoblike tentacles of the genus *Ricordea* belong to a separate family. They only inhabit the Caribbean.

Ricordea sp., aquarium photo

Ricordea sp.

Fam.: Corallimorphidae

The Corallimorphidae, the coral anemones in the proper sense, are a family within the order Corallimorpharia. Representatives of this group look like small anemones. However, in contrast to true anemones, they are not colonial. Although they may live in groups, there is no contact between individual animals. Additionally, the anatomy of the Corallimorphidae corresponds more to coral polyps than to true anemones. An easily recognizable characteristic of the Corallimorphidae are spherical tentacle tips. They are sometimes called button tentacles. Representatives of this family are not only found in tropical seas, but in subtropical and temperate regions as well. The species presented here, *Corynactis californica* from the Gulf of California and *C. viridis* from the Atlantic, prefer temperatures below 20°C.

Corynactis californica   CARLGREN, 1936
Californian coral anemone

Hab.: Eastern Pacific, Gulf of California.

Sex.: Not distinguishable from external characteristics.

Soc.B./Assoc.: Colonial animals. Can be associated with most invertebrates and small fishes (see p. 440).

M.: Rock aquarium with a moderate current. The water temperature must remain below 20°C.

Light: Moderate light.

B./Rep.: Under good conditions, individuals are constantly dividing. Large colonies can be divided with a sharp cut.

F.: C, FD; feed substitute plankton or crumbled tablet foods delivered with a feeding tube.

S.: Not suitable for tropical marine aquaria.

T: up to 18°C, Ø: 1 cm, **TL:** from 80 cm, **WM:** m, **WR:** b-m, **AV:** 3, **D:** 3 (chiller!)

Corynactis californica

Corynactis californica

Corynactis viridis

Corynactis viridis

Corynactis viridis   ALLMAN, 1846
Jewel coral anemone

Hab.: From the northeast Atlantic to the southern coast of Spain.

Sex.: Not distinguishable from external features.

Soc.B./Assoc.: Colonial animals. Easily kept with invertebrates and small fishes from the Mediterranean. Tube anemones do not make good companions.

M.: Rock aquarium. The temperature should not exceed 20°C. The water temperature should be kept below 18°C in the winter.

Light: Shaded areas.

B./Rep.: The colony constantly enlarges as individual animals divide.

F.: C, FD; feed with a feeding tube. Finely chopped frozen foods, substitute plankton, and crumbled tablet foods can be given; flake foods on occasion. Feed in moderation!

S.: Large variations in color are possible (see photos). Individuals of one colony are always the same color, however. Not suitable for tropical marine aquaria.

T: to 20°C, **Ø:** 1 cm, **TL:** from 80 cm, **WM:** m-s, **WR:** m-t, **AV:** 3, **D:** 2

Fam.: Corallimorphidae

Pseudocorynactis caribbeorum   DEN HARTOG, 1981
Orange ball corallimorph

Hab.: Caribbean islands.

Sex.: No external differences.

Soc.B./Assoc.: Not a colonial animal. They get along well with most invertebrates and small fishes (see below).

M.: Reef aquarium. Anemones are either introduced on a stone or loosely tied to one with a piece of nylon string. They prefer vertical rock formations.

Light: Moderate light.

B./Rep.: This species divides much less frequently than the previously described *Corynactis* species.

F.: C, FD; finely chopped frozen foods, substitute plankton, and crumbled tablet foods delivered with a feeding tube.

S.: Unknown.

T: 22°-26°C, Ø: 3 cm, **TL:** from 80 cm, **WM:** m, **WR:** m, **AV:** 3, **D:** 2

COMBINING DISC AND CORAL ANEMONES WITH OTHER ANIMALS IN THE AQUARIUM

Most species of the order Corallimorpharia are hardy inhabitants of tropical marine tanks. They are easily combined with most invertebrates. However, in regard to crustacea, be aware that shrimp from the genera *Saron* and *Rhynchocinetes* as well as large crabs, particularly hermit crabs, are not proper companions. The anemones can be associated with tube anemones and other highly toxic anemones when a safety distance is maintained between the two. However, STEINER (1983) reports that *Corynactis viridis* does not multiply when associated with tube anemones. A few cowries and nudibranchs are considered predators.

All filtering animals such as sponges, sea fans, soft corals, tubeworms, mussels, and sea squirts as well as shrimp of the genera *Periclimenes*, *Lysmata,* and *Stenopus*, small hermit crabs, starfishes, and algivorous sea urchins make good companions. With the exception of pygmy angelfishes, they can be housed with small to medium sized fishes. BROCKMANN (TI, Sept./1982, pp. 26 ff.) even reported that butterflyfishes (*Heniochus acuminatus* and *Chaetodon auriga*) which eagerly consume *Aiptasia* do not disturb disc anemones.

I myself confirmed this as I watched *Chaetodon lunula* and *C. kleini* ignore disc anemones while divesting the aquarium of *Aiptasia* to such an extent that the only rock anemones left were those in inaccessible corners.

Pseudocorynactis caribbeorum

Pseudocorynactis caribbeorum

A gorgeous "Dutch" marine aquarium. Every week the algae have to be pruned. However, these algae help guarantee optimal water quality for the animals. The turquoise colonial

anemone belongs to the genus *Zoanthus*.

Class: Anthozoa
Order: Zoantharia

ABOUT THE ORDER ZOANTHARIA

These six-rayed anthozoans are not difficult to care for. In their natural habitat they even live in organically polluted areas. They colonize a wide assortment of substrates, even hermit crab shells, but rarely sandy bottoms. Colonial anemones are small animals that barely reach a diameter of 1-2 cm. Their coloration varies from bright red to lemon yellow, orange, green, and turquoise. In the aquarium, the animals will even tolerate direct metal halide lighting and propagate asexually. A mother polyp produces daughters that grow to be the same size and color within about 6 months. Plankton substitutes must be offered, even though the symbiont algae provide nourishment (see p. 446). Filamentous algae are very problematic for colonial anemones. If they are not promptly controlled, they cover and asphyxiate these anthozoans. Aquaria with growing red calcareous algae offer the best living conditions to successfully

maintain these organisms for long periods of time. A varied current keeps them open and searching for food at all times. In a well established aquarium, colonial anemones can be kept with hard (stony) and leather corals. However, there should always be a certain safety distance between the polyp colonies so that they do not sting or kill each other. Generally, they can only be identified to genus based solely on external characteristics.

Two colonial anemones growing intermingled with each other. The larger of the two belongs to the genus *Palythoa* ; the smaller is a member of the genus *Zoanthus*.

Fam.: Zoanthidae

Palythoa sp.
Large colonial anemone

Hab.: Indian Ocean, in clear waters.

Sex.: Not present.

Soc.B./Assoc.: Colonial animals. Only associate with small peaceful coral reef fishes, shrimp, and small hermit crabs. Small surgeonfishes are recommended to control the green filamentous algae which are detrimental to *Palythoa*.

M.: Reef aquarium. The colonies should occasionally be exposed to a strong current. The daughter colonies will need enough substrate. A dense stand of higher algae, such as *Caulerpa*, must be avoided, since they remove important nutrients needed by the colonial anemones. Place other Cnidaria at a respectable distance. One colony of 20-40 animals per ca. 100 l of water.

Light: Moderate light. Frequently the animals are intolerant of direct metal halide illumination. Fluorescent Lumilux 11 tubes are a better choice. Black light fluorescent tubes induce fluorescing of the single polyps, but limit their daily usage to 3 hours. In contrast, actinic tubes should remain on 24 hours (see "Illumination" on p. 109).

B./Rep.: The single polyps are connected by flat runners. These later give rise to daughter or secondary polyps.

F.: C, FD; feed generously with small to moderate sized food particles. Frozen as well as dry foods can be dispensed with a feeding tube. Very fine substitute foods and liquid suspensions are usually encased in mucus and then expelled. An especially high propagation rate is achieved through regular offerings of newly hatched *Artemia* nauplii.

S.: Well suited for tropical marine aquaria.

T: 22°-28°C, **Ø:** 2 cm, **TL:** from 80 cm, **WM:** s, **WR:** m, **AV:** 1, **D:** 2

Symbiosis Between Plants and Animals

The bright colors of many colonial anemones are usually not the product of their own pigments, but those of unicellular algae contained within their tissue, the **zooxanthellae**. They have a true symbiotic (mutualistic) relationship. That is, both organisms benefit from the association. This relationship is so developed that each is incapable of life without the other. With light, the algae release oxygen like all plants. However, it is not released into the water. Instead, it and other metabolic products are absorbed by the anemones. The algae in turn feed on the anemone's catabolites (primarily phosphorus and nitrogen). A perfect cycle! However, note that colonial anemones containing zooxanthellae require sufficient illumination for their associated algae.

Not only colonial anemones have zooxanthellae as symbionts. Sponges, anemones and, especially, reef forming (hermatypical) stone corals also harbor these algae. In the latter, skeleton formation is enhanced when the algae remove CO_2.

Aquaria with good algae growth, especially those with red calcareous algae and few *Caulerpa*, are a basic condition for the growth of zooxanthellae-dependent colonial anemones. Avoid phosphorus and nitrogen over-fertilization (nitrate). Iron, iodine, and other supplemented trace elements should be added in regular, small amounts. Excessive *Caulerpa* growth should be controlled by pruning.

Red and brown smear algae are controlled with chloramphenicol at 1 gram per 100 l water (according to WILKENS, 1987); after three days add half this amount. Suspend activated carbon filtration during this treatment.

Upper anemones, *Palythoa* sp.; below, the yellow colonial anemone, *Parazoanthus* sp.

Palythoa sp.

Fam.: Zoanthidae

Palythoa sp.
Green colonial anemone

Hab.: Indonesia, Singapore.

Sex.: None.

Soc.B./Assoc.: Colonial animals. Only associate with small, peaceful coral reef fishes and sessile invertebrates. Stocking a small surgeonfish or a herbivorous blenny is recommended to control green filamentous algae. Do not place near sea anemones or tube anemones. Higher algae such as *Caulerpa* should be absent or limited, since they remove vital nutrients from the water.

M.: Reef aquarium with good water quality. Strong illumination and good current are preferred.

Light: Sunlight. Best results are achieved with metal halide and actinic lamps.

B./Rep.: With good maintenance, it regularly propagates through budding.

F.: C; newly hatched *Artemia* nauplii are the food of choice. Substitute foods are frequently rejected. Trials with frozen water fleas or mosquito larvae are sometimes successful. The animals are considered trained to these foods after one success.

S.: As soon as an accepted food is found, they are easily maintained. At night they retract their tentacles like all *Palythoa* species.

T: 24°-30°C, **Ø:** 2-3 cm, **TL:** from 100 cm, **WM:** s, **WR:** m-t, **AV:** 1, **D:** 2

Various colonial anemones in an aquarium; center, *Goniopora* sp. (stony coral); upper left, yellow-fringed disc anemone; lower right, a leather coral (*Sarcophyton* sp.).

449

Fam.: Zoanthidae

Palythoa tuberculosa   (ESPER, 1791)
Large Indo-Pacific colonial anemone

Hab.: Indo-Pacific, Red Sea.

Sex.: None.

Soc.B./Assoc.: Colonial animals. Do not associate with aufwuchs feeders or large crustacea such as crabs, lobsters, or spiny lobsters. Small fishes which feed on filamentous green algae are recommended (surgeonfishes, herbivorous blennies), since filamentous green algae are detrimental to colonial anemones.

M.: Reef aquarium with strong current. Filamentous algae must be avoided. *Caulerpa* algae must be absent or limited to small quantities. A sufficiently large distance must be maintained between colonial anemones and other Cnidaria such as sea anemones and tube anemones to allow the colony room to grow. The colony should be fastened to a vertical rock wall with a piece of nylon string. The upper individuals are exposed to direct light and the lower animals are in the shade. Depending on the light requirement, the upper or lower animals will propagate better.

Light: Moderate light to sunlight. Do not expose to direct metal halide illumination.

B./Rep.: The animals multiply by budding (daughter polyps), constantly enlarging the colony.

F.: C; feed the animals with *Artemia*, mussel milk, and crumbled FD tablets using a feeding tube.

S.: Well suited for tropical reef aquaria. Open polyps and regular budding indicate healthy colonies. After the lights are turned off, the polyps close. This anthozoan stores palythoxin, a toxin, in its body tissues.

T: 22°-28°C, Ø: 2 cm, **TL:** from 100 cm, **WM:** s, **WR:** m, **AV:** 3, **D:** 2

Palythoa sp., Caribbean

Palythoa sp., Red Sea

Parazoanthus axinellae with *Halimeda opuntia*, a calcareous green alga from the Mediterranean

Fam.: Zoanthidae

Parazoanthus axinellae　　　　　　　　　　　　　　　　(O. SCHMIDT, 1862)
Yellow encrusting sea anemone

Hab.: Mediterranean and temperate zones of the eastern Atlantic. On hard substrates starting at a few meters depth. Sometimes they also colonize *Axinella* antler sponges.

Sex.: Not present.

Soc.B./Assoc.: Colonial animals. Easily kept with fishes, but not with aufwuchs feeders.

M.: Rock aquarium with overhangs to provide shade. The water temperature should be temporarily dropped to 20°C (winter).

Light: Dim light.

B./Rep.: Reproduces asexually by budding. Overhangs frequently support growth of protuberances that hang into the open water several centimeters.

F.:C; regular feedings using a feeding tube are needed. The polyps are closed during the day, even when food is available, which means nocturnal feedings have to be provided. Feed like *Palythoa* species. Once in a while, *Tubifex* can be fed; place them directly upon the open polyp with forceps.

S.: Not for the tropical saltwater aquarium (temperature). Easy to keep.

T: 15° to 23°C (see above), Ø: 1.5 cm, **TL:** from 80 cm, **WM:** w-m, **WR:** b, **AV:** 2, **D:** 1

Parazoanthus parasiticus   (DUCHASSAING & MICHELOTTI, 1860)
Parasitic colonial anemone, sponge zoanthid

Hab.: Caribbean islands and the Bahama and Bermuda Islands. In clean waters, usually on sponges.

Sex.: Do not exist.

Soc.B./Assoc.: Singly or in colonies. They regularly colonize the surface of *Cliona delitrix* and other sponges.

M.: A reef aquarium with good water quality. This zoanthid should be placed in the current.

Light: Moderate light.

B./Rep.: In the aquarium, they only propagate asexually by budding.

F.: C, FD; feed every other day with various frozen or dry foods using a feeding tube.

S.: In their natural habitat, they are exclusively found on sponges. The relationship between these two animals has not been completely defined. Parasitism (note both the common and scientific name) cannot be ruled out, but a symbiotic relationship is assumed: the sponge offers an algae-free substrate, and the colonial anemone excretes toxins which protect the sponge against sponge-feeding fishes. This species can be kept without a sponge in aquaria.

T: 21°-30°C, Ø: 1 cm, **TL:** from 80 cm, **WM:** m, **WR:** m, **AV:** 2, **D:** 2

Fam.: Zoanthidae

Parazoanthus swiftii (DUCHASSAING & MICHELOTTI, 1860)
Golden zoanthid, yellow Caribbean colonial anemone

Hab.: Caribbean islands; on red and green finger sponges.

Sex.: Not known.

Soc.B./Assoc.: Colonial. In its natural habitat it only colonizes red and green finger sponges. Limit its tankmates to peaceful crustacea and small fishes, e.g., herbivorous blennies.

M.: Reef aquarium. The living sponge or its skeleton (see below) where the colonial anemones are attached is placed in the current.

Light: Sunlight to moderate light, depending on where it lives in its natural habitat. If the polyps do not open in direct light, provide shade for the animals. They can be gradually accustomed to light.

B./Rep.: Occurs asexually through budding. With good food and high water quality, secondary polyps develop rapidly. They remain connected to the mother polyp for a time before separating.

F.: C, FD; microplankton, frozen plankton, red North Sea plankton, or crushed tablet foods (TetraTips) fed with a feeding tube. Feeding every other day is sufficient.

S.: In the aquarium they settle on the keratin-silica skeletons of dead sponges.

T: 20°- 30°C, Ø: 1 cm, **TL:** from 100 cm, **WM:** w-m, **WR:** t-m, **AV:** 2, **D:** 3

Parazoanthus sp.
Yellow Indonesian polyp

Hab.: Indonesia, Lake Java.

Sex.: Not present.

Soc.B./Assoc.: Colonial animals. Associate with small damselfishes, small pygmy angelfishes, and surgeonfishes. Large angelfishes feed on its tentacles with predilection.

M.: Reef aquarium. Polyps colonize rocks, dead corals and, especially, porous fired clay. They prefer strong current. If a current cannot be offered, use a stream of water to clean them of adhering metabolites every second day. Maintain a large distance between these animals and other Cnidaria, especially poisonous sea anemones or tube anemones.

Light: Sunlight to moderate light, depending on origin.

B./Rep.: Asexual propagation through budding. As found in other colonial anemones, these form daughter polyps off runners which later separate.

F.: C, FD; *Daphnia*, *Cyclops*, *Bosmina*, minced *Mysis*, mussel and fish flesh, and crumbled tablet foods delivered with a feeding tube. One feeding per day is absolutely necessary to maintain good reproduction.

S.: Found in several colors. The tentacles of this colonial anemone often vary in length. Healthy colonies have tentacles up to 4 cm long (photo on top of p. 458). Newly acclimated or stung polyps have much shorter tentacles (photo on bottom of p. 457).

T: 22°-30°C, Ø: 1.5 cm, **TL:** from 60 cm, **WM:** s (see above), **WR:** t-m, **AV:** 1, **D:** 1-2

Parazoanthus swiftii

Parazoanthus sp.

Fam.: Zoanthidae

Zoanthus sp.

Zoanthus sp.

Zoanthus sp.
Green-yellow colonial anemone

Hab.: Indonesia, Singapore.

Sex.: None.

Soc.B./Assoc.: Colonial animals. Can easily be placed in company of small coral reef fishes and shrimp, but not with large crustacea or aufwuchs feeders (e.g., large angelfishes and some butterflies like to nibble on the tentacles). Small surgeonfishes or herbivorous blennies as well as tilefishes, sword gobies, damselfishes, and small planktivorous dottybacks are recommended.

M.: Reef aquarium. They are an easy charge when provided with good water quality. Ensure that filamentous algae do not become established in the tank. Enough hard substrates must be available for daughter polyps to settle on. Porous fired clay is especially appreciated.

Light: Sunlight with metal halide and actinic lights.

B./Rep.: They regularly reproduce by budding.

F.: C; planktivores which are difficult to train to substitute foods. However, under favorable lighting, their primary, and even exclusive, source of nourishment are the by-products produced by their symbiotic zooxanthellae (see p. 440).

S.: Like all colonial anemones, these secrete a mucus layer where sand, foraminiferan shells, and similar items get trapped. This layer is then overgrown by skin and turned towards the inside. Therefore, the name "encrusting anemone" is also occasionally used. Sometimes solitary polyps separate from the colony. Place these in small rock crevices. There they will adhere and multiply.

T: 24°-30°C, Ø: 2-3 cm, **TL:** from 80 cm, **WM:** m, **WR:** t, **AV:** 1, **D:** 2

Fam.: Epizoanthidae

Epizoanthus arenaceus (DELLE CHIAJE, 1836)
Gray encrusting anemone

Hab.: Mediterranean.

Sex.: Absent.

Soc.B./Assoc.: Colonial animals. Only associate with small peaceful fishes and invertebrates.

M.: Rock aquarium. Maintain average water quality values. Only reproduction is proof of their health. The daughter anemones need sufficient hard substrates; gastropod shells are especially appreciated. Once in a while either the pump discharge should be directed towards them or the water above the colony strongly stirred by hand to remove dirt particles that have settled among the individual polyps.

Light: Moderate light.

B./Rep.: Small daughter polyps are formed through asexual propagation (budding). With good water quality, this occurs continuously.

F.: C, FD; liquifry marine and crumbled flake or tablet foods are as readily accepted as frozen plankton, newly hatched *Artemia* nauplii, and mussel milk. These animals generally need to be fed with a feeding tube.

S.: Only suitable for a Mediterranean aquarium.

T: up to 21°C, Ø: 1-1.5 cm, **TL:** from 60 cm, **WM:** m, **WR:** m, **AV:** 2, **D:** 2-3

Epizoanthus paxii ABEL, 1955
Brown encrusting anemone

Hab.: Mediterranean; on hard substrates at all depths.

Sex.: None.

Soc.B./Assoc.: Colonial animals. Can be associated with other animals. However, active fishes should only be introduced after the colony has begun to spread.

M.: Rock edifications. The colonies like to sit on slanted surfaces beneath shady overhangs. They do not place any particular demands on water quality, but the water should be cooler than 20°C. They appreciate a slight current.

Light: Dim light.

B./Rep.: With good food, they multiply regularly by budding. Individual polyps can separate and form new colonies at distant locals.

F.: C, FD; like the anemone above. Closed polyps should be enticed to open with small quantities of food.

S.: Based on the temperature requirements of this species, it is not suitable for tropical marine aquaria. They frequently occupy large surfaces of algae-free rocks in display tanks.

T: 15°-20°C, Ø: 1-1.5 cm, **TL:** from 80 cm, **WM:** m-s, **WR:** b-m, **AV:** 3, **D:** 2

460

Epizoanthus arenaceus

Epizoanthus paxii

Taxonomy

Phylum: ARTHROPODA		Jointed Foot
Subphylum: BRANCHIATA = DIANTENNATA		With Two Antennae
Class: CRUSTACEA		Crustacea
Subclass: MALACOSTRACA		

Order	Decapoda	Ten-footed crustacea
Suborder	Nantantia	Shrimp
Family	Hippolytidae	Cleaner shrimp
		BATE, 1888
Genera	*Lysmata*	RISSO, 1816
	Parhippolyte	BORRADAILLE, 1899
	Saron	THALLWITZ, 1891
	Thor	KINGSLEY, 1878
	Tozeuma	SIMPSON, 1860
Family	Alpheidae	Pistol shrimp
		RAFINESQUE, 1815
Genera	*Alpheus*	FABRICIUS, 1798
	Synalpheus	BATE, 1888
Family	Gnathophyllidae	Harlequin shrimp
		DANA, 1852
Genera	*Gnathophyllum*	LATREILLE, 1819
	Hymenocera	LATREILLE, 1819
Family	Palaemonidae	Rock shrimp, anemone shrimp
		RAFINESQUE, 1815
Genera	*Palaemon*	WEBER, 1795
	Leandrites	HOLTHUIS, 1950
	Periclimenes	COSTA, 1844
	Stegopontonia	NOBILI, 1906
Family	Pandalidae	Deepwater shrimp
		HAWORTH, 1825
Genera	*Pandalus*	LEACH, 1814
	Plesionika	BATE, 1888
Family	Rhynchocinetidae	Dancing shrimp
		ORTMANN, 1890
Genus	*Rhynchocinetes*	MILNE-EDWARDS, 1837
Family	Stenopodidae	Boxing shrimp
		HUXLEY, 1879
Genus	*Stenopus*	LATREILLE, 1819
Suborder	Reptantia	Lobsters and crabs
Family	Palinuridae	Spiny lobsters
		LATREILLE, 1803
Genera	*Palinurus*	WEBER, 1795
	Palinurellus	VON MARTENS, 1878
	Panulirus	WHITE, 1847
Family	Scyllaridae	Slipper lobsters
		LATREILLE, 1825
Genera	*Arctides*	HOLTHUIS, 1960
	Scyllarides	GILL, 1898
	Scyllarus	FABRICIUS, 1775

Family	Nephropidae	Lobsters
		DANA, 1852
Genera	*Enoplometopus*	A. MILNE-EDWARDS, 1836
	Homarus	WEBER, 1795
	Nephrops	LEACH, 1814
Family	Diogenidae	Hermit crabs
		ORTMANN, 1892
Genera	*Aniculus*	DANA, 1852
	Calcinus	DANA, 1851
	Cancellus	H.MILNE-EDWARDS, 1836
	Dardanus	PAULSON, 1875
	Paguristes	DANA, 1852
	Petrochirus	STIMPSON, 1858
	Trizopagurus	FOREST, 1952
Family	Paguridae	Hermit crabs
		LATREILLE, 1803
Genera	*Pagurus*	FARBRICIUS, 1775
	Manucomplanus	McLAUGHLIN, 1981
Family	Galatheidae	Squat lobsters
		SAMOUELLE, 1819
Genera	*Allogalathea*	BABA, 1969
	Galathea	FABRICIUS, 1793
Family	Porcellanidae	Porcelain crabs
		HAWORTH, 1825
Genus	*Neopetrolisthes*	MIYAKE, 1937
Family	Dromiidae	Sponge crabs
		DE HAAN, 1833
Genera	*Dromidiopsis*	BORRADAILLE, 1900
	Dromia	WEBER, 1795
Family	Calappidae	Box crabs
		DE HAAN, 1833
Genus	*Calappa*	WEBER, 1795
Family	Leucosiidae	Purse crabs
		SAMOUELLE, 1819
Genus	*Leucosia*	FABRICIUS, 1798
Family	Majidae	Spider crabs
		SAMOUELLE, 1819
Genera	*Loxorhynchus*	STIMPSON, 1857
	Maja	LAMARCK, 1801
	Stenorhynchus	LAMARCK, 1818
Family	Portunidae	Swimming crabs
		RAFINESQUE, 1815
Genera	*Carcinus*	LEACH, 1814
	Lissocarcinus	ADAMS & WHITE, 1848
Family	Trapeziidae	Coral crabs
		MIERS, 1886
Genera	*Trapezia*	LATREILLE, 1825
	Quadrella	DANA, 1851
Family	Xanthidae	Mud and stone crabs
		MACLEAY, 1838

Taxonomy

Genera	*Atergatis*	DE HAAN, 1835
	Liomera	DANA, 1851
	Lybia	H.MILNE-EDWARDS, 1834
Family	Pinnotheridae	Pea crabs
		DE HAAN, 1833
Genera	*Pinnotheres*	BOSC, 1801
	Xanthasia	WHITE, 1846
Family	Grapsidae	Marsh crabs
		MACLEAY, 1838
Genera	*Grapsus*	LAMARCK, 1801
	Pachygrapsus	RANDALL, 1839
Family	Cancridae	Cancer crabs
Genus	*Cancer*	
Family	Ocypodidae	Fiddler crabs
		RAFINESQUE, 1815
Genera	*Ocypode*	WEBER, 1795
	Uca	LEACH, 1814
Family	Mictyridae	Soldier crabs
		BORRADAILLE, 1907
Genus	*Mictyris*	LATREILLE, 1806
Order	Stomatopoda	Mantis shrimp
Family	Gonodactylidae	Smashing mantis shrimp
Genera	*Gonodactylus*	BERTHOLD, 1827
	Odontodactylus	BIGELOW, 1863
	Hemisquilla	HANSEN, 1895
Family	Lysiosquillidae	Spearing mantis shrimp
Genus	*Lysiosquilla*	DANA, 1852

Aeger tipularius, Malm, Solnhofen, Germany, ca. 160 million years

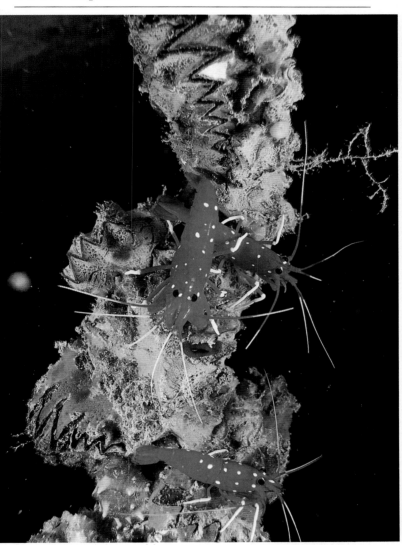

Scarlet cleaner shrimp, *Lysmata debelius,* in their natural habitat in the Maldives. When viewed from above, you can easily see that the white dots extend onto the abdomen. The same species imported from the Philippines and Indonesia has white dots only on the carapace.

Order: Decapoda

The systematics of the more than 30,000 known species of crustacea can only be handled by specialists. About $^2/_3$ of the species are higher crustacea which are again divided into 14 orders. One of these orders, the Decapoda, is dealt with in detail in this chapter for obvious reasons: decapods (shrimp and crabs) primarily live in reef regions which can be reached by the diver and a camera. Many shrimp and crabs can be found in shallow waters by fishermen and collectors and can then be introduced into the international pet trade. Aquarists see the animals for the first time at the retailers without knowing much about their natural habitat, even though this knowledge is an essential condition to successfully maintain these animals. A photographer should also be familiar with this group if he wants to fully portray their beauty.

First some general indications about crustacea before dealing with the two suborders Natantia (shrimp) and Reptantia (lobsters and crabs) in as much detail as possible: what the insects are to land, the crustacea represent for the marine habitat. Crustacea inhabit a wide variety of habitats, from the shore to the deep sea, and the tropics to arctic waters. This class includes both planktivores and large predatory crabs with everything in between. With the exception of the Mollusca, Crustacea is the most diverse animal group. They play an important role as scavengers, coral gardeners, and represent food for whales and other inhabitants of the high seas. They occupy a significant position in the ecology of the oceans.

In most higher crustacea, the gill chamber is covered by the chest armor, the carapace, which protects the gills but also significantly hampers the gills' contact with new, oxygenated water. To compensate, the crustacea have developed a special "pump," the scaphognathite (gill bailer), that fans the gills like a fin and provides a constant stream of oxygenated water to the gill chamber. Like vertebrates, crustacea have an oxygen-binding blood pigment which transports this vital element to the sites of use. It is hemocyanin, so named because of its light blue color in its oxygen-laden form.

The dorsally oriented heart lies in the carapace and pumps the blood coming from the gills into two main arteries which serve the head region and the tail musculature. The circulatory system of crustacea is open. That means that a significant part of the blood does not flow in vessels but must find its way back through sinuses.

The open circulatory system assumes an integral, undamaged body envelope, since blood not flowing in vessels would be pushed through any perforations in the shell. However, crustacea have prepared themselves for these instances: every leg has a break off point which is outfitted with a septum that has a small opening through its center for the nerve and the blood to pass through. When the leg is injured, the crustacean uses a special muscle to bend the leg at the base with a jerking motion, thereby breaking the leg. The small opening in the septum quickly closes and the leg begins to regenerate with the next molt. This active process of dismemberment is called autotomy and may also be used by crustacea to free themselves when a predator has caught them by a limb.

Higher crustacea have separate sexes and occasionally display sexual dimorphism. For example, male fiddler crabs have a larger pincher, and male shrimp remain smaller than females. Higher crustacea undergo various larval stages and metamorphosis, similar to that of tadpoles. Most of these stages are planktonic; they make up a hefty proportion of the total mass of plankton. Advanced crustacea are capable of producing huge numbers of planktonic eggs.

What makes the crustacea (decapods) different from their numerous relatives? The species are not overly similar when you compare shrimp, crabs, and lobsters. The reason is the differently shaped anterior body (carapace), which is elongated posteriorly or significantly widened laterally. The specific characteristic of this order, however, is the 5 pairs of legs with 10 feet on the thorax. Now the common name ten-footed crustacea is better understandable. The layperson sometimes counts wrong, since the first pair of legs is often more developed, in many cases, such as lobsters, they have even been modified into claws. The Japanese sea spider, *Macrocheira kempferi,* is the largest known species of the approximately 10,000 decapods. With extended legs, this crustacean has a diameter of about 3 m and a shell length of 0.5 m. However, the majority of all decapods have a relatively "compact" body. These smaller crustacea are highly suited for both the marine aquarium and the photographer who uses macrolenses. Particularly small Decapoda from tropical seas tend to be much more attractively colored than their large relatives. Many decapods are so talented and enchanting that they make a mockery of invertebrates being called "lower animals."

Fam.: Hippolytidae

Members of the family Hippolytidae, the cleaner shrimp, are probably the most commonly imported shrimp of the marine aquarium hobby. The cleaner shrimp genus *Lysmata* is especially popular, not only because of the attractiveness of the species, but because they help other tankmates. What does a fish do when he is itching? He would like to scratch that itch if he could. But those possibilities are slim. This, in turn, makes him dependent on the help of other sea inhabitants to free him from disturbing parasites. Some wrasses specialize in cleaning large fishes; many juvenile coral reef fishes also clean.

However, it is also known that especially large and stationary-living species such as sea basses, groupers, and morays let themselves be cleaned by shrimp. These shrimp not only pick off skin parasites, they may even stroll into the mouth of large fishes to remove feed remains from between their teeth. Consequently, they have become known by the generic term "cleaner shrimp" and are recognized by underwater photographers as well as crustacea fans by this name. This group is made up of shrimp from different families, but they clean willing fish clients equally well. We are talking about shrimp from the genera *Lysmata, Leandrites*, *Periclimenes,* and *Stenopus*.

Members of the genus *Lysmata* are not only found in tropical seas, but also in temperate and cold waters. Two species are even found in the Mediterranean. Almost all are cleaners and are appreciated as such by their fish clientele. This means that a fish willing to be cleaned puts its predatory instincts aside and lets the juicy morsel do its job. Even on its palate!

Cleaning behavior from the genus *Saron*, commonly called marble shrimp, is unknown. Its species live much of the time secluded, often in coral debris, dark caves, or rock niches. Their sparkling body is frequently very enticingly colored. Species of the genus *Thor,* like the marble shrimp, are found in all tropical seas. Divers should search for them hiding around or in invertebrates. Anemones are particular favorites of this genus.

Cleaner Shrimp

MOLTING OF THE CLEANER SHRIMP *LYSMATA AMBOINENSIS*

The carapace of shrimp does not grow. When practicing husbandry of *Lysmata* shrimp, you sometimes witness molting, since they often molt in the open part of the aquarium. Not all details are known about this complex process. The following is a simplified version: prior to actual molting, the shell begins to separate from the epidermal cells underneath. Simultaneously, a liquid is secreted that dissolves part of the old shell. The freed calcium salts return to the blood. Part of the chitin is also dissolved in this manner and stored in the blood. A new skeleton forms beneath the old. When it is completed, the old skin usually ruptures along the top of the carapace and the animal crawls out of the old shell. After molting, the new shell is soft and folded. The shrimp now swells by taking in water, so much so that the new exoskeleton is stretched to its maximum. When the animal has finished stretching, the new exoskeleton begins to harden. The hardening is a result of protein transformation in the exoskeleton and the uptake of calcium salts from the blood. The calcium reservoir in the blood is then supplemented by heightened absorption of calcium salts from the seawater. Crustacea can only grow when molting because, the exoskeleton neither stretches nor grows after it hardens.

Fam.: Hippolytidae

Lysmata amboinensis　　　　　　　　　　　　　　　　　　　(DE MAN, 1888)
Indo-Pacific white-striped cleaner shrimp, ambon shrimp

Hab.: Entire Indo-Pacific, Red Sea.

Sex.: Not distinguishable from external characteristics.

Soc.B./Assoc.: These shrimp can be kept in small groups. They associate well with other aquarium residents.

M.: Reef aquarium with corresponding hiding places.

Light: Dim light.

B./Rep.: Possible when suitable feed (marine zooplankton) is available in sufficient amounts.

F.: O, FD; easily satisfied. Various frozen and dry foods are accepted.

S.: This species is the most imported cleaner shrimp throughout the world. It likes to clean various fish species in the aquarium. In their natural habitat, these shrimp are almost always found in pairs, but occasionally, groups of up to 100 individuals are encountered. This species is often called *Hippolysmata grabhami* in older literature (see below). Since it is very difficult to distinguish from *L. grabhami*, you should inquire at the time of purchase if the import came from the Indo-Pacific (= *L. amboinensis*) or the Atlantic (= *L. grabhami*).

T: 20°-27°C, **L:** 6 cm, **TL:** from 50 cm, **WM:** w, **WR:** b, **AV:** 1, **D:** 1-2

Lysmata grabhami　　　　　　　　　　　　　　　　　　　(GORDON, 1935)
Atlantic white-striped cleaner shrimp, Grabhami shrimp

Hab.: Entire tropical and warm temperate areas of the east and west Atlantic.

Sex.: Not distinguishable from external characteristics.

Soc.B./Assoc.: Can be kept singly, in pairs, or, even better, in small groups. Gets along well with other crustacea and fishes.

M.: Reef or rock aquarium with sufficient hiding places. Easily maintained.

Light: Dim light.

B./Rep.: This shrimp is regularly bred at American breeding facilities.

F.: O, FD; very easily satisfied. Feeds on practically anything; a wonderful scavenger.

S.: The old literature and aquarists often called this species *Hippolysmata grabhami*. Later, *L. amboinensis* and this species fell under the same name. These two species were just recently separated. Attempts to cross them were not successful, which speaks in favor of the independence of the two. They will clean fishes in the aquarium. Some have been kept for more than 3 years in captivity. Individuals originating from islands in the east Atlantic (Canary and Cape Verde) appear more graceful than those from the Caribbean.

T: 18°-26°C, **L:** 6 cm, **TL:** from 50 cm, **WM:** w, **WR:** b, **AV:** 2, **D:** 1

Exterior differences between *Lysmata amboinensis* (left) and *Lysmata grabhami* (right) can clearly be seen.

Lysmata amboinensis

Lysmata amboinensis cleans the angelfish *A. xanthotis*

Fam.: Hippolytidae

Lysmata californica
Catalina cleaner shrimp

(STIMPSON, 1866)

Hab.: West coast of North America.

Sex.: Not distinguishable from the exterior.

Soc.B./Assoc.: In their natural habitat they are found in groups of up to several hundred individuals.

M.: Provide a rock aquarium with dark areas. If possible, these shrimp should be kept in small groups.

Light: Dim light.

B./Rep.: Breeding is nonproblematic. Feed the newly hatched larvae with free-swimming marine rotifers, since the larvae are unable to eat small *Artemia* nauplii (also see *L. seticaudata*, p. 476).

F.: O, FD; frozen food, *Mysis, Artemia,* and dry foods. If housed with rapid-feeding fishes, they will need to be fed with a feeding tube.

S.: One of the few cleaner shrimp that comes from temperate seas. On the Californian coast these shrimp are often seen with moray eels, which they clean in their caves. However, since they are commonly seen without "cleaning clients," it is assumed that they are only facultative cleaners.

T: 10°-20°C, **L:** 4 cm, **TL:** from 50 cm, **WM:** w, **WR:** b, **AV:** 3, **D:** 1-2

Photo on opposite page:
In a rock crevice on the coast of California, two large moray eels live peacefully with hundreds of Catalina cleaner shrimp, *Lysmata californica*. The moray eels protect their guests from aggressive wrasses, and in exchange, the shrimp keep them clean of parasites.

Lysmata californica

Fam.: Hippolytidae

Lysmata debelius   BRUCE, 1983
Scarlet cleaner shrimp, blood shrimp

Hab.: In the Indo-Pacific among the Society Islands, Japan, and the Maldives. Animals from the Maldives have a somewhat different design than those from the Indonesian region.

Sex.: No external differences.

Soc.B./Assoc.: Best kept in pairs. They defend their territories but are otherwise peaceful towards invertebrates and small fishes.

M.: Reef aquarium with hiding places. Requires shaded overhangs. Several animals maintained together will lose their shyness faster than if kept singly.

Light: Dim light.

B./Rep.: Not known.

F.: O, FD; flake, live, and frozen foods. Broken tablet food (TetraTips) is readily taken. In large tanks they should be fed with a feeding tube.

S.: Although this species has been imported for a long time, it just recently became known to science. As a watchful aquarist, one of the two authors (H.D.) wanted to know the scientific name, collected some specimen off Philippine islands and sent them with uw-photos to a specialist who recognized it as a new species! It generally lives at depths of 20 m and below. In the aquarium, it is more timid, and its cleaning behavior is less pronounced than that of *L. amboinensis* or *L. grabhami*.
There are two more color morphs: the photo on p. 465 shows a specimen from the Maldives, the picture page 479 from the Line Islands, East Pacific.

T: 22°-28°C, **L:** 3 cm, **TL:** from 50 cm, **WM:** w, **WR:** b, **AV:** 1-2, **D:** 2

Lysmata debelius, scarlet cleaner shrimp

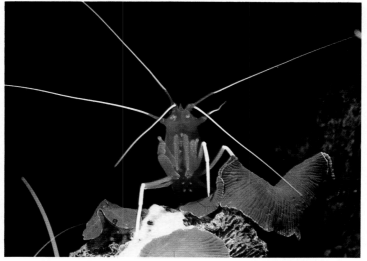

Lysmata debelius, see also page 479

Fam.: Hippolytidae

Lysmata galapagensis
Galapagos cleaner shrimp

SCHMITT, 1924

Hab.: West coast of South America, Galapagos Islands.

Sex.: No external differences.

Soc.B./Assoc.: Usually in pairs or small groups, rarely singly.

M.: Reef and rock aquarium with dark areas. These areas are their preferred habitat.

Light: Dim light.

B./Rep.: Not known.

F.: O, FD; flake and frozen foods.

S.: Little information is available about keeping this species in an aquarium.

T: 15°-20°C, **L:** 3 cm, **TL:** from 50 cm, **WM:** w, **WR:** b, **AV:** 4, **D:** 2

Lysmata galapagensis

Lysmata kükenthali
Kükenthal's cleaner shrimp

(DE MAN, 1902)

Hab.: Indian Ocean.

Sex.: No external differences.

Soc.B./Assoc.: Lives singly or in pairs.

M.: Reef aquarium with good hiding places which they rarely leave (unfortunately). Nocturnal.

Light: Dim light.

B./Rep.: Not known.

F.: O, FD; flake and frozen foods. Best given in small quantities prior to turning the lights off.

S.: Rarely imported.

T: 21°-27°C, **L:** 3-4 cm, **TL:** from 50 cm, **WM:** w, **WR:** b, **AV:** 3, **D:** 2

Lysmata kükenthali

Lysmata sp. from the southern coast of Australia

Fam.: Hippolytidae

Committed aquarists have successfully reproduced *Lysmata seticaudata* in an aquarium. Like other *Lysmata* species, this species sexually transforms from male to female. Conditions from their biotope were closely copied: hiding places were offered; the salinity was maintained. The attempt was made during their natural spawning season, the first months of summer. After fertilization, the eggs are attached to the abdomen between the swimmerets by mucus threads. At the end of embryonal development, the larvae are released. They still differed in body shape from the adult animal. After 25 to 35 days the young begin to look like miniature adults. There are three basic problems during rearing: maintaining clean aquarium water, procuring food, and providing sufficient nourishment during the night.

Lysmata seticaudata

Lysmata seticaudata (RISSO, 1816)
Monaco cleaner shrimp

Hab.: Mediterranean and northern temperate Atlantic.

Sex.: These shrimp undergo a sexual change during the course of their lives: they are initially ♂♂ and then convert to ♀♀. This is why functional ♀♀ are always larger than functional ♂♂.

Soc.B./Assoc.: Solitary animals or pairs are common, but an occasional group may be seen. They get along well with tankmates.

M.: Rock edifications with deep hiding places, where, unfortunately, they frequently retire.

Light: Dim light.

B./Rep.: Breeding has been accomplished by some aquarists. It is described in detail by BÜSCHER (Aquarien Magaz. 5/1982, pp. 311 ff.) or COUTURIER-BHAUD (Vie Milieu, 24, 1974, pp. 413 ff.). You have the greatest chance of success if you start with berried ♀♀ from the wild. In the Mediterranean, July is the best month for this. However, do not even attempt to raise these larvae if you do not have sufficient food.

F.: O, FD; easy to feed. Feeds on leftovers, and usually does not need to be fed separately.

S.: The only cleaner shrimp known from the Mediterranean. It was described scientifically just a few years ago (PATZNER: Helgol. Meeresunters. 35/1982, pp. 227 ff.). They are frequently observed cleaning moray eels, sometimes seen cleaning conger-eels, and only once seen cleaning a blenny. The shrimp that engage in cleaning activities always live with their host and do not lure their clients as most tropical cleaners do. Often, however, they are found without cleaner clients, which indicates that this species, like *L. californica*, is a facultative cleaner. It is common, but very fast and very difficult to capture with a hand net. A small wire basket baited with a piece of liver is significantly more effective. Transport is not difficult when they are well cooled, since the animals are sensitive to oxygen deficiency. This species is sensitive to changes in salinity, so use caution when transferring it into the aquarium. The other *Lysmata* species from the Mediterranean, *L. nilita*, has never been observed cleaning.

T: 15°-23°C, **L:** 4 cm, **TL:** from 50 cm, **WM:** w, **WR:** b, **AV:** 2, **D:** 1-2

Lysmata seticaudata with the moray eel *Murena helena*

The East Pacific distribution of *Lysmata debelius* (photo the Line Islands) shows red feet.

Fam.: Hippolytidae

Lysmata rathbunae   CHACE, 1970
Rathbun's cleaner shrimp

Hab.: East coast of North America, Caribbean.

Sex.: No external differences.

Soc.B./Assoc.: These shrimp live singly or in pairs and are peaceful towards their tankmates.

M.: Reef or rock aquarium with dark hiding places.

Light: Dim light.

B./Rep.: Not known.

F.: O, FD; flake and frozen foods.

S.: Not known.

T: 20°-24°C, **L:** 3 cm, **TL:** from 50 cm, **WM:** w, **WR:** b, **AV:** 2-3, **D:** 2

Lysmata rathbunae

Lysmata vittata   (STIMPSON, 1860)
Australian cleaner shrimp

Hab.: East coast of Australia.

Sex.: No external differences.

Soc.B./Assoc.: Lives singly or in pairs.

M.: Reef aquarium with a few hiding places. Since this species appreciates direct light, it can easily be observed in the aquarium.

Light: Sunlight to moderate light.

B./Rep.: Not known.

F.: O, FD; flake and frozen foods. These foods have to be administered with a feeding tube when there is competition from other tankmates.

S.: Not known.

T: 23°-28°C, **L:** 3-4 cm, **TL:** from 50 cm, **WM:** w, **WR:** b, **AV:** 3, **D:** 2

Lysmata vittata

Lysmata wurdemanni   (GIBBES, 1850)
Caribbean cleaner shrimp, peppermint shrimp, veined shrimp

Hab.: Caribbean to Brazil.

Sex.: No external differences.

Soc.B./Assoc.: Lives alone or in pairs. Often lives with sponges. Gets along well with other shrimp and small fishes.

M.: Reef aquarium with hiding places. It prefers vertical, pipe-shaped caves that are open at the top (pipe sponges in nature), but they are also content with crevices and small holes.

Light: Dim light.

B./Rep.: Regularly bred in the U.S.A. The larvae feed on free-swimming marine rotifers (e.g., *Brachionus*) at first. Later, *Artemia* nauplii are consumed.

F.: O, FD; flake and frozen foods.

S.: Although this is a commonly kept species in the U.S.A., it is rarely imported into Europe. It is mainly found in large pipe sponges of the Caribbean. They can live quite well without them in the aquarium.

T: 20°-26°C, **L:** 3-4 cm, **TL:** from 40 cm, **WM:** w, **WR:** b, **AV:** 2, **D:** 1-2

Lysmata wurdemanni

Fam.: Hippolytidae

Parhippolyte uveae
Sugar cane shrimp
(BORRADAILLE, 1899)

Hab.: Entire Indo-Pacific region.

Sex.: No visible differences.

Soc.B./Assoc.: Lives singly, in pairs, or in small groups.

M.: You should ask your dealer the origin of the import. Animals from Hawaii search for hiding places protected from light, while those from east Africa also venture into strongly illuminated areas.

Light: Sunlight or dim light.

B./Rep.: Not known.

F.: O, FD; tablet, flake, and frozen foods.

S.: Although animals imported from Hawaii largely prefer to remain hidden as they do in nature, they are a more intense red than those coming from the tidal pools of Kenya. However, the latter are more often visible in the aquarium. Their common name is derived from the cross-stripes which resemble sugar cane trunks.

T: 22°-27°C, **L:** 3 cm, **TL:** from 40 cm, **WM:** w, **WR:** b, **AV:** 2, **D:** 2-3

Parhippolyte uveae

Saron marmoratus
Common, marble shrimp
(OLIVIER, 1811)

Hab.: Entire Indo-Pacific, form Hawaii to the Red Sea.

Sex.: The first pair of walking legs are elongated in full-grown ♂♂. ♀♀ have strong pinchers, but they are much shorter. In addition, ♂♂ have large bunches of bristles on the upper side of the body, and the abdomen is more upwardly convex.

Soc.B./Assoc.: They are almost always in pairs, rarely found singly. Although these shrimp are peaceful, towards other crustacea and fishes, two animals of the same sex in an aquarium will usually fight till death.

M.: Reef aquarium with sufficient hiding places. Coarse coral gravel where the animals can hide.

Light: Dim light.

B./Rep.: Not known.

F.: O, FD; frozen food, *Artemia,* and *Mysis.* At first these shrimp will need to be fed at night. After a certain acclimation period, they will also venture out during the day.

S.: This species is the most frequently imported marble shrimp. The genus is easy to recognize by their particular bristle bunches. In their natural habitat, they are usually found in protected lagoons of fringe reefs where they hide in the coarse coral gravel. Occasionally they are found among the long thorns of diadematid sea urchins. Since these shrimp are nocturnal, they are rarely seen in the aquarium at first. Only after an extended acclimation will they appear during the day. Their color change is interesting: the diurnal coloration is a marble brown; their nocturnal coloration is a bright red.

T: 22°-28°C, **L:** 4 cm, **TL:** from 50 cm, **WM:** w, **WR:** b, **AV:** 1, **D:** 1-2

Parhippolyte uveae

Saron marmoratus ♂

Saron marmoratus ♀, see text on previous page

Saron rectirostris ♀

Saron rectirostris ♂

Saron rectirostris   HAYASHI, 1984
Purple-leg marble shrimp

Hab.: Indo-Australian region.

Sex.: The first pair of walking legs in full-grown ♂ ♂ is elongated.

Soc.B./Assoc.: Can be kept singly but does better in pairs. Gets along with other shrimp and fishes, but do not place in tanks that contain live corals.

M.: Use a reef aquarium with hiding places. Rarely seen during the day.

Light: Dim light.

B./Rep.: Not known.

F.: O, FD; frozen food, *Artemia*. Should only be fed after turning off the illumination, since they only leave their hiding places at night.

S.: This species is not suitable for aquaria with live coral. Nocturnal animals.

T: 21°-26°C, **L:** 3-4 cm, **TL:** from 40 cm, **WM:** w, **WR:** b, **AV:** 3, **D:** 2

Fam.: Hippolytidae

Saron inermis ♂

Saron inermis　　　　　　　　　　　　　　　　　　　HAYASHI, 1983
Pine cone marble shrimp

Hab.: Indo-Pacific and tropical Australia.

Sex.: The ♂'s abdomen is darker, and the first pair of walking legs is longer (see picture).

Soc.B./Assoc.: Singly or in pairs. As the illustration on the right shows, several individuals can be housed in one tank. Good companions for other crustacea, even congeners.

M.: Reef aquarium with sufficient hiding places.

Light: Dim light.

B./Rep.: Not known.

F.: O, FD; frozen food, *Artemia*, and tablets. If the animals do not appear during the day, feed only after the lights are turned off.

S.: This species was described in 1984 by HAYASHI of Japan. A German aquarist who was unable to identify the shrimp sent him several specimens. It differs from other *Saron* species by its color pattern, shorter rostrum, and smaller body. The species has smaller bristle bunches on its back than most other *Saron* species.

T: 22°-27°C, **L:** 3 cm, **TL:** from 40 cm, **WM:** w, **WR:** b, **AV:** 2-3, **D:** 1-2

Saron inermis ♀ ♀

Fam.: Hippolytidae

DE MAN, 1902

Saron neglectus
Green marble shrimp

Hab.: Indo-Pacific.

Sex.: The first pair of walking legs on the ♂ is significantly longer than that of the ♀.

Soc.B./Assoc.: Singly or in pairs, but never in groups. They get along well with other crustacea and fish species.

M.: Reef aquarium with corresponding hiding places.

Light: Dim light.

B./Rep.: Unknown.

F.: O, FD; frozen food, *Artemia,* and *Mysis.* It will have to be fed with a feeding tube if housed with tankmates that beat them to the food.

S.: The dark ocelli on the posterior body and the tail fan are prominent. It is not clear whether or not they are designed to mimic the eyes of a larger animal and, by doing so, act as a defense. Such ocelli are known from a number of other crustacea and also from fishes and insects. However, with few exceptions, it has not been investigated whether or not they really are a defense or only a color pattern.

T: 21°-27°C, **L:** 3 cm, **TL:** from 50 cm, **WM:** w, **WR:** b, **AV:** 2-3, **D:** 2

Saron neglectus

Saron sp.
Starlet marble shrimp

Hab.: Indonesia.

Sex.: As in all the species of the genus *Saron*, here, too, the first pair of walking legs of the ♂♂ is longer than that of the ♀♀.

Soc.B./Assoc.: They live singly or in pairs and are amiable towards other crustacea and fishes.

M.: Reef aquarium with corresponding hiding places.

Light: Dim light.

B./Rep.: Not known.

F.: O, FD; frozen food, *Artemia,* and *Mysis.*

S.: This marble shrimp has only been imported since 1980. They are nocturnal animals, but have been known to venture from their hiding places during the day after a proper acclimation period has passed.

T: 22°-27°C, **L:** 3 cm, **TL:** from 50 cm, **WM:** w, **WR:** b, **AV:** 3, **D:** 2

Saron neglectus

Saron sp.

Fam.: Hippolytidae

Thor amboinensis
Squat anemone shrimp
(DE MAN, 1888)

Hab.: Found throughout the tropical Indo-Pacific region.

Sex.: No external differences.

Soc.B./Assoc.: Different sized animals live in small groups. Compatible with other crustacea and fishes. They usually live with anemones (e.g., *Heteractis*). Sometimes they are found on an anemone with anemone shrimp of the genus *Periclimenes* (p. 524).

M.: If possible, they should always be housed with an anemone. It prefers flat disc-shaped anemones, but other species that lie horizontal on the substrate will be accepted.

Light: Dim light.

B./Rep.: Not known.

F.: O, FD; frozen food, dry food is occasionally accepted. Does not need to be fed specifically, since there is enough food for the shrimp from the food given to the anemone.

S.: They inhabit the shallow water and like to stay on or directly beside various anemones, including tube anemones. On the latter they do not sit among the tentacles but on the outside of the tube. This species is easily recognized by their coloration and the characteristic way their posterior body is held higher than the head. They often preform whipping motions with their abdomen.

T: 22°-27°C, **L:** 2 cm, **TL:** from 40 cm, **WM:** w, **WR:** b, **AV:** 1-2, **D:** 2

Tozeuma sp.
Pipefish shrimp

Hab.: Southern coast of Australia.

Sex.: No external differences.

Soc.B./Assoc.: Singly or in small groups. They get along well with other species.

M.: Reef or rock aquarium. A few hiding places are needed.

Light: Moderate light.

B./Rep.: Not known.

F.: O, FD; frozen food, *Artemia*, and *Mysis*.

S.: Lives in algae and seagrass lawns. Their eyelike design on the end of their abdomen and their elongated shape closely resembles a pipefish. This impression is enhanced because the shrimp often moves backwards. Detailed studies about this mimicry behavior have not been undertaken. It is suspected that they clean fishes in their natural habitat, but this could not be confirmed.

T: 16°-20°C, **L:** 4 cm, **TL:** from 60 cm, **WM:** w, **WR:** b, **AV:** 3-4, **D:** 2-3

Thor amboinensis

Tozeuma sp.

Fam.: Alpheidae

Members of the family Alpheidae, the pistol shrimp, have two morphological features that separates them from other shrimp. First, the eyes are on very short eyestalks and are recessed under their carapace which makes them less noticeable and gives the shrimp a "sleepy" appearance. Second, one pincher of the shrimp is enlarged and capable of generating sound. The sound has been compared to that of a pistol shot and is produced when the claw opens and closes. Whether above or below the water, the sound can be clearly heard by the human ear (see p. 498).

Pistol shrimp are widely distributed. Most species live in tropical waters of the three oceans, a few in the Mediterranean, but only two species live in the North Sea. Their vertical distribution extends from the shallow waters to the deep sea, where at times they grow quite large. The best known genera of the family Alpheidae are *Alpheus, Synalpheus,* and *Athanas.* Only the first two reach the aquarium trade. *Athanas* species are very small and plainly colored.

The behavior of those *Alpheus* pistol shrimp that live in symbiotic relationship with gobies is notorious. Such symbiotic relationships, however, have only developed in warmer seas. It is hypothesized that the poorly seeing pistol shrimp are informed about dangers by the partner fishes in front of their common cave entrance. Studies in marine aquaria have shown that pistol shrimp are in constant contact with the gobies. The advantage to the fishes from this symbiotic relationship is obvious: they use the caves built and maintained by the pistol shrimp and are protected therein from approaching predators.

However, most pistol shrimp lead a "normal" lifestyle and sit pairwise by the thousands in the tropical coral reefs without contact to other inhabitants. Since they live a very secluded life, sometimes it escapes notice that pistol shrimp are by far the most common family of shrimp along the reef. Like all nonpredatory marine inhabitants, they also feed by the rule "everything good comes from above." In other words, falling detritus and microorganisms are eaten from the bottom.

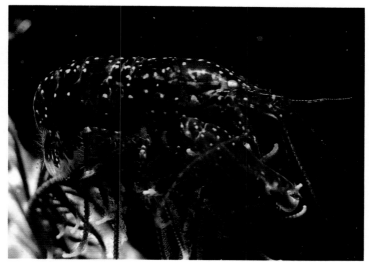

Synalpheus sp.

Alpheus sp.

Fam.: Alpheidae

Alpheus bisincisu   DE HAAN, 1850

Hab.: Indian Ocean, Red Sea, Japan.

Sex.: It is not known if ♂♂ have larger pinchers than ♀♀, as is found in *A. randalli.*

Soc.B./Assoc.: These animals live singly with one or two gobies and dig a cave to house themselves and their goby partner(s). These shrimp continue their symbiotic relationship in the aquarium. The pictured goby is *Istigobius ornatus.*

M.: The aquarium should have coral debris and a rock cave. Caution—the shrimp can bring rockwork tumbling down with their digging.

Light: Dim light.

B./Rep.: Not known.

F.: O, FD; tablet, dry, and frozen foods.

S.: These organisms are photophobic and require an extended period of time to become accustomed to aquarium illumination. The partnership between pistol shrimp and gobies is a true symbiosis in which both partners benefit from the association: the goby warns the shrimp, who has poor eyesight, of predators, while the shrimp constantly maintains the cave in which they both live. In Japan, this species lives in a cave with a pair of *Apocryptodon bleekeri* gobies. TAKEMURA & MIZUME (Bull.Fac.Fish. Nagasaki, 26; 1968, pp. 37 ff.) provide a detailed description of how this shrimp generates sound with its claw (see p. 498).

T: 21°-26°C, **L:** 3 cm, **TL:** from 60 cm, **WM:** w, **WR:** b, **AV:** 3, **D:** 2-3

Alpheus djeddensis   COUTIERE, 1897
Djibouti pistol shrimp

Hab.: Entire Indo-Pacific and Red Sea.

Sex.: It is not known if ♂♂ have larger pinchers than ♀♀, as is found in *A. randalli.*

Soc.B./Assoc.: A pair of these shrimp lives in caves with various goby species. They are pictured with *Amblyeleotris steinitzi* (right) and with *A. wheeleri* (p. 496, top right).

M.: Provide rubble, a sandy bottom and shell debris with a rock cave where the crustacean and the goby can retire. If a suitable cave is not available, the shrimp will dig in the sand. If a flat stone is lying on a sandy bottom, they will usually place their tunnels beneath it. Caution—they may prey on small fishes and shrimp.

Light: Moderate light.

B./Rep.: Not known.

F.: O, FD; dry and frozen foods, which usually have to be delivered with forceps or a feeding tube. They readily pull on algae.

S.: *A. djiboutensis* is a synonym of DE MAN, 1909. In their natural habitat they are often found in shallow water. However, since these shrimp are highly skittish and cautious of divers, they are difficult to see and photograph. They quickly become accustomed to an observer in an aquarium. Their relationship with the gobies is considered to be a true symbiosis.

T: 22°-27°C, **L:** 3 cm, **TL:** from 60 cm, **WM:** w, **WR:** b, **AV:** 2, **D:** 2-3

494

Alpheus bisincisu together with the goby *Istigobius ornatus*

Alpheus djeddensis

Fam.: Alpheidae

Alpheus sp.

Alpheus djeddensis with A. wheeleri

Alpheus sp.

Alpheus randalli
Randall's pistol shrimp

BANNER, 1981

Hab.: Indo-Pacific.

Sex.: The ♂♂ usually have a larger "pistol" pincher than ♀♀.

Soc.B./Assoc.: These shrimp normally live in pairs with a goby in a cave. Here *Alpheus randalli* is pictured with an undescribed goby of the genus *Amblyeleotris* at Bali/Indonesia.

M.: Coral gravel and coarse sand substrates with caves. They like to dig under stones they find laying on the sand.

Light: Moderate light.

B./Rep.: Not known.

F.: O, FD; flake and frozen foods.

S.: Lives together with various gobies of the genera *Amblyeleotris* and *Stenogobius*. Although a pair of shrimp live together in the cave, usually only one of the two is visible. However, it cannot be assumed that all *Alpheus* species live symbiotically with gobies. Most species found in tropical and temperate seas live singly or in pairs in narrow rock cervices, within sponges, etc. *A. armatus,* a Caribbean species, is an obligatory symbiont to the anemone *Bartholomea annulata.* According to research on various Japanese species of *Alpheus* by TAKEMURA & MIZUE (Bull. Fac. Fish. Nagasaki, 26, 1968, pp. 37 ff.), these shrimp are responsible for the constant knocking sounds that are especially audible in the upper water strata of tropical seas. The duration of the sound is about 18 milliseconds, and the frequency is above 7 kHz. The bang frequency of one individual is less than 1 second. The origin of this sound is described on page 498.

T: 22°-28°C, **L:** 3 cm, **TL:** from 50 cm, **WM:** w, **WR:** b, **AV:** 3, **D:** 2

Fam.: Alpheidae

Alpheus strenuus   DANA, 1852
Snowflake pistol shrimp

Hab.: Eastern Pacific, Hawaii.

Sex.: It is not known if ♂ ♂ have larger pinchers than ♀ ♀, as is found in *A. randalli*.

Soc.B./Assoc.: Loner.

M.: They need caves and overhangs as hiding places; however, they do not need a sandy bottom.

Light: Dim light.

B./Rep.: Not known.

F.: O, FD; frozen food, krill, and tablets.

S.: Since the animals are loners, they should not be kept with conspecifics in the same tank. Like most pistol shrimp, they may prey on small shrimp at night.

T: 22°-27°C, **L:** 4 cm, **TL:** from 60 cm, **WM:** w, **WR:** b, **AV:** 3, **D:** 2-3

Alpheus sp.
Pistol shrimp

Hab.: Indo-Australian region.

Sex.: It is not known if ♂ ♂ have larger pinchers than ♀ ♀, as do some *Alpheus* species.

Soc.B./Assoc.: These shrimp live in pairs in a symbiotic relationship with gobies.

M.: They need sand and rock caves.

Light: Dim light.

B./Rep.: Not known.

F.: O, FD; frozen food, *Artemia*, and *Mysis*. Food has to be delivered to them with a feeding tube.

S.: Lives in pairs, either in rock caves or, much more commonly, on muddy bottoms where they dig tunnels. They live together with the goby *Amblyeleotris gymnocephala*. This species is primarily nocturnal. Often times the sounds it produces are the only evidence the animal is alive. The source of these bang sounds is explained on the bottom of this page.

T: 22°-27°C, **L:** 3 cm, **TL:** from 60 cm, **WM:** w, **WR:** b, **AV:** 3-4, **D:** 2-3

Ordinarily the left pincher in pistol shrimp is very enlarged. If it is lost in the course of a fight, it is regenerated. Since the claw regenerates a bit with each molt, the undamaged right pincher is adapted into a pistol pincher and the left pincher remains small. The large pincher is used to produce the bang that is so typical of this family. The pinchers of decapoda have a static (propodus) and a movable (dactylus) part. The dactylus has an appendage which exactly fits into an indention in the propodus. When a sudden muscle tension closes the pincher, a strong stream of water is ejected. A loud bang or knocking sound reminiscent of breaking glass results. Quite a few aquarists have jumped up in alarm expecting to find a broken aquarium, only to remember the presence of the pistol shrimp. The same sound occurs again when the pincher is opened. The opening and closing occurs in alternate intervals of about 1 second. TAKEMURA and MIZUE have documented the process in detail (Bull.Fac.Fish. Nagasaki, 26, 1968, pp. 37 ff.). The stream of water serves both as defense and a weapon. They reportedly use the water jet to prey on small fishes and shrimp.

Alpheus strenuus

Alpheus sp.

Fam.: Alpheidae

Alpheus sp.

Hab.: Indo-Pacific, in tropical as well as warm temperate regions.

Sex.: It is unknown whether or not ♂ ♂ and ♀ ♀ have pinchers of different size.

Soc.B./Assoc.: These shrimp live singly or in pairs. So far it is unknown if this species lives with gobies.

M.: Provide a sandy bottom and rockwork with hiding places.

Light: Dim light.

B./Rep.: Not known.

F.: O, FD; frozen food, tablets and, occasionally, algae. They usually do not need to be fed with a feeding tube, since they readily eat leftovers and detritus at night.

S.: Because this species has a very retiring lifestyle, there is a paucity of information about its biology.

T: 18°-22°C, **L:** 3 cm, **TL:** from 60 cm, **WM:** w, **WR:** b, **AV:** 4, **D:** 2-3

Alpheus sp.

Alpheus sp.

Alpheus sp.

Fam.: Gnathophyllidae

Members of the family Gnathophyllidae, the harlequin shrimp, are extremely stout, short, and broad bodied. The rostrum is usually small and barely reaches beyond the eyes. The second pair of walking legs is clearly larger than the first. In the genus *Hymenocera,* these legs may even be twice the length of the carapace.

The family Gnathophyllidae is divided into 4 genera. Of these 4, only *Gnathophyllum* and *Hymenocera* are familiar to aquarists. A little is known about the living customs of the Mediterranean species *Gnathophyllum elegans*: the brown to red colored shrimp inhabits hard substrates and has been seen in bare caves or free rock formations in water depths as shallow as 1 m. However, the tropical species, of which *G. americanum* is the best known, live in dead coral stalks and feed off detritus. They are all solitary animals that have never been observed in community with other crustacea. Since the anatomy of harlequin shrimp of the genus *Hymenocera* is not easily discernible, let it be noted again that they have 5 pairs of legs on their thorax like all Decapoda, even if they look different. The last segment of the first pair is shaped like a tweezer. It is usually covered by the second tweezerlike pair of legs which is proximally flaplike widened. The following 3 pairs of legs are exclusively for locomotion. The head of all *Hymenocera* shrimp seems to consists of appendages of the anterior edge of the thorax, out of which the first antennae are particularly protrusive. These shrimp are notorious for their flag-shaped widening on the shaftlike basal segment of the antennae which they constantly swing back and forth. The eyes next to them are stalked and can move in all directions. The second pair of antennae is thread-thin and translucent. These lie along the side of the carapace.

Hardly any other ten-footed crustacean has been so intensely observed by behaviorists as the harlequin shrimp *Hymenocera elegans*, especially by the Max Planck Institute for Behavioral Physiology in Seewiesen/Bavaria. "Will a shrimp save the Australian Barrier Reef?" was a headline which came about from the research. Since it was observed that this harlequin shrimp killed the starfish *Acanthaster planci,* a lot of attention was generated by regions that have this starfish. Why? This starfish, commonly called the crown-of-thorns starfish, had reproduced epidemically in several parts of the Indo-Pacific. The animals fed on coral polyps and had managed to eat some sites on the reef absolutely bare. Since the dead reef zone is avoided by other organisms and destroyed by wave action, it was feared that a catastrophe was imminent. The only potential enemy of the crown-of-thorns, the large triton snail, had been decimated to a large extent by shell collectors. The hope was that the harlequin shrimp could come to the rescue of the coral reefs. This belief was based on a film by the Max Planck Institute which showed the following:

A *Hymenocera* female runs towards a small *Acanthaster* starfish, climbs on top of it, and searches the surface with its tiny first pincher for a wound. The starfish continues to crawl about and climbs on a stone. Now the male shrimp enters the picture, and both it and the female try to turn the starfish over. The male sits on an arm of the starfish and lifts the arm and itself by pushing against the bottom with the anterior edges of the large pinchers. The feeding pinchers now enter into the ampullae channel that runs along the bottom of the starfish arm. As a consequence, the tube feet pull back and release their hold on the bottom. While the shrimp keeps pushing, the starfish continues to crawl, but the shrimp matches it step for step, always lifting with its large pinchers. Finally it turns the crown-of-thorns over. The starfish tries to right itself and extends its ampullae. But both shrimp grab it and pull out a long intestinal segment from a wound they have made on the starfish. This is guided to their mouth and torn with their sharp feeding pinchers. Later, additional pieces of tissue are sawed off and eaten from the disintegrating starfish.

However, *Hymenocera* were never used against the *Acanthaster* plague. Not only are they much too rare, but they prefer other starfish when they are hungry. Further research by the Australian government showed that the crown-of-thorns plague was locally limited, and the danger to infested reefs remained lower than first feared. In addition, drilling samples from the barrier reef revealed that there must have been previous mass propagations of *Acanthaster* over geological time which the reef has survived. You can see how careful the term "catastrophe" has to be used, since what seems to be a disaster may in fact be nothing more than part of a natural cycle.

Fam.: Gnathophyllidae

Gnathophyllum americanum   GUERIN, 1857
Striped harlequin shrimp

Hab.: Widely distributed in the tropical Indo-Pacific, from Japan to Hawaii and Australia.

Sex.: The ♂♂ have chelipeds that are significantly longer than those of the ♀♀.

Soc.B./Assoc.: These shrimp live singly or in pairs. They get along well with other tankmates. Often together with echinoderms such as short-spined sea urchins and sea cucumbers (e.g., *Paracucumaria tricolor*).

M.: Provide a reef or rock aquarium with good hiding places. Although not necessary, you can provide a host.

Light: Dim light.

B./Rep.: Not known.

F.: C; various frozen foods. Otherwise, they primarily feed on the tube feet of echinoderms.

S.: This species can be easily distinguished by its characteristic striations. It has a broad depth distribution. They can be found both in the tidal zones as well as in deep reefs with large rocks. They have been observed there at times living with starfish, sea cucumbers, and sea urchins. Various color morphs are known which vary with the habitat. Morphs that come from profound depths are less intensely colored. In the aquarium these animals are initially shy and timid, but they soon learn to search for food. This species is a relatively common aquarium animal.

T: 21°-26°C, **L:** 2-3 cm, **TL:** from 60 cm, **WM:** w, **WR:** b, **AV:** 1, **D:** 2-3

Gnathophyllum panamense   FAXON, 1893
Panama harlequin shrimp

Hab.: Caribbean.

Sex.: ♂♂ have longer chelipeds than ♀♀.

Soc.B./Assoc.: Not known.

M.: They prefer rockwork with sufficient hiding places.

Light: Dim light.

B./Rep.: Not known.

F.: C (O?); chopped frozen foods.

S.: Not known.

T: 22°-26°C, **L:** 2-3 cm, **TL:** from 50 cm, **WM:** w, **WR:** b, **AV:** 3, **D:** 2-3

Gnathophyllum sp

Gnathophyllum panamense

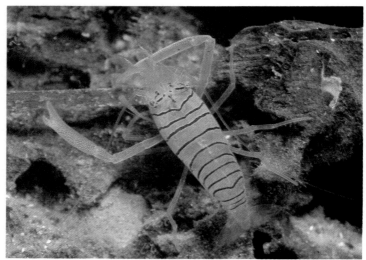

Gnathophyllum americanum

Gnathophyllum elegans, Mediterranean (no text)

Hymenocera picta
Eastern harlequin shrimp

DANA, 1852

Hab.: Central Pacific.

Sex.: ♂ ♂ are smaller than ♀ ♀. The ♀ ♀ have a pronounced dorsal spot on each of the first abdominal body segments. The second body flap on the ♂ is pale or colorless. The ♀'s abdominal legs are blue tipped, while those of the ♂'s are transparent.

Soc.B./Assoc.: These shrimp live in pairs and should only be kept as such. Like *H. elegans*, the ♀ releases a scent. These two species are two of the few invertebrates that recognize their partner as an individual. Do not keep with echinoderms (except as food).

M.: Reef aquarium with corresponding cover.

Light: Moderate light.

B./Rep.: These animals were bred in the framework of the previously mentioned research. The difficulty in this endeavor, as with all shrimp, lies in acquiring food for the larvae.

F.: C (feeding specialist!); these shrimp feed exclusively on echinoderms. Though they primarily feed on starfish, they will also consume some species of sea urchins. They can be fed *Asterias rubens* and *A. vulgaris,* two starfish from the North Sea. Be sure to remove them after they die so that the water is not fouled.

S.: *H. picta* differs from *H. elegans* by its intense red coloration. ♂ ♂ and ♀ ♀ accompany each other when hunting.

T: 24°-29°C, **L:** 3 cm, **TL:** from 60 cm, **WM:** w, **WR:** b, **AV:** 1, **D:** 3-4

Fam.: Gnathophyllidae

Hymenocera elegans HELLER, 1861
Western harlequin shrimp

Hab.: Red Sea and the Indian Ocean to Indonesia.

Sex.: ♂♂ are larger than ♀♀. See *H. picta* for additional differences.

Soc.B./Assoc.: These shrimp live pairwise in their natural habitat, and they should always be kept in pairs in the aquarium. Under no circumstances should two animals of the same sex be kept in the same aquarium. The ♀♀ release a sexual lure (pheromone) that allows the ♂ to recognize specific individuals! Do not house with starfishes or sea urchins.

M.: Needs a reef aquarium with hiding places where the pair can retire.

Light: Moderate light.

B./Rep.: Can be bred like *H. picta.*

F.: C (feeding specialist!); their natural food is starfish. They rarely accept other foods in an aquarium. Only persons that can procure starfish (e.g., *Asterias rubens*) every once in a while should keep these animals.

S.: This species is more brownish than *H. picta*. Like *H. picta*, it only feeds on echinoderms (see p. 504).

T: 22°-28°C, **L:** 3 cm, **TL:** from 60 cm, **WM:** w,
WR: b, **AV:** 3, **D:** 3-4

H. picta, Photo off Mani, Hawaii

Hymenocera picta, Indonesia

Hymenocera elegans, aquarium

Fam.: Palaemonidae
Subfam.: Palaemoninae

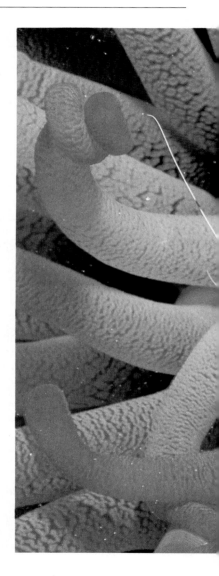

The clown anemone shrimp, *Periclimenes yucatanicus*, likes to live among the tentacles of the anemone *Condylactis gigantea*.

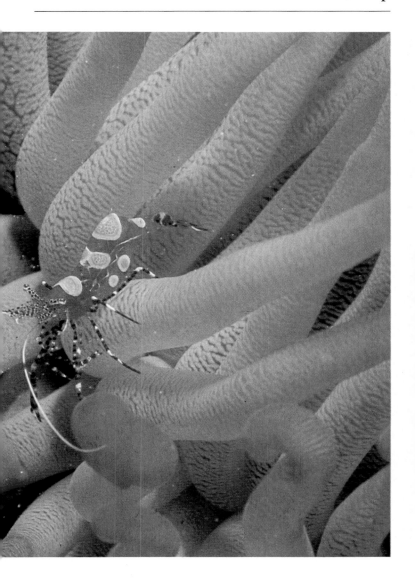

Fam.: Palaemonidae

The species-rich family Palaemonidae is divided into two subfamilies, the rock shrimp (Palaemoninae) and the anemone shrimp (Pontoniinae). Rock shrimp principally come from temperate or cold water, while anemone shrimp mainly live in tropical seas. When you look closely, you can see droves of the almost transparent rock shrimp on all of the Mediterranean's rocky coasts to the shallow water zones. Juveniles spend the entire day searching for food; however, larger specimens stay in the shade of rock walls and caves during the bright daylight hours. They are easily recognized by their long rostrum (forehead appendage) that is serrated on both the dorsal and ventral edges.

In contrast, anemone shrimp are, with few exceptions, commensals. That is, they live in constant, obligatory, non-parasitic community with other animals. Commensalism is not limited to shrimp; other crustacea practice this interspecific relationship. It is the main factor in increasing species diversity on coral reefs. Many sessile invertebrates, largely anemones and other coelenterate species, offer niches for commensals that are absent for the most part in temperate waters. Anemone shrimp can adapt perfectly to the color of their host animal to take optimal advantage of these niches. The color pattern of their host can be exactly matched. This is the result of the way several types of chromatophores, special epidermal cells which contain various pigments, are distributed. Through expansion and contraction, these chromatophores can increase or decrease the intensity of their coloration and, by doing so, change the overall appearance of the animal. A much used example, which is looked at in detail in this chapter, is the anemone shrimp, *Periclimenes imperator*, which appears totally different on a sea cucumber host than it does on a feather star or a nudibranch. But whatever its outward dress, it is the same species, of course.

More recent research by BIRKHOLZ (Das Aquarium, 7/1989) questions the common name "anemone shrimp" for members of the subfamily Pontoniinae, since he discovered two Mediterranean species (*P. scriptus* and *P. amethysteus*) that nibble on their host anemone. Therefore, they should be designated parasites rather than commensals. It has not yet been investigated to what extent this applies to *P. yucatanicus* or other tropical species, if at all.

Palaemon elegans
Glass prawn

RATHKE, 1837

Hab.: Mediterranean, eastern Atlantic.

Sex.: No external differences.

Soc.B./Assoc.: Maintain these animals singly or in groups. May nibble on delicate tankmates and even fishes.

M.: *P. elegans* is a content, undemanding species. They can tolerate large temperature and salinity fluctuations. This species is conditionally suitable for a coral tank.

Light: Sunlight.

B./Rep.: Can be successfully bred as described for *P. serratus* (p. 518). The larvae are positively phototactic (swim towards light) and will feed on finely ground dry foods that drift in the water. The spawning season in the Adriatic Sea is from May to August; they spawn from June to September in the western Mediterranean.

F.: O, FD; an omnivore that consumes all leftovers.

S.: Still known to many by the name *Leander squilla*. There are several similar species in the same distribution area of the Mediterranean. Because this species is extremely robust and transparent, they are appreciated experimental animals. They like to nibble on legs of swimmers and hands of aquarists; however, they have not been observed acting as cleaners.

T: 10°-23°C, **L:** 5 cm, **TL:** from 30 cm, **WM:** w, **WR:** b, **AV:** 2, **D:** 1

Fam.: Palaemonidae
Subfam.: Palaemoninae

Palaemon intermedius (STIMPSON, 1860)

Hab.: Australia.

Sex.: No visible differences.

Soc.B./Assoc.: Keep singly or in small groups. A rather shy shrimp that is easily housed with other tankmates.

M.: Do not have special demands. They like current.

Light: Moderate light.

B./Rep.: Not known.

F.: O, FD; omnivorous and an excellent scavenger when it is not being dominated by aggressive tankmates.

S.: Lives in seagrass lawns in shallow bay waters that have relatively strong tidal currents. A robust aquarium animal which is rarely imported into Europe, even though it is an appreciated addition to Australian aquaria.

T: 18°-24°C, **L:** 3-4 cm, **TL:** from 60 cm, **WM:** m-s, **WR:** b, **AV:** 3, **D:** 1-2

Palaemon intermedius

Palaemon intermedius

Palaemon intermedius

Fam.: Palaemonidae
Subfam.: Palaemoninae

Palaemon serenus   (HELLER, 1862)
Yellow-spotted glass shrimp

Hab.: Southern Australia.

Sex.: ♂♂ have longer chelipeds than ♀♀.

Soc.B./Assoc.: They live singly as well as in larger groups and are compatible with other small aquarium inhabitants.

M.: While these animals have no special requirements, they may retire into hiding places for extended periods of time, especially during acclimation.

Light: Moderate light.

B./Rep.: Not known.

F.: O, FD; an omnivore that is an excellent scavenger.

S.: They live in rocky regions as well as in seagrass lawns. These, like other representatives of this subfamily, are appreciated scavengers. But because other *Palaemon* are easier to capture, this species is rarely imported into Europe.

T: 10°-24°C, **L:** 4 cm, **TL:** from 40 cm, **WM:** w, **WR:** b, **AV:** 3, **D:** 1-2

Palaemon serratus

Palaemon serenus

Fam.: Palaemonidae
Subfam.: Palaemoninae

Palaemon serratus, also see top of p. 520

Palaemon serratus   (PENNANT, 1777)
Common prawn

Hab.: Mediterranean, temperate eastern Atlantic, e.g., coast of Ireland.

Sex.: No visible external differences.

Soc.B./Assoc.: Maintain singly or in groups. Sensitive tankmates may be disturbed by their constant searching and pulling.

M.: No special requirements. Temperature and salinity can vary greatly. Though 10° to 25°C is the suggested range, values both significantly below and above are tolerated for a short time. Therefore, it is well suited also for tropical tanks.

Light: Sunlight.

B./Rep.: Relatively simple. The greatest chance of success is with freshly caught berried ♀♀. These shrimp usually spawn twice a year in the Mediterranean. In the Adriatic Sea they spawn from May to June and from August to September; in the western Mediterranean they spawn from January to March and from August to November. Algae collected from tidal pools and placed in shallow vats under strong illumination will produce planktonic food for the larvae. After a short time, crumbled flake food can be fed. These shrimp will often breed unnoticed in the aquarium or the filter box.

F.: O, FD; they are easily satisfied omnivores and excellent scavengers.

S.: The older name, *Leander serratus,* is no longer valid. There are several similar species in the Mediterranean. They are differentiated based on their rostrum and the development of the first pair of walking legs. Since the animals like to inhabit tidal pools and are also found in more polluted regions, they are some of the most robust aquarium animals. Transport is simple, even wet rags are sufficient. Occasionally, animals caught in the open water will be infested with parasitic isopods; however, these parasites will not spread to any other aquarium inhabitants.

T: 10°-25°C, **L:** 6 cm, **TL:** from 30 cm, **WM:** w, **WR:** b, **AV:** 2, **D:** 1

Palaemon xiphias
Glass prawn

RISSO, 1816

Hab.: Mediterranean.

Sex.: No external differences.

Soc.B./Assoc.: Keep singly or in small groups.

M.: This is a robust aquarium animal that has no special requirements.

Light: Sunlight.

B./Rep.: Not known; however, breeding this species should be as easy as breeding the other Mediterranean species, *Palaemon elegans* and *P. serratus*. Spawning season in the Adriatic Sea is from May to June, while spawning extends from June to September in the western Mediterranean.

F.: O, FD; omnivore.

S.: This species has a lifestyle similar to *P. elegans*.

T: 10°-24°C, **L:** 6 cm, **TL:** from 40 cm, **WM:** w, **WR:** b, **AV:** 2, **D:** 1

Fam.: Palaemonidae
Subfam.: Pontoniinae

Palaemon serratus, text on p. 518

Leandrites cyrtorhynchus   FUJINO & MIYAKE, 1869
Cleaning anemone shrimp

Hab.: Entire Indo-Pacific region.

Sex.: Not known.

Soc.B./Assoc.: Although this species usually has a gregarious lifestyle, it can be kept singly.

M.: Provide a reef aquarium with hiding places. They get along well with other invertebrates, but not with overly large fishes.

Light: Dim light.

B./Rep.: Not known.

F.: O, FD; tablet and frozen foods.

S.: In nature it cleans large fishes; however, do not keep with large fishes in the limited space of an aquarium.

T: 20°-27°C, **L:** 3 cm, **TL:** from 60 cm, **WM:** w, **WR:** b, **AV:** 3, **D:** 2-3

Leandrites cyrtorhynchus, Maldives

Leandrites cyrtorhynchus shares this genus with several unidentified species. They not only clean small coral reef fishes such as small groupers and butterflies, but also large moray eels. Droves of shrimp wait under overhangs for their cleaning clients.

Leandrites sp., Thailand

Leandrites cyrtorhynchus cleaning butterfly fish

Leandrites sp. in a care off Bali, Indonesia

Fam.: Palaemonidae
Subfam.: Pontoniinae

Periclimenes aesopius   (BATE, 1863)
Southern anemone shrimp

Hab.: Southern coast of Australia.

Sex.: No external differences.

Soc.B./Assoc.: Maintain singly, in pairs, or in small groups on anemones and sea cucumbers. The number of animals depends on the size of the host.

M.: Only keep with anemones or sea cucumbers.

Light: Moderate light.

B./Rep.: Not known.

F.: O, FD; varied frozen foods.

S.: This species is probably the southern-most *Periclimenes* species. It is suspected that it also cleans fishes. The animals that live on anemones are protected against their stings. This protection has to be regenerated over and over (see **S.** of species below).

T: 16°-22°C, **L:** 1-2 cm, **TL:** from 60 cm, **WM:** w, **WR:** b, **AV:** 3, **D:** 2-3

Periclimenes brevicarpalis   (SCHENKEL, 1902)
Pacific clown anemone shrimp

Hab.: Indo-Pacific, Australia.

Sex.: ♂ ♂ are smaller than ♀ ♀.

Soc.B./Assoc.: They live singly or in pairs with various species of anemones (e.g., *Stoichactis*) and sea cucumbers. They are sometimes found together with *Thor amboinensis* on an anemone.

M.: Should only be kept with a host (anemone or sea cucumber).

Light: Moderate light.

B./Rep.: Not known.

F.: O, FD; dry and frozen foods. They also devour leftovers.

S.: This is the most frequently imported *Periclimenes* species. Although it is easily maintained, it should not be kept with large fishes. Either a sea cucumber or, better, an anemone should be present to act as host. If there are no fishes in the aquarium, the shrimp feels safe and often leaves its host for extended periods of time. If the species lives on an anemone, it is protected from its toxic stings. This holds true for other *Periclimenes* and crustacean species which live with anemones. The outer shell of the crustacean is covered by mucus secreted by the anemone. This chemically prevents the release of the nematocysts. However, this protection is lost when the old shell is shed (ecdysis) as the shrimp molts to grow. Shortly before this happens, the shrimp leaves the anemone and looks for a hiding place in the rocks. After the new shell has hardened, they slowly regain their protection by making very slight contact with the anemone's tentacles at first.

T: 23°-28°C, **L:** 2 cm, **TL:** from 60 cm, **WM:** w, **WR:** b, **AV:** 1, **D:** 2

Periclimenes aesopius

Periclimenes brevicarpalis

Fam.: Palaemonidae
Subfam.: Pontoniinae

Periclimenes brevicarpalis, Australia

Periclimenes brevicarpalis, Indonesia

Periclimenes amethysteus, Mediterranean

Periclimenes sagittifer, Mediterranean

Fam.: Palaemonidae
Subfam.: Pontoniinae

Periclimenes imperator
Emperor shrimp

BRUCE, 1967

Hab.: Entire Indo-Pacific, Red Sea.

Sex.: Sex cannot be determined from external characteristics.

Soc.B./Assoc.: Lives singly or in pairs on hosts such as the large nudibranch *Hexabranchus sanguineus*, sea cucumbers such as *Stichopus* and *Synapta*, or feather stars.

M.: If possible, a host should be offered. However, this species will leave its host for extended periods of time if there are no predators in the tank.

Light: Moderate light.

B./Rep.: Not known.

F.: O, FD; these shrimp primarily feed on particles adhering to the slimy skin of their host. In the aquarium, however, they also accept small chopped frozen and tablet foods.

S.: This shrimp can perfectly match its host's coloration. Therefore, its coloration may vary a great deal. Observations in an aquarium have shown that its bond to *Hexabranchus* is especially strong; the nudibranch is rarely left. The bond it forms to feather stars and sea urchins is significantly weaker. Since artificial hosts are not accepted, it is suspected that the shrimp are bound to their host through their olfactory senses (chemical). Extensive research has been done by SCHUHMACHER (Mar. Biol. 22/1973, pp. 355 ff.).

T: 22°-28°C, L: 2 cm, TL: from 60 cm, **WM**: w, **WR**: b, **AV**: 2, D: 2-3

Periclimenes imperator

Periclimenes imperator

The giant nudibranch, *Hexabranchus sanguineus* (Spanish dancer), is host to the emperor shrimp.

Within this order, there is hardly another animal that can better adapt itself to its host's coloration than the emperor shrimp, whether living on a feather star, a giant *Hexabranchus*, or a sea cucumber

Fam.: Palaemonidae
Subfam.: Pontoniinae

Periclimenes holthuisi   BRUCE, 1969
Holthuis' cleaner shrimp

Hab.: Indo-Pacific, Australia.

Sex.: No distinguishable external characteristics.

Soc.B./Assoc.: Usually lives in groups on various coelenterates, such as anemones (*Dofleinia*), mushroom corals (*Fungia*), other corals (*Goniopora, Catalaphyllia*), and mangrove jellyfish (*Cassiopeia*). In nature, they are sometimes found with *Amphiprion* on an anemone; however, it is not recommended that these two animals be maintained together in an aquarium.

M.: Only keep with the appropriate coelenterates.

Light: Moderate light.

B./Rep.: Not known.

F.: O, FD; no specific feeding is necessary, since they feed off of detritus and leftovers.

S.: Besides *P. brevicarpalis* (p. 524), it is the most frequently imported shrimp species. Both in nature and the aquarium, it cleans fishes. It will leave its host during these activities and climb, sometimes in groups, on the fish to clean. They are specifically protected against the poison of the nematocysts of anemones and corals (see p. 524). In most cases, the protection against stings is species specific. That means that the shrimp is only immune towards one species of anemone or coral, and others are avoided.

T: 23°-28°C, **L**: 2 cm, **TL**: from 50 cm, **WM**: w, **WR**: b, **AV**: 1, **D**: 2

Periclimenes lucasi   CHACE, 1937
Lucas' anemone shrimp

Hab.: Eastern Pacific, west Mexico.

Sex.: ♂♂ and ♀♀ cannot be distinguished from external features.

Soc.B./Assoc.: Occurs on various anemones either singly, in pairs or, less commonly, in groups.

M.: Only maintain with anemones.

Light: Moderate light.

B./Rep.: Unknown.

F.: O, FD; easy to feed. Leftovers. Small pieces of frozen or dry foods.

S.: Lives on anemones which are occasionally abandoned in its quest for food. They are protected against the poison of their host animals.

T: 21°-26°C, **L**: 2 cm, **TL**: from 60 cm, **WM**: w, **WR**: b, **AV**: 3, **D**: 2-3

Periclimenes holthuisi on *Entacmaea quadricolor*

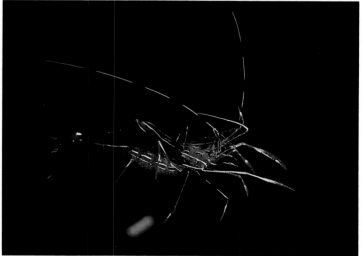

Periclimenes lucasi

Fam.: Palaemonidae
Subfam.: Pontoniinae

Periclimenes pedersoni　　　　　　　　　　　　　　　　　CHACE, 1958
Caribbean anemone shrimp, Pederson's cleaner shrimp

Hab.: Western tropical Atlantic and islands of the Caribbean, but not the Bermudas.

Sex.: No external differences.

Soc.B./Assoc.: Usually found singly or in pairs, but small groups of up to 36 specimens may occasionally be seen on an anemone. *Bartholomea annulata* is the anemone of choice, though *Condylactis gigantea, Hetreactis lucida,* or *Lebrunia danae* may also be used. They are compatible with the cleaner goby *Gobiosoma oceanops*, but not with clownfishes (*Amphiprion*).

M.: Always keep with anemones.

Light: Moderate light.

B./Rep.: Not known. Egg carrying ♀♀ have been observed on the Virgin Islands from February to August.

F.: O, FD; they do not need to be fed individually.

S.: This is a true cleaner shrimp that lures fishes with its long antennae and climbs on them to clean. It is even allowed to enter the mouth of a predator while cleaning. Like other *Periclimenes* species that live on anemones, this species is immune to the stinging cells of the anemone. The *modus operandi* of this protection is explained under **S.** of *P. brevicarpalis* (p. 524). Behavioral observations in nature have shown that several animals inhabiting one anemone have developed a hierarchy (social order) among themselves.

T: 21°-28°C, **L:** 2 cm, **TL:** from 50 cm, **WM:** w, **WR:** b, **AV:** 2-3, **D:** 2

Periclimenes pedersoni

Periclimenes pedersoni , cleaning grouper

Fam.: Palaemonidae
Subfam.: Pontoniinae

Periclimenes yucatanicus (IVES, 1891)
Clown anemone shrimp, spotted cleaner shrimp

Hab.: Western tropical Atlantic, Caribbean islands.

Sex.: No external differences.

Soc.B./Assoc.: This species lives singly, in pairs or, rarely, in small groups in community with the anemones *Bartholomea annulata*, *Condylactis gigantea* or, sometimes, *Lebrunia danae*. WILLIAMS & WILLIAMS (Crustaceana, 42, pp. 318 f., 1982) discuss this shrimp living with a single specimen of *Discosoma sanctithomae* in the Virgin Islands (Caribbean).

M.: Needs a reef aquarium with one of the above mentioned anemones.

Light: Moderate light.

B./Rep.: Not known. In the Caribbean, the ♀ ♀ carry eggs in July and August on their abdomen.

F.: O, FD; flake food and *Artemia*.

S.: They probably clean fishes they lure with their waving antennae. Unlike other *Periclimenes* species, almost constant contact with the bottom is maintained while they clean. These shrimp are especially protected against the anemone's stinging cells, which are deadly to other crustacea (see p. 524).

T: 20°-26°C, **L:** 2 cm, **TL:** from 50 cm, **WM:** w, **WR:** b, **AV:** 2-3, **D:** 2

Stegopontonia commensalis NOBILI, 1906
Sea urchin anemone shrimp

Hab.: Indo-Pacific, Australia.

Sex.: ♀ ♀ are larger than ♂ ♂.

Soc.B./Assoc.: Lives singly or in pairs commensally with various species of sea urchins.

M.: Only maintain with sea urchins whose spines are longer than the body of the shrimp.

Light: Moderate light.

B./Rep.: Not known.

F.: O, FD; easy to feed; feeds on leftovers and detritus and searches the sea urchin's spines for edibles with its thin pinchers. It is unclear whether or not they "clean."

S.: This diminutive 2 cm shrimp is especially adapted both in shape and color to life between sea urchin spines. They are normally found on diadem sea urchins (*Echinothrix diadema*), even throughout the night. FRICKE has done decoy experiments in nature and determined that it prefers vertical substrates rather than horizontal structures as well as more structures versus fewer. There is a Caribbean shrimp (*Tuleariocaris neglecta*) whose behavior is very similar. It was recently discovered in the eastern Atlantic at Madeira (WIRTZ et. al., Cour. Forsch. Inst. Senckenb. 105, pp. 169 ff., 1988).
Stegopontonia commensalis is found in all tropical seas. Its camouflage is uncanny enough to fool even the human eye when it is adhered to a sea urchin spine. The white stripes help dissolve the contour of the shrimp. This species accepts any sea urchin as host in the aquarium as long as the spines are longer than its body.

T: 22°-28°C, **L:** 2 cm, **TL:** from 60 cm, **WM:** w, **WR:** b, **AV:** 2-3, **D:** 3

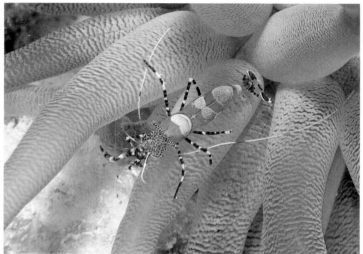

The clown anemone shrimp, *Periclimenes yucatanicus,* likes to live between the tentacles of the anemone *Condylactis gigantea.*

Stegopontonia commensalis

Fam.: Pandalidae

It is not easy for the layperson to differentiate Pandalidae from other shrimp families like, Palaemonidae (rock shrimp) or Hippolytidae (cleaner shrimp). All three families have a standard shrimp body and a well developed rostrum. However, pandalids have the longest rostrum, especially species of the genus *Plesionika*. If you want to ensure that you are dealing with a deepwater shrimp you have to work scientifically. The first pair of legs is the basis for positive identification. The claws on this first pair are either microscopically small or totally absent in members of the Pandalidae. So if the shrimp you are trying to identify has a large claw on the first leg, it is definitely not a member of this family. Additionally, members of this family are usually readily identified by their long rostrum, as mentioned above.

The family Pandalidae is composed of approximately 15 genera worldwide. The commonly encountered *Pandalus* and *Plesionika* are two of the six genera from this family that are found in European seas. Especially in cold waters around the coastline of Great Britain, Ireland and Norway, e.g., in the North and Baltic Seas, they have commercial value. Around Iceland and Greenland, they reach the impressive length of 10 cm and enter nets by the drove. The vertical distribution extends to the deep sea. Species of the genus *Pandalus* can easily be kept in a coldwater aquarium. These sociable animals should be kept in groups.

The genus *Plesionika* is common in the Mediterranean and around the islands of the east Atlantic. It is somewhat rarer in the Red Sea and Indo-Pacific. In shallow water, large groups of these shrimp sit among rubble and rocks and can be found in almost every cave. The large forest of antennae is often reminiscent of waving flags. They feed on algae and microorganisms which are deposited on the bottom. Filmdocuments by the scientist Hans FRICKE show that an unknow *plesionica*-species off the Comoros, Indian Ocean, lives together with the famous coelacanth in a depht of 250 m.

Pandalidae have never been seen living with other organisms. But they, like other shrimp, serve as host to *Bopyrus*. These parasitic isopods live in the shrimp's gill chamber and can not be expelled, even after molting. Whether or not this infestation leads to death could not be determined.

Pandalus montagui, Ireland

Pandalus montagui
Aesop prawn

LEACH, 1814

Hab.: Northern Atlantic. The southern limit of their range is the German Bay and English Isles.

Sex.: ♂ ♂ are smaller than ♀ ♀.

Soc.B./Assoc.: Usually in great droves.

M.: Only difficult to maintain because of its need for high salinity and low temperatures.

Light: Dim light.

B./Rep.: The larvae have been repeatedly reared in scientific laboratories. At first the eggs are green; later they turn green-violet. The hatching larvae (zoea) have a length of 2.4 to 3.4 mm. After the animals pass through 11 very similar stages, the shrimp is an adult. Spawning extends from the beginning of November to February. The shrimp undergo a sexual transformation from ♂ ♂ to ♀ ♀.

F.: C, FD; frozen foods.

S.: This species is the most common edible shrimp of the European seas. *P. montagui* is captured at depths of 50 to 100 m with bottom trawls. In the spring, they are found in shallow waters; in the fall, preceding spawning, they are in deeper waters. They live up to 3 or 4 years.

T: max. 18°C, **L:** 7 cm, **TL:** from 100 cm, **WM:** w, **WR:** b, **AV:** 3, **D:** 3-4

Fam.: Pandalidae

Pandalus kessleri (CHERNIAVSKY, 1878)

Hab.: Northern Japan. Have been experimentally released by Soviet scientists in the Black Sea.

Sex.: Not known.

Soc.B./Assoc.: This species lives in loose groups.

M.: Requires a large tank with a sandy bottom.

Light: Dim light.

B./Rep.: The larvae are caught and raised in tanks to provide seed stock for commercial mariculture projects.

F.: C, FD; various frozen foods.

S.: These animals are of great economic importance in Japan (KURATA, Proc. Int. Pandalid Shrimp Symp., Kodiak, 1979, pp. 89 ff.). They are poorly suited for an aquarium.

T: 15°-21°C, **L:** 6-12 cm, **TL:** from 150 cm, **WM:** m, **WR:** b, **AV:** 3, **D:** 2-3

Plesionika narval (FABRICIUS, 1787)
Narval

Hab.: Mediterranean and temperate and northern regions of the Atlantic.

Sex.: No external differences.

Soc.B./Assoc.: This crustacean is found in large groups of more than 100 individuals.

M.: Provide a large tank with a flat bottom and a back wall of rocks. They only feel comfortable in a group; therefore, do not keep singly.

Light: Dim light.

B./Rep.: The various larval stages have been raised by scientific institutions; however, actual breeding behavior is unknown.

F.: C, FD; frozen foods.

S.: A beautiful but difficult aquarium animal. Typically found on open sandy bottoms at several hundred to almost a thousand meters depth. They are commercially harvested with bottom trawls as food shrimp. However, many also live at shallower depths of about 10 m where they colonize both the floor and walls of caves. At night they leave their shelter to search for food. Their extremely long rostrum is characteristic of the species. Synonym: *Parapandalus narval*.

T: 5°-21°C, **L:** 5 cm, **TL:** from 120 cm, **WM:** w, **WR:** b, **AV:** 3-4, **D:** 3

Pandalus kessleri

Plesionika narval

Fam.: Rhynchocinetidae

The large bulging eyes and the humpback are obvious morphological characteristica that differentiate this family from other decapod species. Other than these two visible characteristics, there is another of particular importance to taxonomists: Dancing shrimp have a foldable rostrum. The rostrum is the serrated appendage that extends forward from the forehead. All the previously mentioned shrimp have a fixed rostrum. But Rhynchocinetidae have a hinged rostrum that can fold down. The importance of this movable appendage for the animals is shown in pictures of *Rynchocinetes kuiteri* molting on the following pages. For the first time, individual stages of molting for the Rhynchocinetidae are documented.

Aquarists named these shrimp after watching their unusual movements. They strut around carefully and pause after a few movements. The abrupt stop is reminiscent of a tango dancer. However, that is the extent of the similarity. They are typically sluggish animals that somehow escape being boring.

Today, scientists are convinced that Rhynchocinetidae have separate sexes: males have larger chelipeds. There is no dichromatism. Dancing shrimp are quite gregarious crustacea. In their natural habitat you often encounter groups of up to 100 animals. It is not uncommon to see anemone and boxing shrimp in the same vicinity, which leads one to deduce that there is a certain degree of compatibility among them.

However, dancing shrimp are quarrelsome towards other invertebrates: colonial and disc anemones and leather and flower corals, all appreciated inhabitants of today's marine aquaria, are disturbed when dancing shrimp pull on them and pinch off polyps with their chelae. Hardly any of these delicate animals can survive this abuse for long. Dancing shrimp can be maintained without problems with stinging anemones and bubble corals.

Opposite page:
A pair of undescribed dancing shrimp from the Caribbean begin their ascent on a sponge. The coloration of the abdomen and the hunch clearly show that this species is not *Rhynchocinetes rigens*, which is present throughout the Atlantic.

Rhynchocinetes sp., Caribbean

Fam.: Rhynchocinetidae

Rynchocinetes uritai off Thailand

Rynchocinetes uritai   KUBO, 1942
Rosy dancing shrimp

Hab.: Entire Indo-Pacific.

Sex.: ♂ ♂ have elongated chelipeds.

Soc.B./Assoc.: They live gregariously in groups of 10 or more ♀ ♀ and 1 ♂. Keep pairs or, better, a small group. However, even if a group is kept, there should only be one ♂. They get along well with other shrimp such as *Lysmata* or *Palaemon* species. Keeping these shrimp in the same aquarium as colonial anemones and soft corals is not recommended, since the shrimp tend to bother them. More toxic anemones and bubble corals are left in peace.

M.: Requires a reef aquarium with shaded walls and hiding places.

Light: Dim light.

B./Rep.: Not known.

F.: O, FD; frozen foods and tablets. These animals have the capacity to quickly learn to identify the feeding tube and its significance. TetraTips broken into quarters and delivered with the tube are greatly appreciated. *R. uritai* come directly towards the end of the pipe and feel the opening for edibles. Other shrimp usually flee from the pipe.

S.: This is the only frequently imported dancing shrimp. Their jerking movements (name) are very uncommon and cute. Since the animals are sensitive to fluctuations in salinity, beware when transferring. During the day they are shy and avoid brightly lit regions of the aquarium. They are especially pleased if they have small niches to hide in. After an acclimation phase, they will come out of their hiding places during the day to search for food. Life expectancy is about 2 years, rarely longer.

T: 23°-28°C, **L:** 4 cm, **TL:** from 50 cm, **WM:** w, **WR:** b, **AV:** 1, **D:** 2

Rynchocinetes durbanensis, GORDON 1936

Rynchocinetes durbanensis, the common dancing shrimp

Fam.: Rhynchocinetidae

Rhynchocinetes sp.
Caribbean dancing shrimp

Rhynchocinetes sp.
Red Sea dancing shrimp

Rhynchocinetes sp.
Indonesian dancing shrimp

UNDESCRIBED DANCING SHRIMP:

LINNAEUS (1758) is the father of today's classification system for both plants and animals. He introduced the "binomial nomenclature," i.e., every species has a two-part name consisting of the genus and species name. During his time, exactly 4,236 animal species were known. It was recently estimated that there are more than 1 million animals worldwide. But according to new sources of information, there may be as many as 30 million! More than 90% of these are insects from the tropical rain forests. Undescribed animal species are regularly found. With the exception of the tropical forests, surely the ocean is the most promising place to discover new species. A whole range of undescribed species is known to divers and aquarists. The *Rhynchocinetes* species pictured here are an example. Either scientists are ignorant about the existence of these animals (and therefore need the help of aquarists and divers), or the taxonomists that describe new species are simply overworked.

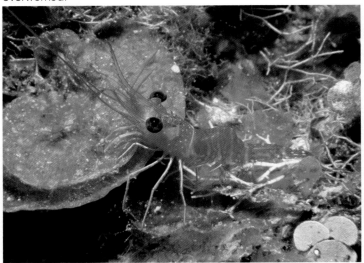

Rhynchocinetes sp., Caribbean (also see p. 541!)

544

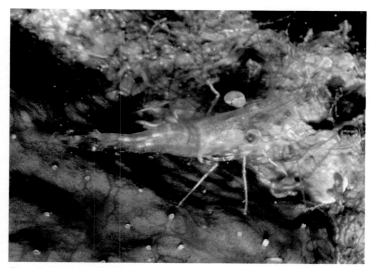

Rhynchocinetes sp., Red Sea

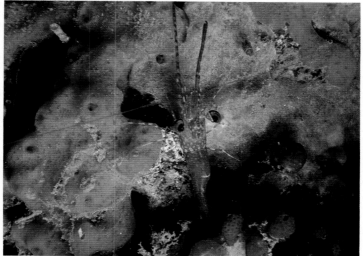

Rhynchocinetes sp., Indonesia

Fam.: Rhynchocinetidae

The photographs below show the Australian dancing shrimp *Rhynchocinetes kuiteri* in the process of molting. The folded rostrum (photo 1) is clearly visible.

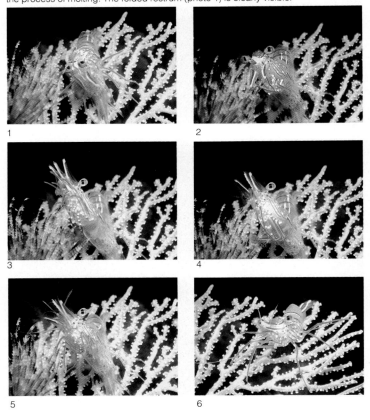

1

2

3

4

5

6

Rhynchocinetes kuiteri
Kuiter's dancing shrimp

TIEFENBACHER, 1983

Hab.: Southern coast of Australia, Tasmania.

Sex.: ♂♂ have significantly larger chelipeds than ♀♀.

Soc.B./Assoc.: Found singly, in pairs, or in small groups. Gets along well with other shrimp and fishes of moderate size.

M.: House in a rock aquarium that has plenty of hiding places.

Light: Dim light.

B./Rep.: Not known.

F.: O, FD; frozen foods and tablets.

S.: One of the few dancing shrimp found in temperate seas.

T: 16°-21°C, **L:** 3-4 cm, **TL:** from 60 cm, **WM:** w, **WR:** b, **AV:** 3, **D:** 2-3

Fam.: Rhynchocinetidae

Rhynchocinetes rigens   GORDON, 1936
Red dancing shrimp
Hab.: The entire tropical Atlantic and the Caribbean islands.

Rhynchocinetes australis   HALE, 1941
Australian dancing shrimp
Hab.: Temperate waters around Australia and New Zealand.

Rhynchocinetes rugulosus   STIMPSON, 1860
Color changing dancing shrimp
Hab.: Indo-Pacific, Australia.

Sex.: In most species the ♂'s chelae are larger than those of the ♀ (exception: *R. rigens*).

Soc.B./Assoc.: Found singly, in pairs, or in small groups.

M.: Requires a reef or rock aquarium with good hiding places. They may bother colonial anemones and soft corals.

Light: Dim light.

B./Rep.: Not known.

F.: O, FD; frozen and dry foods.

S.: None known.

T: 21°-26°C; *R. australis:* 17°-21°C, **L:** 2-4 cm, **TL:** from 50 cm, **WM:** w, **WR:** b, **AV:** 3-4, **D:** 2-3

Rhynchocinetes rigens

548

Rhynchocinetes australis

Rhynchocinetes rugulosus

Fam.: Stenopodidae

The first three pairs of walking legs of the boxer shrimp have small claws. But it is the noteworthy third pair of legs that gave them their common name. It has especially large pinchers which are generally the same color as the body and held extended. Its long white antennae are notorious both in their natural habitat and the aquarium. These antennae often "peek" out of their hiding place, giving their observer a valuable clue as to the occupant of the grotto. Although boxer shrimp are reclusive, even a snorkeler can find them: they are found directly below the low tide mark along some tropical coasts such as Kenya.

The most famous member of this family is the banded boxing shrimp, *Stenopus hispidus*. It is one of the few known shrimp distributed throughout the tropics. That is, it has been described from all three oceans of the earth. It must, therefore, have crossed into the Caribbean part of the Atlantic prior to the closing of the Central American Isthmus about 10 million years ago. Experts consider it impossible that these crustacea could have survived the trip around the southern tip of the American or African continent into the Atlantic. The water temperature in these regions is too low.

Courtship behavior of boxer shrimp is very developed, and these animals begin their search for a partner at a very early age and then grow and mature together. Once they have chosen a site, it is not willingly abandoned. If possible, they remain in the shade. Most of their time is spent hanging from the ceiling of their cave in their natural habitat as well as in the reef aquarium. If you are curious whose job it is to acquire food, you are in for a surprise. Only the female is conspicuously inactive in the aquarium; it is waiting to be served by the male! Immediately following the acquisition of food, the male returns to the female which has been patiently waiting for him. The female tries to take a piece with her pincers. She is always successful because the grasping action triggers the male to transfer the food. However, if the male is also hungry, the transfer threshold may be raised. Although he offers the food, he holds it fast and begins to eat it himself. One speaks of a heightened threshold. That is, the hungry male has two instincts fighting against each other (hunger and feeding instinct), and the stronger, more active tendency prevails (hunger is the most powerful).

Boxing shrimp have another uncommon behavioral characteristic which can be observed in the aquarium: the courtship ritual. The

Stenopus scutellatus from the Caribbean

male progressively begins a rhythmic lateral walk. Initially the female remains motionless. After the first lateral dance steps, the female begins to move her pinchers as if she wants to embrace the male. This is normally followed by coupling. The male climbs onto the back of the larger female and presses the posterior end of his abdomen laterally against her. The female stores the sperm in a special pouch. Soon after copulation, the first portion of eggs are fertilized and deposited. The eggs are then adhered to her swimmerets. The sperm packet is sufficient—for Stenopodidae as well as other shrimp—for several ovipositions. If the male dies for any reason prior to its partner, she can still fertilize eggs for a limited time.

Stenopus cyanoscelis GOY, 1984
Blue-legged boxing shrimp

Hab.: Indo-Pacific.

Sex.: No external differences.

Soc.B./Assoc.: Lives singly or in pairs.

M.: Needs a reef aquarium with a large cave to hide in. Nothing is known about water quality requirements.

Light: Dim light.

B./Rep.: Not known.

F.: O, FD; frozen and tablet foods.

S.: *S. cyanocelis* was described in 1984. Since then it has been rarely but repeatedly imported into Europe and the U.S.A.

T: 21°-26°C, **L:** 3 cm, **TL:** from 50 cm, **WM:** w, **WR:** b, **AV:** 2, **D:** 2

Stenopus devaneyi GOY & RANDALL, 1984
Devaney's boxing shrimp

Hab.: The Indo-Pacific region from Hawaii to the Maldives.

Sex.: No sexual dimorphism or dichromatism. Both sexes have two red spots on their back.

Soc.B./Assoc.: The species demonstrates a marked pairing behavior.

M.: *Stenopus deyaneyi* is quite robust; molting occurs in relatively clean water (NO_3 max. 50 mg/l; phosphate max. ca 3,0 mg/l), usually without problems. Smaller specimens can live up to 6 years in an aquarium.

Light: Dim light.

B./Rep.: ♀ ♀ carry whitish/yellow eggs under their abdomen. Egg development requires about 14 days; more exact data are hard to acquire due to the animal´s extreme timidity. The larvae are difficult to raise. Besides food procurement, maintaining water quality is problematic. The water in the rearing tank cannot contain nitrates!

F.: O, FD; tablet, live, and frozen foods.

S.: This species has only been recently described (1984), although it has been in the hobby for a long time. The pictured pair on p. 553 has not yet regenerated its pinchers since they were imported; caution is advised when dealing with specimens that have fully developed pinches, since they can pinch hard.

T: 21°-27°C, **L:** 6 cm, **TL:** from 60 cm, **WM:** w, **WR:** b, **AV:** 3, **D:** 2

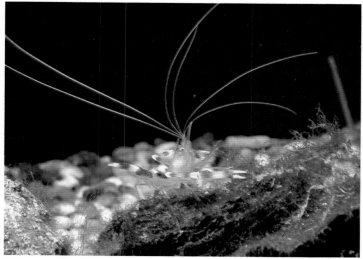

Stenopus cyanoscelis

Stenopus devaneyi

Fam.: Stenopodidae

Stenopus hispidus   (OLIVIER, 1811)
Banded boxing shrimp

Hab.: One of the few crustacea found in all tropical seas.

Sex.: ♀ ♀ are larger than ♂ ♂ , but rarely is the difference so pronounced as on the photo on the facing page. In addition, adult ♂ ♂ are more slender than ♀ ♀ and their carapace is more brownish dorsally (also see **B./Rep.**).

Soc.B./Assoc.: Though they always live in pairs in their natural habitat, they can be kept singly in the aquarium. Never keep animals of the same sex together.

M.: They need a reef aquarium with a large cave. Usually they are found inside, hanging on the ceiling. Either keep one animal or a ♂ and ♀ , since animals of the same sex kill each other. This species is not as sensitive as *S. scutellatus* (p. 556). On a pylon (bridge post of a harbor walk), I have observed 25 full-grown animals at various water levels from 0.5 to 3 m depth. Each pair obviously had its mini territory (observation by H.B. [Nassau]). The antennae of large specimens are extremely long. Therefore, if you wish to house them with stinging anemones, they should be put in really large aquaria. Otherwise the antennae are always touching the tentacles of the anemones. Aquarists frequently report that they capture small fishes and kill them. They may also turn aggressive towards other small shrimp species. They are sensitive during molting. The KH value during this time must be above 10.

Light: Dim light.

B./Rep.: The ♀ ♀ often carry greenish eggs under their abdomen. After 6 weeks and usually at night, the larvae hatch. Rearing the larvae is difficult. They usually starve after 10 days. Success is dependent on a well functioning *Brachionus* set-up.

F.: O, FD; frozen foods and mussel and shrimp meat. There is a report by TSCHÖRTNER (TI, March/1981, pp. 32 f.) exploring the interesting behavior of one partner feeding the other.

Continued on p. 556:

Stenopus hispidus, ♀

Fam.: Stenopodidae

Continuation of *Stenopus hispidus* from p. 554:

S.: This large cleaning boxing shrimp was one of the first species to be imported for the tropical marine aquarium hobby. It is regularly found in all tropical seas, and there it uses its long antennae to entice its clients. Usually maintains contact with the substrate while cleaning. Depending on water temperature and nutrition, they molt every 3 to 8 weeks.

T: 21°-28°C, **L:** 6 cm, **TL:** from 60, 100 cm for large specimens, **WM:** w, **WR:** b, **AV:** 1, **D:** 1-2

Stenopus pyrsonotus   GOY & DEVANEY, 1980
Ghost boxing shrimp

Hab.: Entire Indo-Pacific region, especially Hawaii, New Guinea, Mauritius, and the east coast of Africa.

Sex.: No external differences.

Soc.B./Assoc.: Lives singly or in pairs.

M.: Robust animals, but the great majority of these rarely imported shrimp are full-grown. The live expectancy in captivity is often only 1-3 years; juveniles, in contrast, would live about 6 years. *S. pyrsonotus* lives in deeper regions beginning at a depth of 10 m in itsnatural habitat. Because of this, *S. pyrsonotus* is less able to adapt to life in aquaria in comparison to other *Stenopus* species. Nitrate levels should not exceed 30 mg/l, and the temperature should not be above 29°C. During the day these shy animals remain hidden. For ideal maintenance, offer a large cave with the opening situated in such a fashion that you can see the animals during the day.

Light: Dim light.

B./Rep.: Reproduction is similar to that of other *Stenopus.*

F.: O, FD; tablets, *Artemia*, and mussel meat.

S.: Although it is relatively rare in nature, it is repeatedly imported. It, like *S. hispidus,* has been observed cleaning fishes. In nature, and perhaps in the aquarium, it leads a significantly more secretive life than other cleaning *Stenopus* species. It was known to aquarists prior to scientists.

T: 19°-26°C, **L:** 3 cm, **TL:** from 50 cm, **WM:** w, **WR:** b, **AV:** 2, **D:** 2

Stenopus scutellatus   RANKIN, 1898
Caribbean boxing shrimp

Hab.: Western Atlantic, Caribbean islands.

Sex.: No external differences.

Soc.B./Assoc.: Only keep in pairs.

M.: A reef aquarium that has large hiding places where they can retire together is required. The animals are sensitive to fluctuations in salinity. It is equally important to maintain low nitrate levels.

Light: Dim light.

B./Rep.: It is regularly bred in the U.S.A. When sufficient planktonic food can be provided, rearing is nonproblematic.

F.: O, FD; tablet and frozen foods. Mussel and shrimp meat should be given often to insure sufficient iodine.

S.: This species is easily differentiated by the two red dots around the mouth. It is not an easy animal to maintain because it is sensitive to fluctuations in salinity and excessive nitrate levels. The latter condition combined with an iodine deficiency usually inhibits molting. When cleaning, they barely leave their cave and never climb on top of their clients. This species cleans smaller fishes than *S. hispidus.* It and *S. hispidus* will happily share the tank if it is large enough.

T: 21°-27°C, **L:** 3-4 cm, **TL:** from 50 cm, **WM:** w, **WR:** b, **AV:** 2, **D:** 2-3

Stenopus pyrsonotus

Stenopus scutellatus ♀

Fam.: Stenopodidae

Stenopus tenuirostris   DE MAN, 1888
Blue boxing shrimp

Hab.: Entire Indo-Pacific region.

Sex.: During spawning season the egg stalks that attach the blue eggs to the ♀ are visible through the dorsal carapace.

Soc.B./Assoc.: Usually in pairs, rarely singly. They get along well with other shrimp and small fishes, even though they chase them away from their cave.

M.: Provide a reef aquarium with a large cave and shady overhangs. Contrary to most other *Stenopus* species, this species seems to be less sensitive to sudden fluctuations in salinity. Nothing is known about special requirements in regard to nitrate concentrations.

Light: Dim light.

B./Rep.: Not known.

F.: O, FD; tablet, flake, and frozen foods.

S.: Its diminutive 2 cm length makes this one of the smallest *Stenopus* species. It is easily kept. Initially very shy. Months are needed before it dares to emerge 10 cm from its cave. Molts every 4 to 5 weeks. The life expectancy in the aquarium is, at most, about 6 years. In large aquaria, the animals are rarely seen.

T: 21°-27°C, **L:** 2 cm, **TL:** from 40 cm, **WM:** w, **WR:** b, **AV:** 3, **D:** 2

Stenopus zanzibaricus   BRUCE, 1976
Red antennae boxing shrimp

Hab.: Indo-Pacific, especially Micronesia and Kenya.

Sex.: No external differences.

Soc.B./Assoc.: Lives in pairs, rarely singly.

M.: Reef aquarium with shady overhangs and hiding places.

Light: Dim light.

B./Rep.: Not known.

F.: O, FD; frozen food and live *Artemia*.

S.: Juvenile animals have a red stripe above their tail fan which adults do not.

T: 21°-27°C, **L:** 3 cm, **TL:** from 50 cm, **WM:** w, **WR:** b, **AV:** 3, **D:** 2

The Mediterranean boxing shrimp *Stenopus spinosus* (photo on the bottom of p. 560) can be found in caves and dark hiding places.

Both tropical boxing shrimp from the Indo-Pacific, *Stenopus earlei* and *Stenopus* sp., are very rarely imported. Both are pictured on p. 561. These 2 cm dwarfs live around rubble and dead coral.

Stenopus tenuirostris

Stenopus zanzibaricus, adult

Fam.: Stenopodidae

Stenopus zanzibaricus, see p. 558 for text

Stenopus spinosus

Stenopus earlei

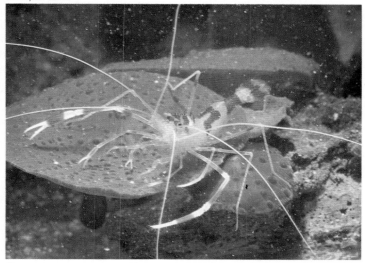

Stenopus sp.

Fam.: Palinuridae

Spiny lobsters are one of the most beautiful and impressive crustacea. The absence of claws separates the Palinuridae from other lobsters. The first pair of walking legs, which many crustacea have transformed into pinchers or claws, is still undeveloped and primitive in spiny lobsters. If you look closely, you will see the thorn on the second to last leg segment. When the thorn is enlarged, it distinctly resembles the propus, the nonmovable finger of the claw. Science assumes that lobsters with large claws evolved from spiny lobsters. A clear differentiating characteristic are the spines between the eyes. Spiny lobsters have two rostra, while lobsters only have one rostrum. The first antenna is not whiplike as in lobsters, but forked close to the tip like hermit crabs and shrimp. The second antenna is long and has a strongly developed basal segment. By rubbing the antennae segments against each other, spiny lobsters can produce creaking noises.

Palinurus elephas is widely distributed along European coasts. In the early days of the marine aquarium hobby, it was brought home by Mediterranean vacationers. Today the more attractively colored tropical species are found in the trade. However, those who did their first dives in the Mediterranean will have fond memories of the conspicuous cave inhabitants that lived along less polluted coastal regions. This species also occurs in the neighboring Atlantic to the west coast of Ireland, where the fishermen capture 40 cm specimens with their weir traps. Spiny lobsters, contrary to lobsters, are gregarious animals which are commercially exploited in many parts of the world. One of the authors (H.D.) had the opportunity to witness the native species from the Western Australia coast at the Abrolhos Islands, *Panulirus cygnus,* being fished. The state controls these activities. Since research showed that reproduction begins in June, spiny lobsters can only be caught from November to June. After its indiscriminate capture in the 1940's only standard capture cages that allow smaller specimens to escape can be used. Nevertheless, every spiny lobster lifted onto the specially constructed fishing boats has to be measured, and its carapace length must be at least 76 mm. It is illegal to keep smaller animals or egg-carrying females.

A 15 cm European spiny lobster, *Palinurus elephas* (note its genus as compared to the tropical genus *Panulirus*), in its natural habitat at the Mediterranean island of Elba. This same species is pictured on p. 565, but it comes from the west coast of Ireland in the Atlantic. This specimen is an impressive 40 cm long.

Palinurus elephas, Mediterranean

Fam.: Palinuridae

Nevertheless, there are several weekly transport ships that are filled with bags of spiny lobsters destined for gourmets around the world. *Panulirus versicolor* is distributed in the entire Indo-Pacific and is considered to be the most often imported spiny lobster of the marine aquarium hobby. After this species achieves a length of 10 cm, it is impossible to house it with invertebrates, because at this size it begins to prey on small fishes, tubeworms, and shrimp.

Palinurus elephas   (FABRICIUS, 1787)
European spiny lobster

Hab.: Mediterranean, northern Atlantic.

Sex.: No secondary sexual differences. The external sexual organs can be seen on the lower side of the abdomen (p. 584), just like in *Enoplometopus*.

Soc.B./Assoc.: If the tank is large enough, various specimens can be kept together. It can be housed with large fishes, but not with sensitive invertebrates.

M.: Rock aquarium with large hiding places. These animals can grow more than 30 cm in length in a relatively short time. Excessive nitrate levels inhibit molting (p. 570). If they cannot molt, they die. The temperature in the winter has to be below 18°C.

Light: Dim light.

B./Rep.: Has not been successfully bred in an aquarium. In the western Mediterranean they spawn in September and October.

F.: C, FD; easily fed with large pieces of frozen food; but earthworms, lean beef heart, and tablet food can be fed occasionally.

S.: Though an easily kept species, it is not suitable for the tropical marine aquarium (temperature). Large specimens are often kept in restaurant aquaria in Mediterranean countries. Older literature frequently calls this species *Palinurus vulgaris*.

T: 16°-24°C (see above), **L:** 40 cm, **TL:** from 100 cm, **WM:** m, **WR:** b, **AV:** 2, **D:** 1

Palinurus elephas, Ireland

Fam.: Palinuridae

Panulirus cygnus
Australian spiny lobster

GEORGE, 1962

Hab.: Australian side of the Indo-Pacific.

Sex.: There are no differentiating characteristics. On the ventral side of the abdomen, the exterior sexual organs can be recognized as in *Enoplometopus* (p. 584).

Soc.B./Assoc.: Several specimens can be kept together if the aquarium is large enough.

M.: Rock aquarium with sufficiently large hiding places.

Light: Dim light.

B./Rep.: Has not been successfully bred in an aquarium. In its natural biotope the spawning season begins in June.

F.: C, FD; large pieces of fish, mussel, and crustacean meat.

S.: Large numbers are commercially fished (photo on bottom of facing page).

T: 20°-25°C, **L:** 35 cm, **TL:** from 100 cm, **WM:** m, **WR:** b, **AV:** 2-3, **D:** 1

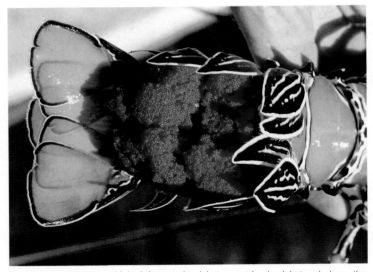

In higher crustacea, to which shrimp, crabs, lobsters, and spiny lobsters belong, the abdomen has swimmerets where the female fastens her eggs until they hatch.

Panulirus cygnus

Lobster fishermen, Western Australia

Fam.: Palinuridae

Panulirus inflatus, western Mexico

In Europe, the most frequently imported lobster is *Panulirus versicolor*. This species is widely distributed in the Indo-Pacific and is clearly recognizable by its azure blue longitudinal stripes on its walking legs. Once acclimated, it will abandon its hiding place in the reef aquarium during the day. According to the authors' experiences, maintaining this species in a fish community tank is nonproblematic. Of course, tanks containing large predators and triggerfishes are exceptions.

Panulirus versicolor

Panulirus versicolor
Blue spiny lobster

(LATREILLE, 1804)

Hab.: The entire tropical Indo-Pacific.

Sex.: No secondary sexual differences. The external sexual organs, as in *Enoplometopus* (p. 584), can be seen on the ventral side of the abdomen.

Soc.B./Assoc.: Several specimens can be kept together in a large tank. They get along well with other large crustacea and robust fishes. Use caution when housing with sensitive animals.

M.: Reef aquarium with large hiding places. The animals retire to these sites during the day, but come out to feed. They do not place special requirements on water quality; however, excessive nitrate inhibits molting. Keep the concentration low.

Light: Dim light.

B./Rep.: Has not been accomplished in an aquarium.

F.: C, FD; they feed on large pieces of fish, mussel, and crustacean meat. Once in a while tablet foods can also be given.

S.: They produce sounds that resemble a cicada's. People from the Indo-Pacific consider them a delicacy.

T: 22°-26°C, L: 35 cm, TL: from 100 cm, **WM:** m, **WR:** b, **AV:** 1, **D:** 1

Fam.: Palinuridae

Not all details are known about the complex molting process. The following is a greatly simplified version: prior to the actual molting, the exoskeleton begins to separate from the dermis beneath. At the same time a liquid is secreted which dissolves part of the old shell. The released calcium salts return to the blood. Part of the chitin is also dissolved in this manner and stored in the blood. Now a new shell is formed underneath the old. Once it is totally finished, the old shell breaks open along the dorsal side of the carapace, and the animal crawls out of the old shell. After molting, the new shell is soft, and the body absorbs water to stretch the new exoskeleton to its maximum size.

Panulirus regius, Atlantic, Cape Verde Islands

Panulirus marginatus, Hawaii

Panulirus penicillatus, Maldives

Fam.: Palinuridae

Palinurella wieneckii   DE MAN, 1881
Indopacific dwarf spiny lobster

Hab.: Indopacific region.

Sex.: No secondary sexual differences. As for *Enoplometopus*, the external sexual organs can be recognized on the ventral side of the abdomen.

Soc.B./Assoc.: It can be easily housed with most fishes. Do not place with small shrimp; however, there have been positive results when this species was combined with the banded coral shrimp, *Stenopus hispidus*.

M.: Reef aquarium with hiding places. It likes a thick layer of coarse sand or shell debris to dig in.

Light: Dim light.

B./Rep.: Has not been accomplished in an aquarium.

F.: C, FD; they are nonproblematic feeders and accept all leftovers from the bottom; any kind of frozen and tablet foods.

S.: They are easily distinguished from other spiny lobsters. They have pinchers on the first pairs of walking legs and short antennae. This lobster is of no use commercially since its maximal size is rather diminutive.

T: 22°-26°C, L: 15 cm, TL: from 80 cm, **WM:** m, **WR:** b, **AV:** 1-2, **D:** 1-2

SOUND GENERATION IN SPINY LOBSTERS

The production of sounds in lobsters was studied by MULLIGAN & FISCHER (Crustaceana 32, 1977, pp. 185 ff.) using the Caribbean spiny lobster, *Panulirus argus*.

Popping, flapping, and scraping noises are generated. All sounds were found to be pulsations with an abrupt onset and gradual, irregular decay. Although behavioral observations showed no relationship between specific behavior and the type of sound, the sounds seem to express the general level of stimulation. Scraping sounds are primarily produced when the animals are in an excited state. Flapping sounds occur when the animals are calm, and popping noises are heard when the animals are in a state of moderate excitation.

Palinurella wieneckii, aquarium picture

Palinurella wieneckii, in its natural habitat, Hawaii

Fam.: Scyllaridae

About the Family Scyllaridae

There are a lot of weird looking representatives among the decapoda, but the slipper lobsters take the cake: their primeval appearance is due to their flattened carapace and a distinct, sharp edge that separates the dorsal and ventral side of the animal. The large, conspicuous antennae seen on its close relatives are totally absent in slipper lobsters. Quite to the contrary, the second pair of antennae is modified into shovellike structures. Slipper lobsters, with the aid of these modified antennae, can quickly bury their entire body into the sandy or muddy bottoms they live on. However, they also use these "shovels" to lift loose rubble and coral gravel and dig for worms, molluscs, and snails. With astonishing speed the prey is caught with the clawed walking legs, pressed against the ventral side of the carapace and guided to the mouth. Since each segment of the walking legs is much shorter than those of spiny lobsters, they are often invisible when the animals are walking.

Some members of the family Scyllaridae are colorful and have drawn the interest of aquarists. Typically, genera of slipper lobsters from temperate seas, *Scyllarus* and *Scyllarides,* are less colorful than members of the genus *Arctides* from tropical regions. These lobsters are nocturnal for the most part and are slow to acclimate to an illuminated aquarium. Not even mussel meat tempts them from their cover. But as soon as the lights are turned off they emerge from their hiding places - either deep in the sand or from a cave. They will demonstrate their nimbleness at twilight or during the night when offered frozen fish or tablet food. They never attack their tankmates,

Arctides regalis   HOLTHUIS, 1963
Red-banded slipper lobster

Hab.: Tropical Indo-Pacific.

Sex.: No external differences.

Soc.B./Assoc.: Since they do not get along with conspecifics, keep them singly. Can be easily housed with free-swimming fishes. Do not place larger specimens with small sea urchins, lest they are smashed and eaten.

M.: A rock aquarium with a large cave for shelter. A cover is advisable to prevent the animals from jumping out of the tank at night.

Light: Dim light; nocturnal crustacean.

B./Rep.: Has not been accomplished in an aquarium.

F.: C, FD; mussel and frozen crab meat. Tablet foods (TetraTips) can be given as supplemental nourishment.

S.: They lead a nocturnal life and are usually hidden during the day.

T: 22°-25°C, **L:** 12 cm, **TL:** from 80 cm, **WM:** w, **WR:** b, **AV:** 2, **D:** 1

The tropical red-banded slipper lobster, *Arctides regalis,* is a cave dweller that avoids muddy and sandy bottoms. Groups of up to 10 animals have been observed around Hawaii at night. Its orange-red coloration has evolved to help it blend in with *Tubastrea* coral that grows in its hiding place.

Fam.: Scyllaridae

even if they are fragile cleaner or anemone shrimp. Only short-spined sea urchins are in peril, since these animals are one of their main foods in their natural habitat. They use their sharp claws to rip them open starting at the oral opening.

Slipper lobsters and spiny lobsters are both gregarious animals in their natural habitat. Underwater photographs taken in various seas have shown these relationships. *Scyllarides latus*, which inhabits the Mediterranean and east Atlantic, emerges at night to congregate with conspecifics. Neither courtship, reproductive behavior, nor aggressions could be discerned. Is it an attempt to protect themselves against predatory octopi while searching for food? If you feed slipper or spiny lobsters cephalopods, especially tentacles of octopi, these lobsters race around nervously or retire into their hiding places. Larger specimens respond to the scent by executing pseudofights with their claws until they finally realize that their worst enenig is dead.

Scyllarus arctus   (LINNAEUS, 1758)
Little Cape Town lobster

Hab.: Mediterranean, eastern Atlantic.

Sex.: No external differences between ♂♂ and ♀♀.

Soc.B./Assoc.: Should be kept singly to avoid fights. However, they can live peacefully with most other invertebrates and many fishes.

M.: Rock aquarium with deep, dark crevices as hiding places. The water temperature should be less than 20°C during part of the year (winter).

Light: Dim light; nocturnal crustacean.

B./Rep.: Has not been successful in an aquarium. Ripe ♀♀ are found in the western Mediterranean from February to April and July to September.

F.: C, FD; they accept tablet foods. Since they are almost exclusively nocturnal, they should be fed after the lights are turned off.

S.: They are sometimes sold live at fish markets. These nocturnal animals are rarely seen during the day.

T: max. 23°C (see above), **L:** 10 cm, **TL:** from 80 cm, **WM:** w, **WR:** b, **AV:** 2-3, **D:** 1

An unidentified slipper lobster from the Maldives

Scyllarus arctus, Mediterranean

Fam.: Scyllaridae

Scyllarides latus (LATREILLE, 1803)
Cape Town lobster

Hab.: Mediterranean, eastern Atlantic.

Sex.: No external differences.

Soc.B./Assoc.: Keep singly. The picture on the top right was taken in its natural habitat where such group formations are very rare. In an aquarium, it will occasionally fight with other large crustacea such as hermit crabs. They can be housed with large fishes.

M.: Roomy rock aquarium with a cave. Since these strong animals like to dig with their modified antennae, the rocks in the aquarium must be very massive. A glass or lattice cover is recommended. In the winter the temperature should be less than 20°C.

Light: Dim light; nocturnal crustacean.

B./Rep.: Has not been accomplished in an aquarium.

F.: C, FD; frozen food, but tablet and flake foods are also eaten off the bottom during the night.

S.: Because these animals can reach a length of more than 30 cm, they are only recommended for very large aquaria. Large specimens are sometimes offered live at fish markets.

T: max. 23°C (see above), **L:** 30 cm, **TL:** from 120 cm, **WM:** w, **WR:** b, AV: 3, **D:** 1-2

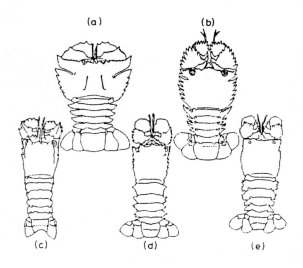

Body shapes of 5 different genera of slipper lobsters: (a) *Ibacus*, (b) *Parribarus*, (c) *Scyllarus*, (d) *Scyllarides*, and (e) *Arctides*.

Scyllarides latus, Mediterranean

Scyllarides latus, east Atlantic

Fam.: Scyllaridae

Scyllarides astori, Gulf of California

Scyllarides astori
Californian slipper lobster

HOLTHUIS, 1960

Hab.: Eastern Pacific, Gulf of California.

Sex.: No recognizable exterior differences.

Soc.B./Assoc.: Do not keep with conspecifics or other crustacea. Sea urchins are crushed and eaten.

M.: Rock aquarium with good hiding places. Because they often dig, all edifications must be stable.

Light: Dim light; nocturnal crustacean.

B./Rep.: Has not been successful in an aquarium.

F.: C, FD; they are easily fed with fish and mussel meat. Flake food is also happily eaten.

S.: Only conditionally suitable for tropical aquaria.

T: 18°-22°C, **L:** 25 cm, **TL:** from 120 cm, **WM:** w, **WR:** b, **AV:** 3, **D:** 1

Scyllarides astori

Scyllarides haanii, Hawaii

Since they rarely flee, slipper lobsters are choice animals for divers to observe. On these pictures you can also see the uncommon anatomy of this decapod. Above, *Scyllariedes haanii* from Hawaii; top of facing page, *Scyllarides astori* in the Gulf of California (Mexico). Note *S. astori*'s shovellike purple antennae.

Fam.: Nephropidae

Knebelia bilobata , a fossil of a lobster from Fort Peck, Montana, USA (80 million years)

About the Family Nephropidae

In the last decade, various lobsters from tropical seas have been discovered. Many are enchantingly colored, and their size and temperature requirements coincide with conditions prevailing in a tropical tank. Although members of the genera *Homarus* and *Nephrops* are also seen in aquaria, they are generally kept to tempt restaurant patrons to grace their plates with them, not their aquarium. Species from these genera tolerate temperatures as low as -1°C and are already uncomfortable at 15°C. Their tasty meat is a sought commodity on the world market and is sold by the ton. Their desirability is understandable despite their rather drab appearance, since the two largest species, *Homarus americanus* and *Homarus gammarus*, attain a length of over 60 cm.

All members of the family Nephropidae can be easily identified by their first pair of walking legs that are modified into powerful claws. Coldwater lobsters use them to crack mussels, whereas tropical reef lobsters use them to capture and guide other foodstuffs to their mouthparts. All species of lobsters have claws longer than one third of their total body length.

Enoplometopus debelius

ABOUT THE GENUS *ENOPLOMETOPUS*

The tropical reef lobsters of the genus *Enoplometopus* rarely grow longer than 15 cm and are real eye catchers - provided you even catch a glimpse of these reclusive animals. As can be deduced from a revision of the genus, the first tropical reef lobster, *Enoplometopus occidentalis*, was known to science in the previous century. It is still considered the most widely distributed reef lobster. This species is usually imported from Hawaii; that is why it was named the Hawaiian lobster (also known as the red dwarf lobster). However, it is distributed throughout the Indo-Pacific.

Fam.: Nephropidae

At first glance there are no noticeable sexual differences in tropical reef lobsters. However, with a closer look the animals can easily be sexed. The male's first pair of swimmerets (pleopods) is modified into copulatory organs that transfer the sperm. They are two half-cylinders that form a whole when placed together. This looks like a small pin at the base of the fifth pair of legs in the photo. The female has an exterior spermatheca, which is a longitudinal structure between the posterior three pairs of legs (refer to photo). The median longitudinal slit receives the male's sex organ. A small peg of the second pair of pleopods is introduced from behind into the cylinder and acts like a piston to expel the sperm out the anterior opening. This action concludes the copulation and the lobsters separate. The female fertilizes the eggs by passing the eggs from the sexual opening at the base of the third pair of legs, past the spermatheca, and then to the swimmerets, where they are adhered and carried until they hatch.

♂   ♀

Enoplometopus debelius

Enoplometopus debelius, ♀ with eggs

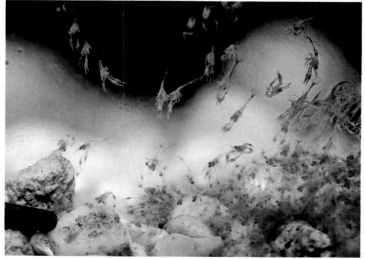

Copulation occurs after the ♀ molts. After 6 days, the larvae hatch during the night.

Fam.: Nephropidae

Enoplometopus antillensis

Enoplometopus antillensis
LÜTKEN, 1865
Caribbean red reef lobster

Hab.: From the Caribbean to the islands of the east Atlantic.

Sex.: No secondary sexual characteristics.

Soc.B./Assoc.: Gets along well with most tropical and Mediterranean fishes.

M.: Rock aquarium with deep hiding places.

Light: Dim light.

B./Rep.: Has not been successful in an aquarium.

F.: C, FD; like other *Enoplometopus* species.

S.: Like other species of reef lobsters, they are easily seen during nocturnal dives.

T: from 18°C, **L:** 10 cm **TL:** from 80 cm, **WM:** w-m, **WR:** b, **AV:** 2, **D:** 1-2

Enoplometopus daumi
HOLTHUIS, 1983
Daum´s reef lobster

Hab.: Indo-Australian region, the Philippines, and Indonesia.

Sex.: No secondary sexual characteristics. The external sexual organs can be seen on the ventral side of the abdomen.

Soc.B./Assoc.: Ideal scavenger for large fish aquaria that do not contain triggerfishes or others that may crack their exoskeleton and devour them. Although there are few negative experiences, they have been known to take advantage of small, slow fishes. The same applies to smaller crustacea. They can be housed with spiny lobsters, large hermit crabs, and tube and other large anemones. Do not keep with conspecifics of the same gender.

M.: Reef aquarium with deep hiding places.

Light: Dim light.

B./Rep.: Has not been successful in an aquarium.

F.: C, FD; accepts all meat-based foods and tablets (TetraTips).

S.: Just recently scientifically described.

T: 20°-24°C, even above 30°C for short durations, **L:** 11 cm, **TL:** from 80 cm, **WM:** w-m, **WR:** b, **AV:** 1, **D:** 1-2

Enoplometopus antillensis, Cape Verde Islands

Enoplometopus daumi, aquarium

Fam.: Nephropidae

Enoplometopus debelius   HOLTHUIS, 1983
Debelius' reef lobster

Hab.: Pacific, from Hawaii to Indonesia.

Sex.: No secondary sexual characteristics. The sexual organs can be seen on the ventral side of the abdomen.

Soc.B./Assoc.: They can be kept in pairs; cohabit well with fishes. Although they move about at night, they do not bother wrasses buried in the sand. Sensitive invertebrates, however, are sometimes disturbed.

M.: A reef aquarium with good hiding places. Caves can be arranged so that the lobsters are visible during the day also.

Light: Dim light. With subdued illumination (e.g., one small actinic tube) the animals will also search for food during the day.

B./Rep.: As with most crustacea, copulation occurs after the ♀ molts. During molting, chemical attractants (pheromones) are released to entice the ♂. As long as the ♀ has eggs on her abdomen, the ♂ should be kept out of the tank. Six days after fertilization, the larvae hatch. Rearing is only successful if live marine plankton is offered.

F.: C, FD; content to feed on any leftovers it finds on the substrate.

S.: The author kept this species almost 9 years in his tanks.

T: 20°-26°C, **L:** 10 cm, **TL:** from 80 cm, **WM:** w-m, **WR:** b, **AV:** 1, **D:** 1

Homarus gammarus, European lobster; text on p. 593

Enoplometopus debelius, aquarium photo   *Enoplometopus debelius* in its biotope

Enoplometopus debelius during molting; the old exoskeleton is in front

Fam.: Nephropidae

Enoplometopus holthuisi   GORDON, 1968
Holthuis reef lobster

Hab.: Entire tropical Indo-Pacific, from Hawaii to east Africa.

Sex.: No secondary sexual characteristics. The external sexual organs can be seen on the ventral side of the abdomen.

Soc.B./Assoc.: It can be associated with fishes, but it is less successfully housed with other crustacea. Always engages in injurious fights with conspecifics of the same gender.

M.: Reef aquarium with deep hiding places. Sensitive to high nitrate concentrations.

Light: Dim light; nocturnal crustacean.

B./Rep.: Has not been successful in an aquarium.

F.: C, FD; a good scavenger. This species searches the tank at night and will eat any food found on the bottom.

S.: More slender than most *Enoplometopus* species. Its conspicuous design makes it easily discernible from other species.

T: 22°-27°C, **L:** 12 cm, **TL:** from 80 cm, **WM:** w-m, **WR:** b, **AV:** 2, **D:** 1-2

Enoplometopus occidentalis   (RANDALL, 1840)
Hawaiian, reef lobster

Hab.: The entire Indo-Pacific region.

Sex.: No secondary sexual characteristics. The external sexual organs can be seen on the ventral side of the abdomen.

Soc.B./Assoc.: This lobster gets along with most fishes. Small, slow-moving fishes, however, might be considered prey. It should not be associated with conspecifics of the same sex.

M.: Reef aquarium with deep hiding places. It is sensitive to excessive levels of nitrate.

Light: Dim light. If the illumination is not excessive, these nocturnal animals will venture forth during the day to feed.

B./Rep.: After acclimation, the ♀ may repeatedly carry eggs. Rearing is possible, but it usually fails because of the lack of procurable food for the larvae (marine plankton).

F.: C, FD; they accept any frozen or tablet foods. Since they have well developed senses, they find all types of leftovers.

S.: With good care, the Hawaiian regal lobster molts approximately every 6 weeks.

T: 20°-25°C, **L:** 12 cm, **TL:** from 80 cm, **WM:** w-m, **WR:** b, **AV:** 2, **D:** 1-2

Enoplometopus occidentalis

Enoplometopus holthuisi off Hawaii

Enoplometopus occidentalis, aquarium

Fam.: Nephropidae

Enoplometopus voigtmanni   TÜRKAY, 1989
Voigtmann's reef lobster

Hab.: Has only been found along the outer reef of the island of Maayafushi, in the Ari Atoll of the Maldives, and probably Sri Lanka.

Sex.: No secondary sexual characteristics. The sexual organs can be seen on the ventral side of the abdomen.

Soc.B./Assoc.: *E. voigtmanni* usually live in pairs in their biotope, but sometimes they are found singly.

M.: This species has not yet been kept in aquaria. Maintaining them in the manner suggested for other members of the genus is probably adequate. These animals seclude themselves away in grottos along the reef drop-off.

Light: Dim light.

B./Rep.: Current observations suggest that the spawning time in the Maldives begins in September.

F.: C, FD; nothing is known, but it can be assumed that this species should be cared for like other members of the genus.

S.: The species was not scientifically described until the end of 1989! Its color pattern is distinctive.

T: 24°-26°C, **L:** 10 cm, **TL:** from 80 cm, **WM:** w, **WR:** b, **AV:** 4, **D:** 2

Homarus americanus   H. MILNE-EDWARDS, 1837
American lobster, Maine lobster

Hab.: American side of the Atlantic. The southern boundary is the Bermuda Islands.

Sex.: ♂♂ grow larger and usually have stronger pinchers.

Soc.B./Assoc.: Quarrelsome towards conspecifics and other invertebrates. Best kept singly or with large, free-swimming fishes.

M.: Massive rock aquarium with large caves to hide in.

Light: Dim light.

B./Rep.: Has not been accomplished in an aquarium.

F.: C, FD; frozen food, fish and crustacean meat, mussels (with or without shells).

S.: Occasionally found live at fish markets. Only suitable for large show aquaria. Regularly available at seafood importers (except during the protected period).

T: 10°-20°C, **L:** 40 cm, **TL:** from 120 cm, **WM:** m, **WR:** b, **AV:** 1, **D:** 1-3 (chiller!)

Homarus gammarus (see p. 588 for photo)   (LINNAEUS, 1758)
European lobster

Hab.: Mediterranean, Atlantic to Norway.

Sex.: ♂♂ have larger claws.

Soc.B./Assoc.: If several animals are kept, their claws are tied to prevent them from injuring each other.

M.: Only in restaurant aquaria. Stony bottom with hiding places when possible. Strong filtration with added oxygen.

Light: Dim to moderate light.

Continued on p. 594:

Nephrops norvegicus   LINNAEUS, 1758
Norway lobster, Dublin Bay prawn

Hab.: Mediterranean and Atlantic to Norway.

Sex.: ♂♂ have stronger pinchers than ♀♀.

Soc.B./Assoc.: Keep singly or with large fishes. Their nocturnal activity disturbs invertebrates.

M.: Provide a sandy substrate with a flat stone plate on top. Build a cavern under the stone. The water temperature should not exceed 18°C.

Light: Dim light.

B./Rep.: Has not been successful in an aquarium. The main spawning season in the Mediterranean extends from July to February, but there are always a few ♀♀ with eggs. The eggs are initially green, but turn reddish later.

F.: C, FD; they take any frozen food as well as tablet food.

S.: Often found in fish markets in Mediterranean countries; however, they are rarely alive.

T: 10°-22°C (see above), **L:** 15 cm, **TL:** from 100 cm, **WM:** w, **WR:** b, **AV:** 3, **D:** 2

Continuation of *Homarus gammarus* from p. 593:

B./Rep.: Impossible in an aquarium. In nature the lobsters spawn at more profound depths. The larvae are pelagic for a few weeks.

F.: C, O; carrion, fish, mussels, sea urchins, tablet foods, salmon (trout) pellets, etc.

S.: Protected species! It is forbidden to sell these animals for aquaria—but you can buy and sell it for human consumption. What a paradoxical law for species protection!

T: 24°-29°C, **L:** 50 cm, **TL:** 100 cm, **WM:** m, **WR:** b, **AV:** 2, **D:** 2 (chiller!)

About the Family Diogenidae

All members of the hermit crab family Diogenidae have a totally transformed abdomen which is not surrounded by the crustacean-typical calcareous chitin shell. To better live in the merciless predator/prey world, the hermit crabs have searched for a way to protect their soft abdomen. Empty gastropod shells or hollow pieces of coral branches were used, and slowly the abdomen adopted a curved shape to better follow the windings of the gastropod shell.

What the layperson particularly notes about the family Diogenidae is that it is left-handed. The chela on the left side is larger than the right. All other hermit crabs, including members of the family Paguridae introduced later in the book, are right-handed; right-handed hermits are less popular among aquarists and divers. Hermit crabs, which are omnipresent in coastal regions of tropical and temperate seas, are not particular about the type of snail shell they use, even freshwater gastropod shells carried to the sea by rivers are accepted. The only condition the crustacean places on housing is size suitability. Houses of inappropriate size, whether too large or small, are exchanged as soon as a more fitting one is found. Since crustacea grow when they molt, it is quite possible that the hermit crab will outgrow its old shell when it molts and have to find another. Its unprotected abdomen is especially vulnerable to predators at this time.

Research has shown that hermit crabs fix themselves into the snail shell with, among other structures, the last pair of legs. The distal edge of the legs is concave and covered with tubercles that are arranged more or less in parallel rows. The last legs are carried at a forward slant, which means the bristles point towards the head and prevent the body from being pulled out of the shell as they press against the inside. A hermit crab tears along the delicate line between its abdomen and thorax before it permits itself to be forcibly removed from its shell. Never try to remove a hermit crab from its shell.

Many Diogenidae are diurnal. You can observe them while diving or in front of the aquarium reef. Members of this family of hermit crabs are not gregarious, rather each adult is independent of the other. However, groups of juveniles of the genus *Diogenes* have been observed in the shallow waters of the Mediterranean. Strangely, they all used shells of *Bittium reticulatum*, a gastropod. Their days are passed avoiding the currents. The species of the family Diogenidae are omnivores: they will eat anything from algae to all types of carrion. They search large areas and graze on encountered foods that have fallen to the substrate. They are the reef cleaners for tropical and temperate seas.

However, in nature they—like other crustacea—have a number of enemies. Included among these are strong-toothed predators such as porcupinefishes and puffers, stomatopods and their relatives, and the box crab that opens the shell like a can opener using its pinchers. To resist its main enemy, the *Octopus*, the hermit crab carries venomous anemones on its house. An octopus hates nothing more than nematocysts, which are shot by the anemone on contact. This living community has been studied in detail: the sessile anemone gains a pair of legs which helps it locate food. The hermit crab seems to be aware of the advantages of the relationship. It actively strokes the anemones. The anemone responds by releasing its hold. The crab then places them on its house. Hermit crabs have even been seen transplanting anemones from their old shell onto a new one. The stroking seems to identify the crab as a friend because nematocysts are not shot at their future "housemate."

This snap shot of an unprotected hermit crab abdomen was successfully taken while the crab was in the process of changing houses. It was quite amusing how fast it grabbed the new snail shell and pushed its soft abdomen inside.

This unknown *Dardanus* species was photographed during a diving expedition along Australia's Great Barrier Reef. This species was seen in old decrepit shells as well as new, shiny shells (small photo).

Fam.: Diogenidae

Aniculus maximus
Large hermit crab

EDMONDSON, 1952

Hab.: Tropical Indo-Pacific.

Sex.: No external differences between the sexes.

Soc.B./Assoc.: Based on its body size and rambunctious behavior, they are unsuitable for invertebrate aquaria. In a large tank, they can be kept with large fishes (e.g., triggers).

M.: Massive rockwork and a sandy bottom. There should always be several larger empty snail shells to choose from.

Light: Dim light.

B./Rep.: Has not been successful in an aquarium.

F.: C, FD; they accept all frozen foods as well as tablet foods (TetraTips).

S.: Very robust animals which only get along with a few other species. Even free-swimming fishes are not safe.

T: 20°-25°C, **L:** 10 cm, **TL:** from 120 cm, **WM:** m, **WR:** b, **AV:** 2-3, **D:** 1

Aniculus hermits, which inhabit the entire Indo-Pacific, are brightly colored. This picture was taken during the day on a reef by Maui, Hawaii.

Aniculus maximus

Aniculus maximus

Fam.: Diogenidae

Calcinus ornatus
Ornate hermit crab

(ROUX, 1830)

Hab.: Mediterranean, east Atlantic.

Sex.: No external differentiating characteristics.

Soc.B./Assoc.: These small, delicate animals are nice scavengers for the invertebrate and fish aquarium. Do not keep with large crustacea, triggers, or wrasses.

M.: Rock aquarium with or without a sandy bottom. Always have empty snail shells lying around.

Light: Moderate light.

B./Rep.: Not yet successful in an aquarium.

F.: C, FD; they accept all types of frozen, tablet, and flake foods. Since they always feed on leftovers, they do not need to be individually fed.

S.: Also suitable for the tropical marine aquarium. In the Mediterranean, this is the only species often found in fastened shells of *Vermetus* snails or calcareous tubeworms. They do not abandon these shelters. How they acquire a larger shell is unknown.

T: 16°-24°C, **L:** 2 cm, **TL:** from 50 cm, **WM:** w-s, **WR:** b-m, **AV:** 3, **D:** 1

Cancellus sp.
Sandstone hermit crab

Hab.: Southern Australian coast.

Sex.: No external differentiating features.

Soc.B./Assoc.: Can be kept singly or in a small group. They are peaceful and rather shy. See *Calcinus ornatus* for acceptable tankmates.

M.: Shallow sand or gravel bottom with pieces of sandstone (see photo).

Light: Dim light.

B./Rep.: Has not been successful in an aquarium.

F.: C, FD; if there are leftovers from feeding other occupants of the aquarium, you need not worry about feeding this crab individually.

S.: This species drills holes in sandstone pebbles and then carries these self-made houses around instead of a snail shell.

T: 18°-23°C, **L:** 2 cm, **TL:** from 50 cm, **WM:** m, **WR:** b, **AV:** 3, **D:** 1

Fam.: Diogenidae

Dardanus calidus   (RISSO, 1827)
Mediterranean hermit crab

Hab.: Mediterranean.

Sex.: No external differences.

Soc.B./Assoc.: Based on their size, follow the advice given for *Aniculus maximus*.

M.: Rock aquarium with a sand bottom.

Light: Dim light; nocturnal.

B./Rep.: Has not been successful in an aquarium.

F.: C, FD; nonproblematic. Frozen and tablet foods are accepted.

S.: Puts anemones on his house just like *D. pedunculatus* (see below). Not suitable for tropical aquaria.

T: 16°-22°C, **L:** 10 cm, **TL:** from 120 cm, **WM:** m, **WR:** b, **AV:** 3, **D:** 1

Dardanus deformis   (H. MILNE-EDWARDS, 1836)
Rock hermit crab

Hab.: The entire Indo-Pacific region.

Sex.: No external differences.

Soc.B./Assoc.: Larger specimens should not be kept with delicate invertebrates.

M.: Reef aquarium with a sand bottom. Rockwork must be stable.

Light: Dim light.

B./Rep.: Has not been successful in an aquarium.

F.: C, FD; nonproblematic. Any frozen, flake, and tablet foods are accepted. Once in a while earthworms can be given.

S.: The left pincher is so large that it can be used to totally close the opening of the snail shell. A stinging anemone, *Calliactis polypus*, is usually adhered to the shell. These are nocturnal crabs which do not move much during the day.

T: 22°-28°C, **L:** 10 cm, **TL:** from 100 cm, **WM:** m, **WR:** b, **AV:** 1, **D:** 1

The strong left pincher identifies *Dardanus deformis* as a member of the Diogenidae. Both aquarium photos show that hermit crabs can be kept in an aquarium with many invertebrates. Invertebrates were ignored. However, every once in a while the crab attacked the copious growing *Caulerpa* algae. The anemones, which were imported on the crab's shell, remained with the crab in the aquarium.

Dardanus calidus

Dardanus deformis

Fam.: Diogenidae

Dardanus lagopodes   (FORSKÅL, 1775)
Blade eyed hermit crab

Hab.: All of the Indo-Pacific region and the Red Sea.

Sex.: No external differences.

Soc.B./Assoc.: Since this species does not grow as large as some of the others, it is easier to combine with other species. Does well in a fish aquarium. Delicate invertebrates are greatly disturbed.

M.: Reef aquarium with shallow areas. Growing animals will need progressively larger empty gastropod shells.

Light: Dim light.

B./Rep.: Not yet successful in an aquarium.

F.: C, FD; excellent scavengers which, however, will occasionally desire something more substantial. They also like to feed on filamentous green algae.

S.: *Dardanus lagopodes* is often imported and can easily be distinguished from other species by its white eyestalks. The uncommon snail shell was three times larger than the crab itself and was brought from the Maldives to Germany. This clumsy elephant was finally transferred to a fish tank since its unremitting activity injured disc and colonial anemones. The fishes benefited from its presence, as its sloven feeding behavior whirled up the food, and they only needed to join the party and eat.

T: 21°-28°C, **L:** 6 cm, **TL:** from 80 cm, **WM:** w-m, **WR:** b, **AV:** 2, **D:** 1

Dardanus deformis, aquarium photo

Dardanus lagopodes

Dardanus lagopodes

Fam.: Diogenidae

Dardanus megistos   (HERBST, 1789)
White-spot hermit crab

Hab.: The Indo-Pacific region.

Sex.: No distinguishing external features.

Soc.B./Assoc.: Only associate with fishes and very robust invertebrates (e.g., other strong crustacea such as crabs, lobsters, and spiny lobsters). Several specimens in the same tank will fight.

M.: Reef aquarium with massive decorations. Because these crabs are messy feeders, a good filter will be needed.

Light: Dim light.

B./Rep.: Has not been successful in an aquarium.

F.: C, FD; large amounts of mussel, fish, and shrimp meat are consumed. Tablet foods, *Tubifex*, and earthworms are also accepted.

S.: Especially active at night.

T: 21°-28°C, **L:** 10 cm, **TL:** from 120 cm, **WM:** m, **WR:** b, **AV:** 2, **D:** 1

Dardanus pedunculatus   (HERBST, 1804)
Coral hermit crab

Hab.: Indo-Pacific region.

Sex.: No differentiating external features.

Soc.B./Assoc.: The larger the specimens, the more difficult they are to house with other animals. They constantly search for food. Almost all small invertebrates are devoured. Larger specimens are best kept alone or with large fishes (including triggers and wrasses).

M.: Provide a rock aquarium. They will clamber about on the rocks during the night. Keep several large gastropod shells available to allow them to change.

Light: Dim light.

B./Rep.: Although they will occasionally mate in an aquarium, they have not been successfully reared.

F.: C, FD; they eat all foods of animal origin as well as carrion, algae, and tablets.

S.: To protect themselves from their primary enemy, *Octopus*, many *Dardanus* species place stinging anemones on their house. It is very interesting to watch them transfer both themselves and their anemones to their new shell. Unfortunately, this is almost always a nocturnal event.

T: 20°-25°C, **L:** 6 cm, **TL:** from 80 cm, **WM:** m, **WR:** b, **AV:** 3, **D:** 1

Dardanus megistos

Dardanus pedunculatus

Paguristes cadenati
Red reef hermit

FOREST, 1954

Hab.: Caribbean and western Atlantic.

Sex.: There are no external differences.

Soc.B./Assoc.: They get along well with many invertebrates and almost all fishes. Several specimens can be kept in larger tanks.

M.: Reef aquarium. It has no special requirements.

Light: Dim light.

B./Rep.: Not yet successful in an aquarium.

F.: C, FD; nonproblematic. They accept any type of food. Good scavengers for the fish aquarium.

S.: Nocturnal crab which likes to inhabit gastropod shells that are overgrown with encrusting red algae (red calcareous algae). This alga gives a pink color to the shell.

T: 20°-27°C, **L:** 3 cm, **TL:** from 80 cm, **WM:** w-s, **WR:** b-m, **AV:** 1-2, **D:** 1

Petrochirus diogenes
Giant hermit, stony finger hermit

(LINNAEUS, 1758)

Hab.: Caribbean and western Atlantic.

Sex.: No external differences.

Soc.B./Assoc.: Same as other large *Dardanus* species (pp. 602 - 606). Caution—small specimens grow quickly.

M.: A reef and rock aquarium with massive decorations. No special water quality requirements.

Light: Dim light.

B./Rep.: Has not been accomplished in an aquarium.

F.: C, FD; large pieces of mussel, fish, and shrimp meat. Tablet food is also readily accepted.

S.: The largest Caribbean hermit. It often inhabits the shells of the large conch *Strombus gigas*. In contrast to *Dardanus* species, both pinchers are usually the same size. Largely similar to *P. californiensis* from California.

T: 20°-27°C, **L:** 12 cm, **TL:** from 120 cm, **WM:** m-s, **WR:** b, **AV:** 2, **D:** 1-2

Trizopagurus strigatus   (HERBST, 1804)
Striped hermit crab

Hab.: Indo-Pacific and Red Sea.

Sex.: No external differences.

Soc.B./Assoc.: *T. strigatus* is a medium-sized hermit which should only be associated with robust invertebrates and fishes.

M.: A reef aquarium with a sand substrate.

Light: Dim light.

B./Rep.: Not yet successful in an aquarium.

F.: FD; they accept any kind of frozen and tablet foods.

S.: Unknown.

T: 22°-28°C, **L:** 6 cm, **TL:** from 80 cm, **WM:** m, **WR:** b, **AV:** 2, **D:** 1

Most species of the Paguridae family live in temperate waters. The picture on the right was taken on the west coast of Ireland. The right-handedness of pagurids is clearly shown (larger chela on the right). A live snail has climbed onto the hermit's house. The photo on the top of page 612 shows the same species along the Dutch coast examining another house, which, unfortunately, was already occupied.

About the Family Pauridae

Like the previous family (Diogenidae), these animals also have a soft abdomen that they stick into a gastropod shell. However, their right pincher is clearly larger than the left. A species-rich family whose representatives are usually smaller than species of Diogenidae.

Pagurus bernhardus   (LINNAEUS, 1758)
Soldier hermit

Hab.: North Atlantic and the North and Baltic Seas.

Sex.: There are no external differences.

Soc.B./Assoc.: Large specimens need to be kept singly or exclusively with free-swimming fishes or strong invertebrates, e.g., crabs.

M.: Sandy bottom with stones. The temperature should not exceed 20°C.

Light: Dim light.

B./Rep.: Not yet successful in the aquarium.

F.: C, FD; mussel, fish, and crab meat. Tablet food and earthworms are also eaten.

S.: Only suitable for the coldwater aquarium. This species is normally found in empty *Buccinum* shells.

T: 15°-20°C, **L:** 9 cm, **TL:** from 100 cm, **WM:** m, **WR:** b, **AV:** 2, **D:** 1

Pagurus bernhardus

Pagurus bernhardus

Pagurus cuanensis

Manucomplanus varians
(BENEDICT, 1892)
Coralhouse hermit

Hab.: Pacific.

Sex.: No external differences.

Soc.B./Assoc.: They get along well with many invertebrates and fishes.

M.: Reef aquarium. They are relatively sensitive to poor water quality.

Light: Dim light.

B./Rep.: Has not been successful in an aquarium.

F.: C, FD; they accept all foods and are good scavengers for the fish tank.

S.: Their house is covered with hydroids or bryozoans. They use their oversized right pincher to close the shell entrance.

T: 22°-28°C, **L:** 3 cm, **TL:** from 80 cm, **WM:** w-m, **WR:** b, **AV:** 3, **D:** 1

Manucomplanus varians

Pagurus cuanensis   BELL, 1846
Wool-hand hermit

Hab.: Mediterranean, North Sea, and east Atlantic.

Sex.: There are no external differences.

Soc.B./Assoc.: They can be easily associated with most invertebrates. Only particularly delicate animals should be barred from their tank. Good scavengers in the fish aquarium.

M.: Rock aquarium with a sand substrate. Few demands are placed on water quality. However, the temperature should be moderate.

Light: Dim light.

B./Rep.: Ha not yet been successful in an aquarium. The spawning season in the western Mediterranean occurs between July and September.

F.: C, FD; they accept any kind of food.

S.: Conditionally suitable for the tropical marine aquarium.

T: 16°-24°C, **L:** 3 cm, **TL:** from 80 cm, **WM:** w-m, **WR:** b, **AV:** 2-3, **D:** 1

Fam.: Galatheidae

About the Family Galatheidae

The Galatheidae, or squat lobsters, have a very peculiar body shape. They have two large, long pinchers, a carapace that extends from the rostrum to the center of the body, and an abdomen that is folded beneath the thorax. Just image an egg with two pinchers. The walking legs are comparatively small and short, and the posterior legs are invisible at rest, since they are folded away. Although squat lobsters resemble true crabs, the differences become evident under closer observation: squat lobsters only have three active pairs of walking legs behind their pinchers; crabs have 4. This "missing" pair of legs, however, is located in the gill cavity of the lobster. It is modified to constantly clean the sensitive gills of dirt and foreign bodies. The oversized pinchers rarely capture prey. Instead they are used for courtship and defense.

The squat lobsters are divided into three large groups: the munides, the munidopsines, and the galagheines. There are only a few known species in the first two groups because they are almost exclusively found in the deep sea. However, the chewing squat lobster, *Munida rugosa*, from the western European coast and the striated *Munidopsis polymorpha* from the "Jameos del Aqua" cave on the Lanzarote Island of the Canaries, a tourist attraction, should be mentioned.

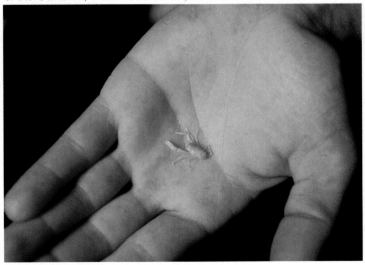

Munidopsis polymorpha, Lanzarote, Canary Islands

Allogalathea elegans
Feather star squat lobster

(ADAMS & WHITE, 1848)

Hab.: The entire tropical Indo-Pacific.

Sex.: No recognizable external differences.

Soc.B./Assoc.: They always live together with feather stars and are often imported with them. Otherwise, a substitute host should be offered. Do not keep with predatory crustacea.

M.: Reef aquarium with a feather star(s). There must be small crevices that they can take refuge in when needed.

Light: Dim light.

B./Rep.: Has not been done in an aquarium.

F.: C, FD; they feed on dry and frozen foods that have settled on the bottom.

S.: They live commensally (two organisms living in community to the benefit of one, but without harm to the other) on feather stars and change their color to match their host. They usually sit on their arms, only searching for a rock crevice during danger.

T: 22°-27°C, **L:** 2 cm, **TL:** from 80 cm, **WM:** m-s, **WR:** m, **AV:** 3, **D:** 2 (feather star 3-4!)

Galathea strigosa
Spinous squat lobster

(LINNAEUS, 1767)

Hab.: Mediterranean, northern Atlantic.

Sex.: The sexes cannot be differentiated from external features.

Soc.B./Assoc.: Many fishes and other crustacea make suitable companions for this species. Several individuals of the same species should not be put together, since it usually leads to fights.

M.: Rock aquarium with a large cave you can peer into. Though the crabs are nocturnal, they do not always remain hidden during the day. The temperature should drop below 20°C in the winter.

Light: Dim light.

B./Rep.: Has not been successful in an aquarium. In the Mediterranean, the spawning season extends from December to April.

F.: C, FD; easily fed. They accept any frozen and flake foods.

S.: Not suitable for the tropical aquarium. There are several related, but smaller, species in its area of distribution. Similar species of the *Munida* genus can be differentiated by their extremely long pinchers.

T: 17°-23°C (see above), **L:** 8 cm, **TL:** from 80 cm, **WM:** w-m, **WR:** b, **AV:** 3, **D:** 1-2

Allogalathea elegans, see text on previous page

Galathea strigosa, Mediterranean

Fam.: Porcellanidae

The notoriety of this species-rich family is due to the frequently imported members of the genus *Neopetrolisthes*. They are commonly called anemone crabs because they live either at the base or in the tentacles of stinging anemones. They can be found in this niche in all tropical seas by the attentive diver. They defend their protective site against vicious clownfishes of the genus *Amphiprion,* even in a marine aquarium. Although they are planktivores, their care and feeding is not difficult. Algae quickly use their exoskeleton as a substrate if the tank is excessively illuminated. Molting will restore their beauty.

When the layman uses the expression "crab," you should realize that it does not refer to a taxonomic term, but rather to a body type. Crabs are decapods that carry their thin abdomen folded forward against the ventral side of their cephalothorax. If you look closely at the abdomen, you can clearly see the various segments. The last segment is very mobile and can be opened at will to defecate without exposing its entire abdomen. It is different, however, when the animals want to reproduce. The other segments are permanently attached to the lower thorax with two snaplike structures. Using the basal musculature, the male stretches his abdomen and inseminates willing females. Afterwards the snaplike structures are re-aligned! These snaps significantly aid the abdominal musculature, because even though the abdominal muscles can close the abdomen, they are too reduced to keep it shut.

In the Porcellanidae, this mechanism does not exist. Here a strong folding muscle maintains the abdomen protectively folded underneath the shelled carapace. This is highly advantageous for anemone crabs, because during danger, they can flip their abdomen to propel themselves backwards. True crabs, which have to use their walking legs to move, are slower. The anemone crabs, as the porcelain crabs presented in this chapter are called, have much less reason to flee than other porcellanids because they are protected by their hosts, stinging anemones. In contrast, the closely related species of the genera *Petrolisthes* and *Petrocheles* live in deeper zones and must protect themselves.

While members of these two genera filter feed while well hidden in coral rubble or rock crevices, anemone crabs can filter their foods from sunlit shallow waters that are often only 50 cm deep.

Neopetrolisthes sp.

So far, three species of anemone crabs of the genus *Neopetrolisthes* are known. This is an additional, as yet undescribed species. The picture was taken in front of the Maldive Islands in the Indian Ocean.

Fam.: Porcellanidae

Their third maxillipeds have very long, fine bristles that are spread fanlike to filter out food. When folded, a considerable amount of water is pressed through the bristles. The suspended solids remain trapped on the third maxillipeds. The second maxillipeds remove the filtered food and guide it to other mouthparts. But these crabs can also feed on large pieces of food, e.g., krill, that they pick up off the ground with their chelipeds. They hold on to the substrate for hours with their chelipeds while cleaning themselves or feeding. The fifth pair of walking legs is held close to the body, originating approximately where the abdomen folds in. This pair of walking legs is only used for cleaning. In a folded state, the anemone crab can reach from its gill cavity almost any point on its body. The two cleaner legs alternatedly clean by passing over pincher legs, body and underneath the carapace. All while the crab continues filtering for food in the current!

Anemone crabs are usually true to their host, especially when a sexually mature pair has nested there. The male anemone crab has to wait for the female to molt before he can mate with her. Copulation is otherwise impossible because the female's hard chitinous shell closes the genital opening. Newly molted females release pheromones into the water to attract males. Some porcelain crabs insure that they don't miss the opportune moment by carrying their chosen female around on their back until she molts.

Neopetrolisthes alobatus (LAURIE, 1925)
Blue-spotted anemone crab

Hab.: Western Indo-Pacific, Mauritius, and Madagascar.

Sex.: Not recognizable based on external characteristics.

Soc.B./Assoc.: They usually live in pairs in various species of anemones. Do not associate with large crustacea or aggressive fishes. They are ideal companions for invertebrates.

M.: Reef aquarium with a host anemone (e.g., *Heteractis* or *Stichodactyla*). *Caulerpa* algae are recommended.

Light: Moderate light.

B./Rep.: Has not been successful in an aquarium.

F.: C, FD; the crustacea are planktivores which can be fed various plankton substitutes (e.g., mussel milk) or ground flake or tablet foods administered with a feeding tube (e.g., TetraTips rubbed through an *Artemia* sieve and then wetted).

S.: This is an uncommon, rarely imported species.

T: 22°-26°C, **L:** 2 cm, **TL:** from 50 cm, **WM:** m, **WR:** m, **AV:** 3-4, **D:** 2

Fam.: Porcellanidae

Neopetrolisthes maculatus   (MILNE-EDWARDS, 1837)
Dotted anemone crab

Hab.: Entire tropical Indo-Pacific.

Sex.: Not distinguishable from external features.

Soc.B./Assoc.: They live in pairs exclusively in a commensal relationship (living together to the advantage of one) with large host anemones of the genera *Entacmaea, Gyrostoma, Stichodactyla, Cryptodendrum,* and *Heteractis.* Tube anemones are not suitable alternative hosts, since they will sting anemone crabs to death. Good companions for delicate invertebrates like small shrimp, brittle starfish, etc. Although they are often seen sharing an anemone with clownfishes (*Amphiprion*) in nature, this congeniality does not extend to the aquarium.

M.: A reef aquarium with one of the above mentioned anemones.

Light: Moderate light. With excessive illumination, the animals hide beneath the anemone.

B./Rep.: Has not been successful in an aquarium.

F.: C, FD; planktivore that accepts all kinds of zooplankton and crumbled flake foods. Small pieces of food administered with tweezers can also be given. Because they only feed at night when in new surroundings, at first they will have to be fed after the lights are turned off.

S.: In the aquarium literature this species is often described as *N. ohshimai*; however, that species has much larger dots (see p. 624).

T: 20°-24°C, **L:** 2-3 cm, **TL:** from 50 cm, **WM:** m, **WR:** m, **AV:** 1, **D:** 1-2

One of the two *Neopetrolisthes maculatus* just molted in an aquarium (top of facing page). The lower anemone crab still has its algae-encrusted shell. Without the disturbing presence of clownfishes, both anemone crabs roam in and about the anemone.

Neopetrolisthes maculatus

Neopetrolisthes maculatus

Fam.: Porcellanidae

Neopetrolisthes ohshimai   MIYAKE, 1937
Spotted anemone crab

Hab.: Indo-Australian region and Pacific islands.

Sex.: Not distinguishable from external features.

Soc.B./Assoc.: They almost exclusively live in pairs and do not get along with conspecifics of the same sex. They live together with various species of anemones. Usually they hide among the tentacles, but they can also be found beneath the anemones. An appropriate animal to keep with delicate invertebrates and shy fishes. *Amphiprion* usually chase them from their anemone. Establishing *Caulerpa* algae is strongly recommended.

M.: Reef aquarium with a host anemone.

Light: Sunlight region.

B./Rep.: Not yet successful in an aquarium.

F.: C, FD; as for *N. maculatus* (p. 622). If tablet food (TetraTips) is placed next to the anemone, they fan it with their maxillipeds, dissolving part for themselves.

S.: Confusion with *N. maculatus* can easily be avoided by studying the dots. The coloration can vary depending on geographic origin.

T: 20°-25°C, **L:** 2-3 cm, **TL:** from 60 cm, **WM:** m, **WR:** m, **AV:** 2, **D:** 1-2

Neopetrolisthes ohshimai

Neopetrolisthes ohshimai

Neopetrolisthes ohshimai

Fam.: Dromiidae

ABOUT THE FAMILY DROMIIDAE

Dromiidae, the sponge crabs, are quite easily recognized by their hairy, spherical body. The crabs usually have a pair of strong pinchers with different colored tips. They are normally light colored. The Mediterranean species, *Dromia personata*, has conspicuous pink tips. The distribution of sponge crabs, which are some of the most original crabs, extends from the tropical belt to the temperate latitudes. As their common name indicates, these crabs live together with sponges. The last pair of walking legs hold and carry the sponges above the carapace. The shape of the sponge adapts to the rounded carapace. The chelae and walking legs are not covered by the sponge. This behavior is an attempt to better camouflage and protect itself from predators. A few *Dromia* species carry a mussel shell instead of a sponge. There are parallels between the behavior of sponge crabs and hermit crabs.

Dromia personata (LINNAEUS, 1758)
Sleepy sponge crab

Hab.: Mediterranean and the temperate east Atlantic.

Sex.: The sexes can be distinguished on the ventral side: in the ♂♂, the folded abdomen is triangular, while it is broad and rounded in ♀♀.

Soc.B./Assoc.: Keep singly. Larger specimens should only be kept with robust invertebrates and fishes.

M.: Rock aquarium. The decor must be massive since the crabs are very strong. The temperature should be allowed to fall below 20°C in the winter. They do not place any special demands on water quality.

Light: Dim light.

B./Rep.: Has not been done in an aquarium. Breeding in the western Mediterranean takes place in July and August.

F.: C, FD; frozen or fresh mussel, fish, and shrimp meat and tablet foods are accepted.

S.: They always cover their carapace with a sponge or a colony of sea squirts which are held fast with the last pair of legs. Not suitable for the tropical marine aquarium.

T: 16°-22°C (see above), **L**: 8 cm, **TL**: from 100 cm, **WM**: m, **WR**: b-m, **AV**: 2, **D**: 1

Dromia sp.

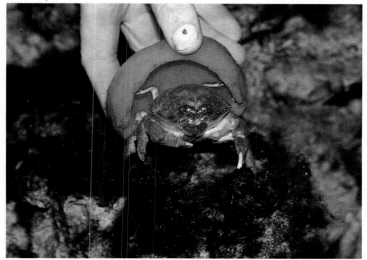

Dromia personata, aquarium photo

Fam.: Calappidae

About the Family Calappidae

The representatives of the Calappidae, the shame-faced crabs, are rarely mentioned in aquarium literature. Two genera, *Hepatus* and *Calappa*, however, are irregular imports or encountered by divers in the reef. Shame-faced crabs get their name because they hold their large claws in front of their face "in shame." Only the eyes and a slender crack that allows water to pass to the mouth remain open. The carapace width of these brightly colored crabs sometimes reaches 20 cm.

During the day they are often hidden in the sand. But at night, the shame-faced crabs come out of the sediment to search for snails, their favorite food. The crab uses its characteristic large chelae to open the snails. Both its movable and opposite static finger have a flattened, anvil-like tooth. The small pincher holds the snail by the tip of its shell and places its opening on the anvil. The large pincher closes and a piece is broken away from the opening. The small pincher rotates the snail and another piece is broken off. This procedure is repeated along the spiral winding until the crab reaches the soft body of the snail, which it then devours. You can justifiably say that *Calappa* "invented" the can opener!

Calappa sp.
Shame-faced crab

Hab.: On sand substrates of temperate and tropical seas.

Sex.: Recognizable on the ventral side: in the ♂ ♂, the forward folded abdomen is triangular; it is broad and rounded in ♀ ♀.

Soc.B./Assoc.: Keep singly. Do not associate with delicate invertebrates. They get along well with large sand-dwelling fishes (e.g., gobies).

M.: Bottom of loose, 5 cm deep, moderately fine sand.

Light: Dim light.

B./Rep.: Not yet successful in an aquarium.

F.: C, FD; they take any frozen foods or tablets.

S.: A nocturnal crustacean that burrows in the sand during the day. They are capable of using their broadened claws to bury themselves lightning fast.

T: 20°-28°C, **L:** 3-8 cm, **TL:** from 100 cm, **WM:** m, **WR:** b, **AV:** 2-3, **D:** 1

Calappa calappa

Calappa convexa, west Mexico

Hepatus epheliticus, Vanuatu

Hepatus sp.

Fam.: Leucosiidae

ABOUT THE FAMILY LEUCOSIIDAE

Members of the family Leucosiidae, the Purse crabs, always have a circular or rhomboidal carapace. It moves about on relatively thin legs; the pinchers are also quite slim. The carapace is mostly covered with dense spines, although the genus *Leucosia* is an exception. Contrary to the calappids, the mouthparts of Purse crabs are not made for hunting or cutting up large prey. They usually form colonies and bury themselves in the sand, keeping a channel open for water circulation. Only rarely do Purse crabs change their site, and then it is usually under the protection of darkness.

Purse crabs are distributed almost worldwide and there are even several species that live in colder climes. The most beautiful and colorful forms, as usual, live in the tropics, not only in the coral reef, but also in lagoons with fine sediments and nutrient-rich water. You will need a sand substrate to keep these crabs in the marine aquarium, and strong-toothed fishes will have to be barred. They become accustomed to substitute foods and will eat everything that falls to the substrate.

Leucosia sp.; perhaps *Persephona subovata*, western Mexico

Purse Crabs

Ilia nucleus (LINNAEUS, 1758)
Nut crab

Hab.: Mediterranean.

Sex.: Recognizable on the ventral side: in ♂ ♂, the abdomen is triangular; in ♀ ♀, it is broad and rounded.

Soc.B./Assoc.: Can be easily housed with most invertebrates and peaceful fishes.

M.: Sand bottom with hiding places. Allow the temperature to fall below 20°C during the winter.

Light: Moderate light.

B./Rep.: Has not yet been successful in an aquarium. The ♀ ♀ carry a large number of small, red eggs during the spawning season (May to August).

F.: C, FD; small pieces of frozen foods and tablets. Since they are relatively slow, you must insure that faster tankmates are unable to consume all of the foodstuffs first.

S.: Perfect camouflage artists; these crabs let themselves become overgrown with sponges, algae, bryozoans, etc.

T: 16°-22°C (see above), **L:** 2 cm, **TL:** from 80 cm, **WM:** w, **WR:** b, **AV:** 3, **D:** 1-2

Fam.: Majidae

ABOUT THE FAMILY MAJIDAE

Out of this family, only members of the genus *Stenorhynchus*, the arrow crabs, interest aquarists. But since this atlas is also used by divers to identify members of the subaquatic world, the notorious sea spiders are also mentioned. The largest crab of the Mediterranean and the neighboring Atlantic, *Maja squinado,* belongs to this family. Generally this is a solitary abiding animal that lives in seagrass beds or on sandy substrates. The cephalothorax may grow up to 20 cm in breadth. It is triangular with the apex pointed cranially. Numerous spines cover the body, particularly along the dorsal edge of the carapace. It is often camouflaged with algae. The legs are comparatively long and yellow to red in color. Eyes and antennae are covered by a cephalic shell, where, besides algae, hydrozoids also grow as camouflage. They feed on sea urchins and detritus.

Loxorhynchus grandis, the Californian sheep crab, appears larger than *Maja squinado* because of its sturdier legs. Until the following report, this crab was always thought to lead a solitary life. A diver happened upon a curious, previously unknown behavior which even surprised scientists - including the author of a doctoral dissertation on *Loxorhynchus grandis*: "I sit in disbelief watching a video that shows a mountain of spider crabs. My diving partner, who filmed this event one afternoon in April along the Californian coast, estimates that there were about 500 animals. Throughout my 23 years of diving experience along the southern Californian coast I have never seen more than a few solitary sheep crabs! All *Loxorhynchus grandis* I have ever seen combined would not account for half this mountain of crabs.

Upon counting, we saw that there were 25 females per male. We also saw some of the animals coupling: back to back with the last pair of walking legs intertwined. When we came closer, the male stretched towards us and raised his pinchers. Since we were not intimidated by this display, he fled, carrying the female. A little bit further away from the large mountain of crabs we saw about another 100 sheep crabs, also in formation. Here the males were on the top of the pile trying to pair with a fitting partner. All of these females were carrying eggs beneath their carapace. We were as still as death until we had photographed and documented everything."

The origin of the common name for members of the genus *Stenorhynchus* is readily apparent to those who take the time to look at the animals. Their body bears a distinct resemblance to terrestrial

Loxorhynchus grandis mating

Fam.: Majidae

spiders, which have similarly long stilted legs. This is the reason these crabs are called spider crabs in Germany. However, in English-speaking regions, members of this genus in particular are called arrow crabs because of their body shape. The body shape itself is triangular- to onion-shaped and terminates cranially in a point, like the tip of an arrow. It appears uncharacteristically small in comparison to the 10 overly long legs. The eyes are to the left and right of the posterior third of the rostrum. This puts them in an exposed, unprotected position, and make them look as if they are glued to the top of the head. The first pair of legs are modified into two long chelipeds which look strong compared to their long, thin walking legs. The mouth is located ventrally. *Stenorhynchus* are rather drably colored. In the Atlantic species at least, the dorsum and legs are rust brown with narrow beige stripes. Coloration is largely dependent on their biotope, which happens to be algae-covered rocks, pale sponges, and corals.

The attentive diver will note that arrow crabs are frequently found around stinging anemones; for example, they are found around anemones of the genus *Bartholomea* in the Caribbean and in the vicinity of tube anemones of the genus *Pachycerianthus* in the Gulf of California. If not for these organisms that often colonize open sandy substrates, arrow crabs would be bereft of shelter from predators. They walk along the bottom using their pinchers to dig for worms and small buried animals. As a diver approaches with a camera, they slowly retreat towards the anemone, looking for protection amongst the stinging tentacles. This fosters the believe that species of the genus *Stenorhynchus* are immune to the stings of anemones. There is a lot of information on immunity of the clownfishes of the genus *Amphiprion* towards their host animals, but little of arrow crabs. At least the Mediterranean species, *Inachus phalangium*, has been observed and studied. It seeks protection within the tentacles of the anemone *Anemonia sulcata*. *Inachus* spider crabs are not inherently protected against the stings of its host. The protective mucus of its poisonous host is rubbed on its body with its chelipeds before it hides among the tentacles (see p. 636).

The Commensal Relationship of *Inachus phalangium* with *Anemonia sulcata*

This partnership can occasionally be observed when diving and snorkeling in the Mediterranean. However, these spiderlike crabs are

Loxorhynchus grandis   STIMPSON, 1857
Californian sheep crab

Hab.: West coast of North America.

Sex.: Recognizable on the ventral side: on the ♂ ♂, the folded abdomen is triangular; the abdomen is broad and rounded ♀ ♀.

Soc.B./Assoc.: Loner; it very rarely congregates in large groups. Only associate with a few robust invertebrates and free-swimming fishes.

M.: Rock aquarium with stable structures.

Light: Dim light.

B./Rep.: Has not been accomplished in an aquarium.

F.: O, FD; unproblematic omnivore.

S.: Large specimens are only suitable for show aquaria. See accompanying text for additional information.

T: 18°-20°C, **L:** up to 20 cm, **TL:** from 150 cm, **WM:** m, **WR:** b, **AV:** 3, **D:** 1

not easily seen. They can perfectly camouflage themselves with algae from their biotope. Especially interesting is their protection from the poisonous nematocysts of *A. sulcata*. A study done by WEINBAUER et al. (Mar. Ecol. 3, 1982, pp. 143 ff.) explained some of the unsolved mysteries. If the surface of the crab is cleaned, the protection against

Fam.: Majidae

the nematocysts is lost. After the first stings, the anemone was carefully approached and touched with the pinchers and first walking legs. Only then did they dare to come closer to the tentacle region. Experiments used individually marked animals to show that *Inachus* crabs are true to their site, and can even find their way back to their anemone when placed quite a distance away.

Inachus phalangium and *Anemonia sulcata*

Inachus phalangium   FABRICIUS, 1775
Mediterranean ghost crab

Hab.: Mediterranean, especially the western Mediterranean and eastern Atlantic.

Sex.: In adult animals, the sexes are recognized from the ventral side: in ♂♂, the folded abdomen is triangular; in ♀♀, it is broad and rounded.

Soc.B./Assoc.: They live singly, in pairs, or in small groups of up to 5 individuals with *Anemonia sulcata*. Can be kept with other invertebrates and most Mediterranean fishes.

M.: Rock aquarium. If possible, an anemone should be offered as a host. They do not have special water quality requirements.

Light: Moderate light.

B./Rep.: Has not been successful in an aquarium.

F.: O, FD; unproblematic omnivore.

S.: They live in partnership with *Anemonia sulcata* and have interesting social and reproductive behavior (WIRTZ & DIESEL: Z. Tierpsychol. 62, 1983, pp. 209 ff.). Its temperature requirement makes it unsuitable for tropical marine aquaria.

T: 16°-22°C, **L:** 2 cm, **TL:** from 80 cm, **WM:** w, **WR:** b, **AV:** 3, **D:** 1

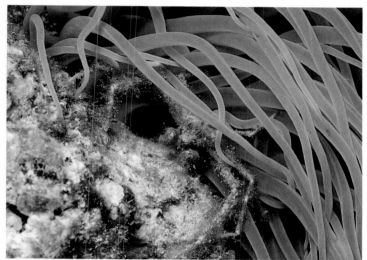

Inachus phalangium and *Anemonia sulcata*

Maja squinado

Fam.: Majidae

Maja squinado   (HERBST, 1788)
Spiny spider crab, Great spider crab

Hab.: Mediterranean and the eastern Atlantic.

Sex.: Recognizable on the ventral side: in ♂♂, the abdomen is triangular, and in ♀♀, it is broad and rounded.

Soc.B./Assoc.: They can only be kept with large fishes.

M.: Rock aquarium with stable rockwork. Allow the temperature to fall below 20°C in the winter.

Light: Moderate light.

B./Rep.: Has not been accomplished in an aquarium. Spawning in the Mediterranean occurs in March and April. During this time, they often migrate in small groups to shallower, more vegetation-rich areas.

F.: O, FD; omnivore that pulls on filamentous green algae.

S.: Often available live at fish markets of Mediterranean countries. Only suitable for large show aquaria. Contrary to the small spider crab, *M. v. rucosa,* the spiny spider crab's carapace is devoid of organisms growing on it.

T: 16°-20°C (see above), **L:** 20 cm, **TL:** from 200 cm, **1:** m, **WR:** b, **AV:** 3, **D:** 1

The east Atlantic spider crab, *Stenorhynchus lanceolatus*, crawls beneath the spines of a sea urchin for protection. If you see a pair in its natural habitat, you quickly notice that the male is significantly larger than the female.

Stenorhynchus lanceolatus　　　　　　　　　　　　　　　　　(BRULLE, 1837)
Atlantic arrow crab

Hab.: Islands in the Atlantic such as the Canary and Madeira Islands, but not the Azores.

Sex.: Recognizable on the ventral side: in ♂♂, the folded abdomen is triangular; in ♀♀, it is broad and rounded. ♀♀ are usually significantly larger than ♂♂.

Soc.B./Assoc.: Though they can be housed with large fishes, they will remain very shy. Do not keep with delicate invertebrates.

M.: Rock aquarium with long-spined sea urchins. If these sea urchins cannot be offered, other refuge options have to be provided.

Light: Moderate light.

B./Rep.: Has not been successful in an aquarium.

F.: C, FD; small pieces of frozen or tablet foods and *Tubifex*.

S.: Beware of the pointed rostrum.

T: 20°-24°C, **L:** 2 cm, **TL:** from 80 cm, **WM:** m, **WR:** b-m, **AV:** 2, **D:** 1

Fam.: Majidae

Stenorhynchus seticornis (HERBST, 1788)
Caribbean arrow crab

Hab.: Caribbean Sea.

Sex.: Recognizable on the ventral side: in ♂♂, the forward folded abdomen is triangular; in ♀♀, it is broad and rounded.

Soc.B./Assoc.: Appropriate additions for aquaria with small fishes (e.g., damselfishes and clownfishes), anemones, and tube anemones. Fragile invertebrates are often disturbed and/or chewed on. Although it has long been suspected that the rostrum plays a role in the crab's predatory lifestyle, no one had actually reported it. I (H.B.) have seen it. I set up a 50 l tank during my vacation in Nassau, Bahamas, and collected an arrow crab from my "front yard" in shallow water about 50 m away from the beach. Besides various damselfishes, I also added a small group of 5 cardinalfishes (*Apogon maculatus*) to the tank. The crab chose to sit in a small cave made of rocks. Suddenly, it darted into the school of cardinalfishes, thrusting its rostrum forward. It successfully speared one animal in the center of the body. The fish remained on its "spear" the whole day and was later completely eaten. The length of the rostrum of the crab was over 2.5 cm; the fish was about 3 cm long. The natives have a healthy respect for this crab's rostrum. It causes a painful, slow-healing wound that is prone to infection.

M.: Reef aquarium with anemones (e.g., *Bartolomea*, *Condylactis*).

Light: Moderate light.

B./Rep.: Has not been successful in an aquarium.

F.: C, FD; takes all animal foods and tablet foods.

S.: Full-grown arrow crabs do not molt, so lost legs or pinchers cannot be regenerated. *S. debilis* (lower right photo) lives commensally with anemones in the Gulf of California, just like *S. seticornis* in the Caribbean.

T: 22°-25°C, **L:** 2 cm (without rostrum), **TL:** from 80 cm, **WM:** w-m, **WR:** b, **AV:** 1, **D:** 1

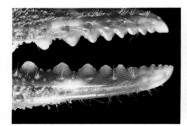

Chela of a cheliped

The long rostrum of the Californian arrow crab

Stenorhynchus seticornis ♀. When you look close, the strong claws and the ventral mouthparts are easily seen.

The Caribbean *S. seticornis* in front of its host, the anemone *Bartolomea anulata*.

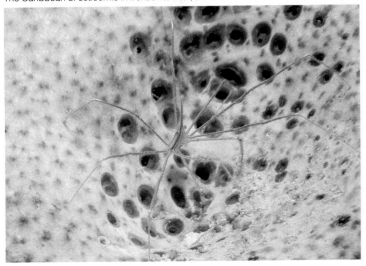

Stenorhynchus seticornis likes to hide in sponges

Stenorhynchus seticornis

A perfect camouflage: *Stenorhynchus debilis*, Gulf of California

Fam.: Portunidae

About the Family Portunidae

Swimming crabs are some of the fastest, most mobile crabs. As their common name already indicates, they are able to literally swim. Their ability to swim, and their willingness to abandon the protection of the sea floor is totally atypical for crabs. What makes these crabs different? The two distal segments of the fifth pair of walking legs have evolved into flattened paddles. By turning the axis of the leg in relation to the body, portunids can move the legs up and down and swim relatively speedily in open water.

Portunids are not bound to any particular biotope. Instead, they represent a "fringe group," colonizing rocky as well as sandy substrates and flitting from one to the other according to their desire and need. Rocky areas are often colonized by mussels, while schools of goatfishes swim above sandy substrate. Both are tasty morsels for swimming crabs. To catch their prey, they cover themselves with sand, then erupt from their hiding place and grab a fish with their sharp chelae. Caution - this technique is also used to the detriment of snorkeler's and nature observer's bare feet. Serious cuts followed by an infection may result. Swimming crabs have the unpleasant habit of not letting go after pinching!

These crabs are detested by net fishermen. Within a few hours, droves can devour the night's catch.

Carcinus maenas   (LINNAEUS, 1758)
Common shore crab

Hab.: North and Baltic Seas, and the northern Atlantic.

Sex.: Recognizable on the ventral side: in ♂♂, the abdomen folded underneath the carapace is triangular, but in ♀♀, it is broad and rounded.

Soc.B./Assoc.: Aggressive, quarrelsome, and very active; therefore, they should only be associated with robust animals. Adult animals will often fight. Even animals larger than themselves are very ably caught. Predator!

M.: Sandy bottom with a back wall of rocks that the animals can clamber on to leave the water. A well-fitting cover is a necessity. There are no special water quality requirements.

Light: Sunlight region.

B./Rep.: Rearing their larvae in scientific laboratories is repeatedly performed.

F.: C, FD; unproblematic omnivore.

S.: Largely similar to *C. aestuarii* (*C. mediterraneus*), a common crab from the Mediterranean. Neither species has the last segment of the fifth pair of legs developed into a paddle.

T: 10°-22°C, **L:** 6 cm, **TL:** from 80 cm, **WM:** w-m, **WR:** b-t, **AV:** 2, **D:** 1

Carcinus maenas

Carcinus maenas, swimming

Fam.: Portunidae

Lissocarcinus laevis
Tube anemone swimming crab

MIERS, 1886

Hab.: Indo-Pacific.

Sex.: Recognizable on the ventral side: in ♂♂, the folded abdomen is triangular, but in ♀♀, it is broad and rounded.

Soc.B./Assoc.: They commonly live singly among the tentacles of tube anemones or other toxic anemones. They are protected against the nematocysts. Can be housed with invertebrates that are not overly sensitive and small fishes.

M.: Reef aquarium with tube anemones or other anemones.

Light: Moderate light.

B./Rep.: Has not been successful in an aquarium.

F.: C, FD; they accept any kind of animal-based foods and tablets.

S.: Not known.

T: 22°-28°C, **L:** 3 cm, **TL:** from 80 cm, **WM:** w-m, **WR:** b, **AV:** 3, **D:** 1

Lissocarcinus orbicularis
Sea cucumber swimming crab

DANA, 1852

Hab.: Indo-Pacific, Red Sea.

Sex.: Recognizable on the ventral side; the abdomen is folded beneath the cephalothorax and is triangular in ♂♂ and broad and rounded in ♀♀.

Soc.B./Assoc.: They live singly or in pairs, mostly in community with sea cucumbers.

M.: Reef aquarium with a sand bottom and hiding places. A host sea cucumber should be present.

Light: Moderate light.

B./Rep.: Has not been successful in an aquarium.

F.: C, FD; feeding is simple since they are voracious feeders; frozen and tablet foods.

S.: Not known.

T: 22°-28°C, **L:** 3 cm, **TL:** from 80 cm, **WM:** m, **WR:** b, **AV:** 2, **D:** 1

Lissocarcinus orbicularis

Species of swimming crabs from the genus *Lissocarcinus* live in tropical seas and are often seen living commensally with poisonous tube anemones. Alhough they live on sandy substrates, *Lissocarcinus* do not bury themselfs. They depend on their commensal host for protection and remain close to its tube. *Lissocarcinus* are immune to the potent stings of tube anemones.

Lissocarcinus laevis

Portunus sebae, a true swimming crab, Caribbean

Fam.: Trapeziidae

ABOUT THE FAMILY TRAPEZIIDAE

It is not easy to differentiate trapeziids (coral crabs) from xanthids (mud crabs). Previously, they were even one family. They have a trapezoidal body, and instead of the typical black-tipped chelae found in xanthids, they have multicolored chelae. Coral crabs are generally beautifully colored, and many species even have a dotted carapace, claws, and walking legs. Others have reticulated surfaces that look as if they are "painted" different colors.

Coral crabs are broadly distributed in the tropics, almost identically paralleling the world's coral reef distribution. The coral reefs supply many hiding places for these crabs. *Acropora* or *Pocillopora* stone corals always shelter coral crabs in their branches. The diver may also find wrasses of the genus *Gomphosus*, which are feeding specialists. Coral crabs abandon their protective surroundings at night to forage for food, particularly settled organic matter. Whether it is of vegetable or animal origin is unimportant. Carrion is especially relished.

In contrast to the Xanthidae, Trapeziidae tend to school. Several conspecifics may live on one stalk of coral in a communitylike relationship. Heterospecifics are not tolerated on the coral stalk. Smaller refuges support pairs.

An unidentified coral crab from Kenya, Africa

Trapezia sp.
Coral crab

Hab.: Red Sea and the entire Indo-Pacific region.

Sex.: Recognizable on the ventral side; the abdomen is folded beneath the cephalothorax and is triangular in ♂ ♂ and broad and rounded in ♀ ♀.

Soc.B./Assoc.: They live singly or in pairs on coral stalks. Can be housed with moderately large fishes.

M.: Reef aquarium with stalks of *Acropora* or *Pocillopora* where they can hide.

Light: Moderate light.

B./Rep.: Has not been successful in an aquarium.

F.: O, FD; an omnivore which will readily take filamentous algae off the decorations. Small pieces of frozen and tablet foods. May need to be fed with a feeding tube.

S.: There are several species which are quite similar, both in behavior and appearance.

T: 23°-28°C, **L:** 2 cm, **TL:** from 80 cm, **WM:** m, **WR:** m, **AV:** 1, **D:** 1

Fam.: Xanthidae

Representatives of this family have an "ideal crab shape": a round-ish-oval body, two harmonically-fitting pinchers, and proportionate legs. Mud crabs are identified by the dark brown to black tips on their claws, as the pictured species of various genera clearly show. Even relatively colorless species have distinctly marked chelae tips.

By present-day classification, the family Xanthidae was split into several families such as Pilumnidae and Trapeziidae. The now reduced family of mud crabs, however, is still comprised of heter-ogenous species: compare *Liomera* and *Lybia*. Xanthids are the most common crabs of the coral reef. But since their carapace width rarely exceeds 5 cm, they are infrequently seen by divers. Hundreds of these small crabs (often only 2 cm) live in pieces of dead coral. The genus *Liomera* normally lives above sandy bottoms in front of the reef, and *Atergatis* is also found in stalks of coral.

The most fascinating species of mud crabs are found in the genus *Lybia* and are commonly called boxing crabs. Similar to hermit crabs, boxing crabs use small anemones to defend themselves against predators. But they do not carry them on their body. They are carried instead on the chelae of their chelipeds. Where does the name boxing crab come from? As soon as *Lybia* perceives danger, it lifts its anemone-covered chelae. A "left-right combination" fol-lows. To anyone familiar with boxing, the anemones are reminiscent of boxing gloves. Few scientists have studied the phenomenon, so the following comes from studies done at the turn of the century:

Lybia species are not particular about what species of anemone they use. Three different anemones were found on the claws of the studied animals (*Lybia tessellata*): *Bunodeopsis, Sagartia,* and *Triactis.* The way the boxing crabs acquire their anemones is intriguing. Once they locate a small anemone, it is closely studied to see if it is too large. Although the investigation is carried out with the claws that will later carry the anemone, their first walking legs and maxillipeds are used to separate the anemone from its substrate. *Lybia* skillfully pushes the walking legs and maxillipeds between the substrate and the foot of the anemone until it looses its hold. Only then does the boxing crab use its chela to hold the anemone. Experiments have shown that a *Lybia* crab ignores the anemone it so diligently removed if a larger, preferred anemone is offered. The spinelike teeth of the chelae release the anemone when the crab molts. After molting, the anemone is again grabbed with the chelae. This phenomenal feat, transferring the anemone with the chelae without injuring it, amazes scientists. Is it instinct or intelligence that drives these actions?

Each contact with other organisms elicits the defensive posture— "boxing gloves" raised and ready, and anemones directed towards the antagonist. But whether the chelae have one, several, or no anemones makes no difference. The defensive posture of *Lybia* species is assumed when they perceive a threat. The pinchers remain open as if they were carrying an anemone. Do *Lybia* crabs actively use their chelipeds, for example, to procure food? It has been determined that

Fewale *Lybia edmondsoni* with eggs

they only use their anterior walking legs to guide detritus to their mouth with the aid of their maxillipeds. The chelipeds do not actively help to acquire food as some individuals claim. However, boxing crabs will help themselves to any food its anemones have found, even if it has been half swallowed already. All tasty morsels such as *Mysis* are fair game. The crab's walking legs reach into the anemone, pluck the morsel from its tentacles, and place it in the crab's mouthparts. Nonedible items caught by the anemone did not elicit a response. Thieves!

But don't worry. The anemones are in no danger of starving, since all smaller planktonic foodstuffs are ignored by the crab. The active movements of the *Lybia* crabs ensures enough food for both "boxing gloves."

Unknown mud crab

Atergatis sp.

Lybia edmondsoni
Pompom boxing crab

TAKEDA & MIYAKE, 1970

Hab.: Pacific, especially around Hawaii.

Sex.: Recognizable on the ventral side; the abdomen is folded beneath the cephalothorax and is triangular in ♂ ♂ and broad and rounded in ♀ ♀.

Soc.B./Assoc.: Lives a solitary life in partnership with various species of anemones. Follow housing recommendations given for *L. tessalata*.

M.: Reef aquarium with a sandy bottom and small hiding places.

Light: Moderate light.

B./Rep.: Has not been accomplished in an aquarium.

F.: C, FD; they accept any animal-based food. However, it usually has to be administered with a feeding tube.

S.: The interesting symbiotic relationship with anemones is described on pp. 650 ff.

T: 23°-28°C, **L:** 1-2 cm, **TL:** from 80 cm, **WM:** w-m, **WR:** b, **AV:** 3-4, **D:** 1

Fam.: Xanthidae

Lybia tessalata
Common boxing crab

(LATREILLE, 1812)

Hab.: Entire Indo-Pacific region.

Sex.: Recognizable on the ventral side; the abdomen is folded beneath the cephalothorax and is triangular in ♂♂ and broad and rounded in ♀♀.

Soc.B./Assoc.: They usually live singly. Welcome tankmates for invertebrates and small fishes. However, the animals are rarely seen in a heavily stocked aquarium.

M.: Sand bottom reef aquarium with hiding places.

Light: Moderate light.

B./Rep.: Has not been bred in an aquarium.

F.: C, FD; small pieces of frozen foods and chunks of tablet foods. May have to be fed with a feeding tube.

S.: Interesting partnership with various species of anemones.

T: 22°-28°C, **L:** 1-2 cm, **TL:** from 80 cm, **WM:** w-m, **WR:** b-m, **AV:** 2-3, **D:** 1

Lybia tessalata

Lybia tessalata

Liomera sp.
Red boxing crab

Hab.: Red Sea and the entire Indo-Pacific region.

Sex.: Recognizable on the ventral side; the abdomen is folded beneath the cephalothorax and is triangular in ♂♂ and broad and rounded in ♀♀.

Soc.B./Assoc.: Usually lives singly. Only keep with robust invertebrates. Bottom-dwelling fishes (e.g., gobies and flatfishes) are especially bothered during the night.

M.: Sand bottom with rocks as hiding places.

Light: Moderate light.

B./Rep.: Has not yet been successfully accomplished in an aquarium.

F.: C, FD; eagerly takes any animal-based or tablet foods.

S.: Unknown.

T: 22°-28°C, **L:** 3-4 cm, **TL:** from 80 cm, **WM:** m, **WR:** b, **AV:** 2, **D:** 1

About the Family Pinnotheridae

Representatives of this family live in mussels, sea cucumbers, and tunicates. It requires an observant eye on the part of the diver to discover the small commensals in their hosts. The females are larger than males and have a soft, pliable body; the male's exoskeleton is hard like that of other crustacea. They often colonize gill chambers of mussels during their larval phase and may even stay throughout their life. During breeding season, the males wander about searching for females. They go from mussel to mussel to fertilize every willing female. Pea crabs, as they are commonly called, live in tropical as well as temperate seas. While the females profit from food gained from their host, males live off detritus.

The clam-guard, *Xanthasia murigera* in a giant clam

Pinnotheres pisum, North Sea

Pinnotheres pisum   (LINNAEUS, 1767)
Pea crab

Hab.: Mediterranean, eastern Atlantic.

Sex.: Recognizable on the ventral side; the abdomen is folded beneath the cephalothorax and is triangular in ♂ ♂ and broad and rounded in ♀ ♀. ♀ ♀ have a thinner carapace, since they never leave their host.

Soc.B./Assoc.: They (♀ ♀) live singly or in pairs in mussels and sea squirts. They are almost always coincidental guests in the aquarium.

M.: Dependent on their host.

Light: Moderate light.

B./Rep.: Has not yet been successful in an aquarium. Spawns in April and May as well as October, November, and December.

F.: C, FD; they do not need to be individually fed.

S.: Their relationship with mussels has been described as both parasitic and symbiotic. Both are probably wrong. They live commensally with their host; that is, they are protected but neither harm nor benefit their host. There is no known information on husbandry in a tropical marine aquarium.

T: 16°-24°C, **L:** 1.5 cm, **TL:** from 80 cm, **WM:** m, **WR:** b, **AV:** 3-4, **D:** 1

Fam.: Grapsidae   Rock Runners, Spray Crabs, Marsh Crabs

ABOUT THE FAMILY GRAPSIDAE

The typical flat, quadratic body differentiates these crabs from other amphibious crabs (living both on land and water). Grapsidae have evolved towards terrestrial life so well they can stay out of water for several hours. Many of them, however, continue to live in the sea, especially the smaller species. Their bond to the sea remains, and they must return to release their larvae.

Although most of this family inhabits tropical marine waters, a few are also found in cooler habitats or freshwater. The largest species, the 10 cm Chinese mitten crab, *Eriochir sinensis*, which was introduced to Europe from China at the turn of the century, is now found in the North and Baltic Seas. This species has been studied and found to follow strict reproductive decorum: in the fall, the males converge and form large groups in riverine estuaries. They assemble in long lines waiting to fertilize passing females. The females then wander into the flats where the larvae hatch the next spring. The large, beautifully-colored *Grapsus* species live on rocky coasts where they are protected from their primary enemies, birds. These crabs are so adapted to terrestrial life that they only visit the water to fill their gill chambers, which are always kept humid, and to release their larvae. Smaller species, which make nice aquarium residents, live hidden among coral rubble or on the top of the reef. *Pachygrapsus* species are found in the Mediterranean and Atlantic, where they dart around at great velocities underwater. Members of this family should be kept in a terrarium so they can maintain their amphibious lifestyle.

Grapsus sp.

Grapsus sp.

Fam.: Grapsidae

Pachygrapsus marmoratus (FABRICIUS, 1787)
Runner crab

Hab.: Mediterranean, eastern Atlantic.

Sex.: As for other crabs.

Soc.B./Assoc.: Do not house with sensitive invertebrates.

M.: A rock aquarium that allows them to live out of the water. Well-fitted cover!

Light: Sunlight.

B./Rep.: Not known.

F.: O, FD; omnivore.

S.: Very fast and agile.

T: 16°-24°C, **L:** 3 cm, **TL:** from 80 cm, **WM:** m, **WR:** t, **AV:** 3, **D:** 1-3 (aquaterrarium)

Pachygrapsus marmoratus at the water line

Geograpsus sp.

Grapsus grapsus

Grapsus grapsus, Galapagos; a fully-colored specimen (♂)

Grapsus grapsus, Galapagos; ♀♀ are not as brilliantly colored

Cancer pagurus, a cancer crab, Atlantic to the Mediterranean; an edible crab that grows to be 20-30 cm wide and weigh 6 kg; not an aquarium animal.

Harpactocarcinus punctulatus, Eocene, Monte Bolca, Italy, ca. 50 million years. A fossilized fiddler crab.

ABOUT THE FAMILY OCYPODIDAE

Only the two most familiar genera of the Ocypodidae, *Ocypode* and *Uca*, will be discussed. The first is comprised of ghost crabs. Various species inhabit moist, sandy regions in the tropics where they constantly build on their subterranean tunnels and caves. *Ocypode saratan*, which lives in the Red Sea, even builds high sand pyramids. There is a dual purpose to this type of architecture: it lures females and keeps competing males at a distance. In general, ghost crabs are gregarious animals which have developed a social system in the course of their evolutionary development. This makes it possible for several individuals to inhabit a small space without constant bickering. The humid beach, a necessary factor for building their dwellings, is really a very limited habitat. Ocypodidae communicate by chemical, visual, and acoustical stimuli. Scientists have found a serrated strip called the stridulation organ on the anterior side of the large claw. When the small claw and large claw rub against each other, they produce knocking, grating, or scratching sounds. But this system is not complete without an "ear." Fiddler crabs have a myochordotonal organ in their legs that fulfills this purpose.

Ocypode ceratophthalma

Fam.: Ocypodidae

Ocypode ceratophthalma (PALLAS, 1772)
Indo-Pacific ghost crab

Hab.: The entire tropical Indo-Pacific region.

Sex.: Recognizable on the ventral side; the abdomen is folded beneath the cephalothorax and is triangular in ♂♂ and broad and rounded in ♀♀.

Soc.B./Assoc.: They can only be kept singly or in pairs in a species tank.

M.: Terrarium with at least 10 cm of fine sand for substrate so that the animals can dig their caves. A small water surface suffices. The humidity of the air should not fall below 80%. Cover the aquarium well!

Light: Sunlight.

B./Rep.: Has not been successful.

F.: O, FD; an omnivore that accepts frozen, tablet, and flake foods.

S.: Extremely fast beach runners which leave their caves at low tide. At high tide, they remain in their submerged hiding places. Their raised eyes give them 360° field of vision!

T: 22°-30°C, **L:** 4 cm, **TL:** from 120 cm, **WM:** not necessary, **WR:** b, **AV:** 3, **D:** 2

Ocypode gaudichaudii, Galapagos

Ocypode gaudichaudii MILNE-EDWARDS & LUCAS, 1843
Pacific ghost crab

Hab.: Eastern Pacific, Galapagos Islands.

Sex.: Recognizable on the ventral side: the ♂'s abdomen is narrower than the ♀'s.

Soc.B./Assoc.: Based on their natural habitat, they should not to be housed with other species. Only large set-ups can support several specimens.

M.: As for *O. ceratophthalma*.

Light: Sunlight.

B./Rep.: Has not been successful in captivity.

F.: O, FD; an easily fed omnivore.

S.: As for *O. ceratophthalma*.

T: 22°-30°C, **L:** 4 cm, **TL:** from 120 cm, **WM:** not necessary, **WR:** b, **AV:** 3, **D:** 2

The Ocypodidae are recognizable by the following characteristics: well-developed thickened or inflated eyestalks which may even extend above the eye in some species, giving the crab a ghostlike appearance. Males of the genus *Uca* have an overdimensioned claw they wave at the females during courtship; they look like a fiddler fiddling, hence their common name. Ocypodidae are typical beach inhabitants which only depend on the sea to reproduce and occasionally fill the reservoir of their branchial chamber.

665

Fam.: Ocypodidae

Uca anullipes, Maldives

Uca anullipes   (MILNE-EDWARDS, 1837)
Lagoon fiddler crab

Hab.: In lagoons and mangrove swamps of the Indo-Pacific.

Sex.: The ♂ ♂ have one extremely large claw and one that is very small; ♀ ♀ have two small claws.

Soc.B./Assoc.: As for *U. crassipes*.

M.: As for *U. crassipes*.

Light: Sunlight region.

B./Rep.: Has not yet been successful in captivity.

F.: O; FD, as for *U. crassipes*.

S.: In the tropical Indo-Pacific and western Atlantic there are over 60 similar species. In Europe, *U. tangeri* can be found around Gibraltar and Portugal.

T: 22°-30°C**, L:** 3 cm; **TL:** from 100 cm, **WM:** w, **WR:** b, **AV:** 2, **D:** 1-2

Species of the genus *Uca* build their caves closer to the sea than *Ocypode*. Easy to recognize, as the males have an oversized, usually gorgeously colored claw. They normally colonize intertidal zones. The entrance is plugged before each high tide to keep air in and water out.

Uca crassipes
Mangrove fiddler crab

(ADAMS & WHITE, 1848)

Hab.: In the tropical Indo-Pacific, especially around mangrove swamps.

Sex.: ♂ ♂ have one extremely large claw and one that is very small; ♀ ♀ have two small claws.

Soc.B./Assoc.: Since they are very peaceful, they can be easily associated with fishes from the same habitat (e.g., *Periophthalmus* mudskippers). Aquaria less than 1 m long should house one ♂ and two ♀ ♀ at the most.

M.: Marine aquaterrarium with a deep layer of fine sand. At least half of the habitat should be land. A high tide/low tide set-up really allows you to watch the interesting habits of these animals. Even in this intricate set-up, flat emergent stones will always be needed. The water has to be filtered or frequently exchanged.

Light: Sunlight.

B./Rep.: Has not been accomplished in an aquarium.

F.: O, FD; omnivores which, besides the usual frozen, dry, and flake foods, also readily accept pieces of banana.

S.: Very interesting courtship behavior.

T: 22°-30°C, **L:** 3 cm, **TL:** from 100 cm, **WM:** w, **WR:** b, **AV:** 2, **D:** 1-2

Uca sp. ♀

Uca vomerus

ABOUT THE FAMILY MICTYRIDAE

Mictyridae are semiterrestrial crabs which might remind you of a spider at first glance because of their spherical body and stiltlike legs. Interested observers on Asian and Australian beaches will note that Mictyridae walk forward—not laterally like other crabs.

Systematically, Mictyridae and Ocypodidae are closely related. Soldier crabs, as the former are commonly called, live in burrows also. They stay in their burrows during high tide and the hottest times of the day. As the tide waters recede, the crabs exit and form a giant moving carpet of animals. This behavior protects them from bird predation. From an aerial view, they look like one very large animal. In formation they search the newly exposed beach for edible microparticles the sea left behind. The incoming high tide makes them retreat into their burrows again.

Mictyris sp.

Mictyris longicarpus   LATREILLE, 1806
Soldier crab

Hab.: Tidal zones of the Indo-Pacific.

Sex.: Recognizable on the ventral side; the abdomen is folded beneath the cephalothorax and is triangular in ♂♂ and broad and rounded in ♀♀.

Soc.B./Assoc.: They usually live in large dense groups (top photo). Do not keep too many animals in an aquaterrarium.

M.: As for *Uca crassipes* (p. 667).

Light: Sunlight.

B./Rep.: Has not been successful in an aquarium.

F.: O, FD; omnivores which readily take a piece of fruit with their carnivorous foodstuffs.

S.: They frequently execute groupwise wheeling maneuvers.

T: 22°-30°C, **L:** 3 cm, **TL:** from 100 cm, **WM:** w, **WR:** b, **AV:** 3, **D:** 1-2

An uncommon snapshot: startled by the diver, *Odontodactylus scyllarus*, the peacock mantis shrimp, pushes its tail fan forward to intimidate the would-be predator with its large eyespots. Note the insectlike faceted eyes.

Order: Stomatopoda

All the Crustacea presented so far have belonged to the order Decapoda, the ten-footed crustacea. Members of the Stomatopoda hold interest for both aquarists and divers because they are sold as aquarium animals and can be found in their natural habitat. Mantis shrimp are so called because of their superficial similarity to the predatorial, terrestrial praying mantis insects (family Mantidae). These insects' large anterior legs are folded as they sit patiently waiting for their prey. Lightning fast the legs unfold, snap forward, and grab the prey.

Capture techniques of mantis shrimp closely parallel those applied by praying mantises. Their five pairs of thoracic appendages are pincher-bearing raptorial feet, whereby the second pair is greatly enlarged. Of the more than 300 known Stomatopoda species, all are predators. They can be divided into two groups, smashers and spearers, based on how they use their second pair of legs.

Mantis shrimp are ambush predators which lie in wait in their cave. Smashers ambush shelled crabs, hermit crabs (in their gastropod shell), and any kind of mollusc. The crab's defensive instict of burying itself is of little help: the second pair of raptorial legs split the shell in two and kill the prey. Only four or five blows with the hammerlike legs are normally needed to break open a gastropod shell. The modified legs are also used in territorial disputes: generally the attacked cave inhabitant is more motivated than the attacker and can beat the assailant unconsious.

To protect their cave, smashers will even attack octopi ten times their size. To measure the exact strength of these incredible append-ages, a Californian scientist connected an osceloscope to a rubber sand bag. The results were astonishing: the force of a blow was only slightly less than the impact of a .22-caliber bullet. Fascinating slow-motion pictures demonstrated the ease these animals have break-ing a pane of glass.

Spearers, whose main prey happens to be softer-bodied shrimp and fishes, also use the second pair of legs to catch their quarry. While darting forward, the raptorial legs are extended, and the sharp spines thereon stab into the prey.

Prey recognition is mainly visual. They have highly-developed, stalked eyes. These crustacea have three-dimensional vision, a necessity to capture fishes that unsuspectingly swim within their reach. The large, faceted eyes are on mobile stalks that can move independent of each other like turnable telescopes and follow prey that have entered their field of vision. Caretakes notice that the animals follow movements outside the aquarium, recognize foods such as *Mysis* or krill, and quickly respond by leaving their cave to gather the food.

The cleaning behavior of mantis shrimp is interesting, regardless of which group they belong to. When they are not stalking prey, they continously groom themselves with their bristled walking legs. The uropods function as a rudder. Mantis shrimp can not only run and climb on the reef, but are also nimble swimmers. When danger threatens, their abdomen is suddenly folded forward and the uropods and telson jet-propel the animals backwards. Why is the tail particularly beautiful? Extensive observations have lead scientists to deduce that the frequently present ocelli are used to startle pursuers. Usually hidden, the eyespots can be quickly exposed.

Mantis shrimp exist in many sizes. Small species barely reach 5 cm body length, while the largest species can grow to be 40 cm. Most live in tropical regions, but some species occur in temperate

Gonodactylus sp.

latitudes. All this information can only lead you to the obvious conclusion—it is next to impossible to find appropriate tankmates for these animals. Mantis shrimp are so superior to all other crustacea that their tankmates hardly have a chance to survive. A single specimen, however, can provide great joy when housed either in an acrilic or thick glass tank. These animals show much more "personality" and "communication skills" than you would hope for from an invertebrate.

Unknown mantis shrimp from the Maldives, Indian Ocean

Hemisquilla ensigera californensis   STEPHENSON, 1959
Panamic mantis shrimp

Hab.: East Pacific; soft and rubble bottoms at depths of 20 to 200 m.

Sex.: Hard to distinguish. Only possible from the ventral side of the abdomen.

Soc.B./Assoc.: They should be kept singly, since they prey on invertebrates as well as fishes.

M.: Gravel bottom with rock edifications where the animals can retire.

Light: Dim light.

B./Rep.: Has not been successful in an aquarium. Development includes three planktonic larval stages.

F.: C; though they prefer live foods such as snails and earthworms, frozen foods (shrimp, mussels) will also be eaten. After briefly feeling the food with their antennae, they quickly strike.

S.: *H. ensigera californensis* is a subspecies of *H. ensigera* OWEN, 1832.

T: 20°-22°C, **L:** 12 cm, **TL:** from 50 cm, **WM:** m, **WR:** b, **AV:** 3, **D:** 1

Peacock mantis shrimp in an aquarium

Odontodactylus scyllarus   (LINNAEUS, 1758)
Peacock mantis shrimp

Hab.: Throughout the Indo-Pacific; sandy and rubble bottoms at depths of 2 to 70 m.

Sex.: The anatomical differences of the posterior body are difficult to distinguish. The ♀ ♀ carry the eggs at spawning time.

Soc.B./Assoc.: All mantis shrimp should be kept singly. Because of their predatory lifestyle, they do not get along with fishes or invertebrates. However, there are reports of housing them with large fishes.

M.: Sandy bottom with caves and other protected areas.

Light: Dim light.

B./Rep.: Although the animals sometimes carry eggs, they have not been successfully reared in an aquarium.

F.: C; primarily live food, snails (with shell). They can also be easily taught to accept frozen foods. If feeding by hand, caution has to be exercised.

S.: The animals have very good vision. Their posterior body is extremely flexible, allowing them both to turn around in their narrow caves and to "swim."

T: 22°-26°C, **L:** 14 cm, **TL:** from 60 cm, **WM:** m, **WR:** b, **AV:** 1, **D:** 1

Odontodactylus scyllarus, Great Barrier Reef

Odontodactylus scyllarus, Maldives

Fam.: Lysiosquillidae

Lysiosquilla maculata   (FABRICIUS, 1793)
Spotted giant mantis shrimp

Hab.: Indo-Pacific region from Japan to east Africa; soft and rubble bottoms between coral reefs at depths of 2 to 50 m.

Sex.: Barely recognizable.

Soc.B./Assoc.: Solitary maintence is especially recommended for larger specimens.

M.: Sand or gravel bottom with rock edifications that offer sufficient cover for the animals.

Light: Dim light.

B./Rep.: Not known.

F.: C; live and frozen foods.

S.: The largest species of mantis shrimp.

T: 21°-26°C, **L:** up to 40 cm, **TL:** from 60 cm, **WM:** m, **WR:** b, **AV:** 2, **D:** 1-4 (kept singly)

Lysiosquilla maculata

Lysiosquilla sulcirostris with its spear clearly visible

Lysiosquilla sulcirostris   KEMP, 1913
Marble mantis shrimp

Hab.: In the Indo-Pacific region from Japan to Madagascar; soft and rubble bottoms at depths of 5 to 50 m.

Sex.: Only recognizable by the anatomy of the posterior body (uropods and telson).

Soc.B./Assoc.: Not for the community tank! They prey on fishes and large crustacea.

M.: Sandy bottoms with rock constructions that have long, built-in galleries.

Light: Dim light.

B./Rep.: Has not been successful in an aquarium.

F.: C; they readily accept live foods, but quickly become accustomed to various frozen foods. Usually their prey is seized from the entrance of their cave.

S.: A large species with very well-developed compound eyes. Normally they walk over the bottom, but they can also swim. The uropods and telson propel them through the water.

T: 21-26°C, **L:** up to 33 cm, **TL:** from 60 cm, **WM:** m, **WR:** b, **AV:** 2, **D:** 1

Anthias anthias, one of the most beautiful Mediterranean fish species

Taxonomy

Phylum: CHORDATA — Chordates
Subphylum: VERTEBRATA — Vertebrates
Class: OSTEICHTHYES — Bony Fishes
Superorder: TELEOSTEI — True Bony Fishes

Order	Perciformes	Perches
Family	Acanthuridae	Surgeonfishes
Subfamily	Acanthurinae	Tangs
Genera	*Acanthurus*	FORSSKÅL, 1775
	Ctenochaetus	GILL, 1885
	Paracanthurus	BLEEKER, 1863
	Zebrasoma	SWAINSON, 1839
Subfamily	Nasinae	Unicornfishes
Genus	*Naso*	LACÉPÈDE, 1802
Subfamily	Prionurinae	Bladefishes
Genus	*Prionurus*	LACÉPÈDE ,1804
Family	Siganidae	Rabbitfishes
Genus	*Siganus*	FORSSKÅL, 1775
Family	Zanclidae	Moorish idols
Genus	*Zanclus*	CUVIER & VALENCIENNES, 1831
Family	Labridae	Wrasses
Subfamily	Bodianinae	Hogfishes
Genera	*Bodianus*	BLOCH, 1790
	Choerodon	BLEEKER, 1847
Subfamily	Cheilininae	Splendour wrasses
Genera	*Cheilinus*	LACÉPÈDE, 1802
	Novaculichthys	BLEEKER, 1861
	Xyrichthys	CUVIER, 1815
Cirrhilabrus Group	*Cirrhilabrus*	TEMMINCK & SCHLEGEL, 1845
	Paracheilinus	FOURMANOIR, 1955
	Pseudocheilinus	BLEEKER, 1861
Subfamily	Corinae	Sand wrasses
Genera	*Anampses*	QUOY & GAIMARD, 1824
	Cheilio	LACÉPÈDE, 1802
	Coris	LACÉPÈDE, 1801
	Gomphosus	LACÉPÈDE, 1801
	Halichoeres	RÜPPELL, 1835
	Hemigymnus	GÜNTHER, 1861
	Hologymnosus	LACÉPÈDE, 1801
	Macropharyncgodon	BLEEKER, 1861
	Stethojulis	GÜNTHER, 1862
	Thalassoma	SWAINSON, 1839
	Xenojulis	DE BEAUFORT, 1939
Subfamily	Labnichthyinae	Cleaner fishes
	Diproctacanthus	BLEEKER, 1862
	Labrichthys	BLEEKER, 1854
	Labroides	BLEEKER, 1851
	Labropsis	SCHMIDT, 1930
	Larabicus	RANDALL & SPRINGER, 1973

Taxonomy

Subfamily	Pseudodacinae	chiseltooth wrasses
Genus	*Pseudodax*	BLEEKER, 1861
Family	**Scaridae**	**Parrotfishes**
Genus	*Cetoscarus*	SMITH, 1956
Family	**Serranidae**	**Sea Basses**
Subfamily	Anthiinae	Fairy basslets
Genera	*Anthias*	BLOCH, 1792
	Luzonichthys	HERRE, 1936
	Pseudanthias	BLEEKER, 1873
	Serranocirrhitus	WATANABE, 1949
Family	**Pseudochromidae**	**Rock basslets**
Genera	*Cypho*	MYERS, 1940
	Labracinus	BLEEKER, 1876
	Ogilbyina	FOWLER, 1931
	Pseudochromis	RÜPPELL, 1835
	Pseudoplesiops	BLEEKER, 1858
Family	**Grammidae**	**Basslets**
Genus	*Gramma*	POEY, 1868
Family	**Plesiopidae**	**Longfius**
Genera	*Assessor*	WHITLEY, 1935
	Calloplesiops	FOWLER & BEAN, 1930
	Paraplesiops	BLEEKER, 1875
	Plesiops	CUVIER, 1816
	Trachinops	GÜNTHER, 1861
Family	**Malacanthidae**	**Tilefishes**
Genera	*Hoplolatilus*	GÜNTHER, 1887
	Malacanthus	CUVIER, 1829
Family	**Cirrhitidae**	**Hawkfishes**
Genera	*Cirrhitichthys*	BLEEKER, 1856
	Cirrhitus	LACÉPÈDE, 1803
	Oxycirrhites	BLEEKER, 1857
	Paracirrhites	BLEEKER, 1875
Family	**Gobiidae**	**Gobies**
Genera	*Amblyeleotris*	BLEEKER, 1874
	Amblygobius	BLEEKER, 1874
	Bryaninops	SMITH, 1959
	Cryptocentrus	VALENCIENNES, 1857
	Ctenogobiops	SMITH, 1959
	Discordipinna	HOESE & FOURMANOIR, 1978
	Eviota	JENKINS, 1903
	Fusigobius	WHITLEY, 1930
	Gnatholepis	BLEEKER, 1874
	Gobiodon	BLEEKER, 1856
	Gobius	LINNAEUS, 1758
	Istigobius	WHITLEY, 1932
	Lotilia	KLAUSEWITZ, 1960
	Lythrypnus	JORDAN & EVERMANN, 1896
	Signigobius	HOESE & ALLEN, 1977
	Stonogobiops	POLUNIN & LUBBOCK, 1977
	Trimma	JORDAN & SEALE, 1906
	Valenciennea	BLEEKER, 1868
	Vanderhorstia	SMITH, 1949

Family	Microdesmidae	Dart gobies
Genera	*Gunnelichthys*	BLEEKER, 1858
	Nemateleotris	FOWLER, 1938
	Oxymetopon	BLEEKER, 1861
	Ptereleotris	GILL, 1863
Family	Pholidichthyidae	Convict blennies
Genus	*Pholidichthys*	BLEEKER, 1856
Family	Callionymidae	Dragonets
Genera	*Callionymus*	LINNAEUS, 1758
	Diplogrammus	BLEEKER, 1858
	Synchiropus	GILL, 1859
Family	Opistognathidae	Jawfishes
Genus	*Opistognathus*	CUVIER, 1816

Schools of makarels near the reef, Red Sea

Order: Perciformes

All fishes presented in this volume of the Marine Atlas belong to the Perciformes (perchlike fishes).

No other order of fishes is as varied in relation to their body conformation and ecology as the Perciformes. This is not surprising when you consider this is the largest of all vertebrate orders. It is comprised of over 20 suborders, 150 families, and almost 8000 species, a great number more than all the mammals and almost as great as all the known species of birds. When dealing with such a large group, which surely cannot be traced back to a common ancestor, it is not surprising that the opinions of specialists largely diverge about their classification. Clear diagnostic characteristics have not been found for all Perciformes thus far. However, the group can be characterized in the following way: Perciformes have spines in the dorsal, anal, and ventral fins. The dorsal fin was originally divided into two sections, hard rays in the anterior and soft rays in the posterior segment; often the two segments are joined. There is never an adipose fin. The body is usually covered with ctenoid scales; some families, however, have very reduced scales. The intestine is normally short, but it can be quite long in some herbivores. The swimbladder is closed; it is not connected to the intestine.

The oldest fossil finds of Perciformes belong to the Cretaceous period (about 100 million years ago). Throughout their long evolutionary pathway, they successfully colonized the most varied habitats. Accordingly their body shapes vary just as greatly. The long-barbeled goatfishes (Mullidae) inhabit shallow waters above sandy substrates; damselfishes and butterflies (Pomacentridae and Chaetodontidae, respectively) usually inhabit reefs; fusiliers and rabbitfishes (Caesionidae and Siganidae, respectively) colonize open waters near reefs; jacks (Carangidae) inhabit the upper regions of the open sea, while bandfishes (Cepolidae) live in the deep water. About $3/_4$ of all species inhabit shallow coastal regions, with the greatest densities in tropical and subtropical areas. The smallest species barely reach 30 mm in total length, while the largest can reach over 3 m.

Reproductive behavior of the Perciformes is just as varied as body shape and habitats. Almost all species are egg layers. Demersal or planktonic eggs and sperm are either released into the open water, or the eggs are adhered to a substrate. Numerous groups practice brood care; many cardinalfishes (Apogonidae) are mouthbrooders. Surfperches (Embiotocidae) of the North Pacific are livebearers. Until recently, hermaphroditism and sex changes in vertebrates were considered oddities. However, newer studies have shown this to be more the norm than the exception for Perciformes. Several variations of hermaphroditism are represented: synchronous, protogynous sequential, and protandrous sequential. Synchronous hermaphroditism is characterized by one fish having ripe male and female gonads simultaneously. Protogynous sequential hermaphrodites undergo a sex change—functional females turn into functional males. To the contrary, protandrous sequential hermaphrodites were functional males before turning into functional females. Examples of each of these variations can be found in the familial descriptions.

Acanthonemus subaureus de Blainville (ca. 14 cm) of the mid-Eocene from Bolca, Italy. Original: British Museum of Natural History, London, GB (P 16201). [From Frickhinger, FOSSIL ATLAS].

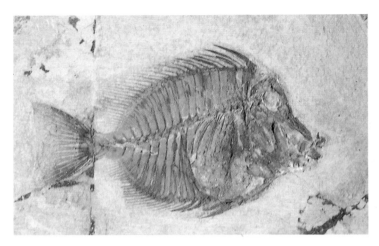

Naseus rectifrons Agassiz (ca. 10 cm) of the mid-Eocene from Bolca, Italy. Original: Museo Civico di Storia Naturale, Verona, Italy.

Acanthurus ovalis Agassiz (ca. 14 cm) of the mid-Eocene from Bolca, Italy. Original: Museo Civico di Storia Naturale, Verona, Italy.

This *Naso* sp. from the museum in Verona was catalogued as *Chaetodon* sp.

Surgeonfish fossils dating back more than 50 million years to the Tertiary period (Eocene) have been found. The most beautiful finds probably come from Monte Bolca, Italy. The pieces pictured here are in the Verona Museum. An Acanthuridae representative was identified more than 100 years ago as "*Chaetodon.*" You can "discover" new fish species even in fossil collections. The coauthor, BAENSCH, asked FRICKHINGER for a fossil of a butterflyfish to use in this book. Immediately he noticed that far from being a fossil of a Chaetodontid (butterflyfish), this was an excellently preserved fossil of an Acanthurid (surgeonfish). The museum paleontologists in Verona will probably rename their fossil. Surgeonfishes no longer inhabit the Mediterranean. Two species of *Siganus*, however, have migrated through the Suez Canal from the Red Sea into the eastern Mediterranean.

Fam.: Acanthuridae

ABOUT THE FAMILY ACANTHURIDAE

The majority of all tropical reef fishes are predators, either active piscivores such as sea basses, or planktivores such as dottybacks and tilefishes. However, there are also fish families which predominantly ingest plant fare they find by grazing the reef. The best known, most colorful, and most widely distributed is the surgeonfishes. Algae grow especially well on sunny, shallow reefs, and the diver as well as the snorkeler can admire these elegant, nimble swimmers as they graze these locals. Surgeonfishes can fairly easily be surrounded with nets by fish collectors. This is why surgeonfishes are almost always available in stores. Their common name is derived from a characteristic which clearly distinguishes Acanthuridae from other fish families: the base of the tail fin has "scalpels," either foldable or fixed spines on each side of the body. Based on this characteristic, the family Acanthuridae was subdivided: the first four genera described (subfamily Acanthurinae) generally have bright colors outlining their spines (warning coloration) which are flipped outward during danger and used to slit adversaries. Important: studies have shown that this is not a direct response. There is no musculature between the spine and the fish's body. However, the spine is erected when the tail fin twists at an angle of 80°. This sequence of movements is easily followed when a mirror is placed in front of an aquarium housing a territorial surgeonfish. As soon as it discovers the "adversary," it spreads all its fins, darts towards the mirror image, and whips its caudal peduncle at the imagined new arrival. The scalpel only emerges on the outward curve of the posterior body. Use caution when handling surgeonfishes lest these spines cause painful flesh wounds.

Detailed studies have been unable to confirm reports that these spines are poisonous. Both of the later described genera (subfamilies Nasinae and Prionurinae) use their fixed blades in a similar manner. Particularly older specimens have long, knife-sharp and, therefore, very effective spines. Extensive experiments have proven that the spines or their surrounding tissue are poisonous. All fishes with injuries inflicted by the spine of a *Prionurus* surgeonfish died.

An algae-grazing school of powder blue tangs (*Acanthurus leucosternon*); p. 704.

Fam.: Acanthuridae

There are few differences between males and females. Males generally grow larger. In the genus *Naso,* males of some species grow a larger horn than females. Sexual dichromatism only exists during spawning season. The rest of the time the sexes are the same color. Spawning is tied to the lunar cycle; some surgeonfishes spawn on a new moon, while others spawn around the full moon. Many surgeonfishes spawn together in a group, and others spawn strictly in pairs. The male pesters the female and demonstrates his readiness to spawn by changing color and shimmying. Side by side the pair rises from the bottom, swimming towards the surface. At the apex of an imaginary U, both simultaneously release their gametes into the open water. Divers, especially those diving at sunset around reefs, will perhaps witness this event.

Sexually mature female surgeonfishes can spawn about once a month. After hatching, the larvae are pelagic and use up their egg yolk in two days. After four days, the larvae start feeding on plankton. The body becomes compressed and large thorns develop on the dorsal and ventral fins. The thorns are probably poisonous and help protect the defenseless planktonic larvae. Before the larvae settle in the reef, the acronurus stage is reached. At this point the young organisms can be recognized as developing surgeonfish. The body is now oval, the thorns on the fins disappear, and the bladelike spines on the caudal peduncle develop. The young are still transparent at a length of 25 mm. The planktonic stage lasts about 10 weeks. Afterwards, the young surgeonfishes settle in the shallow reef waters. Young surgeonfishes are very territorial, but mature animals often form large schools that widely roam the reef. Surgeonfishes reach sexual maturity after about 2 years. Although some species have spawned in large public aquaria, reproduction in home aquaria has not been reported.

This is the first book that tries to introduce all the known surgeonfishes. You may find that a few species grow too large for home aquaria, placing them out of consideration of the aquarist. However, divers will greatly appreciate the completeness of the section.

The retractable, knife-sharp spines on the subfamily Acanthurinae are posteriorly fastened to the body like a hinge. The anterior end of the spine can be opened, and a precise flick of the tail can inflict a respectable wound.

ABOUT THE GENUS *ACANTHURUS*, FORSSKÅL, 1775

This is the largest genus of the six genera of surgeonfishes. It includes 40 species and is the only genus present in all three oceans. Five *Acanthurus* species have even colonized the tropical Atlantic. Individual species have wide ranges. Divers quickly recognize that extensive reefs are colonized by large schools of *Acanthurus* surgeonfishes. They play a crucial role in maintaining shallow reefs healthy by grazing the algae and keeping them short.

Schooling behavior of the algae grazers is always a fascinating and worthwhile behavior. Why? Well, other algivores such as damselfishes are not migratory. Instead they stake out and energetically defend their "turf." A pair of surgeonfish would not be a match against them. But efforts to keep, say, a school of *Acanthurus leucosternon* (powder blue tang) away from the algae would be futile. Unfortunately, the limited space in an aquarium makes it impossible to house several conspecifics from this genus in one tank. Territorial aggressions immediately break out among them. The weaker animal, unable to flee, may be killed.

Acanthurus, unlike the similar *Ctenochaetus*, have firmly attached teeth. The teeth of *Ctenochaetus* are mobile. The picture shows the mouth of the largest species, *A. xanthopterus*, which grows up to 50 cm long. The rows of small teeth are especially well suited for rasping algae.

Not all *Acanthurus* are herbivores. Two exceptions are *Acanthurus thompsoni* and *Acanthurus mata*. They feed exclusively on zoo-plankton from the open water above the reef. This is carried out within the protection of schools, which aids against predators. In contrast, *Acanthurus lineatus*, one of the most beautiful surgeonfishes, is territorial. Its aggressiveness is a dreaded personality quirk for aquarists who wish to place this fish in their community tank. Its aggression increases with age.

Acanthurus triostegus, see p. 726 for text.

Fam.: Acanthuridae

Acanthurus achilles   SHAW, 1803
Achilles tang

Hab.: Pacific Plate; inhabits extended parts of the Pacific Ocean from the Caroline Islands and the Torres Strait to Hawaii and the Marquesas Islands; usually only imported from Hawaii. At depths to 10 m.

Sex.: None.

Soc.B./Assoc.: *A. achilles* usually live singly, forming territories in shallow-water areas of reefs. Only in Polynesia, where it is more common than in other regions, will it also live in groups and schools.

M.: Even single animals will need large aquaria. It needs plenty of room and clean, oxygen-rich water. When maintained under good conditions, it will prove to be a very robust charge.

Light: Sunlight area.

B./Rep.: Unknown.

F.: H; *A. achilles* prefers vegetable fare. But animal-based foods introduced for other fishes, such as mussel meat, shrimp, flake foods, and similar, are also eaten. When the aquarium does not offer sufficient algae, the algae can be grown on stones under strong illumination in separate tanks and occasionally placed in the aquarium.

S.: Sometimes hybrids between *A. nigricans* and *A. achilles* are seen. The young do not have an orange spot on the caudal peduncle.

T: 26°-28°C, **L:** 20 cm, **TL:** from 150 cm, **WM:** m-s, **WR:** b-t, **AV:** 1-2, **D:** 3

The intense orange spot around the scalpellike spine on *A. achilles* is probably warning coloration. This should deter and caution potential aggressors to keep their distance from this formidable weapon. If surgeonfishes swam with snakelike body movements like trout, the spines would be thrust out alternately from each side as the fish swam. But since surgeonfishes swim like parrotfishes and only use their pectoral fins, this is not the case. Although very maneuverable, forward motion is slow. When fleeing or attacking and speed is needed, the typical snaking body movements are used, and the spines are exposed. They may even be directed towards the victim. If the victims lack an escape or hiding place, lethal multiple stab wounds may be inflicted. This outcome is more frequent in an aquarium than in nature.

Acanthurus achilles off Hawaii

Acanthurus achilles

Fam.: Acanthuridae

Acanthurus bahianus
Ocean surgeon
CASTELNAU, 1855

Hab.: Western Atlantic, from Massachusetts to Brazil. At depths of 2 to 25 m.

Sex.: None.

Soc.B./Assoc.: Usually lives pairwise, and although schools are also seen, they are less frequent. Sometimes found with *A. chirurgus*. *A. bahianus* can be associated with other fishes relatively easily, especially if they are nimble swimmers or capable of defending themselves.

M.: It is comparatively peaceful and can be kept singly. Besides sufficient swimming space, it needs a place to hide, but like most surgeonfishes, a sandy bottom is not necessary.

Light: Sunny areas.

B./Rep.: Not known.

F.: *A. bahianus* is not very choosy. It accepts plant as well as animal fare.

S.: *A. bahianus* is predominately a bottom oriented fish which swims more between the aufwuchs than above it. Therefore, they are found everywhere aufwuchs-covered reefs, rocks, or calcareous rocks are present. It rasps plenty of calcareous material into its muscular stomach in addition to the low-growing algae. There are several color morphs. They range from dark brown to golden brown, similar to the algae they feed on the entire day. *A. bahianus* is easily differentiated from other Caribbean species by a notorious white posterior edge on the caudal peduncle and the absence of striations on the body.

T: 21°-25°C, **L:** 35 cm, **TL:** from 180 cm, **WM:** w, **WR:** b, **AV:** 2, **D:** 3

Acanthurus bariene
Black-spot surgeon
(LESSON, 1830)

Hab.: Indo-Australian region from east Africa to Japan, the Barrier Reef, and the Solomon Islands. At depths of 5 to 35 m.

Sex.: None; only large ♂♂ develop a convex frontal hump which extends to the tip of the nose.

Soc.B./Assoc.: Lives either singly or in pairs in clear waters of outer reefs.

M.: This quarrelsome loner requires very clean water, plenty of swimming space, and robust tankmates.

Light: Area of sunlight.

B./Rep.: Not known.

F.: H; besides algae and plant fare, *A. bariene* feeds on flake food, shrimp, and many other items.

S.: Some peculiarities in coloration differentiate *A. bariene* from similarly-colored species: white lips; a round black shoulder spot exactly behind the eye, sometimes with a light blue edge; and an oblique, light brown band posterior to the shoulder spot running downward. The entire base of the dorsal fin is blue, the knife is dark, and the white band on the tail narrows into a slender stripe by the time it reaches the edge of the caudal fin.

T: 23°-29°C, **L:** 30 cm, **TL:** from 180 cm, **WM:** w, **WR:** b, m, **AV:** 3-4, **D:** 3-4

Acanthurus bahianus, aquarium

Acanthurus bariene, Indo-Pacific

Fam.: Acanthuridae

Acanthurus chirurgus
Doctorfish
(BLOCH, 1787)

Hab.: Tropical and subtropical regions of the Atlantic, from the coast of the USA (Massachusetts) to Brazil and the west African coast. At depths of 2 to 15 m.

Sex.: None.

Soc.B./Assoc.: Lives singly, in pairs, or sometimes in groups that may include *A. bahianus*.

M.: Can be maintained singly in an aquarium where it may live for over 5 years. It likes current. Do not associate with invertebrates.

Light: Sunlight zone.

B./Rep.: Unknown.

F.: H; herbivore, but it will accept fish and mussel meat as well as seagrass after habituation.

S.: *A. chirurgus* is probably the most common surgeonfish in the tropical Atlantic and is readily recognizable by its dark brown bands. It can present itself in different color phases depending on mood and substrate. Animals from sandy bottoms are significantly lighter than those from reefs. The young are brown. Although *A. chirurgus* and *A. bahianus* feed in a similar manner, the former swims more above the aufwuchs than among it. They have a strong muscular stomach, and they scrape the algae in such a way that large quantities of calcareous material are also ingested.

T: 22°-25°C, **L:** 30 cm, **TL:** from 180 cm, **WM:** m, **WR:** b, m, **AV:** 2, **D:** 3

Acanthurus chirurgus, juvenile

Acanthurus coeruleus
Blue tang
BLOCH & SCHNEIDER, 1801

Hab.: Caribbean, from the Bermudas along Florida to Brazil. At depths of 2 to 18 m.

Sex.: None.

Soc.B./Assoc.: Lives in pairs or small groups; rarely forms schools of more than 10 fish.

M.: *A. coeruleus* requires a lot of swimming space; therefore, large aquaria and single maintenance are required. It is a robust charge and can be well maintained. Only in sufficiently large aquaria can it achieve the intense blue adult state that gives it its name.

Light: Sunlight region.

B./Rep.: Unknown.

F.: H; it quickly accepts substitute foods, especially green algae, *Mysis*, and Enchytraeidae. After adaptation, it accepts almost all foods ranging from plants to flakes (e.g., Tetra Conditioning Food Large Flakes).

S.: In contrast to the other two west Atlantic species, this species has a very thin-walled stomach. Therefore, it carefully pulls on the algae to limit the amount of ingested detritus and calcareous material. Juveniles are yellow with blue fin edges. Transitional forms have a blue body and yellow fins. In contrast to other Caribbean species that always have a dark frame around their spines, the caudal spine in this species is always yellow.

T: 24°-26°C, **L:** 35 cm, **TL:** from 200 cm, **WM:** w, **WR:** b, m, **AV:** 2, **D:** 3

Acanthurus coeruleus, juvenile

Acanthurus chirurgus, adult

Acanthurus coeruleus, adult

Fam.: Acanthuridae

Acanthurus dussumieri   VALENCIENNES, 1835
Dussumier's surgeonfish

Hab.: In the Pacific, from east Africa to Hawaii, the Line Islands, Japan (N), the southern Great Barrier Reef, and New Caledonia (S); absent in the central Pacific. At depths of 9 to 130 m.

Sex.: None.

Soc.B./Assoc.: *A. dussumieri* is usually found alone in outer reef waters deeper than 10 m. Sometimes found in small groups along shallow reefs or in sand bottomed lagoons.

M.: *A. dussumieri* is aggressive towards conspecifics and new introductions; therefore, keep singly. Requires sufficient hiding places and current. This species is poorly suited for home aquaria because of the respectable mature size they attain.

Light: Sunlight region.

B./Rep.: Unknown; a pair was observed spawning in the sea.

F.: H; in nature, *A. dussumieri* feeds on the surface film of fine green and brown algae and diatoms and detritus it finds lying on the sand; less frequently it scrapes this material from hard surfaces. In the aquarium, it prefers flake and frozen foods and "sucks" the bottom.

S.: The white spine has a dark outline. This characteristic and the yellow band through the eye are good identifying marks. Dark spots in the central part of the caudal fin and lack of a yellow edge on the pectoral fins differentiate it from very similar species such as *A. mata, A. blochii,* and *A. xanthopterus.*

Acanthurus dussumieri, juvenile

T: 24°-28°C, **L:** 40 cm, **TL:** from 200 cm, **WM:** m, **WR:** b, **AV:** 2-3, **D:** 3

Acanthurus fowleri   BEAUFORT, 1951
Fowlers surgeonfish

Hab.: West Pacific; east India and the Philippines. At depths of 2 to 20 m.

Soc.B./Assoc.: Unknown.

Sex.: None.

M.: Unknown; because of its size, it is little suited for the home aquarium.

Light: Sunlight zone.

B./Rep.: Not known.

F.: H (?); unknown.

S.: *A. fowleri* is only found in a limited area around east India. In contrast to other species that have a bright tail fin base, this species has a shoulder spot that starts in line with the top of the operculum and terminates above the pectoral fin axis. Its shape varies from triangular to semicircular. The thorn has a black outline.

T: 24°-28°C, **L:** up to 40 cm, **TL:** from 200 cm, **WM:** w, **WR:** b, m, **AV:** 3-4, **D:** 3-4

Acanthurus dussumieri from Hawaii

Acanthurus fowleri, Indonesia

Fam.: Acanthuridae

Acanthurus gahhm   (FORSSKÅL, 1775)
Monk tang

Hab.: Arabian Sea, Red Sea, and the Gulf of Aden. At depths of 5-40 m.

Sex.: None.

Soc.B./Assoc.: *A. gahhm* lives in groups or loose schools above sand and rubble at the base of the reef, both on the lagoon and outer, exposed side.

M.: *A. gahhm* grows very fast and is, therefore, unsuitable for the home aquarium. It requires a correspondingly large swimming space and hardy tankmates. Its behavior towards them can be considered rough but not aggressive.

Light: Sunlight region.

B./Rep.: Not known.

F.: O; *A. gahhm* has a strong muscular stomach. It ingests sand as it feeds on the detritus and algae layer that covers the sandy and rubble substrates. Invertebrates found in the substrate and zooplankton from the water column are also consumed. It eagerly tears meats of all kinds from the diver's hand; in the aquarium it is a voracious omnivore.

S.: *A. gahhm,* unlike the very similar but somewhat smaller *A. nigricauda,* does not have a black line extending from the tail spine cranially. The dark zone is limited to the knife. The dark shoulder band of both species is about the same and is absent in young animals. Adults like to catch large zooplankton from the water column, but they rarely venture beyond the protection of the reef. In front of exposed capes, for example, Ras Muhammed (Sinai), Shaab Roumi, and Sanganeb (Sudan), they join schools of circling barracudas, using the school to protect themselves and penetrate farther than usual into the open water. Food is more abundant away from the reef and its associated feeding competitors.

T: 25°-27°C, **L:** 50 cm, **TL:** from 250 cm, **WM:** w, **WR:** b, m, **AV:** 3, **D:** 3

Acanthurus japonicus
White-faced surgeonfish

(SCHMIDT, 1930)

Hab.: Western Pacific Ocean, from the Philippines to Japan. At depths of 5 to 15 m.

Sex.: Not known.

Soc.B./Assoc.: Lives singly or in small groups along outer reefs or in lagoons full of coral.

M.: Since it is aggressive and tends to be waspish towards conspecifics, it should be maintained singly. However, it is normally peaceful towards other fishes. Sensitive to *Oodinium*!

Light: Sunlight zone.

B./Rep.: Unknown.

Acanthurus japonicus

F.: H; usually accepts food immediately. *A. japonicus* grazes the algae lawn and eats small crustacea, tablet, live, or flake foods.

S.: It is very similar to *A. nigricans*, but this species has a white band that runs from the eye to the upper lip.

T: 24°-28°C, **L:** 18 cm, **TL:** from 150 cm, **WM:** w, **WR:** b, **AV:** 2, **D:** 3

Acanthurus japonicus, Philippines

Fam.: Acanthuridae

Acanthurus leucosternon (BENNETT, 1832)
Powder blue tang

Hab.: Indian Ocean, from Africa to Indonesia. At depths of 0 to 25 m.

Sex.: None.

Soc.B./Assoc.: Usually live singly and maintain a territory in shallow moving water around reef terraces and reef edges. Sometimes form groups or schools (see p. 689).

M.: Aggressive territorial defender; therefore, only single animals can be kept. Besides a lot of swimming space, these animals must have moving, oxygen-rich water. It has proven to be a robust aquarium animal. Housing it with other surgeonfishes and/or large blue fishes is not recommended.

Light: Sunlight.

B./Rep.: Unknown.

F.: H; *A. leucosternon* feeds almost exclusively on vegetable fare in the sea, but in an aquarium, it accepts algae and lettuce as well as *Mysis*, Enchytraeidae, grindal worms, shrimp, mussels, flesh from marine fishes, and flake foods.

S.: Sometimes forms gigantic schools, especially when free algae territories are absent. This allows it to penetrate the territories of other fishes (e.g., damsels) to graze their algae lawns. Like many other species, *A. leucosternon* changes its coloration depending on its mood. If it is pale blue with a gray-black head, it feels poorly and leaves its tankmates in peace. If the head is jet black and the body is dark blue, it is in top form and its aggressive nature emerges as it patrols the aquarium. If light cross-stripes appear on the body and the forehead lightens—caution—the other tankmates, especially butterflies, are in danger. Attack and use of the spine are imminent.

T: 23°-28°C, **L:** 30 cm, **TL:** from 150 cm, **WM:** m-s, **WR:** b-t, **AV:** 1-2, **D:** 2-3

Acanthurus leucocheilus HERRE, 1927
Pale lipped tang

Hab.: West central Pacific: Indonesia, Philippines, Palau, and Micronesia to the Line Islands south of Hawaii. At depths of 3 to 30 m.

Sex.: None; with age large ♂ ♂ develop a frontal hump which may protrude beyond the tip of the snout.

Soc.B./Assoc.: *A. leucocheilus* occurs singly along sharply sloped outer reefs. Only suitable for fish community tanks that contain other species capable of defending themselves.

M.: Since this fish becomes quite large, it is barely suitable for the home aquarium. It requires clean water and plenty of swimming space.

Light: Sunlight region.

B./Rep.: Unknown.

F.: Besides flake food and small crustacea, *A. leucocheilus* needs plant fare and algae.

S.: It differs from similar species by its reddish lips which are surrounded by a pearl white line followed by a black band. The throat and thorn are white.

T: 23°-27°C, **L:** 30 cm, **TL:** from 200 cm, **WM:** w, **WR:** b, m, **AV:** 3-4, **D:** 3-4

Acanthurus leucosternon, Maldives

Acanthurus leucocheilus, Indonesia

Acanthurus leucopareius, Acanthurus nigrofuscus and *Acanthurus triostegus*

Acanthurus leucopareius   (JENKINS, 1903)
Whiteband tang

Hab.: Pacific islands; from the Mariana Islands to Japan, Hawaii (N), New Caledonia, Rapa, Tuamotu, and the Easter Islands (S). At depths of 1 to 85 m.

Sex.: None.

Soc.B./Assoc.: *A. leucopareius* normally lives in groups and large schools in the surf, especially where there are steep basalt cliffs (calcareous rocks are avoided). It can be kept alone, in groups, or with numerous other fishes.

M.: A rock aquarium with appropriate refuges suits it well. At least initially, it will need a dense layer of filamentous algae.

Light: Areas with sunlight to moderate light.

B./Rep.: Not known; group spawning in open water has been observed.

F: H; primarily feeds on filamentous algae. These algae must be present in the tank. Later it will accept substitute foods, lettuce, and spinach.

S.: Other than its white tail base, this species is identified by a black framed white crossband.

T: 24°-28°C, **L:** 20 cm, **TL:** from 50 cm, **WM:** m-s, **WR:** b-t, **AV:** 2, **D:** 3

On a Hawaiian reef, convict surgeonfish (*A. triostegus*) mix with whiteband surgeonfish (*A. leucopareius*) and spot-cheeked surgeonfish (*A. nigrofuscus*). *A. triostegus* holds the lowest strata in the pecking order of the Acanthuridae because of its comparatively small size and less developed spines. Rarely is it able to defend its territories; so, it "gangs up" with conspecifics in groups and schools and penetrates the territories of almost all territorial herbivorous species. When they school with stronger and larger surgeonfishes, any territories belonging to other herbivorous are undefendable against their invasion. The population existing around Hawaii has somewhat different coloration and an oblique line instead of one or several dots below the pectoral fin. The Hawaiian subspecies is *A. triostegus sandwichensis,* and the remaining Pacific specimens are *A. triostegus triostegus*.

Fam.: Acanthuridae

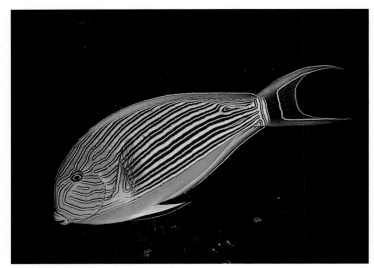

Acanthurus lineatus, adult

Acanthurus lineatus   (LINNAEUS, 1758)
Lined tang

Hab.: Indo-Pacific, from east Africa to the Marquesas. At depths of 0 to 15 m.

Sex.: None; ♂♂ grow larger than ♀♀.

Soc.B./Assoc.: *A. lineatus* lives alone or in small groups made up of a large territorial and aggressive ♂ and several ♀♀. These groups live in shallow moving waters at the reef edge.

M.: Not only is it aggressive towards conspecifics, it is also bellicose towards all equal-sized or larger fishes. This problematic feeder needs a large tank with current. Once acclimated, it is easily cared for if you consider it unimportant that it will attack all new introductions as well as the caretaker.

Light: Sunlight region.

B./Rep.: Not known; in the sea this is a group spawner that spawns above a steep reef edge shortly after sunrise during a new moon. The animals rapidly swim towards the surface, twisting spiral-like, and release the eggs and sperm into the open water just below the surface.

F.: H; primarily feeds on filamentous algae; later, flake foods and tablets will be accepted.

S.: This species' wide yellow longitudinal stripes distinguishes it from the similar Arabian species *A. sohal* (p. 725).

T: 24°-30°C, **L:** 20 cm, **TL:** from 200 cm, **WM:** m, **WR:** b, m, **AV:** 1-2, **D:** 3

Acanthurus lineatus, juvenile

A. lineatus only has territories outside of the spawning season. These vary in size from 4 to 12 m², depending on the population density. It is thought that the borders are outlined by optical reference points. The fish constantly patrols its territory, usually along an established pathway. After observing the fish for about an hour, you know the exact outline of the territory. Borders next to conspecifics are almost constantly monitored. When the neighbor approaches the border, the fish is already prepared and in a state of slight excitement. If the neighbor refuses to retreat, its demeanor changes to "furious" and it and its neighbor swim parallel to each other, as if sizing up their opponent. If the neighbor is still not intimidated, the pair begins to circle faster and faster until they are practically swimming head to tail. Victory is usually conceded to one of the participants when they finish circling. The loser flees into the distance or a nearby refuge.

Their coloration during the confrontation and fighting changes, reflecting their mood. The most notorious is the central part of the tail fin which changes from black during tranquil phases to white during excitement. Not just conspecifics are treated inhospitably. Other fishes, particularly herbivores such as other surgeonfishes, rabbitfishes, and sometimes damselfishes and butterflyfishes, are also threatened and chased away when possible.

Acanthurus lineatus in shallow water (Maldives)

Acanthurus maculiceps, Bali

Acanthurus maculiceps (AHL, 1924)
Whitespot tang

Hab.: Tropical west Pacific from the Christmas Island in the Indian Ocean to northwest Australia, the Philippines, Japan, Micronesia, and Samoa. At depths of 3 to 15 m.

Sex.: None; however, very large ♂ ♂ develop a convex frontal hump which can reach beyond the tip of the snout.

Soc.B./Assoc.: Little known; lives singly or in small groups, preferably on outer reef terraces and slopes that have coral.

M.: Little known; requires a large tank that offers the necessary free space to swim and grow.

Light: Sunlight zone.

B./Rep.: Unknown.

F.: H; other than plant fare such as algae and lettuce, it is said to also accept live, frozen and flake foods.

S.: A rarely seen fish with a limited range.

T: 24°-28°C, **L:** 35 cm, **TL:** from 200 cm, **WM:** w, **WR:** b, m, **AV:** 3-4, **D:** 3-4

Acanthurus mata
Elongate tang

CUVIER, 1829

Hab.: Indo-Pacific; from the Red Sea and east Africa to Japan and through all of Micronesia to the Marquesas and Tuamotu. At depths of 5 to 45 m.

Sex.: None.

Soc.B./Assoc.: Found singly or in schools above coral reef slopes, often in strong current. Also lives above sand bottoms of lagoons.

M.: Requires a lot of space, oxygen, light, and current; grows too large for the home aquarium.

Light: Region of sunlight.

B./Rep.: Not known.

F.: O; in its natural habitat, *A. mata* feeds less on algae from the bottom and more on zooplankton from the open water than other related species. While flake and frozen foods are eaten, small, live crustacea are definitely the preferred fare.

S.: *A. mata* has a rather straight tail fin without filaments. In contrast, similar fishes such as *A. dussumieri* and *A. xanthopterus* all have crescent-shaped tail fins. The spine on the caudal peduncle is dark; the yellow zone around the eye presents itself as two parallel bands anteriorly.

T: 23°-28°C, **L:** 50 cm, **TL:** from 250 cm, **WM:** m-s, **WR:** b-t, **AV:** 3, **D:** 3-4

Fam.: Acanthuridae

Acanthurus monroviae   STEINDACHNER, 1876
Monrovian tang

Hab.: East Atlantic from Guinea to Cape Verde. At depths of 5 to 40 m.

Sex.: None.

Soc.B./Assoc.: Schooling fish; its social behavior towards conspecifics probably carries over to the aquarium.

M.: It is reported to be fairly robust and sociable; requires a large tank.

Light: Sunlight zone.

B./Rep.: Unknown.

F.: H (?); unknown.

S.: The spine is framed in yellow, making it easily distinguishable from *A. bahianus*. *A. monroviae* is the only species that solely inhabits the eastern tropical Atlantic. Even though it is the closest species of surgeonfish to European hobbyists, little is known about the fish and next to nothing is known about its lifestyle. Divers' reports are needed!

T: 20°-25°C, **L:** 45 cm, **TL:** from 200 cm, **WM:** w, **WR:** b, **AV:** 4, **D:** 3

Acanthurus nigricauda   (DUNKER & MOHR, 1929)
Epanlette tang

Hab.: Indo-Pacific, from east Africa to Japan and through all of Micronesia to Tuamotu. At depths of 2 to 15 m.

Sex.: None; large ♂♂ develop a frontal hump.

Soc.B./Assoc.: *A. nigricauda* usually lives in small groups in clear lagoons and along outer reefs, especially close to coral blocks or rocks which lie on terraces or sandy bottoms. Juveniles school in shallow lagoons and tidal pools.

M.: *A. nigricauda* is somewhat more peaceful than territorial species. It is easily associated with other coral reef fishes. However, its size makes it inappropriate for most home aquaria.

Light: Sunlight zone.

B./Rep.: Unknown.

F.: O; beside algae, it feeds on all kinds of plankton substitutes, since it catches zooplankton from the open water in its natural habitat.

S.: *A. nigricauda* can quickly change its coloration from dark gray to light gray to indicate moods such as courtship, belligerence, or its willingness to be cleaned. It is closely related to A. *gahhm* from the Red Sea which also has a dark shoulder stripe, but not an anteriorly elongated spot around the tail spine. In addition, *A. gahhm* grows much larger. Above open areas of submersed terraces, adult animals may swim in schools that include *A. olivaceus,* other surgeonfishes, and parrotfishes.

T: 23°-28°C, **L:** 30 cm, **TL:** from 180 cm, **WM:** w, **WR:** b, m, **AV:** 2, **D:** 3

Acanthurus monroviae

Acanthurus nigricauda

Fam.: Acanthuridae

Acanthurus nigricans　　　　　　　　　　　　　　　　(LINNAEUS, 1758)
Gold-edge tang

Hab.: Eastern Indian Ocean and the entire Pacific from the Christmas Island to Japan, Hawaii, Galapagos, and Mexico. At depths of 2 to 67 m.

Sex.: None.

Soc.B./Assoc.: *A. nigricans* is a territorial species which usually lives alone; it rarely forms schools. It claims hard bottoms in clear lagoons or outer reefs from the surge zone downward.

M.: *A. nigricans* is aggressive in the aquarium and has to be kept singly. It requires a lot of swimming space and oxygen-rich, clean water.

Light: Sunlight region.

B./Rep.: Not known.

F.: H; *A. nigricans* almost exclusively feeds on filamentous algae in nature. In the aquarium it tends to be omnivorous. It accepts a wide range of foods including algae, shrimp, and flake foods.

S.: This species was previously known as *A. glaucopareius*. The similar *A. japonicus* lacks the horizontal white stripe below the eye and the vertical white stripe on the edge of the mouth. Sometimes hybrids of this species and *A. achilles* are found.

T: 21°-29°C, **L:** 22 cm, **TL:** from 150 cm, **WM:** w, **WR:** b, **AV:** 1-2, **D:** 3

A. nigricans has an enormous distribution area. The picture on the top right was taken in the east Pacific at the Cocos Islands; the photo on the bottom right was taken at the Christmas Island in the eastern Indian Ocean.

Acanthurus nigricans

Acanthurus nigricans

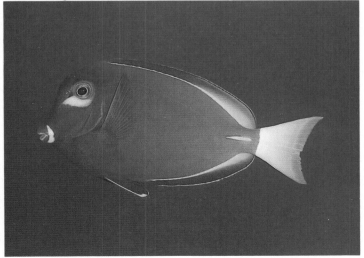

Acanthurus nigricans

Fam.: Acanthuridae

Acanthurus nigrofuscus   (FORSSKÅL, 1775)
Brown tang

Hab.: Indo-Pacific, from the Red Sea to Japan, New Caledonia, Hawaii, and Tuamotu. At depths of 2 to 25 m.

Sex.: None.

Soc.B./Assoc.: *A. nigrofuscus* rarely lives alone or in pairs. Usually found in large migrating schools above shallow hard bottoms of lagoons and outer reefs from the lower surge zone downward.

M.: This relatively large and, unfortunately, rather plain species of Acanthuridae is comparatively peaceful and therefore can be easily kept in a home aquarium if offered sufficient swimming space.

Light: Region of sunlight.

B./Rep.: Not known.

F.: H; in the sea *A. nigrofuscus* almost exclusively feeds on fine filamentous algae scraped from hard substrates. In the aquarium, it prefers to scrape the algae layer from the glass. Tablet and flake foods will also have to be offered.

S.: Orange dots on the head and pupil-sized black dots on the posterior corner of the base of the dorsal and anal fins make these fish easy to identify. The dots tend to fade in preserved specimens, so fresh specimens and preserved specimens were originally classed as two different species. *A. nigrofuscus*, like *A. triostegus*, is a small surgeonfish barely able of defend its own territory. That is why it often forms gigantic schools, sometimes with *A. triostegus*. Within the protection of the school, it invades the territories of other herbivores.

T: 24°-28°C, **L:** 20 cm, **TL:** from 120 cm, **WM:** w, **WR:** b, m, **AV:** 2, **D:** 3

Acanthurus nubilus   FOWLER & BEAN, 1929
Pinstripe tang

Hab.: Indo-Pacific; probably from east Africa through Indonesia, the Philippines, Celebes, Micronesia, and the Solomon and Cook Islands. At depths of 5 to 40 m.

Sex.: None.

Soc.B./Assoc.: Only solitary animals living well apart from others have been observed. Almost nothing is known about its behavior.

M.: Unknown; since the animals have been observed swimming a few meters above the bottom in the open water, it is assumed that they catch zooplankton. There is a distinct paucity of information concerning this fish's maintenance. Nothing other than its need for a large swimming space is known

Light: Sunlight zone.

B./Rep.: Not known.

F.: C; it is likely that *A. nubilus* can be fed live foods such as *Mysis*, small crustacea, and *Tubifex*. Flake foods will be consumed if they are suspended in the water.

S.: Originally described from Celebes, this species has been sporadically captured in the Pacific. A specimen found in the Mozambique Channel at South Africa widened its distribution to the entire Indian Ocean. Whether or not the African animals will continue within this species remains to be seen. The number of dorsal fin rays tends to be different. Only a larger number of specimens will bring about a final decision.

T: 24°-28°C, **L:** up to 30 cm, **TL:** from 180 cm, **WM:** w, **WR:** m, t, **AV:** 4, **D:** 4

Acanthurus nigrofuscus

Acanthurus nubilus

Fam.: Acanthuridae

Acanthurus olivaceus
Orange-epaulette tang

SCHLOCH & SCHNEIDER, 1801

Hab.: Indo-Pacific, from the eastern Indian Ocean (Christmas Island) to Japan, Hawaii, and the Marquesas Islands. At depths of 4 to 45 m.

Sex.: None.

Soc.B./Assoc.: Lives singly, in pairs, or in groups; at times, they may form large schools which occasionally include other species.

M.: Because of its bellicose nature, it can only be kept alone, even as a juvenile (over 6 cm length). Robust and easily cared for. It has reportedly been kept for over 5 years in an aquarium.

Light: Sunlight region.

B./Rep.: Not known; young fish are found singly or in small groups in shallow, protected bays and lagoons at depths less than 3 m.

F.: H; in the ocean, *A. olivaceus* feeds on the film of diatoms, detritus, and delicate filamentous algae which cover the sand and naked rocks. In the aquarium, it eats algae growing in the tank and "sucks" detritus from the bottom; also eats flake foods.

S.: *A. olivaceus* is closely related to *A. tennenti*, which inhabits the western Indian Ocean. Coloration is virtually the only difference between the two.

T: 24°-28°C, **L:** 30 cm, **TL:** from 180 cm, **WM:** w, **WR:** b, **AV:** 3, **D:** 3

Acanthurus olivaceus, juvenile

This species is subject to dramatic color changes. Up to 6 cm in length it is yellow; the typical spot above the pectoral fin is somewhat darker. These yellow juveniles can easily be confused with juveniles of other species such as *A. pyroferus*. At 12 cm, they are greenish-brown. The posterior half of the body appears somewhat darker. At a length of 25 cm, some animals are dark brown with a pronounced orange shoulder spot.

Acanthurus olivaceus, subadult, aquarium

Acanthurus olivaceus, adult, Hawaii

Fam.: Acanthuridae

Acanthurus pyroferus　　　　　　　　　　　　　　　　　　KITTLITZ, 1834
Mimic tang

Hab.: Indo-Pacific; from the Seychelles to Japan, the Community Islands, the Marquesas and Tuamotu. At depths of 5 to 40 m.

Sex.: None.

Soc.B./Assoc.: This rare loner prefers deep lagoons and outer reefs. It can be found in areas with mixed corals or above coral rubble and sand at the base of reefs.

M.: Fully colored specimens are difficult to acclimate. Juveniles generally become accustomed to their captive environment easily; severaljuveniles can usually be kept in a reef aquarium. As they mature, they will become incompatible, however. Usually solid yellow juveniles from the Philippines and Singapore are offered. Animals similar to *Centropyge eibli* are regularly offered from Sri Lanka. The Pacific color variants, which are similar to *Centropyge flavissimus* and *C. vroliki*, are rarely found in aquaria. Juveniles can easily live 5 years. In contrast to most other *Acanthurus* species, *A. pyroferus* is no more sensitive to *Cryptocarion* than other coral reef fishes, even in reef aquaria.

Light: Sunlight zone.

B./Rep.: Unknown.

F.: O; during acclimation, feed the animals algae from the reef tank and *Artemia*; difficult specimens may demand live adult *Artemia*, spinach, moistened (!) rolled oats, small krill, and glassworms. Cautiously feed flake foods until the animals are accustomed to them.

S.: Juveniles live in the same habitat as adults, but they have a different color, form, and behavior to camouflage themselves. They tend to mimic pygmy angelfishes.

T: 26°-28°C, **L:** 25 cm, **TL:** from 150 cm, **WM:** w, **WR:** b, **AV:** 2, **D:** 3

Uncommon phenotypes of *Acanthurus pyroferus* are worth considering more extensively in the following context: in its juvenile state it imitates the coloration of pygmy angelfishes of the genus *Centropyge* that live in the same biotope. Since juveniles of *A. pyroferus* often enter the aquarium trade, buyers interested in purchasing a pygmy angelfish should be aware of this phenomenon. Science calls it mimicry when an animal imitates the appearance of another which either lacks predators or is avoided because of other reasons (poison, foul taste, etc.). There is a model and an imitator. If you want to know why *Acanthurus pyroferus* mimics, we need to know what benefit is obtained from imitating a pygmy angelfish. What makes species such as *Centropyge eibli, C. flavissimus,* or *C. vroliki* good models? Even the filaments on the caudal fin of surgeonfishes are rounded like those of pygmy angelfishes. Are pygmy angelfishes unpalatable? The answer lies in the strong spine on the operculum and the extremely aggressive nature of the angelfish. As long as its own caudal peduncle spine is immature and ineffective, its mimicry provides protection; later the fish is capable of defending itself.

Acanthurus pyroferus, juvenile

Acanthurus pyroferus, subadult

Acanthurus pyroferus, adult

Acanthurus pyroferus mimics *Centropyge heraldi* (top). Both animals are compatible!

Acanthurus pyroferus

Acanthurus pyroferus

Mimicry color forms of *Acanthurus pyroferus*
- upper left: *Centropyge flavissimus*
- upper right: *Centropyge eibli*
- bottom: *Centropyge vroliki*

Acanthurus pyroferus

Fam.: Acanthuridae

Acanthurus sohal
Arabian tang
(FORSSKÅL, 1775)

Hab.: Arabian Sea, from the Red Sea to the Arabian Gulf. At depths of 0 to 20 m.

Sex.: None.

Soc.B./Assoc.: Normally a loner that requires a relatively small territory. Several solitary animals densely populate reef plateaus close to the edge. Sometimes seen in large aggregations.

M.: *A. sohal* is one of the most beautiful surgeonfish, but also one of the most dominating. In the aquarium they become enormously aggressive as they grow. Old tankmates are usually left in peace, but new arrivals are normally molested. While this bellicose behavior is not out of the ordinary for surgeonfishes, their strong mandibles and larger than average caudal spines enables this species to kill other aquarium inhabitants with ease. Oddly, many specimens pursue of small wrasses. Other aspects of their care are easily fulfilled and these animals will easily become sizable charges. Only suitable for larger reef aquaria. A large swimming area is needed.

Light: Sunlight zone.

B./Rep.: Unknown.

F.: O; accepts the usual foodstuffs.

S.: Unlike *A. lineatus,* this species has slender light blue and black longitudinal stripes. *A. sohal* is an extremely nimble swimmer. This can be seen even in nature: in the breaker zone, these fish can be observed from land through the front side of breakers as they race back and forth at the reef edge.

T: 24°-30°C, **L:** 40 cm, **TL:** from 200 cm, **WM:** m-s, **WR:** b-t, **AV:** 2, **D:** 3-4

Acanthurus sohal, aquarium picture

Acanthurus tennenti
Spinecircle tang
GÜNTHER, 1861

Hab.: Western Indian Ocean from east Africa to the Maldives and Sri Lanka. At depths of 3 to 25 m.

Sex.: None.

Soc.B./Assoc.: *A. tennenti* lives singly or in small groups and prefers shallow reef terraces with coral rocks, coral rubble, and sand overgrown with algae.

M.: Since it quickly reaches a length of 45 cm, maintenance in the home aquarium is not recommended.

Light: Sunlight zone.

B./Rep.: Unknown.

F.: H; in nature, *A. tennenti* feeds on the thin layer of algae, detritus, and diatoms. In an aquarium this fish acts like a vacuum cleaner. It sucks up small animals and flake and tablet foods.

S.: *A. tennenti* differs from *A. olivaceus* only in the number of pectoral fin rays and coloration.

T: 24°-28°C, **L:** 45 cm, **TL:** from 200 cm, **WM:** w, **WR:** b, **AV:** 3, **D:** 3

Acanthurus sohal

Acanthurus tennenti

Fam.: Acanthuridae

Acanthurus thompsoni   (FOWLER, 1923)
Whitetail tang

Hab.: Indo-Pacific; from east Africa to Japan, the southern Barrier Reef, Hawaii, and the Ducie Islands east of Tuamotu. At depths of 5 to 70 m.

Sex.: None.

Soc.B./Assoc.: *A. thompsoni* lives in loose groups in the open sea above deep coral terraces or in front of steep drop-offs in shallower locals.

M.: Large tanks with a lot of swimming space facilitate the maintenance of these moderate-sized animas.

Light: Sunlight zone.

B./Rep.: Not known.

F.: C; *A. thompsoni* eats fish eggs, crustacea, and zooplankton in the sea, particularly large gelatinouslike forms. It can be acclimated and taught to feed in captivity on *Mysis* and other small, live crustacea as well as other foods that are whirled around in the current.

S.: One of the most important distinguishing characteristics is a dark brown spot below the base of the pectoral fin. The white tail fin cannot be used as a distinguishing feature, since animals from Hawaii and east Africa reportedly have dark caudal fins and juveniles of other species may also have a white tail fin. *A. thompsoni* is capable of great color transformations: it can quickly change from black to light blue.

T: 24°-27°C, **L:** up to 25 cm, **TL:** from 150 cm, **WM:** w-m, **WR:** m, t, **AV:** 3-4, **D:** 3

Acanthurus triostegus   (LINNAEUS, 1758)
Convict surgeonfish

Hab.: The entire Indo-Pacific from east Africa to Mexico and Panama. At depths of 0 to 90 m.

Sex.: None.

Soc.B./Assoc.: Usually found in gigantic schools of up to 1000 specimens in lagoons with a hard bottom and along outer reefs from the surface to profound depths. The school may include other herbivorous fishes.

M.: The less pronounced aggressiveness of *A. triostegus* allows a small group of juveniles to be kept. However, they are difficult to train to food and quite sensitive to suboptimal water conditions.

B./Rep.: Unknown. In the sea they spawn in small groups along reef edges or canal openings. These groups separate out of large schools, rise above the school with quick movements, and spawn into the open water. The larval phase lasts two and a half months. The young are then sedentary in the tidal zone of reef terraces and banks.

Light: Region of sunlight.

F.: H; in the sea it primarily feeds on filamentous algae, but it is also interested in *Mysis*, grindal worms, and flake foods.

S.: It likes to join other surgeonfishes, rabbitfishes, and parrotfishes to penetrate territories of other herbivores. They strip the feeding grounds like a horde of locusts.

T: 24°-26°C, **L:** 20 cm, **TL:** from 200 cm, **WM:** w, **WR:** b, m, **AV:** 1-2, **D:** 3

Acanthurus thompsoni

Acanthurus triostegus

Fam.: Acanthuridae

Acanthurus xanthopterus
Yellow fin tang

VALENCIENNES, 1835

Hab.: Indo-Pacific, from east Africa to Mexico, towards Japan and Hawaii in the north and the Barrier Reef and New Caledonia in the south. At depths of 5 to 90 m.

Sex.: None.

Soc.B./Assoc.: Lives singly or in loose aggregations in deeper waters of outer reefs, but they also live in sandy bottomed lagoons and bays. Will never be found over hard bottoms or corals. Should only be housed with fishes that can defend themselves, such as rabbitfishes and angelfishes.

M.: These are rapid growing fishes which quickly outgrow the home aquarium. They cannot be recommended for the home aquarium.

Light: Region of sunlight.

B./Rep.: Unknown; in nature it has been observed spawning during the new and full moons. The young inhabit shallow protected areas that have strong water movement.

F.: O; in the sea the animals feed on diatoms and the thin layer of detritus on the sand. Filamentous algae and animal matter such as hydrozoans and pieces of fish are also eaten. In the aquarium they are omnivores which eat algae, small crustacea, flake food, tablet food, and many other substances.

S.: Yellow pectoral fins, the absence of a shoulder spot, and a rather dull colored caudal peduncle distinguishes it from similar species.

T: 24°-28°C, **L:** 60 cm, **TL:** from 250 cm, **WM:** juv.: s, adult: w, **WR:** b, **AV:** 3-4, **D:** 3-4

Acanthurus xanthopterus

About the Genus *Ctenochaetus* GILL, 1885

The specialized mouth and feeding behavior are characteristic of the genus *Ctenochaetus* and make these animals relatively easy to distinguish from other surgeonfishes: their movable, bristlelike teeth cover and rasp algae from reefs or, likewise, from aquarium fixtures. The protrusive, pouting mouth is characteristic of *Ctenochaetus*. From comparative studies done on the larvae, it has been determined that these animals evolved from surgeonfishes.

While bristletooths are normally found in pairs, they will school, especially during spawning season. Keep this in mind when maintaining them. Since the sexes are indistinguishable, procure single specimens. The juvenile coloration of this genus is often striking, but disappears at 7 to 8 cm. When angered, the uniform brown adult *Ctenochaetus* surgeonfishes display luminous lateral stripes. As in their natural habitat, they constantly graze on algae from the artificial reef. Flake food, krill, and *Artemia* will be eaten from the water column. They feel most at home in strong currents and are peaceful towards tankmates that bear no resemblance to surgeonfishes.

Ctenochaetus mainly differ from *Acanthurus,* which have well attached spatulate teeth, by their larger number of mobile teeth that are somewhat indented at the tip and have lateral teethlets. Not only are they able to scrape attached algae from the bottom, but they can also ingest the fine film of detritus and unicellular algae from the surface of dead corals, rocks, algae, and seaweeds. When this film contains high concentrations of blue-green algae, the poison contained therein (ciguatoxin) concentrates in the surgeonfishes and can lead to ciguatera poisoning if consumed by humans.

C. strigosus, Hawaii

Ctenochaetus strigosus from the Maldives

Fam.: Acanthuridae

Ctenochaetus binotatus
Two-spot bristletooth

RANDALL, 1955

Hab.: Indo-Pacific; from east Africa to Tuamotu, Japan, and the southern Barrier Reef. At depths between 10 and 50 m.

Sex.: Not known.

Soc.B./Assoc.: *C. binotatus* lives singly or in pairs. While found primarily above rubble or coral covered surfaces in deep lagoons, it may also be seen along outer reefs.

M.: Requires sufficient space, plentiful light, hiding and resting sites, and a slight current.

Light: Sunlight area.

B./Rep.: Not known.

F.: H; requires a tank that has a slight algae cover. It is tirelessly grazed, especially from the glass panes. Detritus and feed remains are sucked off the bottom.

S.: *C. binotatus*'s notable characteristics are a black spot on the posterior base of the dorsal and anal fins as well as a blue ring around the eye.

T: 24°-26°C, **L:** up to 15 cm, **TL:** from 120 cm, **WM:** w, **WR:** b, m, **AV:** 2, **D:** 3

Ctenochaetus binotatus

Ctenochaetus hawaiiensis
Hawaiian bristletooth

RANDALL, 1955

Hab.: Central Pacific, in the region of the so-called Pacific Plate from Australia to Hawaii and the Marquesas. At depths of 5 to 40 m.

Sex.: None.

Soc.B./Assoc.: *C. hawaiiensis* is rare and almost always seen singly along deep outer reefs. Small groups were seen in front of Pagan above shallow basalt blocks in a somewhat protected region.

M.: This rare loner is quarrelsome and only exported from Hawaii. It is less dependent on coral reef aquaria than it is on crevice riddled rock formations with hiding places.

Light: Sunlight zone.

B./Rep.: Unknown.

F.: H; little is known concerning the maintenance of this animal. Like related species, it primarily feeds on fine algae which are sucked from the glass panes and bottom. It will also take flake food.

S.: Young of *C. hawaiiensis* are quite different from adults: not only do they have a deeper body, but their coloration with the species-typical herringbone design is especially spectacular. The adults appear to be a rather uniform black when seen from a distance. Only up close can you recognize dark green longitudinal stripes.

T: 25°-27°C, **L:** 25 cm, **TL:** from 150 cm, **WM:** w, **WR:** b, m, **AV:** 3-4, **D:** 3-4

Ctenochaetus hawaiiensis, adult

Ctenochaetus binotatus

Ctenochaetus hawaiiensis, juvenile

Fam.: Acanthuridae

Ctenochaetus strigosus in an aquarium

Ctenochaetus strigosus   (BENNET, 1828)
Spotted bristletooth

Hab.: Indo-Pacific, from east Africa to Hawaii (with the exception of the Red Sea). At 10 to 45 m depth.

Sex.: None.

Soc.B./Assoc.: Solitary animals or pairs are most common. Groups are rare. They live in deep lagoons or outer reefs. In contrast to *C. binotatus,* it is always found in locales with plentiful coral growth.

M.: With sufficient algae growth, *C. strigosus* is relatively easy to keep. It is said to be amiable, even when kept in small groups. Some aquarists, however, consider it particularly sensitive and difficult to train to food in captivity.

Light: Sunlight zone.

B./Rep.: Most surgeonfishes spawn in groups; however, this species has been observed spawning in pairs.

F.: H; *C. strigosus* depends on large quantities of minute algae to remain healthy, but it will accept animal fare and flake food.

S.: *A. strigosus* exhibits a high degree of variability in coloration in relation to age and geographical distribution. Juveniles have a distinctive yellow-gold dress, while adults only retain the yellow coloration around the eye. Only animals from the Pacific have elongated tail fins and a blue longitudinally striped body (similar to *C. striatus*). Specimens from Polynesia have a white caudal fin but are lacking the yellow eye ring.

T: 21°-27°C, **L:** 18 cm, **TL:** from 120 cm, **WM:** w, **WR:** b, m, **AV:** 2, **D:** 3-4

Ctenochaetus strigosus, juvenile

Ctenochaetus strigosus, adult

Fam.: Acanthuridae

Ctenochaetus striatus   (QUOY & GAIMARD, 1824)
Striped bristletooth

Hab.: Indo-Pacific; from the Red Sea to Tuamotu, Japan, and the southern Barrier Reef. At depths of 3 to 30 m.

Sex.: None.

Soc.B./Assoc.: *C. striatus* lives singly or in small to large aggregations (especially at spawning time), but may also be found associated with other species over corals, rocks, or coral rubble of reef terraces, lagoons, and outer reefs.

M.: A large tank (at least 1 m long) with a crevice riddled rocky reef will allow small groups of young animals to be kept. The constant danger with this type of arrangement is that the strongest animal will slowly decimate its conspecifics with deadly cuts from its spines.

Light: Bright sunlit area.

B./Rep.: These animals breed in large groups, notably at places such as canal openings of lagoons where the current washes into the open sea.

F.: H; *C. striatus* sucks the thin covering of diatoms and poisonous blue-green algae from the bottom, making it one of the few herbivorous species that can be poisonous (ciguatera). It represents an important link in the ciguatera food chain. In the aquarium they graze on fine algae and accept all kinds of substitute foods.

S.: Juveniles are very beautifully colored, but the brilliant colors pale after just a few weeks when the fish reaches a length of 5 cm. Occasionally there are solid yellow (xanthic), solid white (albinic), or black (melanic) animals.

T: 24°-28°C, L: 22 cm, TL: from 150 cm, **WM**: w, **WR**: b, m, **AV**: 1, **D**: 2-3

Ctenochaetus striatus, adult

Ctenochaetus striatus, frontal view

Ctenochaetus striatus, juvenile

Ctenochaetus striatus, subadult

Fam.: Acanthuridae

Ctenochaetus tominiensis   RANDALL, 1955
Tomini bristletooth

Hab.: Indo-Australian Archipelago, from Bali to the Philippines, Micronesia and the Solomon Islands. At depths of 3 to 25 m.

Sex.: None.

Soc.B./Assoc.: *C. tominiensis* lives singly or in small groups along steep reef drop-offs of protected bays full of coral.

M.: Due to its lively swimming habits and its solitary and somewhat aggressive personality, *C. tominiensis* requires a large, relatively clean tank and robust tankmates. These needs and personality traits make it a difficult fish to maintain.

Light: Sunlight area.

B./Rep.: Not known.

F.: H; this species, as others of the genus, grazes on algae. But it also eats animal fare and flake foods in the aquarium.

S.: *C. tominiensis* is a brightly colored fish and the only species of the genus that has an acute dorsal and anal fin. All other species have rounded dorsal and anal fins.

T: 24°-27°C, **L:** 12 cm, **TL:** from 90 cm, **WM:** w, **WR:** b, m, **AV:** 4, **D:** 3-4

Ctenochaetus tominiensis, adult

Ctenochaetus tominiensis, juvenile

About the Genus *Paracanthurus* BLEEKER, 1863

With only one species, this is the smallest genus in the surgeonfish family. Nevertheless, this species, *Paracanthurus hepatus*, is widely distributed. It is found in the Pacific from east Africa to Japan and Samoa. The blue surgeonfish lives secluded and sheltered among the branches of the coral *Pocillopora eydouxi*. Its life is more perilous than other surgeonfishes' because it forages for plankton in the open water far above the bottom. The hectic swimming pattern seen in its natural biotope extends to the aquarium. Small groups of up to 10 animals of the same size can be kept simultaneously. Of course, under these circumstances the aquarium should have a volume of at least 400 l.

Paracanthurus hepatus

Fam.: Acanthuridae

Fish community aquarium with several *Paracanthurus hepatus*.

Paracanthurus hepatus   LINNAEUS, 1766
Blue surgeonfish

Hab.: Indo-Pacific, from east Africa to Japan, the southern Barrier Reef, and the Line Islands south of Hawaii. At depths of 10 to 40 m.

Sex.: None.

Soc.B./Assoc.: *P. hepatus* inhabits clear, current-rich outer reef terraces. Young fish live in free-swimming groups until they reach sexual maturity, catching zooplankton 1-2 m above isolated coral stalks (*Pocillopora eydouxi*). When threatened, they flee into the coral and press close to its branches. Adults are solitary abiding animals.

M.: Juveniles can be kept in groups. They require hiding places similar to those of *P. eydouxi*. They need a lot of light, very clean water, and current. These fish are susceptible to ectoparasites. Adult specimens are better kept alone; they can live for years as long as they are supplied with plenty of algae.

Light: Sunlight.

B./Rep.: Not known.

F.: O; in the sea the animals feed on zooplankton; in the aquarium they accept small, live shrimp such as *Mysis*, but any other food such as Enchytraeidae, grindal worms, and flake foods suspended and moving in the water column are also accepted. The fish will also eat algae and lettuce.

S.: *P. hepatus* is a relatively rare fish, limited as it is by its requirements. But because young specimens are colorful and easily kept, they are a sought aquarium fish. Commercial fish collectors should always leave a few fish on each coral tree!

T: 24°-26°C, **L:** 30 cm, **TL:** from 80 cm (juv.), 150 cm (adult), **WM:** w, m, **WR:** b-t, **AV:** 2, **SG:** 2-3

About the Genus *Zebrasoma* SWAINSON, 1839

The seven species of sailfin surgeonfishes can be found in every sea except the Atlantic. In their natural habitat they are found in pairs. Very rarely, small groups of up to 6 animals are seen. They, too, live off of attached benthic algae, tugging from morning to evening along great stretches of sunlit reef. Its fondness for swimming is carried over into their aquarium habitat. Therefore, *Zebrasoma* should always be housed in tanks with a volume of at least 300 l. They are rather slow swimmers, and when in danger, they spread their enlarged saillike dorsal and anal fins. Young sailfin surgeons appear twice their actual size when their fins are open. The mouth is thick-lipped and, in comparison to other genera, protrudes outward. *Zebrasoma* surgeons are known for their hardiness. In other words, they have a great capacity to adapt to unfavorable aquarium conditions.

School of *Zebrasoma flavescens*

Fam.: Acanthuridae

Zebrasoma desjardinii and *Z. veliferum* have identical body shapes, but their coloration, especially their adult coloration, is totally different. While the young of both species are mainly black and white striped with a beautiful design on the giant dorsal and anal fins, this contrasting design disappears in *Z. desjardinii* as the fish approaches adulthood. Just the dark body with light rows of dots or pinstripes remains. But the attractive juvenile stripes remain in *Z. veliferum,* even when the animal reaches maturity (see p. 748).

A brief glance at these two pictures and the difference between juvenile and adult *Z. desjardinii* becomes obvious: the dorsal and anal fins are relatively larger in juveniles than in adults and have an attractive striation design following that of the body. Adult animals are rather dark, and their beautiful pattern can only be seen when close. It consists of tiny white or yellowish-brown dots which are clearly delineated, especially on the head and belly. The high density of dots along the snout and behind the eye appears as stripes from a distance. There are very light pinstripes along the back. The design on the dorsal and anal fins is limited to varying hues of brown.

Zebrasoma desjardinii, adult, Maldives

Zebrasoma desjardinii, subadult, Red Sea

Zebrasoma desjardinii, juvenile

Zebrasoma desjardinii   (BENNETT, 1835)
Desjardin's sailfin tang

Hab.: Red Sea and western Indian Ocean. At depths of 2 to 30 m.

Sex.: None.

Soc.B./Assoc.: Juveniles live singly between rocks and corals both in protected bays and areas with current. Adults usually swim in pairs.

M.: *Z. desjardinii* is a lively swimmer which requires a lot of illumination, a large tank, some current, and good water quality.

Light: Sunlight zone.

B./Rep.: Unknown; pairwise spawnings have been observed.

F.: H; *Z. desjardinii* is exclusively herbivorous in nature and tends to feed continuously in the aquarium if sufficient green food is available. Limit your purchases to well fed animals (5-8 cm). Only these can be acclimated and expected to live for years. Adults are usually unable to adapt to the aquarium environment.

S.: This species was previously considered synonymous to *Z. veliferum,* but the adults were found to differ in coloration and have a lesser number of soft rays in the dorsal and anal fins. Depending on the author, there are two geographic species: one western and one eastern species, *Z. desjardinii* and *Z. veliferum* respectively. The giant dorsal and anal fins are approximately the same size as the body. These fins in juvenile animals have an exceptionally beautiful color and design. They are spread to their full extent when the animals are upset.

T: 24°-28°C, **L:** 40 cm, **TL:** from 150 cm, **WM:** w, **WR:** b, m, **AV:** 2, **D:** 3

Zebrasoma flavescens (BENNETT, 1828)
Yellow sailfin tang

Hab.: Pacific Plate, north of the equator from Japan to Hawaii. At 3 to 46 m depth.

Sex.: None.

Soc.B./Assoc.: *Z. flavescens* occurs singly, in pairs, and in loose groups. They live in lagoons and along outer reefs within dense coral stands from 0 - 50 m depth.

M.: Its congenial behavior towards invertebrates and other fishes, slow growth rate, and lively coloration have made this tang an appreciated aquarium fish. It is probably the only *Zebrasoma* that can be kept with conspecifics when added young enough.

Light: Sunlight area.

B./Rep.: In nature they usually spawn in groups, but a kind of pairwise spawning has been observed where a territorial ♂ will court passing ♀ ♀, individually spawning with each.

F.: H; *Z. flavescens* requires plenty of vegetable fare for its well being. Lettuce and spinach alone are not sufficient. Filamentous algae it can scrape from the substrate are especially important. Where permitted, these animals will graze the entire day. A full stomach is a sure indication of a healthy animal. Paper thin specimens need immediate aid, i.e., placing them into an algae tank. *Mysis*, shrimp, *Tubifex*, mosquito larvae, fish meat, beef heart, tablet food, etc., will also be eaten.

S.: *Z. flavescens* is **the** export fish of Hawaii. One of the hardiest and most beautiful surgeonfishes! Poor water conditions seem to be its only weakness. Its hardiness is shown in the following example: without previously placing it in a quarantine tank, a friend put a *Z. flavescens* in his 800 l community tank. The fish had not reached a protected hiding place when an old inhabitant, a powder blue tang, *A. leucosternon*, attacked and inflicted a deep wound with its spine. The gash was so severe that its intestines hung out of the open slit along its side. It was not possible to catch him, so the yellow sailfin was left to its fate. For 7 days it did not eat anything but often swam out of its hiding place and eluded other attacks. With the ingestion of food, it then began to defecate out of the wound, which took an additional 3 months to close again. This particular *Z. flavescens* lived an additional 5 years in that aquarium!

T: 24°-28°C, **L:** 18 cm, **TL:** from 100 cm, **WM:** w, **WR:** b, m, **AV:** 2, **D:** 2

Zebrasoma flavescens

743

Fam.: Acanthuridae

Zebrasoma gemmatum   (VALENCIENNES, 1835)
Spotted sailfin tang

Hab.: Southwestern Indian Ocean from the southern coast of Africa (Durban, Sodwana Bay) to the Mascarene Islands, Madagascar, and Mauritius. At depths of 10 to 60 m.

Sex.: None.

Soc.B./Assoc.: *Z. gemmatum* is a rare territorial loner. It is, nevertheless, amiable, making it possible to house it with invertebrates or even other surgeonfishes.

M.: *Z. gemmatum* requires hiding places and is sensitive towards diseases and parasites. Therefore, it has to be classified as a difficult charge.

Light: Moderate light.

B./Rep.: Not known.

F.: H; besides algae, it also accepts flake and frozen foods.

S.: *Z. gemmatum* is an extremely rare fish that is only imported from Mauritius. Hardly more than 10 specimens are caught per year. Its exorbitant price and rarity are probably why there isn't any information on maintaining it with conspecifics. They should not be imported!

T: 24°-28°C, **L:** 15 cm, **TL:** from 120 cm, **WM:** w, **WR:** b, **AV:** 3, **D:** 4

Zebrasoma gemmatum

Zebrasoma rostratum   (GÜNTHER, 1873)
Longnose sailfin tang

Hab.: Central Pacific, Society Islands, and Tuamotu. At depths of 8 to 35 m.

Sex.: None.

Soc.B./Assoc.: Lives singly or in pairs on coral reefs. Only found around a few islands.

M.: *Z. rostratum* is amiable towards fishes and invertebrates. Its congenial personality makes it a welcome addition to community tanks.

Light: Sunlight area.

B./Rep.: Unknown.

F.: H; *Z. rostratum* feeds on layers of algae from the glass or uses its long snout to pluck algae from tight crevices that are inaccessible to other fishes. These fish are omnivores in aquaria after they are fully acclimated and will accept live, flake, and frozen foods.

S.: The dark coloration and highly elongated snout make *Z. rostratum* easily recognizable. Certain similarities to long-nosed butterflyfishes, which also have an elongated snout, lead you to believe that all of these fishes share a common feeding niche; but luckily this is not so. *Z. rostratum* neither feeds on coral polyps nor sea anemones. Instead, it proves to be an extremely peaceful herbivore whose habits can be compared to *Z. flavescens.* Its dark coloration places it at a distinct disadvantage to colorful species. Definitely a Cinderella. Only healthy, acclimated fishes show the jet black coloration.

T: 23°-28°C, **L:** 25 cm, **TL:** from 150 cm, **WM:** w, **WR:** b, m, **AV:** 2-3, **D:** 2-3

Zebrasoma gemmatum

Zebrasoma rostratum

Fam.: Acanthuridae

Zebrasoma scopas, adult

Zebrasoma scopas (CUVIER, 1829)
Brown sailfin tang

Hab.: Indo-Pacific, from east Africa to Japan and Tuamotu. At 1 to 60 m depth.

Sex.: None; ♂♂ grow larger than ♀♀.

Soc.B./Assoc.: *Z. scopas* lives singly or in groups in lagoons or along outer reefs rich in coral.

M.: Despite its similarity to *Z. flavescens,* this species is not very amiable. It claims a territory and defends it with its caudal peduncle spines. Large tanks (from 80 cm length) allow this species to be kept with invertebrates and other surgeonfishes.

Light: Sunlight area.

B./Rep.: Not known; in the sea, spawning occurs in pairs or groups.

F.: H; same requirements as *Z. flavescens*; besides animal, flake, and dry foods, vegetable fare has to be provided. Do not limit its menu to lettuce and spinach. Filamentous algae are a must.

S.: As in most surgeonfishes, juveniles are more colorful than adults. Since their coloration has a lot of yellow, mostly in the form of fine lines and dots, it was previously assumed to be merely a color variation of *Z. flavescens*. More than 150 years ago CUVIER recognized that *Z. scopas* was an autonomous species with a body shape deceptively similar to *Z. flavescens*. The adults can be found in two hues, gray and brown. The white spine is a common characteristic of all color variants.

T: 25°-28°C, **L:** 17 cm, **TL:** from 120 cm, **WM:** w, **WR:** b, m, **AV:** 1, **D:** 3

Zebrasoma scopas, juvenile, aquarium photo

Zebrasoma scopas, yellow form

Zebrasoma scopas, mutation

Fam.: Acanthuridae

Zebrasoma veliferum   (BLOCH, 1797)
Pacific sailfin tang

Hab.: Pacific, from the Indonesia-Australian area to Japan, Hawaii, and Tuamotu. At depths of 5 to 30 m.

Sex.: None, but ♀ ♀ grow larger than ♂ ♂.

Soc.B./Assoc.: This sailfin surgeonfish grows very large. It lives singly or in pairs in lagoons and outer reefs from the lower surge area downward.

M.: Young are relatively easy to acclimate, but they are fast growing fish that are aggressive towards conspecifics and newly added animals. They require a lot of room; therefore, a large, clean tank with hiding possibilities is needed. Under favorable conditions they may live for years.

Light: Sunlight zone.

B./Rep.: Not known; pairs have been observed spawning in the sea.

F.: H; like *Z. desjardinii*, *Z. veliferum* is primarily an algivore which constantly grazes on algae stands in the aquarium. It also feeds on lettuce, dry foods, and animal fare.

S.: Although this fish has fallen somewhat out of fashion, it used to be frequently kept. It was mainly imported from Indonesia and the Philippines. *Z. veliferum* is similar to *Z. desjardinii*, but while the latter's striations dissolve into faint rows of dots as it ages, the former largely retains its attractive contrasting stripes throughout its life.

T: 24°-28°C, **L:** 40 cm, **TL:** from 150 cm, **WM:** w, **WR:** b, m, **AV:** 1, **D:** 3

Zebrasoma desjardini

Zebrasoma veliferum, Kerama (Japan)

Zebrasoma veliferum, Great Barrier Reef

Zebrasoma xanthurum in an aquarium

Zebrasoma xanthurum   (BLYTH, 1852)
Yellowtail sailfin tang

Hab.: Arabian Sea; originally only known from the Red Sea, but it has been found in latter years around the Arabian Peninsula, from the Red Sea to the Persian Gulf. At depths of 2 to 20 m.

Sex.: None.

Soc.B./Assoc.: Usually lives singly, but pairs are only slightly less common. Schools (in the southern part of the Red Sea) are more infrequent.

M.: Because this species is often imported too large, it is difficult to adapt. Its general demeanor is one of aggression and bellicosity. A great deal of experience and diplomacy are needed to find it the proper tankmates. Once this is achieved, it will prove to be a robust charge that will live for years.

Light: Sunlight zone.

B./Rep.: Not known.

F.: O; when imported young enough, *Z. xanthurum* is easily adapted. It is most likely to accept live foods such as *Mysis* and small shrimp. Later mussel meat, *Tubifex*, mosquito larvae, Enchytraeidae, and frozen, flake, and dry foods will be eaten. Vegetable fare is only occasionally taken.

S.: When in good health, *Z. xanthurum* has a dark blue body, a bright yellow tail, and proves to be a nimble active swimmer which requires a lot of space. When ill, its activity diminishes, its blue color fades to brown, and the tail fin turns a dirty yellow-brown. Imported animals should be 6 -10 cm long.

T: 24°-28°C, **L:** 25 cm, **TL:** from 150 cm, **WM:** w, **WR:** b-t, **AV:** 2, **D:** 3-4

Zebrasoma xanthurum in a reef

Zebrasoma xanthurum, aquarium photo

Zebrasoma xanthurum

Fam.: Acanthuridae

About the Genus *Naso*
LACÉPÈDE, 1802

Few species of this genus are suitable for the home aquarium. As can be seen from the maximum length indications, they simply grow too large. The common differentiating characteristic between the genus *Naso* and other surgeonfishes is the two securely attached sharp spines on each side of the caudal peduncle. Few members of the genus develop a frontal horn; therefore, "unicorn-fish" is a rather inappropriate common name for this genus. In two species, the forehead protuberance is limited to males. *Naso* surgeonfishes are capable of growing more than 1 m in length. They generally swim in large schools while feeding on zooplankton (H.D.).

A school of *Naso* surgeonfishes

Fam.: Acanthuridae

A notable exception is the colorful *Naso lituratus* which generally is found in pairs rather than schooling. Since its rare schooling behavior is fascinating, it is documented in detail here. The orange-spined unicornfish is regularly imported. It, like all *Naso* surgeon-fishes, has a late larval phase called keris, which is pictured below. The tiny *Naso lituratus* is covered with thorns for protection. The acronurus phase, which refers to the subfamily Acanthurinae, looks similar. Juveniles of the 16 *Naso* species are difficult to distinguish, since their body, including the horn and coloring, has not developed; they all look very similar.

Late larval phase of *Naso lituratus*

Naso lituratus, Hawaii

Fam.: Acanthuridae

Naso annulatus (QUOY & GAIMARD, 1825)
Giant unicornfish

Hab.: Indo-Pacific, from east Africa to Japan, Lord Howe Island, Hawaii, Tuamotu, and the Marquesas Islands. At depths of 25 to 60 m.

Sex.: None.

Soc.B./Assoc.: Young fish live in groups and prefer the shallow waters of lagoons; adults are found in pairs or groups and are virtually never seen in waters less than 25 m deep. Found along outer reef drop-offs.

M.: Not known.

Light: Area of sunlight.

B./Rep.: Unknown; a spawning was observed in front of Palau on the reef drop-off of the interior corner of the barrier reef around the new and full moon.

F.: C; primarily feeds on zooplankton that it snaps from the open water.

S.: *N. annulatus* is similar to *N. brevirostris* in its juvenile form; the horn, however, starts further back on its flatter head. Normally only 30-40 cm specimens with a short horn, like the one pictured here, are seen. Only older fish about 50 cm long develop a larger horn which may extend as much as 10 cm past the snout. It was only after 1960 that juveniles and adults were matched. Long-nosed adults were previously thought to be an autonomous species (*N. herrei*). But no animal less than 50 cm in length was ever found.

T: 24°-28°C, **L:** 100 cm, **TL:** from 300 cm, **WM:** w, **WR:** b, **AV:** 3-4, **D:** 4

Not an aquarium fish

Naso brachycentron (VALENCIENNES, 1835)
Humpback unicornfish

Hab.: Indo-Pacific; from east Africa to the central Pacific, Japan, the Marquesas, and the Society Islands. At depths of 2 to 20 m.

Sex.: ♂ and ♀ animals are different. While the ♂♂ develop a large horn that extends beyond the snout, the ♀♀ have none. The body of ♀ fish is less deep, and they develop a small hump in front of the eye.

Soc.B./Assoc.: *N. brachycentron* occurs regularly but is not commonly seen. It lives in pairs or small groups in shallow waters in front of reef edges in lagoons, especially in the proximity of large mushroomlike coral blocks which offer sufficient shelter.

M.: Grows too fast and large for the home aquarium.

Light: Sunlight area.

B./Rep.: Not known.

F.: C; feeds on zooplankton from the open water.

S.: In coloration and certain developmental stages, *N. brachycentron* is similar to *N. unicornis*, but they are easily distinguished beyond a length of 15 to 20 cm. Beginning at that size, *N. brachycentron* forms a hump on the anterior dorsum. It appears as if the animal has a humpback, but it is only a fat cushion which increases in size at sexual maturity. At the same time the tips of the caudal fin grow long filaments.

T: 25°-28°C, **L:** 90 cm, **TL:** from 300 cm, **WM:** w, **WR:** m, t, **AV:** 3-4, **D:** 4

Not an aquarium fish

Naso annulatus

Naso brachycentron ♂

Fam.: Acanthuridae

Naso brevirostris   (VALENCIENNES, 1835)
Spotted unicornfish

Hab.: Indo-Pacific; from the Red Sea to Japan, Lord Howe Island, Hawaii, the Marquesas, and Ducie Island. At depths of 4 to 46 m.

Sex.: None.

Soc.B./Assoc.: While *N. brevirostris* may be found solitarily or in pairs, it usually lives in loose aggregations. The species prefers moderate water depths in front of steep reefs, both in lagoons and along the outer reef.

M.: The fish and its horn will only grow to their full potential when a tank large enough to permit the fish to sedately swim is provided. Once acclimated, it can be kept for years, but its size restricts it to large show aquaria.

Light: Sunlight zone.

B./Rep.: Not known; spawning in pairs has been observed in its natural biotope.

F.: H (Juv.), O (adult); young and half-grown animals feed primarily on algae from the substrate; adults snap zooplankton from the open water. These finicky animals are best fed with algae, *Mysis,* and grindal worms; nevertheless, successful care remains pure luck.

S.: Young animals lack a horn. A horn begins to develop after the fish is 15 to 20 cm long. Animals kept in small aquaria never achieve these lengths. Only 50 cm animals that have a horn reaching far beyond their mouth are true show specimens.
Naso brevirostris is sometimes seen in show aquaria. Both sexes have the typical horn and are not distinguishable by external characteristics. Pair spawning is known from the unicorn tang (*Naso unicornis*). Young juveniles about 15 cm long only have a hint of a horn. At this time, the animals look like *N. annulatus,* but the base of their horn is closer to their mouth. The horn of *N. annulatus* is set somewhat further back, leaving a larger area around the mouth free. In addition, their coloration is very different.

T: 24°-28°C, **L:** 60 cm, **TL:** from 250 cm, **WM:** w, **WR:** b, **AV:** 3, **D:** 4

Naso brevirostris in a show aquarium

Naso brevirostris in the open water

Fam.: Acanthuridae

Naso hexacanthus   (BLEEKER, 1855)
Blacktongue unicornfish

Hab.: Indo-Pacific, from the Red Sea to Japan, Lord Howe Island, Hawaii, the Marquesas, and Ducie Island. At depths of 10 to 137 m.

Sex.: None.

Soc.B./Assoc.: Usually lives in schools in front of steep reefs.

M.: This large, restless swimmer can only be housed in an aquarium for a brief time as a juvenile.

Light: Sun and moderate light zones.

B./Rep.: Not known.

F.: O; in the sea it feeds on large zooplankton like crab larvae, arrowworms, etc., and filamentous algae.

S.: Neither ♂ nor ♀ animals develop a horn. Courting ♂ ♂ have a large luminous pale blue spot on head and neck as well as blue stripes and dots on the sides.

T: 25°-28°C, **L:** 75 cm, **TL:** from 250 cm, **WM:** w, **WR:** b, m, **AV:** 3-4, **D:** 3-4

Naso hexacanthus

Naso lituratus   (BLOCH & SCHNEIDER, 1801)
Orange-spine unicornfish

Hab.: Indo-Pacific, from the Red Sea to Japan, New Caledonia, Hawaii, the Marquesas, and Tuamotu. At depths of 5 to 90 m.

Sex.: None.

Soc.B./Assoc.: *N. lituratus* lives singly, in pairs or, more rarely, in groups or schools. Their habitat is above coral rocks or rubble in lagoons and outer reefs from the lower surge area downward.

M.: *N. lituratus* requires a lot of swimming space and a shady hiding place such as a table coral. Once acclimated, it is quite peaceful and can be kept for years.

Light: Sunlight zone.

B./Rep.: Not known. Spawning in pairs was observed in the sea.

F.: H; *N. lituratus* primarily feeds on leafy brown algae such as *Sargassum* and *Dictyota* in its natural habitat. In the aquarium, it is hard to train. Commence with tender lettuce. Later *Mysis*, mosquito larvae, *Tubifex*, mussel meat, and freeze-dried suspended foods are also accepted.

S.: *N. lituratus* is a conspicuous, beautiful surgeonfish; the bright orange tail spines quickly place it into the proper genus. Juveniles are normally imported from Hawaii. Pacific populations deviate somewhat in color from those of the Indian Ocean. The dorsal fin is mostly black.

T: 24°-26°C, **L:** 50 cm, **TL:** from 200 cm, **WM:** w, **WR:** b, m, **AV:** 1-2, **D:** 3-4

Naso hexacanthus

Naso lituratus

Fam.: Acanthuridae

Naso thynnoides (VALENCIENNES, 1835)
Single-spined unicorn

Hab.: Indo-West Pacific; from east Africa to the Philippines and Japan. At depths of 20 to 100 m.

Sex.: None.

Soc.B./Assoc.: This rarely seen species lives in dense schools above deep coral banks and along outer reefs.

M.: Not known; *N. thynnoides'* schooling behavior lends testimony to its social abilities. This combined with its smaller size make it the best suited *Naso* for the aquarium. Unfortunately, its rarity makes it an uncommon aquarium fish.

Light: Moderate light zone.

B./Rep.: Unknown.

F.: O; in the sea it feeds on algae, sessile benthic animals, and zooplankton.

S.: *N. thynnoides* was previously in its own genus, *Axinurus,* since, unlike all other species of this genus, it only has one knife on the caudal peduncle which does not end in a point but only protrudes slightly, forming an irregular keel. While the even rarer *N. (Axinurus) minor* also only has one spine on the caudal peduncle, the thin vertical line along the entire body and a dark spot around the eye clearly identify *N. thynnoides.*

T: 22°-24°C, **L:** 35 cm, **TL:** from 200 cm, **WM:** w, **WR:** b, **AV:** 4, **D:** 3

Naso unicornis (FORSSKÅL, 1775)
Unicorn tang

Hab.: Indo-Pacific, from the Red Sea to Japan, the Rapa Islands, Hawaii, Tuamotu, and the Marquesas. At depths of 5 to 80 m.

Sex.: Adult ♂♂ usually have a better developed horn, stronger tail spines, and more elongated filaments on the tail fin than equal sized ♀♀.

Soc.B./Assoc.: *N. unicornis* rarely occurs alone. It is usually found in schools which navigate shallow, moving water of inner and outer reefs as well as canals.

M.: Since it likes to swim, provide this tang with a large swimming area and some cover.

Light: Sunlight zone.

B./Rep.: Unknown; pair spawnings were observed along the fringes of the feeding schools, especially during the new and full moon.

F.: H; *N. unicornis* primarily feeds on leafy brown algae in the sea; in the aquarium it is difficult to entice it to accept substitute food, but once successful, the fish can be kept for years. Tanks best suited to successfully maintain this fish have heavy algae growth that allows it to constantly scrape the algae stand with its rasping teeth. It also feeds on *Mysis,* shrimp, mosquito larvae, grindal worms, Enchytraeidae, *Tubifex,* mussel meat, etc.

S.: As an adult, *N. unicornis* is easily recognizable by its horn. In this species the horn sits extremely posterior and does not extend beyond the tip of the snout; it grows when the fish is about 15 cm long. Until then the fish is similar to other species such as *N. annulatus.*

T: 26°-29°C, **L:** up to 60 cm, **TL:** from 250 cm, **WM:** w, **WR:** b, m, **AV:** 1, **D:** 3-4

Naso unicornis   *Naso unicornis*

Naso thynnoides

Naso unicornis

Fam.: Acanthuridae

Naso vlamingii
Vlaming's unicornfish

(VALENCIENNES, 1835)

Hab.: Indo-Pacific, from east Africa to Japan, the Great Barrier Reef, New Caledonia, and the Line, Tuamotu and Marquesas Islands. At depths of 1 to 50 m.

Sex.: None.

Soc.B./Assoc.: Although *N. vlamingii* is occasionally found singly or in pairs, it normally lives in loose aggregations and schools in front of steeply sloped lagoons and outer reefs during the day. However, it always stays within 10 to 20 m of the reef, so that it can quickly seek shelter when needed.

M.: Since the fish grows fast and very large, it can only be kept in correspondingly sized tanks. It is more suited for show aquaria than home aquaria.

Light: Sunlight zone.

B./Rep.: Not known.

F.: C; in nature *N. vlamingii* finds its prey (zooplankton) in the open water. In the aquarium it is relatively easily trained to substitute foods such as *Mysis*, shrimp, mosquito larvae, mussel and fish flesh, and many others. All are expertly snapped as they drift by in the water.

S.: Adult animals develop a conspicuous convex snout and enlarged dorsal and anal fins. They have numerous blue stripes and dots which flash like lightning in courting ♂ ♂ and individuals submitting to cleaner fishes. At diving posts where fish are being fed, *N. vlamingii* becomes very pushy, often coming dangerously close to divers with its strong blades.

T: 24°-28°C, **L:** 70 cm, **TL:** from 250 cm, **WM:** w, **WR:** b-t, **AV:** 3, **D:** 3

The unicorn surgeonfishes mostly spawn in pairs in the open water (pelagic). The males can change at least part of their body into a brilliant color, such as light blue, to impress the females (mentioned under **S.** above). The same color changes are used to indicate anger and dominance. Therefore, coloration is a barometer of the mood. Changes occur almost instantaneously. If the fish goes to a cleaning station, it demonstrates its willingness to be cleaned by body posture, spread fins, and the steel blue coloration it adopts. When cleaning is completed or is interrupted by a diver, it reverts to its normal coloration and swims away.

Naso vlamingii in an aquarium

Naso vlamingii, Maldives

Fam.: Acanthuridae

ABOUT THE GENUS *PRIONURUS* LACÉPÈDE, 1804

This genus is fairly unknown to divers and aquarists, but it is part of the surgeonfishes. In contrast to the genus *Naso*, *Prionurus* usually has 3 blades on each side of the caudal peduncle, and some species even have 6. Divers from the Gulf of California to the Galapagos Islands will encounter these fishes. Some of the 6 known species live in the cooler waters around Japan and Australia. Members of this genus swim in groups. Occasionally there are schools of hundreds of *Prionurus laticlavius* around the Galapagos Islands.

I (H.D.) first saw *Prionurus* surgeons in show aquaria on the west coast of the USA. Surely these 30 cm long *Prionurus punctatus* I saw schooling in giant tanks came from the Gulf of California. This species is regularly seen in American aquarium stores. Specimens that reach the European market are generally nice 10 cm fish, though their presence there is sporadic. *P. punctatus* is the only species of the genus suitable for surgeonfish fanciers, because *Prionurus* generally cannot be acclimated to temperatures above 22°C. This is due to cool waters the Humboldt Current brings up to the Galapagos Islands from the south and the California current brings down to California from the north.

An adult *Prionurus maculatus*, see page after next for text

Prionurus laticlavius   (VALENCIENNES, 1846)
Galapagos sawtail

Hab.: East Pacific, between the Galapagos Islands and the coast of South America. At depths of 3 to 25 m.

Sex.: None.

Soc.B./Assoc.: *P. laticlavius* usually live in large hordes, especially where there is plenty of food. These schools can be comprised of more than 200 specimens.

M.: This peaceful fish adapts quickly and is long-lived. Supposedly there are specimens that have lived for more than 10 years in an aquarium.

Light: Sunlight zone.

B./Rep.: Not known.

F.: C; *P. laticlavius* feeds on plankton in the open water. After it becomes accustomed to the aquarium, it is not choosy and feeds on any plankton substitutes such as *Mysis,* shrimp, and grindal worms. Suspended dry foods, mussels, etc., are also accepted.

S.: *P. laticlavius* is similar to *P. punctatus.* While both of these species are found in the same region, have the same number of green spines on the caudal peduncle, and a similarly colored caudal fin, this species lacks black spots on the head and body.

T: 12°-15°C, **L:** 30 cm, **TL:** from 200 cm, **WM:** w, **WR:** b, m, **AV:** 3-4, **D:** 3

Fam.: Acanthuridae

Prionurus microlepidotus LACÉPÈDE, 1804

Hab.: Southeast Australia, from the southern Barrier Reef southward.

Sex.: None.

Soc.B./Assoc.: Not known.

M.: Unknown; the fish is too large for standard home aquaria.

Light: Daylight zone.

B./Rep.: Not known.

F.: C; feeds on zooplankton in the sea, especially shrimp from the water column; it can be fed appropriate plankton substitutes.

S.: *P. microlepidotus* has 10 spines on each side of the caudal peduncle. You will repeatedly find in the literature that younger animals have fewer spines than older animals, and that additional spines develop in front of the others. This is not entirely true. Young fish already have a total of 10 plates, 6 of which are large, conspicuous, and lie consecutively in a row. As the animal ages, large spines not only develop on the 6 main plates, but the smaller thorns fuse into a blade at an angle to the others. A 7th large spine (see photo) may appear later. The body shape also changes with age: the fish becomes relatively more elongated, and above the snout, a small hump develops. This surgeonfish is rarely for sale except in Sydney. Young animals are blue. Some authors erroneously consider this species to be *P. scalprus*; however, it is easily distinguished by its distribution and more numerous spines.

T: 15°-20°C, **L:** 45 cm, **TL:** from 250 cm, **WM:** w, **WR:** m, **AV:** 3-4, **D:** 3

Prionurus maculatus (OGILBY, 1887)
Spotted sawtail

Hab.: Southeast Australia and Lord Howe Island.

Sex.: None.

Soc.B./Assoc.: Unknown.

M.: Not only does it need a lot of swimming space, but also hiding places such as crevices and caves. Peaceful towards its tankmates.

Light: Daylight zone.

B./Rep.: Not known.

F.: O; *P. maculatus* eats just about everything offered in an aquarium: krill, mussels, beef heart, liver, fish meat, spinach, algae, tablet food, carp pellets, etc.

S.: *P. maculatus* only develops its contrasting orange and blue coloration with age. One of the most attractive species of the genus. It has three spines on each side of the caudal peduncle in the form of low keels. The posterior knife has the largest plate.

T: 20°-24°C, **L:** 45 cm, **TL:** from 300 cm, **WM:** w, **WR:** b, m, **AV:** 3-4, **D:** 3

Prionurus microlepidotus, Sydney

Prionurus maculatus, subadult, Sydney, see picture of adult on p. 766

Fam.: Acanthuridae

Prionurus punctatus
(GILL, 1862)
Yellowtail sawtail

Hab.: East Pacific, from California to El Salvador and the Revillagigedo Islands. At depths of 5 to 35 m.

Sex.: None.

Soc.B./Assoc.: *P. punctatus* forms loose schools in the sea and large schools above algae-covered substrates of rocky reefs.

M.: Provide a lot of swimming space and algae-covered rocks. Best kept in a fish community tank.

Light: Sunlight zone.

B./Rep.: Not known.

F.: H; *P. punctatus* eats the algae cover from hard substrates which keeps the tank clean; it also accepts substitute foods such as shrimp.

S.: In the Steinhart Aquarium in San Francisco, this species has been seen swimming in large tanks with *P. laticlavius* for the past 10 years. The gray head and body of *P. punctatus* are densely covered with black spots. This and its bottom-oriented swimming behavior differentiate it from *P. laticlavius,* which also has a yellow tail fin and three spines on each side of the caudal peduncle, but swims in the open water. Young fishes can go from completely yellow to the punctated adult coloration within one week. This transformation occurs gradually: transitional forms have vertical striations of yellow as well as gray stripes with black spots.

T: 12°-22°C, **L:** 35 cm, **TL:** from 200 cm, **WM:** w, **WR:** b, **AV:** 3-4, **D:** 3

Aquarium photo of *Prionurus punctatus*

Prionurus scalprus
(CUVIER & VALENCIENNES, 1835)
Blackthorn sawtail

Hab.: Northwest Pacific between China, Japan, and the Philippines. At depths of 2 to 20 m.

Sex.: None.

Soc.B./Assoc.: *P. scalprus* lives singly, in small groups, or in schools along coastal reefs.

M.: This animal's size and feed requirements make it a poor candidate for the home aquarium.

Light: Sunlight zone.

B./Rep.: Unknown; in Japan the breeding season is in the spring.

F.: H; *P. scalprus* feeds primarily on calcareous algae in the sea; they are hard to provide in any quantity in an aquarium. Feeding is extremely problematic.

S.: *P. scalprus* has at least 4 bony plates with spines on both sides of the caudal peduncle. Large animals can develop a fifth spine anteriorly to the others. It is rather blandly colored; the dark spots along the lateral line and the black plates are the only distinct markings on the olive-blue body. The clearly marked spines are interpreted as being warning coloration. *P. scalprus* is not available in Germany and only occasionally offered in Japan. The species is often confused with the southeastern Australian *P. microlepidotus.*

T: 24°-28°C, **L:** 40 cm, **TL:** from 200 cm, **WM:** w, **WR:** b, **AV:** 3-4, **D:** 4 (calcareous algae)

Prionurus punctatus

Prionurus scalprus

Fam.: Siganidae

The tropical Indo-Pacific is home to another family related to the surgeonfishes, the rabbitfishes. It is limited to about 30 species which are all considered members of the genus *Siganus*. Rabbitfishes live in the same habitat and feeding niches as surgeonfishes. They gnaw algae from flat reefs or search at more profound depths for tunicates and sponges. These bright yellow fishes predominately swim in groups as juveniles (rarely schools) and pairs as adults. Heterogeneous schools of rabbitfishes and surgeonfishes have been sighted.

Four species of the genus *Siganus* have an elongated snout and were previously placed in the genus *Lo*. Since other morphological data do not support this split, these appreciated aquarium fishes have been returned to the genus *Siganus*. There is also dissent between experts on whether or not *Siganus vulpinus* and *Siganus unimaculatus* are two autonomous species. Morphologically, these fishes are identical, yet one, *S. unimaculatus*, has a black lateral spot that the other lacks. Because all rabbitfishes have a similar morphology and most criteria on species identification within the genus as a whole are based on different coloration, this book will treat the species as two autonomous species until proof to the contrary is shown. These two rabbitfishes have independent regions of distribution that overlap in the Philippines. If they are found to interbreed in regions where they coexist, this would be sufficient reason to consider them one and the same species.

Divers and aquarists should wear working gloves when handling these fishes (catching, transferring, etc.), as rabbitfishes have thin rays with poison glands at their base. The resulting wounds are extremely painful and require medical attention (see p. 788!).
Sexes cannot be differentiated on the basis of color in rabbitfishes. In a few species the female is somewhat larger. Like surgeonfishes, spawning depends on the lunar rhythm. Some spawn in the shallow waters among mangroves, while others spawn at 20 m depth. Large numbers of *Siganus canaliculatus* around Palau have been seen congregating and spawning along certain portions of the reef.

It is a pleasure to watch a foxface in an aquarium. Like all members of the genus, it is peaceful towards tankmates. However, it can very aptly defend itself. It faces a frontal attack by placing its dorsal fin rays towards the enemy; rear attacks are handled by harmless bites delivered with its pipe-shaped mouth.

The foxface is easily trained to any substitute food. Time is passed by unflaggingly rasping at the green and red algae it finds in well illuminated aquaria. The specimen owned by the author (H.D.) for the past 4 years has the inexplicable habit of putting its snout above the water, sucking up air, carrying it to the bottom, and then releasing a steady stream of bubbles.

Rabbitfishes gained their common name from the pronounced harelike upper lip. As a rule, they swim in pairs in the upper regions of the reef. However, some juveniles and some species are marked schooling fishes which mostly live in the shallow waters of lagoons.

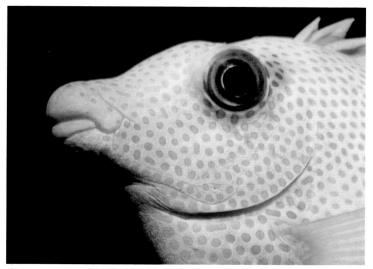

Siganus corallinus from the Great Barrier Reef

Fam.: Siganidae

Siganus vulpinus   (SCHLEGEL & MÜLLER, 1844)
Foxface

Hab.: Tropical southwest Pacific from Indonesia to the southern Barrier Reef, New Caledonia, and the Caroline and Marshall Islands. At depths of 1 to 30 m.

Sex.: None.

Soc.B./Assoc.: *S. vulpinus* lives singly or in pairs in lagoons and outer reefs ridged in coral. Young and half-grown animals will occasionally appear in large schools around antler corals (*Acropora*).

M.: While juveniles can manage with a modicum of space, adult animals require a large swimming area and rock and coral edifications with corresponding hiding possibilities. *S. vulpinus* can be associated with similar, able-bodied fishes such as surgeonfishes or unicornfishes. Since it is aggressive towards conspecifics, it should either be kept singly or in pairs.

Light: Sunlight zone.

B./Rep.: Not known.

F.: H, O; young of this species mainly graze algae from dead lower branches of corals. Adults also feed on zooplankton. *S. vulpinus* readily eats available live foods such as *Mysis*, shrimp, *Daphnia*, mosquito larvae, Enchytraeidae; but plant foods such as algae and lettuce are also accepted.

S.: Previously from the entire Indo-Pacific area, but only one very variable species was listed. This species has been split into 4, essentially based only on color variations: *S. magnificus* from the Andaman Islands, *S. uspi* from the Fiji Islands, an undescribed species from Tonga, and *S. unimaculatus* from the Philippine-Japan area. All of these animals are long snouted, which is quite usual for rabbitfishes. Like all rabbitfishes, they have poisonous fin rays: 13 in the dorsal fin, 4 in the ventral fins, and 7 in the anal fin. They are quite capable of defending themselves and should not be handled with bare hands.

T: 26°-28°C, **L:** 25 cm, **TL:** from 120 cm, **WM:** w, **WR:** b, m, **AV:** 1, **D:** 3

Siganus unimaculatus   (EVERMANN & SEALE, 1907)
One spot foxface

Hab.: Northwestern tropical Pacific, from the Philippines to Japan. At depths of 1 to 30 m.

Sex.: None.

Soc.B./Assoc.: Like *S. vulpinus*.

M.: As with *S. vulpinus*.

Light: Daylight zone.

B./Rep.: Not known.

F.: H; it feeds on algae and all types of live foods.

S.: *S. unimaculatus* is sometimes considered a race of *S. vulpinus*. The primary difference is its large, dark, roundish spot underneath the soft rayed section of the dorsal fin.

T: 26°-28°C, **L:** 20 cm, **TL:** from 120 cm, **WM:** w, **WR:** b, m, **AV:** 2, **D:** 2-3

Siganus vulpinus, Indonesia

Siganus unimaculatus, aquarium photo

Fam.: Siganidae

Siganus uspae   (GAWEL & WOODLAND, 1974)
Brown-yellow foxface

Hab.: Central Pacific, especially around the Fiji Islands. At depths of 3 to 30 m.

Sex.: None.

Soc.B./Assoc.: Juveniles usually live in schools, but adults either live singly or in pairs. More gregarious than *Siganus vulpinus*.

M.: Much more peaceful among themselves than *S. vulpinus*. In brightly lit reef aquaria, these animals are somewhat shy. Slightly sensitive during acclimation, which may be due to the long transport to Europe. These animals are usually routed through wholesalers in Los Angeles.

Light: Moderate light, sunlight zone.

B./Rep.: Unknown.

F.: H ; not choosy after acclimation. All foxfaces relish *Caulerpa*, especially pinnate forms (fleshy forms are less appreciated). Those of you that have an overabundance of *Caulerpa* only need to buy a foxface to watch your problems disappear. Microalgae and filamentous alga are not well liked.

S.: *S. uspae* was not considered an autonomous species until 1974. Primarily split from *S. vulpinus* because of its dark body coloration.

T: 24°-28°C, **L:** up to 20 cm, **TL:** from 120 cm, **WM:** w, **WR:** b, m, **AV:** 3, **D:** 3

Siganus magnificus   (BURGESS, 1977)
Andaman foxface

Hab.: Eastern Indian Ocean, the Andaman Islands, and Christmas Island. At depths of 3 to 30 m.

Sex.: None.

Soc.B./Assoc.: As with *S. vulpinus*.

M.: Rarely found in pet stores. Its contrasting coloration makes this foxface a notable inhabitant of the reef aquarium. Unfortunately, this species is not totally benevolent towards invertebrates. Besides algae, anthozoans (organpipe corals, *Xenia*) are sometimes eaten. Unlike *Siganus uspae*, *S. magnificus* is noticeably oblivious to bright light.

Light: Sunlight zone.

B./Rep.: Not known.

F.: O; besides all kinds of algae (including crusting species), this species also consumes animal fare. Foods such as *Artemia*, oats (moistened), spinach, mosquito larvae, and squid can be fed.

S.: Like all the aforementioned species, *S. magnificus* was previously considered part of *S. vulpinus*, like all the above species and separated into an autonomous species 1977 based on its coloration.

T: 24°-28°C, **L:** 20 cm, **TL:** from 120 cm, **WM:** w, **WR:** b, m, **AV:** 3, **D:** 3

Four species of foxfaces were previously considered to be one species, *S. (Lo) vulpinus*. Preserved specimens are virtually indistinguishable, since the coloration washes out and meristic characteristics (countable and measurable) are equal in all 4 species. Live animal comparisons allowed the separation in the '70's. Normally, autonomous species are not based solely on coloration, but as all foxfaces are practically identical with the exception of color, color had to be the criterion of classification. A computer analysis of the compiled data did show minor differences, at least for *S. uspae*.

While the coloration differences would have only attributed these fishes a separate standing of race or subspecies in any other family, four independent species emerged within Siganidae.

S. unimaculatus : a large dark spot laterally on its dorsum.

S. uspae : majority of the body dark, white stripe on cheek.

S. magnificus : only the dorsal region is dark. The ventral area is light. The proportion of dark to light varies from animals to animal.

Siganus uspae

Siganus magnificus

Fam.: Siganidae

Siganus argenteus   (QUOY & GAIMARD, 1825)
Streamlined spinefoot

Hab.: Indo-Pacific, from the Red Sea to Japan, the southern Barrier Reef, the Marquesas, and Tuamotu. At depths of 1 to 30 m.

Sex.: None.

Soc.B./Assoc.: *S. argenteus* usually lives in large schools in lagoons and along outer reefs that have a mixed substrate of coral, rocks, and rubble.

M.: An amiable fish. Small groups can be kept. However, because of its respectable mature size and the large swimming area it demands, it can only be adequately kept in large show aquaria.

Light: Sunlight zone.

B./Rep.: In the Red Sea, pairs or groups of these animals spawn during the new moon of July/August. The eggs and larvae are pelagic. On the Mariana Islands, the final larval state forms large "balls" on the reef terrace (especially in the last quarter of the moon of April and May), and in three days, they metamorphose into completely pigmented, herbivorous juveniles.

F.: H; but also feeds on live and flake foods.

S.: *S. argenteus* has the longest larval stage. The largest larvae grow up to 8 cm long. This is the most widely distributed species of the genus.

T: 25°-29°C, **L:** 37 cm, **TL:** from 200 cm, **WM:** w, **WR:** b-t, **AV:** 2-3, **D:** 3

Siganus corallinus   (SCHLEGEL, 1852)
Blue-spotted spinefoot

Hab.: Indo-West Pacific, from the Seychelles to Papua New Guinea, Japan, and the Great Barrier Reef. At depths of 5 to 30 m.

Sex.: None.

Soc.B./Assoc.: Adult specimens live singly or in pairs in coral-rich regions of lagoons and outer reefs. Small groups of young school among antler corals (*Acropora*).

M.: Since *S. corallinus* constantly browses and has a respectable growth rate, it requires plenty of space. Both young and adult animals like to hide between dense branches of antler corals in nature. Therefore, these or similar structures should be offered as cover. It is amiable towards tankmates, but capable of defending itself against aggressors.

Light: Daylight zone.

B./Rep.: Not known.

F.: H; juveniles in the sea primarily feed on algae and small animals found on lower dead sections of antler and table corals as well as on the bottom substrate. Adults not only feed on bottom growth, but also consume plankton. This makes them relatively receptive to substitute foods such as shrimp, *Mysis*, and frozen and flake foods. But never forget the supplemental plant food.

S.: *S. corallinus* is closely related to *S. trilospilos* from northwest Australia. It has three dark spots in the upper half of the body.

T: 24°-27°C, **L:** 25 cm, **TL:** from 150 cm, **WM:** w, **WR:** b, m, **AV:** 2, **D:** 3

Lower right hand photo:
S. corallinus and *S. puelloides* are very similar. However, the former has an elongated spot through the eye that extends upward (sometimes downward) and dense dark and light blue spots on the head.

Siganus argenteus

Siganus corallinus in an aquarium

Fam.: Siganidae

Siganus corallinus in its natural biotope

Siganus guttatus   (BLOCH, 1787)
Yellow-blotch spinefoot

Hab.: Indo-Pacific area from Malaysia to the Australian Barrier Reef, the Philippines, the Ryukyu Islands (southern Japan), and Belau and Yap in Micronesia.

Sex.: No visible differences.

Soc.B./Assoc.: Lives in large schools at mouths of rivers and mangrove swamps. A peaceful species, yet it cannot be housed with small crustacea.

M.: Since *S. guttatus* enters brackish water, it is insensitive to variations in salinity. A powerful filter and regular partial water changes are recommended. Offer a lot of swimming space!

Light: Moderate light to sunlight zones.

B./Rep.: They probably spawn in schools in the open water—especially in mangrove swamps.

F.: H, O; omnivore, feeds mostly on algae and aufwuchs. Flake food, *Mysis*, and *Artemia* are accepted. Feed foods low in fat and protein, rich in fiber.

S.: Can be well maintained in large tanks. House with scats. The geographical distribution and habitat of *Siganus guttatus* and *S. lineatus* overlap, but the former will enter brackish water. They are the same color down to the yellow spot anterior to the tail. *S. lineatus* has linear markings, while *S. guttatus* mainly has dots.
BLOCH calls this fish the "spotted rabbitfish" in German.

T: 24°-28°C, **L:** 33 cm, **TL:** 200 cm, **WM:** m, **WR:** all, **AV:** 3, **D:** 2-3

Siganus guttatus, adult, in its natural biotope.

Siganus guttatus, juvenile (top) and subadult (night or fright coloration), in an aquarium.

Fam.: Siganidae

Siganus javus   (LINNAEUS, 1766)
Streaked spinefoot

Hab.: Indo-West Pacific, from Sri Lanka to Tahiti. At depths of 2 to 20 m.

Sex.: None.

Soc.B./Assoc.: This schooling fish is rarely observed or caught.

M.: Not known.

Light: Area of sunlight.

B./Rep.: Unknown.

F.: C; *S. javus* is said to be a feeding specialist which only feeds on jellyfish.

S.: *S. javus* schools in the open water in front of reefs. The dorsum of the fish has numerous, dense dots, while the lower body half has undulating longitudinal lines. Indian specimens have a dark spot in the middle of the tail fin, dots on the ventral half of the body, and are a slightly different color than animals from the Pacific.

T: 25°-28°C, **L:** 25 cm, **TL:** from 150 cm, **WM:** w, **WR:** t, **AV:** 4, **D:** 4

Siganus lineatus   (VALENCIENNES, 1835)
Golden-lined spinefoot

Hab.: Indo-Australian region, from the eastern Indian Ocean (Sri Lanka) to the Philippines, the southern Barrier Reef, and New Caledonia. At depths of 0 to 20 m.

Sex.: None.

Soc.B./Assoc.: *S. lineatus* prefers shallow waters close to shore, especially areas close to mangrove swamps. Of course, these locals are often polluted

M.: While *S. lineatus* does not place high demands on water quality, it has high oxygen requirements and requires plenty of swimming space. It is a peaceful, suitable companion for other fishes.

Light: Daylight zone.

B./Rep.: In Indonesia the animals congregate in giant schools under mangroves and then migrate together to the mouth of canals where they spawn on the 9th or 10th day after the new moon. They primarily spawn from March to June and in November; some animals, however, spawn throughout the year.

F.: H, O; *S. lineatus* feeds on animal and vegetable fare as well as flake and frozen foods.

S.: *S. lineatus* is often confused with *S. guttatus*.

T: 25°-29°C, **L:** 40 cm, **TL:** from 200 cm, **WM:** m, **WR:** b, m, **AV:** 3, **D:** 2-3

Siganus javus feasting on jellyfish

Siganus lineatus

Fam.: Siganidae

Siganus puellus   (SCHLEGEL, 1852)
Decorated spinefoot

Hab.: Indo-Australian Archipelago, from the eastern Indian Ocean (Cocos-Keeling) and South China Sea to the southern Barrier Reef and New Caledonia. At 2 to 30 m depth.

Sex.: None.

Soc.B./Assoc.: When young, groups of this colorful rabbitfish inhabit regions of lagoons and outer reefs densely grown with coral; adults are usually found in pairs.

M.: *S. puellus* is relatively peaceful and can be kept singly or in pairs. Needs a lot of swimming space and some current.

Light: Daylight zone.

B./Rep.: Unknown.

F.: H; accepts all kinds of live foods as well as vegetable fare and flake food.

S.: *S. puellus* is closely related to *S. puelloides* from the eastern Indian Ocean.

T: 22°-27°C, **L:** 30 cm, **TL:** from 150 cm, **WM:** m, **WR:** b, m, **AV:** 2, **D:** 3

Siganus puelloides from the Andaman Sea and the Maledives is very closely related to *S. puellus*, however, *S. puelloides* does not have wide clear blue lines and a mask. Essentially only a dark eyespot remains. It is, therefore, rather similar to *S. corallinus*. But the latter has dark, usually blue, spots at least on the head and lacks a dark eyespot.

Siganus puelloides, Maldives

Siganus puellus

Siganus puellus

Fam.: Siganidae

Siganus spinus (LINNAEUS, 1758)
Little spinefoot

Hab.: Indo-West Pacific, from the Persian Gulf to Japan, the southern Barrier Reef, and the Society Islands. At depths of 1 to 20 m.

Sex.: None.

Soc.B./Assoc.: In certain areas *S. spinus* is the most abundant rabbitfish. It routinely swims in giant migrating schools and prefers reef terraces and shallow lagoons with mixed bottoms of sand, coral rubble, or seaweed.

M.: The fish's affable nature allows juvenile to adult animals and small groups of up to 5 fish to be housed together.

Light: Daylight zone.

B./Rep.: Unknown. In the sea (along the Mariana Islands) the last larval stage congregates in masses on the terraces during the last quarter moon of April and May. Sometimes their numbers are so great that all the filamentous algae are shortly gnawed off and they starve to death.

F.: H; in nature, *S. spinus* is a herbivore who will also consume benthic organisms; in the aquarium it feeds on vegetable and animal fare.

S.: Juveniles from the post larval state and adult animals are an important, traditional protein source, especially in Micronesia. Many authors consider the Red Sea species, *S. rivulatus* (which also migrates into the Mediterranean), part of *S. spinus*, although it never has such a winding linear design.

T: 24°-28°C, **L:** 23 cm, **TL:** from 150 cm, **WM:** w, **WR:** b, m, **AV:** 1-2, **D:** 3

Siganus stellatus (FORSSKÅL, 1775)
Brown-spotted spinefoot

Hab.: In the Red Sea and the Indian Ocean. At depths of 5 to 30 m.

Sex.: None.

Soc.B./Assoc.: Always lives in pairs.

M.: The mature size of *S. stellatus* combined with its browsing behavior demands large aquaria. It is only suitable for show aquaria, though its graceful movements may lead you to think otherwise.

Light: Sunlight zone.

B./Rep.: Not know.

F.: H; eats animal and vegetable fare equally well.

S.: There are color variations between animals from the Red Sea and those from the Indian Ocean. The former have a yellow-green spot anterior to the dorsal fin and a yellow fringe on the posterior of the dorsal, anal, and caudal fins. These fringes are white in the Indian forms. *S. stellatus*, like most rabbitfishes, is capable of quick color changes. The fish may take on opposite color designs from one moment to the next. When resting or hiding, the dark dots suddenly become white and brown shadings and designs appear on the body.

T: 24°-28°C, **L:** up to 40 cm, **TL:** from 200 cm, **WM:** w, **WR:** b, m, **AV:** 2-3, **D:** 3-4

Siganus spinus

Siganus stellatus, Maldives

Fam.: Siganidae

Siganus virgatus   (VALENCIENNES, 1835)
Double-barred spinefoot

Hab.: Indo-Australian Archipelago, Indonesia. At depths of 1 to 20 m.

Sex.: None.

Soc.B./Assoc.: These rare fish normally live in pairs among coral growth in lagoons and along outer reefs. Sometimes they can be found in schools above shallow coral reefs.

M.: It is said to reach 50 cm in length, which makes it an inappropriate addition to all but the largest tanks. However, the fish is extremely peaceful.

Light: Sunlight zone.

B./Rep.: Unknown.

F.: H, O; *S. virgatus* is easily trained to feed in captivity; it accepts almost anything, but do not forget "green stuff" such as algae and lettuce.

S.: *S. doliatus* (not presented in this volume) is confusingly similar to this species. Numerous errors in identification have resulted. *S. doliatus* has fine yellow, sometimes wavy, lines on the head and back that this species lacks. Animals from between the Philippines, northwest Australia, the Great Barrier Reef, and New Caledonia are often called *S. virgatus,* but they are not. *S. virgatus* is probably absent throughout Micronesia.

T: 23°-28°C, **L:** 30 (up to 50?) cm, **TL:** from 200 cm, **WM:** w, **WR:** b, m, **AV:** 3, **D:** 3

If rabbitfishes are attacked, e.g., by a surgeonfish, they adopt a typical defense posture—body downward, dorsal rays towards the attacker. The 13 dorsal, 4 ventral, and 7 anal fin rays all have poison glands. When these rays stab into their victim, poison flows through a fine groove on the anterior and posterior edges of the ray and into the puncture wound. The 1st dorsal fin ray is the weapon of choice. The poison is felt immediately. The prick is significantly more painful than a normal stab. The pain amplifies quickly to an unbearable level and persists for several hours. Such wounds are not fatal unless you have a very labile circulatory system or an allergic reaction. If hot compresses are applied immediately, the heat denatures the poison (the molecular structure of a protein is changed and the natural properties of the protein are lost) and the pain is minimized. At night, rabbitfishes stand motionless in a niche or lie on the bottom and adopt designs and colors that differ from their day coloration. To a certain degree they will imitate the color patterns of their surroundings.

Siganus virgatus

Siganus virgatus, nocturnal coloration

Fam.: Zanclidae

About the family Zanclidae

The sole representative of this monotypic family is a close relative to surgeonfishes, *Zanclus cornutus*. *Zanclus cornutus*, the Moorish idol, has one of the broadest distributions of all fishes because its native habitat embodies all the tropical reefs of the Indo-Pacific. However, its distribution does not extend into the Atlantic. Its vertical distribution is also quite expansive: it has been sighted at depths of up to 180 m.

These magnificent fish are yellowish white with two broad, black crossbands. The anterior band is broader and encompasses a large part of the face, making the eye invisible at first sight. The snout is elongated, orange dorsally, and black ventrally. The area of the eye to the chin is yellowish white. The caudal peduncle is yellow at the base, while the caudal fin is black, but outlined front and back by white stripes. As the fish mature, two hornlike structures develop between the eyes. Although Moorish idols seem a respectable size, few grow to be more than 17 cm long. The long extension of the dorsal fin makes the fish seem larger.

Snorkelers or divers can observe small groups or pairs of Moorish idols at depths of 1-50 m. Throughout their vertical distribution, they search the rocks and corals for food using their pointed snout. The preferred food for *Z. cornutus* is invertebrates, principally sponges. Little is known about the reproductive behavior of *Z. cornutus* despite its notoriety. Pairs of Moorish idols have been seen swimming in long circles towards the surface to spawn during the evening hours. Pelagic eggs are produced. The larval phase is similar to the acronurus stage of surgeonfishes. However, surgeonfish larvae do not have an elongated third dorsal fin ray nor do they have a thorn on the mouth like *Zanclus*. When the larvae settle on the bottom at a length of about 7 cm, the thorn on the mouth disappears. This postlarval phase of *Zanclus cornutus* is pictured for the first time in this book. The Moorish idol and surgeonfishes both have deep, compressed bodies, equal sized dorsal and anal fins, and similar sized scales. But Moorish idols lack the spine(s) that is (are) typically found on each side of the caudal peduncle of surgeonfishes. *Z. canescens* is a synonym of *Zanclus cornutus*.

Zanclus cornutus

Fam.: Zanclidae

Zanclus cornutus   (LINNAEUS, 1758)
Moorish idol

Hab.: Indo-Pacific, from Africa to Japan, Lord Howe Island, Hawaii, and Mexico. At 5 to 180 m depth.

Sex.: None.

Soc.B./Assoc.: Z. cornutus usually lives in small groups of 2-5 animals everywhere there are hard substrates, from inner harbors, lagoons, and reef terraces to the deep outer reefs. Sometimes schools of over 100 specimens are seen.

M.: Despite its popularity as an aquarium animal, Z. cornutus is a fragile resident. It requires a lot of swimming space and cover. Its relatively peaceful nature allows groups to be housed in very large tanks. If that is your preference, all the animals should be introduced simultaneously. Each fish will command a shelter that becomes the center of its territory. Even when schooling, each fish is dominant in its respective territory.

Light: Daylight zone.

B./Rep.: Unknown. Z. cornutus has a very long larval stage and is at least 6 cm long before it settles in a reef. This helps explain its wide distribution.

F.: O; though Z. cornutus chiefly feeds on sponges, other foodstuffs of animal or plant origin are also consumed in its natural habitat. In an aquarium it scrapes algae and the layer of microorganisms from stones and prefers to take its food from the bottom. These fish can be trained to feed on a "feeding stone" covered with mussel meat, etc. Training these fish to feed in the open water takes a bit of patience and time. It likes varied fare such as crustacean meat, frozen *Artemia*, and flake food. Algae!!! Fiber rich foods. The sponges from a slow flowing foam filter!

S.: Z. cornutus is more sensitive than most surgeonfishes. Its body structure allows little if any reserve against starvation. Slightly undernourished specimens, even if they begin eating again, rarely recover. Therefore, note the stomach outline when purchasing; if there is an indention anterior to the anal fin, the fish is hopelessly undernourished.

T: 24°-28°C, **L:** 23 cm, **TL:** 120 cm (150 cm for a group), **WM:** l, **WR:** b, **AV:** 1-2, **D:** 2-3

Protected species. It cannot be imported into Germany. Most specimens are feeding specialists, requiring sponges which cannot be offered in the aquarium. Some animals, however, are algivores - these can be kept for long periods of time.

The Moorish idol is sometimes confused with whimpelfishes since it vaguely resembles some of them. But *Z. cornutus* has a black tail fin, almost vertical bars, and a distinctly colored elongated snout. The posterior cross-stripe on whimpelfishes is always slanted towards the back, as if the 2 cross-stripes would meet in a triangular fashion dorsally. The whole fish looks somewhat triangular. In addition, the tail is light colored.
The nocturnal coloration of the Moorish idol is quite opposite to the colors it adopts during the day.

Late larval phase of *Zanclus cornutus*

Zanclus cornutus, adult

Zanclus cornutus, juvenile

School of *Zanclus cornutus* in their natural habitat.

Halichoeres richmondi in an aquarium.

Wrasses

Wrasses are one of the most widely distributed and prominent fishes of the world's coral reefs. Only the Gobiidae (gobies) surpass them in species diversity. Since color, size, and body shape can be so different, it is often difficult to imagine one being closely related to the other. Some dwarf species only grow a few centimeters, while others reach lengths of over 2 m. Some are slender and tall, while others are very massive. However, the majority of wrasses are cigar-shaped, streamlined, and powerfully built fishes. Even with all these deviants, they have common characteristics that tie them together:

a) All wrasses normally only swim with their pectoral fins. The tail fin can be used to produce extra thrust.

b) Although the mouth opening is never very wide, they have strong lips with large, protruding, pointed teeth. While the roof of the palate is toothless, the pharyngeal teeth have developed into a mill with round teeth which is used to crush tough foods.

Every tropical wrasse is a protogynous hermaphrodite; that is, most all males have developed from functional females. Although wrasses—like all vertebrates—have two normal sexes (male and female), the patterns of sexuality in this family are so peculiar that they require an explanation. The key to development is the male: there are "primary males," which are fish born males, and there are "secondary males," which are animals born females and function as such until they transform into males. The gonadal structure of the two types of males is unequal: the testis of primary males are similar to those of nonhermaphroditic fishes—cylindrical and white with a seminal duct. The testis of secondary males reflect their ovarian origins. Whether or not females convert to secondary males is directed by social considerations. For example, females of the genus *Labroides* are suppressed from being secondary males by the dominant male of the harem. As long as the situation remains *status quo* all wrasses within the harem are females except the single male. But as soon as the male is caught, eaten, or otherwise meets its demise, the highest ranking female exteriorly transforms into a male. This process takes just a few hours. This secondary male has enough strength to prevent other male contenders from encroaching on its harem. As little as 2 weeks are needed for this fish to release sperm. Most species have dramatic color variations between males and females, and each may undergo several color changes before it establishes its adult coloration. Dominant, primary males are the most flamboyant, whereas others are either less intensely colored or have a totally different color pattern. These forms are more reclusive than the "leader." Science labels the developmental phases as initial and terminal when trying to distinguish the different sexes and their respective stages of development. This undertaking has proved to be embarrassingly difficult in some cases and fraught with errors. For instance, males and females of *Anampses chrysocephalus* from Hawaii were originally described as two autonomous species. The female of *A. chrysocephalus* on the bottom of page 845 was originally described as *Anampses rubrocaudata*.

Wrasses reproduce year-round, but breeding is most active during the warmest time of the year. This, of course, depends on geographic location. The seasonal breeding peaks for Japan and the Mediterranean are opposite to the peak season for the Easter Islands or Mauritius.

The lunar cycle plays an influential role in stimulating the fishes of this family to spawn. Many species search for particular sites along the outer reef slopes, and spawn when the tide is going out and the water flows into the open sea. Time of day is unimportant. Nocturnal spawnings are excluded because wrasses are diurnal. At night they rest in the reef, often buried in the sand. This family spawns by two methods.

The first method involves several females and initial phase males, but rarely mature terminal phases of the specific wrasse species. Groups can consist of anywhere from a dozen to several hundred specimens. Subgroups within the schools can also form. The initial males greatly outnumber the females. The group of fish swims towards the surface and expels eggs and sperm. These in turn are quickly carried away by the current. Spawning by this "free-pairing" system is very fast. Afterwards the groups dart back into the protective reef. Similar behavior occurs in the genera *Thalassoma, Halichoeres,* and *Stethojulis.*

The second type of spawning is more common within this family because of its predilection to form pairs, especially at spawning time. Courtship is a fascinating spectacle to behold. The colors that the primary males display when their spread fins are flaunted in front of the females are only seen during this courtship rite. The courtship dance with its circling participants is difficult to document with a camera, but the author (H.D.) successfully recorded the courtship of *Pseudocheilinus octotaenia* from the Red Sea after trying for one hour. Never has a picture depicted this species in all its glory! When the pair spawns, the so-called looping occurs: closely together both swim parallel to the surface and spawn at the apex of the curve. Within seconds they return to the protective cover of the reef. The fertilized, pelagic eggs take one day to hatch. The larvae remain planktonic for about a month. The smallest juvenile form of wrasses found in a reef were only 1 cm long and slightly pigmented. This stage is very vulnerable to predation. Consequently they live secluded within the reef and may even search for protection in sea anemones, even though they are not immune to their stings like clownfishes. Many juvenile wrasses clean ectoparasites from larger reef inhabitants.

Rearing wrasses in an aquarium has not been successful even though spawning has been reported. The problem originates from the fact that the reduced space of a seawater aquarium usually prevents wrasses from developing to their terminal size. Peak sexual activity is only achieved at this stage. On the continuation of the subject of reproduction, it should not be forgotten that wrasses from temperate seas, such as the Mediterranean, do not spawn pelagically, but build nests of algae to protect their brood therein.

The menu of wrasses is quite extensive. Some species live off benthic (bottom living) invertebrates and fishes. Others dine on plankton. A few eat coral polyps, whereas others live from parasites they clean off large fishes. Crustacea, snails, mussels, sea urchins, starfish, bristleworms, and corallike invertebrates are among the organisms that are purposely freed and eaten from the coral rubble. Their nimble movements allow them to chase and surprise other defenseless fishes, especially juveniles. Some wrasses are even specialized at robbing nests of substrate spawners such as damselfishes.

Training these fishes to accept food in the aquarium is generally unproblematic, as they are not finicky eaters. Animal fare such as meat from crustacea, *Mysis*, krill, *Artemia*, mosquito larvae, fish meat, and beef heart are eagerly accepted. Of course, processed foods like tasty tablet foods and flake foods are likewise eagerly eaten. Even feeding specialists such as the bird wrasses, *Gomphosus,* or the cleaner wrasses, *Labroides,* quickly convert over to substitute foods.

Not all wrasses presented in this chapter are suitable for the home aquarium. However, size is not the only reason this is so. Smaller species may be so restless and active that a large aquarium with corresponding swimming space is the first condition to successfully care for these colorful fishes. Refuges in the reef aquarium and a deep layer of sand many species use to burrow in also plays a significant role in making this species "fit" in the home aquarium. The decisive question of which species you want to care for should be answered before buying the animal: Do I want a traditional fish community tank, or an aquarium with a combination of small fishes and invertebrates? If you answered the latter, the majority of the wrasses presented are unsuitable. Only *Cirrhilabrus* or *Labrichthys* are suggested for this type of biotope. For a fish community tank, however, any of the introduced subfamilies make suitable additions. Wrasses need a clean environment. They have a large energy requirement; therefore they like to eat a lot. This stresses the filtration system and causes a subsequent drop in water quality. Filtering pure fish aquaria is addressed in the technical section of this book. Since wrasses' movements are restrained by the confines of the home aquarium, aggressions build and are expended, unfortunately, on tankmates. Carefully select cohabitants. Keeping conspecifics is not recommended.

Labroides dimidiatus cleans a member of the Pomadasyidae (sweetlips).

Fam.: Labridae

About the Genus *Bodianus* Bloch, 1790

Wrasses can be divided into two large groups: those who burrow and those that do not. None of the genera of the subfamily Bodianinae bury themselves in the substrate. Only two of the nine genera are kept in aquaria: *Bodianus* and *Choerodon* (30 and 25 species, respectively). Wrasses of the genus *Bodianus* are very territorial. To help circumvent this trait, stock the tank with equal-sized animals and introduce all animals simultaneously. This prevents the first animals from claiming territories. They accept all kinds of foods and relish hiding places such as caves, tunnels, and overhangs in mini-reef tanks.

Bodianus anthioides, adult

Bodianus anthioides (BENNET, 1831)
Lyretail hogfish

Hab.: Indo-Pacific; from the Red Sea to the Line Islands, Tuamotu, Japan (N), and New Caledonia (S). At depths of 6 to 60 m.

Sex.: None.

Soc.B./Assoc.: *B. anthioides* lives singly or in small loose groups. It prefers steep reefs, especially outer reefs at depths of 25 m and below.

M.: It requires a protected resting place and sufficient swimming space. Almost the entire day is spent cruising the tank in search of food. Limit yourself to one animal and house it with robust fishes. Do not associate with invertebrates. This fish continually tugs and pulls on them before finally eating them.

Light: Sunlight zone.

B./Rep.: Not known.

F.: C; like all related *Bodianus*, it feeds on molluscs, crustacea, and the occasionally brittle star.

S.: This spectacular species has an uncommonly large tail fin. Furthermore, it is distinctively marked with two dark longitudinal stripes. The lyretail hogfish, in contrast to most wrasses, goes through minute color changes as it grows; the bicolored body becomes more pronounced with age as does its black outline; the juvenile's white snout changes to match the rest of the anterior body.

T: 23°-27°C, **L:** 24 cm, **TL:** from 150 cm, **WM:** w, **WR:** b, **AV:** 2, **D:** 3

Bodianus anthioides, juvenile

Bodianus anthioides, subadult

Fam.: Labridae

Bodianus axillaris　　　　　　　　　　　　　　　　　(BENNET, 1831)
Coral hogfish

Hab.: Indo-Pacific; from the Red Sea to the Line Islands, the Marquesas, the Pitcairn Group, Japan (N), and Lord Howe and Rapa Islands (S). At depths of 2 to 40 m.

Sex.: Young and sexually mature animals from the Indian Ocean are spotted. Only secondary ♂♂ evolving from ♀♀ are bicolored. All sexually mature animals from the Pacific are bicolored.

Soc.B./Assoc.: The animals live a solitary existence in the sea, but form small loose groups along reefs of clear lagoons and outer reefs with tranquil water; limit tankmates to robust fishes.

M.: Provide clean, new water (sensitive to old water), and shelters (see *B. anthioides*).

Light: Sunlight zone.

B./Rep.: Not known.

F.: C; young animals sometimes act as cleaner fish and clean large fishes of parasites, including predators such as groupers. Later they feed on snails and mussels they break open against hard substrates (or against the glass of the aquarium). Small sea urchins are eaten, but only after each spine is individually torn off. Crustacea and brittle stars are also accepted.

S.: *B. axillaris* changes its coloration markedly in the course of its growth. But at least among fish in the Pacific there is no sexual dichromatism. Juveniles and adults of *B. axillaris* from the Pacific can be confused with *B. mesothorax*. Young of the former have a row of 4 white spots running dorsally and ventrally as well as a white snout. *B. mesothorax* has more dots dorsally than ventrally, and they tend to be more yellowish. Besides the large spot on the base of the pectoral fin (hence the name), the spot on the dorsal fin and that on its anal fin are important characteristics. Juveniles from the Red Sea are black, whereas those from the Indian Ocean are brown.

T: 24°-27°C, **L:** 20 cm, **TL:** from 120 cm, **WM:** w, **WR:** b, **AV:** 1, **D:** 3

Bodianus axillaris, juvenile, Indonesia

A juvenile *Bodianus axillaris* cleaning a grouper.

Bodianus axillaris, Indonesia

Fam.: Labridae

Bodianus diana
Diana's hogfish

(LACÉPÈDE, 1801)

Hab.: Indo-Pacific; probably from the Red Sea to Samoa, Japan (N), New Caledonia, and Tonga (S). At depths of 6 to 25 m.

Sex.: None.

Soc.B./Assoc.: In nature, juveniles live either solitarily or in small groups, often hidden among branches of black corals or gorgonians. Adults are solitary in habit and live along coastal areas and outer reefs that have dense coral growth. Do not house with invertebrates.

M.: *B. diana* is probably the only representative of the genus that can be kept in small groups, at least when young. It requires plenty of swimming space, clean water, and sufficient shelters.

Light: Area of sunlight.

B./Rep.: Not known.

F.: C; training these fish to accept food in the aquarium presents no difficulties. Almost all foods offered are gladly eaten: mussels, snails, *Mysis*, shrimp, *Artemia* (shrimp are essential for its health), pieces of earthworms, water fleas, *Tubifex*, Enchytraeidae, fish meat, finely chopped beef heart, calf liver, FD tablets (TetraTips), etc.

S.: *B. diana* is somewhat similar to *B. axillaris*. The former is neither totally red nor bicolored. Only the lower fins have large, dark ocelli. There are 3 to 4 white dots dorsally. Young fish have white spots covering their body and bear only the slightest resemblance to the parents; only the ocelli and the ventral and anal fins are similar. *B. diana*'s ecological niche is filled by *B. nielli* in the western Indian Ocean around Sri Lanka and *B. prognathus* in the eastern Pacific (Line Islands). Young *B. nielli* have significantly fewer and larger white spots than *B. diana* (see *B. nielli*).

T: 24°-28°C, **L:** 25 cm, **TL:** from 120 cm, **WM:** w, **WR:** b, **AV:** 1, **D:** 3

Bodianus diana

Bodianus diana, juvenile

Bodianus diana

Fam.: Labridae

Bodianus bimaculatus   ALLEN, 1973
Twospot hogfish

Hab.: Indo-West Pacific; originally only known from the western Pacific (Japan, Palau, New Guinea), but now it is also found in the western Indian Ocean (east Africa, Madagascar, and Mauritius). At depths of 30 to 60 m.

Sex.: Not known.

Soc.B./Assoc.: This solitarily living fish inhabits deep outer reefs; it is rarely encountered.

M.: Unlike other *Bodianus* species, this notoriously smaller species is extremely aggressive towards other yellow wrasses. Small fishes are occasionally attacked but not as zealously. Therefore keeping these animals with small wrasses is problematic. Quite peaceful towards sessile anthozoans; however, small crustacea are hunted. *Bodianus bimaculatus* is capable of handling relatively large prey for its size.

Light: Sunlight areas are tolerated.

B./Rep.: Not known.

F.: C; all substitute foods are suitable, but usually only animal fare is accepted.

S.: This species was named for the ocelli on the caudal peduncle and the operculum; however, in the aquarium, *Bodianus bimaculatus* is chiefly known for its incredibly bright shiny yellow color. Almost all of the few imported animals come from Sri Lanka.

T: 22°-27°C, **L:** 10 cm, **TL:** from 50 cm, **WM:** w, **WR:** b, **AV:** 2-3, **D:** 3

Bodianus diplotaenia   (GILL, 1863)
Mexican hogfish

Hab.: East Pacific; from the Galapagos to the coast of North America and the Gulf of California. At depths of 5 to 40 m.

Sex.: Primary ♂♂ and ♀♀ are a nondescript brown color with two faint longitudinal stripes. Large secondary ♂♂ are a solid gray-brown with a shiny yellow crossbar at the center of the body. ♂♂ grow filaments on the fins and develop a frontal hump as they age.

Soc.B./Assoc.: A loner that grows rapidly and soon disturbs its tankmates. Not a recommended aquarium fish.

M.: *B. diplotaenia* is a robust and easily acclimated fish, but it grows much too large for the home aquarium.

Light: Area of sunlight.

B./Rep.: Not known.

F.: C; this species has a nonselective, voracious appetite.

S.: The fish are a solid lemon yellow up to a length of 2.5 cm; afterwards, the yellow changes to a brown with two broken longitudinal stripes. ♂ animals from greater depths (more than 50 m) are reddish with a yellow crossbar. Young often sleep in a mucus cocoon.

T: 20°-22°C, **L:** 80 cm, **TL:** from 250, **WM:** w, **WR:** b, **AV:** 3-4, **D:** 3

Not an aquarium fish

Bodianus bimaculatus, juvenile

Bodianus diplotaenia ♀

Fam.: Labridae

Bodianus diplotaenia ♂

Bodianus izuensis, juvenile

Bodianus loxozonus
Trotter's hogfish

(SNYDER, 1908)

Hab.: Indo-Australian Archipelago; from Indonesia to Japan and the Mariana and Marshall Islands. At depths of 3 to 40 m.

Sex.: None.

Soc.B./Assoc.: *B. loxozonus* is a solitary animal that prefers clear lagoons and outer reefs.

M.: *B. loxozonus'* rapid growth and unsocial behavior limit its suitability at best to large aquaria inhabited by other robust tankmates; not recommendable for the home aquarium.

Light: Sunlight zone.

B./Rep.: Not known.

F.: C; feeds on snail and mussel meat and crustacea. It is easily trained to substitute foods of all kinds (with the exception of lettuce).

S.: There are two differently colored populations, so two subspecies are being described. One population, *B. loxozonus loxozonus*, is more western and is comprised of fishes from Japan and the Mariana and Marshall Islands. The other more eastern subspecies, *B. loxozonus trotteri* (common name), is found around the Line Islands, the Marquesas, the Society Islands, Tuamotu, and Rapa Island. The fish reported from southeast Africa and Mauritius are probably *B. bilunulatus* (trade name *B. hirsutus*). Juveniles of this species have a broad vertical black stripe that extends into the dorsal and anal fins. The stripe disappears with age until just a dark spot behind the dorsal fin remains.

T: 25°-28°C, **L:** 40 (90 ?) cm, **TL:** from 150 cm, **WM:** w, **WR:** b, **AV:** 2-3, **D:** 3

Bodianus izuensis
Striped hogfish

MASUDA, ARAGA & YOSHINO 1973

Hab.: Australia.

S.: There are practically no biological data available.

Bodianus loxozonus

Fam.: Labridae

Bodianus mesothorax   (SCHNEIDER, 1801)
Eclipse hogfish

Hab.: Indo-Australian Archipelago; from the Christmas Island west to Australia, Indonesia, Japan, and the southern Barrier Reef. At depths of 5 to 20 m.

Sex.: None.

Soc.B./Assoc.: *B. mesothorax* lives singly along outer reefs with rich coral growth, especially in the vicinity of caves.

M.: Make sure juveniles have a hideaway. The best choice is a cave with a sandy bottom where it will lie and rest. Since the fish search all day for food, a large swimming area is a prerequisite for their care. Keep single specimens; do not maintain with invertebrates.

Light: Area of sunlight.

B./Rep.: Not known.

F.: C; the eclipse hogfish is a greedy, jealous feeder. It is covetous of any foods dropped in the tank with the exception of plant foods.

S.: Young and adult animals are similar to their counterparts in *B. axillaris*, and they are often confused. While juveniles (see side photo) are the same brown color but with slightly more yellowish spots, adults are the same down to the black spot on the base of the pectoral fin. The only valuable distinguishing mark between the two species is the wide black stripe between the anterior brown section of the body and the posterior white body half. This species lacks the ocelli on the dorsal and anal fins as is found in *B. axillaris*.

T: 24°-28°C, **L:** 20 cm, **TL:** from 120 cm, **WM:** w, **WR:** b, **AV:** 2, **D:** 3

Bodianus neilli
Neill's hogfish

Hab.: Central Indian Ocean; Sri Lanka, Maldives. At depths from 10 to 30 m.

Sex.: None.

Soc.B./Assoc.: Like *B. diana*.

M.: As for *B. diana*.

Light: Sunlight area.

B./Rep.: Not known.

F.: C; all kinds of animal foods, especially mussels, crustacea, minced fish fillets, beef heart, etc.

S.: *B. nielli* is extremely similar to *B. diana* and may fill its ecological niche in the Indian Ocean. Young fish mainly differ by their fewer but larger white spots.

T: 25°-28°C, **L:** up to 20 cm, **TL:** from 100 cm, **WM:** w, **WR:** b, **AV:** 3, **D:** 3

Bodianus mesothorax

Bodianus neilli, juvenile

Fam.: Labridae

Bodianus pulchellus (POEY, 1860)
Spotfin hogfish

Hab.: West Atlantic, from the Bahamas to South America. At depths of 20 to 120 m.

Sex.: Unknown.

Soc.B./Assoc.: Surprisingly peaceful among themselves; however, the high price this fish commands and its sporadic availability precludes group maintenance. These fish can be kept in reef aquaria, but small crustacea are in danger as the fish grow. Otherwise, this fish can be considered docile.

M.: Large tanks, including reef aquaria. Slow growing.

B./Rep.: Unknown

F.:C.: particularly crustacea; feed *Artemia*, krill, and pieces of squid. The red coloration may pale and become more brown, particularly in animals that are either kept singly or poorly fed.

S.: *B. pulchellus* is similar to *B. rufus*, differing only in its coloration. The most important differences are the dark upper fringe on the pectoral fins and the red background coloration (purple to blue in *B. rufus*). Young fishes go through drastic color transitions: first they are yellow, and only the anterior half of the hard dorsal fin is black; at 5 cm they become gray anteriorly and white ventrally; when over 12 cm long, the red along the back spreads until full adult coloration is obtained.

T: 24°-28°C, **L:** 30 cm, **TL:** 150 cm, **WM:** w-m, **WR:** all, **AV:** 2-3, **D:** 3

Bodianus rufus (LINNAEUS, 1758)
Spanish hogfish

Hab.: Tropical Atlantic; from the Gulf of Mexico to the Bermudas, and Brazil to the east Atlantic islands (St. Helena, Ascension). At depths of 3 to 70 m.

Sex.: None.

Soc.B./Assoc.: Peaceful among themselves unless two ♂ ♂ are kept together. Harmless towards heterospecifics, but its size makes it unsuitable for reef aquaria.

M.: Maintain in large tanks. Small, shy fishes are not appropriate tankmates.

Light: Area of sunlight.

B./Rep.: ♀ ♀ keep most of their juvenile coloration, but may lose a bit of their contrast. The entire body of the ♂ becomes blue-yellow. The snout area turns yellow and, during spawning, the body becomes darker and more contrasting. The yellow region around the mouth becomes lighter. Spawning is similar to other reef fishes that lay pelagic eggs. However, largely due to the shallow depth of the tank, the fish rarely spawn in the aquarium.

F.: C; all kinds of animal fare satisfy its large, hardy appetite. Young often act as cleaner fishes and feed on parasites and loose skin particles of other fishes, even marked predators such as groupers.

S.: In contrast to *B. pulchellus*, *B. rufus* does not go through major color changes. Small specimens are dark anteriorly (bluish or violet) and yellow posteriorly. Adult specimens from deeper regions (30 m and deeper) may be red dorsally, which makes them more similar to *B. pulchellus*. The meat of this species and some of the other wrasses is poisonous! Therefore, it is avoided by fishermen. The toxic flesh probably results from fishes eating poisonous jellyfish and accumulating that poison (Bahamian fishermen; H.B.).

Around the Bahamas, a 1 mile protected zone has been established in which fishes cannot be speared. This species is very common in the outer reefs there.

T: 22°-28°C, **L:** 30 (up to 60) cm, **TL:** from 100 cm, **WM:** w, **WR:** b, **AV:** 1-2, **D:** 2

Bodianus pulchellus

Bodianus rufus, juvenile, 5 cm

Bodianus rufus, juvenile, cleaning a grouper.

About the Genus *Cheilinus* LACÉPÈDE, 1802

Only a few of the 15 *Cheilinus* species are recommended for the hobby. After all, its largest representative, *Cheilinus undulatus*, grows to be 2.30 m long and weigh 190 kg! Their habitat extends from shallow coastal waters to deep drop-offs. They live off crustacea and other invertebrates. The smaller *Cheilinus,* however, are attractively colored, easily kept fishes.

Cheilinus celebicus from Indonesia

Cheilinus celebicus   (BLEEKER, 1853)
Celebes wrasse

Hab.: West central Pacific; from Indonesia to Japan and the Marshall and Solomon Islands. At depths of 5 to 30 m.

Sex.: No significant ones.

Soc.B./Assoc.: Rare loner that lives in protected lagoons and along coral covered reefs.

M.: See *C. fasciatus*.

Light: Sunlight zone.

B./Rep.: Unknown.

F.: C; feeds on gastropods, crustacea, etc.

S.: None.

T: 24°-28°C, **L:** 22 cm, **TL:** from 120 cm, **WM:** w, **WR:** b, **AV:** 3, **D:** 3

Fam.: Labridae

Cheilinus fasciatus
Redbreasted wrasse
(BLOCH, 1791)

Hab.: Indo-Pacific; from the Red Sea to Samoa, Japan (N), and New Caledonia (S). At depths of 4 to 40 m.

Sex.: None.

Soc.B./Assoc.: *C. fasciatus* lives alone over mixed bottoms of live coral, pieces of dead coral, and rubble in lagoons and outer reefs. It cannot be housed with invertebrates.

M.: A hardy fellow that "cleans" the aquarium, perhaps to reach hidden animals. It requires a hiding place, a large swimming space, and clean water. Show aquaria are more appropriate for these animals than home aquaria.

Light: Area of sunlight.

B./Rep.: Unknown.

F.: C; in nature it feeds on small animals found in the sand and rubble. In the aquarium, it accepts all kinds of live foods.

S.: *C. fasciatus* likes to rove with substratum-digging fishes to catch animals that are whirled up. It follows divers for the same reason. Exposed food particles are immediately eaten.

T: 23°-27°C, **L:** 40 cm, **TL:** from 180 cm, **WM:** w, **WR:** b, **AV:** 2-3, **D:** 3

Cheilinus fasciatus ♂

ABOUT THE GENUS *CHOERODON* BLEEKER, 1847

All 25 species of this genus occur in the Indo-Pacific. Some reach lengths of up to 1 m, making them essentially unsuitable for aquarists. Generally loners that lead a reclusive life. Their monstrous teeth can even crack open gastropod shells. *Choerodon fasciatus*, the harlequin tuskfish, is imported from the Philippines and Australia.

Choerodon fasciatus
Harlequin tuskfish

(GÜNTHER, 1867)

Hab.: West Pacific, from Australia to Japan. At depths of 5 to 35 m.

Sex.: None; in contrast to *Bodianus,* coloration does not change significantly with age and sex.

Soc.B./Assoc.: It lives singly above sand and coral rubble; limit its tankmates to those capable of standing their ground.

M.: Requires a hiding site for sleeping and plenty of swimming space. Often very quarrelsome towards other tankmates.

Light: Area of sunlight.

B./Rep.: Not known.

F.: C; has a typical set of 4 fanglike, protrusive teeth, 2 from the lower mandible and 2 from the upper. The teeth of the upper mandible exactly fit into the space between the teeth on the lower mandible. Its diet is typical for wrasses; mussels, crustacea, minced squid, etc.

S.: Like all *Choerodon* species, its distribution is limited to the Australia-Japan area. It likes to use its strong teeth to turn over stones and other bottom material in its quest for food.

T: 25°-28°C, **L:** 40 cm, **TL:** from 180 cm, **WM:** w, **WR:** b, **AV:** 2, **D:** 3

Choerodon fasciatus, juvenile

Choerodon fasciatus, 25 cm long

Choerodon azurio
Scarbreast tuskfish

(JORDAN & SNYDER, 1901)

Hab.: West Pacific; between China, Japan, and Korea. At 8 to 50 m depth.

Sex.: None known.

Soc.B./Assoc.: Lives singly along deep rock banks and coral reefs.

M.: Keep singly in a fish community.

Light: Area of sunlight.

B./Rep.: Not known; spawns in June.

F.: C; usual wrasse fare. Provide dead coral and calcareous algae so these animals can keep their teeth worn down. Otherwise, the teeth will rapidly grow out of the mouth, and the fish will have to go to the "dentist."

S.: The cephalic hump and the dark oblique band (dark anteriorly, light posteriorly) that stretches from the dorsal fin to the pectoral fin are distinctive characteristics.

T: 23°-28°C, **L:** 40 cm, **TL:** from 180 cm, **WM:** w, **WR:** b, **AV:** 3-4, **D:** 3

About the Genera *Novaculichthys* Bleeker, 1861 and *Xyrichtys* Cuvier, 1815

Juveniles from these genera are highly regarded aquarium fishes. Most members of these genera inhabit open sand or algae biotopes. They are very shy. In response to danger, they quickly dive into the sand. The first rays of the dorsal fin are often very long, dissolving the outline of the body. Juvenile *N. taeniourus*, a common species, drift above the substrate of the seas like pieces of algae. They escape notice of predators and prey alike. Adults live in pairs and have developed behavioral patterns accordingly. When searching for crustacea or molluscs, one of the two will turn pieces of coral over while the other grabs exposed prey. They alternate duties. *Xyrichtys* species are called razorfish. They live in tropical seas and the Mediterranean. Many of these fishes have an uncommon adaptation: the ventral skin over the ovaries is transparent. As soon as the eggs ripen, the females display their readiness to spawn to their sexual partner!

Novaculichthys taeniourus, adult

Fam.: Labridae

Novaculichthys taeniourus (LACÉPÈDE, 1802)
Dragon wrasse, redbelly wrasse, rockmover wrasse

Hab.: Indo-Pacific; from the Red Sea to Panama, Japan (N), Lord Howe Island, and Tuamotu (S). At depths of 0.5 to 14 m.

Sex.: None.

Soc.B./Assoc.: Lives singly along reef terraces and in lagoons and outer reefs that have mixed sand and rubble bottoms. Do not associate with invertebrates.

M.: *N. taeniourus* requires at least a 10 cm deep layer of sand to dive into during danger. It is accustomed to water movement and wave action; therefore, it likes strong current in the aquarium.

Light: Sunlight zone.

B./Rep.: Not known.

F.: C; in nature it catches most of its food by turning stones and corals over. There it finds mussels, sea urchins, brittle stars, bristleworms, crustacea, etc. Its English name, rockmover, comes from this habit.

S.: Young and old animals are quite different in appearance. Young look like pieces of algae and imitate them by swaying back and forth in the waves. An interesting fish to observe in an aquarium; large animals, however, are troublemakers.

T: 24°-28°C, **L:** 30 cm, **TL:** from 150 cm, **WM:** s, **WR:** b, **AV:** 2, **D:** 3

Xyrichtys pavo (VALENCIENNES, 1839)
Peacock wrasse

Hab.: Indo-Pacific; from the Red Sea to Mexico, Japan, Hawaii (N), and the Lord Howe and Society Islands (S). At depths of 1 to 20 m (down to 100 m).

Sex.: None.

Soc.B./Assoc.: Lives singly above sandy bottoms, especially in protected lagoons. Do not associate with conspecifics or invertebrates.

M.: Requires at least 10 cm of sand to dig its spade-edged head into.

Light: Sunlight zone.

B./Rep.: Unknown.

F.: C; *X. pavo* feeds on sand inhabitants in the sea which it digs up, but it is not above grabbing tidbits whirled up by other diggers or divers. In the aquarium it eats any live and substitute foods, especially crustacea, mussels, and pieces of worms.

S.: Young are said to imitate leaves that have fallen into the water. They let themselves drift around in the current, lying on their side just above the bottom.

T: 24°-28°C, **L:** 35 cm, **TL:** from 180 cm, **WM:** w, **WR:** b, **AV:** 2-3, **D:** 3

Two other species have like behavioral adaptations:

The fivefinger wrasse, *Xyrichtys pentadactylus* (LINNAEUS, 1758), inhabits the Indo-Pacific and the Red Sea like the above species.

The pearly razorfish, *Xyrichtys novacula* (LINNAEUS, 1758), inhabits the Mediterranean and the Atlantic. It can tolerate temperatures down to 15°C.

Novaculichthys taeniourus, juvenile

Xyrichtys pavo from Mauritius

Xyrichtys pentadactylus ♂, see p. 822

Xyrichtys novacula ♂, see p. 822

About the Cirrhilabrus Group

One special characteristic separates the following three genera of the subfamily Cheilininae from all other wrasses: the central part of the cornea is divided. It is believed that this is a close-up lens that enables them to see small organisms. All species of these genera have very small mouths. *Cirrhilabrus* and *Paracheilinus* feed on zooplankton, while *Pseudocheilinus* searches the substrate for food. None of these genera grow longer than 10 cm. The coloration of these fishes looks like something out of your wildest dreams. Many of this group are undescribed recent discoveries.

ABOUT THE GENUS *CIRRHILABRUS* TEMMINCK & SCHLEGEL, 1845

This genus has significant sexual dichromatism. During courtship, males really show their colors. Males are larger and less numerous than females. This speaks in favor of sex change and harems.

Cirrhilabrus lubbocki ♂, text on next page.

Fam.: Labridae

Cirrhilabrus cyanopleura   (BLEEKER, 1851)
Blue-sided fairy wrasse

Hab.: Indo-Australian Archipelago; from the Christmas Island (Indian Ocean) to New Guinea. At depths of 5 to 20 m.

Sex.: ♂ ♂ are larger and more intensely colored than ♀ ♀, their ventral fins are elongated, and their tail fin is pointed. Their colors may be iridescent during courtship. The ♀ ♀ are smaller and have a black dot on the caudal peduncle.

Soc.B./Assoc.: *C. cyanopleura* lives in harems consisting of a secondary ♂ and numerous ♀ ♀ in its natural biotope. They prefer lagoon edges, canals, and outer reef drop-offs. There they remain 1 to 2 m above the substrate catching plankton. Best maintained singly or in pairs in an aquarium with either fishes or invertebrates.

M.: The animals require cover and plenty of swimming space as well as clear, well-oxygenated water.

Light: Sunlight zone.

B./Rep.: Not known.

F.: C; a planktivore in nature; in the aquarium it feeds on all kinds of plankton substitutes, especially frozen and flake foods.

S.: Like most wrasses, ♀ ♀ are less colorful than ♂ ♂. Secondary ♂ ♂ (terminal phase) developing from these ♀ ♀ are larger and significantly more intensely colored.

T: 25°-28°C, **L:** 15 cm, **TL:** from 90 cm, **WM:** w, **WR:** b, m, **AV:** 2, **D:** 3

Cirrhilabrus lubbocki   RANDALL & CARPENTER, 1980
Lubbock's wrasse

Hab.: Indo-Australian Archipelago. At depths of 5 to 30 m.

Sex.: See photos: while the ♂ is primarily red, the ♀ is decorated with two burgundy colored striations. The first runs along the hard-rayed section of the dorsal fin, and the second runs to the caudal peduncle in two segments of different length. This second line lies one scale width under the first and begins where the first terminates.

Soc.B./Assoc.: It can be kept relatively well either singly or pairwise with invertebrates and/or fishes.

M.: Likes to seclude itself away in appropriately sized caves and crevices where it will lie and rest. Prefers to swim under overhangs.

Light: Area of sunlight.

B./Rep.: Not known.

F.: C; in the sea it feeds on plankton. In aquaria it can be easily nourished with small crustacea (*Mysis*, pieces of shrimp), mussel meat, mosquito larvae, etc.

S.: Like many species of this genus, these animals have just recently been described. Some species are still waiting to be named.

T: 24°-28°C, **L:** 8 cm, **TL:** from 50 cm, **WM:** w, **WR:** b, **AV:** 3, **D:** 3

Cirrhilabrus cyanopleura ♀

Cirrhilabrus lubbocki ♀, ♂ pictured on p. 825

Fam.: Labridae

Cirrhilabrus jordani   SNYDER, 1904
Jordan's fairy wrasse

Hab.: Northeast Pacific, especially around Hawaii. At depths of 5 to 30 m.

Sex.: Secondary ♂ ♂ are yellow ventrally and orange dorsally with a red stripe that starts at the eye and runs along the back (see picture). The ♀ ♀ are red, white ventrally, and have a faint dark stripe extending from the eye along the upper back.

Soc.B./Assoc.: *C. jordani* may be found alone, but it prefers to live in groups (harems) in deep, rocky reefs. Can be successfully housed with fishes and invertebrates.

M.: Requires good water conditions (every 14 days exchange about 20% of the tank volume), caves, and cover (e.g., table corals; slate plates can be built into the mini-reef in lieu of corals!). The horizontal cover provides the preferred shaded, protected swimming areas. The fiberglass coral figures by INSTANT OCEAN (see pp. 46 f.) can be used.

Light: Sunlight zone.

B./Rep.: Not known.

F.: C; *C. jordani* primarily feeds on small crustacea in the wild. In the aquarium, it eats *Mysis*, *Tubifex*, mosquito larvae, water fleas, mealworms, calf heart, etc., as well as hard-shelled animals such as snails, mussels, and crabs. Provide a varied diet.

S.: This small wrasse goes merrily along its way, seemingly oblivious to its surroundings. Even invertebrates are ignored.

T: 25°-28°C, **L:** 10 cm, **TL:** from 80 cm, **WM:** w, **WR:** b, **AV:** 2-3, **D:** 2-3

Cirrhilabrus melanomarginatus   RANDALL & SHEN, 1978
Blackedge fairy wrasse

Hab.: West Pacific; Taiwan and the Philippines. At depths of 8 to 25 m.

Sex.: Not exactly known; the pictured animal is probably a secondary ♂.

Soc.B./Assoc.: Not known.

M.: Not known, but probably like all other *Cirrhilabrus* species.

Light: Sunlight zone.

B./Rep.: Unknown.

F.: C; it feeds on zooplankton; it will probably accept all kinds of plankton substitutes in the aquarium.

S.: Sometimes confused with *C. temmincki,* but *C. temmincki* has very fine dark lines at the edge of the dorsal and anal fins.

T: 24°-28°C, **L:** 10 cm, **TL:** from 80 cm, **WM:** w, **WR:** b, **AV:** 3, **D:** 3

Cirrhilabrus jordani ♂

Cirrhilabrus melanomarginatus

Fam.: Labridae

Cirrhilabrus rubriventralis   SPRINGER & RANDALL, 1974
Social fairy wrasse, redfin wrasse

Hab.: Northern half of the Red Sea. At depths of 3 to 43 m.

Sex.: The ♀♀ are orange-red with some blue longitudinal stripes and a black spot at the top of the caudal peduncle. The ♂♂ (secondary) are red, with red, highly elongated ventral fins (hence its Latin name); the first 2 rays of the dorsal fin end in long filaments, and the dorsal and ventral edge of the tail fin terminates in pointed tips (rounded in ♀♀).

Soc.B./Assoc.: In nature, *C. rubriventralis* lives along reefs that provide cover and caves and have a substratum of coral rubble. Here they form harems made up of 1 ♂ and numerous ♀♀. It can be associated with fishes and many invertebrates (but not small molluscs or crustacea).

M.: Needs swimming areas under overhangs as well as shelters where it can totally disappear (there it will sleep). Rarely found in open water.

Light: Sun and moderate light zones.

B./Rep.: Not known.

F.: C; in the sea they feed on zooplankton and small, hard-shelled organisms such as snails, mussels, and crustacea. In captivity, feed it small animals like shrimp, *Cyclops,* and *Mysis* as well as mussel meat, frozen foods, and a little algae.

S.: Although it comes from the northern Red Sea, the animals are imported from Sri Lanka. Do these animals also occur there, or do the roads of commerce move in mysterious ways?

T: 24°-28°C, **L:** 10 cm, **TL:** from 180 cm, **WM:** w, **WR:** b, m, **AV:** 2, **D:** 3

Cirrhilabrus rubriventralis ♀

Cirrhilabrus ryukyuiensis ♀

Cirrhilabrus ryukyuiensis   ISHIKAWA, 1904
Ryukyu fairy wrasse

Hab.: West Pacific; from the Philippines to Hawaii. At depths of 4 to 15 m.

Sex.: The ♀♀, that is, animals in their initial phase, have a conspicuous yellow spot on their side and a dark violet-blue blotch above it starting at the head. This blotch is slanted on the ventral side. Secondary ♂♂ are less attractive.

Soc.B./Assoc.: Lives in large groups in the sea, most often within the protection of corals.

M.: Unknown; like all members of the genus, it probably needs a hiding place, oxygen-rich water and sufficient swimming space.

Light: Sunlight zone.

B./Rep.: Not known.

F.: C; in the sea it feeds on zooplankton it catches from the open water above soft corals; accepts a variety of finely chopped foods it grabs from the water column.

S.: There is still a deficit of information on this wrasse. ♀♀ are especially colorful.

T: 23°-28°C, **L:** 10 cm, **TL:** from 90 cm, **WM:** w, **WR:** b-t **AV:** 4, **D:** 3

Cirrhilabrus rubriventralis ♂

Cirrhilabrus ryukyuiensis

Fam.: Labridae

Cirrhilabrus temmincki   SCHULTZ, 1960
Temminck's wrasse, threadfin wrasse

Hab.: West Pacific; from Indonesia to Japan and the Great Barrier Reef. At depths of 5 to 30 m.

Sex.: Almost without exception, the ♀♀ are orange-red and paler than ♂♂. ♂♂ have lengthy ventral fins and brilliant blue striations in the dorsal and anal fins that are "turned on and off" during courtship.

Soc.B./Assoc.: *C. temminicki* lives singly or in small groups (harems?) in shallow reefs of clear lagoons and outer reefs. They can be kept in a fish and/or an invertebrate aquarium.

M.: Requires good hiding places and clean water.

Light: Sunlight zone.

B./Rep.: Not known.

F.: C; it relishes a variety of foods of animal origin and snaps at everything that drifts by in the water.

S.: The animals are similar to *C. rubriventralis*; however, the light ventral half of the body begins higher above the pectoral fins, and the dorsal as well as the anal fins have fine blue lines.

T: 23°-28°C, **L:** 9 cm, **TL:** from 80 cm, **WM:** w, **WR:** b, **AV:** 2-3, **D:** 3

Cirrhilabrus punctatus

Hab.: East Australia. At depths of 5 to 28 m.

Sex.: Not known; assumably this specimen is a secondary ♂.

Soc.B./Assoc.: Not known.

M.: Unknown.

Light: Sunlight zone.

B./Rep.: Not known.

F.: C.

S.: This attractive species is waiting to be identified.

T: 24°-28°C, **L:** 10 cm, **TL:** from 80 cm, **WM:** w, **WR:** b, **AV:** 4, **D:** 3

Cirrhilabrus temmincki ♂

Cirrhilabrus punctatus

Fam.: Labridae

This genus is closely related to *Cirrhilabrus*. Likewise, *Paracheilinus* feed on zooplankton from the open water above the reef. In the '80's new species from the Indonesian region were discovered. The beautiful coloration of these fishes is unsurpassable. However, they have not yet been scientifically described. ♂♂, in contrast to the known species, have 2 elongated dorsal fin rays.

So far, *P. mccoskeri* has only been found in the Indian Ocean. Its single extended dorsal fin ray makes its identification straightforward. Meanwhile it has probably also been found in Indonesia. *P. octotaenia*, which occurs in the Red Sea, is the type-species of the genus; however, it has a totally different silhouette. *Paracheilinus* wrasses are well suited for the invertebrate seawater aquarium that has a sparse fish population. As per their feeding habits in their native waters, they will eat substitute foods from the water column. The circulating pump will keep the foods in suspension.

Paracheilinus carpenteri   RANDALL & LUBBOCK, 1979
Carpenter's wrasse

Hab.: Indonesia, Philippines to Japan. At depths of 27 to 45 m.

Sex.: The ♂♂ are reddish to orange and have 2 to 4 very elongated soft rays in the dorsal fin; the ♀♀ are yellow-beige colored, and the same 2 to 4 rays that are very elongated in ♂♂ may be slightly drawn out in ♀♀. The light blue longitudinal stripes are present in both sexes. ♂♂ have large round blue dots in the dorsal and anal fins. In contrast, ♀♀ have fine whitish dots and lines on the dorsal and anal fins.

Soc.B./Assoc.: The animals live in loose groups over deep mixed substrates with hard and soft corals as well as coral rubble with some sand. They only reach the trade as by-catches, and little is known about what fishes they can be housed with. Because they feed on plankton, they can be maintained in an invertebrate aquarium.

M.: *P. carpenteri* requires rocks and sand as well as moderate illumination and a constant temperature, since it is unaccustomed to dealing with temperature fluctuations in its native waters.

Light: Moderate light zone.

B./Rep.: Unknown.

F.: C; in the sea it feeds primarily on plankton. Easiest to train using small crustacea, mussel meat, etc.

S.: This rare fish is exclusively imported from the Philippines. It is easily recognized by the 2 to 4 elongated soft dorsal fin rays (1.3.5.7. ray).

T: 24°-26°C, **L:** 10 cm, **TL:** from 80 cm, **WM:** w, **WR:** b, **AV:** 3, **D:** 3

Paracheilinus carpenteri ♀

Paracheilinus carpenteri ♂

Fam.: Labridae

Paracheilinus filamentosus
Filament-fin wrasse
ALLEN, 1974

Hab.: Indo-Australian Archipelago; from Indonesia to New Guinea and the Solomon Islands. At depths of 5 to 35 m.

Sex.: The ♂♂ have an elongated sickle-shaped tail fin and 2 to 6 soft dorsal fin rays. The tail fin of the ♀♀ is not as elongated, and a few of the dorsal rays are only slightly longer than the rest. The five reddish to purple longitudinal stripes on the body beneath the lateral line converge at the head and are essentially equal in ♂♂ and ♀♀.

Soc.B./Assoc.: Live in groups over mixed bottoms with coral growth. Appropriate companions for other fishes and many invertebrates.

M.: The animals require hiding places and free swimming space.

Light: Sunlight area.

B./Rep.: Unknown.

F.: C; adults catch plankton in the open water. In the aquarium, feed them plankton substitutes and an assortment of other foodstuffs.

S.: *P. filamentosus* is the only species of the genus that has an elongated caudal fin. This facilitates identification, since the other species have rounded tail fins. The species is very variable. For example, ♀♀ from the Philippines lack longer soft dorsal fin rays.

T: 24°-28°C, **L:** 9 cm, **TL:** from 80 cm, **WM:** w, **WR:** b, **AV:** 3-4, **D:** 3

Paracheilinus filamentosus

Paracheilinus hemitaeniatus
Mauritius wrasse
RANDALL & HARMELIN-VIVIEN, 1977

Hab.: This species, which is known from Mauritius and the Mascarene Islands, also occurs along the coast of east Africa, in the Red Sea, and is possibly even found around the Maldives. At depths of 10 to 30 m.

Sex.: The ♀♀ are primarily pink, with a whitish ventral side and translucent pink, framed in red pectoral fins. A dark red irregular spot extends from the dorsal fin to the base of the anal fin. The pictured fish is a typically colored secondary ♂. Note the blue lines.

Soc.B./Assoc.: Single specimens can be associated with fishes and invertebrates.

M.: Needs hideaways, swimming space, and good water quality (frequent water changes!).

Light: Area of sunlight.

B./Rep.: Not known.

F.: C; feeds on all kinds of "plankton substitutes" such as *Mysis*, shrimp, and mosquito larvae. But it will also consume cut up mussels and squid meat.

S.: Although the species comes from Mauritius and is even occasionally imported from there, the name was unknown.

T: 23°-27°C, **L:** 10 cm, **TL:** from 80 cm, **WM:** w, **WR:** b, m, **AV:** 2, **D:** 3

Paracheilinus filamentosus ♂

Paracheilinus hemitaeniatus

Fam.: Labridae

Paracheilinus mccoskeri
McCosker's wrasse

RANDALL, HARMELIN & VIVIEN, 1977

Hab.: Indian Ocean from east Africa to Thailand. At depths of 5 to 40 m.

Sex.: The ♂'s most notable distinguishing characteristics are its single elongated soft fin ray and a wide dark zone at the base of the tail fin. Juveniles and ♀♀ have no such dark zone, are less colorful, and have very narrow, faint red and blue striations.

Soc.B./Assoc.: This small wrasse often lives in large groups above sandy bottoms covered with shells or seagrass. Here the ♀♀ live secluded while the colorful secondary ♂♂ patrol 0.5 to 1 m above the substratum. *P. mccoskeri* can either be kept singly or in small groups.

M.: Use rockwork to provide hideaways and sand or rubble as substrate.

Light: Moderate light and sunlight zones.

B./Rep.: Not known.

F.: C; primarily feeds on plankton, but small benthic animals are also consumed. Offer *Mysis*, grindal worms, shrimp, minced mussels, etc.

S.: *P. mccoskeri*, like most members of the genus, is extremely shy. The ♀♀ are so secretive that they are rarely seen. ♂♂ are wary and maintain a few meters distance from divers. An immeasurable reward is in store for those who have the patience to wait, because when two ♂♂ encounter each other, they spread all their fins and let an explosion of color shine.

T: 25°-28°C, **L:** 9 cm, **TL:** from 80 cm, **WM:** w, **WR:** b, **AV:** 3, **D:** 3

Paracheilinus octotaenia
Eightline wrasse

FOURMANOIR, 1955

Hab.: The Red Sea. At depths of 5 to 45 m.

Sex.: Both sexes are equally orange-red. Only ♀♀ have 4 to 5 blue longitudinal lines. ♂♂ have 8.

Soc.B./Assoc.: *P. octotaenia* lives in loose congregations and large groups above coral rubble or live corals, usually swimming 1 m above the bottom. It can be kept in groups, even with invertebrates.

M.: Rocky hiding places and plenty of open swimming space are conditions to successfully care for this species. However, it is rarely imported.

Light: Daylight zone.

B./Rep.: Not known.

F.: C; in the sea it catches plankton from the open water; in the aquarium it accepts all small drifting foods.

S.: *P. octotaenia* is easily recognized by its roundish head and uniform, tall dorsal and anal fins. Since there are significantly more ♀♀ than ♂♂, it is assumed that all *Paracheilinus* species live in harems with one large, colorful secondary ♂ and numerous ♀♀.

T: 24°-28°C, **L:** 9 cm, **TL:** from 80 cm, **WM:** w, **WR:** b-t, **AV:** 3-4, **D:** 3

Paracheilinus octotaenia

Paracheilinus mccoskeri ♂, Flores (indonesia)

Paracheilinus octotaenia

Fam.: Labridae

Species within the genus *Pseudocheilinus* have colonized the entire Indo-Pacific. They are secretive fishes that hide among stands of coral, darting around coral rubble and sandy sections of tropical reefs. Their rapid movements and small size make them difficult for divers to recognize. The normal depth range is 6 to 40 m. These colorful species are popular pets. They are famous for their amiable attitude towards cleaner, marble, and coral shrimp, and it is quite feasible to place them in tanks with larger crustacea. Picking on live rock is a particular love of theirs, although frozen foods and some dried commercial foods will also be accepted. They forget themselves and leave the security of the bottom when the circulation pump hurls krill past them.

These animals may have problems in tanks containing rapid feeding, competitive fishes. Therefore, do not associate these *Pseudocheilinus* wrasses with dottybacks or coral perches. None of the members of the cirrhilabrus group (*Pseudocheilinus, Paracheilinus, Cirrhilabrus*) will harm coral or colonial anemones.

Pseudocheilinus hexataenia

Pseudocheilinus evanidus

Pseudocheilinus evanidus
Disappearing wrasse

JENKINS, 1901

Hab.: Indo-Pacific; from the Red Sea to Hawaii, Tuamotu, and Japan (N). At depths of 6 to 40 m (rarely shallower than 20 m).

Sex.: None.

Soc.B./Assoc.: *P. evanidus* lives singly or in pairs hidden along outer reefs that have a substratum of rocks and coral pieces. Do not place with invertebrates or large, aggressive fishes.

M.: Set up the aquarium with plenty of cover, hiding places, and shaded swimming areas so it can maintain its hidden lifestyle.

Light: Moderate light.

B./Rep.: Not known.

F.: C; it searches for small organisms among coral rubble. Very small pieces of crab and mussel meat are your best chance of successfully training these fishes to accept substitute foods.

S.: The very fine longitudinal stripes which look like one white bar extending from the corner of the mouth to the cheek are distinctive characteristics of this solid orange animal. Like some closely related fish genera (*Cirrhilabrus, Paracheilinus*, and others), *Pseudocheilinus* has a two-part pupil. This feature probably allows the animals to see small crustacea better (eagle eye!).

T: 23°-28°C, **L:** 8 cm, **TL:** from 80 cm, **WM:** w, **WR:** b, **AV:** 2, **D:** 3

Fam.: Labridae

Pseudocheilinus hexataenia   (BLEEKER, 1857)
Sixstripe wrasse

Hab.: Indo-Pacific; from the Red Sea to Tuamotu, Japan (N), and Lord Howe Island (S). At depths of 4 to 35 m.

Sex.: None.

Soc.B./Assoc.: It mostly lives singly and in pairs but is occasionally sighted in small groups along outer reefs, especially among branches of live corals.

M.: Requires good hiding possibilities and covered swimming spaces. Juveniles can be kept with conspecifics. Refrain from housing it with either aggressive or heavy-bodied species or invertebrates.

Light: Sunlight and moderate light zones.

B./Rep.: Unknown.

F.: C; especially appreciative of fish eggs as well as small benthic organisms such as crustacea, mussels, snails, and crab larvae. Feed it a wide variety of foods, including flake foods. Caution: it is sensitive during acclimation.

S.: *P. hexataenia* is one of the commonest Pseudocheilinae, but because of its low key lifestyle, it is rarely seen. Important characteristics are a black ocellus at the top of the caudal peduncle and the numerous longitudinal stripes (6 blue stripes alternating with 6 yellow-orange stripes) which extend into the lower body.

T: 24°-28°C, **L:** 10 cm, **TL:** from 100 cm, **WM:** w, **WR:** b, **AV:** 1-2, **D:** 3

Pseudocheilinus tetrataenia   SCHULTZ, 1960
Four-lined wrasse

Hab.: Pacific Plate; from Indonesia and Australia to Hawaii and Tuamotu. At depths of 6 to 44 m.

Sex.: None.

Soc.B./Assoc.: *P. tetrataenia* lives a reclusive life either alone or pairwise among living corals and coral rubble in outer reefs. Do not associate with rough fishes or invertebrates.

M.: Provide it with rockwork that has incorporated shelters.

Light: Sunlight or moderate light zones.

B./Rep.: Not known.

F.: C; in the sea it feeds on small organisms such as crustacea, fish (and other) eggs, molluscs, and all kinds of "worms." It needs a varied animal diet and eats just about anything offered after it becomes accustomed to its environment.

S.: The alternating 4 blue and 4 red striations on the upper body distinguishes this species from the slightly similar *P. hexataenia*; the pointed snout separates it from the round-headed genus *Paracheilinus*, which also includes a few longitudinally striped species.

T: 25°-28°C, **L:** 9 cm, **TL:** from 80 cm, **WM:** w, **WR:** b, **AV:** 2-3, **D:** 3

Pseudocheilinus hexataenia

Pseudocheilinus tetrataenia

Fam.: Labridae

About the Genus *Anampses* QUOY & GAIMARD, 1824

Fishes of this genus reside in the Indo-Pacific. There are 13 species which almost all undergo extreme color changes that correlate to their passage to adulthood. *Anampses* species can be distinguished from other wrasses by a pair of protruding teeth in both the upper and lower mandibles. They hack on corals and rocks with their teeth to remove food. Small groups swim spryly throughout the reef. Juveniles have ocelli on the ends of the dorsal and anal fins. When swimming normally, tamarins look like a large face with their two ocelli as the eyes. Small, recommendable fishes for the aquarium.

Anampses caeruleopunctatus pp. 850-851

Anampses chrysocephalus   RANDALL, 1958
Red-tailed tamarin

Hab.: Pacific; around Hawaii and the Midway Islands. At depths of 15 to 50 m.

Sex.: The initial phase is faintly spotted; these dots are very dense on the head and back; the dorsal fin is bright with a small posterior ocellus. Terminal ♂♂ have a red head and a few dots. Dorsal and ventral areas (including the fins) are dark, while the center of the body is light. The tail fin is dark posteriorly.

Soc.B./Assoc.: *A. chrysocephalus* usually lives in pairs above mixed bottoms of rocks and sand. It is best associated with peaceful fishes.

M.: Requires rocky bottoms and sand to dig in and an open area for swimming.

Light: Sunlight area.

B./Rep.: Not known.

F.: C; in nature it feeds on various small animals, but in the aquarium, it accepts almost all kinds of substitute foods such as shrimp, mussels, crab meat, and moderately sized flakes.

S.: All of the few imported specimens come from Hawaii.

T: 24°-28°C, **L:** 15 cm, **TL:** from 120 cm, **WM:** w, **WR:** b, **AV:** 2, **D:** 3

Anampses chrysocephalus

Anampses chrysocephalus ♂ and ♀

Anampses chrysocephalus 2 ♀♀

Fam.: Labridae

RANDALL, 1972
Blue-striped orange tamarin

Hab.: Tropical south Pacific. At depths of 10 to 30 m.

Sex.: The initial phase is anteriorly yellow-orange with wavy blue longitudinal lines. The posterior fins have with ocelli in the dorsal and anal fins. Terminal phase (secondary ♂♂) animals have a blue head with bright blue lines (especially at spawning time). The posterior half of the body is yellow, often with a dark overlying shadow. Only the posterior fins are blue.

Soc.B./Assoc.: The animals live singly or in pairs above substrates of sand and rocks. Little is known about interactions with other fishes or invertebrates.

M.: A sandy layer to dig in and rock edifications fulfill the necessary requirements.

Light: Sunlight zone.

B./Rep.: Not known.

F.: C; offer a variety of foods, including small pieces of mussel, crustacean, and fish flesh, and small crustacea. Flake and frozen foods are also eaten.

S.: Because the animals live in a remote region off the main fish export lanes and lead a reclusive life, the rare import is attributed to being a coincidental by-catch. Observational information would be valuable, since aquaristic data for this fish are scarce.

T: 24°-28°C, **L:** 12 cm, **TL:** from 100 cm, **WM:** w, **WR:** b, **AV:** 3-4, **D:** 3

Anampses lennardi, pp. 850-851

Anampses lineatus RANDALL, 1972
Line wrasse, line tamarin

Hab.: Indian Ocean; from the Red Sea and east Africa to Indonesia. At depths of 10 to 30 m.

Sex.: Slight; coloration and shape change insignificantly with growth and sex. Only the ♂♂ which evolved from the initial phase ♀♀ are somewhat larger.

Soc.B./Assoc.: *A. lineatus* lives singly or in pairs in deeper outer reefs.

M.: Besides a rocky bottom with hiding places, it needs a section with at least 3 cm of sand substrate where it can hide during danger and sleep at night. It will bury itself when not at ease in its surroundings, i.e., when newly introduced into an aquarium.

Light: Sunlight zone.

B./Rep.: Unknown.

F.: C; in the sea it looks for small benthic organisms which it catches with its protruding teeth. In the aquarium it takes the usual feeds offered to wrasses such as *Mysis*, krill, other shrimp, mosquito larvae, water fleas, mussels, crabs, fish flesh, and flake foods.

S.: The animals have a light blue spot on each scale. Each spot becomes a stripe through the scale as the fish ages, and they join to form longitudinal lines. The tail is anteriorly white and posteriorly black.

T: 23°-28°C, **L:** 10 cm, **TL:** from 100 cm, **WM:** w, **WR:** b, **AV:** 2, **D:** 3

Anampses femininus

Anampses femininus ♀

Anampses meleagrides, juvenile, p. 848

Anampses lineatus

Anampses twisti, text on p. 850

Fam.: Labridae

Anampses melanurus   (BLEEKER, 1857)
Yellow tailband wrasse

Hab.: West Pacific; from Indonesia through Micronesia to Japan. At depths of 15 to 40 m.

Sex.: The animal's form and color only undergo slight changes as they grow; little sexual dimorphism. Secondary ♂ ♂ are somewhat larger.

Soc.B./Assoc.: The animals live singly or in pairs around outer reefs with sandy deposits. Relatively rare. They are suitable for traditional fish aquaria.

M.: Provide rockwork and a sandy layer where the fish can bury itself.

Light: Sunlight zone.

B./Rep.: Not known.

F.: C; feeds on a variety of animal foods, ranging from shrimp and gastropods to flake foods.

S.: *A. melanurus* is closely related to *A. lineatus*, although the latter is limited to the Indian Ocean. The two were separated in 1983 by RANDALL. Prior to this, both were considered subspecies (*A. melanurus lineatus* and *A. m. melanurus*). Unlike *A. lineatus*, the light blue spots remain limited to the center of the scale. Rows of dots (not longitudinal lines) result. The tail fin is yellowish at the base (not white) and black at the edge.

T: 23°-28°C, **L:** 10 cm, **TL:** from 80 cm, **WM:** w, **WR:** b, **AV:** 2, **D:** 3

Anampses meleagrides   VALENCIENNES, 1839
Yellow-tailed tamarin

Hab.: Indo-Pacific; from the Red Sea to Tuamotu and Japan (N). At 5 to 50 m depth.

Sex.: Form and shape only change slightly with age and sex. Juveniles have a rounded tail fin, while adults have a straight to slightly convex caudal fin. The initial phase has a reddish brown snout and a small round white dot on each scale. The tail fin is yellow. Secondary ♂ ♂ are dark orange-brown with oblong, vertical blue dots. Dorsal and anal fins are a matte orange with blue stripes. The tail fin is orange with round blue spots and a typical blue V in front of the pale translucent triangular center.

Soc.B./Assoc.: The animals live singly or in pairs on reefs with mixed coral growth but also above rubble, calcareous rocks, and sand on outer reefs. Keep with fishes that are not too rough.

M.: *A. meleagrides* makes a nice addition for the sandy bottomed reef aquarium.

Light: Sunlight zone.

B./Rep.: Not known.

F.: C; the species eats *Mysis*, krill, shrimp, water fleas, mussels, crab meat, etc.

S.: The solid yellow tail fin distinguishes ♀ ♀.

T: 24°-28°C, **L:** 17 cm, **TL:** from 150 cm, **WM:** w, **WR:** b, **AV:** 2, **D:** 3

Anampses melanurus ♂

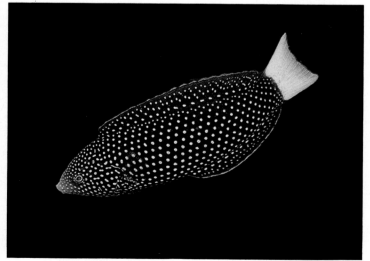

Anampses meleagrides ♀

Fam.: Labridae

Anampses neoguinaicus, Montague Island, New South Wales

The New Guinea tamarin, *A. neoguinaicus* BLEEKER, 1878, inhabits the Indo-Australian Archipelago and grows to a length of 8 cm. The picture is slightly overexposed; the fish is dorsally brown, whereas the remainder of the body is white with white dots and stripes.

The yellowbreasted tamarin, *A. twisti* BLEEKER, 1856, occurs from the Red Sea to Tuamotu and Japan and prefers protected reefs (see p. 847 for photo).

Lennard's tamarin, *A. lennardi* SCOTT, 1959, lives around west Australia and grows to a length of 25 cm. This fish has an atypical appearance in comparison to others of the genus. It is decorated with irregular orange and blue lines.

The bluespotted tamarin, *A. caeruleopunctatus* RÜPPELL, 1828, has strong coloration differences between initial and terminal phase animals. It inhabits the Red Sea to the Easter Islands. The secondary ♂ ♂ are dark blue-green with dark blue-green vertical lines on the scales and horizontal stripes on the fins. The initial phase (see picture) has shiny blue spots on each scale (name).

Anampses lennardi

Anampses caeruleopunctatus

Fam.: Labridae

About the Genus *Cheilio* LACÉPÈDE, 1802

This monotypic genus only contains *Cheilio inermis*, the cigar wrasse. Its broad distribution explains its presence in pet stores. Found in the Red Sea and along the Easter Islands, this extremely cylindrical wrasse reaches a length of 50 cm! Juveniles have longitudinal stripes that disappear with age. Its red, yellow, or multicolored spots behind the pectoral fins are striking. While juveniles like to swim in small groups, full-grown cigar wrasses are only seen singly. They are found at depths down to 30 m above fields of seagrass or algae-covered reefs. They feed on sea urchins, snails, and crustacea.

Cheilio inermis
Cigar wrasse
(FORSSKÅL, 1775)

Hab.: Indo-Pacific; from the Red Sea to Hawaii, the Easter Island, Japan (N), and Lord Howe Island (S). At 2 to 30 m depth.

Sex.: None; large ♂ ♂ can develop a shiny yellow, orange, black, white, or multicolored spot behind the pectoral fin.

Soc.B./Assoc.: *C. inermis* lives singly above seagrass lawns or subtrates that are densely covered with algae; may also be found in lagoons and outer reefs. Even very young specimens have to be associated with robust fishes.

M.: Its rapid growth and penchant for eating invertebrates limits its prospective homes. Perhaps it fits into large conventional fish aquaria, but it can never be trusted with invertebrates. It requires a lot of swimming space.

Light: Sunlight zone.

B./Rep.: Not known.

F.: C; in nature it eats benthic animals such as crustacea, snails, mussels, and sea urchins. After acclimation, almost all substitute foods are eaten.

S.: Young usually are brown or green mottled. This allows them to blend into the seagrass and algae. Some animals have a broad longitudinal center stripe (see picture); others are totally yellow.

T: 24°-27°C, **L:** 50 cm, **TL:** from 200 cm, **WM:** w, **WR:** b, **AV:** 2-3, **D:** 3

Cheilio inermis

About the Genus *Coris* LACÉPÈDE, 1801

There are about 20 species in this genus, one of which even occurs in the Mediterranean. Some species can be identified based on size. The smallest is a mere 10 cm, whereas the largest achieves a length of more than 1 m. Juvenile *Coris* wrasses are extremely desirable aquarium fishes. During the day these brightly colored species swim tirelessly, but at night, they bury into the substrate to sleep. The substrate also offers a safe haven in the face of danger. Taking this into consideration, provide a deeper than normal sandy layer. In nature they feed on shelled molluscs, sea urchins, and hermit crabs they pull from their shells. Forward positioned fanglike teeth are used by adult *Coris* to flip over pebbles and stones in their search for food.

Fam.: Labridae

Coris aygula
Clown coris

(LACÉPÈDE, 1801)

Hab.: Indo-Pacific; from the Red Sea to the Line and Ducie Islands, Japan (N), and Lord Howe and Rapa Islands (S). At 2 to 30 m depth.

Sex.: Goes through an unbelievable color transformation in the course of growth. The initial phase is greenish; head and anterior body are somewhat lighter with red spots. Secondary ♂ ♂ are dark green to blue-green (appear black from a distance) with 1 or 2 pale green bars in the center of the body. They develop a large frontal hump, a long first dorsal fin ray, and a frayed tail.

Soc.B./Assoc.: *C. aygula* lives a solitary existence in lagoons, on outer reef drop-offs, and along reefs with coral rubble and a sand substrate.

M.: It likes rockwork rich in hiding places. Requires at least a 5-10 cm layer of sand to burrow in.

Light: Sunlight zone.

B./Rep.: Not known.

F.: C; in nature it feeds on hard-shelled invertebrates such as molluscs, crustacea, and sea urchins. It uses its anterior, protruding teeth to flip stones and coral pieces to reach small organisms hiding underneath. In an aquarium, it quickly becomes a greedy feeder that accepts anything from small fishes to beef heart, flake, and tablet foods.

S.: *C. aygula* is a welcomed aquarium fish when young, but space restrictions will preclude it from changing into a giant with a cephalic hump. You should renounce keeping this fish in an aquarium!

T: 24°-28°C, **L:** 120 cm, **TL:** from 250 cm, **WM:** w, **WR:** b, **AV:** 1, **D:** 3

Coris aygula, juvenile, 5 cm

Coris aygula, adult ♂

Coris aygula, juvenile, about 10 cm

Coris aygula, adult

Fam.: Labridae

Coris frerei (previously *C. formosa*)   (GÜNTHER, 1866)
Queen coris

Hab.: Indian Ocean; from south and east Africa to Australia. At depths of 2 to 50 m.

Sex.: From the white-spotted red juveniles, initial phase ♂♂ and ♀♀ result. These animals are gray or gray-brown with small black dots. The head is yellowish with blue stripes through the eye; the tail fin is intensely red proximally, white distally. Secondary ♂♂ (originating from initial phase ♀♀) have a reddish body and a caudal fin with numerous small, dark-edged blue-green dots. They have a solid orange-red fringe on the caudal fin.

Soc.B./Assoc.: *C. frerei* lives singly; young may form groups over mixed bottoms of rocks, corals, and sand.

M.: *C. frerei* needs rocks with passages it can swim through and a sandy bottom to hide in (at least 3-4 cm deep). An internal clock prompts him to retire in the sand at the same time each evening and reappear at the same time each morning; both of these activities are totally independent of the aquarium's illumination.

Light: Sunlight zone.

B./Rep.: Not known.

F.: C; the animal feeds on small, hard-shelled animals which are grabbed with its strong teeth. In the aquarium it can be fed crustacean meat, mussels, snails, pieces of meat, etc.

S.: *C. frerei* is similar to *C. gaimard*, especially as a juvenile; however, a broad, black-fringed, white crossband posterior to and extending below the eye and a large ocellus in the center of the dorsal fin clearly define it as a different species.

T: 24°-27°C, **L:** 50 cm, **TL:** from 100 cm, **WM:** l, **WR:** b, **AV:** 1, **D:** 3

Coris frerei

Coris frerei

Coris frerei

Fam.: Labridae

Coris gaimard
Clown wrasse

(QUOY & GAIMARD, 1824)

Hab.: Indo-Pacific; from the Red Sea to Hawaii, Tuamotu, the Marquesas, Japan (N), and New Caledonia (S). At 1 to 50 m depth.

Sex.: Besides dramatic color changes during growth, large ♂♂ develop a light green stripe on the body above the anal fin.

Soc.B./Assoc.: The animals live singly; young may form groups over mixed bottoms of coral, rubble, and sand found on exposed reef terraces, lagoons, and outer reefs. Limit their companions to robust fishes.

M.: Its most notable necessity is a sandy substrate: young need 3 cm, while older specimens need a minimum of 5 cm so they can burrow during danger or at night to sleep.

Light: Sunlight zone.

B./Rep.: Unknown.

F.: C; animals in the sea primarily feed on hard-shelled invertebrates such as molluscs, hermit crabs, crabs, sea urchins, and the occasional tunicate and foraminiferan. In the aquarium it quickly accepts all kinds of substitute foods.

S.: Juvenile *C. gaimard* are particularly similar to juvenile *C. frerei* (previously called *C. formosa*). However, the first white crossband of the former only descends to the eye (not below as in the latter), and it lacks an ocellus in the dorsal fin. *C. gaimard* is often divided into 2 subspecies. *C. g. gaimard*, whose adults have much stronger colors, corporal brilliant blue spots, and a shiny yellow tail fin, hails from the Pacific. The Indian subspecies, *C. g. africana*, lacks these attributes.

T: 24°-28°C, **L:** 40 cm, **TL:** from 150 cm, **WM:** w, **WR:** b, **AV:** 1, **D:** 3

Coris gaimard

Coris gaimard

Coris gaimard

Coris gaimard

Fam.: Labridae

Coris julis   (LINNAEUS, 1758)
Mediterranean rainbow wrasse

Hab.: East Atlantic, from the Bay of Biscay to Guinea, including the Mediterranean. At 0-120 m depth.

Sex.: Primary animals (juveniles, ♀ ♀, and ♂ ♂) are a plain inconspicuous brown with light and dark longitudinal stripes. Only secondary ♂ ♂ have one orange and one dark zig-zag longitudinal band in the center of the body.

Soc.B./Assoc.: The Mediterranean rainbow wrasse is a gregarious fish that lives over all types of substrata. It can be successfully housed with most fishes.

M.: As a fast, continuous swimmer, *C. julis* requires a large tank with rockwork full of passageways that can challenge its swimming ability and a few centimeters of sandy substrate to burrow into.

Light: Area of sunlight.

B./Rep.: Difficult since it spawns into the open water. The pelagic eggs and resulting larvae drift in the current.

F.: C; in the sea it feeds on a number of invertebrates, from sponges and worms to crustacea and snails. Not a finicky eater. Almost all kinds of substitute foods will be accepted.

S.: Young fish often act as cleaners, cleaning parasites from conspecifics as well as heterospecifics. Secondary ♂ ♂ from the Atlantic and extreme western Mediterranean have a dark posterior body.

T: 18°-22°C, **L:** 25 cm, **TL:** from 120 cm, **WM:** m, **WR:** b-t, **AV:** 1, **D:** 2-3 (chiller)

Coris caudimacula   (QUOY & GAIMARD, 1834)
Spottail coris

Hab.: Indian Ocean, from the Red Sea to Indonesia, Mauritius, and the South African Cape Province. At depths of 3-25 m.

Sex.: Not significant. The patterns always remain relatively equal; only primary animals look red-orange; secondary ♂ ♂ are mostly blue-violet, sometimes yellowish green.

Soc.B./Assoc.: *C. caudimacula* lives singly or in groups over mixed bottoms of rocks, corals, and sand. An active fish that should not be housed with delicate fishes.

M.: Requires a large swimming area, sand to burrow in, and rocks with numerous passages.

Light: Sunlight zone.

B./Rep.: Not known.

F.: C; feeds on a number of small invertebrates, especially crustacea, mussels, snails, bristleworms, etc. In the aquarium it accepts just about all that is offered, including flake and frozen foods.

S.: The indistinct spot on the caudal peduncle is the origin of the scientific name. The small, dark spot at the front of the dorsal fin is another distinctive feature.

T: 24°-28°C, **L:** 20 cm, **TL:** from 120 cm, **WM:** m, **WR:** b-t, **AV:** 2-3, **D:** 3

Coris julis

Coris caudimacula

Fam.: Labridae

Coris batuensis   (BLEEKER, 1856)
Dapple coris

Hab.: Central and western Pacific. At depths of 2-15 m.

Sex.: In contrast to most other species within this genus, this coris has no clear sexual dimorphism.

Soc.B./Assoc.: *C. variegata* lives singly. Young may form groups in lagoons and on outer reefs. Not aggressive; it can be associated with most other fishes.

M.: As a fast, continuous swimmer, *C. variegata* requires a large tank with hiding places. Make sure it also has rockwork with passages and a sand substrate deep enough to burrow in.

Light: Area of sunlight.

B./Rep.: Not known.

F.: C; primarily feeds on small crabs and snails in its natural waters. It quickly learns to take substitute foods in the aquarium, including flake and frozen foods.

S.: Animals from the Australian region are dark brown with a few slender bright crossbands. Those from the Indian Ocean (for instance, the Maldives) are light, frequently almost totally white.

T: 24°-28°C, **L:** 20 cm, **TL:** from 150 cm, **WM:** m, **WR:** b-t, **AV:** 2, **D:** 3

Coris picta   (SCHNEIDER, 1801)
Combfish

Hab.: Australian Archipelago; in the seas around Australia and New Zealand. At 3-25 m depth.

Sex.: Slight; the primary phase is white and has a broad, dark longitudinal stripe. A large proportion of the white immediately adjacent to the black stripe is violet in secondary ♂♂. The net result is a violet stripe following the dorsal line and another along the center of the body. The ventral side of the latter is jagged. Frequently they also have a red-violet stripe along the ventral side.

Soc.B./Assoc.: *C. picta* is a social fish that usually makes a good companion for other fishes on rocky coasts, reefs, or sand. It is peaceful and can be associated with a wide variety of fishes.

M.: According to its natural biotope, this species needs a sandy layer several centimeters deep and rockwork with navigable passageways.

Light: Area of sunlight.

B./Rep.: Not known.

F.: C; like other *Coris*, it feeds on all kinds of invertebrates, especially bristleworms, crustaceanlike organisms, snails, mussels, and echinoderms. It quickly learns to accept substitute foods such as shrimp, *Mysis*, grindal worms, mosquito larvae, mussel meat, crab meat, fish flesh, and worms. Frozen and dry foods are also eaten.

T: 20°-26°C, **L:** 25 cm, **TL:** from 150 cm, **WM:** m, **WR:** b-t, **AV:** 2-3, **D:** 3

Coris batuensis

Coris picta

Fam.: Labridae

About the Genus *Gomphosus* LACÉPÈDE, 1801

Both species of bird wrasses have, without a doubt, one of the most uncommon body shapes found within this family. The long snout informs us this is a feeding specialist. It uses this long snout to probe between branches of coral to reach its favorite prey: crabs, crinoids, and molluscs. However, juveniles lack the long snout. Both species, *G. varius* and *G. caeruleus*, seem to be very similar. The former inhabits the eastern Atlantic to the Marquesas in the Pacific, while the latter is known from the Red Sea and the western Indian Ocean.

Gomphosus varius   LACÉPÈDE, 1801
Bird wrasse

Hab.: From the Indian Ocean to Hawaii. At 2 to 30 m depth.

Sex.: Only the primary ♂ ♂ turn dark blue.

Soc.B./Assoc.: This solitary, tireless fish swims all day. Other tankmates are driven batty by its restless behavior. Refrain from purchasing these fish if you have a small aquarium. It blunders into the infrastructure and incessantly bothers cohabitants in small tanks.

M.: *G. varius* requires clean water (frequent water exchanges), plenty of swimming space, and rock edifications with many passageways.

Light: Sunlight zone.

B./Rep.: Not known.

F.: O; *G. varius* feeds on foods hidden in crevices and cracks. In the aquarium, it first has to learn to take food from the open water. Training is often difficult and laborious. Begin by continuously offering bite-sized pieces which sink to the bottom. To avoid deficiencies, provide plant foods as well. Housing the animals in tanks with a nice algae layer precludes the need for the latter.

S.: The long snout develops when the fish are about 8 to 10 cm long. The Indian Ocean has another, very similar species: *G. caeruleus caeruleus*. The other subspecies, *G. c. klunzingeri*, lives in the Red Sea.

T: 24°-28°C, **L:** 30 cm, **TL:** from 150 cm, **WM:** w, **WR:** b-t, **AV:** 1-2, **D:** 3

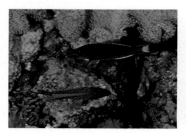
Gomphosus caeruleus klunzingeri ♂

Gomphosus caeruleus klunzingeri ♀

Gomphosus varius, top ♂, bottom ♀

Gomphosus varius ♀

Fam.: Labridae

ABOUT THE GENUS *HALICHOERES* RÜPPELL, 1835

This is the largest genus of wrasses. New species are constantly being added to the over 60 known species. The two fishes pictured on the opposite page are newly discovered, as yet undescribed species. Scientists have always had a difficult time matching males with corresponding females. The dramatic color changes these fishes undergo as they grow confounds the situation to no small degree. *Halichoeres* usually remain smaller than 20 cm in length and are distributed throughout the world. All members of the genus need a deep layer of sand to sleep in. Several congenerics as well as other family members can be kept in one aquarium. Be forewarned: tubeworms and shrimp are too tempting to resist. Whether in an aquarium or its natural biotope, these invertebrates rank as their favorite foods and will be devoured as such.

Note the ocelli on the dorsal fin of juveniles and initial ♂ ♂. When the fin is spread, the ocelli fool potential predators into thinking these large eyespots have a correspondingly large mouth just below them. When threatened, juvenile *Halichoeres* irritate their pursuer with whipping motions of their body. Then they suddenly dart away. The author (H.D.) has observed juvenile *H. chrysus* swimming with clownfishes in an anemone, but it is unknown whether or not they are protected from the stings.

Halichoeres chrysus swims within the anemone *S. mertensii* just like the clownfishes.

Halichoeres sp. ♂

Halichoeres sp. ♀

Fam.: Labridae

Halichoeres biocellatus   SCHULTZ, 1960
Red-lined wrasse

Hab.: West Pacific; from the Philippines to the Fiji Islands, Japan (N), and the Great Barrier Reef. At depths of 7 to 35 m.

Sex.: With the exception of the loss of the eyespots as the fish matures, the color differences between juveniles and sexually mature individuals are minimal.

Soc.B./Assoc.: *H. biocellatus* lives singly or in pairs over mixed bottoms of corals, rocks, and sand, especially along outer reefs. A pleasant tank inhabitant that pays little notice to tankmates; like all *Halichoeres,* it is unsuitable for tanks that contain invertebrates.

M.: It requires rock formations rich in hiding places and a sand substrate as cover.

Light: Area of sunlight.

B./Rep.: Not known.

F.: C; in the sea it feeds on small benthic organisms. In the aquarium it relishes a varied diet (see *H. hortulanus*).

S.: Two eyespots on the juvenile's dorsal fin are characteristic for *H. biocellatus.*

T: 25°-28°C, **L:** 10 cm, **TL:** from 80 cm, **WM:** w, **WR:** b, **AV:** 2, **D:** 3

Halichoeres biocellatus, adult

Halichoeres hortulanus   (LACÉPÈDE, 1801)
Checkerboard wrasse

Hab.: Indo-Pacific; from the Red Sea to the Line Islands, Tuamotu, the Marquesas, Japan (N), and the southern Barrier Reef (S). At 1 to 30 m depth.

Sex.: *H. hortulanus* undergoes surprising color changes during growth until the checkered adult coloration is adopted.

Soc.B./Assoc.: It lives singly and usually establishes its territory on shallow reef terraces, in lagoons, or along outer reefs.

M.: While the young prefer broken coral, caves, or crevices in rocks near sandy bottoms, adults appreciate extensive sand substrates. Therefore, provide them the sand, rubble, and rock substrates they prefer.

Light: Area of sunlight.

B./Rep.: Not known.

F.: C; *H. hortulanbus* feeds on small sand inhabitants such as snails, mussels, hermit crabs, bristleworms, and fishes in the wild. In the aquarium it relishes a varied menu consisting of mussel meat, shrimp, mosquito larvae, and tablet foods.

S.: Juveniles are remotely similar to juvenile *H. biocellatus*, but *H. hortulanus* only has one ocellus on each side of the dorsal fin.

T: 24°-28°C, **L:** 35 cm, **TL:** from 200 cm, **WM:** m, **WR:** b-t, **AV:** 1-2, **D:** 3

Halichoeres hortulanus, adult

Halichoeres biocellatus

Halichoeres hortulans

Fam.: Labridae

Halichoeres chrysus   RANDALL, 1980
Golden rainbowfish

Hab.: West central Pacific from the Christmas Island in the Indian Ocean to the Solomon and Marshall Islands, Japan (N), and Rowley Shoals (S). At 15 to 60 m depth.

Sex.: Almost none; secondary ♂ ♂ lose the eyespot from the center of the dorsal fin.

Soc.B./Assoc.: *H. chrysus* lives singly or in pairs within established territories. They choose deep isolated coral blocks surrounded by sand. Their sleeping site is in the center of their territory and is defended against conspecifics; other species are ignored.

M.: Requires a varied "landscape" with rockwork, shelters, and passageways. They need a sand substrate to rest in.

Light: Sunlight zone.

B./Rep.: Unknown.

F.: C; like most *Halichoeres, H. chrysus* feeds on small living organisms it digs from beneath coral pieces and the sand. In the aquarium it feeds on all kinds of substitute foods as soon as it overcomes its bottom oriented feeding habits.

S.: There are practically no corporal differences between this species and *H. leucoxanthus,* yet they are differently colored.

T: 24°-27°C, **L:** 10 cm, **TL:** from 80 cm, **WM:** w, **WR:** b, **AV:** 3, **D:** 3

Halichoeres leucoxanthus   RANDALL & SMITH, 1982
Indian rainbowfish

Hab.: Central and eastern Indian Ocean from the Maldives to Java. At 15 to 50 m depth.

Sex.: *H. leucoxanthus* does not undergo marked color changes as it grows or passes through different sex phases. Terminal ♂ ♂ do not lose the dark spots on the dorsal fin like *H. chrysus.*

Soc.B./Assoc.: This species lives singly or in pairs along small isolated reefs or around coral blocks on open sand bottoms of lagoons. Limit its tankmates to peaceful fishes.

M.: *H. leucoxanthus* is bashful (the diver rarely comes close enough to photograph them). Set up the aquarium with rockwork containing hiding places and a sand substrate where it can sleep or dart during danger.

Light: Sunlight zone.

B./Rep.: Unknown.

F.: C; *H. leucoxanthus* feeds on small animals it digs out of the sand and other hiding places; in the aquarium it prefers a variety of substitute foods.

S.: If this and the previous species would be geographically separated, they would be considered subspecies. But since their distribution areas overlap in Indonesia, they are considered two separate species. The name *leucoxanthus* (white-yellow) was derived from the two-tone coloration.

T: 25°-28°C, **L:** 12 cm, **TL:** from 100 cm, **WM:** w, **WR:** b, **AV:** 3, **D:** 3

Halichoeres chrysus, adult

Halichoeres leucoxanthus, adult

Halichoeres chrysus, juvenile

Halichoeres leucoxanthus, juvenile

Fam.: Labridae

Halichoeres garnoti
Yellowhead wrasse

(CUVIER & VALENCIENNES, 1839)

Hab.: Caribbean and west Atlantic. At depths of 4 to 60 m.

Sex.: Not only is there a strong color difference between juveniles and adults, there is also sexual dichromatism. Juveniles are yellow and have an outlined longitudinal band in the center of the body. The initial phase looses this longitudinal stripe and develops wavy oblique lines behind the eye. It is yellowish brown dorsally and lighter ventrally. Terminal ♂ ♂ have a black crossbar in the center of the body which continues over the dorsum (the picture to the right shows two such ♂ ♂ during a "mouth fight").

Soc.B./Assoc.: These territorial animals are quarrelsome towards conspecifics. Other species are ignored, which is why they can be successfully maintained in a traditional fish community.

M.: *H. garnoti* requires clean water with some movement, varied decoration with plenty of swimming space, and sand to rest in.

Light: Sunlight zone.

B./Rep.: Not known.

F.: C; *H. garnoti* searches for invertebrates in and on the substrate. Its main obstacle to accepting prepared foods is learning to take them from the water column. Train them using sinking foods they can pick from the bottom.

S.: None.

T: 23°-27°C, **L:** 15 cm, **TL:** from 100 cm, **WM:** m, **WR:** b-t, **AV:** 2, **D:** 3

Halichoeres garnoti, juvenile

Halichoeres radiatus
Puddingwife

(LINNAEUS, 1758)

Hab.: Caribbean and western Atlantic; from the Bermudas to Brazil. At depths of 5 to 45 m.

Sex.: While juveniles have a large ocellus, a longitudinal dorsal stripe, and white crossbars, ♂ ♂ do not. The initial phase, as shown in the lower photo, is colorful. The terminal ♂ ♂ are primarily blue or green, often with light blue stripes, lines, or dots and a small black dot at the base of the pectoral fin (picture to the right).

Soc.B./Assoc.: Live singly or in pairs within their territories over mixed bottoms of sand and corals. They can be housed with fishes, but not with invertebrates.

M.: *H. radiatus* requires clean water ($^1/_4$ water exchange every 3 weeks), a rocky reef richly decorated with crevices and holes, and sand to burrow in.

Light: Area of sunlight.

B./Rep.: Not known.

F.: C; in nature it feeds on benthic invertebrates, especially crustacea and gastropods. Needs a varied mixed diet.

S.: The dark dorsal spots appear progressively with age. Young specimens only have the ocellus in the dorsal fin. Next the spot on the base of the tail fin appears. One or two additional spots appear at a length of 7 to 10 cm beneath the soft rayed section of the dorsal fin. These fish can reach enormous proportions.

T: 23°-27°C, **L:** 45 cm, **TL:** from 200 cm, **WM:** w, **WR:** b, **AV:** 2, **D:** 3

Halichoeres garnoti

Halichoeres radiatus, adult

Fam.: Labridae

The green wrasse, *Halichoeres chloropterus* (BLOCH, 1791), reaches a length of 12 cm and inhabits protected lagoon reefs of the Indo-Australian Archipelago that have sand, corals, rocks, and algae. The initial phase does not have a dark spot behind the pectoral fin. Very large terminal ♂ ♂ turn dark green.

The black-eared wrasse, *H. melanopomus* RANDALL, 1980, reaches a length of 20 cm and colonizes mixed bottoms of coral, sand, and rubble in deep outer reefs of the west and central Pacific. This species' coloration does not change much with growth. Juveniles lose the three ocelli on their dorsal fin. Large ♂ ♂ are slightly more colorful than initial phase animals.

The masked rainbowfish, *H. melanochir* FOWLER & BEAN, 1928, reaches a length of 15 cm and inhabits the west Pacific between Japan and the Philippines. It occurs in depths down to 30 m.

All three species are rarely imported. Besides clean water and secluded places to hide them from view, they also require sandy bottoms where they can hide. They feed on small animals such as benthic crustacea, snails, mussels, and worms. Easily kept animals once they are acclimated to feeding from the water column. They claim the entire aquarium as their territory. All conspecifics are zealously evicted or driven into the sand substrate and dare not emerge. They totally ignore other fishes.

Halichoeres chloropterus, aquarium picture

Halichoeres melanopomus

Halichoeres melanochir

Fam.: Labridae

About the Genus *Hemigymnus* GÜNTHER, 1861

Juvenile *H. melapterus,* one of the two *Hemigymnus* species, are commonly imported. The anterior body is white, and the posterior is black. This species is widely distributed. The bottom photo shows an adult half-and-half thicklip. Like parrotfishes, it sieves coral rubble with its mouth, expelling it through the gills.

Hemigymnus melapterus

Hemigymnus melapterus

Hemigymnus melapterus   (BLOCH, 1791)
Half-and-half thicklip

Hab.: Indo-Pacific; from the Red Sea to the Society Islands, Japan (N), and Lord Howe Island (S). At 5 to 30 m depth.

Sex.: There are large color differences between juveniles and adults; however, there is little sexual dichromatism.

Soc.B./Assoc.: *H. melapterus* is a loner which prefers mixed bottoms of sand, rubble, and coral. Juveniles occur in groups among branches of corals.

M.: Juveniles require hiding places that are reminiscent of branched corals. The massive size the adults attain make them unsuitable for home aquaria.

Light: Sunlight zone.

B./Rep.: Not known.

F.: C; the diet of the animals changes as they grow. Juveniles feed on planktonic crustacea from the water close to the bottom; later, they search the substrate for hard-shelled invertebrates, especially crustacea, bristleworms, brittle stars, sea urchins, molluscs, and foraminifers. Juveniles have to be offered a corresponding "plankton" substitute; later, you can change to a mixed menu of mussel and crab meat, *Mysis*, flake food, etc. In the sea, the fish take large bites from the sandy substrate, rise from the bottom, then spit the sand out. The food is sorted in the mouth, and only the edible component is retained.

S.: The animals grow very large and are easily recognized by their thick lips. Juveniles are white anteriorly, dark posteriorly, and have a yellow tail. The yellow color progressively fades. The pink and blue stripes around the eyes spread as the fish ages until adults are almost entirely covered.

T: 24°-28°C, **L:** 90 cm, **TL:** from 250 cm, **WM:** w, **WR:** b, **AV:** 1, **D:** 4 (size)

Hologymnosus annulatus   (see next page for photos)   (LACÉPÈDE, 1801)
Finescale wrasse

Hab.: Indo-Pacific; from the Red Sea to the Society Islands, Japan (N), and southeast Australia. At 3 to 25 m depth.

Sex.: They change colors during the course of growth. Initial phase adults are olive brown with dark cross-stripes on the body and a white fringe on the tail fin. Terminal ♂ ♂ are blue-green with purple cross-stripes on their sides and have an elongated tail fin.

Soc.B./Assoc.: *H. annulatus* lives singly above sandy bottoms with rocks and rubble.

M.: Do not keep this fish with small fishes lest they are eaten. It needs a lot of swimming space. Only moderately suitable for the home aquarium.

Light: Sunlight zone.

B./Rep.: Not known.

F.: C; in the sea *H. annulatus* primarily feeds on fishes. Crustacea are its second choice. Therefore, feed it small fishes until it has been taught to accept substitute foods such as crustacea and mussel meat.

S.: Juveniles are similar to young *Malacanthus latovittatus*, which also occur above sandy bottoms. It is assumed that we are dealing with mimicry. They are yellow dorsally with a reddish line. There is a very wide brown longitudinal stripe on the ventral side.

T: 25°-28°C, **L:** 25 cm, **TL:** from 150 cm, **WM:** w, **WR:** b, **AV:** 2, **D:** 3-4 (predator!)

Hologymnosus annulatus

About the Genus *Hologymnosus* LACÉPÈDE, 1801

The long body and strong tail fin found in this genus are typical characteristics of ambush predators. These attributes allow the fish to propel itself forward with a sudden burst of speed, facilitating attacks on other fishes. All four known species are over 30 cm long. All go through distinctive color changes during their development. Due to their broad distribution throughout the Indo-Pacific, they regularly reach pet stores. *Hologymnosus* wrasses, however, should

only be housed with equally large fishes in aquaria larger than 500 l. Do not combine with invertebrates.

Hologymnosus annulatus, see p. 877 for care

Hologymnosus doliatus, juvenile; adult on next page

Hologymnosus doliatus   (LACÉPÈDE, 1801)
Ringed wrasse

Hab.: Indo-Pacific; from east Africa to Samoa, the Line Islands, Japan (N), and southeast Australia. At 5 to 30 m depth.

Sex.: Juveniles are longitudinally striped, while adults have crossbars. Adults are differently colored depending on their phase. Initial phase animals are light green, bluish, or pink with 20-23 dark brownish orange crossbands. They lack a white edged caudal fin. Terminal ♂ ♂ are light blue-green to light red with bluish crossbands and a broad pale zone in the pectoral region which is framed in purple. The body is blue to blue-green with irregular pink-orange bands.

Soc.B./Assoc.: Juveniles swim in tight groups just above the bottom. Adults live singly or in loose groups 1 - 2 m above the bottom. Juveniles can be kept in groups; adults singly at best.

M.: *H. doliatus* prefers canals and depressions with a sandy bottom in clear lagoons and outer reefs from the surf zone down. Because of its fast growth and potential size, it cannot be recommended for the home aquarium.

Light: Sunlight zone.

B./Rep.: Not known.

F.: C; *H. doliatus* primarily feeds on fishes and crustacea, but brittle stars and bristleworms are also eaten. After acclimation it can be easily fed with fish, mussels, and crustacean meat, shrimp, and many other foodstuffs.

S.: The young are white with 3 slender, orange longitudinal stripes.

T: 25°-28°C, **L:** 50 cm, **TL:** from 200 cm, **WM:** w, **WR:** b, **AV:** 2, **D:** 3

Hologymnosus doliatus, adult

Macropharyngodon bipartitus ♀, see p. 882 for text

ABOUT THE GENUS *MACROPHARYNGODON* BLEEKER, 1861

This genus is comprised of 10 species. They all remain under 15 cm long and are extremely colorful. That is to say, they are ideal aquarium inhabitants. The genus name refers to the large teeth on each side of the upper mandible which protrude from the edges of the mouth, primarily in males. Defense seems to be their main purpose, since these wrasses cannot be termed aggressive, although occasional fights will break out.

All *Macropharyngodon* are initially females. Only some specimens change into males. Most live in haremlike groups, and pairs are rarely formed. Eggs and larvae are pelagic. But from a length of 1 cm and over, juvenile "macros" colonize their future living space. This is generally coral rubble and sand spots within 20 m of a coral reef. Therefore, they like shallow water. Juvenile *M. meleagris*, the species with the widest distribution, often live in the surf. There they drift close to the bottom with their heads down like pieces of seaweed. Adult animals live in deep sections of sand bottomed lagoons and upper reef slopes where they burrow during the night. The harem behavior can be exploited and several macros can be kept in one aquarium as long as there is only 1 male among the group. If the group is all females, the dominant individual will soon transform into a male. *Macropharyngodon* species are good eaters, neither bothering nor being bothered by other fishes in their proximity. They can even be housed with invertebrates. Use plenty of sand as substrate, and, as always, the animals should be as small as possible. Young specimens seem to adapt to their captive environment the best. It is interesting to observe color changes. Within one year the macros reach adulthood. Some specimens have been kept seven years in aquaria.

M. meleagris, juvenile

M. meleagris, frontal view

Fam.: Labridae

Macropharyngodon bipartitus
Divided wrasse

SMITH, 1957

Hab.: Western Indian Ocean. At depths of 2 to 25 m.

Sex.: Initial phase animals are dorsally and posteriorly orange with white spots. The ventral half of the body is dark with a network of shiny blue dots and lines. Terminal ♂ ♂ have green bands on the head and anterior body and a large U-shaped black spot on the caudal fin.

Soc.B./Assoc.: *M. bipartitus* is found above mixed bottoms of coral, rocks, and rubble, generally singly but occasionally in pairs. Maintain single specimens in a fish community tank.

M.: Rock formations with navigable passageways, some sand, and clean water are basic conditions to successfully maintain this fish.

Light: Sunlight zone.

B./Rep.: Not known.

F.: C; like other representatives of this genus, *H. bipartitus* prefers to feed on hard-shelled animals. Feed it shrimp and similar organisms, mussel meat, etc.

S.: The coloration of the Red Sea inhabitants differs somewhat from the one presented here. Therefore, they are classified as the subspecies *H. b. marisrubri*.

T: 24°-28°C, **L:** 11 cm, **TL:** from 80 cm, **WM:** w, **WR:** b, **AV:** 1-2, **D:** 3

Macropharyngodon bipartitus ♀

Macropharyngodon choati
Choat's wrasse

RANDALL, 1978

Hab.: East Australia; from the Great Barrier Reef to the southeast coast of Australia. At depths of 0.5 to 30 m.

Sex.: While there are some color differences between juveniles and adults, there are no significant differences between the sexes.

Soc.B./Assoc.: *M. choati* is most commonly encountered alone, but occasionally seen in pairs over mixed bottoms of coral, rock, and sand.

M.: Occasionally imported from Australia. *M. choati* can easily be cared for in a reef aquarium and is less sensitive than other *Macropharyngogon* species. Unfortunately, these fish are frequently infested with gill worms.

Light: Sunlight zone.

F.: C; *M. choati* feeds on small hard-shelled invertebrates in the sea. Feed it mussel and crustacean meat, shrimp, etc.

S.: *M. choati* is a species which deviates somewhat from the others. It has a few, mostly orange spots on a very silver-white body, especially when young. Juveniles have black dots on the head, the body, the dorsal and ventral fins, and the caudal peduncle (see small inset photo). Adults, in contrast, only have a black spot on the operculum.

T: 23°-26°C, **L:** 10 cm, **TL:** from 80 cm, **WM:** w, **WR:** b, **AV:** 3-4, **D:** 3

Macropharyngodon choati ♀

Macropharyngodon bipartitus ♂

Macropharyngodon choati ♂

Fam.: Labridae

Macropharyngodon kuiteri
Kuiter's wrasse

RANDALL, 1978

Hab.: East Australia; from the Great Barrier Reef to Sydney and New Caledonia. At 10 to 55 m depth.

Sex.: Initial phase ♀ ♀ are similar to juveniles. They are orange with a bluish white spot on each scale. The black opercular spot has a blue circle around it. There is a small black spot just behind the eye and another in front of the eye, again with a blue circle around it. Dorsal and anal fins have 3-4 rows of dark framed bluish dots. While terminal ♂ ♂ have no blue spots, they do have a lot of orange, and their black opercular spot has an orange and green circle around it (see picture on facing page).

Soc.B./Assoc.: *M. kuiteri* lives singly, usually at greater depths.

M.: Not known.

Light: Sunlight zone.

B./Rep.: Unknown.

F.: C (?); the dentition totally deviates from other *Macropharyngodon* species. This leads to the assumption that this species has a different diet.

S.: This east Australian species, like the previous species, is very different from others of the genus. Small juveniles are matte orange with bluish white spots. Some of these form irregular bands. Dorsal and anal fins contain two ocelli each (see small picture). They fade as the fish grows.

T: 24°-26°C, **L:** 12 cm, **TL:** from 60 cm, **WM:** w, **WR:** b, **AV:** 4, **D:** 3

Macropharyngodon kuiteri ♀

Macropharyngodon meleagris
Guinea fowl wrasse

(VALENCIENNES, 1839)

Hab.: West central Pacific from Cocos-Keeling in the Indian Ocean (not in Indonesia) to the Line Islands, the Marquesas, Japan and Lord Howe Island (S). At 0.5 to 30 m depth.

Sex.: All initial phase animals are ♀ ♀. They are whitish with numerous irregular black dots. Terminal phase ♂ ♂ are orange-red with a green spot on each scale and green bands on the head. They also have a black shoulder spot which has a few small yellow spots.

Soc.B./Assoc.: Solitary individuals are most commonly encountered. Pairs are rarely seen. They live over areas of mixed coral, sand, and rubble in front of somewhat protected reefs and reef terraces.

M.: Requires rocks with hiding places, a substrate of rubble and sand, clean oxygen-rich water, and some current.

Light: Sunlight zone.

B./Rep.: Not known.

F.: C; *M. meleagris* feeds on small hard-shelled benthic invertebrates and foraminiferans in the sea. The best substitute foods are shrimp and mussel meat.

S.: Primary phase animals were previously classified as *M. pardalis*.

T: 24°-28°C, **L:** 14 cm, **TL:** from 100 cm, **WM:** s, **WR:** b, **AV:** 1-2, **D:** 3

Macropharyngodon kuiteri ♂

Macropharyngodon meleagris ♀, ♂ on following page

Macropharyngodon meleagris ♂

Macropharyngodon negrosensis ♀

Macropharyngodon negrosensis ♂

Macropharyngodon negrosensis
Yellowspotted wrasse

HERRE, 1932

Hab.: West central Pacific; from the Philippines to Samoa, Japan (N), and the Great Barrier Reef. At depths of 8 to 32 m.

Sex.: *M. negrosensis* is very variable, and animals from different regions are often different colors. Juveniles and initial phase ♀♀ are basically very similar (see small picture). Terminal ♂♂ are primarily black with blue-green edged scales and light yellow bands on the head and back (see large photo). Ventral and anal fins of ♂♂ and ♀♀ are black; the caudal fin of both is pale and transparent; only ♂♂ have a dark fringed caudal fin.

Soc.B./Assoc.: *M. negrosensis* lives singly above mixed bottoms of rocks and live corals.

M.: Unknown.

Light: Sun and moderately lit areas.

B./Rep.: Not known.

F.: C; not known. Probably like related species.

S.: This rare species is normally found at depths below 15 m.

T: 24°-28°C, **L:** 12 cm, **TL:** from 100 cm, **WM:** w, **WR:** b, **AV:** 3-4, **D:** 3

Fam.: Labridae

An additional Indo-Pacific genus with 8 species. The male's body has blue colored stripes that are typical for the genus. All are less than 15 cm long and live in small groups on top of reefs.

Stethojulis albovittata

Stethojulis strigriventer

The bluelined wrasse, *Stethojulis albovittata* BONATERRE, 1755, reaches a length of 15 cm, inhabits the western Indian Ocean and Red Sea, and is easily distinguished by its dark body and light ventral area. All species of this genus need a varied diet and a layer of sand to burrow in.

The three-ribbon rainbowfish, *S. strigriventer* BENNETT, 1832, reaches a length of 15 cm and inhabits the Indo-Pacific from east Africa to Samoa. The solid blue line running through the dark band is species specific.

The three-lined wrasse, *S. trilineata* BLOCH & SCHNEIDER, 1802, hails from the Indo-Australian Archipelago. At 12 cm it is slightly smaller than other wrasses of the genus. It has 3 solid, roughly parallel, white-blue lines running along its side.

The orange-axil wrasse, *S. bandanensis* BLEEKER, 1851, inhabits the west and central Pacific from the Christmas Island in the Indian Ocean to the Marquesas. It feeds on small bottom oriented planktonic crustacea and invertebrates it finds in the ground. It reaches a length of 15 cm, and its blue lines are characteristically curved in the head and chest region.

Stethojulis trilineata

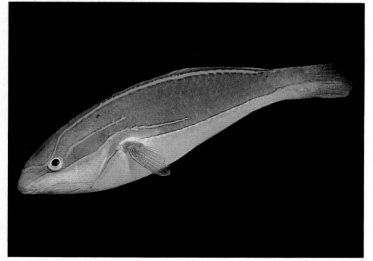

Stethojulis bandanensis

Fam.: Labridae

This genus is represented in all the seas of the world. It contains 22 species. Juveniles and adults are primarily found above shallow, tropical reefs. Their nimble movements are a joy for divers and snorkelers, even in the temperate Mediterranean waters where *Thalassoma pavo,* the rainbow wrasse, lives. The picture on the opposite page also shows the different color stages of the fish. Primary males nervously guard over juveniles and large females to inhibit them from changing into males and taking over the harem. This genus includes juveniles that use stinging anemones for protection (*T. bifasciatum* from the Caribbean and *T. amblycephalum* from the Indo-Pacific). Studies have shown that they coat themselves in the anemone's mucus like Pomacentridae. This apparently raises the firing threshold of the nematocysts. Many *Thalassoma* species pick food particles from the actinians.

Only single specimens can be cared for in an aquarium despite their social behavior in the sea. Although species such as *T. lunare* and *T. bifasciatum* will swim in groups and not display aggressive behavior in large tanks, keeping more than one individual in small home aquaria is simply courting trouble.

Thalassoma species like deep sandy bottoms, but will also retire into a reef. In their natural biotope, they feed on benthic foods as well as zooplankton from the water column above the reef. This characteristic makes them easily trained to frozen *Mysis, Artemia,* or even flake foods floating on the surface. They cannot be trusted with tubeworms, feather stars, colonial anemones, crabs, or snails.

Thalassoma pavo, all developmental stages

Thalassoma amblycephalum (BLEEKER, 1856)
Rainbow wrasse

Hab.: Indo-Pacific; from east Africa to the Marquesas, Tuamotu, Japan (N), and Lord Howe Island (S). At 1 to 15 m depth.

Sex.: Initial phase ♂ ♂ and ♀ ♀ as well as juveniles are basically equal in coloration. They are white with a brown-black jagged longitudinal stripe. Terminal phase individuals are secondary ♂ ♂ that evolved from ♀ ♀. These ♂ ♂ are a riot of color. They have a blue head, a yellow shoulder, and a red body.

Soc.B./Assoc.: Juveniles and initial phase animals live in groups above the pinnacles of isolated coral blocks or along reef edges. Secondary ♂ ♂ occupy large territories and are solitary and aggressive. Juveniles can be kept in small groups; but consider what you will do with the animals when they mature into adults. Their restless movements betray their unease in small aquaria; unlike most fishes, they do not resign themselves to captivity. Hence, they do not make good aquarium fish.

M.: Most *Thalassoma* live in rock hiding places and not in the sand. They are fast swimmers that require plenty of space. Therefore, decorate the aquarium with rock edifications riddled with hiding places and a sand substrate in case you have an unidentified species that may be a burrower.

Light: Area of sunlight.

B./Rep.: Primary ♂ ♂ and ♀ ♀ spawn in groups in the sea; territorial ♂ ♂ spawn in pairs.

F.: C; in the sea, *T. amblycephalum* feeds primarily on crustaceanlike zooplankton such as shrimp, crab larvae, *Mysis*, copepods, and others. It is therefore best to feed it with similar crustacea.

S.: None.

T: 24°-28°C, **L:** 14 cm, **TL:** from 100 cm, **WM: m, WR:** b, m, **AV:** 1-2, **D:** 3

Thalassoma amblycephalum

Thalassoma commersoni (VALENCIENNES, 1839)
Commerson's wrasse

Hab.: Mauritius.

S.: *T. commersoni* lives in the same region as *T. genivittatum,* Mauritius to east Africa. Some authors consider these two species one and the same. See page 898.

Thalassoma amblycephalum ♂

Thalassoma commersoni

Fam.: Labridae

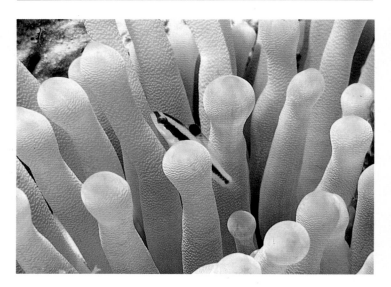

Thalassoma bifasciatum　　　　　　　　　　　　　　　　　(BLOCH, 1781)
Bluehead wrasse

Hab.: Caribbean Sea and tropical Atlantic. At 3 to 30 m depth.

Sex.: Initial phase ♂ ♂ and ♀ ♀ generally maintain the yellow juvenile coloration. But the black stripe along the side of the body usually fades as the fish ages until only a shadow remains. The secondary ♂ ♂, which result from the sexual transformation of ♀ ♀, undergo a dramatic color change and become primarily blue with two black crossbands in the shoulder region.

Soc.B./Assoc.: Juveniles and initial phase animals like to live together in dense groups above reefs with rocks and live coral. Secondary ♂ ♂ are territorial. Juveniles can be kept in groups with most fishes, but not invertebrates.

M.: *T. bifasciatum* is sensitive to poor water quality. Perform frequent partial water exchanges. Sufficient swimming space and rock edifications with hiding places are necessary.

Light: Sunlight zone.

B./Rep.: Initial phase fishes spawn in groups; terminal phase animals spawn in pairs.

F.: C; whereas juveniles are capable of gaining all their nourishment from their cleaning activities along the reef, this is impossible in an aquarium. Feed both juveniles and adults a varied diet strong in small crustacea. *Artemia*! Fish and sea urchin eggs are favorite foods.

S.: None.

T: 23°-26°C, **L:** 15 cm, **TL:** from 100 cm, **WM:** m, **WR:** b-t, **AV:** 1, **D:** 3

Thalassoma bifasciatum ♂

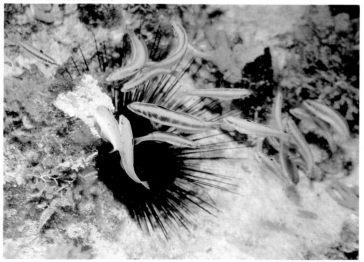

Thalassoma bifasciatum, juveniles surrounding a ♀

Fam.: Labridae

Thalassoma duperreyi
Saddle wrasse

(QUOY & GAIMARD, 1834)

Hab.: Hawaii. At 5 to 25 m depth.

Sex.: Juveniles are uniformly dark dorsally and light ventrally. When the fish are 6 cm long, the adult coloration (initial phase) develops. Three beautiful distinct colors emerge; a blue head, a broad orange band, and a green posterior body. Secondary ♂ ♂ are a dark blue-green (small picture with cleaner fish).

Soc.B./Assoc.: Initial phase animals live singly or in groups on coral and rock reefs. Secondary ♂ ♂ are territorial loners. Since the animals grow quite large, limit yourself to one specimen per fish community. Do not keep with invertebrates.

M.: These fish, like all *Thalassoma*, require clean water, plenty of swimming space, and rocks with numerous hiding possibilities.

Light: Area of sunlight.

B./Rep.: In the sea, initial phase fish are sometimes seen spawning in large groups; terminal ♂ ♂ spawn in pairs.

F.: C; feed a varied diet. These heavy eaters quickly grow into large, bullish tankmates.

S.: At diving bases where fishes are fed, droves of *T. duperreyi* often follow divers to fight over the food. *T. duperreyi* is the most common wrasse on the Hawaiian Islands.

T: 22°-26°C, **L:** 30 cm, **TL:** from 150 cm, **WM:** w, **WR:** b-t, **AV:** 2-3, **D:** 3

Thalassoma duperreyi

Thalassoma duperreyi

Thalassoma duperreyi

Fam.: Labridae

Thalassoma genivittatum   (VALENCIENNES, 1839)
Redcheek wrasse

Hab.: Indian Ocean, from Mauritius to South Africa. At depths from 4 to 25 m.

Sex.: The initial phase is dorsally dark brown changing to yellow on the caudal peduncle. The ventral area is greenish with a red vertical line on each scale. The head is dark red with yellow cheeks and a wide reddish band below the snout. The picture on the right is a terminal ♂ (secondary).

Soc.B./Assoc.: *T. genivittatum* usually lives singly above coral reefs.

M.: *T. genivittatum* is peaceful towards other fishes.

Light: Area of sunlight.

B./Rep.: Not known.

F.: C; feeds on hard-shelled invertebrates. Feed similar substitute foods, including frozen foods.

S.: This species was/is sometimes confused with *T. commersoni*. Some consider these two species one and the same.

T: 21°-24°C, **L:** 20 cm, **TL:** from 100 cm, **WM:** w, **WR:** b-m, **AV:** 2-3, **D:** 3

Thalassoma hardwickii   (BENNETT, 1828)
Sixbar wrasse

Hab.: Indo-Pacific; from east Africa to Tuamotu, Japan (N), and the Australian Islands (S). At 0.5 to 15 m depth.

Sex.: There are no major color differences between juvenile and adult fish. Secondary ♂♂ are slightly more colorful.

Soc.B./Assoc.: Groups of young *T. hardwickii* inhabit shallow lagoons and outer reefs. Adults live singly or in loose groups.

M.: Prefers clear, moving water and mixed bottoms of coral, rubble, and sand along the upper edge of protected reefs. These conditions, if possible, should be offered in the aquarium.

Light: Sunlight region.

B./Rep.: Initial phase animals spawn in groups; secondary ♂♂ usually spawn in pairs.

F.: C; *T. hardwickii* feeds on a great variety of benthic and planktonic crustacea, small fishes, and foraminiferans. It has a hardy appetite and is easily trained to substitute foods. Offer a wide variety of foods to this robust fish.

S.: At diving stations where fishes are fed, even secondary ♂♂ abandon their territories and swarm in large groups around the diver or snorkeler. They eagerly rip offered animal fare from divers' hands; if nothing is offered, they pinch fingers or legs.

T: 24°-28°C, **L:** 20 cm, **TL:** from 110 cm, **WM:** m-s, **WR:** b-t, **AV:** 1-2, **D:** 3

Thalassoma hardwickii

Thalassoma genivittatum

Thalassoma hardwickii

Fam.: Labridae

Thalassoma hebraicum   (LACÉPÈDE, 1801)
Goldbar wrasse

Hab.: Western Indian Ocean to South Africa. At depths of 3 to 30 m.

Sex.: Primary animals are very similarly colored to the pictured terminal phase animal. Initial phase animals are a bit darker and plainer since they have black lines instead of blue lines on a gray body (like the pictured animal). But they do have two longitudinal stripes of diffuse yellowish dots. The yellow crossband is about equal in both phases. Terminal ♂ ♂ often have more yellow on the head and posterior body than the pictured individual.

Soc.B./Assoc.: Usually lives singly on reefs above rocky bottoms.

M.: *T. hebraicum* requires rock formations with hiding places, clean water, and plenty of swimming space.

Light: Sunlight zone.

B./Rep.: Not known.

F.: C; *T. hebraicum* feeds on benthic invertebrates in the sea. In the aquarium it should be fed a broad range of the usual substitute foods.

S.: None.

T: 22°-26°C, **L:** 23 cm, **TL:** from 150 cm, **WM:** w, **WR:** b-t, **AV:** 3-4, **D:** 3

Thalassoma janseni   (BLEEKER, 1856)
Jansen's wrasse

Hab.: Indo-Pacific, from the Maldives to the Fiji Islands, Japan (N), and Lord Howe Island (S). At 1 to 15 m depth.

Sex.: All ages and sexes of *T. janseni* have about the same combination of colors. Secondary ♂ ♂ are, of course, more colorful.

Soc.B./Assoc.: *T. janseni* is quite rare and usually lives singly on the edges of exposed lagoons and outer reefs.

M.: This fish requires very clear, oxygen-rich, moving water. Ensure plenty of swimming space and furnish the aquarium with rock edifications that have good hiding possibilities.

Light: Sunlight region.

B./Rep.: Not known.

F.: C; *T. janseni* prefers crustaceanlike fare which should be offered in a variety of forms.

S.: None.

T: 24°-28°C, **L:** 17 cm, **TL:** from 120 cm, **WM:** s, **WR:** b-t, **AV:** 2-3, **D:** 3

Thalassoma janseni, juvenile

Thalassoma hebraicum

Thalassoma janseni

Fam.: Labridae

Thalassoma klunzingeri   FOWLER & STEINITZ, 1956
Klunzinger's wrasse

Hab.: Red Sea. At 1 to 30 m depth.

Sex.: Juvenile, initial, and terminal phase animals are quite similarly colored; only secondary ♂♂ acquire dark fin fringes.

Soc.B./Assoc.: *T. klunzingeri* are solitary living fish. Young will sometimes live in loose groups above coral reefs. They are good additions for fish community aquaria.

M.: Clean water, some current, and plenty of swimming space as well as some refuges are required for the successful care of this fish.

Light: Sunlight zone.

B./Rep.: Not known.

F.: C; in the sea, *T. klunzingeri* feeds on many different invertebrates. In the aquarium it should be offered a variety of foods. Ensure that crustacea are included.

S.: Secondary ♂♂ form territories that are defended against conspecifics. Even divers are confronted. At diving bases where fishes are fed, they partially relinquish their territoriality and surround the feeder in droves.

T: 24°-28°C, **L:** 25 cm, **TL:** from 150 cm, **WM:** m, **WR:** b-t, **AV:** 2-3, **D:** 3

Thalassoma klunzingeri

Thalassoma lucasanum   (GILL, 1863)
Cortez rainbow wrasse

Hab.: East Pacific, Gulf of California. At 3 to 25 m depth.

Sex.: Juveniles and initial phase animals are yellow with two dark broad longitudinal stripes, one centrally along the body and the other from the forehead along the back. The space between the broad, dark stripes on the head is blue; the stomach is white. With progressing age, the yellow fades, and the lateral stripe on the body becomes ragged and broader. Only secondary ♂♂ present the colorful dress pictured here.

Soc.B./Assoc.: Initial phase ♂♂ and ♀♀ commonly live in small groups. Large groups are occasionally seen above rocky bottoms. Secondary ♂♂ live alone. Associate with other fishes, not with invertebrates.

M.: *T. lucasanum* requires a rock aquarium with many hiding places and plenty of swimming space.

Light: Area of sunlight.

B./Rep.: In the sea, initial phase animals spawn in large groups of 50 or more specimens. Secondary ♂♂ search for ♀♀ and spawn pairwise.

F.: C; juveniles sometimes clean other fishes of parasites. Feed them a variety of foods, especially crustacean or crab meat.

S.: This fish, which is common in the Gulf of California, is rarely imported into Germany.

T: 20°-24°C, **L:** 18 cm, **TL:** from 120 cm, **WM:** w, **WR:** b-t, **AV:** 4, **D:** 3

Thalassoma klunzingeri

Thalassoma lucasanum

Fam.: Labridae

Thalassoma lunare (LINNAEUS, 1758)
Lyretail wrasse

Hab.: Indo-Pacific; from the Red Sea to the Line Islands, Japan (N), and Lord Howe Island (S). At 1 to 20 m depth.

Sex.: Although this fish basically retains the essence of its juvenile coloration, secondary ♂♂ have startling colors.

Soc.B./Assoc.: *T. lunare* usually live in groups composed of one territorial ♂ and several to many initial phase animals in shallow parts of lagoons and coastal and outer reefs.

M.: *T. lunare* prefers clear, moving, oxygen-rich water. It demands a lot of swimming space. A hardy, peaceful creature that makes a choice aquarium animal; only large, territorial secondary ♂♂ may be quarrelsome.

Light: Sunlight zone.

B./Rep.: In the sea, groupwise spawning occurs.

F.: C; *T. lunare* primarily feeds on small benthic invertebrates, especially crustacea. Fish eggs, snail eggs, etc., are also part of its natural diet.

S.: Because of its beautiful colors and swimming habits, *T. lunare* is an appreciated, commonly imported aquarium fish.

T: 24°-28°C, **L:** 20 cm, **TL:** from 110 cm, **WM:** s, **WR:** b-t, **AV:** 1, **D:** 3

Thalassoma lunare ♂

Thalassoma lutescens (LAY & BENNETT, 1839)
Yellow wrasse

Hab.: Indo-Pacific; from Sri Lanka to Panama, Japan, Hawaii (N), and Lord Howe, Ducie, and Rapa Islands (S). At 1 to 30 m depth.

Sex.: While juveniles may be totally yellow, initial phase individuals usually have orange hues and a linear design on the body. Only secondary ♂♂ develop the rich colors seen in the picture on the opposite page.

Soc.B./Assoc.: The animals usually live singly above sand, gravel, or dense coral growth in shallow exposed inner and outer reefs.

M.: *T. lutescens* likes a diversely furnished tank that includes such things as rocks, caves, stones, and sand. Provide water movement and plenty of swimming space.

Light: Sunlight zone.

B./Rep.: Not known.

F.: C; *T. lutescens* feeds on a number of benthic hard-shelled invertebrates such as crabs, shrimp, snails, mussels, brittle stars, sea urchins, and others. It also feeds on fish eggs in its native waters. Offer a diverse menu.

S.: None.

T: 24°-28°C, **L:** 22 cm, **TL:** from 100 cm, **WM:** s, **WR:** b-t, **AV:** 1-2, **D:** 3

Thalassoma lutescens, juvenile

Thalassoma lunare

Thalassoma lutescens ♂

Fam.: Labridae

Thalassoma pavo (VALENCIENNES, 1758)
Rainbow wrasse, peacock wrasse

Hab.: Mediterranean Sea and the east Atlantic. At 1 to 15 m depth.

Sex.: Juveniles and primary phase individuals are yellow with numerous fine crossbands. There are ca. 5 broad bluish crossbands that transect the juveniles along the length of their bodies. One, the broad shoulder band, remains in initial phase animals. Secondary ♂♂ are mostly blue with an elongated tail fin.

Soc.B./Assoc.: Juveniles live singly or in loose groups; secondary ♂♂ establish large territories where juveniles and initial phase animals are free to reside.

M.: The fish like rock formations covered with algae and a sand layer a few centimeters deep. Unlike most *Thalassoma,* they burrow at night.

Light: Area of sunlight.

B./Rep.: The animals spawn in the sea during the summer. The eggs are pelagic.

F.: C; *T. pavo* feeds on numerous small invertebrates that it finds amid the aufwuchs. Feed it a varied animal diet.

S.: *T. pavo* can be kept at significantly lower temperatures than its relatives from tropical seas. It tends to be less sensitive.

T: 18°-22°C, **L:** 25 cm, **TL:** from 100 cm, **WM:** w-m, **WR:** b-t, **AV:** 1, **D:** 3

Xenojulis margaritaceus

About the Genus *Xenojulis* de Beaufort, 1939

Xenojulis is closely related to the genus *Macropharyngodon* and is monotypic; that is, there is only one species, *Xenojulis margaritaceus*. It lives in shallow waters above coral debris and/or seagrass. A surprisingly little imported fish.

Xenojulis margaritaceus   (MACLEAY, 1884)
Pink speckled wrasse

Hab.: West Pacific, from the Philippines to New Guinea. At 2 to 10 m depth.

Sex.: None (?).

Soc.B./Assoc.: Lives singly or in pairs; a suitable addition for a fish aquarium.

M.: It requires a rock aquarium with clean water and many niches.

Light: Sunlight zone.

B./Rep.: Not known.

F.: C; feeds on small invertebrates. Accepts all kinds of foods.

S.: The irregular, sometimes aligned pearly silver spots on its sides are typical for *X. margaritaceus*. The 5 indistinct, dark crossbands on the body and the two black spots, one in front of the hard rayed dorsal fin and the other in the soft rayed section, are hard to distinguish on this photo.

T: 24°-28°C, **L:** 10 cm, **TL:** from 70 cm, **WM:** w, **WR:** b, **AV:** 3-4, **D:** 3

Fam.: Labridae

About the Labrichthys Group

This group is distinguished from the subfamily Corinae by their feeding habits. While some species are facultative cleaners, most are obligate cleaners throughout their life. Some establish cleaner stations that clients visit (large coral reef fishes). Others travel around in the reef and offer their services to territorial fishes in their region. The latter also feed on coral polyps and seem to be the only wrasses that do so. The mouth is terminal, and the lips protrude forward like a pipe, analog to a "kissing mouth." *Aspidontus taeniatus,* the cleaner mimic, looks just like a *Labroides* cleaner wrasse, except it has an inferior mouth.

About the Genus *Labrichthys* Bleeker, 1854

This genus of wrasses only contains one widely distributed species. From east Africa to Samoa in the Pacific, *Labrichthys unilineatus* is found at depths between 0.5 m and 20 m. It is named *unilineatus* because of the line juveniles have along their side. By the time the fish is full-grown and 15 cm long, the line has disappeared and the fish has its adult coloration. This is a facultative cleaner that also eats antler coral polyps. It can be housed with peaceful fishes such as gobies and coral perches. A welcomed addition to invertebrate tanks that do not contain stony corals.

Labrichthys unilineatus, juvenile

Labrichthys unilineatus ♂

Labrichthys unilineatus ♀

Invertebrate aquarium with leather coral and a giant clam—a preview to vol. 2.

About the Genus *Diproctacanthus* BLEEKER, 1862

There is only one species in this genus, *Diproctacanthus xanthurus*. It lives along the Australian Archipelago and only grows to 5 cm. In contrast to species of the genus *Labroides, D. xanthurus* travels around the coral reef to offer its cleaning services to territorial damselfishes and others. It is not as dedicated to cleaning as *Labroides*. It has adopted a more happenstance attitude. Stomach contents have revealed coral polyps.

Diproctacanthus xanthurus
Yellow-tailed cleaner

(BLEEKER, 1856)

Hab.: Indo-Australia, from Java to the Philippines and New Guinea. At 2 to 20 m depth.

Sex.: While juveniles are black with two white longitudinal stripes that continue to the caudal peduncle (the tail fin is mostly black), adults are colored as in the picture above. The black stripes become a more pronounced brown, and the yellow fades.

Soc.B./Assoc.: *D. xanthurus* lives singly and roams within relatively large areas. It can be associated with fishes, but under no circumstances should it be put in an aquarium with live corals.

M.: Decorate a large tank with assorted materials and stock it with moderate-sized fishes. Pomacentrides are a good choice.

Light: Sunlight zone.

B./Rep.: Not known.

F.: C; *D. xanthurus* usually clean for their dinner, but they will also feed on coral polyps. Since it cannot live solely by cleaning aquarium inhabitants, bite-sized substitute foods, especially in the form of small crustacea, have to be offered. The transition is often difficult. Live *Artemia* of any size and, after acclimation, frozen foods become its main diet in the aquarium.

S.: In contrast to most other cleaner fishes, *D. xanthurus* does not establish a cleaner station. Instead, it widely roams the reef in search of clients, primarily territorial species of damsel- and clownfishes (Pomacentridae).

T: 24°-28°C, **L:** 6 cm, **TL:** from 80 cm, **WM:** w, **WR:** b-m, **AV:** 3, **D:** 3

Fam.: Labridae

The most fascinating, well-known cleaner fishes are those that set up a cleaning station that fish enter, communicate their willingness to be cleaned, are cleaned, and then leave. A symbiotic relationship is formed. The patrons are cleaned of disturbing parasites, whereas the wrasse obtains food in the form of the ectoparasites. *L. dimidiatus* is not the only cleaner wrasse. There are five species within this genus that engage in cleaning activities, and they all live in the tropical Indo-Pacific. In contrast to others of the Labrichthys group, these fishes are quite thorough. No stone is left unturned so to speak. Behind the operculum and into the mouth, all nicks and crannies are freed of parasites! The predatory instinct is turned off in the client that is soliciting the cleaner wrasses' services. The recipient of the services seems to fall into a trance; its breathing slows and turns irregular, often its body stands vertically in the water, and its mouth and opercula are spread open. In part, the coloration also changes to help the cleaner fish recognize the ectoparasites. The patrons can readily identify cleaner wrasses by their longitudinal stripes. Cleaner wrasses also perform a "dance" to entice their clientele to accept their services. These whipping body movements are more pronounced in young cleaners. The wrasse slowly swims forward, constantly swinging its hind body with its spread caudal fin up and down. When the patron signals its readiness, the cleaner wrasse swims to him and beats the fish with its ventral fins. It then commences its work by studying the offered body sections. The client tells the wrasse to stop with twitching motions. The wrasse relents. In seawater aquaria, *Labroides* maintain their cleaning instinct that makes them so popular among aquarists. In the reef, a small harem of 1 dominant male and several small females is normal. Cleaning is not necessarily an individual activity. Often the chore is shared. Pairs also form in an aquarium as long as there are different sexes. Since there is little sexual dimorphism, you should buy different sized cleaner fish to avoid quarrels among them. Only *L. bicolor* has sexual dichromatism. The male, which grows over 10 cm, can be recognized by a bright spot on the posterior body which dissolves the line pattern found in females. All *Labroides* species accept substitute foods such as *Mysis* and krill.

Labroides dimidiatus, courtship in an aquarium.

Labroides dimidiatus on a large *Naso.*

Labroides bicolor

Labroides dimidiatus, Fiji form

Labroides bicolor

Labroides bicolor

Labroides bicolor   (FOWLER & BEAN, 1828)
Bicolored cleaner wrasse

Hab.: Indo-Pacific; from east Africa to the Line, Marquesas, and Society Islands, Japan (N), and Lord Howe Island (S). At 2 to 20 m depth.

Sex.: Although there are several color variants, juveniles and adults are essentially equally colored: the posterior body, the caudal peduncle, and the majority of the tail fin are yellowish or white. The tail fin may have a dark fringe. In full-grown animals, the dark stripes merge in the center of the body, forming a uniform black semicircle against a yellow or white posterior body. The yellow or white extends to the black fringe of the caudal fin.

Soc.B./Assoc.: Young animals live singly; adults may be found in pairs. They are appropriate companions for all types of fishes.

M.: Decorate the aquarium with rocks that contain caves and niches. Ensure that there are open and covered swimming areas.

Light: Sunlight area.

B./Rep.: Not known.

F.: C; this cleaner fish also searches for parasites, loose skin particles, and mucus on tankmates. However, it cannot find enough nourishment in this alone. It must be trained to accept substitute foods, which is not always easy. *Artemia* of any kind and flake foods are soon accepted.

S.: Young and half-grown animals normally set up cleaner stations, usually on large overhangs or in caves within rocks or coral blocks near the reef's edge. Adults tend to be more migratory cleaners which, alone or in pairs, patrol large areas and clean by request only.

T: 24°-28°C, **L:** 14 cm, **TL:** from 100 cm, **WM:** w, **WR:** b, **AV:** 2, **D:** 3

Fam.: Labridae

Labroides dimidiatus (VALENCIENNES, 1839)
Bluestreak cleaner wrasse

Hab.: Indo-Pacific; from the Red Sea to the Line, Marquesas, and Ducie Islands, Japan (N), and Lord Howe and Rapa Islands (S). At 1 to 30 m depth.

S.D.: None.

Soc.B./Assoc.: *L. dimidiatus* lives singly, in pairs, or in harems on conspicuous sections of the reef. Do not keep more than two specimens in a fish aquarium; one is probably better.

M.: The fish sleep in small snug holes in rocks and reefs. They should be offered clean water and plenty of swimming space.

Light: Sunlight zone. This cleaner will occasionally jump out of the aquarium (fright reaction?). As a precaution, the tank should either have a good cover or a low water level. These, of course, are appropriate measures for all active, jumping fishes!

B./Rep.: Pairs regulary spawn in the aquarium. Courtship is a beautiful sight. The eggs are released into the open water and are identical in size and appearance to those of pygmy angelfishes (*Centropyge*). Larval rearing has not been successful. Spawning occurs once a day and only during twilight hours.

F.: C; in contrast to many of the cleaner fishes that are difficult to train to substitute foods, *L. dimidiatus* can be acclimated relatively easily. Of course, it pursues its cleaning trade, but it cannot fulfill its nutritional needs from this activity alone in an aquarium. *Artemia*, flake foods, and FD foods are readily taken.

S.: *L. dimidiatus* is the best known and most widely distributed cleaner fish. This species was the first to have its cleaning behavior precisely studied and described. It inhabits all reef areas of inner lagoons, reef terraces, and outer reefs from the surface to profound depths.

T: 24°-28°C, **L:** 10 cm, **TL:** from 80 cm, **WM:** w, **WR:** b-t, **AV:** 1, **D:** 2

CLEANER WRASSES AND MIMICRY (LEFT AND BOTTOM PHOTOS)

L. dimidiatus has regular cleaner stations where fishes wanting to be cleaned of parasites or loose skin particles arrive of their own reconnaissance. There they adopt a totally unnatural posture, often with the head up, down, or in another slanted position. They spread their fins and open their mouth or opercula to indicate their readiness to be cleaned and what spots are the "dirtiest." *L. dimidiatus* cleans small fishes, predators, and large fishes such as groupers, moray eels, eagle rays, and manta rays. It fearlessly swims into their mouth. And it is permitted to come back out! A blenny, *Aspidontus taeniatus,* mimics cleaner wrasses in behavior, shape, and color. The poor unsuspecting fish allows these "cleaner" fish near and, WHAM!, the *A. teniatus* bites a piece of their skin off. Mimicking cleaner fishes gives this (parasitic) fish a good, free meal.

While fishes cannot differentiate *A. taeniatus* from cleaner wrasses, we can see the difference in the mouth position. Its inferior mouth holds saberlike teeth.

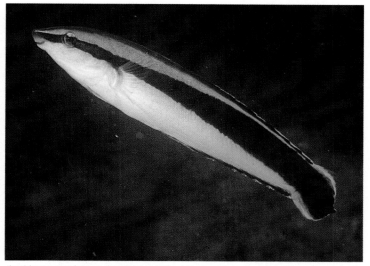

Aspidontus taeniatus, a despised species. However, it can be placed in an invertebrate aquarium without fishes.

Fam.: Labridae

Labroides phthirophagus

The three cleaner fishes on these pages are very similar; however, under closer scrutiny you can easily see significant differences. Additionally, they are geographically separated. However, imported animals require a more exact examination of the chest region to determine species.
Follow maintenance and care suggestions given for *Labroides bicolor*.

The hawaiian cleaner wrasse, *Labroides phthirophagus* RANDALL, 1958, differs from both the others by a distinct, continuous black line and the absence of a spot or line on the chest. The caudal fin has a dorsal and ventral reddish blue to wine red edge. This cleaner fish reaches a length of 10 cm and only occurs in Hawaii.

The false bluestreak wrasse, *L. pectoralis* RANDALL & SPRINGER, 1975, has a black spot beneath the insertion point of the pectoral fins as the main characteristic. It occurs in several color variations, including a bicolored variant with a light anterior body (whitish or yellow) and a dark posterior body and caudal fin. It lacks the anterior black stripe. The longitudinally striped variant (see picture) has a black band through the head and chest region which widens significantly posteriorly. *L. pectoralis* grows to a length of 7 cm and inhabits the western Pacific. Normally a well marked cleaner station is manned in pairs.

The redlip cleaner wrasse, *L. rubrolabiatus* RANDALL, 1958, although similar to *L. pectoralis,* lacks the roundish black chest spot. Instead, it has a slender black longitudinal stripe on the side of the head. The black stripe in the center of the body may be very faint or totally absent in larger animals (see picture). The fish hails from the central Pacific.

Labroides rubrolabiatus

Labroides pectoralis

Fam.: Labridae

About the Genus *Labropsis* Schmidt, 1930

There are more species in the genus *Labropsis* than there are in *Labroides*. All six have a distinctive thick-lipped mouth and are facultative cleaners, especially when young. Full-grown animals feed on coral polyps. *Labropsis xanthonota* is the only species found in the Indian Ocean. The other species are distributed along the Indo-Australian Archipelago. There is clear sexual dichromatism.

Labropsis manabei   (SCHMIDT, 1930)
Oriental wrasse

Hab.: West Pacific, from Japan to the Philippines. At 5 to 20 m depth.

Sex.: Juveniles have black and white striations down the length of their bodies (see picture). Adults of both sexes are a similar uniform dark color.

Soc.B./Assoc.: The animals live singly or in pairs under the protection of branched corals.

M.: Provide clean water, sufficient swimming space, and structures that resemble branched corals, either plastic or rock.

Light: Area of sunlight.

B./Rep.: Not known.

F.: C; *L. manabei* acts as a cleaner fish in the sea, primarily servicing smaller fishes such as damsels and clownfishes. Difficult to train to substitute foods. *Artemia*.

S.: While the young are reluctant to leave the protection of branched corals, adults move 1 m and more from the protection of the substrate to attend their cleaning clients.

T: 24°-27°C, **L:** 9 cm, **TL:** from 80 cm, **WM:** w, **WR:** b, **AV:** 2-3, **D:** 3

Labropsis xanthonota   RANDALL, 1981
Yellowback wrasse

Hab.: Indo-Pacific; from east Africa to Samoa, Japan (N), and the Great Barrier Reef (S). At depths of 7 to 55 m.

Sex.: The young, as pictured here, are black with fine white stripes. ♀♀ are yellowish dorsally. Secondary ♂♂ develop scales with golden centers, blue lines on the head, and a wedge-shaped white spot at the center of the tail fin.

Soc.B./Assoc.: *L. xanthonota* is a rare loner found in outer lagoon reefs and outer reefs rich in corals.

M.: *L. xanthonota*'s diet and high water quality requirements do not make it a model aquarium fish.

Light: Sunlight area.

B./Rep.: Not known.

F.: C; juveniles work as cleaners; adults, however, primarily feed on coral polyps. They are very difficult to train to substitute foods.

S.: None.

T: 24°-27°C, **L:** 12 cm, **TL:** from 80 cm, **WM:** w, **WR:** b-t, **AV:** 3, **D:** 3

Labropsis manabei ♀

Labropsis xanthonota ♀

Labropsis alleni cleans *Cirrhilabrus lubbocki*, Flores

Labropsis alleni ♀

Larabicus quadrilineatus

ABOUT THE GENUS *LARABICUS* RANDALL & SPRINGER, 1973

This monotypic genus is found in the Red Sea. Its behavior is similar to other members of the Labrichthys group.

The fourline wrasse, *Larabicus quadrilineatus* RANDALL & SPRINGER, 1973, inhabits the Red Sea and the Gulf of Aden and can be easily recognized by its solid black and blue longitudinal stripes. However, only juveniles and initial phase animals have this coloring. Secondary males lose the blue stripes and acquire a curved blue band underneath the eye. This species grows to a length of 12 cm, and only juveniles are cleaners; adults primarily feed on coral polyps. Only occasionally imported.

Juvenile Allen's wrasse, *Labropsis alleni* RANDALL, 1981, have the typical longitudinally striped uniform for cleaners. Their coloration and diet changes as the fish reach adulthood, and they begin searching for food along the substrate. It lives at depths of 4 to 52 m and prefers lagoons and outer reefs.

Fam.: Labridae

About the Genus *Pseudodax* Bleeker, 1861

Pseudodax's unique dentition places it in its own subfamily: Pseudo-dacinae. The common name of the only representative of this monotypic genus, chiseltooth wrasse, further emphasizes its note-worthy teeth. The juvenile coloration of 2 blue longitudinal stripes is typical for cleaners from the Labrichthys group. *Pseudodax moluccanus* is distributed from the Red Sea to Japan. It can only be recommended for community fish tanks, since invertebrates of all kinds are its main sustenance.

Pseudodax moluccanus, subadult

Pseudodax moluccanus, adult

Pseudodax moluccanus, juvenile

Pseudodax moluccanus
Chiseltooth wrasse

(VALENCIENNES, 1939)

Hab.: Indo-West Pacific; from the Red Sea and east Africa up to Japan. At depths of 4 to 40 m.

Sex.: While juveniles look like cleaner fishes, initial and terminal phase ♂ ♂ and ♀ ♀ are about equal in coloration. They have a dark stripe on each scale and a white and black striped tail fin.

Soc.B./Assoc.: *P. moluccanus* lives singly or in pairs on clear water reefs. It can be housed with fishes, but not invertebrates.

M.: Little known. It requires rock formations with corresponding hiding places and plenty of swimming space.

Light: Area of sunlight.

B./Rep.: Not known.

F.: C; juveniles not only imitate the coloration of cleaner fishes, but also act as such. Adults feed on hard-shelled benthic organisms and can be fed many types of substitute fare. The teeth have to be watched. If they grow too long, hard-shelled foods such as unshelled shrimp and small whole mussels have to be offered.

S.: None.

T: 24°-28°C, **L:** 25 cm, **TL:** from 150 cm, **WM:** w, **WR:** b, **AV:** 3, **D:** 3

Fam.:. Scaridae

This chapter is purposely kept short since parrotfishes are feeding specialists which are generally not recommended for a seawater aquarium. However, one species, *Cetoscarus bicolor*, is repeatedly imported. We want to introduce this interesting relative of the wrasses. This is truly an interesting family.

Tropical coral reefs of all three oceans are inhabited by parrotfishes. They commonly swim in large schools and gnaw the surface covering of the reef. Most species of this family have fused teeth that look like a parrot's beak. In addition, the pharyngeal teeth are fused into grinding plates. They use their beaks to sever pieces of live or dead coral and grind it into fine sand. Some species also bite or scrape on calcareous algae, which are strongly represented on the reef. Additional nourishment is gained from crabs, bryozoans, and bristleworms.

Their sexual life and reproduction is analogous to the wrasses. Terminal males develop from initial phase females or males. Like the wrasses, terminal males have the most attractive coloration. They spawn in pairs. The courtship is quite interesting to observe: cheek to cheek the partners swim in tight circles in the open water! Mind you, in their natural habitat.

Cetoscarus bicolor undergoes dramatic color changes; bicolored juvenile forms are probably familiar to every aquarist. It does not chew on corals in the aquarium. Like the wrasses, it moves the entire day, sedately swimming along the bottom, then again at the surface. Only after frozen or flake foods are put in the water current will it join other aquarium fishes in their search for food. The bicolor parrotfish remains shyer than, for example, *Thalassoma lunare*. It should not be housed with aggressive tankmates such as triggerfishes. A mature tank is advantageous when keeping this species.

Parrotfishes have developed the ability to put on "payamas" at night. They exude a slimy shell which loosely surrounds their body during the night. It is composed of hardened mucus which is secreted from the gill area when the fishes respire strongly. The gland that produces the cocoon is a morellike growth on the upper edge of the gill chamber. In the morning the parrotfish emerges from its cocoon by using strong strokes of its tail. This mucus cocoon evolved as a defense against nocturnal predation.

Cocoon of a parrotfish . . .

. . . photographed at night

Cetoscarus bicolor ♂

Cetoscarus bicolor ♀

Cetoscarus bicolor, juvenile

Cetoscarus bicolor (RÜPPELL, 1829)
Bicolor parrotfish

Hab.: Indo-Pacific; from the Red Sea to Tuamotu, Japan (N), and the southern Barrier Reef. At depths of 1 to 30 m.

Sex.: Juveniles are a conspicuous white color with a broad red-brown band on the posterior half of the head. Adults are also quite differently colored. Initial phase animals are a dark reddish-black with a yellowish dorsum and scales that are framed in black and spotted. Terminal phase ♂ ♂ are blue-green with orange framed scales and orange dots on the head and anterior body (see photo).

Soc.B./Assoc.: Juveniles as well as adults live singly. But secondary ♂ ♂ can claim large territories and form harems that include several ♀ ♀.

M.: These animals live in clear lagoons and outer reefs and require plenty of swimming space. They grow relatively fast and soon outgrow the home aquarium. Rock formations with good hiding places are required, since the animals sleep in rock niches at night.

Light: Sunlight zone.

B./Rep.: Unknown.

F.: O; in the sea the animals feed on live and algae-covered coral stalks which are scraped with their beak or broken off and ground up. Even pointed branched forms such as *Seriatopora* are not scorned. All of it, including the calcium component, is swallowed. In the aquarium they can be offered coarse, hard-shelled fare like you would offer triggerfishes. For example, give them frozen shrimp (to 5 cm), freeze-dried foods, mussels, beef heart, and others.

S.: Although attractive as a juvenile, it is not an aquarium fish. Because all parrotfishes are regrettably unsuited for aquaria, they have been totally omitted from this book. Not even fishermen appreciate this family. Its flesh lacks texture and is almost inedible. Some species are even poisonous! However, divers always find parrotfishes interesting.

T: 24°-28°C, **L:** 80 cm, **TL:** from 200 cm, **WM:** w, **WR:** b, **AV:** 1-2, **D:** 3

Fam.: Serranidae
Subfam.: Anthiinae

ABOUT THE FAMILY SERRANIDAE

Whether you are talking to aquarists, divers, or ichthyologists, Anthiinae are easily one of the best known and liked members of the enormous grouper family. Contrary to other subfamilies, for example, Serraninae (groupers and sea basses) or Epinephelinae (true groupers), Anthiinae are intimately associated with the substratum. Giant schools of these fishes make a spectacular sight in coral reefs. Their moderate size (<15 cm), colorful body, and planktivorous diet make these, in contrast to their predatory relatives, sought after aquarium fishes. Neither the best underwater photography equipment nor the lens with the widest angle is enough to capture these fishes in all their glory. For example, a school of *Pseudanthias squamipinnis* in the Red Sea in front of a drop-off has such breath that a photo is only capable of capturing a portion of the group. Even single specimens prove to be a challenge. Many photographers will try in vain to photograph a nimble coral perch with a normal or telephoto lens!

In the Gulf of Aqaba, *P. squamipinnis* is the most widely distributed species. Nowhere else can you see such huge numbers of coral perches as on the coast of the Sinai Peninsula. Every cave and every overhang is filled; they even colonize solitary coral blocks below the reef at 35 m depth. Within the groups of several hundred *P. squamipinnis,* you can see three typical forms. The small, sexually mature females comprise 90% of the group. They are reddish orange with a violet iris and do not grow larger than 7 cm. The 12 cm long males are diagnostically colored: their body is violet with a clearly visible violet spot on their pectoral fins. The first rays of the dorsal fin are elongated. The third form is 6 to 9 cm long and is a transitional phase between female and male. Here the female coloration still prevails, but the typical elongated dorsal fin rays of the male are already visible.

In the school there is a tight relationship between the number of females and the number of males. Groups with less than 10 individuals never include a male. But one male is often seen in harems containing more than 10 females. The more females, the more males in the group. Full-grown males normally tolerate transitional animals, but at the beginning of courtship, they are chased away. The pronounced harem behavior of coral perches can be observed throughout the Indo-Pacific. This includes *Pseudanthias cooperi* around Mauritius and *Pseudanthias dispar* in Micronesia.

Pseudanthias squamipinnis

Fam.: Serranidae
Subfam.: Anthiinae

Scientists have closely studied the sexual dimorphism of coral perches and have come to following conclusions: sexual transformation occurs outside of the annual spawning season. If a male is removed from a harem, the largest female changes to a male within 2 days. If several males are removed from larger groups, the same number of females will transform into males.

The courtship and spawning behavior has only been studied in a few species. *P. squamipinnis,* the species with the largest geographical distribution within this genus (from the Red Sea to Japan and the Solomon Islands), is one of them: courtship begins at dusk when territorial males, the guardians of the harem, swim into the open water high above the congregation of females. Following a U-shaped pattern, they dive to the sea floor, spread all their fins, and return to the open water. This zig-zag swim pattern lasts several minutes until a female places herself at the bottom of the U and swims to the surface close to the male. During this maneuver sperm and eggs are released. The females only spawn once before dark, while the males court several females and spawn repeatedly.

The coral perches are the most populous fish family in the Red Sea, bar none. The jewel basslet, *Pseudanthias squamipinnis,* inhabits reef slopes by the thousands.

Despite their attractive colors, manageable size, and other seemingly positive qualities, you should not decide to buy a coral perch as you gaze at their ethereal colors in a pet store. You can get away with this impromptu decision making for some of the easier fishes, but these fishes are not easy to keep! To maintain species of this family successfully, that is, for several months, the aquarium should not be smaller than 500 l. Strong water movement, constant high oxygen levels, and minimum nitrate values are basic conditions for the continued well-being of these sensitive fishes. An artificial reef should provide protection, and dominant large fishes should be excluded from the community. A group of 8 to 12 animals with a maximum of two males is ideal. Once again the seawater aquarist is challenged. Coral perches cannot survive on one meal a day. In the sea they spend the entire day hunting plankton. Therefore, several small feedings during the day brings its captive circumstance more in line with conditions found in its natural habitat. Some species are so fastidious that they only accept small crustacea—live if possible. *Artemia* culturing is recommended, but the cultured animals will have to be fed vitamins. Otherwise, freshly caught *Daphnia* and mosquito larvae are suitable. Frozen krill, *Mysis,* or beef heart are also taken from the water column. Again, a lot of thought should go into whether or not you can appropriately care for these demanding species before you make a purchase. Not only the fish but also the name of the marine hobby as a whole suffers from impulsive buying.

Anthias anthias
Barbier
(LINNAEUS, 1758)

Hab.: Mediterranean, northeast Atlantic north towards Biscay. On rock walls at depths of 30 to 50 m.

Sex.: ♂ ♂ have an elongated dorsal fin.

Soc.B./Assoc.: Groups are suggested, but they can also be kept singly or in pairs.

M.: Rock aquarium with shady areas.

Light: Moderate light.

B./Rep.: Has not been successful in an aquarium.

F.: C, FD; planktivores that are difficult to train to substitute foods.

S.: Not suitable for the tropical seawater aquarium.

T: 16°-22°C, **L:** 15 cm, **TL:** from 100 cm, **WM:** m, **WR:** m, **AV:** 3, **D:** 3

Anthias anthias, also see p. 680.

Anthias anthias

Fam.: Serranidae
Subfam.: Anthiinae

Luzonichthys waitei (FOWLER, 1931)
Pink basslet

Hab.: Indo-Australian Archipelago, east Africa to Micronesia. On steep outer reef slopes at depths of 10 to 55 m.

Sex.: None known.

Soc.B./Assoc.: They always occur in large groups and therefore should not be kept singly. They get along well with almost all invertebrates.

M.: Reef aquarium with vertical rock walls.

Light: Moderate light.

B./Rep.: Has not been successful in an aquarium.

F.: C, FD; planktivore that is difficult to adapt to substitute fare such as frozen *Artemia*.

S.: Unknown.

T: 22°-28°C, **L:** 5 cm, **TL:** from 100 cm, **WM:** m, **WR:** m, **AV:** 2-3, **D:** 3

Pseudanthias bicolor (RANDALL, 1979)
Bicolored coral perch

Hab.: Indo-Pacific, Ryukyu Islands, and Hawaii. On barrier and outer reefs at depths between 5 and 50 m.

Sex.: Unknown.

Soc.B./Assoc.: Occurs in small groups. Gets along with invertebrates. Their association with other free-swimming fishes should be limited to large tanks.

M.: Reef aquarium with steep rock slopes.

Light: Moderate light.

B./Rep.: Has not been successful in an aquarium.

F.: C, FD; a plankton feeder that will adapt to substitute fare.

S.: Unknown.

T: 22°-27°C, **L:** 9 cm, **TL:** from 120 cm, **WM:** m, **WR:** m, **AV:** 2, **D:** 3

Pseudanthias bicolor, Flores at 30 m depth.

Luzonichthys waitei, Flores

Pseudanthias bicolor, Mauritius

Fam.: Serranidae
Subfam.: Anthiinae

Pseudanthias cooperi (REGAN, 1902)
Cooper's coral perch

Hab.: East Africa, the Indian Ocean, Japan, and the east coast of Australia. Near rock walls at depths of 10 to 60 m.

Sex.: The ♂ ♂ have a short bright red vertical stripe on their side (small picture).

Soc.B./Assoc.: They live in small loose congregations. Can also be kept singly or in pairs. Good tankmates for invertebrates.

M.: Reef aquarium.

Light: Moderate light zone.

B./Rep.: Has not been successful in an aquarium.

F.: C, FD; planktivore that accepts finely minced frozen foods.

S.: Unknown.

T: 22°-27°C, **L:** 11 cm, **TL:** from 120 cm, **WM:** m, **WR:** m, **AV:** 2-3, **D:** 3

A harem of *Pseudanthias cooperi*   *Pseudanthias cooperi* ♂

Pseudanthias dispar (HERRE, 1955)
Sickle coralfish

Hab.: Indo-Australian Archipelago and French Polynesia. Shallow sections of coral reefs at depths of 1 to 15 m.

Sex.: The ♂ ♂ have a scarlet red dorsal fin and a long upper lip. They spend most of their time courting ♀ ♀.

Soc.B./Assoc.: In their natural biotope, they live in large groups. Small groups of up to 10 individuals can be kept in an aquarium. Do not keep with large free-swimming fishes. They get along very well with invertebrates.

M.: Reef aquarium.

Light: Sunlight zone. Metal halides (250 W) combined with blue actinic tubes let the intense colors of these fish shine.

B./Rep.: Has not been successful in an aquarium. In their natural biotope, they spawn in the afternoon. Pairs release their sperm and eggs into the open water as they quickly swim up and down in the water column.

F.: C, FD; a plankton feeder which accepts substitute fare relatively easily. Sometimes dry foods are even eaten.

S.: The most common species of shallow waters. Probably the easiest maintained species of all the coral perches.

T: 22°-28°C, **L:** 10 cm, **TL:** from 120 cm, **WM:** m, **WR:** m-t, **AV:** 2, **D:** 2

Pseudanthias cooperi ♂

Pseudanthias dispar ♂

Fam.: Serranidae
Subfam.: Anthiinae

Pseudanthias dispar ♀

Pseudanthias dispar ♂

Pseudanthias evansi
Evans coral perch

(SMITH, 1954)

Hab.: Indian Ocean, east Africa, and Indonesia. On outer reef slopes at 10 to 35 m depth.

Sex.: Unknown.

Soc.B./Assoc.: They always occur in large groups and therefore should not be kept singly. They get along well with almost all invertebrates.

M.: Reef aquarium with vertical rock walls.

Light: Moderately lit areas.

B./Rep.: Has not been successful in an aquarium.

F.: C, FD; plankton feeder which is difficult to train to substitute foods such as frozen *Artemia*. It should be fed at least twice a day.

S.: Unknown.

T: 22°-28°C, **L:** 10 cm, **TL:** from 100 cm, **WM:** m, **WR:** m, **AV:** 2, **D:** 3

Fam.: Serranidae
Subfam.: Anthiinae

Pseudanthias heemstrai   SCHUHMACHER, KRUPP & RANDALL, 1989
Heemstra's coral perch

Hab.: Red Sea. On rock walls at depths of 15 to 40 m.

Sex.: Dorsal fin of the ♂ is elongated.

Soc.B./Assoc.: Lives in groups. Nothing is known about aquarium maintenance.

M.: Reef aquarium.

Light: Areas of moderate light.

B./Rep.: Has not been successful in an aquarium.

F.: C, FD; plankton feeder.

S.: Just described in 1989 as a third species from the Red Sea.

T: 22°-27°C, **L:** 12 cm, **TL:** from 120 cm, **WM:** m, **WR:** m, **AV:** 4, **D:** 3?

Pseudanthias huchtii   (BLEEKER, 1856)
Sea goldie

Hab.: Indian Ocean, Indonesia, Indo-Australian Archipelago, the Philippines, and Micronesia. Around rocky reefs at depths of 5 to 30 m.

Sex.: The third ray of the ♂'s dorsal fin is strongly elongated. ♀♀ do not have a red longitudinal stripe on the head.

Soc.B./Assoc.: Generally found alone or in pairs; rarely occurs in small groups. It gets along well with invertebrates and small free-swimming fishes.

M.: Reef aquarium.

Light: Area of sunlight.

B./Rep.: Has not been successful in an aquarium.

F.: C, FD; planktivore which is difficult to acclimate to substitute foods.

S.: Not known.

T: 22°-28°C, **L:** 12 cm, **TL:** from 100 cm, **WM:** m-s, **WR:** m, **AV:** 2-3, **D:** 3

Pseudanthias evansi ♀ in an aquarium.

Pseudanthias heemstrai ♂

Pseudanthias huchtii ♂

Fam.: Serranidae
Subfam.: Anthiinae

Pseudanthias hypselosoma   (BLEEKER, 1878)
Stout basslet

Hab.: Indo-Australian Archipelago, west to the Maldives. On rock reefs at depths of 10 to 45 m.

Sex.: The ♂♂ do not have an elongated dorsal fin ray.

Soc.B./Assoc.: Live in small groups. They get along well with almost all invertebrates. A large aquarium is needed if the species is kept with other free-swimming fishes.

M.: Reef aquarium with steep rock walls.

Light: Moderate light areas.

B./Rep.: Has not been successful in an aquarium.

F.: C, FD; plankton feeder that is reluctant to eat substitute foods.

S.: Unknown.

T: 22°-27°C, **L:** 12 cm, **TL:** from 120 cm, **WM:** m, **WR:** m, **AV:** 3, **D:** 3

Pseudanthias ignitus   (RANDALL & LUBBOCK, 1981)
Firetail basslet

Hab.: From the Maldives to the Andaman Islands. Along steep rock drop-offs at depths of ca. 30 m.

Sex.: The ♂'s head is white ventrally; ♀♀ are a solid orange-red and have elongated ventral fins.

Soc.B./Assoc.: Live in small groups.

M.: Reef aquarium.

Light: Moderate light zone.

B./Rep.: Has not been successful in an aquarium.

F.: C, FD; planktivore.

S.: None known.

T: 22°-27°C, **L:** 6 cm, **TL:** from 100 cm, **WM:** m, **WR:** m, **AV:** 3, **D:** 3

Pseudanthias ignitus ♀

Pseudanthias hypselosoma ♂

Pseudanthias ignitus ♂

Fam.: Serranidae
Subfam.: Anthiinae

Pseudanthias lori   (LUBBOCK & RANDALL, 1976)
Lori's basslet

Hab.: Indonesia, the Indo-Australian Archipelago, and the western Pacific. In the vicinity of caves and on outer reef slopes at depths of 20 to 70 m.

Sex.: The ♂ ♂ have a slightly protruding upper lip.

Soc.B./Assoc.: They live in small groups.

M.: Reef aquarium.

Light: Moderate light.

B./Rep.: Has not been successful in an aquarium.

F.: C, FD; planktivore.

S.: None known.

T: 22°-27°C, **L:** 7 cm, **TL:** from 100 cm, **WM:** m, **WR:** m, **AV:** 3, **D:** 3

Pseudanthias pleurotaenia ♂

Fam.: Serranidae
Subfam.: Anthiinae

Pseudanthias luzonensis   (KATAYAMA & MASUDA, 1983)
Philippine fairy basslet

Hab.: Philippines, Indonesia, and the northern part of the Great Barrier Reef. On steep slopes at depths of 25 to 45 m.

Sex.: None known.

Soc.B./Assoc.: They live in small groups. In the aquarium they get along well with invertebrates. Only in larger aquaria can they be kept with other free-swimming fishes.

M.: A reef aquarium with steep rock walls.

Light: Moderate light.

B./Rep.: Has not been successful in an aquarium.

F.: C, FD; a planktivore that can be trained to accept substitute foods.

S.: Unknown.

T: 22°-27°C, **L:** 12 cm, **TL:** from 120 cm, **WM:** m, **WR:** m, **AV:** 3-4, **D:** 3

Pseudanthias pleurotaenia   (BLEEKER, 1857)
Purple blotch basslet

Hab.: Indo-Australian Archipelago and western Pacific. Near rock walls at depths of 15 to 180 m. In some areas they are exclusively found at depths below 30 m.

Sex.: The ♂♂ are red and have a bright purple spot on their side; the ♀♀ are yellow with fine red designs.

Soc.B./Assoc.: They live in loose congregations of 6 to 30 individuals. Juveniles swim singly and remain in the vicinity of their hiding places. Affable tankmates for invertebrates.

M.: Reef aquarium.

Light: Moderate light.

B./Rep.: Has not been successful in an aquarium.

F.: C, FD; planktivore which will accept small, chopped frozen foods.

S.: Expensive and rarely available because of the difficulty bringing them up from profound depths.

T: 22°-27°C, **L:** 10 cm, **TL:** from 120 cm, **WM:** m, **WR:** m, **AV:** 3, **D:** 3

Pseudanthias pleurotaenia ♂

Pseudanthias luzonensis ♂

Pseudanthias pleurotaenia ♀

Fam.: Serranidae
Subfam.: Anthiinae

Pseudanthias pictilis   (RANDALL & ALLEN, 1978)
Painted goldie

Hab.: Southern Great Barrier Reef, Lord Howe Island, and New Caledonia. Around corals and rocks at depths of 20 to 30 m.

Sex.: The ♀ ♀ are orange-red. The ♂ ♂ have a light cross-stripe in the vicinity of the anal fin and a large white spot at the base of the tail fin.

Soc.B./Assoc.: They live in large congregations. Good tankmates for invertebrates and bottom oriented fishes.

M.: Reef aquarium.

Light: Moderate light.

B./Rep.: Has not been successful in an aquarium.

F.: C, FD; plankton feeder which is disinclined to accept substitute foods (chopped frozen foods).

S.: None known.

T: 22°-27°C, **L:** 14 cm, **TL:** from 120 cm, **WM:** m, **WR:** m, **AV:** 3, **D:** 3

Pseudanthias randalli   (LUBBOCK & ALLEN, 1978)
Randall's basslet

Hab.: In the western Pacific from the Philippines to the Marshall Islands. Near caves and current-rich steep drop-offs at 15 to 70 m depth.

Sex.: The ♂ ♂ have a slightly protruding upper lip; the ♀ ♀, like juveniles, are uniformly yellow to red-orange and have yellow outer tail fin rays.

Soc.B./Assoc.: They live in small groups. Good tankmates for invertebrates.

M.: Reef aquarium with a strong current.

Light: Moderate light.

B./Rep.: Has not been successful in an aquarium.

F.: C, FD; plankton feeder. Live *Artemia* and finely chopped frozen foods will be eaten.

S.: None known.

T: 22°-27°C, **L:** 7 cm, **TL:** from 100 cm, **WM:** m-s, **WR:** m-t, **AV:** 2-3, **D:** 3

Pseudanthias pictilis ♂

Pseudanthias randalli, Flores

Fam.: Serranidae
Subfam.: Anthiinae

Pseudanthias smithvanizi   (RANDALL & LUBBOCK, 1981)
Smith - Vaniz basslet

Hab.: Indonesia, the Philippines, the Cocos-Keeling Islands, and the western Pacific. On steep outer reef slopes at 6 to 70 m depth.

Sex.: In ♂♂, the third ray of the dorsal fin and the outer rays of the tail fin are elongated.

Soc.B./Assoc.: They usually live in small groups of less than 20 individuals. Good tankmates for invertebrates.

M.: Reef aquarium with steep walls.

Light: Moderate light.

B./Rep.: Has not been successful in an aquarium.

F.: C, FD; planktivores that are difficult to train to substitute foods.

S.: None known.

T: 22°-27°C, **L:** 8 cm, **TL:** from 100 cm, **WM:** m, **WR:** m, **AV:** 2-3, **D:** 3

Pseudanthias smithvanizi

Pseudanthias squamipinnis   (PETERS, 1855)
Jewel basslet

Hab.: Red Sea and the entire tropical Indo-Pacific to southern Japan and the Barrier Reef. At depths of 5 to 35 m.

Sex.: The ♂♂ are purple and have a very long third ray on the dorsal fin. The ♀♀ are reddish orange.

Soc.B./Assoc.: In their natural biotope they live in large groups which are primarily comprised of ♀♀ (see p. 930). In the aquarium they should be kept in small groups of up to 10 animals. Do not keep with other free-swimming fishes. They get along well with invertebrates.

M.: Reef aquarium.

Light: Sunlight to moderate light zones.

B./Rep.: Has not been successful in an aquarium. In the Red Sea, they spawn in the winter; however, around Japan and the Barrier Reef, they spawn in the summer.

F.: C, FD; planktivore. It can be taught to eat substitute foods, sometimes even dry foods.

S.: The most common species in the Red Sea.

T: 22°-28°C, **L:** 16 cm, **TL:** from 120 cm, **WM:** m, **WR:** m-t, **AV:** 1, **D:** 2-3

Pseudanthias smithvanizi ♂

Pseudanthias squamipinnis

Fam.: Serranidae
Subfam.: Anthiinae

Pseudanthias taeniatus   (KLUNZINGER, 1855)
Stripe basslet

Hab.: Red Sea. On rocky slopes at 20 to 40 m depth.

Sex.: ♀♀ are a solid orange-red; ♂♂ have red and white longitudinal striations (photo).

Soc.B./Assoc.: Live in large congregations. Can be kept in pairs or small groups.

M.: Reef aquarium.

Light: Moderate light.

B./Rep.: Has not been successful in an aquarium.

F.: C, FD; plankton feeder.

S.: Sometimes found together with *P. squamipinnis* in large groups.

T: 22°-27°C, **L:** 13 cm, **TL:** from 120 cm, **WM:** m, **WR:** m, **AV:** 2-3, **D:** 3

Pseudanthias tuka   (HERRE & MONTALBAN, 1927)
Purple coralfish

Hab.: Indo-Australian Archipelago and the Pacific. On steep slopes at depths of 10 to 35 m.

Sex.: The ♂'s upper lip is elongated, and its throat is yellow. The ♀♀ have a yellow band that runs along their back.

Soc.B./Assoc.: They swim in small groups and are congenial tankmates for invertebrates and other small free-swimming fishes.

M.: Reef aquarium.

Light: Moderate light.

B./Rep.: Has not been successful in an aquarium.

F.: C, FD; planktivores that are uneager to accept substitute foods.

S.: None known.

T: 22°-28°C, **L:** 12 cm, **TL:** from 100 cm, **WM:** m-s, **WR:** m, **AV:** 2-3, **D:** 3

Pseudanthias tuka ♀

Pseudanthias taeniatus ♂

Pseudanthias tuka

Fam.: Serranidae
Subfam.: Anthiinae

Serranocirrhitus latus   WATANABE, 1949
Sunburst basslet

Hab.: Along the Great Barrier Reef, Indonesia, and the western Pacific. Around caves and on steep slopes at depths of 15 to 70 m.

Sex.: Unknown.

Soc.B./Assoc.: They normally live in small groups, but they can be kept singly or in pairs. They get along very well with almost all invertebrates. Do not keep with other active fishes.

M.: Reef aquarium.

Light: Moderate light.

B./Rep.: Has not been successful in an aquarium.

F.: C, FD; plankton feeders that can usually be accustomed to substitute foods such as frozen *Artemia* or finely chopped frozen foods.

S.: None known.

T: 22°-27°C, **L:** 9 cm, **TL:** from 100 cm, **WM:** m, **WR:** m, **AV:** 3, **D:** 3

Pseudanthias tuka

Serranocirrhitus latus

Pseudanthias tuka ♂

Fam.: Pseudochromidae

The influence of behavioral science on the systematic classification of fishes is shown in this chapter. Besides the morphology of the dottybacks, it is the mode of reproduction that clearly separates this family from the groupers (Serranidae and its subfamilies). While groupers are all pelagic spawners, that is, sperm and eggs are released into the open water, dottybacks and other related perches, which will be dealt with in the following chapters, produce demersal eggs. These eggs are heavier than water and consequently sink to the bottom after they are fertilized. They are adhesive, and dottyback spawns are recognizable as egg clumps stuck to caves or rock crevices. The realization that dottybacks tend towards buccal incubation is an additional characteristic that distinguishes them from groupers. The diminutive size of these species versus groupers of the genera *Epinephelus* and *Cephalopholis* is obviously not the only difference between the families. Since parental care is very rare in fishes, the mouthbrooding behavior has been studied in detail. It is very probable that spawning behavior has developed independently in the families Pseudochromidae, Grammidae, and Plesiopidae, despite the close relationship among them. Taxonomists are now willing to place the jawfishes (Opistognathidae) into this group. All jawfishes are mouthbrooders.

The majority of dottyback species included in this book are very colorful. It is curious that you can distinguish males from females based on color in some species, while it is impossible in others. Dottybacks are hermaphrodites; that is, one individual is capable of adopting either sex. If you find a pair of dottybacks, the **larger** partner is the male, even though they are equally colored. This is opposite of what is found in clownfishes! When sexual dichromatism is present, the males are more brilliantly colored.

Some *Pseudochromis* species have been aquarium bred. But *Labracinus cyclophthalmus,* which reaches a length of about 15 cm, has only been successfully bred once in the Berlin Aquarium. Their notes are of great value to seawater aquarists:

The innate aggressiveness of the dottybacks was diminished by placing five *L. cyclophthalmus* into a large aquarium that was divided by glass panes. The differentiable sexes were placed next to each other. After aggressive behavior subsided, the glass panes were lifted and the fish allowed to intermingle. Ovoposition was imminent when both partners were lying close together in a cave.

Pseudochromis diadema, text on p. 970

Fam.: Pseudochromidae

The female laid thousands of eggs in threads which adhered into a ball and were stuck to a stone. Afterwards, the male fertilized the eggs and immediately chased the female away from what was previously the community cave. It guarded the spawn and fanned the eggs to provide oxygen. The nervous male often transported the egg clump around until it fell apart. Since spawning occurred every 3 weeks, the caretakers placed one spawn with the same water into a rearing aquarium. The water was not filtered, only aerated and kept in motion with a large pore diffuser. At 24°C, the young were freed from their eggshells on the third day by the air bubbles of the diffuser. The hatching dottybacks were about half the size of newly hatched clownfishes. They were fed from the first day with tiny ciliates and mixed plankton raised to feed young clownfishes (*Brachionus, Euplotes*). The few young *Labracinus* from the first spawn died after a few days.

For the next trial, commercial rearing foods were included, and small doses of a large variety of foods were fed 10 to 15 times per day. Many of this batch grew. Food intake and digestion could easily be observed in their transparent bodies. The young grew very slowly and 31 days passed before they could eat *Artemia* nauplii. On the 40th day, large losses were sustained due to fungus. But it was only on the 45th day that the caretakers discovered that the origin of the fungus was not a bacterial infection, but quarrels among the fry. The remaining dottybacks were separated and grew to a length of 3 cm in 4 months.

Cypho purpurescens ♀

Cypho purpurescens ♂

Cypho purpurescens   (DE VIS, 1884)
Purple dottyback

Hab.: West Pacific, from the Great Barrier Reef to the Fiji Islands. At depths of 5 to 35 m.

Sex.: The notorious bright purple color is most prevalent on the posterior body half of the ♂♂; ♀♀ are bluish cranially and reddish caudally.

Soc.B./Assoc.: *C. purpurescens* lives singly in coral reefs; there it establishes territories and displays its aggressive nature primarily towards conspecifics. A good choice for fish community tanks or aquaria with corals.

M.: Requires hiding places corresponding to its size. Until it becomes accustomed to its new home, it will be shy and retiring. Once familiarized with its environment, it leaves its hiding place for extended periods of time and delights observers with its beautiful colors.

Light: Areas of moderate light and sunlight.

B./Rep.: The animals spawn in pairs in the ♂'s cave. The eggs adhere to the rock; the difficult to rear young hatch after a few days.

F.: C; *C. purpurescens* primarily feeds on small crustacea and zooplankton.

S.: This small dottyback is rarely available because of its limited geographic distribution and reclusive lifestyle. Unfortunately, cyanide is repeatedly used to capture this species.

T: 22°-24°C, **L:** 6 cm, **TL:** from 60 cm, **WM:** w, **WR:** b, **AV:** 3, **D:** 3

Fam.: Pseudochromidae

Labracinus cyclophthalmus   (MÜLLER & TROSCHEL, 1849)
Spottysail dottyback

Hab.: West central Pacific, from Indonesia to the Philippines, Japan, and New Guinea. At depths of 10 to 15 m.

Sex.: The ♀ is a rather drab gray with small dots arranged in lines, but it can also be reddish with commalike lines on the dorsal fin. The ♂ is bright red with a dark head and dark, often blue, fin edges. It frequently has a black spot in the middle of the dorsal fin.

Soc.B./Assoc.: *L. cyclophthalmus* lives singly and is territorial and aggressive towards conspecifics, but it can be easily kept with other fishes and invertebrates.

M.: Requires hiding places corresponding to its size and good water quality.

Light: Sun and moderate light zones.

B./Rep.: The animals spawn in pairs in the ♂'s hiding place. The extremely difficult rearing has only been successful at the Berlin Aquarium (see general text on pp. 958-959).

F.: C; young feed on zooplankton. Increase the size as the animals grow. Adults feed on small crustacea. They accept *Mysis*, *Artemia*, mussle meat, and frozen foods in the aquarium.

S.: The ♂ can acquire a light cross-stripe design when frightened. ♂♂ and ♀♀ have a species specific blue to blue-black ring around each eye.

T: 22°-26°C, **L:** 20 cm, **TL:** from 120 cm, **WM:** w, **WR:** b, **AV:** 2, **D:** 3

Labracinus lineatus ♀, text on p. 964.

Labracinus cyclophthalmus ♂, Flores, Indonesia

Labracinus cyclophthalmus ♂, Japan

Fam.: Pseudochromidae

Labracinus lineatus ♂

Labracinus lineatus   (CASTELNAU, 1875)
Lined dottyback

Hab.: Eastern Indian Ocean; tropical and subtropical western Australia. At depths of 5 to 15 m.

Sex.: The ♂ has blue dots in linear arrangements over its entire body; these dots are usually brown in ♀♀. The blue dots and lines on the head are equal on both sexes.

Soc.B./Assoc.: *L. lineatus* is a fairly common species that leads a solitary existence in the protection of caves and crevices. It repeatedly leaves its cave for short periods of time to swim in the open water.

M.: A good fish for the community fish aquarium that has appropriate hiding places and shaded "living rooms."

Light: Sun and moderate light areas.

B./Rep.: The pair spawns in the hiding place of the ♂ which later guards the spawn.

F.: C; feeds on small crustacea, polychaetes, and small fishes; it also accepts mussel meat and frozen foods.

S.: The species is not as timid as most of its relatives. Divers are allowed to closely approach.

T: 20°-24°C, L: 25 cm, TL: from 150 cm, **WM:** w, **WR:** b, **AV:** 3, D: 3

Ogilbyina velifera
Speartail dottyback

(LUBBOCK, 1980)

Hab.: Southwest Pacific; along the Great Barrier Reef. At depths of 12 to 35 m.

Sex.: The ♂ is mainly blue on the head and the anterior dorsal area and fin. The ♀ is yellow-orange.

Soc.B./Assoc.: *O. velifera* occupies territories singly and is bellicose towards conspecifics and occasionally towards Pomacentridae. However, it is a lovely fish to house with corals and anemones.

M.: It requires a rock or reef aquarium full of hiding places.

Light: Sunlight zone.

B./Rep.: The species spawns in pairs in the ♂'s hiding places.

F.: C; it nips passing zooplankton from the water column. Therefore, it readily accepts crustacea such as *Mysis*, krill, and *Artemia* (also frozen) placed in the current.

S.: This is one of the few species of dwarf perches which have a paddlelike, posteriorly pointed tail fin.

T: 24°-26°C, **L:** 9 cm, **TL:** from 80 cm, **WM:** w, **WR:** b, **AV:** 3, **D:** 3

Ogilbyina velifera ♀

Fam.: Pseudochromidae

Ogilbyina novaehollandiae
Newholland dottyback
(STEINDACHNER; 1880)

Hab.: Southwest Pacific; in front of Queensland and Auatralia's Great Barrier Reef, At depths of 10 to 20 m.

Sex.: The ! is bright red with very fuzzy, light crossbands, especially in the caudal half of the body. The fins are edged in blue. The ? has a red head and a body that is dark with light crossbands dorsally and gray to white ventrally. The caudal fin is totally framed in red and its top half is dark. The anal fin is mostly black.

Soc.B./Assoc.: *O. novaehollandiae* lives singly in rock and coral hiding places. An amiable fish that is an appropriate addition to community tanks.

M.: It needs a rock or reef aquarium with sufficient hiding places.

Light: Sunlight area.

B./Rep.: Not known.

F.: C; it feeds on crustacea and other invertebrates as well as freeze-dried foods.

S.: Due to its relatively reduced distribution, *O. novaehollandiae* is rarely found in pet stores.

T: 24°-26° C, **L:** 18 cm, **TL:** from 120 cm, **WM:** w, **WR:** b, **AV:** 3, **D:** 3

Ogilbyina novaehollandiae ♀

Ogilbyina queenslandiae
Queensland dottyback
(SAVILLE-KENT, 1893)

Hab.: West Pacific; from the Great Barrier Reef to the Torres Strait. At depths of 10 to 20 m.

Sex.: The ♀ has a yellow-orange chest which changes to red caudally; the entire fish is framed in blue. The ♂ is red cranially and dark caudally with dark, enlarged, transparent fins.

Soc.B./Assoc.: *O. queenslandiae* lives singly in rock or coral caves as well as in caves it excavates under corals.

M.: Needs rock hiding places commensurate to its size. If it does not find an appealing hole and there are stones, corals, etc., lying on sand or rubble, it will dig out a living area for itself.

Light: Sunlight zone.

B./Rep.: Not known. The species spawns in its cave.

F.: C; it primarily feeds on crustacea. In the aquarium it accepts freeze-dried and, of course, live crustacea.

S.: This beautiful and easily maintainable fish is rarely offered.

T: 24°-26°C, L: 20 cm, TL: from 120 cm, WM: w, WR: b, AV: 3, D: 2-3

Ogilbyina queenslandiae ♀

Ogilbyina novaehollandia ♂, subadult

Ogilbyina queenslandiae ♂

967

Fam.: Pseudochromidae

Pseudochromis aldabraensis   BOUCHOT & BOUTIN, 1958
Aldabra dottyback

Hab.: Gulf of Arabia, Gulf of Oman to Pakistan, and the Aldabra Islands. At depths of 1 to 20 m.

Sex.: None known. See **S**.

Soc.B./Assoc.: *P. aldabrensis* lives singly in caves and crevices appropriate for its size.

M.: Requires a reef or rock aquarium with enough hiding possibilities to allow it to choose its own cave.

Light: Sunlight zone.

B./Rep.: Not known.

F.: C; primarily feeds on small crustacea, but it will also consume frozen foods, chopped mussels, etc.

S.: *P. aldabrensis* is very similar to *P. springeri*, but it is a significantly lighter reddish orange. The blue stripes on the head and back are about equal. The fish is selectively collected in the Persian Gulf and exported from there. This species and *P. dutoiti* are probably synonymous!

T: 24°-28°C, L: 8 cm, TL: from 80 cm, **WM:** w, **WR:** b, **AV:** 2, **D:** 3

Pseudochromis cyanotaenia   BLEEKER, 1857
Blue-striped dottyback

Hab.: Eastern Indian Ocean and west Pacific, from the Lakshadweep to the Fiji and Gilbert Islands, Japan (N), and the southern Barrier Reef. At depths of 0 to 20 m.

Sex.: Only ♂♂ have the blue crossbands the fish are named for. Their unpaired fins may be blue. However, the lower anterior section and the head of the ♀ are yellow-gray to white. They are dark dorsally, and their unpaired fins are largely yellow.

Soc.B./Assoc.: *P. cyanotaenia* lives singly and lurks on advantageous points in the reef for passing prey. In the aquarium it likes to sit on top of the decor.

M.: Provide a rock or reef aquarium with hiding places therein (underneath and on the bottom).

Light: Area of sunlight.

B./Rep.: Not known; it is assumed to spawn in pairs in the ♂'s cave.

F.: C; primarily feeds on small crustacea; freeze-dried foods will be accepted after adaptation.

S.: Besides sexual dichromatism, there are also totally yellow-red or red-orange specimens with dark fins, especially among ♂♂.

T: 24°-26°C, L: 6 cm, TL: from 60 cm, **WM:** w, **WR:** b, **AV:** 2-3●**D:** 3

Pseudochromis cyanotaenia ♀

Pseudochromis aldabraensis ♀

Pseudochromis cyanotaenia ♂

Fam.: Pseudochromidae

Pseudochromis diadema　　　　　　　　　　　　LUBBOCK & RANDALL, 1978
Diadem basslet

Hab.: West Pacific, from the Malayan Peninsula to the Philippines. At depths of 5 to 25 m.

Sex.: The tail fin of the ♂ is elongated along the upper and lower edge.

Soc.B./Assoc.: *P. diadema* lives alone, claims a territory, and is very aggressive towards conspecifics, Pomacentridae, and other tankmates. In some aquaria it develops into a bellicose terror, not even respecting cleaner shrimp.

M.: *P. diadema* requires a rock or reef aquarium with sufficient hiding places and cover.

Light: Sunlight regions.

B./Rep.: Not known.

F.: C; it principally consumes small benthic and planktonic crustacea, but it will also take frozen foods.

S.: *P. diadema*'s yellow color and its blue to purple stripes that run dorsally from the head to its tail fin make it unmistakable. There is another photograph of this fish on page 959.

T: 24°-26°C, **L:** 6 cm, **TL:** from 80 cm, **WM:** w, **WR:** b, **AV:** 3, **D:** 3

Pseudochromis dixurus　　　　　　　　　　　　　　　　　LUBBOCK, 1975
Forktail dottyback

Hab.: Red Sea. At depths of 5 to 60 m.

Sex.: None known.

Soc.B./Assoc.: *P. dixurus* lives singly in caves and among surrounding mud-covered rocks. It will sometimes excavate its own cave under rocks.

M.: Requires a rock aquarium with corresponding cover. *P. dixurus* will also live beneath large shells or, in soft substrates, build its own cave under flat, hard items lying on the bottom.

Light: Sunlight zone.

B./Rep.: Not known.

F.: C; primarily feeds on crustacea which are either snapped from the open water or the bottom.

S.: *P. dixurus* has a lunate tail fin with elongated filaments. Its color varies from olive to yellow or white. They usually have two brownish yellow longitudinal stripes which extend from the head to the tip of the tail fin and enhance the sickle-shaped caudal fin.

T: 24°-26°C, **L:** 9 cm, **TL:** from 100 cm, **WM:** w, **WR:** b, **AV:** 2-3, **D:** 3

Pseudochromis diadema (top)

Pseudochromis dixurus

Fam.: Pseudochromidae

Pseudochromis flavivertex
Sunrise dottyback

RÜPPELL, 1835

Hab.: Red Sea and the Gulf of Aden. At depths of 2 to 30 m.

Sex.: ♂♂ typically have a yellow stripe that extends from the snout dorsally to the upper tip of the tail fin; the remainder of the body is largely blue with a light ventral area. The ♀♀ are gray-blue dorsally and white ventrally with dark dots on the scales; the tail fin is yellow.

Soc.B./Assoc.: *P. flavivertex* lives singly around the base of rocks or coral stalks on sandy bottoms. It is not very aggressive and can be housed with gobies, blennies, corals, and anemones. This species is intimidated by large, robust fishes such as surgeonfishes or angelfishes and will remain shy and retiring in their presence.

M.: Decorate the aquarium with rockwork rich in hiding places. If the aquarium lacks larger fishes, *P. flavivertex* will readily emerge into the open water around its hiding place.

Light: Area of sunlight.

B./Rep.: The animals seem to keep a 14 day, half moon reproduction cycle. They spawn in pairs in the ♂'s cave.

F.: C; it chases zooplankton and small crustacea, but frozen foods are also accepted.

S.: Besides the blue-yellow ♂♂, there are animals with a second yellow stripe along the ventral side. Those 2 yellow stripes can be so broad that they almost cover the entire body, only leaving the blue stripe behind the eye (xanthic form).

T: 24°-28°C, **L:** 8 cm, **TL:** from 80 cm, **WM:** w, **WR:** b, **AV:** 2-3, **D:** 3

Pseudochromis flavivertex ♂ and ♀

P. flavivertex, xanthic form

Pseudochromis flavivertex ♂

Pseudochromis flavivertex ♀

Fam.: Pseudochromidae

Pseudochromis fridmani KLAUSEWITZ, 1968
Orchid dottyback

Hab.: Red Sea. At depths from 1 to 60 m.

Sex.: No significant differences; the ♂ grows somewhat larger than the ♀, and the lower lobe of the tail fin is somewhat more elongated.

Soc.B./Assoc.: *P. fridmani* generally lives singly, but occasionally large numbers are seen on vertical rock walls or under overhangs where it finds protection in crevices and niches.

M.: Requires shelters corresponding to its size as well as shaded overhangs and outcroppings that offer protection from direct sunlight.

Light: Moderate light.

B./Rep.: Aquarium breeding has not been successful; the animals spawn in rock caves, and the ♂ guards the spawn.

F.: C; primarily feeds on free-swimming or benthic crustacea; in the aquarium it will accept shrimp, frozen foods, *Artemia*, and flake foods.

S.: *P. fridmani* 's eye-catching violet-purple color makes it visible from great distances. It has a small dark spot on the operculum and a dark line that starts at the snout, runs through the eye, and ends on the upper end of the operculum.

T: 24°-26°C, **L:** 7 cm, **TL:** from 80 cm, **WM:** w, **WR:** b, **AV:** 2, **D:** 2

Pseudochromis fuscus MÜLLER & TROSCHEL, 1849
Brown dottyback

Hab.: Indo-West Pacific, from Sri Lanka to Palau, the northern Barrier Reef, and the southern China Sea. At depths of 3 to 25 m.

Sex.: The ♂♂ are usually dark with an anteriorly yellow dorsal fin and a whitish transparent tail fin. The ♀♀ are often light gray to yellowish green with a dark dot on every scale.

Soc.B./Assoc.: *P. fuscus* lives singly, either hidden in crevices of rocks or corals or, when rubble or sand are present, beneath corals. It is particularly well suited for a reef aquarium.

M.: When it does not find suitable cover and there is sufficient rubble or sand at the base of rocks or corals, it excavates its own cave.

Light: Area of sunlight.

B./Rep.: *P. fuscus* spawns in pairs in the ♂ 's hiding place. There the egg mass is adhered flatly to the rock. The ♂ guards the spawn until the young hatch.

F.: C; feeds on small crustacea and other invertebrates it either snaps from the water column or off the bottom. It also accepts frozen foods.

S.: Besides the sexual dichromatism, there are totally yellow-orange to red-orange specimens with dark fins, especially among ♂♂.

T: 24°-26°C, **L:** 10 cm, **TL:** from 60 cm, **WM:** w, **WR:** b, **AV:** 2, **D:** 3

Pseudochromis fuscus

Pseudochromis fridmani

Pseudochromis fuscus ♂

Fam.: Pseudochromidae

Pseudochromis olivaceus   RÜPPELL, 1835
Olive dottyback

Hab.: Arabian Sea, from the Red Sea to the Gulf of Arabia. At depths of 1 to 20 m.

Sex.: No significant ones.

Soc.B./Assoc.: *P. olivaceus* is a common territorial shallow water species. It lives either within the branches of live corals or makes a cave under hard objects.

M.: Structures similar to branched corals or hard items on sandy bottoms should be provided. It can dig its own hiding place in the sand substrate. This cave becomes the center of its territory.

Light: Sunlight zone.

B./Rep.: After several approaches, the ♂ guides the ♀ into the cave and nudges her, trying to entice her to spawn. This takes at least 2 hours. After this time, a 2-3 centimeter ball of eggs is formed. This sphere adheres to the genital papilla at first then falls off and sticks to the substratum. The ♂ then chases the ♀ away and begins its brood care which lasts until the young hatch.

F.: C; *P. olivaceus* primarily feeds on benthic and planktonic crustacealike organisms.

S.: *P. olivaceus* is one of the oldest known species of dottybacks. It has elongated tips on its caudal fin and a dark brown, gold framed, circular spot on its operculum.

T: 24°-28°C, **L:** 10 cm, **TL:** from 60 cm, **WM:** w, **WR:** b, **AV:** 2, **D:** 3

Pseudochromis paccagnellae   AXELROD, 1973
Royal dottyback

Hab.: Central west Pacific; from Indonesia to the Solomon Islands, the Philippines, the Great Barrier Reef, and New Caledonia. At depths of 1 to 10 m.

Sex.: No significant differences.

Soc.B./Assoc.: *P. paccagnellae* lives singly in elevated areas, primarily in snug holes within rocks or corals. It has a great affinity for these hideaways and so loaths to leave them that you can remove the rock/coral piece from the water—and *P. paccagnellae* will still be within. You have to shake its hideaway quite hard to get him out. It is territorial and very aggressive.

M.: When good hiding places in a rock or reef aquarium are offered, it proves to be a robust, maintainable fish.

Light: Area of sunlight.

B./Rep.: Not known exactly. The ♂'s cave is used for spawning.

F.: C; feeds on small crustacea; in the aquarium it accepts frozen foods and mussel meat.

S.: It is interesting to note that this bright fish has eluded science for so long, even though it has a relatively broad distribution and lives in shallow zones. Perhaps its similarity to *Gramma loreto* is to blame. *P. paccagnellae*, in contrast to *Gramme loreto*, has totally transparent fins. Sometimes a narrow white line separates the yellow half of the body from the purple half.

T: 24°-26°C, **L:** 7 cm, **TL:** from 80 cm, **WM:** w, **WR:** b, **AV:** 3, **D:** 2-3

Pseudochromis olivaceus ♂

Pseudochromis paccagnellae

Fam.: Pseudochromidae

Pseudochromis pesi
Pale dottyback

LUBBOCK, 1975

Hab.: Red Sea and South Africa (Sodwana Bay). At depths of 10 to 45 m.

Sex.: No significant ones.

Soc.B./Assoc.: *P. pesi* lives singly or sometimes in pairs in isolated rocks or coral stands on sandy bottoms.

M.: Requires rocks that contain caves and crevices to feel secure in its environment.

Light: Sun to moderate light areas.

B./Rep.: They spawn in pairs in the ♂'s cave; he guards the spawn until the young hatch.

F.: C; it chases zooplankton, especially small planktonic crustacea. Suitable substitute foods are shrimp, *Mysis,* etc., placed in the effluent of the pump.

S.: The coloration is often significantly more contrasting than shown in the picture to the right: the ventral side is shiny white with a tint of light blue; dorsally the fish is black with blue edges. The dark brown opercular spot has a yellow frame.

T: 24°-26°C, **L:** 10 cm, **TL:** from 100 cm, **WM:** w, **WR:** b, **AV:** 2-3, **D:** 3

Pseudochromis persicus
Blue-spotted dottyback

MURRAY, 1887

Hab.: Persian Gulf to Pakistan. At depths of 1 to 25 m.

Sex.: No significant ones.

Soc.B./Assoc.: *P. persicus* lives alone in rock and coral hiding places.

M.: Needs a rock or reef aquarium with corresponding cover.

Light: Area of sunlight.

B./Rep.: Not known.

F.: C; like almost all other *Pseudochromis*, this species principally feeds on small crustacea which are picked off the bottom or searched for in its surroundings.

S.: *P. persicus* lives in approximately the same region as the following species and has similar demands and coloration. However, the red on the head and chest region is limited. Otherwise, it is a darker brown with irregular blue dots distributed over the entire body and mainly blue, or at least blue-framed, unpaired fins; the paired fins are red. This rare species is seldom imported.

T: 24°-28°C, **L:** 12 cm, **TL:** from 100 cm, **WM:** w, **WR:** b, **AV:** 3-4, **D:** 3

Pseudochromis pesi

Pseudochromis persicus

Fam.: Pseudochromidae

Pseudochromis porphyreus   LUBBOCK & GOLDMANN, 1974
Magenta dottyback

Hab.: Central west Pacific, from the Philippines to Samoa, Japan (N), and the Moluccas. At depths of 6 to 65 m.

Sex.: None known.

Soc.B./Assoc.: *P. porphyreus* lives singly, forms a territory around its cave, and is aggressive towards conspecifics and, sometimes, pomacentrids.

M.: Needs good hideaways and shelters. Suitable fish for the reef or fish community aquarium.

Light: Sunlight zone.

B./Rep.: Not known; spawns in pairs in the ♂'s cave.

F.: C; it hunts small benthic crustacea as well as zooplankton. In the aquarium it accepts frozen foods that are placed in the effluent of the pump.

S.: Both *P. porphyreus* and *P. fridmani* are bright magenta, but the former lacks the black line that starts at the snout, passes through the eye, and ends at the operculum. In nature they cannot be confused, since they occur in totally different regions. *P. porphyreus* does not lurk, waiting for prey on the bottom. Instead it hovers a few centimeters above it.

T: 24°-26°C, **L:** 5 cm, **TL:** from 50 cm, **WM:** w, **WR:** b, **AV:** 3, **D:** 2

For comparison: *P. fridmani* left and *P. porphyreus* right.

Pseudochromis sankeyi   LUBBOCK, 1975
Striped dottyback

Hab.: Southern Red Sea and the Gulf of Aden. At depths of 2 to 10 m.

Sex.: No significant ones.

Soc.B./Assoc.: *P. sankeyi* lives singly or in colonies within caves or in front of rock hiding places or coral banks. Therefore, it should be possible to keep groups.

M.: It requires a rock or reef aquarium riddled with hiding places.

Light: Area of sunlight.

B./Rep.: Unknown.

F.: C; it feeds on small crustacea and other invertebrates. In the aquarium it also accepts frozen foods and various minced invertebrates.

S.: *P. sankeyi* exhibits a distinct black and white design and has two white longitudinal stripes on its black body. The dorsal fin is transparent. If you discount its totally different coloration and lifestyle and only consider the body shape and fin rays, this fish is practically identical to *P. fridmani*.

T: 24°-27°C, **L:** 8 cm, **TL:** from 80 cm, **WM:** w, **WR:** b, **AV:** 2-3, **D:** 3

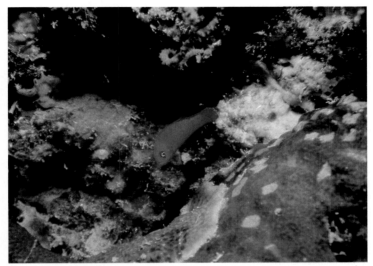

Pseudochromis porphyreus

Pseudochromis sankeyi

Fam.: Pseudochromidae

Pseudochromis splendens

Pseudochromis splendens is probably one of the most beautiful and colorful dottybacks in the world. Its relatively limited habitat in the eastern Indonesian region makes it a rarely seen guest in our aquaria. Almost 20 cm total length makes this species one of the largest of the genus and, as such, makes it a better candidate for the traditional fish community tank. As the photo shows, it likes to inhabit sponges.

Pseudochromis splendens ♂

Pseudochromis splendens   FOWLER, 1931
Splendid dottyback

Hab.: East Indonesia and the northwest coast of Australia. At depths of 20 to 40 m.

Sex.: No significant ones. The ♂ sports the above bright colors; the ♀ is slightly plainer.

Soc.B./Assoc.: *P. splendens* lives singly on coral stalks, rocks, and sponges.

M.: *P. splendens* is suitable for the fish community tank and conditionally suitable for aquaria that house anemones or soft corals.

Light: Area of sunlight.

B./Rep.: Not known. It is assumed that spawning follows the pattern set by other members of the genus: pairs breed in the ♂'s lair.

F.: C; it searches for food, especially crustacea on rocks, corals, and sponges.

S.: This species is one of the most beautiful dottybacks. Its limited geographical distribution makes it a rare import.

T: 24°-26°C, **L:** 18 cm, **TL:** from 120 cm, **WM:** w, **WR:** b, **AV:** 3, **D:** 3

Fam.: Pseudochromidae

Pseudochromis springeri
Springer's dottyback

LUBBOCK, 1975

Hab.: Red Sea. At depths of 2 to 60 m.

Sex.: No significant ones.

Soc.B./Assoc.: *P. springeri* lives a solitary existence in intimate association with corals. It never strays far from the protection of the coral. Pairs are also seen outside the spawning season.

M.: Provide hiding places that correspond to something it might find in its natural biotope.

Light: Sunlight to moderate light zones.

B./Rep.: Not known.

F.: C; primarily feeds on small crustacea. In the aquarium it takes *Mysis*, shrimp, freeze-dried foods, and *Artemia*.

S.: This minute species is easily identified by its gray to black body that has two brilliant blue stripes running from the head to the anterior body.

T: 24°-27°C, **L:** 6 cm, **TL:** from 80 cm, **WM:** w, **WR:** b, **AV:** 3, **D:** 3

Pseudoplesiops multisquamatus
Multi-scaled dottyback

ALLEN, 1987

Hab.: Eastern Indian Ocean (Christmas Island, Cocos-Keeling) and the central Pacific (Indonesia to the Solomon and Fiji Islands). At depths of 15 to 65 m.

Sex.: None known.

Soc.B./Assoc.: *P. multisquamatus* lives singly in rock hiding places. It is particularly suitable for aquaria that contain corals and anemones.

M.: It requires rock or coral formations that are riddled in hideaways.

Light: Moderate light zone.

B./Rep.: Unknown.

F.: C; it feeds on zooplankton and takes plankton substitutes like frozen shrimp, *Mysis*, and live *Artemia*.

S.: None.

T: 24°-26°C, **L:** 5 cm, **TL:** from 60 cm, **WM:** w, **WR:** b., **AV:** 2-3, **D:** 3

Pseudoplesiops typus   BLEEKER, 1858
Pink dottyback

Hab.: Central west Pacific, from Indonesia to the Solomon Islands, northwest Australia, and Queensland. At depths of 15 to 65 m.

Sex.: No significant differences.

Soc.B./Assoc.: *P. typus* lives singly and resides in heads of coral.

M.: It requires either corals or rock scenery rich in lairs.

Light: Moderate light.

B./Rep.: Not known.

F.: C; it lies in wait for zooplankton on prominent sections of the reef. In the aquarium it accepts live as well as frozen crustaceanlike foods.

S.: None.

T: 24°-26°C, **L:** 5 cm, **TL:** from 60 cm, **WM:** w, **WR:** b, **AV:** 3, **D:** 3

Gramma melacara

Fam.: Grammidae

About the Family Grammidae

Grammidae is an independent family comprised of fishes similar to dottybacks. Although closely related, they are geographically separated from each other, since fairy basslets only occur in the Atlantic. In the warm waters of the Caribbean the most numerous representatives, *Gramma melacara* and *Gramma loreto*, live at depths accessible to SCUBA divers, while the third in the pact, *Gramma linki*, can only be found below 40 m. The fairy basslets' striking colors have made them a beautiful, sought aquarium addition.

Several years ago, one of the authors (H.D.) had the opportunity to observe a commercial fish collector based in Miami capture fairy basslets from around the Bahamas Islands. This person was totally obsessed with catching the blackcap basslet because that species was being traded at ten times the price of the royal gramma. It soon became apparent on the reefs of Bimini why *Gramma melacara* brings a higher price: at 10 m depth every crevice and cave contained a *Gramma loreto*. The blackcap was nowhere to be seen. The collector had to dive 30 m, which was quite cumbersome with his system (direct breathing through long hoses connected to a compressor on a boat). Whenever he had outfoxed a *Gramma melacara* and gotten it stored in his plastic container, it was still a long shot that the captured fish would emerge healthy at the surface. A fish, just like humans, has to undergo slow decompression from such profound depths. Time is money, and the few *Gramma melacara* took several hours to reach the boat unharmed.

Maintenance in a salt water aquarium is quite simple for all imported fairy basslets. They are very resistant against disease with the proper water quality and quickly feel at home in artificial caves. If dottybacks or similar small fishes are in the same aquarium, occasional threats ensue; otherwise, they are peaceful. Substrate spawners within this family were the first seawater fishes bred in the U.S.A. *Gramma loreto* was the most notable pioneer fish of the '60's. Several generations of it and *Amphiprion* species were successfully raised in aquaria.

Gramma loreto

Gramma loreto in its natural biotope.

Fam.: Grammidae

Gramma loreto ♂ ♂

Gramma loreto   POEY, 1868
Royal gramma

Hab.: Caribbean islands and the Bermudas. At depths of 1 to 40 m.

Sex.: The sexes cannot be distinguished by external characteristics.

Soc.B./Assoc.: In their natural biotope they sometimes live in groups of up to 100 individuals. Can be kept singly or in pairs. They are peaceful when housed with dottybacks or similar small fishes. Threatening behavior may be discerned, but it is infrequent. *Caulerpa* are recommended (see below).

M.: Reef aquarium with many crevices or caves. Within these lairs is where the fish spend most of their time. An aquarium cover is recommended, since they will occasionally jump out of the water.

Light: Sun to moderate light regions.

B./Rep.: *G. loreto* is one of the few species of aquarium fishes being commercially bred in the United States. It will repeatedly spawn in an aquarium as well. In preparation, the pair cleans the stones and coral rubble from the cave with its mouth. Then *Caulerpa* are placed in the cave as a substrate for the eggs. A stone wall is erected at the cave entrance until just a small opening remains. During this period they are very aggressive towards other fishes. The eggs are laid on the *Caulerpa* and then immediately fertilized by the ♂. Fungal infections of the eggs and procuring food (plankton) for the larvae present the most problematic aspects of rearing.

F.: C, FD; choosey at the beginning, but later learn to accept all frozen foods. Algae are always welcomed while tablet foods are occasionally accepted.

S.: Very suitable as a "beginner fish." It is suggested that it, like other *Gramma* species, should only be kept with west Atlantic and Caribbean species. The fish often swim upside-down with their ventral side towards the roof of the cave.

T: 22°-27°C, **L:** 10 cm, **TL:** from 80 cm, **WM:** m, **WR:** m, **AV:** 1, **D:** 1

Gramma linki

Gramma linki
Yellowlined basslet

STARCK & COLIN, 1978

Hab.: Caribbean islands. At depths of less than 40 m.

Sex.: None known.

Soc.B./Assoc.: Similar to *G. melacara*, but this species is somewhat more timid. They are excellent tankmates for invertebrates.

M.: Reef aquarium with several places to hide. A cover is recommended since the animals occasionally jump.

Light: Moderate light.

B./Rep.: Like *G. loreto*; unfortunately, reproduction on a large scale has not yet been successful.

F.: C, FD; frozen *Artemia* and *Mysis* as well as chopped fish and mussel meat. Broken tablets can also be given.

S.: Sometimes they swim upside-down in their cave.

T: 22°-26°C, **L:** 8 cm, **TL:** from 80 cm, **WM:** m, **WR:** m, **AV:** 2-3, **D:** 2

Gramma melacara

Gramma melacara   BÖHLKE & RANDALL, 1963
Blackcap basslet

Hab.: Caribbean islands. At depths of 20 to 60 m.

Sex..: Not known.

Soc.B./Assoc.: House singly or in pairs. They get along very well with almost all other aquarium inhabitants.

M.: Reef aquarium with several caves as refuges.

Light: Moderate light areas.

B./Rep.: The ♀ deposits eggs from time to time in a cave with a ♂. Reproduction is often successful. Fungal infections of the eggs and procuring food for the larvae are often problematic.

F.: C, FD; frozen *Artemia*, *Mysis*, and chopped mussel meat are readily taken.

S.: Unknown.

T: 22°-27°C, **L:** 10 cm, **TL:** from 80 cm, **WM:** m, **WR:** m, **AV:** 2, **D:** 1-2

Plesiops caeruleolineatus, see p. 1008 for text.

Fam.: Plesiopidae

About the Family Plesiopidae

Members of this reclusive family are appealing to both the aquarist and diver, if he has a sharp enough eye to see them. They live along tropical and temperate reefs in the Indo-Pacific. Both *Assessor* and *Calloplesiops* species are so reluctant to leave their cover that photographing their entire body with its uncommonly large and fascinatingly colored dorsal, caudal, and anal fins demands diligence and patience. This is not to say that the slightly less attractive *Plesiops* are any more outgoing. They, too, are secretive fishes.

Schools of *Assessor* species occur along Australia's Great Barrier Reef. These schools may be comprised of up to 100 fish and are generally found at depths of about 15 m. The blue *A. macneilli* is a cave dweller; therefore, it does not like bright light. It frequently swims just beneath the cave's ceiling and avoids the bright sandy bottom of its surroundings. *A. flavissimus* has a similar lifestyle but is commonly found in pairs or small groups.

Assessor macneilli

Like the jawfish family, *Assessor* species are also mouthbrooders. Observations in an aquarium have shown that the male takes the fertilized egg ball into his mouth and broods it for about 15 days until the larvae hatch.

The close relationship of the Plesiopidae to the Pseudochromidae has already been described. As far as scientists and aquarists were able to determine, the breeding behavior and the parental care of the offspring appears to be very similar in these two families. One Dutch aquarist was able to successfully reproduce the most attractive member of this family, *Calloplesiops altivelis*, in his aquarium in the mid '80's. The following is a synopsis of the event:

Calloplesiops altivelis produce a fairly round egg ball roughly 2.5 cm in diameter which is adhered to the wall of the cave. On average each individual egg has a diameter of ca. 1 mm and has adhesive threads that coalesce the eggs and allow them to adhere to the substrate. A spawn is normally comprised of up to 500 eggs. At 26°C, development takes 5 to 6 days. In the late evening, after the onset of darkness, hundreds of larvae hatch. They are intensely pigmented, about 3 cm long, and have a fin fringe that extends around the tail and part of the body. They have pectoral fins, well developed eyes, and a large mouth. They swim with jerking movements. There is no visible yolk sac, which explains why the larvae begin feeding almost immediately.

The larvae are accomplished swimmers within a few days, moving purposefully through the rearing tank. This is why the food density can be kept relatively low, thereby reducing the danger of water pollution. Young larvae show a predilection for slightly flowing water, and the majority are always located close to the aerator. During the first 14 days, they double in length and their girth increases markedly. Around the 16th day, striking changes occur in design as well as behavior: the black larvae develop a light spot on each side. Examined preserved larvae showed that the black pigment cells are slowly disappearing from that site. The pigment cells continue disappearing until the flanks are totally white, a strong contrast to the black pigmented areas that remain.

However, the changing behavior that comes to pass with the design changes is more notorious. From day 16 on, the initially free-swimming larvae begin transforming into shy, reclusive fish like their parents. They pile into corners of the aquarium trying to hide. After two halved PVC pipes were introduced, all the young roundheads disappeared

Fam.: Plesiopidae

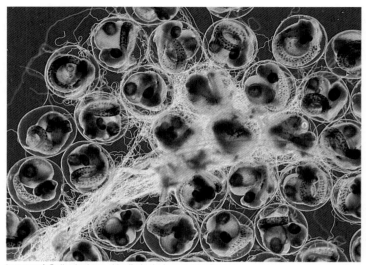

Larvae of *Calloplesiops altivelis* in their egg membranes.

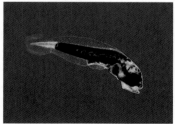

2 months

3 months

4-5 months

beneath them, and the restless swimming immediately stopped. This behavioral change leads you to deduce that the animals underwent a transition and have now adopted their adult lifestyle which is dependent on hiding places. The young remained under the pipes during the day and searched for food in the evenings.

Achieving the full adult coloration is a lengthy process. After the fish is about two months old, white dots begin to spring up on the solid black head. The white flanks remain until about 5 months of age. Once the young have reached 5 months of age, the dorsal, caudal, and anal fins have acquired their characteristic shape that is so typical for the family. In addition, the ocellus has formed. From that time on, the white on the sides progressively fades as black pigment is deposited along the black/white border. By 7 months of age, *Calloplesiops altivelis* has its adult coloration and is about 3 cm long. At this time they forage in the evenings *en masse*, still free of rivalries. Some will claim a refuge after being transferred to a reef aquarium. The sexes are identical. Males and females cannot be distinguished by size or color. Oviposition occurs in seclusion. Pairing must be quite rough because the fins of both animals were damaged. The

Calloplesiops altivelis, subadult, 22 months of age; aquarium-bred animals.

spawn is deposited in a cave and constantly guarded by one parent. If custom follows, it is the male guarding the eggs. Sometimes the "female" marine betta is seen in the cave opening while the "male" shields the egg ball with a spread tail fin. As long as the embryos are developing (5 to 6 days at 26°C), the nest is guarded. The guardian does not eat during this time and chases its partner away. After the larvae have hatched during the night, the hungry parent shows up again at feeding time. A regular spawning pattern, as seen in *Amphiprion* species, does not occur in Plesiopidae. Weeks can pass before there is a new spawn.

While the two *Calloplesiops* species prefer tropical temperatures, there are two genera which feel comfortable in cooler waters. *Paraplesiops* and *Trachinops* can be found exclusively in temperate waters around Australia south of the 30th parallel. The water temperatures there usually remain below 20°C. Most *Paraplesiops* species are bluish and grow quite large, some up to 25 cm. Like *Plesiops* and *Calloplesiops*, they lead a secluded life. But in their habitat there are no coral formations, only algae-covered rock caves and overhangs.

The lifestyle of the hulafishes of the genus *Trachinops*, in contrast, is totally different. Like coral perches, they feed on plankton in the open water and form large schools. Both coldwater genera of the Plesiopidae live about 5 years. They, like their tropical counterparts, adhere their eggs in their hiding places.

Assessor flavissimus
Golden mini-grouper

ALLEN & KUITER, 1976

Hab.: East Australia. At depths of 5 to 20 m.

Sex.: None.

Soc.B./Assoc.: *A. flavissimus* lives singly, in pairs, or in small groups and hides in caves and crevices. Since you cannot differentiate sexes, especially when the fish are purchased young, you are limited to keeping a single specimen in the aquarium.

M.: Needs an aquarium with rocks (coral) and algae. An excellent animal for the fish community aquarium.

Light: Areas of moderate light.

B./Rep.: *A. flavissimus* is a mouthbrooder; it is probably the ♂ that takes the fertilized egg ball and guards it until the larvae hatch.

F.: C; feeds on invertebrates, especially small crustacea. After acclimation it can be fed frozen or freeze-dried foods.

S.: This rare, recently described species has a limited distribution and a secluded lifestyle; in other words, few animals reach pet stores.

T: 24°-26°C, **L:** 6 cm, **TL:** from 60 cm, **WM:** w, **WR:** b, **AV:** 3-4, **D:** 3-4

Fam.: Plesiopidae

Assessor macneilli   WHITLEY, 1935
MacNeill's mini-grouper

Hab.: Southwest Pacific, from the Australian Barrier Reef to New Caledonia. At depths of 2 to 15 m.

Sex.: None.

Soc.B./Assoc.: A social species that lives in schools and resides in caves; therefore, either single specimens or groups can be maintained.

M.: Provide large shaded areas in the form of overhangs, caves, and niches that protect them from direct light.

Light: Moderate to dim light zones.

B./Rep.: *A. macneilli* is a mouthbrooder. Its brood care has been observed in the aquarium. The ♂ takes the fertilized egg ball into his mouth and protects it for about 14 days until all the larvae have hatched. He does not feed during this time.

F.: C; feeds on invertebrates and freeze-dried substitute foods.

S.: None.

T: 24°-26°C, **L:** 6 cm, **TL:** from 50 cm, **WM:** w, **WR:** b, **AV:** 2-3, **D:** 3

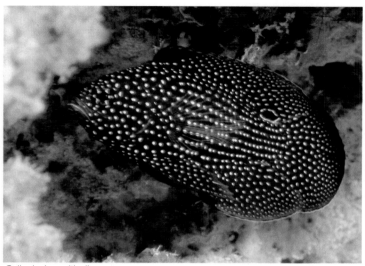

Calloplesiops altivelis

Calloplesiops altivelis   (STEINDACHNER, 1903)
Coral comet, marine betta

Hab.: Indo-Pacific, from the Red Sea to the Line Islands, Japan (N), and the southern Barrier Reef. At depths from 3 to 45 m.

Sex.: None.

Soc.B./Assoc.: *C. altivelis* lives singly in rock hiding places in reef slopes. Keep them singly with other moderate-sized fishes.

M.: It needs a reef or rock aquarium with numerous hiding places.

Light: Areas of moderate light.

B./Rep.: See pages 995-998.

F.: C; feeds on small crustacea and small fishes it captures from the safety of its shelter. After acclimation, frozen and freeze-dried foods are accepted.

S.: During the day the animals usually remain in their hideaway, only appearing at sunset. When threatened, their head is hidden in a hole so that only the posterior body sticks out. The ocelli and finnage look remarkably similar to the head of a moray eel (*Gymnothorax meleagris*).

T: 24°-26°C, **L:** 16 cm, **TL:** from 100 cm, **WM:** w, **WR:** b, **AV:** 2 , **D:** 3

Calloplesiops altivelis

Calloplesiops argus

Calloplesiops argus
Argus comet

FOWLER & BEAN, 1930

Hab.: Western Pacific, especially around the Philippines. At depths of 3 to 50 m.

Sex.: None.

Soc.B./Assoc.: *C. argus* lives singly, usually hidden in rock crevices during the day. Peaceful towards other fishes as long as they are not too small.

M.: Requires a rocky landscape with many hiding possibilities corresponding to its size.

Light: Area of moderate light.

B./Rep.: *C. argus* spawns in pairs in a cave and one of the parents (probably the ♂) cares for the spawn; that is, the eggs adhered to the rock are guarded until they hatch after barely one week. In contrast to the previous species, this one has not been bred in an aquarium.

F.: C; feeds on small crustacea and small fishes or fish larvae when it can get them. Because it is a poor swimmer, it always seems to get the short end of the stick in the presence of tankmates, but left-overs will be eaten from the bottom.

S.: Although *C. argus* is similar to *C. altivelis*, its light dots are significantly smaller and more numerous, the fins are somewhat larger, and there is a light spot on the tip of its caudal fin.

T: 24°-26°C, **L:** 16 cm, **TL:** from 120 cm, **WM:** w, **WR:** b, **AV:** 2-3, **D:** 3

Fam.: Plesiopidae

Paraplesiops alisonae   HOESE & KUITER, 1984
Alison's devilfish

Hab.: Southwest Pacific, south Australia. At depth of 5 to 20 m.

Sex.: None.

Soc.B./Assoc.: *P. alisonae* lives singly in rocky hiding places. A fish community tank presents the least management difficulties.

M.: Needs rock formations that provide cover and hiding possibilities.

Light: Area of moderate light.

B./Rep.: Not known.

F.: C; feeds on crustacea and small fishes, but it can also be acclimated to frozen foods.

S.: Although *P. alisonae* is similar to *P. poweri*, its blue spots on the head are larger and more pronounced and most fins have a blue fringe as well as a second blue band proximal to the first that is separated by a black stripe.

T: 16°-20°C, **L:** 12 cm, **TL:** from 60 cm, **WM:** w, **WR:** b, **AV:** 3-4, **D:** 3

Paraplesiops bleekeri   (GÜNTHER, 1861)
Bleeker's devilfish

Hab.: Southwest Pacific, east Australia. At depths of 5 to 15 m.

Sex.: None.

Soc.B./Assoc.: *P. bleekeri* lives singly in rock caves and holes commensurate to its size.

M.: Requires a rock aquarium outfitted with sufficient refuges.

Light: Areas of moderate light.

B./Rep.: Not known.

F.: C; it feeds on small animals, especially crustacea and small fishes.

S.: This attractively marked species is more colorful than the better known *P. meleagris*; because of its reduced habitat, however, it is infrequently found in pet stores.

T: 18°-22°C, **L:** 23 cm, **TL:** from 150 cm, **WM:** w, **WR:** b, **AV:** 4, **D:** 3

Paraplesiops alisonae

Paraplesiops bleekeri, Bowen Island, New South Wales.

Fam.: Plesiopidae

Paraplesiops meleagris (PETERS, 1869)
Western blue devil

Hab.: Southeast Indian Ocean, around west and south Australia. At depths of 15 to 25 m.
Sex.: None.
Soc.B./Assoc.: *P. meleagris* leads a solitary, secluded life in caves and holes.
M.: Requires a rock aquarium with hideaways that are fitting for its size. It grows relatively fast and becomes quite large.
Light: Moderate light.
B./Rep.: Not known.
F.: C; feeds on crustaceanlike organisms, small fishes, and frozen foods.
S.: Besides *C. altivelis*, this roundhead is one of the most beautiful fishes in the family. Its juvenile coloration of rich blue dots on the head and black dots on the posterior edges of the unpaired fins is an impressive display.
T: 18°-22°C, **L:** 40 cm, **TL:** from 120 cm, **WM:** w, **WR:** b, **AV:** 3-4, **D:** 3

Paraplesiops poweri OGILBY, 1908
Blue-tip longfin

Hab.: Southwest Pacific, east Australia. At depths of 10 to 20 m.
Sex.: None.
Soc.B./Assoc.: Lives alone in caves and crevices. Can be housed with other fishes.
M.: Provide ample refuges and cover.
Light: Moderate light.
B./Rep.: Not known.
F.: C; it feeds on small fishes, all types of crustacea, and frozen foods.
S.: The color of *P. poweri* can vary from reddish to brownish. The blue opercular ocellus, the blue dots on the head, and the blue fin fringes are consistently the same.
T: 20°-26°C, **L:** 20 cm, **TL:** from 120 cm, **WM:** w, **WR:** b, **AV:** 3-4, **D:** 3

Paraplesiops poweri

Paraplesiops meleagris

Paraplesiops meleagris, juvenile

Fam.: Plesiopidae

Plesiops coeruleolineatus
RÜPPELL, 1835
Bluefin devil

Hab.: Indo-Pacific, from the Red Sea to Samoa, Japan (N), and the Great Barrier Reef (S). At depths of 3 to 23 m.

Sex.: None.

Soc.B./Assoc.: *P. coeruleolineatus* lives a solitary, secluded existence along outer reef terraces and reef slopes; suitable for a fish and reef aquarium.

M.: Unfortunately, this fish remains hidden during the day; offer deep shelters and overhangs. It emerges at twilight to search for food.

Light: Moderate light.

B./Rep.: Not known.

F.: C; it feeds on small crustacea, fishes, and snails. Respect its natural feeding behavior and feed during the evening hours.

S.: This dark brown to black fish can be differentiated from all other Plesiopidae by its dorsal fin which has orange to bright red tips distal to the blue longitudinal band.

T: 24°-26°C, **L:** 8 cm, **TL:** from 80 cm, **WM:** w, **WR:** b, **AV:** 2-3, **D:** 3

Plesiops corallicola
BLEEKER, 1853
Ocellated longfin

Hab.: Indo-Pacific, from Madagascar to the Line Islands, Japan (N), and the southern Barrier Reef (S). At 1 to 10 m depth.

Sex.: None.

Soc.B./Assoc.: *P. corallicola* lives singly on reef terraces where it waits for prey under stones or at the bottom of crevices.

M.: Requires a rock aquarium with corresponding overhangs and shelters.

Light: Moderate light.

B./Rep.: Not known.

F.: C; it patiently waits in its hiding place for passing prey (small fishes and crustacea).

S.: The coloration of *P. corallicola* is very variable, ranging from pale gray with black and blue dots to almost entirely black. However, all have a blue ocellus on the edge of the operculum.

T: 24°-26°C, **L:** 15 cm, **TL:** from 120 cm, **WM:** w, **WR:** b, **AV:** 2-3, **D:** 3

Plesiops nigricans
(RÜPPELL, 1828)
Black devil

Hab.: Red Sea. At 5 to 30 m depth.

Sex.: None.

Soc.B./Assoc.: *P. nigricans* is found alone under stones, corals, or in rock crevices.

M.: It needs a rock or reef aquarium with corresponding hiding possibilities.

Light: Moderate light.

B./Rep.: Not known.

F.: C; feeds on small crustacea, fish larvae, and small fishes.

S.: None.

T: 24°-28°C, **L:** 9 cm, **TL:** from 100 cm, **WM:** w, **WR:** b, **AV:** 3, **D:** 3

Plesiops corallicola

The fishes of the genus *Plesiops* differ from the other Plesiopidae by having a more elongated body, a body height less than its head length, and a shorter tail fin which, again, does not exceed the head length. In addition, hard rays of the dorsal fin protrude and stand segregated like little flags. But this is only seen in a spread dorsal fin. The ventral fins are very long. While this is a characteristic common to almost all Plesiopidae, it is by far less obvious in the previously described large-finned species than it is in these small-finned animals. They sit on a tripod made of their two ventral fins and the anal fin. During the day they rest on the substrate within their lair and wait for passing prey. They leave their hideaway in the evening and search for food at night. Small crustacea, fishes, and an occasional snail is the diet of choice.

Plesiops caeruleolineatus

Plesiops nigricans

Fam.: Plesiopidae

Trachinops taeniatus

Species contained within the genus *Trachinops* bear little resemblance to other members of the family. They are small, slender fishes with an interesting caudal fin. Its center rays are longer than the rest and drawn into a distinct tip. All of the three presented hulafishes inhabit the temperate waters around southern Australia and are practically unavailable on the German market. In contrast to their relatives, these are not asocial fishes that live a secluded life. Like coral perches, they are schooling planktivores.

No information is available on maintaining these fishes in an aquarium.

The yellowstripe hulafish, *Trachinops taeniatus* GÜNTHER, 1861, lives in southeast Australia, reaches a length of 10 cm, is beautifully colored, and prefers to live at depths of 20 to 30 m.

The tailspot hulafish, *T. caudimaculatus* MCCOY, 1890, inhabits southeast Australia to Tasmania, also grows to 10 cm in length, and prefers to live at ca. 30 m depth. It is easily identified by its dark spot on the tail fin.

The southern hulafish, *T. noarlungae* GLOVER, 1974, lives along the south and west coasts of Australia and it, like the previous two species, grows to 10 cm and lives at ca. 30 m depth.

Trachinops caudimaculatus

Trachinops noarlungae

Fam.: Malacanthidae

In the '50's and '60's before the advent of reef aquaria, tilefishes were an insignificant part of the hobby. But the desire to combine fishes with invertebrates as well as the discovery of several colorful species during the '70's has brought this family further to the fore. New species are constantly being discovered, as demonstrated by *Hoplolatilus luteus* ALLEN & KUITER, 1989. The genus *Malacanthus* is also a member of this family, but its 3 known species are irregularly imported. While *Hoplolatilus* species rarely top 15 cm, fishes of the genus *Malacanthus* may reach 40 cm in length.

All tilefishes remain very timid in the aquarium. Never house them with aggressive fishes such as triggers or surgeonfishes. They feed on plankton (fish and crustacean larvae) in the open water. Frozen or live *Artemia* and *Mysis* are eagerly taken as they pass by in the current of the recirculating pump. These nimble fork-tailed torpedo-shaped fishes dart through the aquarium while feeding, grabbing their nourishment with precision. A deep sand substratum with a carved-out coral block on top provides an adequate nocturnal resting place.

The most colorful species such as *H. purpureus, H. marcosi,* and *H. luteus* come from the Philippine-Indonesia area. The chameleon tilefish, *H. chlupatyi,* can change its body color from yellow-green to blue-violet and all the colors in between within seconds. All of these fish form a strong bond to a hiding place in the coral above which they "stand" during the day catching plankton. From this position, the round headed tilefishes can recognize possible predators at a distance—the diver is included in this category—and easily dart into their cave as soon as their space is invaded. The underwater photographer's job is not an easy one. Only a macro-telephoto lens helps.

Tilefishes form long term pairs, although there does not seem to be any sexual dimorphism (or dichromatism). Courtship and spawning occurs in the open water. The eggs are pelagic (drift in the current). Tilefishes are uncommon in waters less than 20 m deep. But they are distributed throughout the tropical and subtropical region of three oceans. Pairs are often seen hovering above their shelters in coral rubble or sand slopes. *Malacanthus plumieri,* a species whose distribution is limited to the Atlantic, drew the eyes of ichthyologists when it was seen building small hills with coral branches, mollusc shells, and calcareous algae. It then used these structures like a nest and lived among them. Interestingly enough, *Hoplolatilus geo*, a recently discovered species from profound depths of more than 100 m in the Red Sea, engages in similar activities.

Malacanthus plumieri

Fam.: Malacanthidae

Hoplolatilus chlupatyi   KLAUSEWITZ, McCOSKER, RANDALL &ZETZSCHE,1978
Chameleon tilefish

Hab.: Around the Philippines on sand and gravel bottoms of the fore reef. At about 30 m depth.

Sex.: No external differences.

Soc.B./Assoc.: They live in pairs and should only be kept as such. When possible, do not associate with other fishes. Their extreme timidity becomes more pronounced.

M.: Provide a reef aquarium with a sandy substrate and build several stone or coral caves on it.

Light: Moderate light.

B./Rep.: Has not been accomplished in an aquarium.

F.: C, FD; planktivores which can be easily accustomed to minced frozen foods. Allow the food to drift past them.

S.: Just like the reptilian chameleon, *H.chlupatyi* can undergo fast color changes. It has the capacity to be any color from yellow-green to blue-violet.

T: 22°-27°C, **L:** 11 cm, **TL:** from 80 cm, **WM:** m, **WR:** m, **AV:** 2, **D:** 1-2

Hoplolatilus chlupatyi

Hoplolatilus cuniculus   RANDALL & DOOLEY, 1974
Dusky tilefish

Hab.: From Mauritius to Micronesia on sandy bottoms along the outer coral reefs at depth of 30 to 115 m.

Sex.: No external differences.

Soc.B./Assoc.: They live in pairs or groups. Do not associate with overly active fishes. Its extremely congenial personality allows it to be housed with almost all invertebrates.

M.: Reef aquarium with a sand bottom. Hiding places in rocks as well as on the sand bottom should be offered. Caves are dug underneath stones lying flat on the sand.

Light: Areas of moderate light.

B./Rep.: After fertilization, the eggs drift for some time in the plankton. Larvae and juveniles less than 6 cm in length swim in the open water column. Only afterwards do they start living in the benthic zones and digging caves. Reproduction in captivity has not been successful.

F.: C, FD; frozen or live *Artemia* and *Mysis* as well as chopped mussel and shrimp meat. Place the food so that it drifts past the hovering fish.

S.: The coloration can vary. In their natural biotope they hover in groups above giant hills of sand (up to 5.5 x 3 x 1 m high) they themselves probably built.

T: 22°-27°C, **L:** 11 cm, **TL:** from 80 cm, **WM:** m-s, **WR:** m, **AV:** 2, **D:** 1-2

Hoplolatilus chlupatyi

Hoplolatilus cuniculus

Fam.: Malacanthidae

Hoplolatilus fourmanoiri
Spotted tilefish

SMITH, 1983

Hab.: Vietnam, the Philippines, and the Solomon Islands. On sand and gravel bottoms of coral reefs at depths of about 50 m.

Sex.: No external differences.

Soc.B./Assoc.: Usually found in pairs. These shy fish should not be kept with larger fishes.

M.: Reef aquarium with a substratum of loose sand. Stone caves or halfed flower pots are appropriate refuges.

Light: Area of moderate light.

B./Rep.: Has not been successful in an aquarium.

F.: C, FD; small food pieces are snapped up as they drift past.

S.: In profile, these fish have two black spots—one on the operculum and one in the center of the caudal fin.

T: 22°-28°C, **L:** 15 cm, **TL:** from 100 cm, **WM:** m, **WR:** m, **AV:** 2, **D:** 1-2

Hoplolatilus fourmanoiri

Hoplolatilus luteus
Golden tilefish

ALLEN & KUITER, 1989

Hab.: In Indonesia on sandy rubble bottoms. At depth of 15 to 50 m.

Sex.: Not recognizable from external characteristics.

Soc.B./Assoc.: Their timidness makes a large tank necessary if you care to house them with other fishes.

M.: Reef aquarium with a sand bottom that has several small hiding places arranged upon it.

Light: Area of moderate light.

B./Rep.: Nothing specific is known about this species.

F.: C, FD; small chopped frozen or live foods. Both will have to drift in the vicinity of the fish before they will be eaten.

S.: This species was not scientifically described until 1989.

T: 23°-27°C, **L:** 14 cm, **TL:** from 100 cm, **WM:** m, **WR:** b-m, **AV:** 3, **D:** 1-2

Hoplolatilus fourmanoiri

Hoplolatilus luteus

Fam.: Malacanthidae

Hoplolatilus marcosi　　　　　　　　　　　　　　　　　　　　BURGESS, 1978
Redstripe tilefish

Hab.: From the Philippines to the Solomon Islands. They live over sand and gravel bottoms of coral reefs at depths of 30 to 80 m.

Sex.: No distinguishing external features.

Soc.B./Assoc.: They live in pairs in caves which are dug under stones. Good tankmates for invertebrates. Do not associate with lively fishes.

M.: Reef aquarium that has a substrate of sand and shell with flat stones lying on top. The fish will dig their own caves beneath them.

Light: Moderate light.

B./Rep.: Has not been successful in an aquarium.

F.: *Artemia*, krill, and pieces of squid are particularly appreciated. Healthy animals have an enormous appetite.

S.: This species is easily recognized by its red longitudinal stripe on a white background. Just a few years ago these fish were so ill when imported because of the poison used to capture them that maintaining these animals successfully was hardly possible. Now these animals reach Europe in such good health that the only thing that prevents heatly maintenance is the fish´s own frantic nature. They easily leap out of the aquarium during the night. They probably panic when they are unable to find their cave. Aquaria containing these fish should have a light left on at night and a tight cover. These two measures will allow you to enjoy these unusually personable, tame animals.
Best cared for in large groups. *H. marcosi* is particularly compatible to *Hoplolatilus purpureus*.

T: 22°-28°C, **L:** 8-12 cm, **TL:** from 100 cm, **WM:** m, **WR:** b-m, **AV:** 2, **D:** 1-2

Hoplolatilus purpureus　　　　　　　　　　　　　　　　　　　BURGESS, 1978
Purple tilefish

Hab.: From the Philippines to the Solomon Islands. They live over sand and rubble substrates at depths of 35 to 70 m.

Sex.: No sexual dimorphism.

Soc.B./Assoc.: Since the fish are very timid, they should only be associated with exceptionally peaceful fishes and invertebrates.

M.: A reef aquarium with a sand bottom. Hiding places in the reef zone and on the sand (halved flower pot, etc.) should be offered.

Light: Moderate light.

B./Rep.: Has not been successful in an aquarium.

F.: C, FD; planktivores which eagerly snap at any food that drifts by. Feed a variety of frozen foods and pieces of tablet foods.

S.: See *H. marcosi* above, which gets along very well with *H. purpureus* and should also be kept in groups. If possible, do not keep *Hoplolatilus* singly. Like *H. marcosi*, purple tilefish easily jump out of the aquarium. Previously these fish were anesthetized and captured using poisonous substances and the animals that reached the pet store were both frail and shy and rarely lived more than a few weeks. Now that these animals are no longer captured using these methods, the animals are lively; however, they are rarely available.

T: 22°-28°C, **L:** 15 cm, **TL:** 120 cm, **WM:** m, **WR:** b-m, **AV:** 3, **D:** 3

Hoplolatilus marcosi

Hoplolatilus purpureus

Fam.: Malacanthidae

Hoplolatilus starcki   RANDALL & DOOLEY, 1974
Stark's tilefish

Hab.: Central and western Pacific. On sandy bottoms along outer reef slopes at depths of 20 to 50 m.

Sex.: No sexual dimorphism.

Soc.B./Assoc.: Lives in pairs in its natural habitat and should, if possible, be kept pairwise in an aquarium. Good tankmates for invertebrates.

M.: *H. starcki* is the most demanding species of this genus. While *H. marcosi* and *H. purpureus* readily swim together, H. starcki usually maintains its distance from other species. H. starcki´s head shape is very different from the previously mentioned tilefishes. It is somewhat aggressive towards other tilefishes in the aquarium, but this does not mean that they pursue each other. You may notice when you closely observe these fish that this species tries to maintain a certain distance. While *H.marcosi* and *H. purpureus* frequently use a common cave, H. starcki normally has its own hiding place. H. starcki´s feeding habits are by far not as voracious as those of its relatives. This fish demands more time of its caretaker, largely because of its susceptibility towards bacterial infections and *Cryptocarion*.

Light: Moderate light.

B./Rep.: Has not been successfully bred in an aquarium.

F.: C, FD; as for *H. purpureus*.

S.: During danger they flee into their cave.

T: 21°-26°C, **L:** 9 cm, **TL:** from 80 cm, **WM:** m, **WR:** b-m, **AV:** 2, **D:** 1-2

Malacanthus brevirostris   (GUICHENOT, 1848)
Banded blanquillo

Hab.: Red Sea, Indonesia, and the eastern Pacific to Hawaii. In coral reefs and self-dug caves in the sand.

Sex.: No distinguishing external features.

Soc.B./Assoc.: Pairs live in caves in the sand. Juveniles are suitable tankmates for invertebrates.

M.: A reef aquarium with a sand bottom. Hiding places of stones or coral debris.

Light: Moderate light.

B./Rep.: Has not been successful in an aquarium.

F.: C, FD; planktivores which can easily be trained to accept chopped frozen foods. The food must be suspended and moving in the current.

S.: The genus has a rounder cross-section than *Hoplolatilus*. This species can be recognized by the two black stripes on the tail fin.

T: 22°-28°C, **L:** 30 cm, **TL:** from 120 cm, **WM:** m-s, **WR:** b-m, **AV:** 2-3, **D:** 1-2

Malacanthus brevirostris

Hoplolatilus starcki

Malacanthus brevirostris

Fam.: Malacanthidae

Malacanthus latovittatus, subadult, 20 cm

Malacanthus latovittatus, juvenile, 10 cm

Malacanthus latovittatus   (LACÉPÈDE, 1798)
Blue blanquillo

Hab.: Red Sea, Indonesia, entire Pacific, Hawaii to Japan and South Africa. Makes its home above sandy substrates between coral reefs and on rock reefs at depths of 20 to 65 m.

Sex.: No external differences.

Soc.B./Assoc.: They live singly. Juveniles make good aquarium residents. Do not keep with aggressive fishes or large crustacea.

M.: Reef aquarium with several hiding possibilities.

Light: Moderate light.

B./Rep.: Has not been successful in an aquarium.

F.: C, FD; planktivores which can be easily trained to frozen foods. The food must be suspended in the water column. Food lying on the bottom is ignored.

S.: Conspicuous long snout. Their instinct drives them into the open water rather than a cave during danger. Juveniles look like the cleaner wrasse, *Labroides dimidiatus*. It is even suspected that they mimic that cleaner fish. Larger specimens are edible.

T: 22°-28°C, **L:** may grow over 40 cm!, **TL:** from 120 cm, **WM:** m-s, **WR:** m, **AV:** 2-3, **D:** 1-2

Fam.: Cirrhitidae

Hawkfishes in general are small, colorful fishes which are found on protruding coral blocks or branches in the reef. They sit on their perches using their pectoral fins as support. Why they are called hawkfishes is easily discerned once you watch them procure food. They blend into their background until they sight likely prey—usually a small crustacean or a young fish. At that point they swoop out of their perch and ambush the unsuspecting creature. Cirrhitidae species come in a large variety of sizes. Full-grown animals can be anywhere from 10 cm to 1 m in length. Their heavy body and large head easily separates them from other benthic fish families like the blennies. Besides their stout body, all hawkfishes have tufts of hair, or cirri, on the tips of their dorsal spines. The prominence of these tufts is species dependent. With the exception of two species from the tropical Atlantic, all hawkfishes occur in the Indo-Pacific, including the Red Sea and the Gulf of California. The approximately 35 species contained in the 10 genera of this family are only found in distinct coral reefs.

Sexual dichromatism is largely absent. The longnose hawkfish, *Oxycirrhites typus*, is one of the exceptions. It is assumed that it is the male that has an additional black edge on the ventral and tail fins. Although *Cirrhitichthys oxycephalus* has two color phases, they have nothing to do with sex. They are the result of the fish adapting to its prevailing surroundings. Scientists have surmised that hawkfishes generally live in harems, and the largest fish in each group is the male. These fishes are protogynous hermaphrodites; that is, they change from females to males as males are needed within the group. This is also the norm for wrasses and angelfishes. Courtship and spawning has been observed at twilight. The dominate males defend a territory. The size of the territory depends on how many females belong to the harem (generally 2 to 7). While the male more or less ignores the females during the day, his interest is aroused as the light begins to fade. *C. oxycephalus* males have been observed swimming from one female to another. He visits each female for about one minute at their respective coral blocks, assumably searching for ripe females. Shortly before total darkness, the ripe females move to the end of a coral branch and wait until the male returns. The pair then swims in an upward arch and releases their eggs and sperm together at the apex. The female then abandons her coral branch to rest in the reef, while the male continues to search for other willing partners until it is pitch dark. There is a paucity of information about the pelagic eggs and larvae of hawkfishes, but after 4 cm long larvae of *Amblycirrhites pinos* were found, it is supposed that the pelagic phase takes weeks. The wide distribution of the different species supports this assumption since there is scarcely any other way that juveniles and adults of these benthic territorial animals can become so widespread.

There have been no reports of successfully breeding these animals in a marine aquarium. Pairs are hardly available, although you can assume that the largest animal, if not a male, will transform into a male when several specimens of the same species are placed into a large tank. The most colorful species barely grow over 15 cm long. Their behavior in the fish community tank is no surprise if you are familiar with their behavior in the wild: they sit on exposed areas of the artificial reef, waiting to lunge on passing krill or *Artemia*. While the popular longnose hawkfish is a peaceful inhabitant, smaller fishes or shrimp can never be associated with *C. fasciatus* or *P. forsteri*. Their hunting instinct will always prevail, and small dottybacks as well as cleaner shrimp will be gleefully devoured.

Cirrhitichthys falco

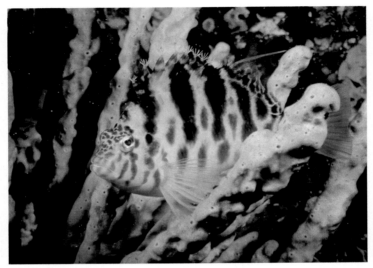

Cirrhitichthys aprinus

The spotted hawkfish (*C. aprinus*) occurs in a whole range of colors. There are light gray, white, green, red, and brown animals with crossbars. The dark crossbars are more pronounced on lighter specimens. At least 4 of the crossbars are very wide and extend from the top of the fish to the ventral half. The 5th stripe, which usually forms an elongated ocellate pattern, is especially interesting. One or two additional crossbars are often found on the caudal peduncle. Other characteristics include a round ocellus behind the eye with another spot immediately above it; this second spot may lie within the first crossband. This species likes to sit on good vantage points. From there they spot their prey—small fishes and crustacea—and pounce.

Cirrhitichthys aprinus
Spotted hawkfish

(CUVIER, 1829)

Hab.: West Pacific, the Philippines, and Indonesia. At depths of 12 to 20 m.

Sex.: None; ♂♂ are larger and developed from ♀♀.

Soc.B./Assoc.: *C. aprinus* is a loner. ♂♂ occupy different size territories. A few ♀♀ reside within its boundaries. The animals always sit alone on open sites ready to pounce on prey.

M.: *C. aprinus* is a robust charge that can be kept with larger fishes.

Light: Area of sunlight.

B./Rep.: In the sea this species spawns in pairs. ♂♂ that own a harem search for ripe ♀♀ at twilight. He swims in an upward arch with each ripe female. Eggs and sperm are released at the apex. Since the eggs and larvae have a long pelagic phase, they are widely distributed.

F.: C; *C. aprinus* is an ambush predator that feeds on passing fishes and crustacea. Shrimp, crustacea, and small fishes are consumed in the aquarium. But this species is fairly easy to train to substitute foods such as fish and crustacean meat and freeze-fried foods.

S.: *C. aprinus* is identified by its dark, usually light-framed ocellus exactly behind the eye and a second, somewhat larger, dark spot immediately above it which may be incorporated in the first crossband. C. aprinus is very aggressive towards other small species in the aquarium. Therefore, placing this fish in a community aquarium is only suggested in the community is composed of species capable of defending themselves.

T: 24°-27°C, **L:** 11 cm, **TL:** from 50 cm, **WM:** w, **WR:** b, **AV:** 2, **D:** 3

Fam.: Cirrhitidae

Cirrhitichthys falco   RANDALL, 1963
Falco hawkfish

Hab.: West Pacific; the Philippines to Japan, Samoa, the Barrier Reef, and New Caledonia. At depths of 10 to 20 m.

Sex.: None.

Soc.B./Assoc.: *C. falco* lives singly on outer reefs that either have little or plentiful coral growth. ♀ ♀ live in harems tended by a somewhat larger ♂. He usually sits at the foot of coral blocks (not on top).

M.: This fish, which requires cover and clear water, adapts well to its captive environment.

Light: Sunlight zone.

B./Rep.: Spawns in pairs at night. Reproduction in an aquarium has not been successful.

F.: C; feed meat of crustacea or fishes.

S.: It can be easily identified by its bright yellow tufts on the dorsal fin rays as well as two typical brownish stripes that descent from the eye.

T: 24°-28°C, **L:** 6 cm, **TL:** from 40 cm, **WM:** w, **WR:** b, **AV:** 1-2, **D:** 3

Cirrhitichthys oxycephalus (BLEEKER, 1855)
Pixy hawkfish

Hab.: Indo-Pacific, from the Red Sea to Panama. At depths of 10 to 25 m.

Sex.: None.

Soc.B./Assoc.: *C. oxycephalus* lives singly in the clear waters of lagoons and outer reefs rich in coral growth. The ♂ ♂ are territorial and form harems.

M.: *C. oxycephalus* does not require much swimming space since it normally sits on coral branches.

Light: Region of sunlight.

B./Rep.: The ♂ spawns in pairs with his ♀ ♀ at twilight.

F.: C; feeds on crustacea and fishes which it hunts from the open water. It can be easily trained to accept frozen foods and all types of animal fare.

S.: *C. oxycephalus* has a distinctive red body with large, round, orange to red colored spots.

T: 24°-28°C, **L:** 10 cm, **TL:** from 50 cm, **WM:** w, **WR:** b, **AV:** 2, **D:** 3

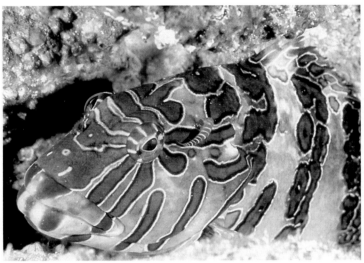

Cirrhitus rivulatus

The **giant hawkfish**, *Cirrhitus rivulatus* VALENCIENNES, 1855, grows to a length of 60 cm. It inhabits the east Pacific from the Galapagos to Colombia and the Gulf of California. Because of its size and predatory lifestyle, it is unsuitable for the home aquarium.

The **soaring hawkfish**, *Cyprinocirrhites polyactis* (BLEEKER, 1875), colonizes the tropical Indo-West Pacific from east Africa to Australia, grows to a length of 10 cm, and prefers depths of 30-120 m. It is easily identified by its orange-brown color and elongated tail fin. Zooplankton is hunted in the open water.

The **brilliant red hawkfish**, *Neocirrhites armatus* CASTELNAU, 1873, inhabits the west Pacific from Japan to Australia and prefers coral blocks of *Pocillopora* and *Stylophora*. It is a timid fish that will promptly choose the deepest crevice to hide in. Despite its beauty (not to mention its price), this fish does not adapt well to captivity. An extremely sensitive fish that needs oxygen-rich, moving water. A species best left in its natural habitat.

Cyprinocirrhites polyactis

Neocirrhites armatus

Fam.: Cirrhitidae

Oxycirrhites typus with prey

Oxycirrhites typus   (BLEEKER, 1857)
Longnose hawkfish

Hab.: Indo-Pacific; from the Red Sea to Panama, Japan, Hawaii (N), and New Caledonia (S). At depth of 10-100 m.

Sex.: Slight; the ♂♂ reportedly have a black fringe on the ventral and tail fins.

Soc.B./Assoc.: *O. typus* lives alone in the branches of large gorgonians, black corals, and *Tubastraea*, especially in deep water areas with localized strong currents.

M.: It requires clear oxygen-rich, moving water and branches similar to those found in its natural habitat.

Light: Sun to moderate light zones.

B./Rep.: *O. typus* spawns in pairs in the open water. The pair will defend its territory from conspecifics. Both the eggs and larvae are planktonic and somewhat larger than those of pygmy angelfishes (*Centropyge*).

F.: C; while it will eat small fishes, it is especially fond of small benthic and planktonic crustacea. In the aquarium it can be fed with "plankton substitutes" such as *Mysis* and other crustacea. Also accepts freeze-dried foods.

S.: The long snout is so unique it is impossible to confuse this species with others. *O. typus* is the most appropriate member of the genus for aquarium care. It is an uncommonly peaceful fish. Caution: do not cover the aquarium. Keep pairs in the aquarium. Animals of the same sex may be aggressive among each other, but strangely enough, it almost always happens that two randomly chosen animals become a harmonnious pair. They will rarely spawn, because the animals cannot rise enough above the decorations. Imports only come from Sri Lanka and are not availabl throughout the year.

T: 24°-26°C, **L:** 13 cm, **TL:** from 50 cm, **WM:** s, **WR:** b, **AV:** 2-3, **D:** 3

Oxycirrhites typus

Oxycirrhites typus

Fam.: Cirrhitidae

Paracirrhites arcatus (CUVIER, 1829)
Arc-eyed hawkfish

Hab.: Indo-Pacific, from east Africa to Hawaii, Japan (N), and New Caledonia (S). At depths of 1 to 33 m.

Sex.: None.

Soc.B./Assoc.: *P. arcatus* occurs singly, especially on corals such as *Pocillopora*, *Acropora*, and *Stylophora*. There it sits on the outer branches observing its surroundings.

M.: *P. arcatus* requires clean water and familiar coral branches or like structures to feel at ease.

Light: Area of sunlight.

B./Rep.: Not known.

F.: C; *P. arcatus* feeds on small crustacea and fishes in the sea; easily trained to substitute foods such as shrimp, crustacean, and fish meats.

S.: This hawkfish is very common. It has several color variants, but all have the typical arch behind the eye which gave it its name. The most common form has a white stripe along the posterior body like the specimen pictured on the right. The stripe is absent in some forms. Olive-green or virtually white animals also occur.

T: 25°-27°C, **L:** 14 cm, **TL:** from 50 cm, **WM:** w, **WR:** b, **AV:** 2, **D:** 3

Cirrhitichthys calliurus

Paracirrhites arcatus

Paracirrhites arcatus in an *Acropora* stone coral.

Fam.: Cirrhitidae

Paracirrhites forsteri   (BLOCH & SCHNEIDER, 1801)
Forster's hawkfish

Hab.: Indo-Pacific, from the Red Sea to Hawaii, the Marquesas and Ducie Islands, Japan (N), and New Caledonia (S). At depths of 5 to 35 m.

Sex.: The coloration of *P. forsteri* varies greatly with age and habitat, but the different colorations do not seem to be sex related.

Soc.B./Assoc.: *P. forsteri* lives singly; ♂♂ have harems with several ♀♀ in their territory, but each fish hunts alone during the day.

M.: *P. forsteri* chooses exposed sites such as the outer branches of *Acropora*, *Pocillopora*, and fire corals where it perches, watching for prey. Such coral skeletons or similar edifications and structures should be offered in the aquarium. Due to its predatory feeding habits, it should not be kept with crustacea or small fishes.

Light: Area of sunlight.

B./Rep.: Not known. ♂♂ spawn pairwise with ♀ members of their harem during the evening hours.

F.: C; in the sea it feeds on crustacea and fishes. It can be fed shrimp, fish meat, and frozen foods in captivity.

S.: Despite the many color variations, this fish is easily recognized by its bullish body shape, its behavior (sitting on open sites), and the irregular black dots on the head.
In the Red Sea, Forester's hawkfish is generally reddish or dark brown with a dark brown dorsum and light stripes down its sides and the center of the back, including the dorsal fin. The dots on the head and anterior body are one of the most typical characteristics of the species. They are usually dark brown but may be red on some fish. Juveniles may be totally red dorsally and dark ventrally. The animals are predatory sprinters which can achieve high speeds for short distances and prey on passing crustaceanlike organisms and fishes. Usually they lie on protruding coral stalks with their head extending into the open water, waiting and watching their surroundings with their large eyes.

T: 24°-27°C, **L:** 20 cm, **TL:** from 100 cm, **WM:** w-m, **WR:** b, **AV:** 1-2, **D:** 3

Juvenile *Paracirrhites forsteri*, Red Sea

Paracirrhites forsteri, Indonesia

Paracirrhites forsteri

Paracirrhites xanthus ⁻ ···

Paracirrhites xanthus   RANDALL, 1963
Golden hawkfish

Hab.: Central Pacific, Society, Tuamotu, and Caroline Islands. At depths of 2 to 10 m.

Sex.: None.

Soc.B./Assoc.: *P. xanthus* lives singly either on corals that jut out into the water or hidden in shaded areas.

M.: *P. xanthus* requires clear, oxygen-rich water and a rocky bottom with several sites to either hide in or perch on. It can be associated with larger fishes.

Light: Areas of sun and moderate light.

B./Rep.: Not known.

F.: C; it feeds on invertebrates, especially crabs and small fishes. It takes shrimp and frozen foods in the aquarium.

S.: Usually an overpowering yellow. There are also reddish-orange specimens. Note the short blue stripe that ascends from the back of the eye.

T: 24°-26°C, **L:** 10 cm, **TL:** from 80 cm, **WM:** w, **WR:** b, **AV:** 2, **D:** 3

Paracirrhites xanthus

Gobiodon histrio, text on p. 1078

Gobiosoma macrodon

Fam.: Gobiidae

ABOUT THE FAMILY GOBIIDAE

This is an extensive family to say the least. Even if this book were solely devoted to gobies, it could not do justice to the over 200 genera and almost 2000 species of this group (some are in other families). Needless to say, new species are constantly being discovered. Gobies have conquered a large variety of substrates: they can be seen above muddy and sandy bottoms, in rocky biotopes, and among corals. Some even live either on or in other organisms such as gorgonians and sponges. Gobies as a whole have adapted to almost every temperature in the sea. They range from the polar circle to the equator.

Many gobies are plain, nondescript animals, but probably an equal number, if not the majority, are attractive, colorful fishes. Basically all gobies are shy, bottom-dwelling individuals. Rarely do they grow longer than 10 cm. Their diminutive size permits them to blend into their background and remain largely out of sight of roving predators. The smallest known vertebrate belongs to the family Gobiidae: *Trimmatom nanus* from the Chagos Archipelago in the Indian Ocean does not grow larger than 8 mm! Most gobies lack an swimbladder, but this organ would be superfluous given their lifestyle. Many of the benthic species have fused ventral fins that form a suction cup. Genera that normally swim above the substrate have retained two individual ventral fins, e.g., *Eviota* or *Valenciennea*. But all gobies have one characteristic that separates them from all others. Note the dorsal fin. Every goby has two dorsal fins, while blennies and other similar fishes only have one.

Most of the goby species covered in this chapter are tropical and reef oriented. There is no sexual dimorphism, especially no dichromatism. However, male and female gobies of temperate waters can be distinguished. Males, including those from the tropics, can be identified by their brighter colors at the onset of courtship. Females can be recognized shortly before spawning when their mature eggs give them a fuller ventral profile.

It seems that most gobies retain their original sex. In genera that form harems, like *Gobiodon* and *Paragobiodon*, the largest animal is a male, and all others are functional females. If that male disappears, a female transforms into a male to replace him. Spawning activities are highly individual; for example, *Gobiosoma* spawns from January to May in the Caribbean. These months correspond to the coldest time of the year in that habitat. *Lythrypus* spawns from May to September in the Gulf of California. Those are the warmest months of the year there.

Goby spawns are adhered to the substrate, whether it be under the roof of a cave, in an empty shell, or just to a rock or piece of coral. Courtship and spawning behavior are similar in all gobies: with the swelling of the ventral region of the female, the male begins to prepare the nest. A spawning site is cleaned and then defended by the male. Usually spawning occurs early in the morning: the male entices the female to the nest by swimming back and forth in between. Once she follows him to the nest, he nudges her posterior body with his snout. All the fins are opened in front of her. When the female seems to welcome his attentions, a courtship dance ensues. The male grunts and the female responds by releasing a liquid from the ovaries which further stimulates the male. Courtship lasts from half an hour to one hour and terminates when the female follows the male to the nest and deposits all her eggs at once. Egg laying and fertilizing take place simultaneously with both partners shivering violently. Anywhere from 10 to 100,000 eggs are laid, depending on the size of the goby species. A normal size spawn for a goby is 300 to 500 eggs. Gobies can spawn 2 to 3 times a week. *Gobiosoma oceanops* has been known to spawn 9 times in 2 weeks. The nest is guarded by the male, even when the female remains close by. The sticky eggs are hard to recognize with the naked eye and are often transparent to yellow, depending on the yolk sac. The larvae hatch after about 5 to 6 days and begin to feed as soon as 12 hours thereafter. The length of the planktonic stage is sketchy for all but a few goby species. In *Paragobiodon* it is 6 weeks, but only 3 weeks in *Gobiosoma*. The life expectancy of *Gobiosoma* is estimated at 1 year, maximum 2 years. Gobies have frequently been bred in captivity, both by serious aquarists and by commercial fish breeders in the USA.

The genera in this book are in alphabetical order for systematic reasons. Consequently, highly interesting species for the aquarium are not grouped together, since they are spread out among such genera as *Amblyeleotris, Cryptocentrus, Ctenogobiops, Lotilia, Stonogobiops,* and *Vanderhorstia.* Why should every aquarist and diver take a closer look at gobies? Among the multitude of interactions between organisms in their natural biotope, there are those relationships between two unrelated species that live in community

Fam.: Gobiidae

with each other. This does not define the relationship as harmful or beneficial. It may be either or both. In contrast to parasitism, where one partner acquires unilateral advantages to the detriment of the other, there is symbiosis (mutualism), which entails both partners benefiting from their association.

The best known examples from marine biology are the interrelationships of hermit crabs or clownfishes with sea anemones.

While protection gained from living near or in the stinging anemone is the most prominent factor of the above mentioned relationships, gobies and their partners, the pistol shrimp of the genus *Alpheus*, each contributes individual services that are to the benefit of both. This symbiotic relationship has been studied for years. Provided they can find both a pistol shrimp and an appropriate goby species, interested persons can view this unique relationship in their own aquarium, as this relationship carries over into these captive environments (see pp. 519-533).

In the Gulf of Aqaba, the part of the northern Red Sea most frequented by Europeans, the sandy beaches often have a faint slope to about 10 m depth where coral growth begins. Sometimes the sandy surfaces are covered with seagrass. However, there are also totally bare parts which at first sight appear bleak and empty. But it was here while snorkeling that one of the authors (H.D.) found gobies the same color as the substrate, sitting in front of a cave with a raised head. Soon a shrimp appeared at the cave's entrance. It was busy dredging sand from the cave. Both animals rapidly disappeared into their hideout when approached. Although approached without much ado, they fled the moment that their safety zone was violated. You could see how the sand and mud slid into the cave and practically closed it. However, after a quarter of an hour, the goby looked out, declaring the area secure, and the shrimp resumed its dredging activity. Only since the end of the '50's has the symbiotic relationship between pistol shrimp and gobies from the littoral zone of tropical seas been known. Scientists familiar with this phenomenon agree that it is a true symbiosis.

The burrows of pistol shrimp are found everywhere in sand substrates and lagoon zones. All are at least 1 m beneath the water surface so that waves do not shift the sand. Quite obviously the shrimp avoid areas where the substrate sediments are moved by water currents. Often the burrow is inhabited by two shrimp, rarely by one.

The two shrimp are always the same size. The burrows are parallel to the surface, 10 cm deep, and about 70 cm long excluding the branches off the main burrow. But the tunnels are never elaborate, highly branched structures.

Symbiotic pistol shrimp are diurnal. Consequently, they are only seen outside their tunnel during the day. At night the entrance of the burrow is sealed by sediments that slide over the opening. Shortly after sunrise the shrimp begin bulldozing the entrance way free of sediments. The outer edges of the pinchers form an upside-down V to push the material about 1 body length from the cave's entrance. If there are two shrimp, they take turns; that is, one digs inside while the other takes the sediment away from the opening. Mussel shells and other obstacles encountered while digging are grabbed with their pinchers and carried out piece by piece.

to be continued on page 1047:

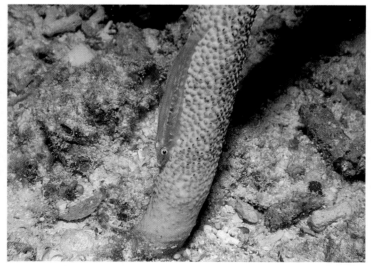

Bryaninops amplus, sea whip goby

Fam.: Gobiidae

Amblyeleotris aurora (POLUNIN & LUBBOCK, 1977)
Pinkbar goby

Hab.: They are only found around the islands of the western Indo-Pacific from the Maldives southward and north of Natal. On sandy bottoms at depths of 5 to 10 m.

Sex.: No sexual dichromatism. The sole external difference is the shape of the genital papilla (p. 1074). However, this is only recognizable in anesthetized or dead animals.

Soc.B./Assoc.: In their natural habitat they are always associated with shrimp of the genus *Alpheus*. They get along well with free-swimming, nonaggressive fishes.

M.: Provide a sandy substrate with flat stones on top. They will construct a cave beneath a stone.

Light: Areas of sun to moderate light.

B./Rep.: Has not been successful in an aquarium.

F.: C, FD; accepts larger pieces of various frozen foods and pieces of tablet foods. The gobies will have to be specially fed with a feeding tube or forceps when free-swimming fishes offer excessive competition.

S.: They live with *Alpheus* pistol shrimp in true symbiosis (see also p. 1042). *A. aurora* is diurnal and retires in its cave for the night.

T: 21°-28°C, **L:** 7.5 cm, **TL:** from 80 cm, **WM:** w, **WR:** b, **AV:** 2-3, **D:** 1-2

Amblyeleotris guttata (FOWLER, 1938)
Orange-spotted prawn goby

Hab.: Western and central Pacific. On sandy bottoms and seagrass lawns at depths of 10 to 40 m.

Sex.: Differ by the shape of their genital papilla (p. 1074). When mature, the ♀♀ can be recognized by their swollen ventral area.

Soc.B./Assoc.: They live in symbiosis with different species of pistol shrimp of the genus *Alpheus*. Only keep single specimens or a pair, since they are aggressive towards conspecifics.

M.: Needs a large area of coarse sand or shell debris. They like to retire into halved flower pots which are immersed into the sand until only a small entry slit remains open.

Light: Areas of sunlight to moderate light.

B./Rep.: Has not been successful in an aquarium, although ♀♀ repeatedly deposit eggs when well fed.

F.: C, FD; they accept all kinds of frozen foods and can be trained to accept tablet foods (Tetra Tips). Provide a balanced menu.

S.: Their spotted body design (name) easily distinguishes them from other symbiotic gobies. A common species throughout their range.

T: 22°-28°C, **L:** 7 cm, **TL:** from 80 cm, **WM:** w, **WR:** b, **AV:** 1, **D:** 1

Amblyeleotris aurora, Villingili, Maldives

Amblyeleotris guttata

Amblyeleotris gymnocephala

Amblyeleotris latifasciata

Amblyeleotris ogasawarensis

Scientists placed an artificial tunnel in an aquarium with its open end towards the front glass pane. The shrimp took up residence and their activities were observed. They carried nutrient rich mud into the cave and masticated it there. As a consequence, the entrance of the burrow moved further and further away from the glass pane as the tunnel collapsed due to these activities. But the tunnel did not shorten, since the shrimp continued their excavation activities on the other end. All feeding, digging, and transporting outside the pipe ended in the evening about 20 minutes after sundown. The pistol shrimp retire for the day at this time and don't reappear even if detritivores such as sea urchins and sea cucumbers are present, although they often end up damaging their burrow.

to be continued on page 1048:

Fam.: Gobiidae

Almost every *Alpheus* shrimp lives in intimate association with a goby. Not only are they co-owners of the cave, but they constantly interact. When the goby appears for the first time in the morning, it sticks its head out of the entrance hole, watches its surroundings for several minutes, then, if the coast is clear, emerges further until it has a better overall view. Its tail fin always remains close to the entrance. Gobies primarily prey on small benthic animals they capture with short, quick dashes. After such an advance, the goby immediately returns to its previous position. When imminent danger looms, the fish quickly flees head first into the cave. If the goby sees predatory fishes or groups of goatfishes approaching, it slowly and nonchalantly retreats tail first into the burrow.

to be continued on page 1052:

Amblyeleotris periophthalmus (BLEEKER, 1853)
Slender shrimp goby

Hab.: Indo-Pacific, Red Sea. On sandy bottoms at depth of 10 to 20 m.

Sex.: No sexual dichromatism. They can be distinguished by the shape of the genital papilla (p. 1074).

Soc.B./Assoc.: Usually live in pairs with various pistol shrimp of the genus *Alpheus*. They can be maintained alone in an aquarium.

M.: Build rock edifications using flat rocks and create several caves or place halved flower pots on the sand substrate. There should always be sand on the floor of the cave.

Light: Sun to moderate light zones.

B./Rep.: Has not been successful in an aquarium.

F.: C, FD; they readily take small pieces of frozen *Mysis*, *Artemia*, and mussels as well as broken tablet foods (TetraTips). If other fishes are in the tank, you will have to feed the gobies with a feeding tube.

S.: In their natural habitat, some individuals use 2 caves simultaneously. They defend both shelters. Others, in contrast, lack a cave and wander from place to place. These "vagabonds" are aggressively chased away by cave owners.

T: 22°-28°C, **L:** 7.5 cm, **TL:** from 80 cm, **WM:** w, **WR:** b, **AV:** 2, **D:** 1-2

Amblyeleotris periophthalmus

Amblyeleotris periophthalmus from Bali

Fam.: Gobiidae

Amblyeleotris randalli   HOESE & STEENE, 1978
Orangestripe prawn goby

Hab.: The entire Indo-Pacific region and along north and east Australia. On sandy bottoms at 25 to 50 m depth.

Sex.: The ♂♂ have a slender cone-shaped genital papilla, whereas ♀♀ have a broad genital papilla. No sexual dichromatism.

Soc.B./Assoc.: The goby lives alone or in pairs in symbiosis with pistol shrimp, usually *Alpheus rapicida*. However, it can be maintained either with or without a symbiotic partner in the aquarium. Can be combined with free-swimming fishes and various crustacea.

M.: Use coarse sand or pulverized shell as substrate. It prefers low caves with a sandy bottom. It is somewhat more demanding towards water quality than most other *Amblyeleotris* species.

Light: Areas of moderate light.

B./Rep.: Has not been successful in an aquarium. ♀♀ repeatedly lay eggs if at ease in their environment. Committed aquarists should be able to successfully rear them.

F.: C, FD; they are easy to feed and accept any frozen foods as well as tablet foods. Some individuals will accept flake foods, but do not base the menu on flakes. Offer them every once in a while to add variety to their diet of frozen or live foods. Several small meals each day are optimal.

S.: Can be easily differentiated from other *Amblyeleotris* species by the slender cross-bands and the pronounced ocellus on the first dorsal fin.

T: 22°-25°C, **L:** 7.5 cm, **TL:** from 80 cm, **WM:** w, **WR:** b, **AV:** 2, **D:** 2

Amblyeleotris wheeleri   (POLUNIN & LUBBOCK, 1977)
Wheeler's prawn goby

Hab.: In the western Indo-Pacific to Sodwana Bay. On sandy bottoms of reef lagoons at 5 to 15 m depth.

Sex.: As for almost all gobies, ♂♂ and ♀♀ can only be distinguished by the shape of the genital papilla (p. 1074).

Soc.B./Assoc.: Lives singly or in pairs with various species of pistol shrimp (*Alpheus*) in caves. Can be associated with invertebrates and peaceful free-swimming fishes.

M.: Provide a large area of coarse dolomite, foraminiferans, or coral sand. A cave below a flat stone plate is usually immediately accepted. They do not place any special requirements on water quality.

Light: Sunlight region.

B./Rep.: These gobies have an interesting courtship and spawning behavior which can be repeatedly observed in an aquarium. YANAGISAWA wrote an elaborate description of this behavior based on *A. japonica* (Jap. J. Ichthyol. 28, 1982, pp. 406 ff.).

F.: C, FD; research by YANAGISAWA (see above) on *A. japonica* in its natural habitat showed small benthic crustacea (e.g., amphipods) to be the main source of food. Large planktonic organisms were second. Various sizes of live *Artemia* come the closest to their natural diet. They also eat frozen and tablet foods.

S.: Largely similar to *A. fasciata*, but *A. wheeleri* has broader crossbands and a red spot on the second dorsal fin.

T: 21°-30°C, **L:** 6.5 cm, **TL:** from 80 cm, **WM:** w, **WR:** b, **AV:** 2, **D:** 1

Amblyeleotris randalli

Amblyeleotris wheeleri

Fam.: Gobiidae

Symbiosis Between Pistol Shrimp and Gobies

The relationship between pistol shrimp and gobies, two highly different animals, is an interesting one. The goby gains a home in the form of a cave that it does not have to maintain. *Amblyeleotris* gobies situate themselves so that their tail remains in contact with the shrimp. Scientists have used an artificial set-up to observe how the shrimp constantly touches the goby with their antennae. Touching the goby, or being unable to, keeps the shrimp informed of the goby's movements. The shrimp can interpret the goby's fin movements either directly or indirectly (water movement) and determine whether or not it is safe to venture forth. When the goby is in a typical look-out position, the shrimp leaves its burrow to dig. However, they quickly disappear into the cave when the fish darts forward for prey or slowly retreats during danger.

The goby gains a home on an open soft bottom it neither has to build nor maintain. This cave slowly changes position as the soft material shifts. The shrimp, in exchange, indirectly uses the goby's superior eyesight to reconnoiter the area for predators. There are some deviations between animals of different seas: the goby's territory often extends beyond the cave's entrance, and the shrimp frequently live on coral debris or lava slack and adapt their coloration accordingly.

This colorful goby of the genus *Amblyeleotris* has not yet been scientifically described. It was found at the northern Indonesian island of Bali at a depth of a few meters. The black sand is of volcanic origin. There is no information on how to maintain this species in an aquarium.

Amblyeleotris sp. nov. with *Alpheus randalli*

Amblyeleotris sp. nov.

Fam.: Gobiidae

Amblygobius albimaculatus   (RÜPPEL, 1830)
Butterfly goby

Hab.: Red Sea, Indian Ocean, and east Africa to Durban; in shallow waters of reef lagoons on sandy bottoms.

Sex.: ♂♂ and ♀♀ are best distinguished by the shape of their genital papilla. The ♂♂ have three black dots on the base of the second dorsal fin; the ♀♀ have a brownish stripe from the tip of the snout to the operculum.

Soc.B./Assoc.: Live in pairs and can be associated with other fishes and invertebrates.

M.: Use coarse sand or shell debris as substrate and place suitable flat stones on top for the fish to construct a cave beneath. No special demands are placed on water quality.

Light: Region of sunlight.

B./Rep.: Has not been successful in an aquarium.

F.: C, FD; easily fed with small pieces of frozen *Artemia*, *Mysis*, krill, and small pieces of tablet foods (Tetra Tips).

S.: In their natural biotope, pairs live in caves they build themselves in the coral sand using their mouth. A second color morph from Mozambique and the Seychelles has a more posterior spot on the dorsal fin, narrower crossbands, and other minor color differences. It may be a different species (*A. semicinctus*) or a hybrid of *A. albimaculatus* and *A. phalaena*.

T: 22°-30°C, **L:** 18 cm, **TL:** from 100 cm, **WM:** w, **WR:** b, **AV:** 2, **D:** 1

Upper and lower right hand photos:

The maintenance requirements of *Amblygobius buanensis* and *A. bynoensis* are similar to those of *A. albimaculatus*. However, they are more sensitive to poor water quality.

Amblygobius buanensis

Amblygobius bynoensis

Fam.: Gobiidae

Amblygobius decussatus   (BLEEKER, 1855)
Orangemarked goby

Hab.: Western and central Pacific. On sand and coral gravel substrates at depths of 3 to 25 m.

Sex.: The sexes can be distinguished by the shape of the genital papilla. However, this is only possible on anesthetized or dead animals with the aid of a magnifying glass.

Soc.B./Assoc.: Singly or in pairs. Can be housed with other fishes and invertebrates.

M.: Bury a 10 cm long acrylic pipe vertically into a deep layer of coarse sand or coral gravel. They masticate fine sand in search of food particles.

Light: Sunlight to moderately lit regions depending on origin. Make sure photophobic animals have a shaded cave entrance. The fish can be slowly acclimated to more light.

B./Rep.: Has not been successful in an aquarium.

F.: C, FD; they readily take frozen and tablet foods that have fallen to the bottom. Often they scoop up sand and chew it in their search for food.

S.: They live in vertical caves which are dug by an unidentified crab species. However, they is no symbiotic relationship between the two.

T: 22°-30°C, **L:** 5.5 cm, **TL:** from 80 cm, **WM:** w, **WR:** b, **AV:** 2, **D:** 1-2

Amblygobius hectori   (SMITH, 1957)
Hector's goby

Hab.: Red Sea and east Africa to the western Pacific. At depths of 5 to 20 m.

Sex.: Recognizable by the shape of the genital papilla.

Soc.B./Assoc.: Maintain singly. They get along well with invertebrates and other fishes.

M.: Reef aquarium with a sandy bottom and flat rocks.

Light: Sunlight regions.

B./Rep.: Has not been successful in an aquarium. The main problem is procuring food for the newly hatched larvae. Rearing should be successful if live marine plankton (*Euplotes* and *Brachionus*) and *Artemia* nauplii are used.

F.: C, FD; they eagerly snap at pieces of frozen and dried foods that slowly drift by in the current. Every once in a while live mosquito larvae or larger *Artemia* should be provided.

S.: They usually swim close to the bottom. Their appearance is largely similar to *A. rainfordi* (p. 1060), but this species is dark blue while *A. rainfordi* is green.

T: 22°-30°C, **L:** 5 cm, **TL:** from 80 cm, **WM:** w-m, **WR:** b-m, **AV:** 2, **D:** 1-2

Amblygobius decussatus

Amblygobius hectori

Fam.: Gobiidae

Amblygobius phalaena   (VALENCIENNES, 1837)
Banded goby

Hab.: Pacific, the Ryukyu Islands, the Philippines, and Bali. On sand and coral gravel in reef lagoons at depths of 2 to 20 m.

Sex.: No sexual dichromatism. The genital papilla is the only way to sex these fish, but even this is difficult.

Soc.B./Assoc.: They live singly or in pairs and get along well with other fishes and crustacea.

M.: Bottom of sand or shell slack with flat stone plates under which they excavate their cave. No special water quality needs.

Light: Sunlight zone.

B./Rep.: Has not been described, but it should not be difficult. Eggs have been laid repeatedly in aquaria. The elongated oval eggs are adhered to the ceiling of the cave by adhesive threads.

F.: O, FD; it happily consumes frozen and dried foods, algae, and detritus. If the aquarium receives sufficient food as a whole, this species will not need to be fed.

S.: They dig a shallow cave in the sand beneath stones using their mouth. This species of goby is easily maintainable, but is rather shy at first and will flee into its cave when the aquarium is approached. Sensitive invertebrates such as tubeworms, colonial anemones, etc., should not be placed in the vicinity of the cave entrance lest the goby's digging activities blanket them with sand.

T: 22°-30°C, **L:** 12 cm, **TL:** from 80 cm, **WM:** w-m, **WR:** b, **AV:** 1, **D:** 1

Amblygobius phalaena, Great Barrier Reef

Amblygobius phalaena, Philippines

Amblygobius phalaena, Bali

Amblygobius nocturnus (bottom photo)   (HERRE, 1945)
Nocturnal goby

Amblygobius rainfordi (upper right hand photo)   (WHITLEY, 1940)
Rainford's goby

Hab.: Both species occur in the Indo-Pacific over fine sand and mud at depths between 3 and 30 m.

Sex.: As in most gobies, the sexes can only be distinguished by the shape of the genital papilla.

Soc.B./Assoc.: They live singly or as a pair and get along well with other small fishes if the tank is sufficiently large.

M.: Sand bottom. For *A. nocturnus*, place flat stones on the bottom where it can excavate a cave. *A. rainfordi* rarely digs. Neither place particular demands on water quality.

Light: Area of sunlight.

B./Rep.: Has not been successfully bred in an aquarium.

F.: O, FD; since they constantly search the sand for food, they make good use of left-overs and do not need to be individually fed. However, they fare especially well when occasionally offered live foods (mosquito larva, *Artemia*).

S.: Both species are well suited for the tropical seawater aquarium.

T: 22°-30°C, **L:** 4-5 cm, **TL:** from 80 cm, **WM:** w-m, **WR:** b, **AV:** 2, **D:** 1

Amblygobius semicinctus (lower right hand photo), like other *Amblygobius* species, can be housed with other fishes and invertebrates.

Amblygobius nocturnus

Amblygobius rainfordi

Amblygobius semicinctus, aquarium photo

Fam.: Gobiidae

Bryaninops amplus
Sea whip goby

LARSON, 1985

Hab.: Indo-Pacific, Hawaii, Japan, and the Great Barrier Reef. On gorgonians at depths of 5 to 20 m.

Sex.: Not known.

Soc.B./Assoc.: Singly, in pairs, or in small groups. Very peaceful.

M.: The same as *B. youngei* (below).

Light: As for *B. youngei.*

B./Rep.: Construct nests on living gorgonians. The eggs are laid in a circular band. The planktonic larvae settle on the gorgonians at a length of 10 mm. After 6 months they are full-grown.

F.: C, FD; as for *B. youngei.*

S.: They generally settle on gorgonians such as *Juncella fragilis* and *J. juncea*, but they are occasionally found on sea whips and some *Acropora* corals.

T: 22°-26°C, **L:** 5 cm, **TL:** from 80 cm, **WM:** m, **WR:** m, **AV:** 3, **D:** 2

Bryaninops youngei
Tiger sea whip goby

(DAVID & COHEN, 1969)

Hab.: Red Sea, Indo-Pacific, Hawaii, the Ryukyu Islands, and the Great Barrier Reef. On steep walls and debris; exclusively found on whip corals (*Cirripathes anguina*).

Sex.: Not known. They undergo a sexual change from ♀ to ♂.

Soc.B./Assoc.: Live in pairs on whip corals. They are extremely peaceful and therefore especially suitable for the invertebrate aquarium.

M.: Reef aquarium. If whip corals cannot be offered, other vertical or oblique structures the diameter of a pencil are suitable. They like current.

Light: Area of dim light.

B./Rep.: They construct a 2 to 3 cm long nest about 15 to 25 cm from the tip of the coral. Before oviposition, they remove the tissue of the whip coral.

F.: C, D; they snap at small particles that drift by in the current. Every once in a while newly hatched *Artemia* nauplii should be offered. Disconnect the pump when feeding nauplii.

S.: They live exclusively on the whip coral *Cirripathes anguina*. However, they are sometimes observed on buoy ropes. It is not known if they also spawn there.

T: 22°-26°C, **L:** 3 cm, **TL:** from 89 cm, **WM:** m-s, **WR:** m, **AV:** 3, **D:** 2

Bryaninops amplus

Bryaninops youngei

Fam.: Gobiidae

Cryptocentrus caeruleopunctatus   (RÜPPEL, 1830)
Ocellated prawn goby

Hab.: Primarily lives in the Red Sea, but sometimes found down to Kenya. On sand surfaces at depths of 2 to 15 m.

Sex.: The ♂♂ have darker fins than the ♀♀. The ♂'s caudal fin has a dark fringe.

Soc.B./Assoc.: They live singly or in pairs and are always associated with a pistol shrimp. Animals of the same sex do not get along. Only associate with small free-swimming fishes, not other bottom-dwelling fishes.

M.: Needs coarse sand, coral debris, or shell gravel. Flat stone plates on the bottom ease cave construction. Only keep with pistol shrimp if possible.

Light: Moderate light.

B./Rep.: Has not been successful in an aquarium.

F.: C, FD; in nature they primarily feed on small benthic crustacea. In the aquarium they quickly become accustomed to frozen foods and small pieces of tablet foods.

S.: Always lives with pistol shrimp, primarily *Alpheus djiboutensis,* in caves on sandy bottoms. This species is characterized by especially small scales.

T: 22°-28°C, **L:** 12 cm, **TL:** from 100 cm, **WM:** w-m, **WR:** b, **AV:** 1, **D:** 1-2

Cryptocentrus cinctus   (HERRE, 1936)
Yellow prawn goby or Banded prawn goby (depending on color morph (see below))

Hab.: West Pacific to the Great Barrier Reef. In lagoons with a sand bottom at depths of 1 to 10 m.

Sex.: Can only be identified by the shape of the genital papilla (see p. 1074). The two animals in the photo are obviously a pair. Sexual differences probably include size and coloration. But which is which? In my opinion, the animal with the thicker belly (top) is the ♀.

Soc.B./Assoc.: They live in pairs symbiotically with various *Alpheus* species. Do not associate with other bottom-dwelling fishes or large crustacea.

M.: Provide a bottom of coarse sand with flat stone plates laid on top. There they excavate their cave. They should not be kept without pistol shrimp.

Light: Areas of sunlight.

B./Rep.: Has not been successful in an aquarium.

F.: C, FD; they adapt very quickly to frozen and dried foods. Left-over food is eaten from the bottom. Uneaten remains must be quickly removed.

S.: There are two color morphs of *C. cinctus.* One has light and dark crossbars; the other is solid yellow. They live symbiotically with 2 species of *Alpheus* shrimp.

T: 22°-28°C, **L:** 6 cm, **TL:** from 80 cm, **WM:** w, **WR:** b, **AV:** 2, **D:** 1-2

Cryptocentrus caeruleopunctatus

Cryptocentrus cinctus

Fam.: Gobiidae

Cryptocentrus spp.
Symbiotic gobies

Hab.: In the tropical region of the Indo-Pacific; on flat sandy bottoms in lagoons or mangrove forests.

Sex.: Only a few species have exterior differences.

Soc.B./Assoc.: They usually live in pairs and always live with various pistol shrimp of the genus *Alpheus*. In the aquarium they are easily bothered by their fellow tankmates. Do not keep with aggressive fishes or crustacea. A pistol shrimp must be present for the fish to feel at ease in its environment.

M.: Bottom of coarse sand, coral gravel, or shell gravel. Flat stones should be placed on top to ease the cave building process for the shrimp.

Light: Area of sunlight.

B./Rep.: Has not been successful in an aquarium.

F.: C, FD; easily fed. Some species have difficulty acclimating to nonliving foods. From time to time, live foods should be provided (various sizes of *Artemia*, large *Daphnia*, mosquito larvae).

S.: The genus *Cryptocentrus* can be relatively easily confused with *Amblyeleotris* (pp. 1044 ff.) and *Vanderhorstia* (pp. 1112 ff.). However, both of the latter genera are more slender and have a broader gill opening. New species are constantly being discovered (bottom right hand photo). They make interesting subjects for behavioral studies.

T: 22°-28°C, **L:** 6-12 cm, **TL:** from 80 cm, **WM:** w, **WR:** b, **AV:** 2-4, **D:** 1-2

Cryptocentrus fasciatus, aquarium photo

Cryptocentrus leonis

Cryptocentrus sp.

Fam.: Gobiidae

Ctenogobiops maculosus   (FOURMANOIR, 1955)
Spotted prawn goby

Hab.: Red Sea and the central and western Indo-Pacific. Over sand bottoms at depths of 1 to 5 m.

Sex.: Can only be distinguished by the shape of the genital papilla (p. 1074). A difficult feat on live animals.

Soc.B./Assoc.: Live symbiotically with *Alpheus* pistol shrimp who dig a cave for them. Animals of the same sex do not get along and are often involved in bitter fights.

M.: Substrate of loose, moderate sized sand. They like to place their cave under a flat stone or a buried, halved flower pot.

Light: Area of sunlight.

B./Rep.: Has not been successful in an aquarium.

F.: C, FD; they quickly acclimate to substitute foods, including small pieces of tablet foods.

S.: The genus has ctenoid scales (name); there are no scales on the head.

T: 22°-28°C, **L:** 7 cm, **TL:** from 80 cm, **WM:** w, **WR:** b, **AV:** 3, **D:** 1-2

Ctenogobiops tangaroai   LUBBOCK & POLUNIN, 1977
Tangaroa goby

Hab.: West Pacific and the Ryukyu Islands. Over bottoms of fine sand at depths of 4 to 40 m. Only found at depths greater than 12 m in Micronesia.

Sex.: Not known.

Soc.B./Assoc.: Live with pistol shrimp (*Alpheus*). It is a true symbiosis in which both partners benefit. Do not associate with bottom-dwelling fishes or crustacea.

M.: Use medium to fine grained sand as substrate. Under a flat stone plate, dig a shallow entrance. The animals will widen it. Place the cave entrance in the shade.

Light: Moderate light.

B./Rep.: Has not been successful in the aquarium.

F.: C, FD; easily cared for with frozen and dried foods. Every once in while provide live foods. Minute quantities of *Tubifex* can also be given, but uneaten worms have to be immediately removed.

S.: Like most symbiotic gobies, these too are often offered in the trade without a pistol shrimp. But this goby only feels comfortable and display its interesting behavior when cohabitating with a pistol shrimp.

T: 22°-25°C, **L:** 6 cm, **TL:** from 80 cm, **WM:** w, **WR:** b, **AV:** 2-3, **D:** 1-2

Ctenogobiops maculosus

Ctenogobiops tangaroai

Fam.: Gobiidae

Discordipinna griessingeri
Griessinger's goby

HOESE & FOURMANOIR, 1978

Hab.: The entire Indo-Pacific, the Cocos Islands, and Tahiti. The holotype comes from the Gulf of Aqaba. They live over sandy substrates at depths of 2 to 15 m.

Sex.: The sexes can only be distinguished by the shape of the genital papilla.

Soc.B./Assoc.: Keep singly or in pairs. Good partners for many invertebrates and peaceful fishes.

M.: Provide a substrate of coarse sand or crushed shells. Hiding places under halved flower pots or within constructions of stone plates should be included in the tank's infrastructure.

Light: Moderate light to sunlight.

B./Rep.: Has not been successful in the aquarium.

F.: C, FD; easily cared for with any kind of frozen or tablet foods.

S.: The extreme anterior projection of the dorsal fin is eye-catching.

T: 23°-27°C, **L:** 5 cm, **TL:** from 80 cm, **WM:** w-m, **WR:** b, **AV:** 3, **D:** 1-2

Eviota pellucida
Pygmy goby

LARSON, 1976

Hab.: Western and central Pacific to Indonesia. At depths of 3 to 15 m.

Sex.: Only recognizable by the shape of the genital papilla.

Soc.B./Assoc.: Singly or in pairs with peaceful fishes. Do not house with large crustacea.

M.: Reef aquarium with overhangs and small hiding places.

Light: Moderate to dim light.

B./Rep.: Has not been successful in the aquarium.

F.: C, FD; they are easily trained to frozen and tablet foods (broken). If other fishes are present in the aquarium, *E. pellucida* must be fed with a feeding tube.

S.: There are 60 known species that belong to the genus *Eviota*. All are diminutive fishes. Species identification often uses the position of sensory papillae on the head and body coloration rather than meristic characteristics. At first glance, this fish can be confused with cardinal fishes, but note the position of the eyes and the mode of swimming. A clear giveaway.

T: 22°-25°C, **L:** 3 cm, **TL:** from 80 cm, **WM:** w, **WR:** m, **AV:** 2, **D:** 2

Discordipinna griessingeri

Eviota pellucida

Fam.: Gobiidae

Fusigobius neophytus (GÜNTHER, 1877)
Dusky fusegoby

Hab.: Indo-Pacific to Hawaii; large numbers are found in shallow lagoons at depths of 1 to 5 m and in tidal pools.

Sex.: No known sexual dichromatism.

Soc.B./Assoc.: Several specimens can be kept in aquaria that have a large surface area. Do not associate with other benthic fishes or crustacea. They get along well with free-swimming fishes like pomacentrids and surgeonfishes.

M.: Substrate of coarse sand or coral gravel. Halved PVC pipes which are partially buried in the substrate are eagerly accepted shelters. They do not place any special demands on water quality.

Light: Sunlight areas.

B./Rep.: Has not been successful in an aquarium, although the fish spawn repeatedly. The primary problem lies in the small size of the larvae or, more to the point, in the acquisition of food for them.

F.: C, FD; they accept frozen and dried foods. Since they initially do not care for food that has fallen to the bottom, it has to be promptly removed.

S.: This species can be recognized by the small black dot between the 1st and 2nd dorsal fin ray. J. L. B. SMITH described a new subspecies in 1959 from the east African coast: *F. n. africanus.* It occurs in the Red Sea and the western Indo-Pacific.

T: 21°-30°C, **L:** 8 cm, **TL:** from 80 cm, **WM:** w-m, **WR:** b, **AV:** 1, **D:** 1

Fusigobius signipinnis HOESE & OPIKA, 1988
Signalfin goby

Hab.: Central Pacific, Samoa, and the Cook Islands. On sandy bottoms at depths of 5 to 25 m.

Sex.: It is not known if these fish display sexual dimorphism or dichromatism.

Soc.B./Assoc.: As for *F. neophytus.*

M.: As for *F. neophytus.*

Light: Areas of moderate light.

B./Rep.: Has not been successful in the aquarium.

F.: C, FD; small pieces of frozen and tablet foods.

S.: This genus is often confused with *Favonigobius. F. signipinnis* was just recently scientifically described.

T: 23°-27°C, **L:** 7 cm, **TL:** from 80 cm, **WM:** m, **WR:** b, **AV:** 3, **D:** 1-2

Fusigobius neophytus

Fusigobius signipinnis

Fam.: Gobiidae

ABOUT THE REPRODUCTIVE BIOLOGY OF GOBIES

The reproductive biology of the goby family is just as diverse as the family itself. Although the majority of species have separate sexes, there are also those that are hermaphrodites, either protandrous (from male to female) or protogynous (from female to male). Few species can be sexed from external characteristics such as coloration, elongated fin rays, etc. Usually the only clue as to which sex is which is the genital papilla. The illustrations show a few examples.

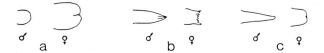

Genital papillae of various goby genera: a) *Amblyeleotris*, b) *Eviota*, and c) *Gobius*

The male genital organs are peculiar. Next to the testicles you can see large "semen bladders," which contain a sticky secretion. Its purpose is unknown. Some species have a "testicle gland" adjacent to their testicles that produces hormones (pheromones) that serve to attract females. In most cases, the male searches for or builds a cave where the female deposits her eggs. Almost all goby eggs are oval and have adhesive threads on one end. These threads attach the eggs to the ceiling of the cave. In most species the male guards the spawn, but in some species, the female or even both of the parents participate in brood care. After hatching, the larvae are planktonic for a while and then descend to the bottom.

A goby egg

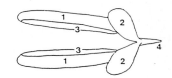

Genital organs of a male goby
1. Testicle, 2. Semen Bladder,
3. Testicle Gland, 4. Genital Papilla

Gnatholepis scapulostigma
Shoulderspot goby

HERRE, 1933

Hab.: Indo-Pacific, the Ryukyu Islands, and the Maldives; on fine sand at depths of 2 to 20 m.

Sex.: Sexual dichromatism is unknown.

Soc.B./Assoc.: Usually lives singly. Only house with small fishes and peaceful invertebrates.

M.: Provide a sandy substrate with stones. They will live in a halved PVC pipe that has been partially buried in moderately coarse sand.

Light: Sunlight zone; the entrance of the cave, however, should not be in direct light.

B./Rep.: Has not been successful in an aquarium.

F.: C, FD; place small frozen and dried foods directly into the cave with a feeding tube. Once in while small live foods should be given.

S.: *Gnatholepis* is easily confused with *Istiogobius*. This genus contains ambiguities and should be revised.

T: 22°-26°C, **L:** 4 cm, **TL:** from 80 cm, **WM:** w, **WR:** b, **AV:** 3, **D:** 1-2

Gobiodon citrinus (RÜPPEL, 1838)
Citron goby

Hab.: Red Sea, Indo-Pacific, and the western Pacific to southern Japan and the Great Barrier Reef. In coral stalks at depths of 2 to 20 m.

Sex.: Exterior sexual differences are unknown. The shape of the genital papilla can usually only be seen on dead animals (see p. 1074).

Soc.B./Assoc.: Do not associate with fast feeding fishes such as pomacentrids. They are ideal partners for sessile invertebrates such as tubeworms, stone corals, and disc and colonial anemones. Pipefishes and dottybacks are also appropriate tankmates.

M.: Reef aquarium with branches of *Acropora* coral. They often rest on animals that sting weakly such as soft corals and disc and colonial anemones. Their ventral fins form a suction disc that allows them to maintain their place in strong currents.

Light: Areas of moderate light.

B./Rep.: They are consecutive hermaphrodites; in other words, they undergo a sexual change in the course of their lives. ♀♀ regularly spawn in an aquarium, but larvae rearing has not been successful. Attempts have probably been frustrated by their diminutive size.

F.: C, FD; newly imported specimens usually only accept live foods. But they soon become accustomed to frozen and dry foods. Some individuals will never eat flake foods.

S.: A rather sedentary species that may lie among branches of coral for hours on end. *G. citrinus* has 2 to 4 vertical stripes on the head, but none on the body. Many members of this genus have not been scientifically described (lower right hand photo).

T: 22°-27°C, **L:** 6 cm, **TL:** from 80 cm, **WM:** m, **WR:** m, **AV:** 1, **D:** 1-2

Gobiodon citrinus

Gobiodon citrinus

Gobiodon sp.

Fam.: Gobiidae

Gobiodon histrio   (VALENCIENNES, 1837)
Blue-spotted coral goby

Hab.: In coral reefs of the Indo-Pacific, Melanesia, and Polynesia. Usually motionless between the branches of *Acropora* at depths of 2 to 15 m.

Sex.: Does not seem to have any sexual dimorphism.

Soc.B./Assoc.: Only associate with peaceful, slow-swimming fishes, small crustacea, and invertebrates.

M.: Reef aquarium with branches of *Acropora* (not necessarily live) where the fish will retire. When they feel secure in the tank, they attach themselves to elevated locations with their suction discs.

Light: Areas of moderate light.

B./Rep.: Has not been successful in an aquarium.

F.: C, FD; after a brief training period, they will take small pieces of frozen and dry foods. May need to be fed with a feeding tube.

S.: Every species within this genus secretes a poisonous epidermal mucus. It has a bitter taste which deters predators. *G. histrio* has 2 vertical stripes at the base of the pectoral fins. There are several color patterns, including the pictured *G. h.* var. *erythrospilus* (lower photo).

T: 22°-28°C, **L:** 8 cm, **TL:** 80 cm, **WM:** w-m, **WR:** b, **AV:** 2-3, **D:** 2

Gobiodon histrio var. *erythrospilus*

Gobiodon histrio

Gobiodon histrio and a hawkfish

Fam.: Gobiidae

Gobiodon okinawae   SAWADA, ARAI & ABE, 1973
Yellow coral goby

Hab.: South Japan, the Great Barrier Reef, and Micronesia. At depths of 2 to 15 m in coral reefs, usually on branches of *Acropora* stone corals.

Sex.: No known sexual dichromatism.

Soc.B./Assoc.: They live singly among branches of *Acropora*. Ideal fish for the invertebrate tank. Do not house with fast swimming fishes or very active crustacea.

M.: Reef aquarium with *Acropora* (not necessarily live). However, they also rest in soft corals, colonial anemones, and other animals with capability of administering slight stings (photo).

Light: Areas of moderate light.

B./Rep.: Has not been accomplished in an aquarium.

F.: C, FD; they will generally eat small pieces of frozen foods and crushed tablet foods. Flake foods are almost always avoided.

S.: This species leads a secluded life. Its lifestyle combined with its diminutive size insures that it is rarely seen.

T: 20°-25°C, **L:** 3 cm, **TL:** from 50 cm, **WM:** m, **WR:** m, **AV:** 3, **D:** 2

About the Coral Gobies of the Genus *Gobiodon*

Although fishes of this genus are beautiful, they do not have many fans among aquarists. They lead a secretive, sedentary life in the aquarium. A poisonous, bitter-tasting, predator deterring mucus is secreted by their epidermis (outer skin). This explains their ability to claim elevated positions on the coral reef and not become a tasty morsel as a consequence. When kept with fast swimming, rapid feeding fishes, they rarely get their share of the food. These animals are most content in tanks that contain soft corals, colonial and disc anemones, and a few small crustacea.

Gobiodon okinawae

Gobiodon unicolor

Fam.: Gobiidae

Breeding Neon Gobies of the Genus *Gobiosoma*

The neon gobies are found in all the tropical regions of the western Atlantic. They are divided into two groups—cleaner gobies and noncleaner gobies. The latter almost always live on or near large tube sponges. Here, however, we will only address the cleaner gobies, since they hold more interest for aquarists and divers. The coloration of these gobies is quite similar to the *Labroides* cleaner wrasses of the Indo-Pacific.

Spawning season lasts for several months. During this time the ♀ ♀ can spawn several times. They always spawn in pairs. Provide them with a length of PVC pipe that has an inner diameter of about 2 cm as a spawning tube. Either fasten it to rock structures or bury it at a slight angle in the substrate. Make sure the opening is not in direct light. Detailed descriptions of reproductive behavior and development can be found in FEDDERN (Bull. Mar. Sci. 17/1967, pp. 367 ff.) and VALENTI (Copeia 3/1972, pp. 477 ff.). About a week after spawning, the larvae hatch from the oval eggs. Rearing is described by COLIN (1975, see bibliography): the spawning cave (PVC pipe) and one male were transferred to a 120 l glass aquarium. The tank was illuminated 24 hr a day with a Grolux tube. The larvae were fed every 8 to 12 hours with 56 to 200 μm zooplankton (easily reared unicellular *Euplotes* and *Brachionus* are recommended). The water was well aerated, had a salinity of 32 ppt, and a temperature of 24°C. Fourteen days after the larvae hatched, newly hatched *Artemia* nauplii were added to the plankton. The gobies are fully developed 26 days after hatching.

Gobiosoma evelynae

Gobiosoma evelynae on a brain coral

Gobiosoma evelynae
Sharknose goby

BÖHLKE & ROBBINS, 1968

Hab.: Caribbean. On coral reefs at 1 to 50 m depth.

Sex.: Not recognizable from external characteristics.

Soc.B./Assoc.: They live singly, in pairs, or in groups of up to 20 individuals. They can even be successfully kept with congeners. Larger fishes may be included in the community as long as you allow the gobies time to become adjusted to their surroundings.

M.: Reef aquarium with hiding places they can retire to during the night. PVC pipes about 2 cm in diameter are especially well suited as spawning shelters.

Light: Area of sunlight.

B./Rep.: They regularly spawn in PVC pipes or beneath stones in an aquarium. Breeding is not particularly difficult (see facing page). They have even been crossbred with *G. genie* and *G. oceanops*.

F.: C, FD; this species is the only one of the genus that has had an extensive feeding analysis done. Only parasitic crustacea were found. That means they are obligate cleaners. However, in the aquarium they also take frozen foods. The primary food eaten in the aquarium is live *Artemia*.

S.: Because they act as cleaner fish, they are not eaten by predators. There are three known colorations: yellow, yellow-blue, and white.

T: 22°-27°C, **L:** 3 cm, **TL:** from 80 cm, **WM:** m, **WR:** t, **AV:** 1, **D:** 1

Fam.: Gobiidae

Gobiosoma genie
Genie's cleaning goby

BÖHLKE & ROBBINS, 1968

Hab.: Bahamas and the Cayman Islands. In coral reefs at depths from 1 to 30 m.

Sex.: No distinguishing external characteristics.

Soc.B./Assoc.: They live singly, in pairs, or in groups and get along well with other fishes and crustacea. They, together with *G. evelyne*, have been observed cleaning fishes.

M.: A reef aquarium with hiding places.

Light: Area of sunlight.

B./Rep.: With good care they repeatedly spawn in the aquarium, preferably in PVC pipes. Rearing is relatively easy (see p. 1082).

F.: C, FD; since this species has not been researched, we can only assume that they are obligate cleaners like *G. evelynae*. In the aquarium, however, they quickly learn to accept frozen and tablet foods.

S.: They clean fishes either singly or in groups (picture). This is the only member of the genus that has a well developed swimbladder.

T: 23°-28°C, **L:** 4 cm, **TL:** from 80 cm, **WM:** m, **WR:** t, **AV:** 2, **D:** 1

Gobiosoma illecebrosum   BÖHLKE & ROBBINS, 1968
Coral-dwelling cleaning goby

Hab.: In coral reefs throughout the Caribbean. At depths of 2 to 45 m.

Sex.: No external differences.

Soc.B./Assoc.: They colonize flat coral stalks and rocks singly, in pairs, or in groups. They are an excellent fish to combine with other fishes or crustacea.

M.: Reef aquarium with sleeping shelters.

Light: Regions of sun to moderate light.

B./Rep.: Has not been successful in the aquarium. Neither are there spawning observations from its natural habitat. During the fall spawning season, the ♀ ♀ have exceptionally thick bellies, and the eggs can even be seen.

Continued on next page.

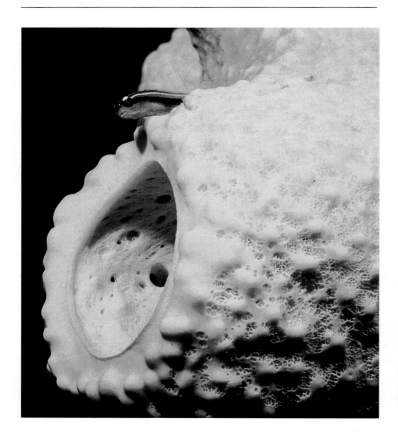

Continuation of *Gobiosoma illecebrosum* (from the previous page):

F.: C, FD; they feed exclusively on parasitic crustacea which are cleaned from other fishes. In the aquarium, they usually accept all substitute foods immediately.

S.: The coloration can be variable; yellow, blue, and white morphs exist. They are found on flat corals and rocks, on and in large sponges (photo), and on mangrove roots.

T: 22°-28°C, **L:** 3.5 cm, **TL:** from 80 cm, **WM:** m, **WR:** t, **AV:** 1-2, **D:** 1

Gobiosoma oceanops

Gobiosoma oceanops (JORDAN, 1904)
Neon goby

Hab.: In coral reefs of Florida and the Caribbean. At depths of 1 to 40 m.

Sex.: No external differences.

Soc.B./Assoc.: Singly, in pairs, or in groups of more than 30 individuals. Tankmates may include other *Gobiosoma* species and larger fishes which they occasionally clean.

M.: Reef aquarium with elevated sites near the water's surface where the gobies usually spend the whole day.

Light: Areas of sunlight.

B./Rep.: They regularly spawn in the aquarium and are relatively easy to raise (see p. 1082). Spawning behavior and the various stages of development are best studied in this species.

F.: C, FD; exclusively feed off parasitic crustacea they clean from their "clients." In the aquarium, however, they also take frozen foods and small pieces of tablets.

S.: Often listed under their previous name, *Elacatinus oceanops*. They spend the night in coral stalks, whereby the extended tentacles completely cover the gobies. This species is the most frequently imported member of the genus.

T: 21°-28°C, L: 3.5 cm, TL: from 80 cm, **WM:** m, **WR:** t, **AV:** 1, **D:** 1

Fam.: Gobiidae

Gobiosoma randalli   BÖHLKE & ROBBINS, 1968
Yellownose goby

Hab.: In coral reefs of the Caribbean islands. At depths of 1 to 50 m.

Sex.: No external differences. The original describers of this species indicated that ♂♂ have a dark snout; however, this is probably inaccurate.

Soc.B./Assoc.: Singly, pairwise, or in small groups. They get along well with larger fishes, which they occasionally clean, and congeners.

M.: Reef aquarium with elevated, flat sites.

Light: Areas of moderate light and sunlight.

B./Rep.: They do not spawn in an aquarium and have not been observed spawning in their natural habitat.

F.: C, FD; it is unknown whether or not these are obligate cleaner fish that feed exclusively on ectoparasites. However, they are easily trained to accept substitute foods.

S.: They clean fishes and are amiable towards congeners.

T: 22°-27°C, **L:** 3.5 cm, **TL:** from 80 cm, **WM:** m, **WR:** t, **AV:** 2, **D:** 1

Gobius auratus   RISSO, 1810
Golden goby

Hab.: Mediterranean Sea, eastern and northern coast of the Iberian Peninsula, the Canary Islands, and the southern coast of Ireland and England. On rocky substrates at depths of 5 to 30 m.

Sex.: The sexes can only be distinguished by the shape of the genital papilla. During the spawning season the ♀'s ventral area is significantly distended.

Soc.B./Assoc.: Live singly or in loose aggregations. Nonaggressive fishes and crustacea are appropriate tankmates.

M.: Provide a rock aquarium with hiding places. PVC pipe caves are accepted with alacrity. The water temperature in the winter should be below 18°C.

Light: Moderate to dim light.

B./Rep.: Spawning may ensue in the spring in the Mediterranean aquarium in which the winter temperature was low and the photoperiod was short. At this time they show their beautiful spawning coloration (photo). The young have not been successfully raised.

F.: C, FD; they readily accept chopped frozen foods and will occasionally eat tablets. Live foods are needed to bring the fish to spawning condition; blood worms are a particular delicacy.

S.: This species is not suitable for the tropical seawater aquarium. The golden yellow spawning coloration is especially striking.

T: 15°-20°C, **L:** 7 cm, **TL:** from 80 cm, **WM:** m, **WR:** b-m, **AV:** 3, **D:** 1-2

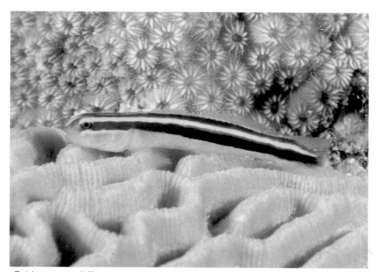

Gobiosoma randalli

Gobius auratus in spawning coloration

Fam.: Gobiidae

Gobius bucchichii STEINDACHNER, 1870
Bucchichi's goby

Hab.: Mediterranean. On rocky bottoms at depths of 1 to 30 m.

Sex.: Only differentiable by the shape of the genital papilla (p. 1074).

Soc.B./Assoc.: Lives singly or in pairs, usually in the tentacle region of *Anemonia sulcata*. Can be kept with invertebrates and other fishes.

M.: Rock aquarium with hiding places. If possible, maintain it with *Anemonia sulcata*. Although the association is not obligatory, it widens the scope of behavior that can be observed in an aquarium. They prefer to live in the transition zone between the sandy bottom and the rocks. Allow the temperature to fall below 20°C in the winter.

Light: Moderate to dim light.

B./Rep.: With good maintenance they will spawn; rearing the 2.2 mm larvae has not been successful.

F.: C, FD; they eagerly snap at larger food pieces. They rarely accept flake foods.

S.: The only "clownfish" of the Mediterranean. As with clownfishes, their skin is protected against the anemone's nematocysts. A few days without an anemone and their protection is lost. More precise research about its behavior has been done by ABEL (Vie Milieu, 11/1960, pp. 517 ff.).

T: 15°-24°C, **L:** 8 cm, **TL:** from 80 cm, **WM:** m-s, **WR:** b-m, **AV:** 3, **D:** 1

Gobius vittatus VINCIGUERRA, 1883
Mediterranean banded goby

Hab.: Mediterranean. On rocky bottoms at depths of 15 to 50 m.

Sex.: The sexes can only be distinguished by the shape of the genital papilla.

Soc.B./Assoc.: Live singly; however, several specimens can be kept in one tank. They are an excellent addition for aquaria with invertebrates and other fishes.

M.: Rock aquarium with a gravel bottom and small hiding places. In the winter the temperature should drop below 18°C.

Light: Dim to moderately lit areas.

B./Rep.: Has not been successful in an aquarium.

F.: C, FD; they take frozen and tablet foods without much ado and will even become accustomed to flake foods; however, flake foods should never be the sole source of nourishment.

S.: They bear an uncanny resemblance to the striped blenny, *Parablennius rouxi*, which is found in the same biotope (HEYMER & ZANDER: Z. zool. Syst. Evol. 16/1978, pp. 132 ff.). It is not clear whether or not this is a case of mimicry (purpose-specific imitation). Committed aquarists may be able to answer the question.

T: 16°-20°C, **L:** 4 cm, **TL:** from 80 cm, **WM:** w, **WR:** b-m, **AV:** 3, **D:** 1

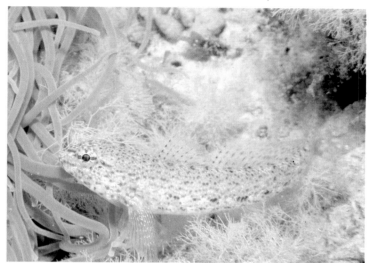

Gobius bucchichii

Gobius vittatus

Fam.: Gobiidae

Istigobius decoratus   (HERRE, 1927)
Decorated goby

Hab.: Red Sea, east Africa to Duban, the Indo-Pacific, and Samoa. On sandy bottoms of shallow bays at depths of 1 to 18 m.

Sex.: Can be sexed by their genital papilla. The ♂♂ are usually darker, and the second dorsal fin is taller.

Soc.B./Assoc.: Always seen alone. Two animals of the same sex cannot be kept together; but many other fishes and crustacea make nice tankmates.

M.: Bottom of coarse sand with stone plates lying on the surface. They build their cave beneath the stone.

Light: In sunlight areas.

B./Rep.: Has not been successful in an aquarium.

F.: C, FD; they take frozen foods such as *Mysis* and *Artemia*. Large pieces of tablet foods are also eaten.

S.: The coloration can be quite variable. Some specimens are pale, while others are dark. All animals from the same geographic local have the same coloration. They rarely flee into their caves during danger in their natural biotope. Often confused with *I. ornatus* (p. 1094).

T: 23°-29°C, **L:** 10 cm, **TL:** from 80 cm, **WM:** w-m, **WR:** b, **AV:** 2, **D:** 1

Istigobius hoesei   MURDY & MCEACHRAN, 1982
Hoese's goby

Hab.: Western south Pacific from Sydney to the Solomon Islands. On fine sand in the proximity of rocks at depths of 5 to 7 m.

Sex.: The second dorsal fin of the ♂ is somewhat taller than that of the ♀. Otherwise, they can only be distinguished by the shape of the genital papilla.

Soc.B./Assoc.: Probably lives singly. In the aquarium they get along well with other fishes.

M.: Provide a substrate of sand that is not overly coarse. They build their caves under stones.

Light: Moderate light.

B./Rep.: Has not been attempted in an aquarium.

F.: C, FD; they feed on all kinds of frozen foods and small pieces of tablet foods. Flake food is usually rejected. Once in a while live foods should be given, for example, blood worms.

S.: None known because the animals have just recently been scientifically described.

T: 22°-27°C, **L:** 6 cm, **TL:** from 80 cm, **WM:** w-m, **WR:** b, **AV:** 4, **D:** 1

Istigobius decoratus

Istigobius hoesei

Fam.: Gobiidae

Istigobius ornatus   (RÜPPEL, 1830)
Ornate goby

Hab.: Red Sea and the Indo-Pacific to Japan; on bottoms of sand and mud as well as in mangrove swamps. Often found in merely a few centimeters of water.

Sex.: The pectoral and anal fins of ♂♂ are darker than those of ♀♀.

Soc.B./Assoc.: Live singly in a small area; however, they are numerous. Best kept singly in an aquarium. They get along well with other fishes.

M.: Bottom of fine sand. Partially buried halved flower pots or PVC pipes are readily used as shelters.

Light: Region of sunlight.

B./Rep.: Has not been accomplished in an aquarium.

F.: C, FD; frozen and dry foods are accepted.

S.: The species is relatively easy to confuse with *I. decoratus* (p. 1093). But *I. ornatus* has 7 to 8 black dots in a horizontal row and is the only *Istogobius* species with three or four free upper pectoral fin rays.

T: 21°-29°C, **L:** 9 cm, **TL:** from 80 cm, **WM:** w, **WR:** b, **AV:** 2-3, **D:** 1

Lotilia graciliosa   KLAUSEWITZ, 1960
White-capped prawn goby

Hab.: Indo-Pacific, Red Sea, and the Ryukyu Islands. Habitats with a sandy bottom at depths of 20 m.

Sex.: Not known.

Soc.B./Assoc.: Lives in community with various species of *Alpheus* pistol shrimp (see pp. 1042 and 519 ff.). Its shy nature means its tankmates should be limited to a few peaceful fishes. Maintaining it as the sole fish species is even better.

M.: Bottom of coarse sand. Flat stones on top of the substrate facilitate cave excavation.

Light: Moderate light. The entrance to the cave should always be shaded.

B./Rep.: Has not been successful in an aquarium.

F.: C, FD; as soon as it has become accustomed to humans, it eagerly snaps at any piece of food (frozen or tablet foods) that sinks to the bottom.

S.: All species of the genus live symbiotically with shrimp of the genus *Alpheus*, and they should always be kept in this manner. They have large fanlike pectoral and anal fins.

T: 22°-26°C, **L:** 3.5 cm, **TL:** from 80 cm, **WM:** w, **WR:** b, **AV:** 3, **D:** 1-2

Istigobius ornatus

Lotilia graciliosa

Fam.: Gobiidae

Lythrypnus dalli (GILBERT, 1891)
Catalina goby

Hab.: East Pacific, Gulf of California. Found in fields of boulders and on rocks at depths of up to 60 m.

Sex.: The ♂ ♂ have a longer first dorsal fin. Sometimes they will display sexual dichromatism in an aquarium.

Soc.B./Assoc.: Singly or in pairs. Ideal partners for sessile invertebrates, peaceful fishes, pipefishes, and small shrimp like *Periclimenes*.

M.: Rock aquarium with a substrate of coarse sand with large shells or halved PVC pipes as caves. Temperature should not exceed 22°C.

Light: Dim light.

B./Rep.: They spawn repeatedly in an aquarium, but larvae rearing has not been successful. BAUER & BAUER (Octopus 1(8)/1974, pp. 6 ff.) described the spawning behavior and the development of the larvae, which only are 2.5 mm long. Spawning takes place during the summer months.

F.: C, FD; they eagerly snap at comparatively "giant" pieces of frozen and tablet foods with their large mouth.

S.: Although very beautiful and lively, this species cannot be kept in a tropical aquarium (temperature). The number of vertical stripes can vary from 2 to 6.

T: 18°-22°C, **L:** 5 cm, **TL:** from 80 cm, **WM:** w-m, **WR:** b-m, **AV:** 2, **D:** 1

Oplopomus oplopomus EHRENBERG, 1837
Spinecheek goby

Hab.: Red Sea, western Indo-Pacific, and Sri Lanka. On fine sand substrates in lagoons at depths of 1 to 20 m.

Sex.: The dorsal fin of the ♂ is taller. In addition, the spots on the head and fins are more distinct.

Soc.B./Assoc.: They live singly or in pairs. Can be associated with medium-sized free-swimming fishes and crustacea.

M.: Provide moderately coarse sand as substrate with acrylic tubes buried at an angle.

Light: Area of sunlight.

B./Rep.: Has not been successful in an aquarium.

F.: C, FD; since they have a relatively small mouth, their diet is limited to small morsels. Frozen and dry foods.

S.: This genus has spines on the operculum (name). *O. oplopomus* principally has ctenoid scales. They do not dig caves, but use those dug by invertebrates. Juveniles have black instead of blue and yellow dots.

T: 22°-29°C, **L:** 8 cm, **TL:** from 80 cm, **WM:** w, **WR:** b, **AV:** 2, **D:** 1

Lythrypnus dalli

Oplopomus oplopomus

Fam.: Gobiidae

Signigobius biocellatus
Two-spot goby

HOESE & ALLEN, 1977

Hab.: Indo-Pacific, Australia, the Philippines, and the Great Barrier Reef. In lagoons and sandy bottomed bays at depths of 2 to 30 m.

Sex.: Not known.

Soc.B./Assoc.: Singly as juveniles, otherwise in pairs. Do not keep with other bottom-dwelling fishes or large crustacea.

M.: Use coarse sand, coral gravel, or shell debris. Halved flower pots partially buried in the sand are used without restriction.

Light: Area of moderate light.

B./Rep.: The reproductive behavior of this species is unique among fishes (HUDSON: Z. Tierpsychol. 43/1977, pp. 214 ff.). The pair digs a spawning cave, and the ♀ deposits the eggs therein. Then the ♂ is sealed in the cave. During the incubation time, the cave is opened every once in a while, both partners clean the cave, and then the ♂ resumes his vigil in the sealed cave once again. After 4 to 5 days, the ♂ leaves the cave and the eggs for a while. Eggs and larvae continue developing in the cave. They feed on "food reserves, their surroundings, and possibly each other." When the parents open the spawning cave again, there is only one juvenile left, and it has already adopted its bottom-dwelling lifestyle. They have also been bred in an aquarium. However, it is unknown if HUDSON's observations are valid for an aquarium setting.

F.: C, FD; feed on small crustacea which are found when masticating the substrate. In the aquarium they take small chopped frozen foods and crumbled tablets.

S.: So far it is the only known species of the genus. The characteristic ocelli on the dorsal fin gave it its common name. The eyespots, the spread black ventral and anal fins, and its gliding swimming behavior along the bottom all combine to create the illusion of a crab. This type of mimicry (purpose-specific imitation) is rarely found in animals other than insects. *S. biocellatus*' behavior and relatively easy maintenance makes it a fascinating aquarium inhabitant.

T: 22°-27°C, **L:** 7.5 cm, **TL:** from 80 cm, **WM:** w, **WR:** b, **AV:** 3, **D:** 1-2

About the Genus *Stonogobiops*

The genus *Stonogobiops* was just recently described in 1977 by POLUNIN & LUBBOCK. As the pictures show, there are still undescribed species. This is one of several genera that live in true symbiosis with various species of *Alpheus* pistol shrimp. *Amblyeleotris*, *Cryptocentrus*, *Lotilia*, and *Vanderhorstia* (see there) also display a like symbiotic behavior.

Signigobius biocellatus

Stonogobiops sp. nov.

Fam.: Gobiidae

Stonogobiops nematodes   HOESE & RANDALL, 1982
Threadfin goby

Hab.: Central Indo-Pacific and the Philippines. On sandy bottoms at depths of 15 to 25 m.

Sex.: No external differentiating characteristics. Both sexes have a highly elongated first dorsal fin.

Soc.B./Assoc.: They always live in pairs in symbiosis with the pistol shrimp *Alpheus randalli*. Always keep with one. Should not be housed with other fishes.

M.: Use coarse sand, coral gravel, or shell debris as substrate. Flat stones placed on the sand aid cave excavation for the shrimp.

Light: Moderate light.

B./Rep.: Has not been successful in an aquarium.

F.: C, FD; they snap at small pieces of frozen foods and tablets that drift by in the current.

S.: There is a paucity of information because since these animals are very rare.

T: 22°-25°C, **L:** 4 cm, **TL:** from 80 cm, **WM:** m-s, **WR:** b, **AV:** 3-4, **D:** 1-2

Stonogobiops nematodes

Stonogobiops nematodes

Fam.: Gobiidae

Stonogobiops xanthorhinica   HOESE & RANDALL, 1982
Yellowsnout goby

Hab.: Indo-Pacific and southern Japan. On sandy bottoms at depths of 3 to 45 m.

Sex.: The first dorsal fin is somewhat longer in ♂ ♂ that in ♀ ♀ (photo).

Soc.B./Assoc.: They live in pairs symbiotically with pistol shrimp of the genus *Alpheus*. In southern Japan they have only been observed with *A. bellulus*. Since most fishes disturb this symbiotic behavior, they should be the sole fish in the aquarium.

M.: Use coarse sand, coral gravel, or shell debris as substrate.

Light: Areas of moderate light.

B./Rep.: Has not been successful in an aquarium.

F.: C, FD; they take small pieces of frozen and tablet foods. Blood worms should be given occasionally.

S.: They usually hover 1 to 4 cm above the entrance to their cave. Individuals from the cool waters of southern Japan grow larger.

T: 21°-27°C, **L:** 3.5 cm, **TL:** from 80 cm, **WM:** m, **WR:** b, **AV:** 3, **D:** 1-2

Trimma naudei   SMITH, 1956
Naude's cave goby

Hab.: Indo-Pacific, the Seychelles, the Ryukyu Islands, and Micronesia. In coral reefs of lagoons at depths of 3 to 30 m.

Sex.: Not recognizable from external characteristics.

Soc.B./Assoc.: They live singly or in pairs. Because of their diminutive size, they should only be kept with other small or very peaceful fishes (e.g., pipefishes). An ideal fish for tanks with sessile invertebrates.

M.: Needs a sand bottomed reef aquarium with flat stones or mussel shells lying on top to act as shelters.

Light: Areas of moderate light.

B./Rep.: Has not been successful in an aquarium.

F.: C, FD; they feed on copepods, ostracods (small crustacea), and small rotifers which are picked from the sand. In the aquarium they can be fed minute pieces of frozen foods and tablets. An occasional meal of *Artemia* nauplii delivered with a feeding pipe is appreciated.

S.: The gill slit extending to the eye is typical for the genus. They have reduced sensory papillae and ctenoid scales. Usually found hovering a few centimeters above their cave in the open water. The species is very similar to *T. caesiura* and *T. okinawae*.

T: 22°-26°C, **L:** 3 cm, **TL:** from 80 cm, **WM:** w-m, **WR:** b, **AV:** 3, **D:** 1-2

Stonogobiops xanthorhinica

Trimma naudei

Fam.: Gobiidae

Trimma tevegae
Tevega's cave goby

COHEN & PAVIS, 1969

Hab.: Tropical west Pacific, the Ryukyu Islands, and Micronesia. On rocks along drop-offs at depths of 10 to 40 m.

Sex.: Not recognizable from external characteristics.

Soc.B./Assoc.: They live singly within a loose congregation. They are quite timid and only emerge when the coast is clear of other fishes.

M.: Reef aquarium with hiding places.

Light: Dim light.

B./Rep.: Has not been successful in an aquarium.

F.: C, FD; they feed on copepods (small crustacea), but in the aquarium, they also eat finely minced frozen foods and small pieces of tablet foods. Once in while *Artemia* nauplii should be given with a feeding tube.

S.: Commonly seen with their head at an upward slant in the open water. This genus is easily confused with *Priolepis*.

T: 22°-26°C, **L:** 4 cm, **TL:** from 80 cm, **WM:** w, **WR:** b-m, **AV:** 3, **D:** 2

Valenciennea helsdingenii
Railway glider

(BLEEKER, 1858)

Hab.: Widely distributed in the tropical Indo-Pacific. In coral reefs and small ports at depths of 1 to 30 m.

Sex.: The ♂♂ have long filaments on the first rays of the dorsal fin.

Soc.B./Assoc.: Always found in pairs in their natural habitat, and only pairs should be maintained in an aquarium. Solitary individuals do not live long. In a large aquarium, they can be kept with other fishes. However, a species tank allows them to readily display their behavior.

M.: Needs a 5 cm layer of loose coarse sand and shell debris. A cave is dug under a flat stone.

Light: Region of sunlight.

B./Rep.: The species repeatedly spawns in a species tank. Rearing is not overly difficult. One ♀ produces about 2000 eggs each month. These are adhered to the ceiling of a cave. In contrast to many other gobies, the ♀ cares for the spawn.

F.: C, FD; they constantly dig in the sand searching for tidbits. Feeding is unproblematic, since they will eat frozen foods and pieces of tablet foods.

S.: The sleeper gobies were previously in their own family, the Eleotridae. The genus *Valenciennea* is currently being revised by HOESE.
V. helsdingenii is extremely timid and can only be kept in well-covered aquaria. During acclimation, the animals are very susceptible to disease, especially bacterial infections. Not suitable for reef aquaria.

T: 22°-27°C, **L:** 16 cm, **TL:** from 100 cm, **WM:** w-m, **WR:** b, **AV:** 2, **D:** 1

1104

Trimma tevegae

Valenciennea helsdingenii

Fam.: Gobiidae

Valenciennea immaculata   (NI, 1981)
and
Valenciennea longipinnis   (LAY & BENNET, 1839)
Sleeper gobies

Hab.: Throughout the tropical Indo-Pacific. Over sand bottoms at depths of 2 to 30 m.

Sex.: The first rays of the dorsal fin are elongated in ♂ ♂ .

Soc.B./Assoc.: Always found in pairs and should be maintained in such a fashion. Do not associate with overly aggressive fishes.

M.: Provide a 6 to 8 cm layer of coarse sand, coral gravel, or shell debris. Caves will be excavated under flat stones or buried halved flower pots.

Light: Areas of moderate light to sunlight.

B./Rep.: *V. immaculata* is regularly raised in aquaria. The larvae, however, must be fed live marine plankton.

F.: C, FD; feed any frozen or tablet food. They must be conditioned on live foods to spawn.

S.: Pieces of sand and gravel up to the size of their head are constantly moved about with their mouth. Their high activity level makes them an interesting fish to watch. *V. longipinnis* is one of the few species of this genus that is simple to care for in an aquarium. However, it is just as unsuitable for the reef aquarium as its relatives. This relatively easily cared for goby will build a mound 20-30 cm high and up to 1 m in diameter. Comparable " castles" are only built by the significantly larger. *V. helsdingenii* and *V. strigata.*

T: 22°-27°C, **L:** 13 cm, **TL:** from 100 cm, **WM:** w, **WR:** b, **AV:** 1-2, **D:** 1

Valenciennea immaculata

Valenciennea immaculata

Valenciennea longipinnis

Valenciennea puellaris (TOMIYAMA, 1965)
Pretty prawn goby

Hab.: Red Sea, Indo-Pacific, Japan, and the Great Barrier Reef. In coral reefs at 5 to 20 m.

Sex.: The ♂'s first dorsal fin has threadlike long rays.

Soc.B./Assoc.: They should always be kept in pairs. Their life span can exceed 5 years in captivity. If one partner dies, the other generally follows suit within a short time. You must have a large aquarium if it is your intention to keep these animals with other fishes.

M.: Reef aquarium with a deep layer of coarse sand or coral gravel. Build a cave with flat stone plates. Caution—digging activities may cause stone structures to collapse.

Light: Dim to moderate light.

B./Rep.: The ♀ adheres over 1000 eggs to the ceiling of the cave every month and guards them for three weeks. During this time the ♂ remains outside the cave. The day the eggs hatch the ♂ seals the ♀ into the cave. The cave is opened again that evening and both the ♂ and ♀ herd the newly hatched larvae into the open water.

F.: C, FD; happily accepts large pieces of frozen and tablet foods. However, insure that they receive a balanced diet.

S.: A pair, once formed, is lifelong.

T: 22°-26°C, **L:** 13 cm, **TL:** from 100 cm, **WM:** w, **WR:** b, **AV:** 2, **D:** 1

Valenciennea puellaris, Red Sea

Valenciennea puellaris, ♂ and ♀

Fam.: Gobiidae

a) *Valenciennea sexguttata*   (VALENCIENNES, 1839)
   Ladder glider
   and
b) *Valenciennea strigata*   (BROUSSONET, 1782)
   Pennant glider

Hab.: The entire Indo-Pacific; *V. sexguttata* is also found in the Red Sea. On sandy bottoms between coral reefs at depths of 1 to 20 m.

Sex.: The first dorsal fin rays of the ♂ are elongated.

Soc.B./Assoc.: They must always have a partner. Rarely will a solitary individual live. A large tank is necessary if you wish to maintain these animals with other fishes.

M.: Decorate a large tank as a reef aquarium on one side and put a deep layer of coarse sand or coral gravel mixed with shell debris on the other side. The gobies excavate a cave under flat stone plates.

Light: Zones of moderate light to sunlight.

B./Rep.: Is possible when unicellular animals (e.g., rotifers and, later, *Artemia* nauplii) can be procured for the larvae.

F.: C, FD; suspended frozen and tablet foods are consumed as well as items found on the substrate.

S.: Unsuitable for normal reef aquarium, since the animals constantly search the sand for edible components. The sand is frequently spit over invertebrates. This is not tolerated for long by stone corals, colonial anemones, or sponges. *V. strigata* is quite sensitive during acclimation. Additionally the fishes must be fed frequently, or they rapidly tend to become emaciated. Do not cover the aquarium.

T: 22°-28°C, **L:** a) 13, b) 18 cm, **TL:** from 100 cm, **WM:** w-m, **WR:** b, **AV:** 1-2, **D:** 1

Valenciennea sexguttata

Valenciennea strigata

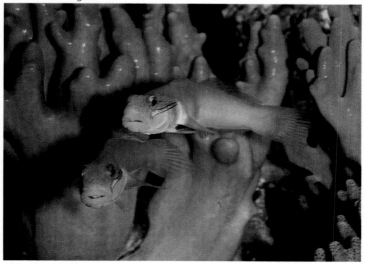

Valenciennea strigata

Fam.: Gobiidae

Valenciennea wardi   (PLAYFAIR & GÜNTHER, 1866)
Ward's glider

Hab.: In the Indo-Pacific, around the Maldives and Mauritius. On sandy bottoms between coral reefs at depths of 5 to 20 m.

Sex.: In ♂♂, the first rays of the dorsal fin are elongated.

Soc.B./Assoc.: Always keep a pair. Only house with other fishes in large tanks. Do not place in an aquarium that has sand-dwelling crustacea.

M.: Needs a deep substrate of coarse material with flat stones lying on top. The gobies use their mouth to dig a cave under a stone.

Light: Areas of moderate light to sunlight.

B./Rep.: While breeding has not been described for this species, it probably deviates little from other *Valenciennea* species (previous pages).

F.: C, FD; unproblematic since it can be fed frozen foods and quartered tablets. Live *Artemia* and blood worms should be occasionally offered.

S.: Their digging may undermine rockwork and cause it to fall. *V. wardi* though regularly available, is only imported from Sri Lanka. This very sensitive, timid fish is difficult to acclimate after it is improted. They must also be handled with care after purchase. Skittish animals. Do not cover the aquarium.

T: 22°-27°C, **L:** 11 cm, **TL:** from 100 cm, **WM:** w-m, **WR:** b, **AV:** 2, **D:** 1

Vanderhorstia ambonoro   (FOURMANOIR, 1957)
Ambonor goby

Hab.: Pacific and New Britain. On sandy bottoms at a few meters depth.

Sex.: No external differentiating characteristics are known.

Soc.B./Assoc.: They live in symbiosis with various species of *Alpheus* pistol shrimp. Try to always keep a pistol shrimp with them in the aquarium. Only associate with other fishes in large aquaria.

M.: Deep sand bottom with hiding possibilities such as flat stone edifications with caves or halved flower pots. There should always be sand on the bottom of the cave.

Light: Region of sunlight.

B./Rep.: Has not been successful in an aquarium.

F.: C, FD; they readily snap at suspended pieces of frozen foods that drift in the current. They also take crumbled tablet foods from the bottom.

S.: They live in symbiosis with *Alpheus* shrimp, which is why many people confuse them with gobies from the genera *Amblyeleotris* or *Cryptocentrus*.

T: 22°-27°C, **L:** 8 cm, **TL:** from 80 cm, **WM:** m, **WR:** b, **AV:** 3, **D:** 1-2

Valenciennea wardi

Vanderhorstia ambonoro

Fam.: Gobiidae

Vanderhorstia mertensi   KLAUSEWITZ, 1974
Mertens' prawn goby

Hab.: In the Red Sea. Sporadically found in the Indo-Pacific to Papua New Guinea, where this picture was taken. On sandy bottoms between coral near reefs at depths of 2 to 10 m.

Sex.: Indiscernible from the exterior.

Soc.B./Assoc.: Live in symbiosis with various species of pistol shrimp from the genus *Alpheus.* Either keep singly or as a pair, since they are aggressive towards conspecifics of the same sex.

M.: Provide a large area of coarse sand or shell debris. They like to retire into halved flower pots which are buried in the sand to the extent that only a small slit remains uncovered.

Light: Sunlight to moderately lit areas.

B./Rep.: Has not yet been successful in an aquarium, although ♀ ♀ repeatedly spawned when well fed.

F.: C, FD; they consume all frozen foods, but they can also be acclimated to tablet foods (TetraTips). However, insure a balanced menu.

S.: They live in symbiosis with pistol shrimp, mostly *Alpheus djiboutensis.* Their interaction is interesting. The taller first dorsal fin can be used to distinguish this species from others.

T: 20°-26°C, **L:** 7 cm, **TL:** from 80 cm, **WM:** w-m, **WR:** b, **AV:** 3, **D:** 1-2

Vanderhorstia ornatissima   SMITH, 1959
Ocellate goby

Hab.: Red Sea, western Indo-Pacific, and the Maldives. On sandy bottoms around coral reefs only a few meters deep.

Sex.: No sexual dichromatism. The only exterior sexual difference is the shape of the genital papilla (p. 1074). However, this can only be recognized in anesthetized or dead animals.

Soc.B./Assoc.: In their natural habitat they are always associated with shrimp of the genus *Alpheus.* In large tanks they get along well with small, peaceful, free-swimming fishes.

M.: Sandy bottom with flat stones under which they can build a cave.

Light: Region of sunlight.

B./Rep.: Has not yet been successful in an aquarium.

F.: C, FD; they accept larger pieces of various frozen foods as well as pieces of tablet foods. If free-swimming fishes reach the food first, the gobies and shrimp must be fed with a feeding tube.

S.: Like *Amblyeleotris, Cryptocentrus, Lotilia,* and *Stonogobiops* (see there), this goby lives in symbiosis with an *Alpheus* pistol shrimp. The ocellated goby is very similar to *V. delagoae,* but has smaller scales.

T: 21°-27°C, **L:** 6 cm, **TL:** from 80 cm, **WM:** w-m, **WR:** b, **AV:** 2, **D:** 1-2

Vanderhorstia mertensi

Vanderhorstia ornatissima

Fam.: Microdesmidae

Microdesmidae typically have a long, slender body. Unlike other gobies, they are not bottom oriented fishes. They swim above their caves as they hunt for zooplankton and dart about to escape predators (which gave them the German common name Pfeilgrundeln = arrow gobies). Two subfamilies, the Microdesminae and the Ptereleotrinae, are recognized.

The genus *Gunnelichthys* belongs to the subfamily Microdesminae. By observing their slender, wormlike bodies and snaking movements, you can immediately see where the idea for their common name, wormfishes, comes from. They differ from other family members by their single fused dorsal fin. Wormfishes usually live in small colonies at depths of 5 to 50 m and spend their time 20 to 100 cm above open sandy bottoms catching planktonic crustacea and fish larvae. When threatened, they dive head first into cavelike shelters in the bottom. Observations made by a Mauritian fisherman that wormfishes, for example, *G. curiosus,* are waspish and injurious to tankmates could not be confirmed.

The remainder of the wormfishes presented here are without a doubt the most sought after species of the marine aquarium hobby. They are members of the subfamily Ptereleotrinae. *Nemateleotris* sword gobies have enthused marine aquarists as well as divers for years. Their common name is derived from a swordlike appendage on the first dorsal fin, which is usually held erect. *Nemateleotris magnifica*, the most widely distributed species of sword goby, has a longer sword then either of the two other known species, *N. decora* and *N. helfrichi.* It is the most established in the trade and the most reasonably priced of the three. Because it is distributed throughout the Indo-Pacific, it is a frequent import. Some friends of mine photographed *N. magnifica* around Tahiti and the Maldives, while I (H.D.) observed them along the Australian Barrier Reef and at the coast of Kenya. Do not assume that the fairly social nature of *N. magnifica* in its natural biotope extends to the aquarium. The limited space of an aquarium brings forth their aggressive nature, and they will pass the day in pursuit of each other. Exhausted individuals are bit and injured with such severity that eventually death results. The maintenance of a single specimen or a pair is recommended, provided you are fortunate enough to acquire a pair in the trade. The sexes cannot be distinguished by external features.

Gobies of the genus *Ptereleotris* are very close relatives of the sword gobies. Both have an elongated body and two separate pectoral fins. Their swimbladder allows them to swim in mid-water without expending excess energy. Some species can frequently be observed in their natural biotope in small schools "standing" above a reef riddled with hiding places. Others form pairs and defend a refuge among the rocks from conspecifics. *Ptereleotris* will search for suitable cracks or crevices in the coral reef at depths down to 70 m rather than dig a cave themselves. This book contains a photo (p. 1132) that shows an *Amblyeleotris*, a *Ptereleotris*, and last but not least, an *Alpheus* pistol shrimp all living in one cave.

Ptereleotris zebra

Fam.: Microdesmidae

Gunnelichthys curiosus   DAWSON, 1968
Yellow-striped worm eel

Hab.: In the Indo-Pacific, Indonesia and Mauritius. Over sand bottoms at depths of 10 to 60 m.

Sex.: Unknown.

Soc.B./Assoc.: Keep pairs or a school if possible.

M.: Reef tank with a large sandy area where an acrylic tube has been buried at a slant.

Light: Region of moderate light.

B./Rep.: Not yet successful.

F.: C, FD; they feed on benthic and free-living crustacea, but in the aquarium, they will accept chopped frozen foods and pieces of tablet foods which drift past them in the current.

S.: *G. curiosus* likes to totally bury itself in sandy, not overly coarse substrate. Fish maintained in groups are significantly less shy, but unfortunately, they frequently jump through the smallest holes and slits left by the aquarium´s cover.

T: 22°-27°C, **L:** 8 cm, **TL:** from 100 cm, **WM:** m, **WR:** b, **AV:** 3, **D:** 1-2

Gunnelichthys monostigma   SMITH, 1958
One-spot worm eel

Hab.: Indo-Pacific, east Africa, the Ryukyu Islands, and the Great Barrier Reef. Over sand bottoms and in lagoons at depths of 6 to 20 m.

Sex.: Unknown.

Soc.B./Assoc.: In nature they live in groups; in the aquarium, ♂ ♂ don't get along. Keep alone or with small fishes.

M.: As for *G. curiosus*.

Light: Areas of moderate light.

B./Rep.: Has not been successful in an aquarium. One ♀ lays approximately 2,000 round eggs that have a diameter of 0.2 mm.

F.: C, FD; as for *G. curiosus*.

S.: Usually hovers a few centimeters above the sand in a slight current. When in danger, they dart head first into their cave.

T: 23°-27°C, **L:** 8 cm, **TL:** from 100 cm, **WM:** m, **WR:** u, **AV:** 3, **D:** 1-2

Gunnelichthys curiosus

Gunnelichthys monostigma

Fam.: Microdesmidae

Gunnelichthys pleurotaenia   BLEEKER, 1858
Black-striped worm eel

Hab.: Western and central Pacific, Java, the Philippines, and the Great Barrier Reef. Generally at depths less than 3 m over sand substrates. Once in a while, however, they venture into depths below 10 m.

Sex.: Unknown.

Soc.B./Assoc.: They live singly, as pairs, or in groups. Nevertheless, animals of the same sex do not get along in the limited space of an aquarium. If possible, do not keep with other fishes unless they are very small and peaceful; otherwise, the gobies will rarely emerge from their cave.

M.: Bottom of coarse sand or crushed shell. Build a long narrow cave of flat stones.

Light: Area of sunlight.

B./Rep.: No reports on captive breeding.

F.: C, FD; they are easily pleased. They will accept chopped frozen foods, *Artemia*, *Tubifex,* and pieces of tablet foods.

S.: Largely similar to *G. copleyi* from the western Indo-Pacific.

T: 22°-27°C, **L:** 8 cm, **TL:** from 80 cm, **WM:** m, **WR:** b, **AV:** 3, **D:** 1-2

Nemateleotris decora   RANDALL & ALLEN, 1973
Decorated firefish

Hab.: Western Pacific, the Ryukyu Islands, and the Great Barrier Reef. Above gravel and rocky bottoms at depths of 25 to 70 m.

Sex.: No differences.

Soc.B./Assoc.: They occur almost exclusively in pairs and should be kept in this manner in an aquarium. Several individuals can be kept in very large aquaria. Very amiable towards small fishes and good tankmates for invertebrates.

M.: Reef aquarium with shaded areas where the caves should be built.

Light: Dim light zone.

B./Rep.: Has not been successfully bred in an aquarium.

F.: C, FD; they feed on zooplankton, but snap at any food that drifts by. Frozen foods, tablets, and flakes are accepted.

S.: This species is usually not as shy as *N. magnifica.* Both in their natural habitat and the aquarium they hover in the current above their cave entrance. They flee head first into their shelter when danger is perceived. As the photographs show, the species exists in a variety of colors.

T: 23°-27°C, **L:** 7 cm, **TL:** from 100 cm, **WM:** m-s, **WR:** m, **AV:** 2, **D:** 1-2

Nemateleotris decora

Gunnelichthys pleurotaenia

Nemateleotris decora

Nemateleotris decora

Nemateleotris helfrichi

Nemateleotris helfrichi, aquarium photo

Nemateleotris helfrichi   RANDALL & ALLEN, 1973
Helfrich's firefish

Hab.: Western Pacific, Samoa, and the Marshall Islands. Above small sandy areas or rock bottoms at depths of 25 to 70 m.

Sex.: No sexual differences.

Soc.B./Assoc.: They are almost exclusively found in pairs and should be kept this way. Only house them with small, rather sedentary fishes and/or invertebrates

M.: Reef aquarium with hiding places. They frequently hover in a strong current.

Light: Moderate to dim light.

B./Rep.: Has not been successfully bred in an aquarium.

F.: C, FD; accepts almost all foods without training. The foods must drift by them in the current. Even live foods will not be taken from the bottom.

S.: Somewhat timid at first in the face of bright illumination. Their cave should be shaded during acclimation.

T: 23°-27°C, **L:** 6 cm, **TL:** from 80 cm, **WM:** s, **WR:** m, **AV:** 3, **D:** 1-2

Fam.: Microdesmidae

Nemateleotris magnifica
Firefish

FOWLER, 1938

Hab.: Indo-Pacific, Hawaii, the Ryukyu Islands, and the Great Barrier Reef. Along the outer fringes of coral reefs at depths of 10 to 70 m.

Sex.: Nonexistent.

Soc.B./Assoc.: Juveniles live in groups within one cave. Adults almost exclusively live in pairs. They will only display normal behavior if kept with small, sedate fishes. Ideal companions for almost all invertebrates.

M.: Reef tank with deep hiding places. They do not place particular demands on water quality, but they prefer a medium to strong current about half a meter above their shelter to hover in.

Light: Areas of moderate light.

B./Rep.: Not yet successful in an aquarium.

F.: C, FD; in nature they feed on planktonic crustacea. In the aquarium they eagerly accept any food up to the size of a *Mysis* as long as it drifts by. Feed live *Artemia* twice a week!

S.: It has the most elongated first dorsal fin of any member in the genus. A popular aquarium species which, although initially shy, soon recognizes its caretaker and quickly overcomes its natural tendency to dive head first into its cave. Due to its coloration and jerky movements, it is usually the most notable inhabitant of the reef aquarium.

T: 22°-28°C, **L:** 8 cm, **TL:** from 80 cm, **WM:** m-s, **WR:** m, **AV:** 1, **D:** 2

Nemateleotris magnifica

Nemateleotris magnifica

Nemateleotris magnifica

Fam.: Microdesmidae

Oxymetropon cyanoctenosum KLAUSEWITZ, 1981
Feathertail sleeper

Hab.: In the Indo-Australian Archipelago. In coral reefs at depths of 10 to 35 m.

Sex.: Not recognizable from the exterior.

Soc.B./Assoc.: Always keep a pair or school; never keep solitary animals.

M.: Reef aquarium with sufficient hiding places.

Light: Areas of moderate light.

B./Rep.: Has not been successful in an aquarium.

F.: C, FD; they snap at any food of animal origin which passes them in the current.

S.: The feathertail sleeper is a very sensitive animal that can only be kept with small, sedate fishes. They are difficult to acclimate. Besides the pictured blue form, there is also a gray form that does not have crossbands on the body, but has red stripes along the upper and lower edge of the tail fin. Both forms are imported from the Philippines.

T: 24°-27°C, **L:** 10 cm, **TL:** from 100 cm, **WM:** m-s, **WR:** b, **AV:** 3-4, **D:** 3

Oxymetropon cyanoctenosum

Ptereleotris evides

Fam.: Microdesmidae

Ptereleotris evides   (JORDAN & HUBBS, 1925)
Spottail gudgeon

Hab.: Red Sea, Indo-Pacific, Japan, and western Pacific. Along outer reef slopes or, occasionally, in bays and lagoons at depths of 2 to 15 m.

Sex.: The sexes can only be distinguished by the shape of the genital papilla.

Soc.B./Assoc.: Juveniles live in groups; adults usually live in pairs. In very large aquaria, several specimens can be kept. Although they can be kept with many moderate sized fishes, they are particularly appropriate tankmates for invertebrates.

M.: Reef aquarium with a sand bottom. Build a cave in the transition zone from sand to rock.

Light: Area of moderate light.

B./Rep.: Even though the gobies spawn regularly with appropriate feeding, rearing has not been successful.

F.: C, FD; they are unproblematic to feed and accept various frozen foods as well as tablet and flake foods. Maintain a varied menu.

S.: Contrary to their relatives, these fish do not flee into their cave. They abandon their territory when in danger. Juveniles can be recognized by the oval spot on the caudal peduncle.

T: 21°-27°C, **L:** 12 cm, **TL:** from 100 cm, **WM:** m, **WR:** m, **AV:** 1, **D:** 1-2

Pterereleotris grammica
Mauritius gudgeon

RANDALL & LUBBOCK, 1982

Hab.: Southern Indo-Pacific. Above gravel and sand substrates along outer reefs at depths of 30 to 50 m.

Sex.: Can only be recognized be the shape of the genital papilla.

Soc.B./Assoc.: Since they are always found in pairs in their natural habitat, they should also be maintained in captivity as such. They are ideal partners for invertebrates, but too timid to house with larger fishes.

M.: Reef aquarium with a sand bottom. Build a shelter of flat stones over the sand substrate.

Light: Areas of moderate light.

B./Rep.: Has not been accomplished in an aquarium.

F.: C, FD; they accept almost any suspended food. Foods eaten from the substrate or surface are an exception, not the rule.

S.: Two differently colored subspecies exist: *P. g. grammica* inhabits the eastern area of distribution and has a dark-brown longitudinal stripe, whereas the black *P. g. melanota* is from Mauritius.

T: 22°-27°C, **L:** 8 cm, **TL:** from 80 cm, **WM:** m, **WR:** m, **AV:** 3, **D:** 1-2

Fam.: Microdesmidae

Ptereleotris hannae (JORDAN & SNYDER, 1901)
Blue hana goby

Hab.: Western and central Pacific, Japan, Korea, the Philippines, Indonesia, and Australia. On sand and gravel substrates near a reef. At depths of 3 to 50 m.

Sex.: Can only be recognized by the shape of the genital papilla.

Soc.B./Assoc.: Usually live in pairs, but individuals can be kept in aquaria. They make good companions for small bottom-dwelling fishes like gobies and blennies. Can be housed with any invertebrate.

M.: Reef tank with coarse sand and acrylic tubes buried at an angle to provide shelter. However, they also accept hiding places among the rocks.

Light: Areas of moderate light.

B./Rep.: The diminutive size of the larvae make it a difficult fish to rear in an aquarium. However, courtship and spawning can be repeatedly observed.

F.: C, FD; not a finicky eater. All foods suspended in the water in their proximity draw interest. They can be easily accustomed to flake food, but do not be tempted to limit their diet to such fare.

S.: This species is frequently observed inhabiting a cave with *Alpheus* pistol shrimp, but it does not develop a symbiotic relationship with it. Difficult to distinguish from *P. arabica,* but note *P. hannae*'s longer caudal fin filaments.

T: 21°-27°C, **L:** 11 cm, **TL:** from 100 cm, **WM:** m, **WR:** m, **AV:** 2-3, **D:** 1-2

Ptereleotris heteroptera (BLEEKER, 1855)
Pale gudgeon

Hab.: Red Sea, Indo-Pacific, Ryukyu Islands, Pacific, and Hawaii. In lagoons and outer reefs above hard substrates as well as over sand. At depths of 5 to 50 m.

Sex.: Can only be recognized by the shape of the genital papilla.

Soc.B./Assoc.: Young fish form small groups; adults are found in pairs which usually swim close to each other. Several pairs can be maintained in very large aquaria. Since they are relatively shy, they should only be associated with invertebrates.

M.: Reef aquarium with sand bottom. Build several crevices and caves among the rocks close to the substrate.

Light: Area of moderate light.

B./Rep.: If the fish are at ease in their environment, they spawn repeatedly. However, there is a paucity of information concerning fry rearing. The larvae begin their bottom-dwelling lifestyle at a length of 3 cm.

F.: C, FD; they feed on zooplankton. In captivity they only eat food particles drifting in the open water column. Frozen foods (*Artemia, Mysis*) are accepted as readily as crushed tablet foods.

S.: In its natural habitat it frequently hovers up to 3 m above the substrate. Nevertheless, when danger approaches, they quickly disappear into their cave. *P. heteroptera* is similar to *P. evides*, but the former has a black spot on the tail fin. This species occasionally shares a cave with a goby and a shrimp (photo on the page after next).

T: 22°-27°C, **L:** 10 cm, **TL:** from 80 cm, **WM:** m, **WR:** m, **AV:** 1-2, **D:** 1-2

Ptereleotris hannae

Ptereleotris heteroptera

Fam.: Microdesmidae

Ptereleotris heteroptera in an unusual living arrangement with a prawn goby that normally lives only with a pistol shrimp.

Ptereleotris hannae shares its care with *Amblyeleotris sp.*

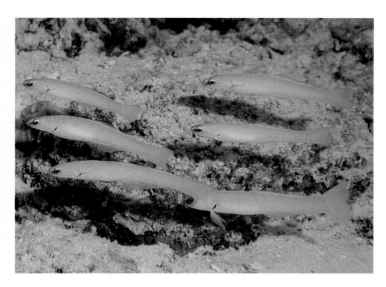

Ptereleotris microlepis
Blue gudgeon

(BLEEKER, 1856)

Hab.: Red Sea, east Africa, the Seychelles, and the Indo-Pacific to Melanesia. On sand and coral gravel in bays and lagoons at depths of 0.5 to 50 m.

Sex.: Can only be recognized by the shape of the genital papilla.

Soc.B./Assoc.: They can be kept in pairs or in small groups made up of several pairs (photo). Since this species is particularly shy, it should only be kept with invertebrates.

M.: Reef aquarium with a sand bottom and hiding places that have to be large enough to accommodate several individuals. When startled, they tend to jump out of the water; a cover for the aquarium is therefore recommended. No strong current.

Light: Sunlight to moderate light areas.

B./Rep.: Has not been successful in an aquarium.

F.: C, FD; they accept almost any foods suspended in the water. Feed that has sunk to the bottom is ignored and should be removed at once.

S.: They are more timid than most other *Ptereleotris* species.

T: 22°-27°C, **L:** 12 cm, **TL:** from 100 cm, **WM:** w-m, **WR:** m, **AV:** 2, **D:** 2

Fam.: Microdesmidae

Pterereotris monoptera
Ghost goby

RANDALL & HOESE, 1985

Hab.: South Japan, Taiwan, Indonesia, the Great Barrier Reef, and the Seychelles. On sand and rock substrates at depths of 6 to 15 m.

Sex.: Can only be distinguished by the shape of the genital papilla. ♂♂ sometimes have longer filaments on the tail fin than ♀♀.

Soc.B./Assoc.: They live in pairs, but frequently form loose aggregations. Only small peaceful fishes and invertebrates are suitable companions.

M.: Sand substrate with rockwork where they can hide.

Light: Moderate light.

B./Rep.: Not yet successful in an aquarium.

F.: C, FD; they quickly grab any feed drifting in the current or sinking to the bottom. Once the food settles on the bottom it is ignored.

S.: Unknown.

T: 22°-27°C, **L:** 11 cm, **TL:** from 100 cm, **WM:** w-m, **WR:** m, **AV:** 3, **D:** 2

Pterereotris uroditaenia
Pacific gudgeon

RANDALL & HOESE, 1985

Hab.: Western south Pacific and the Great Barrier Reef. In coral reefs at 20 m depth.

Sex.: Can only be recognized by the shape of the genital papilla.

Soc.B./Assoc.: They usually live in pairs and should only be kept in this manner. In the majority of cases, animals of the same sex do not get along well. They are ideal for the invertebrate aquarium, but their timid nature makes them poor company for other fishes.

M.: Reef aquarium with various hiding possibilities.

Light: Area of moderate light.

B./Rep.: Has not been attempted in an aquarium.

F.: C, FD; they will only eat finely chopped frozen foods and crumbled tablet foods if they are drifting in the water. Live food (e.g., blood worms) should be fed occasionally.

S.: This species is easily distinguished by the two dark stripes on the tail fin. Next to nothing is known about its biology, since the species is very rare. At the time of its scientific description, only one specimen had been captured and two others photographed.

T: 23°-27°C, **L:** 8 cm, **TL:** from 80 cm, **WM:** w-m, **WR:** m, **AV:** 3-4, **D:** 2

Ptereleotris monoptera

Ptereleotris uroditaenia

Ptereleotris zebra
Chinese zebra goby

(FOWLER, 1938)

Hab.: Red Sea, Indo-Pacific, the Ryukyu Islands, and the Great Barrier Reef. In coral reefs at depths of 2 to 4 m. Occasionally found at depths greater than 30 m.

Sex.: ♂ ♂ and ♀ ♀ can only be distinguished by the shape of their genital papilla (see p. 1074).

Soc.B./Assoc.: According to present observations, this is the only species of the family that can be maintained in small groups in an aquarium. However, this is only possible until sexual maturity. Small groups are formed in its natural waters as well. They may even share the same cave. Good companions for invertebrates and small fishes, e.g., a pair of *Amphiprion*.

M.: Reef tank with sufficient hiding places. A cover is recommended because startled animals sometimes jump out of the water.

Light: Sunlight to moderate light zones.

B./Rep.: During courtship, which can be repeatedly observed, the ♂ approaches the ♀ at an angle from above, dives underneath her, and touches her side with his mouth; then they proceed to swim parallel to each other for a moment. The resulting gray eggs are guarded in a cave. Although the ♂ is tolerated in the cave, it does not seem to participate in brood care (JANDE: Aqu. Magaz. 3/1980, pp. 118 ff.). Since newly hatched larvae are very tiny, rearing them will be difficult.

F.: C, FD; they eagerly snap at all food suspended in the water column, including frozen foods, tablets, and flakes. However, *Tubifex* are avoided by most.

S.: The unpaired chin-barbels are pointed straight down when the animal is threatening another. Because of their conspicuous crossbands (name), they are easily differentiated from other *Ptereleotris* species.

T: 22°-28°C, **L:** 10 cm, **TL:** from 80 cm, **WM:** m, **WR:** m, **AV:** 1, **D:** 1

Ptereleotris zebra

Fam.: Pholidichthyidae   Convict Blennies

The only representative of this family, *Pholidichthys leucotaenia*, the convict blenny, is a common import from the Philippines and Indonesia. The elongated body has a fin virtually encompassing it in its entirety; in other words, dorsal and anal fins are fused with the tail fin. The broad dorsal fin begins just posterior to the head and has 60 rays, while the narrower anal fin only has 40. The divided dorsal fin is actually an important differentiating characteristic between gobies and blennies. Consequently, this goby should be classified as a member of the suborder Blennioidei. Nevertheless, other characteristics predominate and prompted scientists to place it in the suborder Gobioidei. Until additional investigations are made, the final classification cannot be made.

Scientific studies on the larvae of *P. leucotaenia* are interesting enough to be published here: the convict blenny was successfully bred in seven month intervals. In contrast to most other reef fishes, neither the eggs nor the larvae are planktonic. The parents lived in study aquaria that had an extensive system of tunnels in the substrate and caves in the mini-reef. The timid fishes only stuck their heads out of the cave entrances. Any live food, such as water fleas, or animal fare, like mussel and fish meat, were accepted. Courtship and spawning were not observed. However, the appearance of 400 to 500 larvae near the male and female convict blennies made it self-evident that reproduction had ensued. The different design of the young was pronounced, but the four adhesive glands between the eyes were discovered only with the aid of a scanning electron microscope. At night they secrete an adhesive thread they use to fasten themselves either to the bottom or algae in the vicinity of their parents.

Both parents defended the schooling young and attacked other fishes in the aquarium. But this aggressive behavior begins only after breeding. It seems to be normal that the brood remains close to the parents and is defended by them. It can be deduced that convict blennies also live in pairs in nature. Whereas many gobies live in pairs, there are no reports of blennies ever adopting this lifestyle. At an age of two month and a length of two centimeters, the larvae's adhesive glands had atrophied. The young convict blennies grew one centimeter each month while being fed *Artemia* and *Cyclops*. After one year, their longitudinal pattern transformed into the adult's cross-striped pattern. At a length of 15 cm, the convict blennies

Fam.: Pholidichthyidae

turned predatory and attacked other small fishes. In an aquarium, they rarely grow beyond 20 cm. Literature cites the largest convict blenny as being 33 cm long.

Top right hand photo:
Juveniles of the convict blenny, *Pholidichthys leucotaenia,* have a totally different coloration than adults. They are black with a white lateral longitudinal band that extends from the eyes to the base of the tail fin. They are lighter ventrally. With age, the longitudinal design dissolves and forms crossbands. The young usually form dense ball-like schools above the bottom. They are similar in appearance to young coral catfish. Since coral catfish are very poisonous, they are avoided by predators. Due to the similarity in behavior and appearance, young convict blennies are protected through their mimicry (compare photograph on p. 23!).

Pholidichthys leucotaenia   BLEEKER, 1856
Convict blenny

Hab.: Western Pacific around the Philippines, Indonesia, and the Solomon Islands. In coral reefs at depths of 10 to 20 m.

Sex.: Unknown.

Soc.B./Assoc.: Several individuals may be kept in large tanks that allow each animal to have its own shelter. They also get along well with many other fishes and invertebrates. Combining very small fishes and shrimp with this species is a risky venture.

M.: Reef aquarium with a coarse sandy bottom. Their shelters are built in the transition zone from sand to rock. They constantly maintain their refuges, and sand is continuously dug up and piled in small mounds.

Light: Area of moderate light.

B./Rep.: Very rarely successful in an aquarium. Newly hatched larvae are not planktonic like those of gobies or blennies, but sedentary with adhesive glands on their head.

F.: C, FD; they accept flake foods, TetraTips, TabiMin tablets, *Artemia*, *Mysis*, mussel meat, *Tubifex*, *Daphnia*, blood worms, glassworms, and Enchytraeidae. Algae and lettuce are not consumed.

S.: Classification is still unresolved (see p. 1037). Juveniles have a totally different coloration and exhibit interesting behavior.

T: 22°-28°C, **L:** 20 cm, **TL:** from 100 cm, **WM:** m-s, **WR:** b-m, **AV:** 3, **D:** 2

Pholidichthys leucotaenia, juvenile

Pholidichthys leucotaenia, adult

Fam.: Callionymidae

One of the pioneers of the saltwater hobby hails from the family Callionymidae. *Callionymus lyra* has been both maintained and bred in aquaria since before World War II. Its natural habitat is the northeastern Atlantic. Dragonets tend to be deep-water, benthic fishes from continental shelves, slopes, and sea knolls that live in depths of up to 900 m. Some species enter freshwater at the mouth of rivers. The two major genera, *Callionymus* and *Synchiropus,* live nearly circumtropical and in temperate seas. Most Callionymidae are found on sand and mud bottoms; however, there are a few that live in the coral reef among seagrasses.

Dragonet genera have a like body shape, but different colorations. They are relatively large headed small fishes that barely top 6 cm. Their eyes constantly survey their surroundings and are set on top of their heads. The mouth is small and pointed, and the mandibles may protrude. Their feeding is reminiscent of a pecking bird. Their skin is scaleless, but protected by a thick layer of mucus. Particularly heavy secretions occur when the fish feels threatened. It is assumed that these secretions are poisonous. Most dragonets have a spine on the front of the operculum that acts as additional protection against predators. But the spine does not serve as a direct weapon during scuffles between conspecifics. It only intimidates opponents by increasing the breadth of the fish when the opercula are spread. Generally there is extreme sexual dimorphism. Both sexes have two dorsal fins, but the male's dorsal fin is either very elongated or umbrellalike. Needless to say, this characteristic only becomes obvious when the dorsal fins are extended. In Germany, this family is known as the lyre fishes because of the similarity of the shape of the dorsal fin to the musical instrument. The upward extension of the dorsal fin is occasionally larger than the entire fish! During courtship and skirmishes, the males erect their dorsal fins and impress not only their opponent or partner, but their caretaker as well.

Dragonets, especially the mandarin fishes of the genus *Synchiropus,* can be kept in pairs. If the animals are at ease in their biotope, the female soon becomes ripe. The male responds by hopping near the female and displaying its dorsal fin.

While the aquarium is illuminated, both swim upward; the male always follows the female. Shivers rack his body after it descends to the substrate again, and his mouth protrudes. These pseudo-spawnings continue until the lights are turned off. Apparently that is when the true spawning activities occur.

The animals swim with their ventral sides together towards the surface. Eggs and sperm are released as they reach the pinnacle of an imaginary U. This takes about 15 seconds. The male's extended anal fin is notorious. Once the female has released her eggs, both separate and bury themselves in the sandy bottom.

All species of Callionymidae rise vertically from the bottom of the sea in pairs, and reach the pinnacle of their climb with their ventral sides together. The apex of their curve can be more than 2 m above the substrate. This ensures that the fertilized eggs are widely distributed by the current. Some species migrate to regions that have strong currents close to the bottom. Consequently, the planktonic eggs of these animals are distributed far and wide. Such "passive dispersion mechanisms" are frequently found in bottom-dwellers.

There is little information on how much time the eggs and larvae need to develop. In some species the development is fast (7 to 10 days from oviposition to the metamorphosis in *Synchiropus* species). In others, such as the Atlantic *Chalinops* species, it can take more than 40 days for the larvae to fall out of the plankton to the substrate. Besides the passive distribution through pelagic developmental stages, there are rare cases of active migration by adult animals. It is known that *Callionymus filamentosus* from the northern Red Sea has crossed the Suez Canal into the eastern Mediterranean. *Eleutherochir opercularis* is another that migrates. It regularly swims from the sea to river mouths and back.

Divers proudly relate their observations about this family. Their secretive lifestyle and camouflage coloration make them a rare find in their natural habitat. Photos of dragonets in their natural biotope are rare. The small territory they claim make them highly suited to a captive environment. A 100 l aquarium is sufficient. Live rocks with their associated microfauna and microflora are ideal for their care, especially for tropical species. Forward motion is achieved through small, slow jumps and propulsion with their pectorals.

The ventral fins are always touching the bottom of the aquarium, making all attempts at locomotion resemble hops. Every corner of the aquarium is explored, and the small, pointed mouth purposely searches for the smallest crustacea in the substrate and reef. Frozen foods such as *Mysis* and *Artemia* are readily taken as long as the pieces are not too big for the acuminate mouth, the food items are suspended, and they pass the fish in the current.

Fam.: Callionymidae

Callionymus delicatulus
Delicate dragonet

FRICKE, 1982

Hab.: Indo-Pacific, from the Red Sea to the Solomon Islands. At depths of 1 to 20 m.

Sex.: The ♂ ♂ are larger and have two extremely threadlike elongated rays on the 1st dorsal fin. The ventral half of the tail fin is very elongated as well. The ♀ lacks long dorsal fin rays, and the ventral half of the caudal fin is only slightly longer than the dorsal half.

Soc.B./Assoc.: *C. delicatulus* occur singly or in pairs in shallow waters over sand and mud bottoms, especially along lagoon reefs.

M.: *C. delicatulus* requires a few centimeters of sand to bury itself. It is undemanding and peaceful towards other fishes and invertebrates.

Light: Area of sunlight.

B./Rep.: It is assumed that they spawn in pairs during the evening; rearing has not been successful.

F.: C; feeds on small benthic crustacea, *Artemia*, *Mysis*, frozen foods, etc.

S.: A principle characteristic of this species is the long pointed spine on the front operculum. It is finely dentate on top and has one strong barb.

T: 24°-26°C, **L:** ♂ 6 cm, ♀ 4 cm, **TL:** from 60 cm, **WM:** w, **WR:** b, **AV:** 2, **S:** 3

Callionymus lyra
Common dragonet

LINNAEUS, 1758

Hab.: East Atlantic and Mediterranean, from Norway to northwest Africa and the Azores. At depths of 5 to 30 m.

Sex.: ♂ ♂ are significantly larger than ♀ ♀. The first ray of the ♂ 's dorsal fin is longer than the others, and the whole fin is sickle-shaped. Their spawning dress is a conspicuous orange-yellow with green, blue, and violet longitudinal stripes. The ♀ ♀ are beige and lack an elongated first dorsal fin ray.

Soc.B./Assoc.: *C. lyra* lives singly or in pairs on sandy or muddy bottoms. It is quite attached to its home, never venturing far afield. Bellicose towards conspecifics; peaceful towards other fishes and most invertebrates.

M.: *C. lyra* requires a sandy layer of sufficient depth to bury itself. Demands on the tank and water quality are moderate.

Light: Sunlight and moderate light.

B./Rep.: *C. lyra* was observed spawning in aquaria prior to WW II. The animals swim up into the open water column belly to belly. At the apex of the curve, they expel their eggs and sperm. Fertilization occurs in the open water. The eggs and larvae are widely distributed by the current. The young have not been successfully reared.

F.: C; primarily feeds on small crustacea it finds along the substrate. Once in a while it takes substitute foods such as *Mysis*, *Artemia*, shrimp, and frozen foods.

S.: *C. lyra* was the first fish successfully cared for in an aquarium, and not surprisingly, it is the least demanding species of the family. The aquarium must be cooled during the summer or in excessively heated rooms.

T: 16°-20°C, **L:** ♂ 30 cm, ♀ 20 cm, **TL:** from 120 cm, **WM:** w, **WR:** b, **AV:** 2, **S:** 3

Callionymus delicatulus

Callionymus lyra

Fam.: Callionymidae

Callionymus pleurostictus   SMITH, 1963
Bluespot dragonet

Hab.: West Pacific, from Vietnam to the Solomon Islands. At depths of 1 to 20 m.

Sex.: Not known.

Soc.B./Assoc.: *C. pleurostictus* lives singly or in pairs on coral sand in lagoons and can be kept with moderate sized fishes and invertebrates.

M.: *C. pleurostictus* requires at least a few centimeters of sand. This allows them to burrow into the substrate to rest or escape danger.

Light: Region of sunlight.

B./Rep.: It spawns pairwise in the evening hours in the open water. No reported successful spawns.

F.: C; *C. pleurostictus* searches the bottom of the sea for hidden small animals, especially crustacea. In the aquarium it relishes small crustacea such as *Mysis, Artemia*, chopped shrimp, and many other frozen foods.

S.: None.

T: 24°-26°C, **L:** 5 cm, **TL:** from 60 cm, **WM:** w, **WR:** b, **AV:** 2, **S:** 3

Diplogrammus infulatus   SHAW, 1963
Green dragonet

Hab.: Western Indian Ocean, from the Red Sea to South Africa and Mauritius. At depths of 1 to 10 m.

Sex.: Slight; the ♂ is only a little larger than the ♀; the first dorsal fin ray on the ♂ is more elongated. Sexual dichromatism is much more significant. The ♂ has dark blue spots on its sides and, dorsally is golden with silver and dark spots. The ♀ ♀ are a plain leather color.

Soc.B./Assoc.: *D. infulatus* lives singly or in pairs, especially in tidal pools and lagoons overgrown with seagrass.

M.: A very mature tank with corresponding algae growth and a stand of small animals is an absolute necessity to successfully maintain these animals.

Light: Area of sunlight.

B./Rep.: *D. infulatus* spawns during the twilight hours and pairs in the open water; rearing has not been successful in an aquarium.

F.: C; they search the plant stand for small organisms and find enough food in a mature aquarium to satisfy most of their feed requirements. They have also been known to consume small crustacea, even if freeze-dried.

S.: The spine on the front of the operculum is particularly long (up to 10 mm), distally bent, with 5 to 9 barbs curved posteriorly, and two somewhat forward directed teeth proximally.

T: 24°-26°C, **L:** 12 cm, **TL:** from 100 cm, **WM:** w, **WR:** b, **AV:** 2, **S:** 3

Callionymus pleurostictus

Diplogrammus infulatus

Fam.: Callionymidae

Diplogrammus randalli   FRICKE, 1983
Randall's dragonet

Hab.: Red Sea, Gulf of Aqaba. At depths of 1 to 10 m.

Sex.: Not known.

Soc.B./Assoc.: Lives singly or in pairs.

M.: Maintain at a higher specific gravity, since the Red Sea has a specific gravity of 1.028; 48 µs!

Light: Area of sunlight.

B./Rep.: Not known.

F.: C.

S.: Contrary to other dragonets, both species of the genus *Diplogrammus* lack free skin flaps on the posterior operculum. The spine on the anterior operculum is relatively large and sports numerous bent teeth on its dorsal side.

T: 24°-28°C, **L:** 7 cm, **TL:** from 80 cm, **WM:** w, **WR:** b, **AV:** 3, **S:** 3

Synchiropus picturatus ♀

Synchiropus picturatus   (PETERS, 1876)
Psychedelic fish

Hab.: The Philippines and Melanesia. At depths of 0 to 20 m.

Sex.: The ♂♂ and ♀♀ are almost identical in shape and coloration. However, ♂♂ are slightly larger, somewhat more intensely colored, and have more developed dorsal and caudal fins.

Soc.B./Assoc.: The animals live singly or in pairs secluded in coral reefs; therefore, they can be kept in pairs, but two conspecific or congener ♂♂ cannot be kept in one tank lest they fight, perhaps until death.

M.: *S. picturatus* requires a very mature tank with invertebrates and plenty of hiding places.

B./Rep.: Animals maintained in pairs in the aquarium swim to the surface to spawn during evening hours. However, rearing has not been successful.

F.: C; *S. picturatus* prefers to feed among algae growth. It is less interested in the algae than the small organisms living among them. Of course, it may nibble on colonial anemones, but otherwise, it leaves invertebrates in peace.

S.: Because of its secluded lifestyle, this animal, like most related species, is rarely offered. When available, it commands a respectable price. Its difficult maintenance means only experienced aquarists should try their hand at keeping it.

T: 24°-26°C, **L:** 5 cm, **TL:** from 60 cm, **WM:** w, **WR:** b, **AV:** 2-3, **S:** 3

Fam.: Callionymidae

Synchiropus splendidus

Synchiropus splendidus (HERRE, 1927)
Mandarin fish

Hab.: West Pacific, from Java to Japan, the southern Barrier Reef, and the Caroline Islands. At depths of 1 to 18 m.

Sex.: The ♂♂ are somewhat larger than ♀♀, have larger fins, and the first ray of the first dorsal fin is about twice as long.

Soc.B./Assoc.: *S. splendidus* lives singly or in pairs secluded in coral substrates or leaf litter along rocky coastlines. While a ♂ can be kept with one to several ♀♀, two or more ♂♂ cannot be combined, whether they are conspecifics or closely related species. Fights break out that may result in death.

M.: *S. splendidus* requires a heavily decorated reef aquarium that contains live invertebrates and small caves and niches to hide in.

Light: Sunlight and moderate light areas.

B./Rep.: Like other dragonets, these animals form pairs and swim towards the surface to release their sperm and eggs before returning to the substrate.

F.: C; the mandarin fish has a small mouth and feeds on tiny crustacea it finds in the aufwuchs. Although it takes *Artemia, Tubifex,* and other substitute foods in the aquarium, this will not suffice over the long term. Therefore, it needs a mature aquarium where it can find small benthic organisms to feed on.

S.: This appreciated but expensive animal is exported from the Philippines; light red animals are occasionally found.

T: 24°-26°C, **L:** 10 cm, **TL:** from 80 cm, **WM:** w, **WR:** b, **AV:** 2, **S:** 3

Synchiropus splendidus ♀, aquarium form

Synchiropus splendidus ♀

Fam.: Callionymidae

Synchiropus ocellatus (PALLAS, 1770)
Ocellated mandarin fish

Hab.: West central Pacific, from Vietnam to the Caroline and Marshall Islands as well as the southern Barrier Reef. At depths of 1 to 30 m.

Sex.: The ♂♂ are significantly larger than the ♀♀ (up to twice as large) and have a particularly impressive first dorsal fin which has four very long rays and 4 ocelli decorating the membrane between them.

Soc.B./Assoc.: *S. ocellatus* primarily inhabits sandy or rocky regions of lagoons and outer reefs either singly or in pairs.

M.: *S. ocellatus* needs a mature aquarium with good algae growth where it can hide and find nourishment.

Light: Area of sunlight.

B./Rep.: The rearing of *S. ocellatus* has not been successful; however, pairwise spawning during the evening hours has been observed.

F.: C; like all dwarf dragonets, its diet must be based on small organisms it hunts from the aufwuchs in mature aquaria. This menu can be supplemented with small bite-sized pieces of *Artemia, Mysis,* and other crustaceanlike organisms.

S.: There is nothing spectacular about their coloration. It allows them to blend into their surroundings quite well. The eye-catching dorsal fin of the ♂ is only displayed "when needed."

T: 24°-26°C, **L:** 7 cm, **TL:** from 80 cm, **WM:** w, **WR:** b, **AV:** 2, **S:** 3

Synchiropus izimae ♀, text on p. 1152

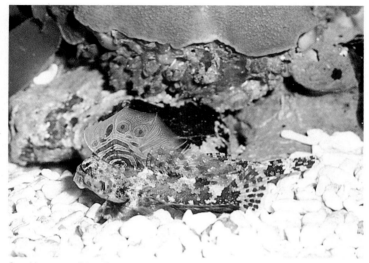

Synchiropus ocellatus ♂

Synchiropus ocellatus ♀

Fam.: Callionymidae

Synchiropus izimae
Fan-fin mandarin fish
JORDAN & THOMPSON, 1914

Hab.: West Pacific, around southern Japan. At depths of 10 to 20 m.

Sex.: Not known.

Soc.B./Assoc.: *S. izimae* can be kept singly or in pairs, and it prefers to hide among algae or within rock caves

M.: It can only be kept in mature aquaria that have corresponding good algae growth and hiding places.

Light: Areas of sun and moderate light.

B./Rep.: Spawns in pairs during the evening in the open water. Aquarium rearing has not been successful.

F.: C; it primarily feeds on tiny benthic organisms in the algae thicket; small crustacea and other sinking animal fare will be picked off the substrate and eaten.

S.: This dragonet, which is only known from Japan, lives on rocky substrates because coral reefs are sporadic in its natural biotope.

T: 18°-22°C, **L:** 9 cm, **TL:** from 80 cm, **WM:** w, **WR:** b, **AV:** 2-3, **S:** 3

Synchiropus morrisoni
Morrison's mandarin fish
SCHULTZ, 1960

Hab.: West central Pacific; from NW Australia and Japan to Samoa. In depths of 12 to 33 m.

Sex.: The ♂♂ and ♀♀ are about the same size; ♂♂ have a very tall, cropped, crown-like first dorsal fin with dark wavy vertical stripes. The first dorsal fin of the ♀ is very short, not even reaching the height of the second dorsal fin.

Soc.B./Assoc.: *S. morrisoni* lives singly or in pairs in deep algae thickets of outer reefs.

M.: It needs a mature aquarium with plenty of algae growth to hide in. The greenish red coloration camouflages it perfectly in these surroundings.

Light: Areas with sun and moderate light.

B./Rep.: The fish spawn in pairs in the open water; rearing has not been successful.

F.: C; it primarily feeds on small organisms found in the algae growth, but it also takes *Mysis, Tubifex,* and small crustacea from the bottom.

S.: The conspicuous dorsal fin is only opened to impress ♀♀ or when the fish is engaged in rivalries with other ♂♂.

T: 24°-26°C, **L:** 8 cm, **TL:** from 80 cm, **WM:** w, **WR:** b, **AV:** 3, **S:** 3

Synchiropus izimae ♂, ♀ on p. 1150

Synchiropus morrisoni

Fam.: Callionymidae

Synchiropus stellatus
Star mandarin fish

SMITH, 1963

Hab.: Western Indian Ocean from east Africa to Sri Lanka. At depths of 10 to 20 m.

Sex.: The first dorsal fin of the ♂ has long rays that extend far beyond the dorsal fin's membrane, which is proximally decorated by concentric semicircles and distally by ocelli. The ♀♀ have a significantly smaller first dorsal fin with a black fringe and fin rays that also extend beyond the membrane.

Soc.B./Assoc.: The animal lives singly or in pairs on coral reefs and among seagrasses in shallow water. They can be kept in pairs, but not with other dragonets.

M.: They need a mature aquarium with a substrate that their reddish brown speckled body can blend into.

Light: Sun and moderately lit areas.

B./Rep.: The animals spawn in pairs during the evening; rearing has not been successful.

F.: C; *S. stellatus* lives off of small benthic animals that it constantly pursues in an aquarium. In addition, it also eats mosquito larvae and small crustacea such as *Mysis,* brine shrimp, and *Daphnia.*

S.: The dorsum of ♂♂ and ♀♀ often have starlike brown spots (name).

T: 24°-26°C, **L:** 6 cm, **TL:** from 60 cm, **WM:** w, **WR:** b, **AV:** 3, **S:** 3

Synchiropus stellatus ♂

Synchiropus stellatus ♂, aquarium form

Synchiropus stellatus ♀

Synchiropus picturatus spawning

SPAWNING BEHAVIOR IN MANDARIN FISHES

Spawning mandarin fishes are quite a spectacle. Courtship, in the form of the male and the female circling each other, is a drawn out, lengthy affair. The male explodes in color to impress the female. After both have accepted overtures from the other, they swim upward in the water column, either back to stomach, stomach to stomach, or circling each other, depending on the species. Up and up they swim until they are several meters above the substrate. Since the depth of aquaria is restrictive, they rise to the water's surface. This process may be repeated several times before the animals actually spawn at the apex of the trajectory. After the animals have spent themselves, they settle back to the substrate exhausted. Actual spawning generally happens at night—or after the lights are turned off. The fertilized eggs are pelagic, and they, as well as the resulting larvae, drift for a long time in the currents that distribute them far and wide. The photo shows a pair of spawning psychedelic mandarin fish.

Opistognathus sp. (Bali). The photographer snapped the picture the precise moment the fish spat sand!

Fam.: Opistognathidae

The systematics of this fish family has long been a controversial issue. Once the breeding behavior was outlined, their close relation to dottybacks and fairy basslets (Pseudochromidae and Grammidae) was discovered. All have an interrupted lateral line, and pectoral fins located at the height of the ventral fins. Furthermore, they all build caves and are mouthbrooders. In contrast to the dottybacks, jawfishes like to colonize sand flats which—besides the caves they excavate in the substrate—offer scant additional protection from attackers.

There is little sexual dichromatism out of spawning season. The blue dotted *Opistognathus rosenblatti* from the Gulf of California has been studied in its natural biotope: at a depth of 20 m, there were several cave-dwelling fish that peered from their homes in typical jawfish fashion. The distance between dwellings was about 1 m. Suddenly, one of the jawfishes rose about 1 m above its cave, spread all fins, and hovered motionless for about 4 seconds in the open water. Quick as a flash, it darted back into its hiding place. This was repeated after a few minutes. The anterior half of this fish was white. To the observer, the diving fish looked like a flash of lightning. Soon a normal-colored neighbor followed "Flash" into its cave. The half white fish was a courting male which fertilized the eggs of the female after she joined him. The eggs were then scooped up into his mouth. The scientist could not observe this process, but when he caught the male with his net, he promptly spit the eggs out. But all was not lost because, amazingly enough, the male picked the eggs back up later that same day after he and the eggs were transferred into an aquarium. He incubated the eggs for one week before releasing them for good.

The most studied jawfish is the yellow head jawfish, *Opistognathus aurifrons,* from the Caribbean. It breeds off the Florida coast from spring to fall. It is a territorial fish that never leaves its home once it is built. The species lives in small colonies. Because there are no rocks or corals within the colonies, only wide open sand, neighbors are within sight of each other. Since jawfishes search for their food in the open water, it is not unusual that courtship occurs there also. When courting, the yellow head jawfish approaches a female swimming in the open water, arches his body, and spreads all his fins. The large mouth is opened wide. Black dots appear on the ventral side of the head. The female follows her courting partner into his cave, or both dive into a neutral cave to spawn. This usually occurs at dawn or dusk. The eggs are guarded by the male. Even in the aquarium, the male opens his mouth so that the egg clump can be easily seen therein. The eggs have a diameter of 0.8 mm, and the young hatch after 7 to 9 days at a temperature of about 25°C. The larvae are 4 mm long and have pigmented eyes, developed mandibles, and rudimentary pectoral and tail fins. The yolk sac is very small.

Young develop quickly: by the ninth day the fins are fully formed and the body contour can be recognized. After 15 days, they search for an open place in the sand and begin to dig. At this time, the yellow head jawfish are already 1.5 cm long. Within one year, the fish has attained its full-grown size of 8 to 10 cm. Crustaceanlike organisms are particular favorites and are conscientiously selected from the passing plankton. This follows in the aquarium. Jawfishes should have an aquarium with a deep layer of coral rubble and sand where they immediately begin building their cave. It is obvious that these naturally timid cave inhabitants should never have fast swimming fishes as tankmates. It is probably advisable to feed these creatures defrosted krill placed directly in front of their cave with a large syringe. A necessary measure since the territorial jawfishes will remain steadfast within their homes, waiting in vain for food to drift within reach.

Opistognathus sp.

Fam.: Opistognathidae

Opistognathus scops
Bullseye jawfish

(JENKINS & EVERMANN, 1888)

Hab.: Tropical and temperate east Pacific, Baja California, and the Galapagos. At depths of about 20 m.

Sex.: During spawning season, the ♂ has more intense colors; otherwise, hardly any differences are apparent.

Soc.B./Assoc.: Every ♂ has his burrow and only permits one ♀ to enter and lay her eggs. Do not keep with small fishes or crustacea!

M.: Needs at least 10 cm of sandy substrate with some small pebbles or snail shells intermingled to help fortify its cave.

Light: Area of moderate light.

B./Rep.: Mouthbrooder; the ♂ incubates the eggs in its mouth for about a week. See p. 1159.

F.: C; the animals must be fed directly with a feeding tube, since they hardly leave their cave. Adult *Artemia*, pieces of mussel meat, raw fish, etc., are consumed. Some also eat pieces of tablet foods as they descend.

S.: Because of its size, the species is an infrequent aquarium fish. However, there are even larger jawfishes, e.g., the 50 cm long *O. rhomaleus* from the same geographical area.

T: 18°-24°C, **L:** 15 cm, **TL:** 120 cm, **WM:** m, **WR:** b, **AV:** 3, **D:** 2

Opistognathus sp.

Opistognathus rosenblatti ALLEN & ROBERTSON, 1991 (courting behavior); east Pacific. See p. 1171 for normal coloration.

Fam.: Opistognathidae

Opistognathus aurifrons   (JORDAN & THOMPSON, 1905)
Yellow head jawfish

Hab.: Caribbean islands and Florida. At depths of 3 to 40 m over a sand substrate.

Sex.: Outside spawning season there are no known sexual differences. During courtship, the ♂ develops black spots on the ventral side of the head.

Soc.B./Assoc.: Can only be kept with free-swimming fishes in large aquaria. Since they rarely venture far from their cave, they make good tankmates for invertebrates.

M.: The substrate should be at least 10 cm deep and consist of a mixture of sand, mussel debris, and coral gravel.

Light: Area of sunlight.

B./Rep.: Mouthbrooder (see p. 1159). Commercially bred in the U.S.A.

F.: C, FD; chopped frozen foods and *Artemia* administered with a feeding tube.

S.: During the day, they usually hover a few centimeters above the entrance to their cave. They quickly dart into their lair when danger threatens.

T: 22°-28°C, **L:** 10 cm, **TL:** from 80 cm, **WM:** m, **WR:** b, **AV:** 1, **D:** 1

Opistognathus aurifrons, ♂ in courtship coloration and a mouth full of eggs

Opistognathus aurifrons

Opistognathus aurifrons

Fam.: Opistognathidae

Opistognathus jacksiensis (MACLEAY, 1881)
Marble jawfish

Hab.: Great Barrier Reef and New Guinea. On bottoms of rubble and rock at depths of 30 to 50 m.

Sex.: Unknown.

Soc.B./Assoc.: Singly or in pairs. But finding a pair presents difficulties because, as stated above, the sexual differences are unknown. They should not be housed with other fishes in small tanks. Good tankmates for invertebrates.

M.: Provide a deep bottom of coarse sand so the animals can build their cave. In an emergency, they will use a long, narrow rock cave.

Light: Moderate light zone.

B./Rep.: Mouthbrooder. Rearing the larvae in an aquarium has not been successful.

F.: C, FD; they take any kind of animal food that either drifts by in the current or is delivered to them with a feeding tube.

S.: Not known.

T: 22°-28°C, **L:** up to 25 cm, **TL:** from 100 cm, **WM:** m, **WR:** b, **AV:** 3, **D:** 1-2

Opistognathus latitabunda WHITLEY, 1944
Spotted jawfish

Hab.: Australia, the Great Barrier Reef and north Queensland. On sand and rubble bottoms off coral reefs at depths of 20 to 50 m.

Sex.: Unknown.

Soc.B./Assoc.: Singly or in pairs. Since the animals are very timid, invertebrates make better companions than fishes.

M.: Deep sand and gravel bottoms wherein the fishes dig their caves. A buried acrylic tube with a diameter of about 3 cm can help.

Light: Areas of moderate light.

B./Rep.: They practice brood care. They have never been bred in an aquarium.

F.: C, FD; frozen foods such as krill, *Artemia,* and chopped shrimp meat are grabbed from the current.

S.: Not known.

T: 22°-27°C, **L:** up to 40 cm, **TL:** from 100 cm, **WM:** m-s, **WR:** b, **AV:** 3, **D:** 1-2

Opistognathus jacksiensis

Opistognathus latitabunda

Fam.: Opistognathidae

Opistognathus muscatensis
Robust jawfish   BOULENGER, 1887

Hab.: Red Sea, Persian Gulf, the Seychelles, and east Africa to Durban. Over bottoms of sand and rubble at depths of 30 to 50 m.

Sex.: Outside spawning season, the sexes cannot be differentiated. It is unknown whether or not ♂♂ develop a different courtship coloration.

Soc.B./Assoc.: Singly or in pairs. Shy creatures that constantly retire into their caves when free-swimming fishes are present. Almost all invertebrates are suitable companions.

M.: Needs a reef aquarium with long, narrow rock caves or a deep bottom of loose sand mixed with shell debris.

Light: Areas of moderate light.

B./Rep.: Mouthbrooder. Rearing in the aquarium has been unsuccessful.

F.: C, FD; they eagerly snap at any kind of animal food that drifts past them in the current.

S.: There are three black spots on the dorsal fin: the first is round and limited to the fin, but the other two extend onto the body.

T: 22°-28°C, **L:** up to 45 cm (♀), **TL:** from 100 cm, **WM:** m, **WR:** b, **AV:** 3, **D:** 1-2

Opistognathus punctatus
Speckled jawfish   PETERS, 1869

Hab.: Pacific American coast to south of Panama. Over bottoms of sand and rubble at depths of 50 to 90 m.

Sex.: Unknown.

Soc.B./Assoc.: Singly or in pairs. They get along with almost all invertebrates; they are so timid in front of free-swimming fishes that they retreat to their burrow and are rarely seen.

M.: Deep bottom of loose sand mixed with coral chunks and shell debris. The animals establish their burrow within.

Light: Areas of moderate light.

B./Rep.: Has not been successful in an aquarium. Interesting courtship behavior.

F.: C, FD; feeding with frozen animal foods is unproblematic. If the current does not carry the food to them, they have to be fed with a feeding tube, because they will not leave the immediate vicinity of their burrow.

S.: There are probably 7 additional species in the Gulf of California. Four of them are not yet scientifically described.

T: 18°-24°C, **L:** up to 40 cm, **TL:** from 100 cm, **WM:** m, **WR:** b, **AV:** 3, **D:** 1-2

Opistognathus muscatensis

Opistognathus punctatus

Bibliography

Allen, G.R. (1978): Die Anemonenfische. Arten der Welt. Haltung, Pflege, Zucht. Mergus Verlag, Melle, Germany.

Allen, G.R. (1979): Falter- und Kaiserfische. Vol. 2. Mergus Verlag, Melle, Germany.

Allen, G.R. (1991): Riffbarsche der Welt. Mergus Verlag, Melle, Germany.

Allen, G.R. & Steene, R.C. (1988): Fishes of Christmas Island. Christmas Island Natural History Association, Australia.

Allen, G.R. & Steene, R.C. (1987): Reef Fishes of the Indian Ocean. T.F.H., Neptune City, N. J., USA.

Amesbury, S.S. & Myers, R.F. (1982): Guide to the coastal resources of Guam 1: The Fishes. University of Guam Press, Guam, USA.

Baensch, H.A. (1987): Neue Meerwasserpraxis 5th ed., Tetra Verlag, Melle, Germany.

Baensch, H.A. & Loiselle, P.V. (1991): Marine Aquarist's Manual. Tetra Press, Morris Plains N. J., USA.

Baumeister, W. (1990): Meeresaquaristik. Ulmer Verlag, Stuttgart, Germany.

Boehlke, J.E. & Chaplin, C.C.G. (1968): Fishes of the Bahamas. Livingston Publishers, Wynnewood, Philadelphia, USA.

Burgess, W.E. & Axelrod, H.R. (1972-1987): Pacific Marine Fishes, Vol. 1 - 10. T.F.H. Publications, Neptune City, USA.

Burgess's Atlas Marine tropical fishes (1988): T.F.H. Publications, Neptune City, USA.

Carcasson, R.H. (1977): A field guide to the coral reef fishes of the Indian and West Pacific Oceans. Collins, London, UK.

Chlupaty, P.: Meine Erfahrungen mit Korallenfischen im Aquarium.

Colin, P. (1975): Neon gobies. T.F.H. Publications, Neptune City, USA.

Colin, P. (1978): Caribbean reef invertebrates and plants. T.F.H. Publications, Neptune City, USA.

Couet, G., Moosleitner, H. & Naglschmid, F. (1981): Gefährliche Meerestiere. Jahr Verlag, Hamburg, Germany.

Debelius, H. (1983): Gepanzerte Meeresritter. Kernen Verlag, Essen, Germany.

Debelius, H. (1986): Fischpartner niederer Tiere. Kernen Verlag, Essen, Germany.

Debelius, H. (1987): Unterwasserführer Rotes Meer. Fische. Naglschmid Verlag, Stuttgart, Germany.

de Graaf, F. (1988): Tropische Zierfische im Meeresaquarium.

de Graaf, F. (1988): Das tropische Meeresaquarium.

Deuvletian, R. (1987): Red Sea fish guide. Nubar Printing, Egypt.

Dunn, D.F. (1981): The clownfish sea anemones. American Philosophical Society, Philadelphia, USA.

Bibliography

Emmens, C.W. (1990): Handbuch der Meeresaquaristik. Bede Verlag, Kollnburg, Germany.

Erwin, D. & Picton, B. (1987): Guide to Inshore Marine Life. IMMEL Publishing, London, UK.

Fosså, S. A. & Nilsen, A. J. (1988): Korallrevs-Akvariet, Band 1 - 3. Göteborgs Papper & Reklam AB, Göteborg, Sweden.

Fricke, H.W. (1972): Korallenmeer. Verhaltensforschung am tropischen Riff. Belser Verlag, Stuttgart, Germany.

Frickhinger, K.A. (1991): Fossilien Atlas -Fische-, Mergus Verlag, Melle, Germany.

Friese, U.E.: Sea anemones. T.F.H. Publications, Neptune City, USA.

Geiss, G. (1990): Weichtiere, Krebse, Stachelhäuter des Mittelmeeres. Natur Verlag, Augsburg, Germany.

George, D. & George, J.: Marine life. An illustrated encyclopedia of invertebrates in the sea. Harrap, London, UK.

Gosliner, T. (1987): Nudibranchs of Southern Africa. E.J.Brill, Leiden, Netherlands.

Gotshall, D.W. (1981): Pacific coast inshore fishes. Challenger, Monterey, USA.

Hargreaves, V. B. (1978): The Tropical Marine Aquarium. McGraw-Hill Book Company, New York, USA.

Hoese, H.D. & Moore, R.H. (1977): Fishes of the Gulf of Mexico. Texas A & M University Press, Texas, USA.

Kipper, H.E. (1986): Das optimale Meerwasser Aquarium. Aquadocumenta Verlag, Bielefeld, Germany.

Klausewitz, W. & Wilkens, P. (1979): Handbuch der Meeresaquaristik. Seewasserfische und Wirbellose. 3 Volumes. Pfriem Verlag, Wuppertal, Germany.

Lange, J. (1986): Korallenfische. Ulmer Verlag, Stuttgart, Germany

Lange, J. & Kaiser, R. (1991): Niedere Tiere tropischer und kalter Meere. Ulmer Verlag, Stuttgart, Germany

McConnaughey, B.H. & McConnaughey, E. (1988): The Audubon Society Nature Guide: Pacific Coast. A. Knopf, New York, USA.

Marcuse, G. & Markuse, F.: Giftige und gefährliche Tiere der Meere.

Masuda, H., Araga C. & Yoshino T. (1975): Coastal fishes of southern Japan. Tokai Univ. Verlag, Tokyo, Japan.

Matthes, D. (1978): Tiersymbiosen und ähnliche Formen der Vergesellschaftung. G. Fischer Verlag, Stuttgart, Germany.

Mayland, H.J. (1979): Niedere Tiere im Aquarium. Philler Verlag, Minden, Germany.

Morton, B. (1989): Partnerships in the sea. Univ. Verlag. Hong Kong.

Myers, R. F. (1989): Micronesian reef fishes. Coral Graphics, Guam, Barrigada, USA.

Bibliography

Nordsieck, F. (1972): Die europäischen Meeresschnecken. G. Fischer Verlag, Stuttgart, Germany.

Patzner, R.A. (1989): Meeresbiologie. Anleitungen zu praktischen Arbeiten.Naglschmid Verlag, Stuttgart, Germany.

Patzner, R.A. & Debelius, H.(1984): Partnerschaft im Meer. Pfriem Verlag, Wuppertal, Germany.

Probst, K. & Lange, J. (1975): Das große Buch der Meeres-Aquaristik. Ulmer Verlag, Stuttgart, Germany.

Randall, J.E.: Indo-Pacific fishes. Bishop Museum, Honolulu, Hawaii.

Randall, J.E. (1983): Red Sea reef fishes. Immel, London, UK.

Randall, J.E. & Myers, F. (1983): Guide to the coastal resources of Guam: Vol. 2, The corals, University of Guam Verlag, Guam, USA.

Reader's Digest (1987): Book of the Great Barrier Reef. Reader's Digest, Sydney, Australia.

Riedl, R. (ed.)(1983): Fauna und Flora des Mittelmeeres. Parey Verlag, Hamburg-Berlin, Germany.

Schmekel, L. & Portmann, A. (1982): Opisthobranchia des Mittelmeeres. Springer Verlag, Berlin, Heidelberg, New York.

Schmid, P. & Paschke, D. (1987): Unterwasserführer Rotes Meer. Niedere Tiere. Naglschmid Verlag, Stuttgart, Germany.

Sefton, N. & Webster, S.K. (1986): Caribbean reef invertebrates. Challengers, Monterey, USA.

Selze, H. & Lemkemeyer, J. (1986): Moderne Meerwasseraquaristik. 2d ed. Selze Labortechnik, Taufkirchen, Germany.

Shirai, S. (1986): Ecological encyclopedia of the marine animals of the Indo-Pacific. Vol. 1, Vertebrata. Tosho, Tokyo, Japan.

Smith, J.B. & Smith, M. (1963): The fishes of Seychelles. Dep. of Ichthyology, Rhodes University, Grahamstown, South Africa.

Smith, M.M. & Heemstra, P.C. (eds.) (1986): Smith's sea fishes. Springer Verlag, Berlin, Heidelberg, New York.

Spies, G. (1989): Praxis Meerwasseraquarium.

Spotte, S. (1973): Marine aquarium keeping. John Wiley & Sons, New York, USA.

Steene, R.C. (1977): Falter- und Kaiserfische. Vol. 1. Mergus Verlag, Melle, Germany.

Steiner, H. (1983): Beobachtungen an Niederen Tieren des Mittelmeeres. Landbuch Verlag, Hannover, Germany

Stephenson, T.A. (1928): The British sea anemones. Ray Society, London, England.

Thresher, R.E. (1984): Reproduction in reef fishes. T.F.H. Publications, Neptune City, USA.

Bibliography

Vine, P. (1986): Red Sea invertebrates. Immel, London, UK.

Walls, J.G. (1974): Starting with marine invertebrates. T.F.H. Publications, Neptune City, USA.

Walls, J.G. (ed.) (1982): Encyclopedia of marine invertebrates. T.F.H. Publications, Neptune City, USA.

Weigel, W. (1969): Aquarianer fangen Meerestiere. Geräte, Hälterung, Transport. Kosmos Verlag, Stuttgart, Germany.

Wickler, W. (1970): Das Meeresaquarium. Kosmos Verlag, Stuttgart, Germany.

Wilkens, P. & Birkholz, J. (1986): Niedere Tiere. Röhren-, Leder- und Hornkorallen. Pfriem Verlag, Wuppertal, Germany.

Wilkens, P. (1987a): Niedere Tiere im tropischen Seewasseraquarium, I. 2nd ed. Pfriem Verlag, Wuppertal, Germany.

Wilkens, P. (1987b): Niedere Tiere im tropischen Seewasseraquarium, II. 2nd ed. Pfriem Verlag, Wuppertal, Germany.

Wilkens, P. (1987c): Niedere Tiere. Steinkorallen, Scheiben- und Krustenanemonen. Pfriem Verlag, Wuppertal, Germany.

Zann, L.P. (1980): Living together in the sea. T.F.H. Publications, Neptune City, USA.

Opistognathus rosenblatti, see pages 1158 and 1161

Bibliography

Algae

Amir, A.P. (1979): Schouwburg der dieren en wieren.

Amir, A.P. (1981): Over wieren gesproken. Het Zeeaquarium 29/9 p. 15 ev - 31/5/27.

Arasaki, S. & Nozowa, K. (1950): On the sexual reproduction of *Caulerpa*. Bot. Mag. Tokyo (3) 1950, 223.

Aubert, M. , Aubert, J. & Gauthier, M. (1979): Marine Algae in Pharmaceutical Science (C). Walter de Gruyter, Berlin, New York.

Basson, Ph.W., Buchard, J.E. & Hardy, J.T. (1976): Biotopes of the Western Arabian Gulf- Aramco.

Bold, H.C. & Wynne, M.J. (1977): Introduction to the algae, structure and reproduction.

Bold, H.C. & Wynne, M.J. (1978): Introduction to the algae, structure and reproduction. Prentice Hall, Englewood Cliffs, New Jersey, 706 pp.

Brons, R. (1982): *Caulerpa paspaloides*. Het Zeeaquarium 82-32/5-141 ev.

Calvert, H.E. & Borowitzska, M.A. (1976): Phytogenetic relationships of *Caulerpa* (Chloro- phyta) based on comparative chloroplast ultrastructure. Journ. Phycol. 12(2), pp. 149-162.

Calvert, H.E. & Dawes, C.J. (1976): Ontogenetic transitions in plastids of the coenocytic algae *Caulerpa* (Chlorophyceae). Phycologia 15(1), pp. 37-40.

Chen, J.W.C. & Jacob, W.D. (1968): The initiation of rhizoid clusters in *Caulerpa prolifera*. Am. Journ. Bot. 55/12-19.

Coppejans, E. (1984): Planten in het Zeeaquarium. Aquariumwereld 37/4, pp. 80-87.

Dawes, C.J. & Goddard, R.H. (1978): Chemical composition of the woundplug and entire plants for species of the coenocytic green algae *Caulerpa*, J. exp. mar. biol. ecol. Vol. 35, pp. 259-263.

Deacon, Charnock & Nierenberg (1979): De Oceanen. Zomer en Keuning, Ede.

Dostal, R. (1929): *Caulerpa allivieri* n. sp.; la seconde espèce europèenne des Caulerpes. Bull. Inst. Oc. Monaco 532, pp. 1-12.

Eubank, L.L. (1946): Hawaiian representatives of the genus *Caulerpa*. Un. Calif. Publ. Bot. 18, pp. 409-432.

Eubank, L.L. (1969): An analysis of the siphonous Chlorophycophyta, Un. Calif. Publ. Bot. 25(5), pp. 325-454.

Ferreira, Correia M., Pinheiro & Vieira, F. (1969): Estudos taxonômicos sôbre o gênero *Caulerpa* Lamouroux, no nord este Brasileiro (Chlorophyta) Caulerpaceae. Arg. Cienc. Mar. 9, pp. 147-161.

Gilbert, W.J. (1941): Notes on Caulerpa from Java and the Philippines, Pap. Mich. Acad. Sci. Arts and Letters 27, pp. 7-26.

Goddard, R.H., Dawes, C.J. (1979): An ultrastructural and histoDchemical study of the wound response of *Caulerpa ashmeadi* (Caulerpales), Journ. Phycol. 15 suppl. 17.

Goldstein, M. & Morrall, G. (1970): Gametogenesis and fertilization in *Caulerpa*. Ann. New York Acad. Sci. 175 (2), pp. 660-672.

Hamel, G. (1930): Les Caulerpes Mediterranéennes. Rev. Algol. 229 pp.

Hering, W. (1969/1974): Die Wunderwelt der Meeresalgen. DATZ 1 t/m 34 of 1969-1974.

Ishiwara, J., Hirose, H. & Enomoto, S. (1981): The life history of *Caulerpa okamurai* (WEBER VAN BOSSE). Proc. Eighth Intern. Seaweed Symposium 1974/1981.

Iyengar, M.O.P. (1940): On the formation of gametes in *Caulerpa*. Journ. Ind. Botan. Soc. 18, pp. 191-194.

Kamperman, Th.C.M. & Stegenga, H. (1983): A new *Caulerpa* species (Caulerpaceae, Chlorophyta) from the Caribbean side of Costa Rica C.A. Acta. Bot. Neerl. 32(4), Aug., pp. 271-275.

Lamouroux, J.V.J. (1809): Memoires sur les Caulerpes, nouveau genre de la famille des algues marines. J. Bot. (Paris) 2: pp. 136-146 - pls 2-3.

Leuring, Hoppe & Schmid (1979): Marine Algae. 390 pp.

Mann-Borgese, E. (1980): Seafarm part. 11 - meadows and fields.

Meinesz, A. & Denizot, M. (1981): Distribution of the algae belonging to the genus *Caulerpa* in French Polynesia (Atoll of Takapoto and Island of Moorea), 4th. Int. Coral Reef Symposium Manila - Reprint.

Meñez, A. & Denizot, M. (1981): The genus *Caulerpa* from central Visayas, Philippines. Smithsonian Contributions to the Marine Sciences 17, pp. 1-22.

Michanek, G. (1975): Seaweed resources of the ocean FIRST 138, Marine Botanical Institute, Göteborg/ Sweden.

Mishra, A.K. (1969): Fine structure of the growing point of the coenocytic algae *Caulerpa sertularioides*. Can. Journ. Bot. 47, pp. 1599-1603.

Muller, W.H. (1966): Botany, a functional approach.

Niel, A. (1983): Biologie et Ecologie des Caulerpes. Aquarama 17e Année nr. 71-3,72-4/ 73-5.

Nizamuddin, M. (1964): Studies on the genus *Caulerpa* from Karachi. Bot. Marine 6 3/4 pp. 204-222.

Peterson, R.D. (1972): Effects of light intensity on the morphology and productivity of *Caulerpa racemosa* (FORSSKÅL), J. Agardh, Micronesica 8 (1-2) pp. 63-86.

Rabanal, H.R. & Trono, G.C. (1983): Seaweeds in Asia, a resource waiting for development (Infofish no.4).

Ricard, M. & Meinesz, A. (1980): Contribution a l'ètude des Caulerpes (Chlorophyta) avec une mention particulière aux espèces de la Mediterranée occidentale. Thèse de doctorat s'ètat en Sciences, Univ. de Nice 262 pp. manuscript Cryptog. Alg. 1(3) pp. 260-261.

Round, F.E. (1971): The taxonomy of the Chlorophyta. 11 British Phycological Journal 6 (2) pp. 235-264.

Sartoni, G. (1964): Ricerche sulla flora algala della Somalic centro meridionale 1 il genera *Caulerpa*. Webbia 32(2), pp. 397-416.

Scullion, D. Littler, Littler, M. M., Bucher, K. E., Norris, J. N. (1989): Marine plants of the Caribbean. Airlife Publishing Ltd., Strewsbury/England with the permission of the Smithsonian Institution.

Taylor, W.R. (1950): Plants of Bikini and other northern Marshall Islands, Univ. Mich. Verlag. Ann Arbor. 227 pp.

Taylor, W.R. (1960): Marine algae of the eastern tropical and subtropical coast of the America's, part. Caulerpaceae.

La Violette, P. & Frontena, T.R. (1967): Temperature, salinity and density of the world's seas, US Naval Oceanographic Off. Wash. DC report no. 67, p. 49.

v. d. Vlugt, P.J. (1980): *Caulerpa racemosa*- knikkerwier, Het Zeeaquarium no. 30/9, p. 47.

Weber van Bosse, A. (1898): Monographie des Caulerpes, Ann. Journ. Bot. Buitenzorg 15, pp. 241-401.

Scedelius, N. (1906): Ecological and systematic studies of the Ceylon species of *Caulerpa*. Ceylon Mar. Biol. Rept. 1(4), pp. 81-144.

General Index

A

Abiotic factors on *Caulerpa*	272
Acclimating fishes	160
Acid binding capacity	139, 190
Acidic	135
Acids	139
Acrylic (Plexiglass) aquaria	41
Acrylic acid	287
Actinic blue light	124
Activated carbon	98, 102, 147
Aerobic conditions	127
Aerobic filters	63
Aerosols	287
Agar	222
Aiptasia	194
Air driven foam filters	35
Air lift	66
Air-driven filter	36
Air-lift pump	34
Alcohol	127, 186
Alcohol as a carbon source	73
Algae	216
Algae aquarium	34
Algae as food	172
Algae culture	273
Algae growth	75, 86, 132
Algae scrubber	34, 75
Algin	219
Algivorous fishes	173
Alkaline	135
Alkalinity	104, 135, 139, 190
Ammonia	16, 129, 283
Ammonium	
	63, 126, 128, 129, 148, 190
Amphipods	192, 193
Amphiroa hancockii	236
Anaerobic conditions	
	52, 127, 132, 146, 187
Anaerobic filters	72
Anaerobic zones	63, 128
Analysis	148
Analytical procedures	148

Anion exchangers	54, 55
Anthozoans	17, 101, 109, 119
	132, 164, 165,192, 197
Antibacterial substances	287
Antibiotic	286, 287
Aquaculture	273
Aquarium equipment	48
Aquarium frames	48
Aquarium water	48
Argulus	209
Artemia	165
Artemia culture	166, 167
Artemia salina	166, 176
Ascarids	209
Ascites	206
Autoinhibitors	288
Automatic refill	36
Automatic compactcontrol	36
Auxospores	217
Availability	213

B

Back pane	156
Background decoration	44
Bacteria	216
Bacterial cultures	290
Bacterial diseases	204
Bacterial fin	204
Bacterial finrot	204
Bacterial lawn	78
Bacterial skin	69
Bacterial tribes	74
Bacteriosis pinnarum	204
Bases	139
Beach sand	42
Berthelina chloris	292
Bicarbonate	101,141
Bind	290
Bioballs	78
Biofilm	78
Biofilter	17, 63, 66
Biological aquarium filters	63

General Index

Biological filters	63
Biological filtration	88, 132
Biomass	17, 264
Biomass of invertebrates	18
Bioporon	84
Bioreactor	63
Biotic factors on *Caulerpa*	272
Black smear algae	214, 216
Blade	251
Bleeding	268
Bloodworms	176
Blue algae	119, 136
Blue smear algae	127
Blue-green algae	214, 216
Body weight	17
Boiling point	48
Botryocladia uvaria	233
Bottom climate	66
Bottom substrate	37, 42, 264
Brachionus	136, 165
Brachionus as food	171
Brachionus culture	170
Brachionus plicatilis	170
Brain coral	46
Breeding	212
Brine shrimp	165
Bristle crabs	192
Bristleworms	195
Bromides	287
Brooklynella hostilis	207
Brown algae	214, 219, 289
Brown algae (seaweed)	119
Brown diatomaceous algae	132
Brown "grease algae"	119
Bryopsis plumosa	240
Bubble algae	111
Buffering capacity	140
Buffering system	135, 139

C

Calanus finmarchicus	176
Calcareous algae	42, 80, 214
Calcarous algae rocks	37
Calcium	86, 132, 141, 221
Calcium bicarbonate	222
Calcium carbonate	132, 140, 141, 222
Calcium hydroxide	142
Calcium phosphate	86, 132
Calcium reactor	36, 101, 102
Calcium water	142, 143
Canister filters	64
Carbohydrates	287
Carbon	98, 134
Carbon dioxide	101, 139, 141, 142
Carbon dioxide supply	188
Carbon filter	102
Carbon pellets	83
Carbon prefilter	52
Carbon replace	52
Carbon source	186
Carbonate hardness	101, 104, 139, 140, 190, 222
Carbonate-bicarbonate system	139
Carbonic acid	101, 139, 141, 284
Carbonyl	287
Care	161
Carnivore	213
Carotene	250
Carrageenan	222
Carrying capacity	16
Catabolites	285
Catching fishes in the aquarium	180
Cation exchanger	54, 55
Caulerpa parasite	293
Caulerpa as food	284
Caulerpa filter	284
Caulerpa juice	284
Caulerpicin	286
Cellulose triacetate	52
Centrifugal pumps	36
Chaetomorpha linum	242
Chelating agent	132, 272
Chemistry	36
Chillers	107

Chlorella	172
Chlorella algae	136, 170
Chlorella culture	172
Chlorine	52
Chloroplasts	216, 259, 266
Choice of animals	16
Choosing a tank	40
Ciliate	202
Cladophora	34
Cladophora profilera	240
Clay	37
Clay rocks	276
Clownfish disease	207
Clorodermis fastigiata	240
CO_2	101, 143, 161, 165
CO_2 - dosage	36
CO_2 concentration	188
CO_2 fertilization	101
CO_2 regulator	102
Cobalt	271
Coccolithophores	220
Colloids	285
Colonial anemones	101
Colorimetric comparisons	148
Colorimetric test	148
Combination aquarium	24, 31
Combination of fishes and invertebrates	17
Common diseases	199
Complete desalination	57
Complete set-up	41
Composition of seawater	49
Conductivity	61, 190
Conductivity meters	151, 153
Control centers	153
Control units	152
Controller maintenance	182
Controlling	152
Convolutriluba	197
Cooling	107
Copper	134, 271
Copper pipes	48
Copper sulfate	201

Coral creations	46
Coral fish disease	200
Coral skeletons	46
Corals	221
Corallina officinalis	236, 237
Corrosive	48
Crabs	192
Crushed coral	86
Crushed dolomite	42, 102, 141, 276
Crushed marble	42
Crushed oyster shells	42
Crushed shell	80, 86
Crust algae	264
Crustacea	17, 192, 209, 462, 465
Cryptocarion	188, 198, 202
Cryptocarion irritans	202
Cyclops	166, 176
Cytology	266

D

Decoration	37, 157
Deionization	133
Dendrophyllia gracilis	281
Denitrification	127, 146
Denitrification bacteria	34, 73
Denitrification filter	72
Denitrification processes	87
Denitrifying bacteria	127, 186
Desulfhydration	72, 87
Detritus	68
Development of *Caulerpa*	276
Diameter	213
Diatom	85
Diatom filter	99
Diatomaceous earth	99, 132
Diatoms	111, 214, 217
Dictyota bartayresii	228
Dim light	119
Dim light zone	111
Dinoflagellates	200, 214, 219, 220
Dinospores	200

General Index

Dissociation of CO_2	278
Dolomite	17, 86, 276
Dolomite rocks	37, 45, 221
Drinking water	54
Drop tests	148

E

Ectoparasites	199
Ectoparasitic infections	198
Effluent	52
Eimeria	206
Electrical meters	182
Electrical safety	123
Electrode	144, 151
Electronic measurements	148
Electronic meters	151
Elements	49
Elkhorn	46
Emersed aerobic filters	70
Epitheca	217
Equipment	37
Ergasilus	209
Escherichia coli	287
Escherichia coli bacteria	287
Ethanol	127
Ethyl alcohol	187
Euplotes	171
Evaporation	54
External parasites	199

F

Fatty acids	287
FD tablets	178
Feed intake	17
Feeding stones	176
Feeding techniques	164
Feeding tube	164
Filamentous algae	34
Filter	37
Filter cleaning	191
Filter materials	78
Filter media	78, 82

Filter medium	264
Filter set-up	17
Filter technology	36
Filtration	63
Filtration methods	220
Fish aquarium	22
Fish diseases	198
Fish tuberculosis	205
Flagellates	200, 216
Flake food	16, 173
Flatworms	196, 209
Floatation reactor	92
Floating switch	62
Flow-through chiller	108
Fluorescent tubes	37, 109, 112, 120, 125
Foam filters	34
Foam fractionation	92
Foam skimmer	94
Foam skimming	92
Foods	165
Freeze dried foods	178
Freezing point	48
Frond	251
Frozen foods	165, 176
Fucus versiculosus	219
Fungal diseases	205
Fungal infections	205

G

Gametes	267
Gelatin	222
Geographic distribution of *Caulerpa*	262
Geographic habitat	259
Gill crustacea	208
Gill worms	208
Gilvin	96, 98, 147
Glass tank	37
Golden algae	214
Golden-brown algae	214, 216
Gracilaria curtissae	230

General Index

Granite	42
Grateloupia filicina	232
Gravity	153
Green algae	
101, 192, 214, 223, 265, 289	
Green filamentous algae	119
Growing *Caulerpa*	270
Growth inhibitors	288
Growth stimulating	290
Growth yield	115, 117
Gymnodinium	220
Gyrotox	208

H

H⁺ ions	55
Habitat	212
Haemogregarina	206
Hanging lamps	122
Hardy animals	158
Heater rating	107
Heater with thermostat	37
Heating	106
Heavy metals	290
Helminths	209
Herbivore	213
Hiding places	37
High speed filter	36
High-tech filter pumps	35
Hydrocarbons	287
Hydrochloric acid	50, 55, 136
Hydrogen	134, 141
Hydrogen peroxide	43, 144
Hydrogen sulfide	66, 146
Hydrolithon boergesenii	237
Hydrometer	37, 60
Hydronium ions	135
Hydroxide ions	135
Hydroxyl ions	101
Hypotheca	217

I

Ichthyophthirius multifilis	202
Ichthyosporidium	205

Illumination	109, 190, 274, 275
	276
Illumination efficiency factor	115
Illumination intensity	117
Illumination intensity	115
Intestinal worms	209
Invertebrate Aquarium	18
Invertebrate tank	75
Invertebrates	17, 165
Iodine	206, 219, 271
Ion exchanger	54, 101, 217
Iron	132, 134, 148, 271
Iron phosphate	132

K

KCl	183
Kelp	227
KH	139
KH test	37
KH value	102

L

Leaf-like red algae	119
Length	213
Lettuce	174
Lewatit S 10061	55
Life cycle of *Caulerpa*	271
Life expectancy of *Caulerpa*	271
Light	274
Light hoods	112
Light intensity	109, 112
Light output	112
Light refraction	274
Light requirement	119, 212
Lighting	37, 109
Liquid food	164, 178
Live mussels	165, 174
Live rocks	45, 222, 264, 276
Low voltage heaters	106
Lumens	109
Lux	109
Luxmeter	109
Lymphocystis	206

General Index

M

Macrocystis pyrifera	227
Macroelements	134
Magnetic drive centrifugal pumps	89
Maintenance	37, 212
Maintenance activities	184
Maintenance checklist	190
Maintenance difficulty	213
Manganese	271
Mantis shrimp	192
Marine algae	286
Marine ich	202
Marine plankton	216
Marine salt	156
Marine water	48
Maturation process	58
Membrane (reverse osmosis)	52
Mercury vapor bulbs	112
Mercury vapor bulbs (HQL)	109
Mercury vapor lamps (HQL)	120
Metabolism	127
Metabolites of the fishes	17
Metal halide bulbs (HQI)	109
Metal halide illumination	125
Metal halide Lamps (HQI)	112, 120
Metal items	48
Micrococcus	216
Microsiemens	62
Millisiemens	62
Mineral colloids	285
Minerals	179
Moderate light	119
Moderate light zone	111
Morphology	258, 265
Mulm	128
Mussel meat	165
Mussels	176
Mycobacterium marinum	205
Mysis	165, 176
Myxobolus	206

N

N concentration	16
Natural filter materials	86
Natural seawater	48
Necessities	38
Necessities, additional	39
Neutral ion exchanger	54
NH_3	66
NH_4	66
Nitrate	16, 50, 54, 63, 101
	126, 131, 140, 148, 186, 190
	216, 271, 283
Nitrate concentration	157
Nitrate Filter	36, 72, 127, 146, 157
	186
Nitrate NO_3 test	131
Nitrate removal	157
Nitrex	72
Nitric acid	55, 140
Nitrification	63, 86, 126
Nitrification phase	157
Nitrifying bacteria	79, 127
Nitrite	16, 101, 126, 128, 129, 148
	157, 161, 164, 186, 190
Nitrite poisoning	42
Nitrite test	37, 157
Nitrobacter	59, 63, 74, 126, 134
Nitrogen	16, 126, 127, 132, 134
Nitrogen cycle	283
Nitrogen-containing catabolites	95
Nitrogenous compounds	283
Nitrosomonas	59, 63, 74, 126
NO_2	66
Nocturnal animals	173
Nudibranchs	197
Number of fishes	75
Nutrient levels	216
Nutrients	99

General Index

O

Omnivore	213
Omnivores	173
Oodinium	198, 200, 220
Oodinium ocellatum	200
Oodinium pillularis	200
Options	38
Organic carbon	127
Organic colloids	285
Organic nitrogen	129
Organic nitrogen compounds	129
Organic wastes	63
Oscillatoria	216
Osmosis	160
Osmotic pressure	50
Ospheres	78
Overfeeding	99
Overflow pipe	34
Overflows	189
Overstocking	99
Oxidation	285
Oxidizer	144
Oxygen	63, 96, 126, 127
	134, 144, 285
Oxygen (O₂) level	190
Oxygen concentration	64
Oxygen content	106
Oysters	174
Ozone	36, 96, 144, 147
Ozone (O₃)	190
Ozone generator	96
Ozonization	96
Ozonizer	36, 182

P

Parasites	100, 214, 220
Patella	197
Pathogenic bacteria	290
Pebbles	42
Permeate	51
Pesticides	50

pH	63, 135, 139, 142
	148, 161, 188, 190
pH controller	104, 182
pH electrode	182, 183
pH fall	290
pH fluctuations	278
pH ranges	136
pH scale	135
pH test	37
pH value	63, 284
Phenol compounds	147
Phenolic compounds	287
Phosphate	50, 54, 132, 148, 186
	191, 216, 271, 283, 289
Phosphorus	17, 134
Photoperiod	125, 259, 274, 289
Photosynthesis	275, 278
Photosynthesizing bacteria	216
Photosynthetic	109
Photosynthetic energy	109
Phycocolloids	285
Phycoerythrin	221
Pillar coral	46
Planarians	196
Planktivores	173
Plankton	220
Plant fare	173
Plant forceps	164
Plant growth	101
Plastic mats	78
Plate coral	46
Plate filters	68
Pollutants	50
Pollution factor	115, 117
Polychaeta	195
Polypeptides	289
Polysaccharides	289
Potassium chloride	183
Powerhead	66, 88

General Index

Predators 19
Pressure filters 71
Protein 16, 287
Protein skimmer
16, 34, 36, 65, 92, 95, 191
Protein foam skimmer 78
Protein level 16
Protein skimming 96, 290
Protozoans 206
Protruding scales 206
Pumice 87
Pump sump 156
Pumps 88
Purified water 51
PVC 48
Pyrenoids 259

Q

Quality of salt 17
Quantity of animals 17
Quarantine tank 161, 200
Quartz gravel 42

R

Raschig rings 80
Reagents 148
Red algae 136, 192, 214, 221, 289
Red calcareous algae 119
Red flatworm 197
Redox 36
Redox meter 144, 187
Redox potential
68, 72, 95, 144, 146, 153, 190, 216
Redox regulator 182
Redox value 73
Reef builders 222
Reflectors 275
Regeneration 56
Removal of nitrates 127, 128
Reproduction 212
Requirements of the invertebrates
17

Reverse osmosis
36, 50, 54, 57, 132, 217
Reverse osmosis module 53
rH value 146
Rhizoids 251, 265, 270, 276
Rhizoidal filaments 276
Rhizome 251
Rocks 37
Root hairs 276
Roundworms 209
Runners 251, 265

S

Safety 122
Salinity 48, 60, 190
Salinity fluctuations 62
Salt 48, 60
Salt content 48
Salt mixes 48
Sea lettuce 173, 175, 223
Sea Salt 48
Sea slugs 197
Sea snails 197
Sea squirts 192
Seawater 48, 58
Seaweed gums 285
Seaweeds 219
Second tank 34
Semipermeable membrane 50
Sepia 176
Set-up 38
Setting up 156
Sex cells 217
Sexual propagation (in *Caulerpa*)
267
Shellfish meat 164, 176
Siemens 62
Silicic 148
Silicic acid 50, 132, 148
Silicon 132, 191
Silicon dioxide 132, 217
Silicon sealed glass tanks 40

Silicone sealers	129
Siporax	80
Siporax ring	83
Skin lesions	204
Smell of ozone	97
Snails	197
Sochrysis galbana	216
Social behavior/association	212
Sodium bicarbonate	142
Sodium chloride	48
Sodium hydroxide	43, 50, 54, 101
	136
Soft corals	101
Softening filter	52, 57
Specific gravity	48, 60, 61, 161
	190
Spectrophotometer	148
Spectrum	274
Spirulina	216
Spirulina food	173
Sponges	192
Sporozoans	206
Sporulation	267
Sprouts	271
Squid	176
Stalks	265
Staphylococcus aureus	287
Sterilization lamps	99
Stocking a tank	34
Stocking an aquarium	156
Stocking of fishes	22
Stocking of invertebrates	18
Stolons	251, 265
Stolon yellowing	271
Strontium	134, 142
Submersed centrifugal pumps	90
Substrate	86, 276
Substrate filters	66
Substrates for *Caulerpa*	280
Sulfate	54
Sulfur	134
Sulfuric acid	55, 136

Sunlight zone	119
Superfluous nitrogen	17
Surface area	117
Surface area of filter media	85
Surface filtration	69
Surface movement	102
Surface skimmer	36
Synonym	212
Synthetic sea salt	48
Systematics	250
Systematics (plants)	250

T

Table of lux	111
Table salt	54, 57
Tablet foods	164
Tank length	213
Tank volume	107
Tankmates	192
Tap water	17, 50, 127, 132
Tapeworms	209
Taxonomy	258
Taxonomy of algae	214
Technical equipment	36
Technology	36
Temperature	161, 190, 213
Temperature control	106
Temperature for *Caulerpa*	273
Terminology	109
Terpenes	287
Testing	148
Testing strips	148
Tetraonchus	208
TFC membrane	52
Thallus	251, 265
Thermometer	37
Thermostat-controlled heaters	106
Thermostat-heater rating	107
Tidal rhythm	88
Timer	182
Titrations	148, 150
Tomites	198, 200

General Index

Toxic nitrogen 129
Toxins removal 57
Trace elements 49, 73, 134, 179
Treatment 201
Trematodes 209
Trickle filter 36, 65, 70, 76, 132
Tubeworms 192
Turnover 191
Types of substrate 42

U

Ultraviolet radiation 99
Undergravel filter 36, 37, 66, 67
Unicellular algae 217
Unwanted guests 192
UV 36
UV lamps 99, 204
UV rays 99

V

Vacation 185
Vanadium 271
Vegetative propagation 269
Venturi jet (injector) 94
Vibriosis 204
Viral infections 206
Vitamins 179, 271

W

Wall reflectors 121
Waste load 22
Waste water 52
Water 135
Water current 102
Water depth 115, 117
Water evaporation 153
Water exchange 127, 141, 157, 191
Water lines 48
Water movement 88, 213
Water quality 264
Water refill 191

Water region 213
Water softening 51
Water supplies 51
Water surface 69
Water temperature 106
Water treatment 50
Water treatment
    chemical-physical 92
Water-lubricated pumps 90
Wavelengths 110
Weir basket 193
White spot, ich 202
"Wire algae" 111, 119
Worms 195

X

Xanthophyll 250

Y

Yellow pigments 147
Yellow-green algae 214, 217

Z

Zinc 271
Zooplankton 217

Zooxanthellae 101, 109, 119, 127
165, 214, 221
Zygotes 217, 270

Unit Conversions

TEMPERATURE

°F = (°C ↔ 1.8) + 32				°C = (°F - 32) / 1.8					
°C	°F	°C	°F	°C	°F	°C	°F	°C	°F
0	32	15	59	21	70	27	81	50	122
10	50	16	61	22	72	28	82	60	140
11	52	17	63	23	73	29	84	70	158
12	54	18	64	24	75	30	86	80	176
13	55	19	66	25	77	35	95	90	194
14	57	20	68	26	79	40	104	100	212

VOLUME

gal = l / 3.785				l = 3.785 ↔ gal					
l	gal	l	gal	l	gal	l	gal	l	gal
1	0.26	15	3.96	70	18.5	250	66	550	145
2	0.53	20	5.28	80	21.1	300	79	600	158
3	0.79	30	7.93	90	23.8	350	92	700	185
4	1.06	40	10.57	100	26.4	400	106	800	211
5	1.32	50	13.21	150	39.6	450	119	900	238
10	2.64	60	15.85	200	79.3	500	132	1000	379

LENGTH

1m = 100 cm = 1000 mm   1yd = 3 ft = 36 in
in = cm / 2.54   cm = in ↔ 2.54   ft = m / 0.305   m = 0.305 ↔ ft

mm	in	cm	in	cm	in	m	ft	m	ft
0.5	0.02	1	0.4	30	12	1	3.28	70	230
1	0.04	2	0.8	35	14	2	6.56	80	262
2	0.08	3	1.1	40	16	3	9.84	90	295
3	0.12	4	1.6	45	18	4	13.1	100	328
4	0.16	5	2.0	50	20	5	16.4	200	656
5	0.20	6	2.4	60	24	10	32.8	300	984
6	0.24	7	2.8	70	28	15	49.2	400	1310
7	0.28	8	3.1	80	31	20	65.6	500	1640
8	0.32	9	3.5	90	35	25	82.0	600	1970
9	0.35	10	3.9	100	39	30	98.4	700	2300
		15	5.9	125	49	40	131	800	2620
		20	7.9	150	59	50	164	900	2950
		25	9.8	175	69	60	197	1000	3280

Animal Index

Italics = Scientific names of genera and species

Normal = Common names

Small Caps = Taxons above genus

The algae are listed in the general

A

Acanthuridae	681, 686
Acanthurinae	681
Acanthurus	681, 691
Acanthurus achilles	694
Acanthurus bahianus	696
Acanthurus bariene	696
Acanthurus chirurgus	698
Acanthurus coeruleus	698
Acanthurus dussumieri	700
Acanthurus fowleri	700
Acanthurus gahhm	702
Acanthurus japonicus	703
Acanthurus leucocheilus	704
Acanthurus leucopareius	706, 707
Acanthurus leucosternon	704
Acanthurus lineatus	708
Acanthurus maculipes	710
Acanthurus mata	711
Acanthurus monroviae	712
Acanthurus nigricans	714
Acanthurus nigricauda	712
Acanthurus nigrofuscus	716
Acanthurus nubilus	716
Acanthurus olivaceus	718
Acanthurus ovalis	686
Acanthurus pyroferus	720
Acanthurus sohal	724
Acanthurus tennenti	724
Acanthurus thompsoni	726
Acanthurus triostegus	693, 726
Acanthurus xanthopterus	692
Acontiaria	326

Actinia	334
Actinia cari	334
Actinia equina	333, 334
Actiniaria	332
Actiniidae	334
Actinodendridae	352
Actinodendron	352
Actinodendron arboreum	352
Actinodendron plumosum	352
Actinopterygii	681
Aiptasia	383
Aiptasia bartholomea	387
Aiptasia diaphana	385
Aiptasia mutabilis	383, 384
Aiptasia sp.	386
Aiptasiidae	383
Alicia	326
Alicia mirabilis	398
Alicia pretiosa	399
Aliciidae	398
Allogalathea	463
Allogalathea elegans	615
Alpheidae	462, 492
Alpheus	462
Alpheus sp. in an aquarium	500
Alpheus bisincisu	494
Alpheus djeddensis	494
Alpheus randalli	497
Alpheus sp.	493, 496, 498
Alpheus strenuus	498
Amblyeleotris	682
Amblyeleotris n.sp.	1053
Amblyeleotris aurora	1044
Amblyeleotris guttata	1044
Amblyeleotris gymnocephala	1046
Amblyeleotris latifasciata	1046
Amblyeleotris ogasawarensis	1047
Amblyeleotris periophthalmus	1048
Amblyeleotris randalli	1050
Amblyeleotris wheeleri	1050
Amblygobius	682
Amblygobius albimaculatus	1054
Amblygobius buanensis	1054

Amblygobius bynoensis	1054
Amblygobius decussatus	1056
Amblygobius hectori	1056
Amblygobius nocturnus	1060
Amblygobius phalaena	1058
Amblygobius rainfordi	1060
Amblygobius semicinctus	1060
Ambonor Goby	1112
Amphiprion clarkii	370, 378
Amphiprion melanopus	344
Amphiprion ocellaris	361, 377
Amphiprion polymnus	377
Amphiroa hancockii	236
Amplexidiscus	415, 432
Amplexidiscus fenestrafer	415
Anampses	681, 844
Anampses caeruleopunctatus	851
Anampses femininus	846
Anampses lennardi	851
Anampses lineatus	846
Anampses melanurus	848
Anampses meleagrides	848
Anampses neoguinaicus	850
Andresia	326
Andresia parthenopea	354
ANDRESIIDAE	354
Anemonia	336
Anemonia rustica	636
Anemonia sulcata	336
Aniculus	463
Aniculus maximus	598
Anthias	682
Anthias anthias	934
ANTHIINAE	682, 930
ANTHOZOA	326, 328, 330, 404, 414
	442
ARACHNACTIDAE	406
Arachnanthus	327
Arachnanthus nocturnus	406
ARAUCARIODEAE	249
Arc-eyed Hawkfish	1034
Arctides	462
Arctides regalis	574, 575
Argus Comet	1003
ARTHROPODA	462
Aspidontus taeniatus	917
Assessor	682
Assessor flavissimus	999
Assessor macneilli	994, 1000
Atergatis	464
Atergatis sp.	652

B

BACILLARIOPHYCEAE	214, 217
Banded Blanquillo	1020
Banded Goby	1058
Barbier	934
Bartholomea	388
Bartholomea annulata	388
Bartholomea lucida	388
Berthelina chloris	292
Bicolor Parrotfish	929
Bicolored Cleaner Wrasse	915
Bird Wrasse	864
Black-eared Wrasse	874
Black-striped Worm Eel	1120
Blackcap Basslet	992
Blackedge Fairy Wrasse	828
Blue Blanquillo	1023
Blue Gudgeon	1133
Blue Hana Goby	1130
Blue-sided Fairy Wrasse	826
Blue-spotted Coral Goby	1078
Blue-striped Dottyback	968
Blue-striped Orange Tamarin	846
Blue-tip Longfin	1006
Bluehead Wrasse	894
Bluelined Wrasse	888
Bluestreak Cleaner Wrasse	916
BODIANINAE	681
Bodianus	681, 802
Bodianus anthioides	802
Bodianus axillaris	804
Bodianus bimaculatus	808
Bodianus diana	806
Bodianus diplotaenia	808

Animal Index

Bodianus izuensis	811
Bodianus loxozonus	811
Bodianus mesothorax	812
Bodianus pulchellus	814
Bodianus rufus	814
BOLOCEROIDARIA	398
Boloceroides mcmurrichi	402
BOLOCEROIDIDAE	402
Botryocladia uvaria	233
BRANCHIATA	462
Brown Dottyback	974
Brown-spotted Spinefoot	786
Brush alga	240
Bryaninops	682
Bryaninops amplus	1043, 1062
Bryaninops youngei	1062
BRYOIDEAE	248
bryon	250
BRYOPSIDACEAE	240
BRYOPSIDALES	250
Bryopsis plumosa	240
Bubble alga	245
Bucchichi's Goby	1090
Bullseye Jawfish	1160
Butterfly Goby	1054

C

Cactus alga	238
Calappa	463
Calappa convexa	629
Calappa sp.	628
CALAPPIDAE	463, 628
Calcareous red alga	235
Calcinus	463
Calcinus ornatus	600
CALLIONYMIDAE	683, 1140
Callionymus	683
Callionymus delicatulus	1142
Callionymus pleurostictus	1144
Calloplesiops	682
Calloplesiops altivelis	996, 997, 1001
Calloplesiops argus	1003
Cancellus	463
Cancellus sp.	601
Cancer pagurus	662
CANCRIDAE	662
Carcinus	463
Carcinus maenas	644
Carpenter's Wrasse	834
Catalina Goby	1096
Caulerpa	249, 251, 278
Caulerpa agardhii	249
Caulerpa alternifolia	249, 305
Caulerpa ambigua	249
Caulerpa anceps	248, 299
Caulerpa arenicola	263
Caulerpa articulata	249
Caulerpa ashmeadii	248
Caulerpa bartoniae	249
Caulerpa biloba	263, 297
Caulerpa biserrulata	248
Caulerpa brachypus	248, 295, 299
Caulerpa brownii	249, 305
Caulerpa clarifera	261
Caulerpa cliftonii	249
Caulerpa certularioides	292
Caulerpa cupressoides	262, 307
Caulerpa cupressoides var. lycopodium	307
Caulerpa distichophylla	249, 310
Caulerpa elongata	248, 297
Caulerpa ethelae	249, 321
Caulerpa falcifolia	248
Caulerpa fastigiata	248, 297
Caulerpa fergusonii	249, 321
Caulerpa filiformis	248
Caulerpa flagelliformis	303, 304
Caulerpa floridana	322, 323
Caulerpa formosa	856
Caulerpa freycinettii	249, 305
Caulerpa harveyii	249
Caulerpa holmesiana	249
Caulerpa hypnoides	249, 308
Caulerpa lentilifera	249
Caulerpa lessonii	249

Animal Index

Caulerpa lycopodium	249
Caulerpa macrodisca	261
Caulerpa mexicana	322
Caulerpa murrayana	297
Caulerpa murrayi	248
Caulerpa nummelaria	324
Caulerpa obscura	249
Caulerpa okamurai	249, 321
Caulerpa ollivieri	262, 273
Caulerpa papillosa	249
Caulerpa parvifolia	248, 299
Caulerpa paspaloides	249, 280
	309, 311, 319
Caulerpa peltata	249, 310, 312, 315
Caulerpa peltata var.	
macrodisca	314
Caulerpa pickeringii	248, 297
Caulerpa pinnata	248, 302, 303
Caulerpa plumaris	248, 302
Caulerpa plumifera	249, 310
Caulerpa prolifera	248, 258
	262, 267, 273, 292, 299
Caulerpa pusilla	248, 297
Caulerpa racemosa	
249, 262, 269, 271, 273, 274, 281	
	282, 292, 310, 312, 317
Caulerpa racemosa var. *peltata*	
	261
Caulerpa remotifolia	248
Caulerpa reyesi	263, 297
Caulerpa scalpelliformis	248, 262
	292, 300, 301
Caulerpa sedoides	249, 321
Caulerpa sertularioides	262, 267
	273, 281, 301, 322
Caulerpa simpliciuscula	249, 321
Caulerpa stahlii	248, 299
Caulerpa subserrata	248
Caulerpa taxifolia	267, 273, 279
	302, 322
Caulerpa trifaria	249
Caulerpa urvilliana	249, 307
Caulerpa uvifera	261
Caulerpa verticillata	248, 297, 324
Caulerpa webbiana	248, 262, 271
	297
CAULERPACEAE	251, 295
Caulerpicin	286
Celebes Wrasse	817
Centropyge heraldi	722
CERIANTHARIA	404
CERIANTHIDAE	403, 405, 406
Cerianthus	327
Cerianthus maua	410
Cerianthus membranaceus	408
Cerianthus sp.	403
Cetoscarus	682
Cetoscarus bicolor	929
Chaetomorpha linum	242
Chameleon Tilefish	1014
CHAROIDEAE	248
Checkerboard Wrasse	868
CHEILININAE	681
Cheilinus	681, 816
Cheilinus celebicus	817
Cheilinus fasciatus	818
Cheilio	681, 852
Cheilio inermis	852
Chinese Zebra Goby	1136
Chiseltooth Wrasse	925
CHLAMYDOMONAS	267
Chlorella	172
CHLOROPHYCEAE	250
CHLOROPHYTA	214, 223, 250
Choat's Wrasse	882
Choerodon	681, 818
Choerodon azurio	820
Choerodon fasciatus	819
CHORDATA	681
CHROMOPHYTA	214, 216
CHRYSOPHYCEAE	214, 216
Cigar Wrasse	852
Cirrhilabrus	681, 825
Cirrhilabrus cyanopleura	826
Cirrhilabrus jordani	828
Cirrhilabrus lubbocki	826, 922

Animal Index

Cirrhilabrus melanomarginatus 828
Cirrhilabrus rubriventralis 830
Cirrhilabrus ryukyukiensis 830
Cirrhilabrus sp. 832
Cirrhilabrus temmincki 832
Cirrhitichthys 682
Cirrhitichthys falco 1025, 1028
Cirrhitichthys oxycephalus 1028
CIRRHITIDAE 682
Cirrhitus 682
Cirrhitus rivulatus 1030
Citron Goby 1076
CLADOPHORA 34
CLADOPHORACEAE 240, 242
Clodaphora profilera 240
Clorodermis fastigiata 240
Clown Coris 854
Clown Wrasse 858
Club caulerpa 259
CNIDARIA 328
COCCOLITHOPHORES 220
CODIACEAE 238
Combfish 862
Comet 1001
Condylactis 326, 340
Condylactis aurantiaca 340
Condylactis gigantea 341, 342
510
Convict Blenny 1138
Coral Hogfish 804
CORALLIMORPHARIA 414
CORALLIMORPHIDAE 327, 436
CORINAE 681
Corallina officinalis 236, 237
CORALLINACEAE 237
Coris 681, 853
Coris aygula 854
Coris caudimacula 861
Coris formosa 856
Coris frerei 856
Coris gaimard 858
Coris julis 863

Coris picta 863
Coris variegata 860
Cortez Rainbow Wrasse 902
Corynactis 327
Corynactis californica 436
Corynactis viridis 438, 439
Cribrinopsis 338
Cribrinopsis crassa 338
Cribrinopsis fernaldi 338
CRUSTACEA 192, 462, 465
Cryptocentrus 682
Cryptocentrus caeruleopunctatus 1064
Cryptocentrus cinctus 1064
Cryptocentrus sp. 1066
Cryptodendrum 326, 380
Cryptodendrum adhaesivum 380
Ctenochaetus 681, 729
Ctenochaetus binotatus 730
Ctenochaetus hawaiiensis 730
Ctenochaetus striatus 734
Ctenochaetus strigosus 729, 732
Ctenochaetus tominiensis 736
Ctenogobiops 682
Ctenogobiops maculosus 1068
Ctenogobiops tangaroai 1068
CYANOPHYTA 214, 216
Cypho 682
Cypho purpurasens 961
Cyprinocirrhites polyactis 1030

D

Dapple Coris 862
Dardanus 463, 597
Dardanus calidus 602
Dardanus deformis 602
Dardanus lagopodes 604
Dardanus megistos 606
Dardanus pedunculatus 606
DECAPODA 462, 465
Decorated Firefish 1120
Decorated Goby 1092

Animal Index

Decorated Spinefoot 784
Diadem Basslet 970
Diana's Hogfish 806
DIANTENNATA 462
DICTYOTACEAE 228
DINOPHYCEAE 214, 220
DIOGENIDAE 463, 595
Diplogrammus 683
Diplogrammus infulatus 1144
Diplogrammus randalli 1146
Diproctacanthus 681, 910
Diproctacanthus xanthurus 911
Disappearing Wrasse 841
Disc caulerpa 259
Discordipinna 682
Discordipinna griessingeri 1070
Discosoma 327
Discosoma neglecta 426
Discosoma nummifere 422
Discosoma sanctithomae 424
Discosoma sp. 420, 423, 426
Discosoma sp. (coeruleus) 430
Discosoma sp. (ferrugatus) 428
Discosoma sp. (malaccensis) 421
Discosoma sp. (marmoratus) 428
Discosoma sp. (plumosa) 427
Discosoma sp. (punctatus) 431
Discosoma sp. (striatus) 429
Discosoma sp. "coeroleo-striatus"
429
DISCOSOMATIDAE 416
Divided Wrasse 882
Double-barred Spinefoot 788
Dragon Wrasse 822
Dromia 463
Dromia personata 626
Dromia sp. 627
Dromidiopsis 463
DROMIIDAE 463, 626
Dusky Fusegoby 1072
Dusky Tilefish 1014

E

Eclipse Hogfish 812
Eightline Wrasse 838
Elacatinus oceanops 1087
ENDOMYARIA 326
Enoplometopus 463
Enoplometopus antillensis 586
Enoplometopus daumi 586
Enoplometopus debelius 588
Enoplometopus holthuisi 590
Enoplometopus occidentalis
583, 590
Enoplometopus voigtmanni 592
Entacmaea 342
Entacmaea quadricolor 343, 344
345
Eozanclus brevirostris 685
EPIZOANTHIDAE 460
Epizoanthus 327
Epizoanthus arenaceus 460
Epizoanthus paxii 460
European lobster 593
EUSIPHONIIDAE 250
Eviota 682
Eviota pellucida 1070

F

Falco Hawkfish 1028
False Bluestreak Wrasse 918
Feather caulerpa 292
Feathertail Sleeper 1126
Filament-fin Wrasse 836
FILICOIDEAE 248
Finescale Wrasse 877
Finger alga 238, 244
Firefish 1124
Fluorescent blue alga 228
Forktail Dottyback 970
Forster's Hawkfish 1036
Four-lined Wrasse 842

Animal Index

Fusigobius 682
Fusigobius neophytus 1072
Fusiogobius signipinnis 1072

G

Galathea 463
Galathea strigosa 616
GALATHEIDAE 463
Genie's Cleaning Goby 1084
Geograpsus sp. 660
Ghost Goby 1134
Gnatholepis 682
Gnatholepis scapulostigma 1075
GNATHOPHYLLIDAE 462, 502
Gnathophyllum 462
Gnathophyllum americanum 504
Gnathophyllum panamense 504
Gobies 1074
GOBIIDAE 682, 1039, 1040
Gobiodon 682
Gobiodon citrinus 1076
Gobiodon histrio 1078
Gobiodon okinawae 1080
Gobiodon unicolor 1081
Gobiosoma 1082
Gobiosoma evelynae 1083
Gobiosoma genie 1084
Gobiosoma illecebrosum 1085
Gobiosoma oceanops 1087
Gobiosoma randalli 1088
Gobius 682
Gobius auratus 1088
Gobius bucchichii 1090
Gobius vittatus 1090
Goby 1085
Goldbar Wrasse 900
Golden Goby 1088
Golden Hawkfish 1038
Golden Mini-Grouper 999
Golden Rainbowfish 870
Golden-lined Spinefoot 782
Gomphosus 681, 864

Gomphosus caeruleus klunzingeri 864
Gomphosus varius 864
GONODACTYLIDAE 464, 674
Gonodactylus 464
Gonodactylus sp. 673
Gracilaria curtissae 230
Gracilaria sp. 230
GRACILARIACEAE 230
Gramma 682
Gramma linki 991
Gramma loreto 990
Gramma melacara 987, 992
GRAMMIDAE 682, 988
Grape caulerpa 259, 292
GRAPSIDAE 464, 659
Grapsus 464
Grapsus grapsus 660
Grapsus sp. 659
Grateloupia filicina 232
GRATELOUPIACEAE 231
Green Wrasse 874
Guinea Fowl Wrasse 884
Gunnelichthys 683
Gunnelichthys curiosus 1118
Gunnelichthys monostigma 1118
Gunnelichthys pleurotaenia 1120

H

HAEMOGREGARINA 206
Half-and-Half Thicklip 877
Halichoeres 681, 866
Halichoeres biocellatus 868
Halichoeres chloropterus 874
Halichoeres chrysus 866, 870
Halichoeres garnoti 872
Halichoeres hortulanus 868
Halichoeres leucoxanthus 870
Halichoeres melanopomus 874
Halichoeres radiatus 872
Halichoeres sp. 867
Halimeda opuntia 238, 279

Animal Index

HALIMEDACEAE	238
Halymenia sp.	232
Halymenia sp. cf. *floresia*	231
Harpactocarcinus punctulatus	662
Hawaiian Cleaner Wrasse	918
Hector's Goby	1056
Helfrich's Firefish	1123
HELMINTHOCLADIACEAE	235
Hemigymnus	681, 876
Hemigymnus melapterus	877
Hemisquilla	464
Hemisquilla ensigera californensis	675
Hepatus epheliticus	629
Heteractis	362
Heteractis aurora	362
Heteractis crispa	364, 366
Heteractis magnifica	329, 357, 360, 361, 368
Heteractis malu	368
Heterodactyla	382
Heterodactyla hemprichi	382
HEXACORALLIA	326
HIPPOLYTIDAE	462, 468
HIPPUROIDEAE	249
Hologymnosus	681, 878
Hologymnosus annulatus	877
Hologymnosus doliatus	879
Homarus	463
Homarus americanus	593
Homarus gammarus	593
Hoplolatilus	682
Hoplolatilus chlupatyi	1014
Hoplolatilus cuniculus	1014
Hoplolatilus fourmanoiri	1016
Hoplolatilus luteus	1016
Hoplolatilus marcosi	1018
Hoplolatilus purpureus	1018
Hoplolatilus starcki	1013, 1020
HYDROZOEN	328
Hymenocera	462
Hymenocera elegans	508
Hymenocera picta	507, 509

I

lia nucleus	631
Inachus phalangium	636
ISOPHELLIDAE	396
Istigobius	682
Istigobius decoratus	1092
Istigobius hoesei	1092
Istigobius ornatus	1094

J

Jansen's Wrasse	900
Jordan's Fairy Wrasse	828

K

Klunzinger's Wrasse	902

L

Labracinus	682
Labracinus cyclophthalmus	962
Labracinus lineatus	962, 964
Labrichthys	681, 908
Labrichthys unilineata	908
Labrichthys-group	908
LABRIDAE	681, 796
Labroides	681, 912
Labroides bicolor	915
Labroides dimidiatus	801, 913, 916
Labroides pectoralis	918
Labroides phtirophagus	918
Labroides rubrolabiatus	918
Labropsis	681, 920
Labropsis alleni	922
Labropsis manabei	920
Labropsis xanthonota	920
Ladder Glider	1110
Larabicus	681, 923

Animal Index

Larabicus quadrilineatus 923
Laurencia sp. 232
Leandrites 462
Leandrites cyrtorhynchus 523
Leandrites sp. 522
Lebrunia 326
Lebrunia danae 400
Leucosia 463
Leucosia sp. 630
LEUCOSIIDAE 463, 630
Liagora sp. cf. ceranoides 235
Lined Cichlops 964
Liomera 464
Liomera sp. 656
Lissocarcinus 463
Lissocarcinus laevis 646
Lissocarcinus orbicularis 646
Little Spinefoot 786
Longnose Hawkfish 1032
Lotilia 682
Lotilia graciliosa 1094
Loxorhynchus 463
Loxorhynchus grandis 633, 635
Lubbock's Wrasse 826
Luzonichthys 682
Luzonichthys waitei 936
Lybia 464
Lybia edmondsoni 651, 653
Lybia tessalata 654
LYCOPODIODEAE 249
Lymphocystis 206
Lyretail Hogfish 802
Lyretail Wrasse 904
Lysiosquilla 464
Lysiosquilla maculata 678
Lysiosquilla sulcirostris 679
LYSIOSQUILLIDAE 464, 678
Lysmata 462
Lysmata amboinensis 469, 470
Lysmata californica 472
Lysmata debelius 465, 474
Lysmata galapagensis 476
Lysmata grabhami 470

Lysmata kükenthali 476
Lysmata rathbunae 480
Lysmata seticaudata 478
Lysmata sp. 477
Lysmata vittata 480
Lysmata wurdemanni 481
Lythrypnus 682
Lythrypnus dalli 1096

M

MacNeill's Mini-Grouper 1000
Macrocystis pyrifera 219, 227
Macrodactyla 326, 346
Macrodactyla doreensis 346
Macropharyncgodon 681, 881
Macropharyngodon bipartitus 882
Macropharyngodon choati 882
Macropharyngodon kuiteri 884
Macropharyngodon meleagris 881, 884
Macropharyngodon negrosensis 887
Magenta Dottyback 980
Maine Lobster 593
Maja 463
Maja sp. 637
Maja squinado 638
MAJIDAE 463, 632
MALACANTHIDAE 682, 1012
Malacanthus 682
Malacanthus brevirostris 1020
Malacanthus lattovittatus 1023
MALACOSTRACA 462
Mantis Shrimp 192
Manucomplanus 463
Manucomplanus varians 613
Masked Rainbowfish 874
Mediterranean Banded Goby 1090
Mediterranean Rainbow Wrasse 860
Mermaid's hard fan 244
Metarhodactis 327

Animal Index

Metarhodactis sp.	416, 418
Metridium	390
Metridium senile	390
METRIIDAE	390
Mexican Hogfish	808
Micrococcus	216
MICRODESMIDAE	683, 1116
MICTYRIDAE	464, 669
Mictyris	464
Mictyris longicarpus	670
Mictyris sp.	669
Miniature caulerpa	295
Moorish Idol	792

N

NANTANTIA	462
Narval	538
NASEUS RECTIFRONS	686
NASINAE	681
Naso	681, 752
Naso annulatus	756
Naso brachycentron	756
Naso brevirostris	758
Naso hexacanthus	760
Naso lituratus	754, 760
Naso sp.	687
Naso thynnoides	762
Naso unicornis	762
Naso vlamingii	764
NEMANTHIDAE	392
Nemanthus	326, 392
Nemanthus nitidus	392
Nemateleotris	683
Nemateleotris decora	1120
Nemateleotris helfrichi	1123
Nemateleotris magnifica	1124
Neocirrhites armatus	1030
Neomeris annulata	238, 244
Neon gobies	1082
Neon Goby	463
Neopetrolisthes alobatus	621
Neopetrolisthes maculatus	622

Neopetrolisthes ohshimai	624
Neopetrolisthes sp.	619
NEPHROPIDAE	463, 582
Nephrops	463
Nephrops norvegicus	594
Nocturnal Goby	1060
Novaculichthys	681, 821
Novaculichthys taeniourus	822

O

Ocellate Goby	1114
Ocellated Longfin	1008
Ocypode	464
Ocypode ceratophthalma	663, 664
Ocypode gaudichaudii	665
OCYPODIDAE	464
Odontodactylus	464
Odontotactylus scyllarus	676
Ogilbyina	682
Ogilbyina novaehollandiae	966
Ogilbyina queenslandiae	966
Ogilbyina velifera	965
Olive Dottyback	976
One-spot Worm Eel	1118
OPISTOGNATHIDAE	683, 1158
Opistognathus	683
Opistognathus aurifrons	1162
Opistognathus jacksiensis	1164
Opistognathus latitabunda	1164
Opistognathus muscatensis	1166
Opistognathus punctatus	1166
Opistognathus scops	1160
Opistognathus sp.	1157, 1159, 1161
Oplet	336
Oplopomus oplopomus	1096
OPUNTIODAE	249
Orange-axil Wrasse	888
Orange-spotted Prawn Goby	1044
Orangemarked Goby	1056
Orangestripe Prawn Goby	1050
Orchid Dottyback	974
Oriental Wrasse	920

Animal Index

Ornate Goby	1094
OSCILLATORIA	216
OSTEICHTHYES	681
Oxycirrhites	682
Oxycirrhites typus	1032
Oxymetopon	683
Oxymetropon cyanoctenosum	
	1126

P

Pachycerianthus	327
Pachycerianthus fimbriatus	405
Pachycerianthus soletarius	410
Pachycerianthus sp.	412
Pachygrapsus	464
Pachygrapsus marmoratus	660
PAGURIDAE	463, 611
Paguristes	463
Paguristes cadenati	608
Pagurus	463
Pagurus bernhardus	611
Pagurus cuanensis	613
Painted Goldie	950
Palaemon	462
Palaemon elegans	513
Palaemon intermedius	514
Palaemon serenus	516
Palaemon serratus	517, 518
Palaemon xiphias	519
PALAEMONIDAE	462, 510
PALAEMONINAE	510
Pale Dottyback	978
Pale Gudgeon	1130
Palinurella wieneckii	572
Palinurellus	462
PALINURIDAE	462, 562
Palinurus	462
Palinurus elephas	563, 564
Palythoa	445
Palythoa sp.	446, 448
Palythoa tuberculosa	450
PANDALIDAE	462, 536

Pandalus	462
Pandalus kessleri	538
Pandalus montagui	537
Panulirus	462
Panulirus cygnus	566
Panulirus inflatus	568
Panulirus jenicillatus	571
Panulirus marginatus	571
Panulirus regius	570
Panulirus versicolor	568, 569
Paracanthurus	681
Paracanthurus hepatus	738
Paracanthus	737
Paracheilinus	681, 834
Paracheilinus carpenteri	834
Paracheilinus filamentosus	836
Paracheilinus hemitaeniatus	836
Paracheilinus mccoskeri	838
Paracheilinus octotaenia	838
Paracirrhites	682
aracirrhites arcatus	1034
Paracirrhites forsteri	1036
Paracirrhites xanthus	1038
Paraplesiops	682
Paraplesiops alisonae	1004
Paraplesiops bleekeri	1004
Paraplesiops meleagris	1006
Paraplesiops poweri	1006
Parazoanthus	327
Parazoanthus axinellae	452, 454
Parazoanthus parasiticus	455
Parazoanthus sp.	456
Parazoanthus swiftii	456
Parhippolyte	462
Parhippolyte uveae	482
PASPALOIDEAE	249
Peacock Wrasse	822
PEDICELLATAE	249
PERCIFORMES	681, 684
Periclimenes	462
Periclimenes aesopius	524
Periclimenes brevicarpalis	
	524, 526

Periclimenes holthuisi	527, 530
Periclimenes imperator	528
Periclimenes lucasi	530
Periclimenes pedersoni	532
Periclimenes yucatanicus	
	510, 534
Petrochirus	463
Petrochirus diogenes	609
PHAEOPHYCEAE	214, 219
Philippine Fairy Basslet	948
PHOLIDICHTHYIDAE	683, 1137
Pholidichthys	683
Pholidichthys leucotaenia	1138
PHYLLANTOIDEAE	248
PHYMANTHIDAE	355
Phymanthus	326
Phymanthus pulcher	355
Pink Basslet	936
Pink Speckled Wrasse	907
Pinkbar Goby	1044
Pinnotheres	464
Pinnotheres pisum	658
PINNOTHERIDAE	464, 657
Pixy Hawkfish	1029
PLEISTOPHORA	206
Plesionika	462
Plesionika narval	538
PLESIOPIDAE	682, 993
Plesiops	682
Plesiops caeruleolineatus	
	993, 1008
Plesiops corallicola	1008
Plesiops nigricans	1008
POLYCHAETA	195
POLYPEPTIDES	289
POLYSACCHARIDES	289
Polysiphonia sp.	235
PONTONIINAE	520
Poplar alga	244
PORCELLANIDAE	463, 618
PORTUNIDAE	463, 644
Pretty Prawn Goby	1108
PRIONURINAE	681
Prionurus	681, 766
Prionurus laticlavius	767
Prionurus maculatus	766, 768
Prionurus microlepidotus	768
Prionurus punctatus	770
Prionurus scalprus	770
PROTOZOANS	206
Pseudanthias	682
Pseudanthias bicolor	936
Pseudanthias cooperi	938
Pseudanthias dispar	938
Pseudanthias evansi	941
Pseudanthias heemstrai	942
Pseudanthias huchtii	942
Pseudanthias hypselosoma	944
Pseudanthias ignitus	944
Pseudanthias lori	946
Pseudanthias luzonensis	948
Pseudanthias pictilis	950
Pseudanthias pleurotaenia	948
Pseudanthias randalli	950
Pseudanthias smithvanizi	952
Pseudanthias squamipinnis	
	931, 932, 952
Pseudanthias taeniatus	954
Pseudanthias tuka	954
Pseudocheilinus	681, 840
Pseudocheilinus evanidus	841
Pseudocheilinus hexataenia	
	840, 842
Pseudocheilinus tetrataenia	842
PSEUDOCHROMIDAE	682, 958
Pseudochromis	682
Pseudochromis aldabrensis	968
Pseudochromis cyanotaenia	968
Pseudochromis diadema	959, 970
Pseudochromis dixurus	970
Pseudochromis flavivertex	972
Pseudochromis fridmani	974
Pseudochromis fuscus	974
Pseudochromis macullochi	26
Pseudochromis olivaceus	976
Pseudochromis paccagnellae	976

Animal Index

Pseudochromis persicus	978
Pseudochromis pesi	978
Pseudochromis porphyreus	980
Pseudochromis sankeyi	980
Pseudochromis splendens	983
Pseudochromis springeri	984
Pseudocorynactis	327
Pseudocorynactis caribbeorum	440
PSEUDODACINAE	682
Pseudodax	682, 924
Pseudodax moluccanus	925
Pseudoplesiops	682
Pseudoplesiops multisquamatus	985
Pseudoplesiops typus	986
Psychedelic Fish	1147
Ptereleotris	683
Ptereleotris evides	1128
Ptereleotris grammica	1129
Ptereleotris hannae	1130
Ptereleotris heteroptera	1130
Ptereleotris microlepis	1133
Ptereleotris monoptera	1134
Ptereleotris uroditaenia	1134
Ptereleotris zebra	1117, 1136
Pterois volitans	1132
Pudding Wife	872
Purple Blotch Basslet	948
Purple Tilefish	1018

Q

Quadrella	463
Queen Coris	856

R

Railway Glider	1104
Rainbow Wrasse	892
Red seaweed alga	231
Red-lined Wrasse	868
Red-tailed Tamarin	844
Redbreasted Wrasse	818
Redcheek Wrasse	898
Redstripe Tilefish	1018
REPTANTIA	462
Rhinomuraena amboinensis	23
Rhipocephalus phoenix,	244
RHODOPHYCEAE	222
RHODOPHYTA	214, 221
Rhynchocinetes	462
Rhynchocinetes australis	548
Rhynchocinetes kuiteri	546, 547
Rhynchocinetes rigens	548
Rhynchocinetes rugulosus	548
Rhynchocinetes sp.	544
RHYNCHOCINETIDAE	462, 540
Ricordea	327
Ricordea florida	434
Ricordea sp.	435
RICORDEIDAE	327, 434
Ringed Wrasse	879
Royal Dottyback	976
Royal Gramma	990
Ruby red alga	230
Rynchocinetes uritai	542

S

Saddle Wrasse	896
Sagartia	326
Sagartia troglodytes	394
SAGARTIIDAE	394
Sargartiogeton	326
Sagartiogeton undulatus	395
Sarcophyton ehrenbergi	281
Sarcophyton trocheiophorum	281
Sargassum fillipendula	228
Saron	462
Saron inermis	486
Saron marmoratus	482
Saron neglectus	488
Saron rectirostris	484, 485

Saron sp.	488
Scarbreast Tuskfish	820
SCARIDAE	682, 926
SCYLLARIDAE	462, 574
Scyllarides	462
Scyllarides astori	580
Scyllarides haanii	581
Scyllarides latus	578
Scyllarus	462
Scyllarus arctus	576
Sea Goldie	942
Sea Whip Goby	1062
SEDOIDEAE	249
SERRANIDAE	682, 930
Serranocirrhitus	682
Serranocirrhitus latus	956
Sharknose Goby	1083
SIGANIDAE	681, 772
Siganus	681
Siganus argenteus	778
Siganus corallinus	773, 778, 780
Siganus guttatus	780, 781
Siganus javus	782
Siganus lineatus	782
Siganus magnificus	776
Siganus puellus	784
Siganus rivulatus	786
Siganus spinus	786
Siganus stellatus	786
Siganus unimaculatus	774
Siganus uspae	776
Siganus virgatus	788
Siganus vulpinus	774
Signigobius	682
Signigobius biocellatus	1098
Sixbar Wrasse	898
Sixstripe Wrasse	842
Slender Shrimp Goby	1048
Social Fairy Wrasse	830
Spanish Hogfish	814
Spinecheek Goby	1096
SPOROZOANS	206
Spotfin Hogfish	814
Spottail Coris	860
Spottail Gudgeon	1128
Spotted Hawkfish	1027
Spotted Prawn Goby	1068
Spotted Tilefish	1016
Spottysail Dottyback	962
Springer's Dottyback	984
Staphylococcus aureus	287
Stark's Tilefish	1020
Stegopontonia	462
Stegopontonia commensalis	534
STENOPODIDAE	462, 550
Stenopus	462
Stenopus cyanoscelis	552
Stenopus devaneyi	552
Stenopus earlei	561
Stenopus hispidus	554
Stenopus pyrsonotus	556
Stenopus scutellatus	551, 556
Stenopus sp.	561
Stenopus spinosus	560
Stenopus tenuirostris	558
Stenopus zanzibaricus	558, 560
Stenorhynchus	463
Stenorhynchus debilis	643
Stenorhynchus lanceolatus	639
Stenorhynchus seticornis	640
Stethojulis	681, 888
Stethojulis albovittata	888
Stethojulis bandanensis	888
Stethojulis strigriventer	888
Stethojulis trilineata	888
Stichodactyla	372
Stichodactyla gigantea	372
Stichodactyla haddoni	374
Stichodactyla mertensii	378
Stichodactylidae	356
STOMATOPODA	671
Stonogobiops	682
Stonogobiops nematodes	1100
Stonogobiops sp.	1098
Stonogobiops xanthorhinica	1102
Streaked Spinefoot	782

Animal Index

Striped Dottyback	980
Strombus gigas	279
Sunburst Basslet	956
Sunrise Dottyback	972
Synalpheus	462
Synalpheus sp.	493
Synchiropus	683
Synchiropus i plendidus	1148
Synchiropus stellatus	1154

T

Tangaroa Goby	1068
TELEOSTEI	681
Telmatactis	326, 396
Telmatactis cricoides	396
Temminck's Wrasse	832
Tetraonchus	208
THALASSIANTHIDAE	380
Thalassoma	681, 890
Thalassoma amblycephalum	892
Thalassoma bifasciatum	894
Thalassoma commersoni	892
Thalassoma duperreyi	896
Thalassoma genivittatum	898
Thalassoma hardwickii	898
Thalassoma hebraicum	900
Thalassoma janseni	900
Thalassoma klunzingeri	902
Thalassoma lucasanum	902
Thalassoma lunare	904
Thalassoma lutescens	904
Thalassoma pavo	906
Thor	462
Thor amboinensis	490
Three-lined Wrasse	888
Three-ribbon Rainbowfish	888
THUYOIDEAE	249
Tozeuma	462
Tozeuma sp.	490
Trachinops	682
Trachinops caudimaculatus	1010
Trachinops noarlungae	1010

Trachinops taeniatus	1010
Trapezia	463
Trapezia sp.	649
TRAPEZIIDAE	648
Triactis	326
Triactis producta	401
Trimma	682
Trimma naudei	1102
Trimma tevegae	1104
Trizopagurus	463
Trizopagurus strigatus	610
Trumpet caulerpa	259
Tufted red calcareous alga	237
Two-spot Goby	1098
Twospot Hogfish	808

U

Uca	464
Uca anullipes	666
Uca crassipes	667
Uca sp.	668
Uca vomerus	668
Udotea spinulosa	244
Ulva lactuca	223
Urticina	347
Urticina felina	347, 348
Urticina lofotensis	350
Urticina piscivora	350

V

Valenciennea	682
Valenciennea helsdingenii	1104
Valenciennea immaculata	1106
Valenciennea longipinnis	1106
Valenciennea puellaris	1108
Valenciennea sexguttata	1110
Valenciennea strigata	1110
Valenciennea wardi	1112
Valonia ventricosa	245
VALONIACEAE	245

Vanderhorstia	682
Vanderhorstia ambonoro	1112
Vanderhorstia mertensi	1114
Vanderhorstia ornatissima	1114
VAUCHERIODEAE	248
VENTRICARIA	221
Ventricaria ventricosa	245
VERTEBRATA	681
VESICULIFERAE	249
Vibriosis	204

W

Western Blue Devil	1006
Wheeler's Prawn Goby	1050
White-capped Prawn Goby	1094
Wire alga	242
Wrangelia argus	233

X

Xanthasia	464
Xanthasia murigera	657
XANTHIDAE	463, 650
XANTHOPHYCEAE	214, 217
Xenojulis	681, 907
Xenojulis margaritaceus	907
Xyrichthys	681, 821
Xyrichthys pavo	822

Y

Yellow Coral Goby	1080
Yellow Head Jawfish	1162
Yellow Prawn Goby	1064
Yellow Tailband Wrasse	848
Yellow Wrasse	904
Yellow-striped Worm Eel	1118
Yellow-tailed Cleaner	911
Yellow-tailed Tamarin	848
Yellowback Wrasse	920

Yellowhead Wrasse	872
Yellowlined Basslet	991
Yellownose Goby	1088
Yellowspotted Wrasse	887

Z

ZANCLIDAE	681, 790
Zanclus	681
Zanclus cornutus	791, 792
Zebrasoma	681, 739
Zebrasoma desjardinii	740, 742
Zebrasoma flavescens	739, 743
Zebrasoma gemmatum	744
Zebrasoma rostratum	744
Zebrasoma scopas	746
Zebrasoma veliferum	748
Zebrasoma xanthurum	750
ZOANTHARIA	442
ZOANTHIDAE	446
Zoanthus	327, 445
Zoanthus sp.	458, 459

Picture Credits

Allen, Gerald R.: 209 r., 689, 715 b., 733 t., 809 t., 837 b., 857 b., 875 t., 901 t., 922 b., 937 b., 944, 945 b., 949 t., 1000, 1011 b., 1045 t., 1121 b., 1122 b., 1154,1215.

Allen, David: 880 b., 1057 b., 1128.

Baensch, Hans A.: 9, 22, 25, 30/31, 37, 43, 45 (5), 46, 58, 65, 70, 80, 81 t.l.+t.r, b.l.+ b.r., 103, 155, 157, 159, 177 (2), 181, 188, 189, 194, 196, 199, 202 (2), 203, 204, 205, 208, 210 (3), 211 (3), 224 t., 225 (4), 226, 233 b.l., 234, 236 b., 237, 241 b., 243 (2), 244, 245, 279, 295, 302 b., 313 t., 314 b., 329, 375 b., 420, 471 t., 479 b., 517 t., 520, 645 t., 661 (2), 722, 815 b., 895 b., 1210

Baker, Patrick: 567 t.

Baumeister, Werner: 527 (2), 636.506

Baumeister, Fred: 339 b., 351 b.

Brons, Robert: 163, 172, 311, 319 t., 996 (5), 997.

Brylla, Robert: 592.

Couet, Heinz Gert, de : 607 t.

Debelius, Helmut: 11, 14, 15, 175, 224 b., 227, 231, 232 b., 233 t.+b.r., 235, 239 t., 261, 299, 301 (2), 302 t.(2), 314 t., 315 (2), 317 b., 323 b., 333, 335 b., 337 t., 339 t., 343 (2), 345 (2), 346, 353 (2), 357, 361 t., 363 (2), 364, 366 t., 367 b., 369 t., 370 b., 371 b., 373 t., 376 (2), 377 (2), 378, 379 (2), 380, 381, 383, 385, 386, 399, 405, 409 b., 415, 416/417, 419 (2), 421 (2), 422, 423, 426 b., 427 (2), 428 (2), 429 (2), 432, 433 b., 434, 435 (2), 437 t., 444/445, 447 (2), 448, 449, 450, 452/453, 457 b., 458 (2), 459, 469, 470 (2), 471 b., 474, 475 b., 477 t., 478, 480 t., 483 b., 484 (2), 386, 488, 491 t., 495 (2), 508, 509 b., 518, 523 b., 525 b., 532, 535 b., 537, 543 (2), 545 (2), 551, 553 (2), 554, 557 b., 559 (2), 560 (2), 561 b., 567 b., 568 b., 571 t., 573 t., 577 b., 580 (2), 584 (3), 585 (2), 589 t.l.+ b., 596, 603 (2), 604, 605 b., 610, 611, 612 t., 623 t., 625 b.l.+ b.r., 627 b., 629 b.r., 643 b., 645 b., 648, 649, 651, 652 (2), 654, 671, 692, 694, 698 b., 699 (2), 702, 705 t., 709 b., 713 t., 717 t., 718, 719 (2), 720, 723 t.l., 724, 727 t., 729 (2), 730 (2), 731 t., 733 b., 734 (2), 735 t., 736 t., 738, 740 b., 740/741, 742, 743, 744, 745 t., 746, 747 b.r., 751 (3), 752 b.l., 755, 757 t., 759 (2), 760, 761 t., 762 b.r., 764, 766, 770, 771 t., 773, 775 t., 780, 785 b., 789 (2), 802, 806, 811, 813 t., 830 l., 831 (2), 838, 839 b., 840 (2), 841, 845 t., 847 m.r.+b.l.+r., 854 (2), 856, 864 (2), 865 t., 866, 868 b., 870 b.r., 871 b., 876 t., 878 b., 883 t., 888 t.l., 890/891, 892, 894, 902, 903 t., 904 t., 905 t., 923 b., 924 b., 925, 927 b., 928 (2), 929, 932/933, 935 (2), 938 l., 941, 943 t., 948, 953 b., 955 t., 956, 964, 968, 969 t., 971 t., 972 (2), 973 (2), 975 t., 979 (2), 980 l., 981 b., 982 (2), 984, 989 (2), 993, 1001, 1002 (2), 1003, 1011 t., 1014, 1015 t., 1019 t., 1020, 1021 t., 1031 b., 1034, 1035 b., 1036, 1037 b., 1053 b., 1054, 1055 b., 1059 t., 1067 (2), 1075, 1076, 1077 t., 1079 b., 1081 t., 1086, 1091 t., 1095 t., 1108, 1109 (2), 1111 b., 1113 t., 1115 b., 1117, 1122 t., 1124, 1125 b., 1127 b., 1129, 1136, 1139 (2), 1149 (2), 1151 (2), 1155 t., 1163 b., 1212

Picture Credits

Douwma, Georgette: 401, 1032.

Erhardt, Harry: 387, 418, 577 t., 588, 631, 637 b., 647 b., 662 t., 680, 748, 1207, 1213

Fiedler, Wolfgang: 528, 615, 703 b., 861 t., 927 t.

Frei, Herbert: 571 b., 659 (2), 660 b.l.

Fricke, Ronald: 1150, 1153 t.

Frickhinger, Karl A.: 209 l., 582, 662 b., 685, 686 (2), 687.

Ghisotti, Andrea: 617.

Gill, Anthony: 966 (2), 1009 b.r.

Göthel, Helmut: 824 b.

Gremblewski-Strate, Otto: 342, 397 b., 407 t., 426 t., 441 (2), 455, 457 t., 535 t., 643 t., 1214

Grüter, Werner: 424, 425 t., 715 t., 725 b., 1083.

Hall, Howard: 344, 351 t., 365, 412, 437 b., 541, 544, 597, 608, 609, 635, 714, 810 t., 819 b., 1029, 1038 t., 1097 t.

Hanauer, Eric: 633.

Hilgert, Klaus: 683, 805 t., 1033 b., 1065 t.

Hoese, Douglas: 1071 t.

Holm, Tony: 594, 647 t., 1028, 1143 b.

Hübner, Reimund: 479 t., 539 b., 548, 638.

Humann, Paul: 400, 425 b., 451 t., 481, 816, 873 t., 987, 990, 991, 1084, 1085.

Johnson, Scott: 561 t., 653.

Jonklaas, Rodney: 783 t.

Burkhard Kahl: 206 (2), 542.

Kerstitch, Alex: 472, 476, 496 b., 499 t., 505 b., 507, 531 b., 568 t., 569, 589 t.r., 629 m+ b.l., 630, 660 b.r., 673, 675, 793 b.r., 844, 857 t., 859 t., 883 b., 954, 959, 1147, 1167 b.

Kochetov, Alexander: 539 t.

Kowallik, K. V.: 218 (6).

Krämer, Gerhard: 229 b., 397 t., 403 (2), 614.

Krupp, Friedhelm: 367 t.

Kuiter, Rudie: 477 b., 480 b., 489 t., 491 b., 493 b., 497, 505 t., 506, 509, 514, 515 (2), 516, 517 b., 523 t., 525 t., 526 t., 529 (2), 546 (6), 547, 549 (2), 555, 601, 646, 655 (2), 670, 697 b., 701 b., 705 b., 708, 709 t., 710, 711, 713 b., 717 b., 721 b., 728, 737, 739, 747 b.l., 749 (2), 769 (2), 771 b., 779 t., 781 t., 783 b., 804, 805 b., 807 b., 810 b., 812, 818, 819 t., 820, 821, 824 t., 825, 833 b., 835 (2), 836, 839 t., 843 t., 847 t.+ m.l., 849 (2), 850, 851 (2), 855 t., 858 (2), 863 (2), 865 b., 867 (2), 868 t., 869 t., 870 b.l., 879, 880 t., 881 b.r., 882 b., 884, 885 (2), 886 (2), 887, 888 t.r., 889 b., 893 t., 898, 899 b., 900, 901 b., 904 b., 905 b., 908, 909 (2), 911, 917, 921 (2), 922 t., 936, 937 t., 938 r., 939 (2), 940 (2), 943 b., 945 t., 946, 947, 949 b., 951 b., 953 t., 957 (2), 961, 963 (2), 965 b., 975 b., 980 r., 983, 985, 994, 999, 1005 (2), 1007 (2), 1010, 1017 b., 1026, 1037 t., 1046 b., 1049 b., 1051 t., 1053 t., 1057 t., 1059 b., 1060, 1066, 1069 b., 1071 b., 1077 b., 1093 (2), 1097 b., 1099 (2), 1100, 1101, 1103 t., 1106, 1110, 1111 t., 1113 b., 1119 (2), 1121 t., 1127 t., 1131 b.,

Picture Credits

Picture Credits

Steiner, Helmut: 335 t., 337 b., 384, 411 b., 438 t., 461 (2).
Terver, Denis: 732, 1013, 1021 b., 1023.
Tetra-Archives: 176.
Thielle, Mike: 1174.
Tomey, W. A.: 18, 19, 20, 21, 24, 26, 27, 28, 29, 32/33, 119, 123, 174, 228, 229 t., 230, 232 t., 236 t., 238, 239 b., 241 t., 277, 307 (2), 313 b., 317 t., 319 b., 323 t. (2), 325, 389 b., 413, 442/443, 871 t., 910.
Türkay, Michael: 513, 519, 600, 612 b., 658, 668 b.
Voigtmann, Herwarth: 382, 433 t., 465, 563, 619, 642 t., 674, 765, 791, 916, 1051 b., 1120, 1155 b., 1211
Weber, Achim: 700.
Werner, Uwe: 853, 878 t.
Wiendl, Horst: 605 t., 640 (2), 691 (2).
Wirtz, Peter: 510/511, 570, 579 b., 586, 587 t., 639, 1082.
Wood, Bill: 677 t., 801, 807 t., 967 t., 977 b., 1043, 1047, 1049 t., 1058, 1061 t., 1133.
Wu, Norbert: 754, 793 t.
Zetzsche, Horst: 992, 1009 b.r.

Drawings:

Patzner, Robert A.: 1074.
Schleid, Gerd
Tomey, W. A.: *Caulerpa*
Walldorf, Volker: 331.

Your MARINE ATLAS
is in
good company

Enjoy your reading
The Authors

Gramma loreto, see page 990

Frickhinger
FOSSIL ATLAS
Fishes

The FOSSIL ATLAS is an especially unique and valuable information source for marine aquarists.

1088 pages with 1000 color pictures, including live fishes, all in a beautifully designed hardback book.

ISBN 3-88244-019-8
ISBN 1-56465-115-0

Rhamphosus aculeatus

Pygaeus gazolei

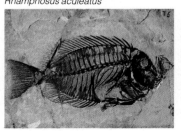

Acanthurus ovalis

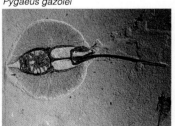

Heliobatis radians

Ceratoichthys pinnatiformis de BLAINVILLE (ca. 50 cm) from the middle Eocene at Bolca, Italy. Original: Museo Civico di Storia Naturale, Verona, Italy.

Cliona delitrix

Amphiprion bicinctus (Red Sea) with beautiful soft corals above and *Entacmaea quadricolor* below.

Plerogyra sinuosa, Indonesia

Spondylus varius, Maldives

Clavelina caerulea

Neoselebastes pandus, a Blenni from western Australia.